Teaching Students with Special Needs in Inclusive Settings

Tom E.C. Smith

University of Arkansas
at Little Rock

Edward A. Polloway

Lynchburg College

James R. Patton

University of Texas

Carol A. Dowdy

University of Alabama
at Birmingham

Nancy Lee Heath

McGill University

Teaching Students with Special Needs in Inclusive Settings

CANADIAN EDITION

Toronto

Canadian Cataloguing in Publication Data

Main entry under title:

Teaching students with special needs in inclusive settings

Canadian ed.
Includes index.
ISBN 0-205-30867-8

1. Inclusive education – Canada. 2. Special education – Canada. 3. Handi-capped children – Education – Canada. 4. Classroom management – Canada.
I. Smith, Tom E. C.

LC1203.C3T42 2001   371.9'046   C00-931013-4

0-205-30867-8

Vice President, Editorial Director: Michael Young
Acquisitions Editor: Kathleen McGill
Marketing Manager: Christine Cozens
Signing Representative: Samantha Scully
Developmental Editor: Laura Paterson Forbes
Production Editor: Sherry Torchinsky
Copy Editor: Kate Revington
Production Coordinator: Peggy Brown
Page Layout: Hermia Chung
Photo Research: Susan Wallace-Cox
Art Director: Mary Opper
Cover Design: Jennifer Federico
Cover Image: Ed Honowitz/Stone
Interior Design: Alex Li

3 4 5   05 04

Printed and bound in Canada.

For all children with special needs and their teachers and parents who provide the supports necessary for them to achieve success; in particular to the children who are special in our personal lives: Jake, Alex, Suni, Lyndsay, Kimi, Cameron, and Meredith

T.E.C.S.
E.A.P.
J.R.P.
C.A.D.

In memory of Dr. Winnifred (Madge) Hall, a caring and insightful educator and researcher.

N.L.H.

BRIEF CONTENTS

CONTENTS

CHAPTER TWO
Designing Inclusive Classrooms 30

CHAPTER THREE
Teaching Students with Learning Disabilities 52

CHAPTER FOUR
Teaching Students with Attention Deficit/Hyperactivity Disorder   88

CHAPTER FIVE
Teaching Students with Emotional and Behavioural Disorders 126

CHAPTER SIX
Teaching Students with Intellectual Disabilities 166

CHAPTER SEVEN
Teaching Students with Sensory Impairments 192

CHAPTER EIGHT
Teaching Students with Autism, Traumatic Brain Injury, and Other Low-Incidence Disabilities   224

CHAPTER NINE
Teaching Students with Communication Disorders   252

BY KATHLEEN FAD

CHAPTER TEN
Teaching Students Who Are Gifted   286

CHAPTER ELEVEN
Teaching Students Who Are at Risk   318

WITH SHARON R. MORGAN

CHAPTER TWELVE
Teaching Students with Special Needs in Elementary Schools   340

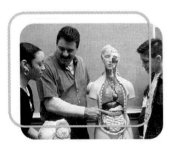

CHAPTER THIRTEEN
Teaching Students with Special Needs in Secondary Schools   374

CHAPTER FOURTEEN
Working with Families of Students with Disabilities 408

About The Authors

Tom E. C. Smith is Professor of Teacher Education at the University of Arkansas at Little Rock. He received his Ed.D. from Texas Tech University and has taught at the University of Arkansas, Fayetteville campus, and the University of Alabama at Birmingham. He is the author of 12 textbooks and has published more than 40 articles in professional journals. He currently serves as the Executive Director of the Division on Mental Retardation and Developmental Disabilities of the Council for Exceptional Children and was appointed by President Clinton in 1994 to the President's Committee on Mental Retardation.

Edward A. Polloway is Professor of Special Education at Lynchburg College in Virginia where he has taught since 1976. He also serves as Dean for Institutional Advancement. He received his Ed.D. from the University of Virginia. He has served on national boards of the Council for Exceptional Children and the Council for Learning Disabilities. Most recently, he was on the committee that revised the definition of mental retardation for the American Association on Mental Retardation. The author of 10 books and more than 70 articles in special education, his primary interests are in the areas of learning disabilities and mental retardation.

James R. Patton the Executive Editor at Pro-Ed in Austin, Texas, and an adjunct professor at the University of Texas at Austin. He received his Ed.D. from the University of Virginia. He has authored more than 80 textbooks and journal articles; his research interests include curriculum development, lifelong learning, science education, and transition. He has served on national boards of the Council for Exceptional Children, Council for Learning Disabilities, and the National Joint Committee on Learning Disabilities.

Carol A. Dowdy is Associate Professor of Special Education at the University of Alabama at Birmingham where she has taught since receiving her Ed.D. degree from the University of Alabama, Tuscaloosa. She has written five books on special education and published more than 25 articles on learning disabilities. Carol has served on the national board of the Council for Learning Disabilities and the Professional Advisory Board for the Learning Disabilities Association of America, and has worked closely with the federal department of Vocational Rehabilitation to assist in their efforts to better serve adults with learning disabilities.

Nancy Lee Heath is Associate Professor of Integrated Education and School Psychology in the Department of Educational and Counselling Psychology at McGill University. She received her Ph.D. from the Ontario Institute of Studies in Education at the University of Toronto. She has taught and worked with students with special needs and consulted with teachers for over fifteen years. She has published 18 articles and presented at more than 30 national and international conferences in the area of social and emotional functioning of children and adolescents with special needs. She is on the editorial board of the *Canadian Journal of Special Education* and is a reviewer for the *Canadian Journal of School Psychology*. She takes pride in continuing to work in the schools as a consultant to teachers and as a member on the governing board of Willingdon Elementary School.

Preface

Since the original edition of *Teaching Students with Special Needs in Inclusive Settings* was published, the delivery of services and supports to students with disabilities and other special needs in general classroom settings has expanded significantly. Research indicates that more and more schools are implementing inclusive education models each year. While the success of inclusion is difficult to validate due to inherent research problems and variant terminology used, research does tend to indicate that including students with disabilities and other special needs in general education classrooms proves both beneficial to these students as well as to students without disabilities. With teacher training programs addressing the need to better prepare general educators to deal effectively with students with diverse learning needs, it is likely that the inclusion movement will continue to move forward.

As with previous editions, we feel that we must indicate our position on inclusion. When the movement first began several years ago, the general interpretation of inclusion was "all or none"—all students, regardless of the severity of disability, all of the time, in general education classrooms. As inclusion has been implemented, this all-or-none position has moderated significantly. It is our belief that inclusion means that all children with disabilities *belong* with their nondisabled, chronological-age peers in the same classes, in the same school they would be attending if they were not disabled. However, it is also our belief that these students must be provided with appropriate educational opportunities. This could include the provision of supports in the general education classroom, but it may also mean the education of some students, at specific times during the day, in specialized settings

CHAPTER **ONE**

CHAPTER OBJECTIVES

- To provide a brief overview of the development of special education services in Canada
- To describe different disabilities served in public schools
- To describe the process for obtaining services for students with exceptionalities
- To discuss formal and informal assessment techniques
- To describe the role of the classroom teacher in assessment and in developing and using individualized education programs (IEPs)

Students with Exceptionalities in an Inclusive Setting: An Introduction

Chapter Objectives are a teaching and learning aid that outline the material to be covered in the chapter.

where they can receive interventions that could not be provided as effectively in the general classroom setting.

It remains our strong belief that students with disabilities and other special needs must be provided educational services that are appropriate for them, as determined by professionals in consultation with parents and family members. The appropriateness of the services definitely includes the location where students will be provided their educational program. Serving students based on educational need rather than clinical label or service delivery model should be the purpose of all special programming; individual student needs must remain the critical element in designing appropriate programs.

Megan is 11 years old and has had many problems in school. In Kindergarten, she already seemed to be behind her peers. She did not start with many of the readiness skills that other students had. In first grade, after she continued to fall behind, her teacher, Mrs. Bland, referred her for an evaluation. The evaluation revealed that Megan was eligible for special education, falling into the mild intellectual disability range. An individualized education program (IEP) was developed, and she was placed in a resource room for half the school day. Megan immediately did better. Her academic skills improved and her social skills progressed. She remained in this type of placement, roughly half-time in a general classroom and half-time in the resource room, for the next two years. By the middle of the third grade, however, Megan's academic performance and behaviour began to decline. For the first time she indicated that she did not like school and got sick in the mornings before school time. At her review in May, the school noted that it was planning to introduce an inclusive service model the next year. Megan's parents were apprehensive. They were concerned that their daughter's behaviour problems would increase and that she would fall further behind her peers. With the urging of school personnel, however, they agreed to try the new arrangement.

At the beginning of Grade 4, Megan seemed out of sorts in the classroom. Although she was provided supports by special education personnel, she had difficulty adjusting to the new classroom and all of her classmates. This situation began to change, however, by the middle of the year. With the cooperative learning activities that her teacher, Ms. Yates, implemented, Megan began to feel more comfortable in the classroom. She did better academically and her social skills improved. She came to enjoy playing with some of her nondisabled peers, who also valued her company. By the end of the fourth grade, Megan was included in all aspects of her class—not only the academic activities.

Now in the fifth grade, Megan is blossoming. She is improving academically and has made many new friends. Her parents are amazed at her attitude toward school. Although there have been many accommodations and modifications made, Megan knows she is a full-fledged member of the class.

1. Why did Megan initially do better when she was placed in a special education classroom?

2. What factors make inclusion successful for students with disabilities and for those without?

Each opening vignette is a case study relating to the topic of the chapter. After studying the chapter, students will be able to answer all of the questions at the end of the vignette with confidence.

FEATURES OF THE CANADIAN EDITION

Too often special education in Canada is taught without reference to or acknowledgment of the substantial differences between the Canadian system of special education and that of the United States. Although Canada has been strongly influenced by the progression of special education services in the U.S., its provincial and territorial educational jurisdictions make it unique. We have twelve different approaches to special education definitions and service delivery. With the emergence of a new territory, Nunavit, which now uses the educational guidelines of the Northwest Territories, we may soon be looking at thirteen different models. A pre-service teacher in Canada needs to be aware of the range of services that exist throughout the country. Throughout this Canadian edition the differences and similarities across the country are highlighted. However, unlike some Canadian editions, this one strives to make pre-service teachers aware of the situation in the U.S. as well; instead of being limited to a review of Canadian service this edition frequently contrasts the Canadian situation to the more generally recognized U.S. system of special education. In this way students are best informed about current special education practices throughout North America.

For this edition a number of changes were made. The first chapter was adapted to focus on Canadian special education policies and definitions of exceptionalities by province/territory; it also includes a summary of the U.S.

special education policy. References to Canadian research, statistics, and prevalence appear throughout the text. The perspective on multicultural education was updated with more current views on approaches to the multicultural classroom. The ethnic diversity represented in the text now reflects Canadian diversity as described by Census Canada. Personal Spotlights in every chapter feature Canadian teachers, parents, and individuals with disabilities. Each chapter now has a list of recommended topical resources that are appropriate for Canadian teachers, including Canadian and international associations, books, videos, and resource guides. Similarly, each chapter provides a short description of recommended relevant Web sites with information and resources that would be helpful to Canadian teachers.

Finally, this edition represents a more concise text appropriate for an undergraduate course on exceptionalities. The first three chapters of the U.S. edition were condensed into two, one introducing exceptionalities, service delivery, and the inclusive classroom, and the second exploring how to design inclusive classrooms. Similarly, the chapters on behaviour management and emotional/ behavioural disorders were consolidated into one chapter on E/BD, with the essential classroom management techniques included.

Margin notes are centred around four themes: Teaching Tip, Further Reading, Cross-Reference, and Consider This.

As in previous editions, the book contains pedagogical features, including chapter opening objectives, vignettes, and chapter summaries. Margin notes are organized around four themes. **Teaching Tip** provides brief, specific suggestions related to the corresponding content in the chapter. **Further Reading** gives the reader a reference to learn more about a particular topic. **Cross-Reference** provides additional information that is found in other chapters in the text. Finally, a margin note called **Consider This** presents issues that call for problem-solving or thinking through particular problems.

Each chapter includes specific boxed features that highlight **technology**, **cultural diversity**, and **inclusion strategies**. These features are intended to provide more depth to a specific topic than is found in the text. **Personal Spotlights** highlight Canadian teachers, parents of children with special needs, and individuals with special needs. These people bring reality to discussions in the text and provide insight into the most important participants pursuing the challenge of inclusion.

The topics presented in these four features are listed on the pages that follow.

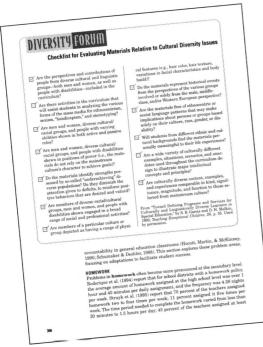

Diversity Forum *boxes provide in-depth information about how a teacher in an inclusive classroom can meet the needs of the culturally diverse students of today.*

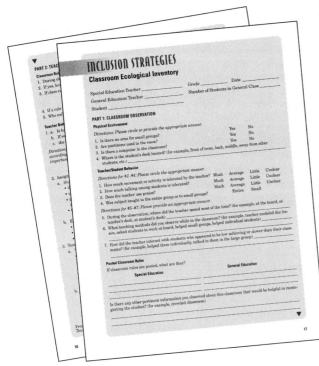

Inclusion Strategies *boxes provide practical strategies for implementing inclusion in the classroom.*

Diversity Forum

Inclusion Strategies

Personal Spotlight

Personal Spotlight boxes highlight teachers, parents of students with special needs, and individuals with special needs, providing insight into the views of people who deal most closely with the challenge of inclusion.

Technology Today

Technology Today boxes feature practical information and discuss the ever-changing technology available to the teachers and students in today's inclusive classrooms.

INSTRUCTOR'S SUPPLEMENT

The Canadian edition of *Teaching Students with Special Needs in Inclusive Settings* is accompanied by an **Instructor's Manual with Test Bank and Transparency Masters**. This supplement provides a chapter overview, teaching outline, focus questions, activities, teaching strategies, and discussion questions for each chapter. It also contains over 1,000 questions—true/false, multiple choice, and essay.

ACKNOWLEDGEMENTS

By the very nature of the Canadian special education situation, this book required the help and cooperation of every provincial and territorial Ministry of Education Special Education branch. I want to thank all those people who went out of their way to answer my questions and send me relevant materials. To all the individuals who shared their personal stories with me, I offer my most sincere appreciation and thanks.

I would like to thank all the people who reviewed the Canadian edition and offered valuable suggestions:

Deborah Butler, University of British Columbia
Don Dworet, Brock University
Lily Dyson, University of Victoria
Noel Williams, University of Windsor

Thanks also to the reviewers of the American text:

Darryl Bauer, Marshall University
Kim S. Beloin, University of Wisconsin at Stevens Point
Patricia A. Connard, The Ohio State University
William E. Davis, University of Maine at Orono
Joan Forsgren-White, Utah State University
Karen N. Janssen, Eastern Kentucky University
Darcy Miller, Washington State University
Gayle Mindes, DePaul University
Gayle L. Nash, Eastern Michigan University
F. Richard Olenchak, The University of Alabama
J. Michael Peterson, Wayne State University
Cynthia Watkins, University of Northern Iowa.

Many thanks to Laura Forbes, my developmental editor, who was both patient and supportive through all my email moods, and to Sherry Torchinsky, production editor. Deepest appreciation to Kate Revington whose remarkable editing and patience made her a valued colleague. Thanks also to Rose Seguin and Ingrid Sladeczek who listened as I learned and whose enthusiasm inspired me. I also must acknowledge all the behind the scenes work done by three outstanding graduate students: Lisa Marie Lanaro who organized the astounding amount of materials from the different provinces and territories; Effie Konstantinopoulos who worked so hard and so cheerfully; Elana Bloom who never said "can't" only "by when?"; and Marla Litvack who always worked to my deadlines without audible complaint. Finally, to Ted Harman my closest collaborator, who served as a sounding board and cheering section throughout, and to Scott and Sophia, for laughter, love, and craziness.

Teaching Students with Special Needs in Inclusive Settings

CHAPTER ONE

CHAPTER OBJECTIVES

- To provide a brief overview of the development of special education services in Canada

- To describe different disabilities served in public schools

- To describe the process for obtaining services for students with exceptionalities

- To discuss formal and informal assessment techniques

- To describe the role of the classroom teacher in assessment and in developing and using individualized education programs (IEPS)

Students with Exceptionalities in an Inclusive Setting: An Introduction

Megan is 11 years old and has had many problems in school. In Kindergarten, she already seemed to be behind her peers. She did not start with many of the readiness skills that other students had. In first grade, after she continued to fall behind, her teacher, Mrs. Bland, referred her for an evaluation. The evaluation revealed that Megan was eligible for special education, falling into the mild intellectual disability range. An individualized education program (IEP) was developed, and she was placed in a resource room for half of the school day. Megan immediately did better. Her academic skills improved and her social skills progressed. She remained in this type of placement, roughly half-time in a general classroom and half-time in the resource room, for the next two years. By the middle of the third grade, however, Megan's academic performance and behaviour began to decline. For the first time she indicated that she did not like school and got sick in the mornings before school time. At her review in May, the school noted that it was planning to introduce an inclusive service model the next year. Megan's parents were apprehensive. They were concerned that their daughter's behaviour problems would increase and that she would fall further behind her peers. With the urging of school personnel, however, they agreed to try the new arrangement.

At the beginning of Grade 4, Megan seemed out of sorts in the classroom. Although she was provided supports by special education personnel, she had difficulty adjusting to the new classroom and all of her classmates. This situation began to change, however, by the middle of the year. With the cooperative learning activities that her teacher, Ms. Yates, implemented, Megan began to feel more comfortable in the classroom. She did better academically and her social skills improved. She came to enjoy playing with some of her nondisabled peers, who also valued her company. By the end of the fourth grade, Megan was included in all aspects of her class—not only the academic activities.

Now in the fifth grade, Megan is blossoming. She is improving academically and has made many new friends. Her parents are amazed at her attitude toward school. Although there have been many accommodations and modifications made, Megan knows she is a full-fledged member of the class.

1. Why did Megan initially do better when she was placed in a special education classroom?

2. What factors make inclusion successful for students with disabilities and for those without?

INTRODUCTION

As recently as the 1960s, many individuals with disabilities were separated from the general public, living and receiving their education in residential facilities. As people began to recognize the debilitating effects of institutionalization, the **normalization movement** emerged (Wolfensberger, 1972). Normalization proponents believed that all individuals, regardless of disability, should be provided with an education and a living arrangement as normal as possible. This conviction led to significant changes for individuals with special needs. People who had been institutionalized for years returned to their communities, and at the same time educational rights for individuals with special needs became a focus of the legal system.

In the United States, the American Rehabilitation Act, Section 504 (1973), "guaranteed the rights of persons with handicaps in . . . educational institutions that receive federal moneys" (Stainback, Stainback, & Bunch, 1989). The Education for All Handicapped Children Act (PL 94-142) was passed by Congress in 1975, requiring each state to educate children with disabilities. This Act was re-authorized in 1990 under the title of Individuals with Disabilities Education Act (IDEA) and states:

> To the maximum extent appropriate, children with disabilities . . . are educated with children who are not disabled, and that special classes, separate schooling, or other removal of children with disabilities from the regular environment occurs only when the nature or severity of the disability is such that education in regular classes with the use of supplementary aids and services cannot be attained satisfactorily.

FURTHER READING

For a more detailed discussion of the history of special education in Canada, read Chapter 1 in *Including Exceptional Students: A Practical Guide for Classroom Teachers, Canadian Edition*, by M. Friend, W. Bursuck, and N. Hutchinson, published by Allyn & Bacon Canada in 1998.

In Canada, the movement toward inclusion was somewhat slower and different in nature. Each province or territory has its own Education Act or School Act governing education in schools within its jurisdiction, including special education services. However, with Canada's adoption, in 1982, of the Constitution Act, which included the **Canadian Charter of Rights and Freedoms** guaranteeing the rights of all individuals with disabilities, Canada became the first country in the world to enshrine the rights of people with disabilities in a constitution. The Charter of Rights and Freedoms, which came into effect in 1985, states in section 15.(1) that

> Every individual is equal before and under the law and has the right to equal protection of the law without discrimination based on race, national or ethnic origin, colour, religion, sex, age, or mental or physical disability.

CONSIDER THIS

What are the advantages and disadvantages of having education under provincial/territorial jurisdiction?

Smith and Foster (1996) describe how all educational policy at every level (provincial/territorial and board/district) must abide by the Charter. Every province and territory has established its own policy documents, but all have moved steadily toward inclusion of students with special needs. Canadian proponents of inclusive education believe that students with disabilities, regardless of severity, should be integrated into the regular classroom (O'Brien, Snow,

Forest, & Hasbury, 1989). They argue that educators are responsible for adapting the regular classroom to meet the students' needs. The provinces and territories adhere to the inclusive model to varying degrees, but all are committed to the principle of inclusion. As a teacher, you will need to learn the current special education guidelines for your own province or territory.

DEVELOPMENT OF SPECIAL SERVICES

Prior to the 1970s and the normalization movement, students with physical disabilities or intellectual disabilities were provided with services, albeit nearly always in self-contained, isolated classrooms. These students rarely interacted with nondisabled students, and their teachers did not routinely come into contact with other teachers in the school. In addition to isolating the students, the existing programs were small. Therefore, very few students were served. Beyond these public school programs, children received services in **residential programs**. Typically, children with intellectual disabilities and with sensory deficits were placed in these settings. These residential programs offered daily living supports as well as some education and training. In 1970, a report by Roberts and Lazure, entitled *One Million Children: A National Study of Canadian Children with Emotional and Learning Disorders*, called for integration and instruction based on learning characteristics, not categories. This landmark report, combined with Wolfensberger's work at the National Institute of Mental Retardation in Toronto (Wolfensberger, 1972) which emphasized the importance of a normal environment for all individuals, contributed to the changes in education in Canada in the 1970s.

Since the mid-1970s, services to students with disabilities have changed dramatically. Not only are more appropriate services provided by schools, but they also are frequently provided in both resource rooms and in general education classrooms by collaborating special education and classroom teachers. Services for students with disabilities evolved in three distinct phases: (1) **relative isolation**, (2) **integration** (or **mainstreaming**), and (3) **inclusion**. In the relative isolation phase, students were either denied access to public schools or were permitted to attend in isolated settings. In the integration phase, which began in the 1970s, students with disabilities were mainstreamed, or integrated, into general education programs when deemed appropriate. Finally, the inclusion phase, introduced in the early 1980s, emphasized that students with disabilities should be fully included in school programs and activities. This phase differed from the integration phase in a minor, but very significant way.

While both integration and inclusion resulted in students with disabilities joining general classrooms, inclusion assumes that these students belong in general classrooms—in the integration phase they were considered to be special education students who were placed in the general classroom part of the time. Recently, the importance of empowerment and self-determination for students with disabilities has been a focus of inclusion efforts, to better prepare students for the highest degree of independence possible (Polloway, Smith, Patton, & Smith, 1996). Figure 1.1 depicts the historical changes in the education of students with disabilities in public education.

CONSIDER THIS

Should all children, even those with very different learning needs, have access to free educational services in public schools? Why or why not? What should be done about the extensive cost that may be incurred?

FIGURE 1.1
Historical Changes in Education for Students with Disabilities

From "Historic Changes in Mental Retardation and Developmental Disabilities," by E. A. Polloway, J. D. Smith, J. R. Patton, and T. E. C. Smith, 1996, *Education and Training in Mental Retardation and Developmental Disabilities, 31,* p. 9. Used by permission.

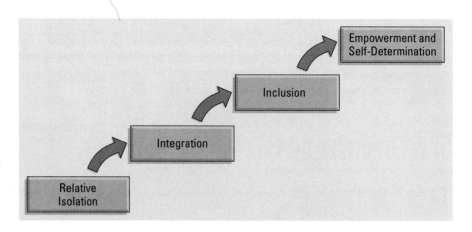

Because all children are eligible for public education in Canada, teachers in today's public schools must provide instruction and other educational services to meet the needs of a very diverse student population. They must develop ways to serve as many students as possible in general education environments (Smith & Smith, 1989). Traditionally, teacher education programs for classroom teachers have focused on teaching students who do not have learning or behaviour problems. However, today's teachers must be prepared to teach all kinds of students. They do not have the luxury of teaching only students who learn easily and behave in a manner that meets teachers' own standards; teachers must be prepared to deal effectively with all students.

STUDENTS WITH SPECIAL NEEDS

Many students do not fit the mold of the "typical" student. Those with identified disabilities, those who are classified as gifted and talented, and those who are "at risk" of developing problems are among them. It has been estimated that, in Canada, approximately 10 percent of school-age children have a recognized exceptionality. Another undetermined number experience learning and behaviour problems, but not significantly enough to be classified as having a disability. Still another group of students who require special attention are those at risk of developing problems. These students include potential dropouts, those from minority cultures, those who speak English as a second language, those from low-income homes, those who abuse drugs or alcohol, those who become pregnant, those from single-parent homes, and those considered "socially maladjusted" (Morgan, 1994).

Adding all these students together, plus those who obviously need assistance but do not fit into any distinct group, results in a group that comprises about half of all students in public schools. Although many of these students do not fit into the specific classification as "disabled"—and are therefore ineligible for special education services—school personnel cannot afford to ignore their special problems (Cosden, 1990; Greer, 1991; Hill, 1991; Morgan, 1994).

Diversity among students in public schools represents the "norm" rather than the exception (Johnson, Pugach, & Devlin, 1990). If our public schools are to be effective, school personnel must address the varying needs of students. They must be able to identify students with special needs and help develop and implement programs. A first step for classroom teachers is to understand the types of students they serve.

Students with Exceptionalities

One of the largest groups of students with special needs in the public school system, also the most visible, consists of students who have been formally classified as having **exceptionalities**.

Students with exceptionalities are defined differently in different provinces and territories. In New Brunswick, students with exceptionalities are defined as "individuals for whom a special education program is considered a necessity. This may be individuals having behavioural, communicational, intellectual, physical, perceptual or multiple exceptionalities" (New Brunswick, 1991). In Saskatchewan, students are defined as having exceptional needs if they have been identified as having "physical and/or intellectual needs that are more specialized than those usually found in the regular classroom" (Saskatchewan, 1996). Similar definitions are found across the country, sharing the characteristic listing of exceptionalities and frequently the statement that the student needs special services.

One other approach to the defining of students with exceptionalities exists in some provincial and territorial education documents, namely, the absence of a definition! For example, in the Education Act (1995) of the Northwest Territories, no mention is made of what constitutes an exceptionality. Instead, the Act focuses on the rights of all students to an inclusive education and support services to meet individual needs. However, even where provincial or territorial guidelines are not provided for identifying exceptionalities, practice at the school level often involves assessment for exceptionalities. Specific categories of exceptionality recognized by the different jurisdictions vary marginally, but the majority of jurisdictions include the following categories:

- Learning disabilities
- Speech or language impairments
- Intellectual disabilities
- Emotional/behavioural disorders
- Multiple disabilities
- Auditory impairments
- Orthopedic impairments
- Other health impairments
- Visual impairments
- Autism (in some, but not all jurisdictions)
- Traumatic brain injury (TBI)

Many different types of students are found in these 11 categories. For example, the broad area of other health impairments includes students with cardiac problems, asthma, and sickle cell anemia. Even the category of learning disabilities comprises an extremely heterogeneous group of students.

The fact that disability categories are composed of different types of students makes simple conclusions about them impossible. Students who need

CONSIDER THIS
What similarities do students with disabilities share with students from racial minorities? Are educational services being offered to both groups of students in a similar fashion?

FURTHER READING
For detailed information about the legal rights of students with exceptionalities in the different provinces and territories, read W. J. Smith and W. F. Foster's *Equal Educational Opportunity for Students with Disabilities: A Source Book for Parents, Advocates and Professionals*, published in 1996 by McGill University's Office of Research on Educational Policy.

special assistance do not all fit neatly into disability categories. Many times it is hard to know into which category a child would best fit. Consider a child with an attention-deficit disorder who has poor academic skills despite high intelligence and who often behaves disruptively. Such a child could be categorized by many provincial/territorial guidelines as having either a behavioural disorder or a learning disability—no jurisdiction has an attention-deficit disorder category.

The majority of students with disabilities experience mild disabilities and join general education classrooms for at least a portion of each school day. A smaller number of students, with more severe disabilities, are more typically educated in segregated special education environments. However, even some students with more severe disabilities are included in general education classrooms part of the time (Hamre-Nietupski et al., 1989; Thousand & Villa, 1990; York & Vandercook, 1991). Most classroom teachers help educate students with disabilities directly. The following section provides a brief overview of each of the major disability categories recognized in most schools.

FURTHER READING

More information on teacher training issues and inclusion can be found in *Winners All: A Call for Inclusive Schools*, published by the National Association of State Boards of Education in 1992.

CROSS-REFERENCE

For more information on intellectual disabilities, and all of the other specific disability categories, see Chapters 3–9.

INTELLECTUAL DISABILITY

The disability category that has been recognized for the longest time in most school districts is **intellectual disability**. Students with intellectual disabilities are usually identified through intelligence tests and measures of adaptive behaviour, which look at a person's ability to perform functional activities expected of age and cultural norms. By definition, they score less than 70–75 on individual intelligence tests and have concurrent deficits in adaptive behaviour (American Association on Mental Retardation, 1992). Their general characteristics include problems in learning, memory, problem solving, adaptive behaviour, and social skills (Beirne-Smith, Patton, & Ittenbach, 1994.

LEARNING DISABILITIES

The disability category that accounts for more than 50 percent of all students served in special education is learning disabilities. This category is beset with problems of definition and programming, but continues to include more children than all other special education categories combined (Smith, Dowdy, Polloway, & Blalock, 1997). In general, students with learning disabilities do not achieve commensurate with their abilities. The cause is unclear, but the assumption, although controversial, is that a neurological dysfunction causes the learning disability (Hynd, Marshall, & Gonzalez, 1991).

EMOTIONAL/BEHAVIOURAL DISORDERS

Students with emotional and behavioural disorders cause disruptions for themselves or others in their environment through inappropriate behaviours or expressions of emotion. Professionals serving children with these problems differ on definitions of the problems and the types of services they provide (Kauffman & Wong, 1991).

SENSORY PROBLEMS

Some students have problems with sensory skills—their visual or auditory abilities. Since the majority of information provided by teachers is presented orally or visually, deficits in these areas can result in significant problems. Visual impairment includes two subcategories: blindness and low vision. The category of auditory impairment covers both deaf and hard-of-hearing students.

ORTHOPEDIC IMPAIRMENTS

Many students experience problems related to their physical abilities. Cerebral palsy, spina bifida, amputations, and muscular dystrophy are a few examples. For these students, physical access to educational facilities and accommodating problems with writing and manipulation are important concerns.

OTHER HEALTH IMPAIRMENTS

This disability category includes a wide variety of problems, for example, cardiac problems, AIDS, diabetes, epilepsy, and asthma. For students with these disabilities, medical needs take precedence. School personnel must work closely with medical and other professionals to provide appropriate services.

AUTISM

Autism is a lifelong disability that primarily affects communication and social interactions. Children with autism typically relate to people, objects, and events in abnormal ways; they insist on structured environments and display many self-stimulating behaviours. Autism is not recognized as a separate category by most provinces and territories.

FURTHER READING
Much information about autism can be found in Chapter 8, which focuses on severe disabilities and health problems.

TRAUMATIC BRAIN INJURY

Traumatic brain injury (TBI) was defined by Savage (1988) as an insult to the brain that often results in impaired cognitive, physical, or emotional functioning. Students with TBI are typically served under the disability category that relates to their functional limitations (e.g., intellectual disability for cognitive deficits and learning disabilities for erratic academic performance).

SPEECH OR LANGUAGE IMPAIRMENTS

For some children, speech difficulties form a serious problem. When the impairment results in a need for special education and related services, children are considered eligible for services under most provincial and territorial jurisdictions. Most of these children need speech therapy. Teachers need to work closely with speech and language specialists when dealing with this group of students.

CONSIDER THIS
Why should students with severe disabilities not be served in institutional or in other segregated settings? Should some children be placed in such settings? Why or why not?

Students Classified as Gifted and Talented

Some students differ from their peers by having above-average intelligence and learning abilities. These students, classified as gifted and talented, were traditionally defined and identified using intelligence quotient test scores (IQ scores). An IQ score of 120, 130, 140, or higher was the primary criterion for identifying a gifted and talented student. Current criteria are much broader. Although definitions vary, most focus on students who are capable of making significant contributions to society in a variety of areas, spanning academic endeavours, creativity, mechanical skills, motor skills, and skills in the fine arts.

Students at Risk of School Problems

Some students who neither fit into a specific disability category nor have an above-average capacity to achieve also present problems for the education system. These students, classified as being at risk, manifest characteristics that could easily lead to learning and behaviour problems (Cosden, 1990; Greer, 1991; Heward & Orlansky, 1992; Johnson, Pugach, & Devlin, 1990). Students considered at risk include the following:

CONSIDER THIS
Should students who are considered at risk of developing learning and behaviour problems be provided with special services? Why or why not?

- Potential dropouts
- Drug and alcohol abusers
- Students from minority cultures
- Students from low-income homes
- Teenagers who become pregnant
- Students who speak English as a second language
- Students who are in trouble with the legal system

These students may present unique problems for teachers who must meet their educational needs in general education classrooms. Since students in the at-risk group are not eligible for special education services, classroom teachers bear the primary responsibility for their educational programs. These will need to be modified to meet student needs.

OBTAINING SERVICES FOR STUDENTS WITH SPECIAL NEEDS

CONSIDER THIS
How can schools deal with the financial impact of special services for students with disabilities? Is there a limit as to how much should be spent on a single child? From province to province this varies. Should it be the same across the country?

The majority of students who receive special services are first identified by the regular classroom teacher. It is usually the classroom teacher at the elementary level who initiates the process that will result in a student receiving special services. This process may involve a number of different school personnel depending on the situation and the specific school, as well as the province or territory. Typically, a school team becomes involved. This team, referred to by different names, generally includes the regular classroom teacher, special education personnel (resource teacher, special education board/district consultant, school psychologist or guidance counsellor), the principal, and specific medical or social service personnel depending on the nature of the student's difficulty. While all of these individuals will take part in a formal identification of a student, the process of obtaining services almost always begins with the teacher. Ideally, it should adhere to the steps outlined in Figure 1.2.

Throughout the process of obtaining special services for a student a variety of assessments are done.

ASSESSMENT

CROSS-REFERENCE
Refer to the Glossary for the meanings of terms associated with assessment.

In the broadest sense, assessment refers to the gathering and analysis of information used to make instructional, administrative, and guidance decisions about individual students (Wallace, Larsen, & Elksnin, 1992). In the context of special education, **assessment** refers to evaluative efforts associated with initial screening, program design, instructional decision making, and the determining of eligibility for special education services.

This information-gathering process should focus primarily on identifying the strengths of children considered "at risk"; appropriate modifications can then be designed to facilitate student success in the inclusive environment of a general edu-

FIGURE 1.2
Steps from Prereferral to IEP and Checklists of the Teacher's Responsibilities

Adapted from *Learning Disabilities* (p. 126), by J. P. Hallahan, J. M. Kauffman, and J. W. Lloyd, 1996, Boston: Allyn & Bacon.

STEPS LEADING TO THE IEP

1. A teacher notices that a student is having serious academic or behavioural difficulty.

2. The teacher consults the student's parents and tries the instructional or behaviour management strategies she or he believes will resolve the problem.

3. If the problem is not resolved the teacher asks for the help of the school team.

4. With the help of the team, the teacher implements and documents the results of strategies designed to resolve the problem.

5. If the problem is not resolved after reasonable implementation of the team's suggestions, the teacher makes a referral for evaluation by the school psychologist.

6. The school psychologist evaluates the student.

7. With the results of the evaluation components in hand, the school team determines whether the student is eligible for special education.

8. If the student is found eligible, then an IEP must be written.

WHAT SHOULD I DO BEFORE MAKING A REFERRAL?

☑ Hold at least one conference to discuss your concerns with the parents (or make extensive and documented efforts to communicate with the parents).

☑ Check all available school records, and interview other professionals involved with the student to make sure you understand the student's history and efforts to help that have already been made.

☑ Ask the school team—or the principal, the school psychologist, and at least one other teacher who knows the student—to help you devise strategies to solve the problem.

☑ Implement and document the results of the academic and behaviour management strategies you have tried.

WHAT INFORMATION SHOULD I BE ABLE TO PROVIDE AT THE TIME OF REFERRAL?

☑ A statement of exactly what you are concerned about

☑ An explanation of why you are concerned

☑ Detailed records from your observations of the problem, including samples of academic work

☑ Records documenting the strategies you have used to try to resolve the problem and the outcomes of those strategies

cation classroom. Later, assessment will measure the success of instructional and behavioural interventions implemented in the general education classroom. Assessment can pinpoint problems that should be addressed in general education classes; it does not necessarily lead to special education placement.

Testing versus Assessment

Polloway and Jones-Wilson (1992) define **testing** as the presentation of tasks or questions to a student within an organized context in order to obtain a score.

PERSONAL SPOTLIGHT

Veteran Mathematics Teacher ■ ROY OHASHI

Retired Secondary Mathematics Teacher

Roy Ohashi taught for 27 years as a secondary school mathematics teacher and department head. He also spent two years at the Saskatchewan Department of Education as an Evaluation consultant conducting workshops for teachers on test setting and standards and as a Mathematics Curriculum consultant for the Department of Education and the Regina Board of Education, developing mathematics curricula. He taught grades 9 to 12, all levels, courses ranging from remedial mathematics to calculus.

Roy's career spans the period from more segregated special education classes to the more inclusive classrooms of the present day. He dealt with students who had hearing impairments (accompanied by sign language interpreters), a student from a juvenile detention centre on a day-pass to attend regular school, and students with cystic fibrosis, cancer, learning disabilities, emotional and behavioural disturbances, and histories of abuse.

Does Roy feel inclusion can work? He sees both advantages and disadvantages to the model. "Integration or inclusion of a student is important if one expects to help the student learn, and in the classroom we encouraged students to help each other. 'By teaching, one learns.' The class accepts individual differences in ability, mobility, and capability. The student becomes one of the class, a member, and is supported by classmates. However, sometimes individuals are labelled as being different by callous students, and vicious slurs humiliate these students. The classroom teacher has a great responsibility to monitor such behaviour and oftentimes this is very difficult with the other demands already on the teacher. Inclusion places a heavy responsibility on the teacher to prepare lessons in a manner which will allow total coverage for *all* students in the class. For example, if Plan A did not work for everyone, swing over to B and try to reach them all and so on."

Roy notes how the cultural diversity of his classes increased throughout his teaching career and observes that teachers of today deal with highly culturally diverse classes, as well as students with exceptionalities. "Cultural differences appear in situations when one least expects them: courtesy in answering questions; 'sir' in response to being addressed; no eye-to-eye contact in one-to-one discussion with First Nations students. All are eventually accepted as normal."

Roy ends by talking about how the labels change, but the job of the teacher stays the same: to accommodate students the best we can. He feels that, as teachers, we can handle these demands. But, says Roy, reflecting on his teaching career, what he was not prepared to handle "was when a bright student regularly requested help after class (despite not really requiring it) then committed suicide before graduation. Or the loner (a good academic student) who got drunk on the night of his graduation party and deliberately drove head-on into another vehicle and took his own life. We were not aware of the 'signs of trouble' and I do think that teachers, both pre-service and in-service, should be made more cognizant of other 'baggage' students are carrying around in their heads. My subject (mathematics) was the least of my concerns when it came to the student's well-being, but I could not take as much time to work with the individual as I should have."

Thus, testing is only one aspect of assessment, which looks at the global evaluative results and the implications of performance. Assessment deals with qualitative as well as quantitative components of performance observed both formally and informally within and outside a given testing setting. Although testing often becomes an end in itself (Wallace et al., 1992), assessment seeks to capture a more complete picture of the student through the determination of current functioning levels. Forming this picture is essential to effective educational planning and instruction.

Formal tests serve two primary functions: surveying ability in an instructional domain and diagnosing difficulties. Survey tests are usually administered to obtain a global score or level of functioning. Numerous tests are used to serve this purpose. Two common survey tests that may be used as part of the special education assessment process are the Peabody Individual Achievement Test—Revised (Markwardt, 1989) and the Wide Range Achievement Test—Revised (Jastak & Wilkinson, 1984).

Diagnostic tests attempt to obtain more specific information about strengths and weaknesses. Two formal diagnostic tests that are often used for instructional program development are the Key Math Test—Revised (Connolly, 1988) and the Gray Oral Reading Test—Revised (GORT-2) (Wiederholt & Bryant, 1986).

Although formal testing does provide quantitative and sometimes qualitative data based on student performance, tests can obtain only a measure of a student's best performance in a contrived situation; they cannot broadly represent a student's typical performance under natural conditions. When considered in isolation, the results of formal tests can lead to poor decisions in placement and instructional planning. Rigid administration and interpretation of test results can obscure, rather than reveal, a student's strengths and weaknesses. Figure 1.3 provides an illustration of this.

Formal Assessment

Formal assessment instruments are generally available commercially. They typically contain detailed guidelines for administration, scoring, and interpretation,

FIGURE 1.3

Illustration of Useful Information Lost During Standardized Testing

From *Improving Educational Outcomes for Children with Disabilities: Principles for Assessment, Program Planning, and Evaluation* (pp. 16–17), by M. Kozloff, 1994, Baltimore, MD: Brookes. Used by permission.

The author makes the following observations:
There are many competent ways to respond to "What is this?" Indra said what potatoes are for and what the duck was doing. Ms. Adams scores Indra's answers incorrect because the test Ms. Adams is using narrowly defines as correct those answers with object-naming function. Thus, Ms. Adams underestimates the size of Indra's object-naming repertoire and does not notice the other functions of Indra's vocabulary.

as well as statistical data on validity, reliability, and standardization procedures. They are most often **norm-referenced**, that is, the tests provide quantitative information comparing the performance of an individual student to others in his or her norm group (determined, for example, by age, grade, or gender). Test results are usually reported in the form of test quotients, percentiles, and age or grade equivalents. These tools are most useful early in an assessment procedure, when relatively little is known of a student's strengths and weaknesses: they may help identify areas in which informal assessment can begin. The ability to compare students to their age and grade peers is also an advantage in making eligibility and placement decisions and in fulfilling related administrative requirements.

Table 1.1 demonstrates various types of scores obtained through standardized testing and the range of scores that may suggest a mild, moderate, or severe deficit.

Professionals can make better informed decisions about the use of formal instruments if they study the instrument and become familiar with its features, benefits, and possible liabilities. One way to do this is to consult one or more of the several excellent resources on tests. Two particularly apt sources are the *Buros Mental Measurements Yearbook* (1998) and *Tests in Print* (1994). Both are periodically revised and updated.

Informal Assessment

Informal assessments are usually more loosely structured than formal instruments and are more closely tied to teaching. Such tools are typically devised by teachers to determine what skills or knowledge a child possesses. Their key advantage is the direct application of assessment data to instructional programs. By incorporating assessment results into the teaching program and by monitoring student responses each day, teachers can achieve reliable measurements that reveal patterns of fluctuation in performance.

Criterion-referenced testing (CRT) compares a student's performance with a criterion of mastery for a specific task, disregarding relative standing in a group. This type of informal assessment can be especially useful when documentation of progress is needed for accountability: the acquisition of skills can be clearly demonstrated. As Wallace et al. (1992) stress, CRTs are quite popular because they focus attention on specific skills in the curriculum, provide measures of progress toward mastery, and assist teachers in designing instructional strategies. Traditionally, most criterion-referenced tests have been produced by teachers, but recently publishers have begun to produce assessment tools of this type.

One important and popular form of criterion-referenced assessment is **curriculum-based assessment**. Unlike norm-referenced tools, it uses the actual curriculum as the standard and thus provides a basis for evaluating and modifying the curriculum for an individual student (McLoughlin & Lewis, 1990). This type of assessment can have a role in many important tasks: identification, eligibility, instructional grouping, program planning, progress monitoring, and program evaluation (Hasbrouck & Tindal, 1992; Marston & Magnusson, 1985). Curriculum-based assessment can focus attention on changes in academic behaviour within the context of the curriculum being

TABLE 1.1

Relation of Various Standard Scores to Percentile Rank and to Each Other

Percentile Rank	Quotients	NCE Scores	T-scores	Z-scores	Stanines	Deficit
99	150	99	83	+3.33	9	
99	145	99	80	+3.00	9	
99	140	99	77	+2.67	9	
99	135	99	73	+2.33	9	
98	130	92	70	+2.00	9	
95	125	85	67	+1.67	8	
91	120	78	63	+1.34	8	none
84	115	71	60	+1.00	7	
75	110	64	57	+0.67	6	
63	105	57	53	+0.33	6	
50	100	50	50	+0.00	5	
37	95	43	47	–0.33	4	
25	90	36	43	–0.67	4	
16	85	29	40	–1.00	3	mild
9	80	22	37	–1.34	2	
5	75	15	33	–1.67	2	moderate
2	70	8	30	–2.00	1	
1	65	1	27	–2.33	1	
1	60	1	23	–2.67	1	severe
1	55	1	20	–3.00	1	

From "The Role of Standardized Tests in Planning Academic Instruction," by D. D. Hammill and B. R. Bryant, 1991. *Handbook on the Assessment of Learning Disabilities,* edited by H. L. Swanson (p. 377). Austin, TX: Pro-Ed. Copyright 1991 by Pro-Ed, Inc. Used by permission.

used, thus enhancing the relationship between assessment and teaching (Deno & Fuchs, 1987). Because curriculum-based assessment encourages reliance on methods keyed to the curriculum and administered by classroom teachers, it is also more realistic than norm-referenced testing (Fuchs & Fuchs, 1986; Fuchs, Fuchs, Hamlett, & Stecker, 1991).

Curriculum-based measures can be developed through systematic analysis of a given curriculum, selection of specific items, and construction of assessment formats (e.g., questions, cloze activities, worksheets). Although manuals and other resources for developing curriculum-based instruments exist, they

Curriculum-based assessment can focus attention on changes in a student's academic behaviour.

serve primarily as guides: instruments used in the classroom should reflect the curriculum being followed there.

Ecological Assessment

Educational assessment has increasingly begun to reflect a trend toward appreciating the ecology of the student. Consequently, data obtained on an individual are now more frequently analyzed in relation to the child's functioning in the various environments in which he or she lives and learns. Although a full discussion of **ecological assessment** is beyond the scope of this chapter, the following section highlights some basic considerations, and the nearby Inclusion Strategies feature provides an example of a classroom ecological inventory.

The focus of ecological assessment is to place the evaluation process within the context of the student's environment. Its central element is functionality—how well the student functions in the current environment or how well a student might function in a proposed environment based on previous ecological assessments. This focus shifts a program's emphasis from correcting deficits toward determining how to build on strengths and interests.

An emphasis on ecological assessment necessarily broadens the assessment process. Additionally, it offers professionals a way of validating findings. The following questions can help teachers better understand the child and why he or she is having difficulty succeeding in school. Answers should help educators develop a positive learning environment and identify specific strategies to reduce negative impacts on learning.

- In what physical environment does the child learn best?
- What is useful, debilitating, or neutral about the way the child approaches the task?
- Can the student hold multiple pieces of information in memory and then act upon them?
- How does increasing or slowing the speed of instruction affect the accuracy of a child's work?

INCLUSION STRATEGIES

Classroom Ecological Inventory

Special Education Teacher _____   Grade _____   Date _____

General Education Teacher _____   Number of Students in General Class _____

Student _____

PART 1: CLASSROOM OBSERVATION

Physical Environment

Directions: Please circle or provide the appropriate answer.

1. Is there an area for small groups?   Yes   No
2. Are partitions used in the room?   Yes   No
3. Is there a computer in the classroom?   Yes   No
4. Where is the student's desk located? (for example, front of room, back, middle, away from other students, etc.) _____

Teacher/Student Behavior

Directions for #1–#4: Please circle the appropriate answer.

1. How much movement or activity is tolerated by the teacher?   Much   Average   Little   Unclear
2. How much talking among students is tolerated?   Much   Average   Little   Unclear
3. Does the teacher use praise?   Much   Average   Little   Unclear
4. Was subject taught to the entire group or to small groups?   Entire   Small

Directions for #5–#7: Please provide an appropriate answer.

5. During the observation, where did the teacher spend most of the time? (for example, at the board, at teacher's desk, at student's desk) _____

6. What teaching methods did you observe while in the classroom? (for example, teacher modeled the lesson, asked students to work at board, helped small groups, helped individual students) _____

7. How did the teacher interact with students who appeared to be low achieving or slower than their classmates? (for example, helped them individually, talked to them in the large group) _____

Posted Classroom Rules

If classroom rules are posted, what are they?

Special Education	General Education
_____	_____
_____	_____
_____	_____

Is there any other pertinent information you observed about this classroom that would be helpful in reintegrating the student? (for example, crowded classroom)

_____

_____

▼

PART 2: TEACHER INTERVIEW

	Special Ed	General Ed
Classroom Rules		

Classroom Rules

1. During class are there important rules? (Yes or No)
2. If yes, how are they communicated? (for example, written or oral)
3. If class rules are *not* posted, what are they?

4. If a rule is broken, what happens? What is the typical consequence?
5. Who enforces the rules? (teacher, aide, students)

Teacher Behavior

1. a. Is homework assigned? (Yes or No)
   b. If so, indicate approximate amount (minutes) of homework, and
   c. the frequency with which it is given.

Directions for #2–#4: Using a 3-point scale (1 = Often, 2 = Sometimes, 3 = Never), rate each item according to frequency of occurrence in class. Place an asterisk (*) in the right-hand margin to indicate important differences between the special and regular education classrooms.

	Special Ed	General Ed		Special Ed	General Ed
2. Assignments in Class			**4. Academic/Social Rewards**		
a. Students are given assignments:			a. Classroom rewards or reinforcement include:		
• that are the same for all			• material rewards (example, stars)		
• that differ in amount or type			b. Classroom punishment includes:		
• to complete in school at a specified time			• time out		
• that, if unfinished in school, are assigned as homework			• loss of activity-related privileges (example, loss of free time)		
b. Evaluation of assignment:			• teacher ignoring		
• teacher evaluation			• reprimands		
• student self-evaluation			• poorer grade, loss of star, etc.		
• peer evaluation			• extra work		
3. Tests			• staying after school		
a. Tests are			• physical punishment (example, paddling)		
• presented orally					
• copied from board					
• timed					

5. To what extent do each of the following contribute to an overall grade? *Estimate the percentage for each so that the total sums to 100%.*

	Special Ed	General Ed
• based on study guides given to students prior to test		
• administered by resource teacher		
b. Grades are:		
• percentages (example, 75%)		
• letter grades (example, B+)		
• both		
• homework		
• daily work		
• tests		
• class participation		

6. Please list skills that have been taught since the beginning of the school year (general education teacher only):

Skill	Will Reteach Later? (Yes or No)

From "Classroom Ecological Inventory," by D. Fuchs, P. Fernstrom, S. Scott, L. Fuchs, and L. Vandermeer, 1994, *Teaching Exceptional Children, 26*, 14–15.

- What processing mechanisms are being taxed in any given task?
- How does this student interact with a certain teaching style?
- With which professional has the child been most successful? What characteristics of the person seem to contribute to the child's success?
- What is encouraging to the child? What is discouraging?
- How does manipulating the mode of teaching (e.g., visual or auditory presentation) affect the child's performance? (Waterman, 1994, pp. 9–10)

Issues of Bias in Assessment

The importance of ensuring fair and equitable assessment procedures cannot be underestimated. When a child to be evaluated does not differ from the norm culturally or in any other significant manner that would preclude the use of traditional tests, evaluation is relatively straightforward. When the child differs, however, other modified approaches must be considered (Zucker & Polloway, 1987). As Wallace et al. (1992) stress, bias in the evaluation of students, particularly those from a minority background, "can and will significantly affect the educational opportunities afforded these youngsters. To minimize the effects of bias in the evaluation, it is absolutely essential that every [professional] . . . be aware of the various ways in which bias is exhibited and take steps to minimize its effects when making educational decisions." (p. 473)

Many sources of possible bias can be found in the assessment process, ranging from administrative practices, such as proximity to student and physical contact, to gender of tester and testee, cultural and ethnic prejudice, and linguistic variance. The nearby Diversity Forum feature provides an example of guidelines for reducing bias in the assessment of students with limited English proficiency. This kind of information should be used when assessing all individuals whose differences might lead to test bias.

Of special concern is the accurate assessment of individuals who experience sensory or motor disabilities. For example, individuals who have hearing impairments may require a nonverbal test, whereas persons who have visual impairments require measures that do not rely on object manipulation and do not include cards or pictures (Hoy & Gregg, 1994). An individual with a severe motor impairment may have limited voluntary responses and may need to respond via an eye scan or blink.

Students who have multiple disabilities compound the difficulties of administering the assessment task. Browder and Snell (1988) note that some individuals simply lack "test behaviours." For example, they may refuse to stay seated for an assessment session or may exhibit interfering self-stimulatory behaviour, such as hand flapping or rocking.

Further, test results should not be unduly affected by disabilities in receptive or expressive language capabilities. Such disabilities may cause the test to measure the problem itself, rather than assess the level of functioning.

Considered collectively, these problem areas can make traditional testing procedures ineffective, resulting in discriminatory practices despite the best intentions of the tester (Browder & Snell, 1988; Luckasson et al., 1992).

Hoy and Gregg (1994) note that **nondiscriminatory evaluation** requires that data be gathered by a school team in a nondiscriminatory fashion, with an awareness of how bias could enter the decision-making process and with the knowledge of how to control it. This general admonition serves as a backdrop

Guidelines for Limiting Bias during Assessment of Students with Limited English Proficiency (LEP)

1. **PREREFERRAL INTERVENTION** — Ensure that the student with LEP has received different types of instruction in the appropriate language in his or her regular environment.

2. **SITUATIONAL ANALYSIS** — Ensure that the referral is appropriate. Confirm that the referral does not reflect a lack of knowledge or a teacher's prejudice concerning culture, race, or income level differences.

3. **DIRECT OBSERVATION** — Directly observe students with LEP in different settings. Discrepant behavior in relation to peers and adults across different school, play, or work settings should be documented.

4. **ESTABLISHING LANGUAGE DOMINANCE** — Carry out formal language assessments in both the native language and in English, prior to any assessment. Assessment of both school language and conversational or interpersonal language is necessary.

5. **DUAL-LANGUAGE TESTING** — Evaluate the student with LEP in both the primary and the secondary language. If a student is tested only in his or her primary language, information about knowledge that might have been stored in the secondary language would not be evaluated.

6. **INFORMED SELECTION OF A TEST BATTERY** — Testing cognitive development for students with LEP should include both formal and informal approaches. Careful consideration should be given to using instruments and methods of assessment that do not contain inappropriate norms or culturally biased tasks.

7. **CAREFUL TEST INTERPRETATION** — Be aware of linguistic and cultural differences when interpreting the assessment results for students with LEP. Unfortunately, linguistic and cultural differences are sometimes ignored during staffings because of lower expectations or prejudice.

From "Assessment of Cognitive Ability," by W. H. Holtzman and C. Y. Wilkinson. In *Limiting Bias in the Assessment of Bilingual Students*, edited by E. V. Hamayan and J. S. Damico, 1991, 248–280. Austin, TX: Pro-Ed. Used by permission.

---

to more specific cautions on assessment procedures. To account for issues of cultural difference as well as other concerns that may arise, the following principles, adapted from Grossman (1993), Turnbull and Wheat (1983), Luckasson et al. (1992), Franklin (1992), and Harry (1992), provide governing procedures:

FURTHER READING

For more information on the role of parents in the education of children with special needs, read issues of *Exceptional Parent* magazine.

- The assessment process should be initiated only when sufficient cause is documented.
- Parents must consent to the assessment, and they have the right to participate in and appeal any determinations made and any program decisions that follow from assessment.
- Assessments are to be undertaken only by fully qualified professionals.

- Assessment procedures must be adjusted to account for specific disabilities in hearing, vision, health, or motor impairment.
- Assessments should be modified to accommodate individuals whose culture or language differs from the population upon whom the instruments were standardized.
- Conclusions and recommendations should be made on the basis of multiple sources of data, including input from people directly acquainted with the person (e.g., parents) and direct observations of the student.
- Periodic reassessments must be made (at least every three years) to re-evaluate previous judgments and to consider necessary programming changes.

As Polloway and Jones-Wilson (1992) note, the cautions that must be considered in assessment can generally be summarized in one key point: The express purpose of undertaking assessment is to provide information that will lead to effective programming. Thus, the utility of the results is measured by how closely they ultimately relate to effective instruction.

Role of the Classroom Teacher

The preceding discussion has outlined the assessment process related to special education. Although much of that information is critical to all professionals who evaluate students with disabilities, this question remains: Which concerns specifically apply to the classroom teacher? The following list suggests ways in which the general education professional can take an active role in the assessment process.

1. Ask questions about the assessment process. Special education teachers and school psychologists should be committed to clarifying the nature of the assessments used and the interpretation of the results.
2. Seek help as needed in conveying information to parents. Special education teachers may offer you needed support during a conference.
3. Provide input. Formal test data should not be allowed to contradict observations in the classroom about a student's ability, achievement, and learning patterns. However, when formal tests indicate higher abilities than seen in the classroom, be willing to re-evaluate your own views of the student. A valid diagnostic picture should bring together multiple sources of data.
4. Observe assessment procedures. If time and facilities (e.g., a one-way mirror) permit, you will find that observing can be educational and can enhance your ability to take part in decision making.
5. Consider issues of possible bias. Since formal assessments are often administered by an individual relatively unknown to the child (e.g., a psychologist), inadvertent bias factors between examiner and examinee may be more likely to creep into the results. Work with other staff to ensure an unbiased process.
6. Avoid viewing assessment as a means of confirming a set of observations or conclusions about a student's difficulties. Assessment is exploratory and may not lead to expected results. Too often, after a student is judged ineligible for special services, various parties feel resentment toward the assessment process. Keep in mind that the purpose is to elicit useful information to help the student, not to arrive at a foregone decision about eligibility that may please the student, parent, or teacher.

CONSIDER THIS
Do you feel that the role of the classroom teacher in the assessment process is realistic? In what areas do you feel comfortable participating? In what areas are you uncomfortable?

TEACHING TIP
When the results of standardized tests differ significantly from your observations of and experiences with a child, consult the examiner. Provide samples of the student's work or report your observations. Additional assessment may be necessary.

INDIVIDUALIZED EDUCATION PROGRAMS (IEPS)

CONSIDER THIS

Should all students be required to have an individualized education program (IEP)? What would be the advantages, disadvantages, and general impact of such a requirement?

FURTHER READING

The development of the IEP should be a team process. For an example of how to do this at the middle school level, read "Middle School Teachers Planning for Students with Learning Disabilities" by S. Vaughn and J. S. Schumm, in *Remedial and Special Education*, published in 1994 in volume 15, pages 152–161.

The results of assessment should be translated into educational plans for instructional goals. The **individualized education program (IEP)**, sometimes referred to as the individualized program plan (IPP) or the individual student support plan (ISSP), is an annual description of services planned for students with disabilities. The IEP is a direct requirement under most provincial and territorial jurisdictions (Smith & Foster, 1996).

The intent of this requirement was to place the focus of intervention on individual needs. The IEP itself is ideally developed by the school team. After analyzing relevant diagnostic data, the team writes an IEP reflecting the student's educational needs. In some provinces and territories the IEP is required independent of any identification process. A team works to develop the IEP ideally, but this is not always possible. In some schools the regular teacher is largely responsible for writing the IEP; in others, the IEP is a collaborative effort of the team; and in others, special education personnel have that responsibility.

Although IEPs may serve varied purposes, Polloway and Patton (1993) list the three most prominent ones. First, IEPs can provide instructional direction. Well-written goals can help remedy an approach to instruction that consists of pulling together isolated or marginally related exercises. Second, IEPs can function as the basis of evaluation; annual goals then serve as standards against which to judge student progress and teacher effectiveness and efficiency. Third, IEPs can improve communication among members of the team. IEPs should facilitate planning and program implementation among staff members, teachers, and parents, and, as appropriate, between teachers and students.

A frequently discussed issue has been the functionality and value of the IEP. Unfortunately, the IEP is often developed simply to comply with the law,

Parental involvement in the development of the individualized education program is both a legal requirement as well as an important aspect in the design of appropriate school programs.

rather than to guide instruction (Smith & Simpson, 1989). Research has indicated the following:

- The needs of students are not always fully addressed by IEP goals (Epstein, Patton, Polloway, & Foley, 1992; Smith, 1990a; Smith, 1990b).
- Correspondence between the instruction that is provided and the student's needs, annual goals, and short-term objectives is low (Lynch & Beare, 1990).
- Goals for academic deficits are overemphasized, while goals in other areas, such as social skills, career development, and functional life skills, are largely overlooked (Epstein et al., 1992; Lynch & Beare, 1990).
- There may be an inadequate number of goals to address the severity of the problem (e.g., two or three goals for a student with severe behaviour or learning deficits) (Epstein et al., 1992; Smith, 1990a).

The generally pessimistic results of research on the validity and utility of IEPs have led many educators to question this instrument's contribution to the development of appropriate programs. Smith (1990b) suggests that the existing research indicates only minimal compliance with the process and thus a failure to achieve "specially designed instruction." If IEPs have only limited functionality, some action for either strengthening the guidelines or deleting the requirement must be entertained (Epstein et al., 1992). Despite data showing that the IEP has not successfully fulfilled its mission, little has been done to correct the situation (Smith, 1990b).

How then should teachers approach the task of formulating and using individualized education programs?

Writing and implementing an IEP, often considered a burdensome or irrelevant task, should instead serve as a catalyst for enhancing the education of the individual child (Turnbull, Strickland, & Hammer, 1978). For the IEP process to function well, teachers must move beyond seeing IEPs as mere paperwork and view them as instruments that help tailor special programs to address areas of instructional need. Teachers need to use the plan as a basis for teaching decisions. Only then can annual goals, which should serve as the basis for determining short-term objectives, be reflected in ongoing instructional planning. The discussion that follows illustrates the principles underlying the development of IEPs.

CONSIDER THIS
Considering the negative research about the use and value of IEPs, do you still see a purpose in their development? How would you improve the process?

Components of an IEP

There are eight required components in the IEP: (1) present level of performance, (2) annual instructional goals, (3) short-term objectives, (4) statement of special services to be provided, (5) description of integration into general education programs consistent with the move toward inclusion, (6) schedules for initiation, (7) evaluation of objectives, and (8) the signed consent and documentation.

Positive goals provide an appropriate direction for instruction. IEPs for students over the age of 16 (and occasionally at earlier ages) should also include the designation of needed transition services (i.e., an individualized transition plan). Once issues of types of services have been resolved, the three components that are central to instruction remain: levels of performance, annual goals, and short-term objectives. These are reflected in the sample IEP for the area of reading decoding shown in Figure 1.4. Teachers should familiarize themselves with the format for IEPs used by their boards.

FURTHER READING
For further information on developing IEPs, order a resource guide entitled *Individual Education Planning for Students with Special Needs*, published in 1996, by writing to the Special Programs Branch of the British Columbia Ministry of Education, P.O. Box 9165 Stn Prov. Govt., Victoria, BC V8W 9H4

AREA: Reading Decoding

ANNUAL GOAL: _____ will improve reading decoding scores to the _____ grade level.

Reading instruction will be designed to improve word recognition skills and strategies in the areas below. Given a variety of level-appropriate text, the student will apply decoding knowledge to complete tasks with 75–80 percent accuracy.

OBJECTIVES:

____ 1. Use Context Clues
  ____ Apply "skip/substitute" strategy
  ____ Predict based on logical meaning
  ____ Predict based on sentence structure
  ____ Predict based on prior knowledge
  ____ Confirm based on word features

____ 2. Use Phonetic Elements
  ____ Consonants   ____ Digraphs
  ____ Short vowels   ____ Vowel combinations
  ____ Long vowels   ____ Consonant variations
  ____ Blends   ____ Silent letters

____ 3. Use Word Analysis Strategies
  ____ Recognize and construct word families
  ____ Identify base words
  ____ Identify prefixes and suffixes
  ____ Apply syllabication rules

____ 4. Recognize High-Frequency Vocabulary
  ____ Dolch word list _____
  ____ Building sight vocabulary _____
  ____ Other: _____

____ 5. Use Information Sources
  ____ Locate words in dictionary/glossary
  ____ Use technology sources
  ____ Request help of others

____ 6. _____
      _____
      _____

EVALUATION:
Gates-MacGinitie
K-TEA
Ekwall
WIAT
Work Samples
Observation

Progress will be monitored every nine weeks and documented on progress report.

FIGURE 1.4
Sample IEP in Reading Decoding
Adapted from N. Dunavant, 1993, Homewood School System, Birmingham, AL.

Levels of performance provide a summary of assessment data on a student's current functioning, which serves as the basis for establishing annual goals. Therefore, the information should include data for each priority area in which instructional support is needed. Depending on the individual student, consideration might be given to reading, math, and other academic skills; written and oral communication skills; vocational talents and needs; social skills; behavioural patterns; self-help skills; or motor skills.

Performance levels can be provided in various forms, such as formal and informal assessment data, behavioural descriptions, and specific abilities delineated by checklists or skill sequences. Functional summary statements of an individual's strengths and weaknesses draw on information from a variety of sources rather than relying on a single one. Test scores in math, for example, might be combined with a description of how the child performed on a curriculum-based measure such as a computational checklist. In general, the phrasing used to define levels of performance should be positive, describing things the child can do. Consider the following statements.

The student can identify 50 percent of times table facts.

The student does not know half of the facts.

The same information is conveyed by the two statements, but the first demonstrates a more positive approach. Appropriately written performance levels provide a broad range of data in order to help generate relevant and appropriate annual goals.

The second, and central, IEP instructional component is annual goals. Each student's goals should address unique needs and abilities. Since predicting the precise amount of progress a student will make in a year is impossible, goals should be reasonable projections of what the student will accomplish. To develop realistic expectations, teachers can consider a number of variables, including the chronological age of the child, the expected rate of learning, and past and current learning profiles.

Annual goals should be measurable, positive, student-oriented, and relevant (Polloway & Patton, 1993). Measurable goals provide a basis for evaluation. Statements should use terms that denote action and can therefore be operationally defined, for example, *pronounce* and *write*. Vague, general language (e.g., know, understand) confounds evaluation and observer agreement. Positive goals provide an appropriate direction for instruction. Avoiding negative goals creates an atmosphere that is helpful in communicating with parents as well as in charting student progress. When goals are oriented to the student, with the development of skills as the intent, the measure of effectiveness becomes what is learned, rather than what is taught. Finally, goals must be relevant to the individual's needs. As noted earlier, research indicates that goals on IEPs frequently do not meet this criterion.

Annual goals should subsequently be broken down into short-term objectives, given in a logical and sequential series to provide a general plan for instruction. The objectives should move a student from the current level of performance through a sequence of objectives toward the relevant annual goal.

Short-term objectives can be derived only after annual goals are written. They should be based on a task analysis process; skill sequences and checklists can be used to divide an annual goal into components that can be shaped into precise objectives. Each broad goal will generate a cluster of objectives. The four criteria applied to annual goals can also apply to short-term objectives. Since objectives are narrower in focus, an objective's measurability should be enhanced with a criterion for mastery. Mastery at 80 percent or above is a commonly used criterion.

CONSIDER THIS

The teacher who developed the IEP in Figure 1.4 made a list of important skills in reading decoding. She could then check off the skills already mastered by the student and circle the areas targeted for this year's goals. What is your opinion of this method of designing an IEP?

FURTHER READING

The use of a computer-generated IEP is still controversial. To explore this issue further, read *Special Education Technology: Classroom Applications* by R. B. Lewis, published in 1993 by Brooks.

TEACHING TIP

As a general education teacher, you should be invited to participate in the IEP meeting of any child in your class. If you were not present, ask the special education teacher for a copy of the student's IEP, including the summary on the child's strengths, weaknesses, and goals, to incorporate into your daily planning.

Numerous computer software programs provide sequenced goal-objective clusters. Although such programs reduce paperwork and time, teachers must be careful to ensure that a student's curriculum and IEP remain consistent with individual needs.

Role of the Classroom Teacher

Although IEPs are supposed to be jointly developed by all those involved in the student's educational program, the task has often fallen to special education teachers. Some abuses of the system have been common. Instances in which general education classroom teachers must ask if they are "allowed to see the IEP," and parents are directed to copy out the IEP so they "would be involved in its 'writing'" (Turnbull & Turnbull, 1986) have been too frequent.

Ideally, the classroom teacher should take part in the IEP meeting. If this is not possible, a different, more informal means of teacher input should be developed; otherwise, the document may not reflect the student's needs in the inclusive classroom. Furthermore, the IEP itself should be readily available as a reference tool throughout the year. In particular, the teacher should keep the goal and objective clusters at hand so that the IEP can influence instructional programs.

FIGURE 1.5
IEP for Student with Learning Disability in the General Education Classroom
From N. Dunavant, 1993, Homewood School System, Birmingham, AL.

Student Name _____ _____ Year _____ Page _____

Area: General Classroom Placement

Annual Goal: _____ will maintain average or above-average grades in all general _____
grade academic classes.

Objectives:

1. _____ will participate in general class activities 5 of 5 days per week.

2. _____ will complete general class assignments on time 5 of 5 days per week.

3. _____ will complete homework assignments 4 of 5 days per week.

4. _____ will average 70 percent or higher on tests taken in the general academic classes.

5. _____ will self-evaluate progress by meeting with a resource teacher a minimum of once per grading period.

Type of Evaluation:

Projected Check Date _____

Date/Degree of Mastery _____

Progress will be monitored every nine weeks, and the report card will document the meeting of objectives.

Note: This student _____ does/ _____ does not require classroom modifications.

An IEP's annual goals and short-term objectives ultimately should be reflected in instructional plans in the classroom. But short-term objectives are not intended to be used as weekly, let alone daily, plans. Teachers should refer to the document periodically to ensure that instruction is consistent with the student's long-term needs. When significant variance is noted, it may become the basis for a correction in instruction or perhaps a rationale for a change in the goals or objectives of the IEP. Figure 1.5 shows a sample IEP.

In concluding their discussion on IEPs, Epstein et al. (1992) counsel teachers not to lose sight of the spirit of individualization that should guide the IEP process. Teachers need to view the documents not just as a process of legal compliance, but rather as tools for meeting students' individual needs. Unless guided by the rationale and spirit that informed the original development of the IEP concept, the process can degenerate into a mere bookkeeping activity. Instead, well-thought-out IEPs should form the foundation for individually designed educational programs for students with disabilities.

CONSIDER THIS

Do you think the IEP in Figure 1.5 is adequate for a student in a totally inclusive setting? What safeguards does it provide to ensure success?

TEACHING TIP

The IEP is a plan, not a contract. If teachers make good faith efforts to implement IEPs, they cannot be held responsible for lack of progress. Ongoing communication with the IEP team is critical, and a revision of the IEP may be necessary.

SUMMARY

- As recently as the 1960s students with disabilities were not provided services in the regular schools.

- In the United States the passage of the Rehabilitation Act, Section 504, and PL 94–142, which later became the Individuals with Disabilities Education Act (IDEA), ensured that individuals with disabilities were included in regular schools and classrooms.

- In Canada, the Charter of Rights and Freedoms, which is part of our Constitution, guarantees the rights of all people, including those with disabilities.

- Canada is the only country in the world that has the rights of individuals with disabilities included in the Constitution.

- Education is the responsibility of the provinces and territories.

- All provinces and territories must adhere to the Charter of Rights and Freedoms and not discriminate on the basis of mental or physical disability.

- All provinces and territories are committed in principle to inclusive education.

- Services for students with disabilities have evolved significantly over the past 20 years.

- Current services for students with disabilities focus on inclusion—including students in general education classrooms as much as possible.

- Today's student population is very diverse and students with a variety of disabilities are part of it.

- A sizeable percentage of students are at risk of developing problems, present learning or behaviour problems, or may be classified as having a disability.

- The largest group of students with special needs in the public school system consists of those formally classified as having disabilities.

- Although recognized categories of disabilities exist, many students do not fit neatly into a specific category.

- Students that are at risk of developing problems, and those considered gifted and talented, also require special attention from school personnel.

- Assessment goes beyond testing, encompassing a broader range of methods that help define a student's strengths and problems. It can lead to the development of educational interventions.

- Formal assessment is based on the administration of commercial instruments, typically for survey or diagnostic purposes.

- Informal assessment includes a variety of tools that can enhance a teacher's knowledge of students' learning needs.

- Curriculum-based measures are tied to the class curriculum and assess a student within this context.

- Ecological assessment places the evaluative data within the context of a student's environment.

- The control of bias in assessment is not only essential to accurate and fair evaluation, but also a legal requirement.

- Classroom teachers may not administer formal assessments, but they contribute in important ways to any assessment process and should be informed about the process.

RESOURCES

Alberta Education, Special Education Branch. (1995). *Awareness Series*. Edmonton, AB.

This series of 15 information brochures helps teachers understand, recognize, and plan for children with a variety of exceptionalities. Examples are Tourette's syndrome, fetal alcohol syndrome, asthma, and visual impairments.

WEBLINKS

Child and Family Studies Program
www.asri.edu/cfsp//
For a Web site that provides an extensive list of all exceptionalities and associations centred on those exceptionalities, visit the Child and Family Studies Program Disability/Exceptionality Web Resource Library Web site, a project that is funded by the U.S. Department of Education, Office of Special Education, through Allegheny University Health Sciences. This site provides an extensive list of exceptionalities and related Weblinks.

Council for Exceptional Children
www.cec.sped.org/
This Web site, which provides information about a variety of exceptionalities, is an excellent starting point for all teachers working with children with exceptionalities or in a diverse classroom.

The Disability Resource Monthly WebWatcher
www.abilityinfo.com/
This site, self-described as "a website for students that are studying in the field of disability, as well as professionals working within it," is a resource centre providing information on other links, news, books, contacts, associations, and forums related to disability. The WebWatcher is a subject guide to all the resources related to disabilities that are available on the Internet. Accessed by alphabetical listing, it is updated monthly and provides relevant sites by disability.

The Special Education Yahoo Subdirectory
dir.yahoo.com/Education/Special_Education/
Many sites related to special education are listed in this directory. Although the majority of sites are American in origin, the material is highly relevant for all special education.

Ability OnLine
www/ablelink.org/public/default/htm
A number of contributors to Ability Network's Young A-Net are members of Ability OnLine—an electronic mail system that connects young people with disabilities or chronic illness to peers and mentors, both disabled and nondisabled. Ability OnLine's introduc-

tion notes: "This easy-to-use network gives 'wings' to thousands of children and adolescents by removing the social barriers that can come with having a disability and illness, and by providing opportunities to form friendships, build self-confidence, exchange information, and share hope and encouragement through email messages." A listing of information for different disabilities also appears here.

Ability Network: Canada's Cross Disability Magazine
www.ability.ns.ca/
Ability Network magazine, originating in Nova Scotia, is an excellent resource for anyone working with individuals with disabilities and for anyone who has disabilities. It should be available in the classroom or library of every school. It improves students' understanding of disabilities while introducing them to positive role models of children, adolescents, and adults with disabilities. There is a special kids' section too. The site also provides some excellent related links.

The Disabilities, Society and Culture, Yahoo Subdirectory
dir.yahoo.com/Society_and_Culture/Disabilities/
Recommended by Canada's Ability Network magazine, this directory of sites related to society and culture of disabilities covers a huge range of issues pertinent to disabilities. For example, some of the directories are relevant to independent living (44 Web sites), education (51 Web sites), children (31 Web sites), parent support, personal experiences, and specific disabilities (568 Web sites).

Instructor's Manual
headlines.yahoo.com/Full_Coverage/World/Disabilities_and_the_Disabled/
Instructor's Manual provides a summary of all recent news stories pertaining to individuals with disabilities. A quick browse on a regular basis will provide readers, especially professors, with the most current issues in the field and good material for discussion in class.

CHAPTER TWO

- To describe the different service delivery models used in meeting the needs of students with special needs

- To describe the advantages and disadvantages of the different service delivery models

- To describe the role of special education and regular classroom teachers in the different service delivery models

- To describe methods that enhance the inclusion of students with disabilities

- To delineate five critical dimensions of inclusive classrooms

- To describe the role of classroom management, curricular options, and accommodative practices in inclusive classrooms

- To discuss the range of personnel supports in inclusive classrooms

- To explain how to create and maintain successful inclusive classrooms

- To describe different methods of maintaining inclusive programs after they are initiated

Designing Inclusive Classrooms

There are two Grade 3 classrooms at the Walker Elementary School, which has an inclusive service model for students with disabilities. Both classrooms include students with disabilities. Both classroom teachers may draw upon similar support services. But the classroom environments vary greatly—as does the success of the students with disabilities.

Before being assigned to a Grade 3 classroom two years ago, Ms. Gnoinski was a special education teacher. She taught students with learning disabilities and mild intellectual disabilities in a resource room. When the school moved to an inclusive education model, she asked for a general classroom since she was also certified as an elementary teacher. Ms. Gnoinski's philosophy is that all students belong and all are capable of success. She uses many cooperative learning activities, arranges social activities for all of her students, and welcomes support services from special education personnel. The students with disabilities in her classroom appear to be doing well.

Across the hall is Mrs. Baker's classroom. Mrs. Baker, who has taught for 25 years, uses "tried and true" methods. Her students sit in neat rows and she expects them to produce neat work on time. Mrs. Baker, unsure about the inclusive education model, does not understand why special education teachers do not teach their students in the special education room—this method worked well for many years. She does not welcome so-called specialists coming into her class, giving her advice about how to teach. The students with disabilities in her classroom are falling behind. Many also have behaviour problems. Some of these students need extra time, and with the distractions that some of their behaviours cause, Mrs. Baker wants to return to the old special education pullout model.

1. What are some basic differences between the two teachers' approaches to teaching children?

2. How can inclusion work when general classroom teachers resist adopting it?

3. How would Ms. Gnoinski feel if the principal began placing all of the students with disabilities in her classroom to avoid placing them with Mrs. Baker?

INTRODUCTION

The setting in which students with disabilities should receive educational and related services is a much discussed, much debated topic. The issue has "received more attention, undergone more modifications, and generated even more controversy than have decisions about how or what these students are taught" (Jenkins & Heinen, 1989, p. 516). The setting affects those who provide those services and the collaborations required to provide them (Smith, Finn, & Dowdy, 1993).

Currently, the majority of all students with disabilities spend a substantial portion of each school day in general education classrooms, where they are taught by general education classroom teachers (Schnailberg, 1994). For at least a portion of each school day, they can mix with their peers. Yet, there are still many students with disabilities who receive most or all of their education in separate, special education settings.

While still raging, the debate about where students should be educated has shifted in favour of more inclusion, which can be implemented in many different ways. Students can be placed in general education classrooms for most of the school day and be "pulled out" periodically for instruction in resource settings by special education teachers. Or, they can be placed full time in general education classrooms, a model commonly referred to as full inclusion. In the latter case, special education teachers may go into general education classrooms and work with students who are experiencing difficulties; they may also work directly with classroom teachers to develop and implement methods and materials that will meet the needs of many students. Schools use the model that best suits their needs. Full inclusion does not occur often. Most proponents of inclusion believe that pulling students out briefly for specific services is appropriate.

CONSIDER THIS

Think about the services that students with disabilities had when you were in school. Did you make contact and interact much with students with disabilities? Why or why not?

FURTHER READING

Several articles related to inclusion of students with special needs can be found in the special December 1994/January 1995 issue of *Educational Leadership*.

PROGRAMS IN WHICH STUDENTS RECEIVE INTERVENTION IN SPECIAL EDUCATION SETTINGS

CONSIDER THIS

What kinds of problems are created when students with disabilities enter and leave general education classrooms over the course of the day? How can teachers deal with these problems?

Traditionally, students with disabilities received their educational programs in either self-contained special classes or resource rooms. Serving students with disabilities in special programs was based on the presumption that general educators did not have the skills necessary to meet the needs of all students representing different learning needs (Shanker, 1994–1995). The result was the removal of students from the general education environment and an education provided by specialists trained specifically to meet their problems.

The Special Education Classroom Approach

In this approach, students receive the majority of their educational program from a special education teacher in a special education classroom. Teachers in

Children with disabilities were often educated in isolated, self-contained classes between 1950 and 1970.

such classrooms are specifically trained to serve students with intellectual disabilities, learning disabilities, or some other specific disability.

Self-contained special education classes were the preferred and dominant service model between 1950 and 1970 (Idol, 1983; Podemski et al., 1995; Smith, 1990; Smith et al., 1986). Special education teachers were trained to teach students with disabilities, but usually only students with one kind of disability, in all subject areas. The primary focus was on a functional curriculum. Students placed in self-contained special education classrooms rarely interacted with their nondisabled peers, often even eating lunch alone. Likewise, the special education teacher interacted very little with nondisabled students or classroom teachers.

Many general education teachers liked the self-contained special class model because they did not have to deal with students who differed from their view of "typical" children. The role of classroom teachers in the self-contained model was extremely limited. Their primary role was to refer students to the special education program, but they rarely had to instruct them. Referrals primarily occurred in lower elementary grades, where the majority of students with disabilities are identified.

The movement away from special class programs has not been without dissent. Advocates for special classes have noted several problems with inclusion. Arguing against including all students with disabilities in general education classes, Fuchs and Fuchs (1994–1995) note that separate settings have several advantages:

- Education is provided by well-trained special educators.
- Education is selected from a variety of instructional methods, curriculums, and motivational strategies.
- The system monitors student growth and progress.

Regardless of these advantages, the self-contained model has had many critics. Special classes, which segregate students with disabilities from their

CONSIDER THIS
Often, parents of students with intellectual disabilities are more supportive of inclusion than parents of students with less severe disabilities. Why do you think this is the case?

CROSS-REFERENCE
Read Chapter 5 to see how modelling appropriate behaviours can have an impact on students with serious emotional disturbances.

FURTHER READING
For an extensive discussion on normalization, read one of the early articles on European approaches and innovations in serving the handicapped, written by K. D. Juul and published in *Exceptional Children*, volume 44, in 1978.

nondisabled age peers, cannot be considered a "normal" school placement and were therefore criticized by adherents to the normalization philosophy of the 1970s. One way to implement the normalization philosophy was through inclusion, which resulted in the widespread reduction of special classes.

One final reason for the decline of the self-contained special class model was a growing awareness of the diversity of students with disabilities. Although the special class was the predominant model, the majority of students with disabilities served in special education were those with mild intellectual disabilities. As exceptional populations, such as students with learning disabilities or emotional problems, became recognized, the number of students needing special education grew significantly. The feasibility of serving all of these students in isolated special classes became less attractive. On the other hand, including these students in general classrooms would benefit all of them (Wang, Reynolds, & Walberg, 1994–1995).

The Resource Room Model

The primary service delivery option used for most students with disabilities (except for those with speech impairments) is the resource room model. The **resource room** is a special education classroom. However, unlike the self-contained special class, students go to the resource room only for special instruction. Students who are served by the resource room model spend part of each school day with their nondisabled, chronological age peers and attend resource rooms for special assistance in deficit areas (Smith et al., 1993). Although all of Canada is committed to the inclusion of students with exceptionalities in the regular classroom, the use of the resource room is still prevalent across the country (Schwean, Saklofske, Shatz, & Falk, 1996; Smith-Myles & Simpson, 1992).

ADVANTAGES OF THE RESOURCE ROOM MODEL

Several obvious advantages make the resource room model preferable to the self-contained, special class. Most important, students with disabilities have an opportunity to interact with their chronological age peers (York, Vandercook, MacDonald, Heise-Neff, & Caughey, 1992). In the special class model, students are isolated from these peers. This difference is extremely important because students tend to see other students as models. Therefore, students who interact only with other students who have exceptionalities may not see more appropriate role models. This lack can result in development of undesirable behaviours and poor study habits. Opportunities for social interactions are enhanced in the resource room model.

The integration of students with disabilities through the resource room model, which became very popular during the early 1980s, can also have a positive impact on nondisabled students. Students in general education classrooms develop a more positive opinion of students with disabilities placed in their classes than they do of students with disabilities who are placed in full-time special classes (Staub & Peck, 1994–1995; York et al., 1992). In a study that investigated the outcomes of integrating students with severe disabilities in general education classes in a junior high school, nearly 90 percent of the nondisabled students thought that the integration should be continued (York et al., 1992).

Another important advantage of the resource room model is that students with disabilities can receive instruction from several teachers. In self-contained special class settings, only special education teachers provide instruction. Students miss the advantage of working with different teachers with diverse expertise. Although this reality may not matter as much at the elementary school level, where most instruction focuses on basic skill development, as students get older and are enrolled in content classes, they need the opportunity to be taught by teachers who are experts in particular content areas.

In the resource room, students with disabilities receive intensive instruction in areas in which they are having difficulties; in general education classrooms, they take part in socialization activities and gain instruction in specific subject areas. The resource room model enables students to receive instruction in basic skills areas twice: in the general education room with their chronological age peers and in the resource room in a one-on-one or small group setting (Rich & Ross, 1989).

DISADVANTAGES OF THE RESOURCE ROOM MODEL

Despite the numerous advantages of the resource room model, this approach does not offer the ultimate answer to the complex question of how to place all students with disabilities in appropriate educational settings (Rich & Ross, 1991). Identifying students as needing special education and requiring them to leave the general education classroom, even for only part of the day, can be detrimental. Students resent being excluded from class activities and feel singled out as being different. Guterman (1995) found these concerns to be the "unifying element" among students interviewed about their special education placement.

ROLE OF SPECIAL EDUCATION PERSONNEL

In the resource room model, special education personnel collaborate with classroom teachers to deliver appropriate programs to students with disabilities. Resource room teachers cannot focus on their students only when they are in the special education classroom. They need to collaborate closely with the classroom teacher to ensure that students receiving instruction in both the special education room and general education classroom are not becoming confused by contradictory methods, assignments, curricula, and so on. The special education teacher should take the lead in opening up lines of communication and in facilitating collaborative efforts.

ROLE OF THE CLASSROOM TEACHER

Unlike the special class model, the resource room model requires that classroom teachers play numerous roles related to students with disabilities. One primary role is referral. The majority of students with mild disabilities and other special needs are referred for services by classroom teachers. General education teachers are often the first to recognize that a student is experiencing problems that could require special education services. Classroom teachers also implement interventions that can ameliorate problems and prevent unnecessary referrals. As a result, fewer students will be labelled with a disability and served in special education programs.

PROGRAMS IN WHICH STUDENTS RECEIVE EDUCATION IN GENERAL EDUCATION CLASSROOMS

FURTHER READING

Read several 1980s articles on the move to integration. Here are a few suggestions: "Effective Special Education in Regular Classes," by M. C. Wang and J. W. Birch, published in *Exceptional Children*, volume 52, 1984; and "Integration versus Cooperation: A Commentary," by Stainback and Stainback, published in *Exceptional Children*, volume 54, 1987.

CONSIDER THIS

How can terms such as *mainstreaming, inclusion,* and *full inclusion* complicate the planning of services for students with disabilities? What could be done to clarify terminology?

FURTHER READING

For more information on defining inclusion, read "The Philosophy and Status of Inclusion," by E. J. Erwin, published in *The Lighthouse* in 1993.

Just as full-time special class placement of students with disabilities received criticism in the early 1970s, resource room programs are now being criticized. Since the mid-1980s there has been a call for dismantling the **dual education system** (general and special) in favour of a unified system dedicated to meeting the needs of all students. Rather than spend much time and effort identifying students with special problems and determining if they are eligible for special education services, proponents of a single education system call for providing appropriate services to all students.

Inclusion Model

The model for more fully including students with special needs in general education programs, referred to as the inclusion model, has been defined in many different ways. Unfortunately, the term *full inclusion* was originally used, suggesting that all students with disabilities, regardless of the severity of the disability, be included full time in general education classes (Fuchs & Fuchs, 1994–1995). This approach was advocated by several professional and advocacy groups, most notably the Canadian Association for Community Living (CACL), The Association for the Severely Handicapped (TASH), and Arc (formerly the Association for Retarded Citizens). Their encouragement of full-time general education classroom placement for all students provoked much criticism and skepticism.

More recently, the term **inclusion** has signified the movement to include students with disabilities in general classrooms, with the provision that, where necessary, some services to students will be provided outside the general education classroom. Proponents suggest that all students with disabilities belong with their nondisabled peers. Smith (1995) states that inclusion means "(1) that every child should be included in a regular classroom to the optimum extent appropriate to the needs of that child while preserving the placements and services that special education can provide; (2) that the education of children with disabilities is viewed by all educators as a shared responsibility and privilege; (3) that there is a commitment to include students with disabilities in every facet of school; (4) that every child must have a place and be welcome in a regular classroom" (p. 1). Rogers (1993) notes that supporters of inclusion use the term "to refer to the commitment to educate each child, to the maximum extent appropriate, in the school and classroom he or she would otherwise attend" (p. 1). When support services are required, these services should be provided in the general education classroom setting as much as possible. In an inclusive model, students attend the schools and classes they would if they did not have disabilities (*Winners All: A Call for Inclusive Schools*, 1992).

The concept of inclusion has a values orientation, "based on the premise that all individuals with disabilities have a right to be included in naturally occurring settings and activities with their neighborhood peers, siblings, and friends" (Erwin, 1993, p. 1). Inclusion, therefore, means more than simply placing students with disabilities in general education classrooms. It means giving students the opportunity to participate, as members, in all school activities and affirming their right to such opportunity.

As early as 1984, Stainback and Stainback suggested the following reasons for supporting inclusion:

1. *"Special" and "regular" students:* The current dual system of general and special education assumes that there are two distinct types of children: special and regular. In reality, all students display a variety of characteristics along a continuum; there is no way to divide all students into two groups. All students exhibit strengths and weaknesses that make them unique.

2. *Individualized services:* There is no single group of children who can benefit from individualized educational programming. The dual system of special and general education adopts the notion that students with disabilities require individual education, whereas other students do not. In fact, some research suggests that students with diverse characteristics do not benefit from different instructional techniques. If future research concludes that individualized instruction does result in improved education, then *all* students should be afforded the opportunity.

3. *Instructional methods:* Contrary to many beliefs, there are not special teaching methods that are effective only with students who have disabilities. Good, basic instructional programs can effectively serve all students.

4. *Classification:* A dual system of education, general and special, requires extensive, time-consuming, and costly efforts to determine which system students fit into. Classification doesn't end there. Once students are seen as eligible for special education, their disability category must be determined. Unfortunately, classification is often unreliable. It can result in stigma and fail to lead to better educational programming.

5. *Competition and duplication:* Perpetuating the general and special systems has resulted in competition between professionals, as well as duplication of

There are numerous advantages to including students with disabilities in general classrooms.

effort. If our education system is to improve, all educators must work together, sharing expertise, effective methods, and educational goals.

6. *Eligibility by category:* In the dual system, extensive effort is spent on determining who is eligible for special services. The programs for students are often based not on their specific needs, but on which category they are placed in. Even curricular options are often restricted on the basis of clinical classification. For example, students classified as having intellectual disabilities may be placed in work-study programs without being able to take part in regular vocational education.

7. *"Deviant" label:* A major negative result of the dual system is the requirement to place "deviant" labels on students. In order to determine that a student is eligible for the special system, a clinical label must be attached to him or her. Few, if any, would argue that clinical labels draw positive reactions. The routine reaction to the labels "intellectual disabilities," "emotionally disturbed," and even "learning disabled" is an assumption that the student cannot function as well as other students.

Although proponents of inclusion have articulated numerous reasons to support the model, many oppose its implementation (Fuchs & Fuchs, 1994–1995). Several professional and advocacy groups support the continued use of a **continuum of services** model. These include the Council for Exceptional Children (CEC), the Canadian National Institute for the Blind (CNIB), the Family Network for Deaf Children, the Learning Disabilities Association of Canada (LDAC), and the Council for Children with Behavior Disorders. The nearby Inclusion Strategies feature provides the CEC position statement on inclusion.

ADVANTAGES OF INCLUSION

Numerous studies have documented some of the advantages of inclusion. In the United States, the National Center on Educational Restructuring and Inclusion (NCERI) conducted a study of inclusion in school districts implementing the model. The study identified 891 schools in 267 districts implementing an inclusive educational model. All 50 states were represented in the study. Findings included the following:

1. The number of school districts reporting inclusive educational programs has increased significantly since 1994.
2. Outcomes for students in inclusive educational programs, both general and special education, are positive.
3. Teachers participating in inclusive educational programs report positive professional outcomes for themselves.
4. Students with a wider range of disabilities are in inclusive educational programs.
5. School restructuring efforts are having an impact on inclusive educational programs, and vice versa. (National Study on Inclusion, 1995, p. 1)

Several studies have concluded that inclusion results in specific benefits for both students with disabilities and those without. A key benefit is developing a better understanding and acceptance of other students (Giangreco, Dennis, Cloninger, Edelman, & Schattman, 1993; Peck, Carlson, & Helmstetter, 1992).

INCLUSION STRATEGIES

CEC Policy on Inclusive Schools and Community Settings

The Council for Exceptional Children (CEC) believes all children, youth, and young adults with disabilities are entitled to a free and appropriate education and/or services that lead to an adult life characterized by satisfying relations with others, independent living, productive engagement in the community, and participation in society at large. To achieve such outcomes, there must exist for all children, youth, and young adults a rich variety of early intervention, educational, and vocational program options and experiences. Access to these programs and experiences should be based on individual educational need and desired outcomes. Furthermore, students and their families or guardians, as members of the planning team, may recommend the placement, curriculum option, and the exit document to be pursued.

CEC believes that a continuum of services must be available for all children, youth, and young adults. CEC also believes that the concept of inclusion is a meaningful goal to be pursued in our schools and communities. In addition, CEC believes children, youth, and young adults with disabilities should be served whenever possible in general education classrooms in inclusive neighborhood schools and community settings. Such settings should be strengthened and supported by an infusion of specially trained personnel and other appropriate supportive practices according to the individual needs of the child.

POLICY IMPLICATIONS

Schools. In inclusive schools, the building administrator and staff, with assistance from the special education administration, should be primarily responsible for the education of children, youth, and young adults with disabilities. The administrator(s) and other school personnel must have available to them appropriate support and technical assistance to enable them to fulfill their responsibilities. Leaders in state/provincial and local governments must redefine rules and regulations as necessary, and grant school personnel greater authority to make decisions regarding curriculum, materials, instructional practice, and staffing patterns. In return for greater autonomy, the school administrator and staff should establish high standards for each child, youth, and young adult, and should be held accountable for his or her progress toward outcomes.

Communities. Inclusive schools must be located in inclusive communities; therefore, CEC invites all educators, other professionals, and family members to work together to create early intervention, educational, and vocational programs and experiences that are collegial, inclusive, and responsive to the diversity of children, youth, and young adults. Policy makers at the highest levels of state/provincial and local government, as well as school administration, also must support inclusion in the educational reforms they espouse. Further, the policy makers should fund programs in nutrition, early intervention, health care, parent education, and other social support programs that prepare all children, youth, and young adults to do well in school. There can be no meaningful school reform, nor inclusive schools, without funding of these key prerequisites. As important, there must be interagency agreements and collaboration with local government and business to help prepare students to assume a constructive role in an inclusive community.

Professional Development. And finally, state/provincial departments of education, local educational districts, and colleges and universities must provide high-quality preservice and continuing professional development experiences that prepare all general educators to work effectively with children, youth, and young adults representing a wide range of abilities and disabilities, experiences, cultural and linguistic backgrounds, attitudes, and expectations. Moreover, special educators should be trained with an emphasis on their roles in inclusive schools and community settings. They also must learn the importance of establishing ambitious goals for their students and of using appropriate means of monitoring the progress of children, youth, and young adults.

Adopted by the CEC Delegate Assembly, 1993, San Antonio, Texas.

From the Council for Exceptional Children, 1920 Association Drive, Reston, VA 22091. Used by permission.

FURTHER READING

For more information on the disadvantages of inclusion, read the articles by Fuchs and Fuchs and by Shanker in *Educational Leadership*, December 1994/January 1995. The articles were part of a special issue on inclusion.

CONSIDER THIS

How can some of the problems caused by inclusion be addressed to facilitate success in school for all students?

DISADVANTAGES OF INCLUSION

Just as there are many supporters of inclusion and reasons for its implementation, there are also professionals and parents who decry the movement. Among the reasons they oppose inclusion are the following:

1. General educators have not been involved sufficiently and are therefore unlikely to support the model.
2. General educators as well as special educators do not have the collaboration skills necessary to make inclusion successful.
3. Limited empirical data support the model. Therefore, full implementation should be put on hold until sound research supports the effort.
4. Full inclusion of students with disabilities in general education classrooms may take away from students without disabilities and lessen their quality of education.
5. Current funding, teacher training, and teacher certification are based on separate education systems.
6. Some students with disabilities do better when served in special education classes by special education teachers.

Although some of these criticisms may have merit, others have been discounted. For example, research indicates that the education of nondisabled students is not negatively affected by inclusion (National Study on Inclusion, 1995). Therefore, though the movement has its critics, research provides support for the idea that inclusion works for most students with exceptionalities.

ROLE OF SPECIAL EDUCATION PERSONNEL

In the inclusion model, special education personnel become much more integral to the broad educational efforts of the school. In the dual system, special education teachers provide instructional programming only to students identified as disabled and determined eligible for special education programs under provincial or territorial guidelines. In inclusive schools these teachers work with a variety of students, including those having difficulties but not identified specifically as having a disability. The special education teacher works much more closely with classroom teachers in the inclusion model.

ROLE OF THE CLASSROOM TEACHER

The role of the classroom teacher also changes dramatically. Instead of focusing primarily on identification and referral, and possibly providing some instructional services to students with disabilities, teachers in the inclusive school become fully responsible for all students, including those with identified disabilities. Special education support personnel are available to collaborate on educational programs for all students, but the primary responsibility is assumed by the classroom teacher.

METHODS THAT ENHANCE INCLUSION OF STUDENTS WITH DISABILITIES

Teachers must develop strategies to facilitate the successful inclusion of students with disabilities in general education classrooms. Neither classroom teachers nor special education teachers want students with disabilities simply "dumped" into general education classes (Banks, 1992), and the successful inclusion of students does not normally happen without assistance. Five essential features characterize successful inclusion of students with special needs (Webber, 1997). These are, as follows: (1) a sense of community and social acceptance, (2) appreciation of student diversity, (3) attention to curricular needs, (4) effective management and instruction, and (5) personnel support. When in place, these features make the general education classroom the best possible placement option. Each of them is discussed in the following sections of this chapter.

Sense of Community and Social Acceptance

In desirable inclusive settings, every student is valued and nurtured. Such settings promote a sense of community in which all members are seen as equal—all have the opportunity to contribute, and all contributions are respected. Deno, Foegen, Robinson, and Espin (1996) describe ideal school settings as "caring and nurturant places with a strong sense of community where all children and youth belong, where diversity is valued, and where the needs of all students are addressed" (p. 350).

Students with special needs will be truly included in their classroom communities only when they are appreciated by their teachers and socially accepted by their classmates. An understanding teacher meets students' instructional and curricular needs more effectively, and social acceptance among classmates contributes to students' self-perception of value. The presence of these two positives is equally critical to creating effective inclusive settings and responsible learning environments. It is imperative that we address the need for acceptance, belonging, and friendship (Schaffner & Buswell, 1996); Lang and Berberich (1995) suggest that inclusive classrooms should be characterized as settings where basic human needs are met. Figure 2.1 highlights critical needs that should be well addressed in an inclusive classroom community.

Teachers play a very critical role in creating a positive classroom environment. Three qualities are essential to establishing a successful inclusive setting (Schulz & Carpenter, 1995):

1. *Teacher attitude:* How does the teacher view students, especially those who are noticeably different in appearance, behaviour, or ability?
2. *Teacher expectations:* What educational and social outcomes does the teacher anticipate for students? Teachers who have high expectations for students are more likely to inspire better performance.
3. *Teacher competence:* What is the teacher's knowledge and skill in teaching students with special needs?

Teachers must have a positive attitude about students with special needs being in their classrooms. If they do not, other students will detect this and be less likely to accept the students. Teachers must also expect students with special needs to perform at a high level. Students often achieve at a level expected of them—if you expect less, you'll get less. Finally, teachers need to know how to meet the instructional needs of students with special needs. Teaching all students the same way will not effectively serve many students with special needs.

FURTHER READING

For more information on the ideal school setting, read "Facing the Realities of Inclusion for Students with Mild Disabilities," by S. L. Deno and colleagues, published in volume 30 of the *Journal of Special Education* in 1996 (pp. 345–357).

FURTHER READING

For more practical suggestions about how to include students with mild disabilities, read *Exceptions: A Handbook of Inclusion Activities for Teachers of Students at Grade 6–12* by Deborah Murphy et al. You can order this publication from the Learning Resources Distributing Centre in Edmonton, AB. (Phone: (403) 427-5775; Fax: (403) 422-9750 Web site: **www.lrdc. edc.gov.ab.ca/**)

FIGURE 2.1
The Basic Needs of
Children in a Learning
Environment

From *All Children Are Special:
Creating an Inclusive Classroom*
(p. 73), by G. Lang and C.
Berberich, 1995, York, ME:
Stenhouse Publishers. Used by
permission.

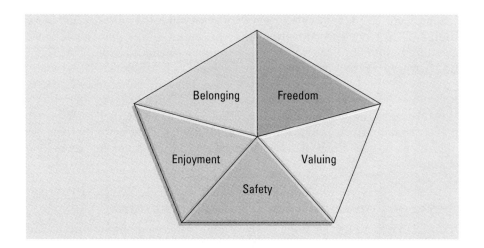

CONSIDER THIS
How likely is it that students with special needs will be successfully included if teachers leave peer acceptance of these students to chance? Why?

TEACHING TIP
When preparing a class for the inclusion of students with special needs, use a variety of techniques. Do not rely on only one method, such as a discussion or the showing of one film.

In addition to exemplifying these positive qualities, teachers must prepare students to interact with others whose physical characteristics, behaviours, or learning-related needs require special consideration. (Specific techniques for doing this will be presented later in the chapter.) To create desirable classroom communities, students in the classroom must be given information and direction to help them understand and value students who are different. Students must acquire competence in two areas to function well in inclusive settings (Schulz & Carpenter, 1995):

Knowledge: They need accurate information about specific differences that students possess and about the effects that these differences will have on the students with exceptionalities and on the whole class.

Peer interactions: They need to develop various informal peer interactions, which lead to peer support and bona fide friendships.

Though 100 percent success cannot be guaranteed in making inclusion work in every classroom, well-prepared students and capable, optimistic teachers can set the stage for a positive educational experience for each person in the class.

Appreciation of Student Diversity

FURTHER READING
For more information on the different types of diversity found in classrooms, read S. E. Schwartz and B. D. Karge's book, *Human Diversity: A Guide for Understanding* (2nd ed.), published by McGraw-Hill in 1996.

To maximize successful learning, a teacher needs to understand each individual in the classroom as well as possible. In addition to recognizing and responding to each student's educational needs, teachers must relate sensitively to the cultural, community, and family values that can have an impact on a student's educational experience. For instance, the nature of teacher-student interactions may be affected directly by certain cultural factors, or the type of home-school contact will be dictated by how the family wants to interact with the school.

Different types of diversity exist within classroom settings. It is important to recognize and celebrate each one. Schwartz and Karge (1996) have identified the following types of differences: racial and ethnic diversity; gender and sexual orientation; religious diversity; physical, learning, and intellectual differences; linguistic differences; and behaviour and personality diversity. Although the following chapters focus on areas of exceptionality, and to a lesser extent cultural diversity, teachers should consider the much broader range of individual variance.

Attention to Curricular Needs

Many discussions of inclusion lose track of an important consideration: what the student needs to be taught. If, for any reason, the individual curricular needs of a student are not being met, the educational placement must be re-examined. A student's learning and life needs should drive programmatic efforts and decisions (Smith & Hilton, 1994). Fortunately, curricular needs can usually be addressed within the context of the general educational classroom.

Curricular concerns take in two issues: (1) content that is meaningful to students in a current and future sense, and (2) approaches and materials that work best for them. Dealing with the first issue helps ensure that what students need to learn (i.e., knowledge and skills acquisition) is provided within the inclusive setting. The second issue involves choosing how to teach relevant content. Scruggs and Mastropieri (1994) found that the provision of appropriate curriculum appeared to be meaningfully associated with success in general education classes.

Effective Management and Instruction

Another essential component of successful inclusive settings is a set of classroom practices conducive to learning for students with a range of needs. There are four key elements to these practices: successful classroom management, effective instructional techniques, appropriate accommodative practices, and instructional flexibility.

CLASSROOM MANAGEMENT

Classrooms that encourage learning are characterized by sound organizational and management systems. Classroom management involves several factors that set the stage for the smooth delivery of instruction. Specific factors include physical management, procedural management, instructional management, and behaviour management. More is said about this topic in Chapter 5.

EFFECTIVE INSTRUCTION

An impressive body of literature validates the effectiveness of certain instructional practices (Brody & Good, 1986; Rosenshine & Stevens, 1986). Mastropieri and Scruggs (1993) have summarized key elements of effective instructional practice: daily review, specific techniques for presenting new information (see Figure 2.2), guided practice, independent practice, and formative evaluation. These concepts are addressed throughout the chapters of this book as they apply to children with various special needs. Chapters 12 and 13 specifically address instructional concerns in elementary and secondary classes, respectively.

ACCOMMODATIVE PRACTICES AND ASSISTIVE TECHNOLOGY

Some students will require special adaptations to the physical environment, the curriculum, the way instruction is provided, or the assignments given to them. Scruggs and Mastropieri (1994) note that instructional supports were a key variable in classrooms where inclusion was successful. Chapters 3 to 9 provide examples of disability-specific accommodations that might be needed.

CONSIDER THIS
If examples of good inclusive classrooms are unavailable in a school board/district, how can teachers find such examples to observe?

CROSS-REFERENCE
For more information on appropriate classroom management techniques for inclusive settings, see Chapter 5.

CONSIDER THIS
How can appropriate accommodative practices benefit all students, including those with special needs?

STRUCTURE		Provide overview and review new information as you proceed. Follow your objective carefully and be sure students understand the sequence and purpose of your presentation.
CLARITY		Avoid unnecessary digressions. Use clearly stated examples. Provide instances and non-instances of new concepts. Use simple, direct, clear language. Avoid vague references (e.g., *"a thing like this," "and so on," "you know"*).
REDUNDANCY		Students usually need to hear, see, and/or experience new concepts several times before they understand them well. Repetition allows new vocabulary or terminology to become more familiar, reinforces new learning as it proceeds, and allows students to practise and test their understanding by predicting what you will say when you are reinforcing previously mentioned concepts.
ENTHUSIASM		Students pay more attention, show more interest, apply themselves better, and learn more when the teacher is enthusiastic. The heightened stimulus arouses their curiosity more, and they will begin to model your attitude toward the subject.
APPROPRIATE PACE		Monitor students' understanding so that you proceed neither too swiftly nor too slowly through the content. If you move too slowly, you will bore them. If you move too fast, you will lose them.
MAXIMIZED ENGAGEMENT		Students learn best when they are directly engaged with the teacher, rather than passively listening. Ask lots of questions directly related to the lesson you are teaching. Ask direct questions about your presentation (e.g., *"What did we say was the major difference between monerans and protists?"*); ask application questions to test comprehension (e.g., *"Give me an example of an insulator that you can see in the classroom"*); and prompt reasoning to promote active thinking (e.g., *"We said that some dinosaurs had 20 rows of teeth. What might that tell us about those dinosaurs?"*). When students answer questions, acknowledge the correctness of response or quality of the thought, give corrective feedback on any part of any response that needs correction, and ask the question again later. Use student responses to guide your instructional delivery.

FIGURE 2.2
How to Present New Information: "SCREAM"

Adapted from A *Practical Guide for Teaching Science to Students with Special Needs in Inclusive Settings* (p. 14), by M. A. Mastropieri and T. E. Scruggs, 1993, Austin, TX: Pro-Ed.

The concept of supports within classrooms, a particularly critical one, refashions inclusion as "**supported education**" (Snell & Drake, 1994). Supports include accommodations and modifications to enhance learning and acceptance in the general education curriculum. **Accommodations** consist of changes in the manner in which students are taught. They include changes in instruction, assignments and homework, and testing. **Modifications**, on the other hand, generally refer to changes in policies that may affect students with disabilities. One example is altering the school curriculum or attendance policy. Whenever possible, accommodative supports should be designed so that they benefit not only students with special needs, but other students in the class as well (Stainback, Stainback, & Wehman, 1997). The idea has merit for three primary reasons. First, it provides support to other students who will find the accommodations helpful. Second, this approach can minimize overt attention to the fact that a certain student needs special adaptations. Third, it enhances the likelihood that teachers will see the specific strategy as feasible, desirable, helpful, and fair.

One support that can have a significant impact on the success of inclusion efforts is the use of **assistive technology**. Ranging from low-tech (e.g., optical devices) to high-tech (e.g., computer-based augmentative communication

TECHNOLOGY TODAY

Examples of Resources Available on the Internet

E-MAIL
Electronic mail allows you to have an address on the information highway. Within an instant you can send or receive messages to any number of the +30 million Internet users around the globe. E-mail can be sent or received despite the Internet service provider to which you are connected. A Compuserve user can just as easily communicate with a university mainframe user, a direct connect user, a BBS user, or an America Online user!

NEWSGROUPS
Newsgroups are essentially message boards. People read messages related to a myriad of subjects and are able to post messages about other people's messages on the Internet. It's kind of an international public forum—a large-scale, electronic town meeting. Everyone can have their say on any given topic and receive feedback on individual thoughts, opinions, and suggestions.

USENET
Usenet consists of a very large collection of newsgroups. Some are very academic and scholarly, others may be amusing and fun, while still others may be adult-oriented and sexually explicit. Users should keep in mind that the Internet is not monitored or policed. Some types of language and/or content expressed in some newsgroups may be considered offensive by some individuals.

MAILING LISTS
These lists are essentially the same as any newsgroup; however, messages are not posted generically. Messages are sent directly to your e-mail address.

WEB SITES
Visiting the Web gives users a break from text-only Net surfing. You can experience refreshing multimedia-based information. Information gleaned from various Web sites may contain pictures, graphics, animation, sound, or video information.

BBS SERVICE
Accessing the Bulletin Board Service entitles you to any/all of the information posted on the select theme of the BBS. The BBS theme is generally established by the SYSOP, or systems operator. A Sysop might be a university professor or a teenage hacker with a passion for mountain bikes. One element that has made the BBS service so alluring is the notion of live chat. Live chat is a form of e-mail; however, you are simultaneously exchanging text based on conversation person-to-person. Live chat lines might be established for academic purposes, entertainment purposes, or social purposes. Keep in mind that live chat is not policed or monitored, and individuals should be wary of divulging personal information online. Both children and adults should be warned of the dangers of live chat, as some criminal elements have met their victims as a result of live chat Internet introductions.

From *Quick Guide to the Internet* (pp. 14–15), by J. D. Rivard, 1997, Boston: Allyn & Bacon. Used by permission.

---

systems) applications, assistive technology can allow students with specific disabilities to participate fully, or even partially, in ongoing classroom activities. Moreover, as Woronov (1996) acknowledges, nondisabled students can benefit from assistive technology as well. The nearby Technology Today feature presents Internet resources that can support inclusion.

FLEXIBILITY
The ability to respond to unexpected and changing situations to support students with special needs is a key characteristic of responsible inclusive settings. As Schaffner and Buswell (1996) note, classroom teachers need to develop the capabilities that families have acquired to react successfully and spontaneously to challenges that arise on a day-to-day basis. Teachers cannot simply

plan certain activities to occur in specific ways. With a diverse group of students in an inclusive classroom, flexibility is critical. Handling behaviour problems, providing extra support during instruction, modifying assessment techniques, and orchestrating social interactions all require teachers to be flexible in their planning and practices.

Personnel Support

Some students with special needs will require personnel supports to allow them to benefit from placement in inclusive settings. These supports would be in addition to the instructional supports noted earlier. Staff who typically provide support to students in inclusive settings include special education teachers, para-educators (teacher aides), and related service professionals, such as speech and language pathologists, occupational and physical therapists, and audiologists. Equally important is administrative support for inclusion, as reflected by attitudes, policies, and practices at the district/board and building levels (Scruggs & Mastropieri, 1994).

FURTHER READING

For more information on collaboration among professionals, read Sharon Cramer's *Collaboration: A Successful Strategy for Special Education*, published by Allyn & Bacon in 1998.

These support service providers work within the inclusive setting in various ways, from indirect collaboration (i.e., working with the teacher outside of the classroom to plan for student needs) to direct collaboration (i.e., working directly with students within the classroom setting) (Bauwens & Hourcade, 1995). Means of providing indirect support to students include collaborative consultation, peer collaboration, and teacher assistance teams. The primary ways to provide direct support to students are cooperative teaching and one-to-one assistance of a more tutorial nature. Table 2.1 presents more detailed information about these approaches.

CONSIDER THIS

How could the use of para-educators be a detriment to the successful inclusion of students with special needs in a general education classroom?

The use of teacher aides to provide direct support to students with significant learning problems is occurring more commonly (Pickett & Gerlach, 1997). If their knowledge of working with students with disabilities is minimal, these para-educators must be trained and supervised carefully if they are to provide critical assistance to students in inclusive classrooms. The practice could have great potential as long as proper safeguards ensure that para-educators implement support services effectively.

TEACHING TIP

Plan to orchestrate opportunities for students with disabilities to act as full members of the classroom. Use methods such as peer support systems.

Establishing a **circle of friends** for students can assist the development of a peer support network. Such a network is particularly important for students who are different and new to a classroom situation. As Pearpoint, Forest, and O'Brien (1996) assert:

> In the absence of a natural circle of friends, educators can facilitate a circle process, which can be used to enlist the involvement and commitment of peers around an individual student. For a student who is not well connected or does not have an extensive network of friends, a circle of friends process can be useful. (p. 74)

The use of a circle of friends is further discussed in Chapter 6.

The five critical dimensions we have discussed are essential to making inclusive settings effective. Appropriate programming for students with disabilities should always be based on an "individual student's needs as determined by an interdisciplinary team and represented by the student's IEP" (Smith & Hilton, 1994, p. 8). Just as important, however, is the need to evaluate those

TABLE 2.1

Types of Collaborative Efforts

Approach	Nature of Contact with Student	Description
COLLABORATIVE CONSULTATION	indirect	General education teacher requests the services of the special education teacher (i.e., consultant) to help generate ideas for addressing an ongoing situation. The approach is interactive.
PEER COLLABORATION	indirect	Two general education teachers work together to identify effective solutions to classroom situations. The approach emphasizes the balance of the relationship.
TEACHER ASSISTANCE TEAMS	indirect	Teams provide support to general education teachers. Made up of core members plus the teacher seeking assistance, [such a team] emphasizes analyzing the problem situation and developing potential solutions.
COOPERATIVE TEACHING	direct	General and special education teachers work together in providing direct service to students. Employing joint planning and teaching, the approach emphasizes the joint responsibilities of instruction.

From *Cooperative Teaching: Rebuilding the Schoolhouse for All Students* (p. 74), by J. Bauwens and J. J. Hourcade, 1995, Austin, TX: Pro-Ed. Used by permission.

instructional settings on the basis of the five critical dimensions. Successful inclusion hinges on them.

Maintaining Effective Inclusive Classrooms

Setting up a responsible inclusive classroom does not guarantee that it will remain effective over time. Ensuring its continued success requires constant vigilance on the critical dimensions of inclusive settings and ongoing re-evaluation of standard operating procedures. Blenk (1995) describes an effective process of ongoing evaluation:

> On a daily basis, teaching colleagues should be observing inclusive procedures and educational techniques. These observations need to be shared among the teacher group to decide whether the practice achieved its intended outcomes, and if not, what changes could occur. Individual staff conferences and meetings, even if they are only two minutes long, need to happen on an ongoing basis to maintain communication in the teaching staff and to share experiences and impressions, sometimes at that moment! (p. 71)

A related method of dealing with ongoing issues is the use of problem-solving sessions (Roach, 1995). With this strategy, teachers meet and work

PERSONAL SPOTLIGHT

Master Classroom Teacher ROGER MORGAN

Secondary Math/Physics/Computer Science Teacher, Kincaid Central School, Kincaid, Saskatchewan

Roger Morgan teaches high school math, physics, and computer science, and coaches volleyball at Kincaid Central School in rural Saskatchewan. His class sizes range from 6 to 35 depending on the classes offered. Each grade in the school has traditionally averaged around 16 students. This situation has led many times to multiple grade/subject classrooms. A typical classroom may hold two different grades, with students taking one or two different classes concurrently. As a result, students, of various ages, with very different abilities and expectations are taking the same class.

Roger states: "Students with exceptional problems and skills are one part of the teaching job that it is vital to deal with. The misconception that students have is that treating them all fairly means treating them the same; if any teacher buys into that philosophy they are dooming the exceptional students. If you have a diabetic in the classroom and you hand out treats at Halloween, should you not have sugar-free candy for the diabetic? Fair is giving all students what they *need*, not giving all students the same thing! On a daily basis a teacher must have alternative strategies and assignments for students of various abilities. The greatest difficulty often is coming up with resources that allow you to meet all the different needs of the students. The greatest reward is that students are encouraged to achieve their potential, which, in essence, is the most important part of our job."

However, for Roger, in a small town with such diversity in his classrooms, how to provide a variety of individualized programs was a challenge. The answer came about during a set of parent-teacher meetings when a specific problem was brought forward by many parents. These parents reported that their older children, recent graduates, had seemed too dependent on the teacher during their high school years. Roger took these comments to heart and tried to create an environment that would allow his students to develop self-discipline, putting the responsibility for success on their shoulders while simultaneously individualizing the assignments.

Roger tells how he did this: "Students were given the complete outline of a unit before it began and there was no deadline on a day-to-day basis to complete assignments. The students were responsible for organizing their time effectively over the next few weeks to ensure that all assignments were completed by the deadline. To keep tabs on the day-to-day understanding of students, a very quick open-book quiz was used at the beginning of classes. Soon various levels of assignments were used in the same class. For each daily assignment, a student would be able to choose between three alternatives; a long, repetitive assignment to build skills for weaker students; a standard assignment with questions at various levels of understanding; and a shorter assignment which quickly goes through the basic skills and moves into analysis and synthesis level questions for the stronger students. This allowed student independence in analyzing their own abilities on a particular assignment and choosing the most appropriate path."

This approach is just one small part of the very detailed curriculum that Roger has developed to individualize the assignments, while giving students both more responsibility and freedom to complete the work in the way that is most helpful to them. Roger has created a truly inclusive high school classroom both at the curriculum level and at the community level. An outstanding teacher, he has won the Saskatchewan Master Teacher Award and the Prime Minister's Award of Achievement.

together to find ways to handle specific inclusion-related situations that have become problematic. In addition to identifying resources that might be helpful, the teachers also generate new strategies to try out. For problem solving to be useful, teachers must have sufficient time to meet and implement the proposed solution. Support from administrators can be very helpful in this area. Principals who are supportive of inclusion and team problem solving often find ways to alter schedules in a way that allows more teaming opportunities.

Maintaining flexibility contributes to long-term success; rigid procedures cannot adequately address the unpredictable situations that arise as challenges to management and instruction. Unforeseen problems will inevitably surface as a result of including students with special needs in general education classrooms. The more pliant a school can be in dealing with new challenges, the more likely it is that responsible inclusion will continue.

FINAL THOUGHT

The concept of inclusion and its practical applications will keep evolving as just one of the changing dynamics in the schools today. According to Ferguson (1995), "The new challenge of inclusion is to create schools in which our day-to-day efforts no longer assume that a particular text, activity, or teaching mode will 'work' to support any particular student's learning" (p. 287). Because the inclusive classroom contains many students with diverse needs, teachers must be equipped to address an array of challenges. To do so effectively, teachers need to create classroom communities that embrace diversity and that are responsive to individual needs.

SUMMARY

- Although current services for students with disabilities focus on inclusion, a range of services still exists in most Canadian schools.

- Key service delivery models are the self-contained, the resource room, and the inclusive.

- There are advantages and disadvantages for each model of service delivery.

- In the self-contained model, special education teachers were trained to teach specific types of students, primarily based on clinical labels.

- Classroom teachers had a very limited role in special education in the self-contained classroom model.

- The role of the regular classroom teacher increases as you move from the self-contained to the inclusive model.

- Inclusion of students with special needs in general education classes has received more attention on a philosophical level than on a practical level.

- Five essential features must be in place to ensure maximum success of inclusion: a sense of community and social acceptance, appreciation of student diversity, attention to curricular needs, effective management and instruction of students, and access to adequate personnel supports.

- The concept of inclusion affirms that students with special needs can be active, valued, and fully participating members of the school community.

- Students with special needs will be truly included in their classrooms only when they are appreciated by their teachers and socially accepted by their classmates.

- Teachers play a critical role in the success of inclusion.

- The curricular needs of students cannot be lost in the philosophical and political debate on inclusion.

- Effective classroom management is an important component in a successful inclusive classroom.

- Accommodative practices that are good for students with special needs are usually good for all students.

- Appropriately trained personnel, in adequate numbers, form a major factor in successful inclusion programs.

- Both staff and students must be prepared for inclusion.

- Once inclusion is initiated, it is important to monitor how well its five essential features are working together to ensure ongoing success.

RESOURCES

Pierangelo, Roger. (1998). *Special Educator's Complete Guide to 109 Diagnostic Tests*. Englewood, NJ: Centre for Applied Research in Education.

The author provides information on how to review evaluation measures, interpret test scores, incorporate results in individualized education programs, and remediate specific disabilities.

Bauer, A. M., & Shea, T. M. (1999). *Inclusion 101: How to Teach All Learners*. Baltimore, MD: Paul H. Brookes Publishing.

Here is a practical hands-on guide that gives teachers the skills to meet the needs of students in the inclusive classroom. Recommended by the Council for Exceptional Children.

WEBLINKS

Alberta Education, Learning Resources Distributing Centre
www.lrdc.edc.gov.ab.ca/
For more resources on inclusion strategies for students with exceptionalities, visit the Centre's site. All of the resources have been reviewed and approved by Alberta's ministry of education.

Alberta Education, Special Education Branch
ednet.edc.gov.ab.ca/
Visit this Web site to gain more information on resources (videos, books, resource guides, and handbooks) on all aspects of students with special needs.

Renaissance Group
www.uni.edu/coe/inclusion/
For an excellent list of teacher strategies, needed teacher competencies, and ways to prepare for in-

clusion as well as resources, visit the Inclusive Education Web site, produced by the Renaissance Group, a consortium of universities noted for their teacher preparation in inclusive education.

Circle of Inclusion
circleofinclusion.org//
For information on inclusion in early childhood (birth through age eight), visit the Circle of Inclusion Web site, a cooperative venture between some U.S. in-service training services, the University of Kansas Department of Special Education, and other associations. The site is funded by the U.S. Department of Education, Office of Special Education. It provides strategies and staffing models, allows you to meet people who are involved in inclusive programs online, enables you to visit inclusive programs online, shares print materials and articles important for inclusive settings, and suggests other helpful links.

Circle and Family Studies Program
www.asri.edu/cfsp//
For a site that provides some information on assistive technology and inclusion, as well as some excellent related links for parents and children, visit the Consortium on Inclusive Schooling Practices on the Child and Family Studies Program which aims to provide information on policy (American), research, and practice related to inclusion. This site is a project funded by a grant from the U.S. Department of Education, Office of Special Education Programs, to Allegheny University of the Health Sciences.

CHAPTER THREE

Teaching Students with Learning Disabilities

Alan was six years old when he eagerly started Kindergarten. Problems began to emerge as the reading program expanded from picture books with lots of repetition to books frequently containing unknown words. Alan had difficulty using context clues, and he had limited phonemic awareness in decoding a new word. His first report card showed "needs improvement" in reading, listening, and following directions. The bright spot in Alan's first-grade achievement was his above-average functioning in math, his ability to attend, and good social skills. Alan was promoted to second grade. Over the summer, his family moved to another province.

Alan adjusted to the new school and worked well for the first nine weeks of review. He then began to have trouble finishing his work. He became frustrated with written assignments and often complained of stomachaches, asking to stay home from school. His teachers felt that he was still adjusting to a new school.

By the middle of the year, his parents and teacher agreed that accommodations were needed as did the school team. The special education teacher put together material to review skills and phonemic elements he had not mastered. Alan's parents agreed to work on this material at home. He also worked with a fifth-grade peer helper who read with him one-on-one three days a week. The classroom teacher agreed to restate oral instructions, to continue working on phonics, and to encourage Alan to predict unknown words based on meaning and evaluate whether the word he guessed fit with the rest of the words in the sentence.

After six weeks the school team still felt that Alan was struggling too much, so they recommended a special education referral. His tests showed average intelligence and deficits in reading skills, writing, and listening. It was determined that Alan had a learning disability, making him eligible for special education services. Although signs of learning disabilities were present, the school proceeded slowly in identifying him as a child with a learning disability, aware that labelling can be detrimental to children.

Alan attended a resource class in third grade. Through these services, his reading of multisyllable words greatly improved as did his writing and listening skills. By fourth grade, he remained in the general education classroom full time, needing only periodic work with the resource teacher.

1. What alerted Alan's teacher to suspect a learning disability?

2. How might his move have been a factor in his school performance?

3. What would have happened to Alan if he did not have special education services in third grade?

INTRODUCTION

Just as it is difficult to distinguish children with **learning disabilities (LD)** from their peers by looks, you cannot distinguish adults with learning disabilities from other adults. You may be surprised to find that many important and famous people have achieved significant accomplishments in spite of experiencing a severe learning disability. Adults with learning disabilities can be found in all professions. They may be teachers, lawyers, doctors, factory workers, or politicians! Read the vignettes that follow, and see if you can identify the names of the individuals with learning disabilities.

During his childhood, this young man was an outstanding athlete, achieving great success and satisfaction from sports. Unfortunately, he struggled in the classroom. He tried very hard, but he always seemed to fail academically. His biggest fear was being asked to stand up and read in front of his classmates. He was frequently teased about his class performance, and he described his school days as sheer torture. His only feelings of success were experienced on the playing field.

When he graduated from high school, he didn't consider going to university because he "wasn't a terrific student, and never got into books all that much." Even though he was an outstanding high-school pole vaulter, he did not get a single scholarship during his senior year. He had already gone to work with his father when he was offered a $500 football scholarship from Graceland College. He didn't accept that offer; instead he trained in track and field. Several years later, he won a gold medal in the Olympics in the gruelling decathlon event! In case you haven't guessed, this story is about Bruce Jenner.

Other famous people with learning disabilities include Leonardo da Vinci, Tom Cruise, Winston Churchill, Woodrow Wilson, F. W. Woolworth, Walt Disney, Ernest Hemingway, Albert Einstein, George Bernard Shaw, and Thomas Edison (Harwell, 1989; Silver, 1995). Like these and others, individuals with learning disabilities are often misunderstood and teased early in life for their inadequacies in the classroom. To succeed in life, they had to be creative and persistent. Adults with learning disabilities rely on sheer determination to overcome their limitations and focus on their talents.

Perhaps the most difficult aspect of understanding and teaching students with learning disabilities is the fact that the disability is hidden. When students with obviously normal intelligence fail to finish their work, interrupt inappropriately, never seem to follow directions, and turn in sloppy, poorly organized assignments, it is natural to blame poor motivation, lack of effort—even an undesirable family life.

However, the lack of accomplishment and success in the classroom does have a cause; the students are not demonstrating these behaviours to upset or irritate their teachers. A learning disability is a cognitive disability; it is a disorder of thinking and reasoning. Because the dysfunction is presumed to be in the central nervous system, the presence of the disability is not visible. There is no prosthetic device to announce the disability (Harwell, 1989).

The individuals with learning disabilities described earlier have experienced the frustration of living with a disability that is not easily identified. Children with learning disabilities look like the other students in their grade.

CONSIDER THIS

Reflect on the students who were your classmates during elementary and secondary school. Do you remember any peers who had good academic abilities in some areas and low achievement in others? Were they ever accused of not trying or being lazy? They may have been misunderstood children with learning disabilities.

They can perform like the other students in some areas, but not in others. Like Alan in the first vignette, a child may have good social skills and make good grades in math, but fail in reading. Another child may be able to read and write at grade level, but fail in math and get in trouble for misconduct. Students with learning disabilities also may perform inconsistently. They may know spelling words on Thursday and fail the test on Friday.

In this chapter you will study the strengths and weakness patterns of children, youth, and adults who experience unexplained underachievement. Professionals from many fields have joined the search for a definition and causes of these disabilities, as well as methods to identify affected children and to successfully accommodate or remedy the disability. The answers are still evolving, but much progress has been made in this exciting field.

BASIC CONCEPTS

Definition

The initial studies of children later described as having learning disabilities were done by physicians interested in brain injury in children. Over the years, more than 90 terms were introduced into the literature to describe these children (Deiner, 1993). The most common include *minimal brain dysfunction (MBD), brain damaged, central process dysfunction*, and *language delayed.* To add to the confusion, separate definitions were also offered to explain each term. The term *specific learning disabilities* was first adopted publicly in 1963 at a meeting of parents and professionals. Kirk (1962) developed the generic term *learning disabilities* in an effort to unite the field, which was torn between individuals promoting different theories on underachievement. The term was received favorably because it did not have the negative connotations of the other terms and did describe the primary characteristic of the children.

In the United States the most widely used definition of learning disabilities is the one featured in the Individuals with Disabilities Education Act (IDEA) (Mercer, Jordan, Allsopp, & Mercer, 1996). This definition was used in the 1990 and 1997 versions of the Act and has two parts. The first part was taken from a 1968 report by a committee appointed by the United States Office of Education (USOE); the second was developed in 1977 to provide guidelines on how to apply the definition. The two parts together comprise the present definition used federally in the United States, which is, as follows:

> "Specific learning disability" means a disorder in one or more of the basic psychological processes involved in understanding or in using language, spoken or written, which may manifest itself in an imperfect ability to listen, think, speak, read, write, spell or to do mathematical calculations. The term includes such conditions as perceptual handicaps, brain injury, minimal brain dysfunction, dyslexia, and developmental aphasia. The term does not include children who have learning problems which are primarily the result of visual, hearing, or motor handicaps, of mental retardation, or emotional disturbance, or of environmental, cultural, or economic disadvantage. (USOE, 1977, p. 65083)

FURTHER READING
Dr. Judith Wiener and Dr. Linda Siegel, two leading Canadian researchers in the area of learning disabilities, wrote a unique article on the Canadian perspective on learning disabilities. To obtain a fuller appreciation of the Canadian approach to learning disabilities, read their 1992 article in volume 25 of the *Journal of Learning Disabilities* (pp. 340–350).

A specific learning disability occurs in a student if (1) s/he does not achieve commensurate with his/her age and ability in one or more of several specific areas when s/he has been given suitable instructional experiences, and (2) the student shows a severe discrepancy between achievement and intellectual ability in one or more of seven areas: (a) oral expression, (b) listening comprehension, (c) written expression, (d) basic reading skill, (e) reading comprehension, (f) mathematics calculation and (g) mathematics reasoning. (Lerner, 1993)

Although this two-part definition is commonly used in the United States, there has been criticism about its use of nonspecific terms (e.g., "perceptual handicaps") and the omission of the acknowledgment that learning disabilities can coexist with other handicaps (Wong, 1996). Therefore, a joint committee of representatives from parent and professional organizations worked together to develop an improved definition of learning disabilities that first emerged in 1981 and was updated in 1997 to read, as follows:

Learning disabilities is a general term that refers to a heterogeneous group of disorders manifested by significant difficulties in the acquisition and use of listening, speaking, reading, writing, reasoning, or mathematical abilities. These disorders are intrinsic to the individual, presumed to be due to central nervous system dysfunction and may occur across the life span. Problems in self-regulatory behaviors, social perception, and social interaction may exist with learning disabilities but do not by themselves constitute a learning disability. Although learning disabilities may occur concomitantly with other handicapping conditions (for example, sensory impairment, mental retardation, serious emotional disturbance) or with extrinsic influences such as cultural differences, insufficient or inappropriate instruction, they are not the result of these conditions or influences. (National Joint Committee on Learning Disabilities, NJCLD, Hammill, 1993, p. 4)

These definitions are the two most frequently used from among many definitions that have been suggested by a variety of organizations (see Hammill, 1990, for review). In Canada, Bernice Wong, a leading author and researcher in the field of learning disabilities, notes that the Canadian definition is closely aligned with the NJCLD definition; however, it emphasizes social and emotional problems to a greater extent (Wong, 1996).

In 1987, the Learning Disabilities Association of Canada (LDAC) defined learning disabilities as follows:

Learning disabilities is a generic term that refers to a heterogeneous group of disorders due to identifiable or inferred central nervous system dysfunction. Such disorders may be manifested by delays in early development and/or difficulties in any of the following areas: attention, memory, reasoning, coordination, communication, reading, writing, spelling, calculation, social competence and emotional maturation.

Learning disabilities are intrinsic to the individual, and may affect learning and behaviour in any individual, including those with potentially average, average, or above average intelligence.

Learning disabilities are not due primarily to visual, hearing, or motor handicaps, to mental retardation, emotional disturbance, or environmental disadvantage, although they may occur concurrently with any of these. (Learning Disabilities Association of Canada Definition, 1987)

Although the above definition has been accepted by LDAC and has influenced the definitions adopted by the individual provinces or territories, the actual identification of children with learning disabilities varies across the country (Wiener & Siegel, 1992).

Prevalence and Causes

In today's schools, there are by far more students with learning disabilities than with any other disability. In both Canada and the United States it is estimated that approximately half of all exceptional students have learning disabilities (U.S. Department of Education, 1995; Wong, 1996).

Experts generally agree that learning is hindered in children with learning disabilities because there is a problem in how the brain processes information (Lerner, 1993). Why this happens generally remains unknown. The literature suggests several causes, primarily genetic factors and trauma induced before birth, during birth, and after birth.

1. *Genetic and hereditary influences:* Some studies have cited the large number of relatives with learning problems in children identified with learning disabilities (Olson, Wise, Conners, Rack, & Falker, 1989). Chromosomal abnormalities and structural brain differences have also been linked to learning disabilities (Geschwind & Galaburda, 1985; Lewis, 1992; Semrud-Clikeman, & Hynd, 1990; Smith, Pennington, Kimberling, & Inge, 1990). Research in this area continues to show promise.

2. *Causes occurring before birth:* Several teratogenic insults that may occur during pregnancy have been linked to learning problems. The most common include use of alcohol, cigarettes, and other drugs, such as cocaine and prescription and nonprescription drugs. Through the mother, the fetus is exposed to the toxins, causing malformations of the developing brain and central nervous system. Although significant amounts of overexposure to these drugs may cause serious problems, such as intellectual disabilities, no safe levels have been identified.

3. *Causes occurring during birth process:* These traumas may include prolonged labour, anoxia, prematurity, and injury from medical instruments such as forceps. Although not all children with a traumatic birth are found to have learning problems later, a significant number of children with learning problems do have a history of complications during this period.

4. *Causes occurring after birth:* The primary accidents and diseases linked to learning problems are high fever, encephalitis, meningitis, stroke, diabetes, and head trauma. Malnutrition and poor postnatal health care can also lead to neurological dysfunction (Hallahan, Kauffman, & Lloyd, 1996).

New areas of research in the causes of learning disabilities include the environmental influences of substances such as lead and the possibility of a chemical imbalance in the brain.

CONSIDER THIS
Often parents will ask teachers what causes a learning disability. You might discuss some of the possible causes and suggest that the single cause is seldom identifiable for individual children. Reassure them that pinpointing the cause is not important in planning and implementing effective intervention strategies.

Characteristics

FURTHER READING
Research has shown that teachers are effective in identifying students at risk of school failure by observing these characteristic differences. For more information, refer to the article by K. A. Salvesen and J. O. Undheim, "Screening for Learning Disabilities with Teacher Rating Scales," published in 1994 in volume 27 of the *Journal of Learning Disabilities* (pp. 60–66).

Learning disabilities are primarily described as a deficit in academic achievement (reading, writing, and mathematics) and/or language (listening or speaking). However, children with learning disabilities may have significant problems in other areas, such as social interactions and emotional maturity, attention and hyperactivity, memory, cognition, metacognition, motor skills, and perceptual abilities. Since learning disabilities are presumed to be a central nervous system dysfunction, characteristics may be manifested throughout the lifespan, preschool through adult (Mercer, 1997).

The most common characteristics of students with learning disabilities are described briefly in the following sections, concentrating on the challenges they may create in a classroom. Students with learning disabilities are a heterogeneous group. A single student will not have deficits in all of these areas. Also, any area could be a strength for a student with learning disabilities, and the student might exceed the abilities of his or her peers in that area. For example, a student with strong abilities in math, metacognition, and social skills may experience limitations in reading, writing, and attention. Another student might have strengths in attention, writing, and reading, and be challenged in math, social skills, and metacognition. An understanding of these characteristics will be important in developing prereferral interventions, in making appropriate referrals, and in identifying effective accommodations and intervention strategies. Figure 3.1 displays the possible strengths and weaknesses of children with learning disabilities.

ACADEMIC DEFICITS

During the elementary years a discrepancy between ability and achievement begins to emerge in students with learning disabilities. Often puzzling to teachers, they seem to have strengths similar to their peers in several areas, but their rate of learning in other areas is slower, and unexpected. In the vignette that began this chapter, Alan provides a typical profile of a child with learning disabilities:

FIGURE 3.1
Areas of Possible Strengths and Deficits of Students with Learning Disabilities

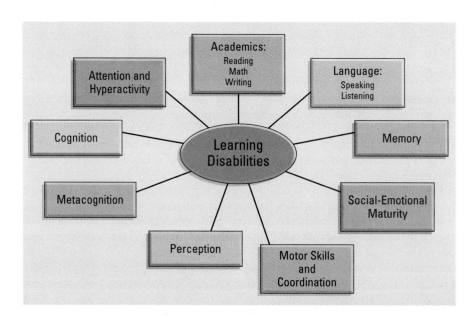

above-average ability in math; average ability in language, attention, and social skills; and severe deficits in reading, written expression, and listening.

The academic problems that serve to identify a learning disability fall into the areas of reading, math, and written expression. The most prevalent academic difficulty for students with learning disabilities is reading. However, this does not mean that a learning disability is the same thing as a reading disability. Although people equate learning disabilities with reading disabilities, reading problems form only one type of academic learning disabilities (Weber, 1994; Wong, 1996). There are also spelling, writing, and mathematics disabilities, as well as nonacademic learning disabilities such as perceptual, memory, and visual-motor. Nevertheless, the majority of learning disabilities observed in the classroom are reading disabilities (Moats & Lyon, 1993). Problems may be noted in *basic reading skills* and *reading comprehension*. Children with learning disabilities may struggle with oral reading tasks. They may read in a strained voice with poor phrasing, ignore punctuation, and grope for words like a much younger child. The oral reading problems cause tremendous embarrassment to these children. Carnine, Silbert, and Kameenui (1990) confirm that a student's self-image and feelings of confidence are greatly affected by reading experience. Deficits in reading skills can also lead to acting-out behaviour and poor motivation.

Some children with learning disabilities may be able to call the words correctly but not remember what they have read. Comprehension problems may include one or more of the following: (1) identifying the main idea, (2) recalling basic facts and events in a sequence, and (3) making inferences or evaluating what has been read (Mercer, 1997).

Another major academic problem area is mathematics. Students with learning disabilities may have problems in *math calculations* or *math reasoning* (LDAC, 1987). These conceptual and skill areas include deficits in the four operations, the concept of zero, regrouping, place value, basic math concepts (e.g., one-to-one correspondence, sets), and solving math problems (Smith, Polloway, Dowdy, & Blalock, 1997). Children may have *abilities* in calculation but have *disabilities* in math reasoning; they may make many errors in calculations but be able to perform calculations to solve a math word problem. Often, the rate of response interferes with success in math; for example, a child may be able to perform the skill, but be unable to complete the number of problems required during the time allowed.

Learning disabilities in the area of *writing* are beginning to receive more recognition as a potentially serious problem. The three main areas of concern are handwriting, spelling, and written expression, including mechanics and creativity. The impact of written language problems increases with a student's age because so many school assignments require a written product.

LANGUAGE DEFICITS

Language deficits are found in the areas of *oral expression* (speaking) and *listening comprehension*. Since these two areas control our ability to communicate with others, a deficit can have a major impact on quality of life—including life in a general education classroom! Studies have found that more than 60 percent of students with learning disabilities have some type of language disorder (Bryan, Bay, Lopez-Reyna, & Donahue, 1991). Common oral language problems include difficulty in retrieving words; children often use a less appropriate word choice because the right word will not come to them (Mathinos, 1991). The response rate and sentence articulation of children with learning disabilities may be slower than that of their nondisabled peers (Ackerman, Dykman, & Gardner, 1990). If ample time is not allowed for a response, the student's behaviour may be misinterpreted as failure to understand or refusal to participate. Children with learning disabilities tend to use simpler, less mature language and confuse sequences in retelling a story. These deficits in expressive language suggest possible difficulties in receptive language or listening, as well (Smith, 1994). Listening problems also can be easily misinterpreted. A child with a disability in listening demonstrates that disability in a negative way, for example, by failing to follow directions or by appearing oppositional or unmotivated. A teacher's careful observation and assessment of a student's language ability is important for ensuring the student's success.

A new area of concern and research pertaining to children with language-learning disabilities is that of **pragmatics**, or use of language in social communication situations. Children with these disabilities are sometimes unsuccessful in fully participating in conversation. They may need extra time to process incoming information, or they may not understand the meaning of the words or word sequences. They may miss nonverbal language cues. They may not understand jokes; they may laugh inappropriately or at the wrong times. Group work is often difficult, as is giving or following directions. Language disabilities can contribute significantly to difficulties in other social situations as well (Lapadat, 1991).

CROSS-REFERENCE

Often students with learning disabilities have social-emotional problems and will present challenges in behaviour management in the classroom. Refer to Chapter 5 for more information in this area.

SOCIAL-EMOTIONAL PROBLEMS

The social and emotional functioning of individuals with learning disabilities has become a focus of investigation only fairly recently. For many years the majority of research on learning disabilities was in the academic or processing areas (Bender, 1998). However, in recognition of the importance of examining the noncognitive functioning of children with learning disabilities, a 1994 issue of a major journal in the field was devoted to the study of the social-emotional development of students with learning disabilities (Bender, 1994).

In a review of the literature Judith Wiener (1987) concluded that students with learning disabilities tend to be rated by their peers as less likeable. Furthermore, in work that she and colleagues at the University of Toronto did (Wiener, Harris, & Duval, 1993; Wiener, Harris, & Shirer, 1990), it was found that labelling of a child as having a learning disability affected peer ratings. Children who were not school-identified as having a learning disability received higher peer ratings than those who were identified even when they otherwise met the same criteria. Therefore, children identified by the school as having a learning disability are at risk of poor social acceptance. Research by Kavale and Forness (1996) demonstrated that 75 percent of students identified as having a learning disability were significantly different from their nondisabled peers on most measures of social competence.

Emotionally, children and adolescents with learning disabilities appear to be at greater risk of depression and negative self-perceptions of academic performance (Bender, 1998). Students with learning disabilities report more depressive symptoms, more severe depression, and more negative self-perceptions than students without learning disabilities (Heath, 1996). Specifically, students with learning disabilities report negative self-perceptions of academic performance, but may report adequate or even high self-perceptions in other areas, such as athletics, physical appearance, and social acceptance (Heath & Wiener, 1996). Nancy Heath, in her self-perception and mood laboratory at McGill University, has studied the self-perceptions and mood of children and adolescents with learning disabilities longitudinally. She has found that frequently students with learning disabilities report inaccurately positive self-perceptions of academic performance, but that these self-perceptions serve to buffer the students from depressive symptoms that often occur in the face of ongoing failure (Heath, 1995). Thus, students with learning disabilities who had a more realistic understanding of their academic difficulties reported higher levels of depression than those who denied having academic difficulties. Dr. Heath's research team is investigating the possible role of teacher feedback in these students' self-perceptions and mood.

By being sensitive to these issues, you can take care to include students with learning disabilities in supportive situations and provide reinforcement for specific successes. General praise statements such as "Good work!" or "You are really smart!" will not have much impact because they are not believable to the students. Commenting on or rewarding specific accomplishments will be more effective. Additional examples of appropriate interventions in this area for inclusive classrooms will be discussed later in this chapter and in future chapters.

ATTENTION DEFICITS AND HYPERACTIVITY

Attention is a critical skill in learning. Conte (1991) suggests that to be effective learners, children must be able to initiate attention, direct their attention in the appropriate direction, sustain their attention according to the task demands, and shift attention when appropriate. Deficits in these areas can have an impact on all aspects of success in school. When children are "not paying attention," they cannot respond appropriately to questions, follow directions, or take notes during a lecture. The excess movement of a hyperactive student can draw sharp criticism when it negatively affects the learning environment. Social problems occur when the student interrupts others and does not listen to

CROSS-REFERENCE
Many students with learning disabilities have attention deficit/hyperactivity disorders. This topic is covered more extensively in Chapter 4.

his or her peers. Students with attention problems often have trouble finishing assignments or rush through their work with little regard for detail. Estimates of the number of students with learning disabilities that have attention problems vary widely based on the stringency of the criteria used to define the attention deficit (DeLong, 1995; Semrud-Clikeman et al., 1992). However, the majority of individuals with learning disabilities do not have attention-deficit disorders (Weber & Bennett, 1999). Attention deficits are covered more thoroughly in Chapter 4.

MEMORY

Several studies have suggested that students with learning disabilities have more deficits in memory than students without learning disabilities (Beale & Tippett, 1992). Students with memory deficits have trouble retaining learned information. They may have difficulty in repeating information recently read or heard, following multiple directions, or performing tasks in the correct sequence. Teachers and parents may also report that the memory skills are inconsistent—for example, such a student may know the multiplication facts on Thursday and fail the test on Friday!

COGNITION

Cognition refers to the ability to reason or think (Hallahan et al., 1996). Students with problems in this area may make poor decisions or frequent errors. They may have trouble getting started on a task, have delayed verbal responses, require more supervision, or have trouble adjusting to change. Understanding social expectations may be difficult. They may require concrete demonstrations. They often have trouble using previously learned information in a new situation.

METACOGNITION

FURTHER READING

Metacognition is the ability to think about thinking. For more information, read the article "The Relevance of Metacognition to Learning Disabilities," by B. Wong in the book *Learning about Learning Disabilities* (pp. 231–258), published by Academic Press in 1991.

Hallahan et al. (1996) refer to metacognition as "thinking about thinking." Metacognitive deficits include the inability to control and direct one's own attention and mental processes (Wong, 1991). Students with problems in this area might have difficulty focusing on listening, purposefully remembering important information, connecting that information to prior knowledge, making sense out of the new information, and using what they know to solve a problem. They often lack strategies for planning and organizing, setting priorities, and solving problems. An important component of metacognition is the ability to regulate one's own behaviour when one perceives that one is acting inappropriately or making mistakes.

PERCEPTION

Perceptual disorders affect the ability to recognize stimuli being received through sight, hearing, or touch and to discriminate between and interpret the sensations appropriately. A child with a learning disability might not have any problems in these areas, or he or she might have deficits in any or all of them. Research has shown that visual perception is more important at very young ages, but is not a major requirement for higher-level academics (Smith, 1994). Identification of deficits and training in the perceptual processes was emphasized in the early 1970s; however, it is no longer a prominent consideration in the education of children with learning disabilities.

MOTOR SKILLS AND COORDINATION

This area has also been de-emphasized in the identification of an intervention for children with learning disabilities because it is not directly related to academics. However, it is common for children with learning disabilities to display problems in gross motor areas; they often cannot throw and catch a ball or may have a clumsy gait. Common fine motor deficits include difficulties with cutting with scissors, buttoning clothing, and handwriting. Occupational therapists refer to this profile as a developmental coordination disorder (DCD) and have acknowledged the overlap between this disorder and learning disabilities for more than a decade (Martini, Heath, & Missiunia, 1999). Consideration of motor skills and coordination is important in the selection of a vocational program and ultimately in the identification of a career.

Identification, Assessment, and Eligibility

In the United States, as mentioned earlier, the federal Office of Education specified criteria for identifying a learning disability (USOE, 1977), stating that there must be a "severe discrepancy" between achievement and intellectual ability. Similarly, the Learning Disabilities Association of Canada definition (LDAC, 1987) indicates that individuals with learning disabilities will have potentially average, average, or above-average intelligence with delays in specific areas (e.g., reading, writing, or arithmetic). In general, definitions of learning disability all suggest a discrepancy between intelligence and achievement; however, the assessment of the discrepancy remains controversial (Bender, 1998), as does the validity of intelligence measures in individuals with learning disabilities (Siegel, 1989). Despite these criticisms, in practice, most school psychologists try to establish that a significant difference, or discrepancy, exists between a student's achievement and intelligence, thereby identifying a learning disability (Weber, 1994).

In a Canadian Council for Exceptional Children survey, it was found that percentages of children identified as having a learning disability varied widely across the country. Quebec identified 10.2 percent of its child population as having a learning disability, Nova Scotia 7.0 percent, Ontario 3.1 percent, Saskatchewan 1.7 percent, and British Columbia 1.3 percent (Wiener & Siegel, 1992). Furthermore, school board to school board the percentage of children identified as having a learning disability can vary.

As Weber (1994) notes in his book, *Special Education in Canadian Schools*, these variations can be explained only by the fact that there must be significant differences in identification procedures from province to province. For example, in Quebec the "learning difficulty" definition stipulates only that the student be one or two years below grade level in any achievement area. In contrast, in Ontario the learning disabilities definition requires an IQ testing and a significant discrepancy between intellectual functioning and achievement; it also requires the exclusion of all other exceptionalities as causes of the low achievement. The Quebec definition uses much less stringent criteria than the Ontario definition does; as a result, a higher number of children are identified as having a learning disability in Quebec.

Ultimately, as a teacher in a Canadian school, you need to familiarize yourself with the criteria used in your province and board. Be aware of characteristics of students with learning disabilities to know when you might want to further document a student's strengths and weaknesses for a possible referral to the school psychologist or school team.

CULTURAL AND LINGUISTIC DIVERSITY

FURTHER READING

The text *Children and Adults with Learning Disabilities* by T. E. C. Smith, C. Dowdy, E. Polloway, and G. Blalock, published by Allyn & Bacon in 1997, devotes a chapter to the important topic of diversity and learning disabilities.

Since learning disabilities are found in approximately 5 percent of the school-age population and the number of school-age children with cultural and language diversity is growing steadily, inevitably many children will fall into both groups (Gerstein & Woodward, 1994). Although the issues related to educating all culturally diverse children apply to the population of children with learning disabilities as well, the existence of a learning disability does bring additional challenges in assessment for identification, program planning, instructional implementation, and personnel preparation.

Accurately identifying a learning disability in the presence of cultural diversity is no small challenge. School personnel must carefully determine that the differences related to diversity are not the primary cause of a student's learning difficulties. Teachers sometimes expect less from students from diverse cultural backgrounds and view special education as the most viable placement option for them (Gerstein, Brengleman, & Jimenez, 1994). As a result, a disproportionate number are referred for assessment and ultimately funnelled into special education settings. Moecker (1992) found that too often a diagnosis of learning disability was based on intelligence and achievement tests administered in English without considering cultural and language difference. Thus, a child's failure to make progress may not be the result of a learning disability but the failure of the education system.

In Canada, we have a large multicultural community as well as a policy of official bilingualism and second language immersion programs (Wiener & Siegel, 1992). Beyond that, 1.3 percent of children in Canada are from First Nations' communities and have specific language, learning, and cultural requirements. Differentiating learning disabilities from problems with English or French as a second language is a major diagnostic issue (Wiener & Siegel, 1992). Furthermore, second language instruction is often problematic for students with learning disabilities (Trites, 1981). In situations where the second language instruction is limited, the problems may be minimal; however, in situations where children are instructed in a second language for most or all of their schooling, the child with a learning disability will encounter significant difficulties (Carey, 1987). New Brunswick francophones and Quebec anglophones, as well as francophones across Canada, are especially subject to these problems.

McGill researcher Maggie Bruck (1982) has argued that, as children with learning disabilities experience difficulty in both their first and second language programs, removing them from an immersion program is not beneficial; what matters is that they can obtain appropriate remedial assistance. Nevertheless, in practice, a common recommendation for students with learning disabilities in an immersion program is to transfer them to a first language instruction program. Also, most students with learning disabilities prefer to be instructed in their first language.

In summary, multicultural and second language components make the identification and instruction of Canadian students with learning disabilities quite complex.

Cultural and Linguistic Considerations Related to IEP Development

SELECTION OF IEP GOALS AND OBJECTIVES

Considerations for IEP Development	Classroom Implications
IEP goals and objectives accommodate the student's current level of performance.	■ At the student's instructional level ■ Instructional level based on student's cognitive level, not the language proficiency level ■ Focus on development of higher-level cognitive skills as well as basic skills
Goals and objectives are responsive to cultural and linguistic variables.	■ Accommodates goals and expectations of the family ■ Is sensitive to culturally based response to the disability ■ Includes a language use plan ■ Addresses language development and second language needs

SELECTION OF INSTRUCTIONAL STRATEGIES

Considerations for IEP Development	Classroom Implications
Interventions provide adequate exposure to curriculum.	■ Instruction in student's dominant language ■ Responsiveness to learning and communication styles ■ Sufficient practice to achieve mastery
IEP provides for curricular/instructional accommodation of learning styles and locus of control.	■ Accommodates perceptual style differences (e.g., visual vs. auditory) ■ Accommodates cognitive style differences (e.g., inductive vs. deductive) ■ Accommodates preferred style of participation (e.g., teacher vs. student-directed, small vs. large group) ■ Reduces feelings of learned helplessness
Selected strategies are likely to be effective for language minority students.	■ Native language and second language instruction ■ Teacher as facilitator of learning (vs. transmission) ■ Genuine dialogue with students ■ Contextualized instruction ■ Collaborative learning ■ Self-regulated learning ■ Learning-to-learn strategies
Second language strategies are used.	■ Modifications to address the student's disability ■ Use of current second language approaches ■ Focus on meaningful communication
Strategies for literacy are included.	■ Holistic approaches to literacy development ■ Language teaching that is integrated across the curriculum ■ Thematic literature units ■ Language experience approach ■ Journals

Adapted from "Toward Defining Programs and Services for Culturally and Linguistically Diverse Learners in Special Education," by S. B. Garcia and D. H. Malkin, 1993, *Teaching Exceptional Children, 26*, pp. 52–58. Used by permission.

When a student is determined eligible for special education services, the process of designing and implementing an appropriate educational plan is critical. Teachers may be uninformed about the short- and long-term goals held by families from different cultures. Therefore, family participation and ongoing communication about progress are essential. The nearby Diversity Forum feature addresses developing educational plans that are sensitive to the needs of culturally and linguistically diverse learners. All teacher-training programs should include discussion of assessment, communication, and service delivery issues related to these students.

STRATEGIES FOR CURRICULUM AND INSTRUCTION

Over the years, treatment procedures for individuals with learning disabilities have been a source of controversy. In the 1970s, advocates for perceptual training of auditory and visual processes debated those who advocated direct instruction in the deficit academic area(s) (Engelmann & Carnine, 1982). A convincing article by Hammill and Larsen (1974) analyzed research showing that perceptual training did little to improve basic academic skills. This triggered a move toward a skills approach in which direct instruction was implemented in the areas of academic deficit. More recently, language, social-emotional, and cognitive-metacognitive areas have received positive attention. Many approaches have gained acceptance as research-based methods for improving the skills and developing the abilities of children and adults with learning disabilities. Other nontraditional approaches have been proposed and some even have a large following, though they may not be supported by research. Teachers need to be well informed on all approaches so that they can provide objective information to parents who seek to understand and address their child's difficulties. The following section discusses the accepted traditional approaches for each age level and provides a brief overview of some of the nontraditional approaches.

Traditional Approaches

CONSIDER THIS

According to Lyon's study, intervention in reading skills in grades 1–3 is critical. Should all students who are behind their peers in reading ability be helped during these years? What are possible positive and negative outcomes of providing a "special education" program for all of these children at risk of later failure?

In a review of various treatment approaches, Lloyd (1988) concludes that no single approach to learning disabilities can be cited as the best. He does suggest that the most effective ones are structured and goal oriented, provide multiple opportunities for practice, including a strategy, foster independence, and are comprehensive and detailed. Many of the following approaches adhere to these principles. They all can be implemented in a general education classroom and may benefit many nondisabled students as well. The strategies are discussed according to age levels—elementary, secondary, and adult. The largest section concerns the elementary school student; however, many elementary-level techniques are equally effective at the secondary level.

THE ELEMENTARY LEVEL

By fifth grade, 76 percent of the children with learning disabilities have been identified; more children are identified during the first and second grades than at any other time (McLesky, 1992). The importance of intervention during the

Most children with learning disabilities are identified during the first and second grades.

early elementary years is validated by a study cited by Lyon (1995), suggesting that 74 percent of the children with a reading disability in the third grade remained disabled in the ninth grade. As discussed in the section on characteristics, many of these deficits remain a problem throughout an individual's life. The intervention begun during elementary years may be equally important at the secondary level and for some adults. Intervention is important in academic and language deficits, social-emotional problems, and cognitive and metacognitive deficits.

Children with learning disabilities may have academic and language deficits in any or all of the following areas:

- Basic reading skills
- Reading comprehension
- Math calculation
- Math reasoning
- Written expression
- Oral expression
- Listening

Since these areas are usually the focus of an elementary curriculum, they can very often be addressed in the general education classroom. Both general and special education teachers have been trained to provide instruction in these areas, so collaborative teaching is possible. Because of the uneven skill development in children with learning disabilities, individualized assessment is often required to identify areas that specifically need to be addressed. Informal methods, such as the curriculum-based assessment discussed in Chapter 1, are usually effective for planning instruction. This assessment should include an evaluation of the student's strengths, which may indicate the most effective method for instruction.

Because student strengths and weaknesses are so diverse, a single method of teaching may not meet the needs of all students with learning disabilities. For example, in the area of reading instruction, the general education teacher

INCLUSION STRATEGIES

Teaching Tips for Use in Learning Strategy Instruction

1. Choose a strategy that matches a task or setting demand for students.

2. Assess the students' current level of strategy use, and teach a strategy that is needed to increase their level of performance.

3. Have students set goals about what they intend to learn and how they will use the strategy.

4. Describe the strategy, give examples, and discuss its applications.

5. Model the strategy for the students. Verbalize your own thinking and problem solving, including ways you monitor, make corrections to, and adjust your task approach and completion.

6. Make sure students can confidently name and explain the strategy.

7. Give sufficient practice of the strategy with materials that are controlled for level of difficulty before expecting use of the strategy in advanced materials.

8. Have students practice the strategy in materials from classes in which they are placed for instruction.

9. Make sure students give examples and actually practice the strategy in various settings in school, at home, and in the community.

From "Promoting Strategic Learning," by V. P. Day and L. K. Elksnin, 1994, *Intervention in School and Clinic*, 29(5), p. 266. Reprinted by permission.

may use a reading approach based on reading literature for meaning; development in areas such as phonics will occur naturally as the reader becomes more efficient. In this method, often referred to as the **whole language method**, the teacher might note difficulty with a phonetic principle during oral reading and subsequently develop a mini-lesson using text to teach the skill. Unfortunately, many children with learning disabilities do not readily acquire the alphabet code because of limitations in processing the sounds of letters. Their reading disability may be the result of a deficit in phonologic awareness (Fletcher, Shaywitz, & Shankweiler, 1994). A large amount of research indicates that these students need a more highly structured **sequential or systematic phonics program** that teaches the application of phonologic rules to print (Duane & Gray, 1991; Lyon, 1991; Rooney, 1995). One strength of the whole language method is its focus on the comprehension of authentic reading material; the teacher using the phonics method must purposely develop those important comprehension skills. These two reading methods are discussed further in Chapter 12.

CROSS-REFERENCE

Reading intervention and strategy instruction are discussed further in Chapters 12 and 13.

Another way to facilitate success for students with learning disabilities in inclusive settings is teaching a **strategy** to apply during the process of learning new information or skills. A strategy is defined by Deshler and Lenz (1989) as an individual's approach to a task. It includes how "a person thinks and acts when planning, executing, and evaluating performance on a task and its subsequent outcomes" (p. 203). Students with learning disabilities may not automatically develop strategies for learning, or the one they develop may be inefficient. Day and Elksnin (1994) provide basic techniques that teachers may use to develop and implement strategies across all grades, within the framework of the regular curriculum. The nearby Inclusion Strategies feature outlines these steps.

An example of a simple strategy is a *personal spelling dictionary*. Students can enter words that they frequently miss or that are important in the environment, and weekly spelling tests can be generated from the entries (Scheuermann, Jacobs, McCall, & Knies, 1994). Lists from a spelling book are often too long for students with learning disabilities; also, the words are taken out of context and may not be transferred to the student's writing. To create a personal spelling dictionary, use a small loose-leaf binder that is tabbed every few pages to designate each letter of the alphabet. When a student encounters a word he or she does not know how to spell, the correct spelling is obtained from the teacher, the dictionary, or a spelling buddy. The word is then entered into the correct section of the dictionary. The dictionary is always available to jog the memory about words learned in the past. This idea can be expanded to create a writing mechanics dictionary or a math dictionary.

Written language is often difficult to master for children and adults with learning disabilities. A study by Palinscar and Klenk (1992) suggests that special education teachers frequently limit students' writing tasks to copying words and filling out worksheets, so it is important in inclusive classrooms that students be exposed to a variety of writing opportunities. Ellis (1994) developed a strategy to improve writing for students with learning disabilities. This strategy, called PASS, shapes the writing process from the creative beginning stages to the editing of the final product (see Figure 3.2).

> **TEACHING TIP**
>
> Many students with learning disabilities will resist the challenge to write because of prior negative feedback. Try giving them multiple opportunities without grading, and then grade only one or two skills at a time. For example, one week you might grade punctuation and the next, spelling. You can also give one grade for content and another for mechanics, and then average the two scores for the final grade.

 PREVIEW, REVIEW, AND PREDICT

Preview your knowledge, audience, and goals.

Review main ideas and details.

Predict best order.

 ASK AND ANSWER QUESTIONS

Topic- and reader-related questions:

> How can I activate the reader's knowledge in the first sentence?
>
> What background knowledge does the reader have that I can link this idea to?
>
> What else can I say? Have I left anything out?
>
> What would be a good example of what I mean?
>
> Does this make sense? Should I explain this idea more?

Problem-solving questions:

> Should I get more information from others?
>
> Where can I look up more information?
>
> Should I rephrase this to make it more clear?

 SUMMARIZE THE MESSAGE IN THE LAST SENTENCE

SEARCH FOR ERRORS AND CORRECT THEM

FIGURE 3.2
Strategy for Teaching Writing Skills

From "Integrating Writing Strategy Instruction with Content-Area Instruction: Part II—Writing Process," by E. S. Ellis, 1994, *Intervention in School and Clinic*, 29 (4), pp. 219–228. Used by permission.

This simple method helps students with learning disabilities complete written assignments more successfully and develop metacognitive skills that will enable them to become active learners.

Improvement in oral language may be stimulated by enriching the language environment. Candler and Hildreth (1990) suggest that relaxation therapy may be needed to open students to more communication opportunities. They also discuss how the classroom can be designed with areas where students are encouraged to talk and how cooperative learning activities promote increased verbal interactions. Providing opportunities for students to share their experiences and expertise will promote use of oral language in a non-threatening way. Listening and praise help reinforce talking.

Poor listening skills also limit individuals with learning disabilities, influencing both success in the classroom and in social interactions. In Heaton and O'Shea's (1995) effective strategy, which can be modified for use with all age groups, students follow these steps:

L   **L**ook at the teacher.
I   **I**gnore the student next to you.
S   **S**tay in your place.
T   **T**ry to visualize and understand the story.
E   **E**njoy the story.
N   **N**ice job! You're a good listener.

Computers and other technology can assist in teaching individuals with learning disabilities in inclusive classrooms. Olsen and Platt (1996) describe the following advantages of technology:

- It is self-pacing and individualized.
- It provides immediate feedback.
- It has consistent correction procedures.
- It provides repetition without pressure.
- It confirms correct responses immediately.
- It maintains a high frequency of student response.
- It builds in repeated validation of academic success.
- It is an activity respected by peers.
- It is motivating.
- It encourages increased time on task.
- It minimizes the effects of the disability.

Writing is an area in which technology can be most helpful. Recommended word-processing programs will be discussed in a later section on accommodations. The computer can also be used effectively for curriculum support in math, language arts, social studies, science, and other areas. Various types of software provide instructional alternatives such as tutoring, drill and practice, simulation, and games. The purpose and strength of these techniques are highlighted in the nearby Technology Today feature. With so many choices available, teachers should carefully evaluate each program for ease of use and appropriateness for exceptional students.

Intervention related to social interactions and emotional maturity is critical for many students with learning disabilities. There is no longer debate regarding the desirability of children with disabilities being included to the greatest degree possible in the general education setting. The question is,

TEACHING TIP

The amount of software available for supporting instruction can be overwhelming, and costly mistakes can be made when ordering a program based on a catalogue description alone. Organize a plan for the teachers in your school to share the names of effective software. Preview a copy before ordering, whenever possible.

Types of Software

Type	Purpose	Strengths
TUTORIAL	1. Designed to present new information 2. Introduces new skills and concepts 3. Prerequisite skills may be necessary	1. Provides practice on new skills and concepts 2. May present sequence of skills 3. Can be used to supplement direct instruction 4. Can be used in student-mediated arrangements
DRILL AND PRACTICE	1. Reinforces skills previously taught 2. Provides practice opportunities on skills and concepts 3. Provides feedback regarding progress	1. Provides the extra practice in skills and concepts that students with learning and behaviour problems may require 2. Can continue providing necessary practice for students to reach mastery
SIMULATION	1. Presents decision-making and cause/effect situations 2. De-emphasizes "right or wrong" answers	1. Gives students opportunities to make decisions and to witness the results of those decisions 2. Provides opportunities to analyze situations and apply problem-solving skills
GAMES	1. Presents learning in a fun situation 2. May use animation and sound to simulate a game format 3. May have points for correct scores	1. May be appealing to some students while reinforcing skills

Adapted from *Special Education Technology: Classroom Application*, by R. Lewis, 1993, Pacific Grove, CA: Brooks/Cole, in *Teaching Students with Learning and Behavior Problems* (3rd ed.) (p. 147), by D. Rivera and D. Smith, 1997, Boston: Allyn & Bacon. Used by permission.

What is the best way to prepare both the children with disabilities and the nondisabled children for positive interactions? Changing a student's self-image, social ability, and social standing is difficult. Until recently, the research and literature on learning disabilities focused primarily on the efficacy of treatments for the most obvious characteristic—academic deficits. The importance of social skills is just now being recognized and given the attention it deserves.

Intervention in the area of social standing and interaction can take two courses: changing the child or changing the environment. Optimally, both receive attention. Good teaching techniques can lead to academic achievement and eventually to higher self-esteem. It is very important to create a positive learning environment, incorporating praise and encouragement for specific accomplishments. Set goals, and be very explicit about expectations for academic work and behaviour in the class. Monitor progress closely, and provide frequent feedback (Mercer, 1997).

Students should be asked higher-level questions that require problem solving and reasoning. Opportunities need to be provided for students to generalize learned information across settings. The most effective learning environment is supportive but encourages independence. Students should be given responsibilities. They should be reinforced for making positive comments about themselves and about other students (Mercer, 1997).

A number of programs are available commercially; however, they may not meet the specific needs of your students. Many techniques may be implemented successfully in either the general or special education classroom. Some teaching strategies for improving social competencies and building self-concept have been summarized by Lerner (1993). She suggests activities that fall into the following four areas:

1. *Body image and perception of self:* Make a scrapbook to tell about each student. Have students make and solve puzzles about the body.
2. *Sensitivity:* Study pictures of faces, gestures, and films to determine the social meaning. Study voices to determine moods.
3. *Social maturity:* Through role-playing and discussion of actual social actions and ethical dilemmas, give students situations and have them determine the consequences. Have students plan and organize weekend activities with friends.
4. *Learning strategies and social skills training:* Teach students strategies about how to stop and think before responding, how to visualize the effects of behaviour options, how to visually or verbally rehearse the chosen response, and how to monitor their own success.

CONSIDER THIS

Describe some situations you have observed in which a child displayed inappropriate social skills or responses in the classroom. How could the FAST strategy have been used to prevent recurring problems?

The overall goal of social programs is to teach socially appropriate behaviour and social skills that are self-generated and self-monitored. The cognitive problems of students with learning disabilities often make this type of decision making very difficult. FAST is an example of a strategy that can be effectively applied to the social skills training curriculum. It aids in interpersonal problem solving by developing questioning and monitoring skills, brainstorming solutions, and developing and implementing a plan to solve the problem. The steps are displayed in Figure 3.3.

FIGURE 3.3
Strategies for Developing Interpersonal Problem Solving

From "FAST Social Skills with a SLAM and a Rap," by R. McIntosh, S. Vaughn, and D. Bennerson (1995), *Teaching Exceptional Children, 28* (1), 37–41. Used by permission.

FAST Strategy

F	**FREEZE AND THINK**	What is the problem? Can I state the problem in behavioral terms?
A	**ALTERNATIVES**	What could I do to solve the problem? List possible alternatives.
S	**SOLUTION**	Which alternatives will solve the problem in the long run? Which are safe and fair? Select the best long-term alternative.
T	**TRY IT**	How can I implement the solution? Did it work? If this particular solution fails to solve the problem, return to the second step and pick another alternative that might solve the problem.

Intervention in cognitive and metacognitive skills has only recently received support from learning disabilities professionals. Powerful techniques are being studied to improve learning. Some of the ideas are relatively simple and require only common sense. Ensuring that a child is paying attention to the stimulus being presented is the first, and most important, one. Dimming the lights, calling for attention, or establishing eye contact might achieve this. Without attention, learning will not take place.

Lerner (1993) suggests that teachers present new information in well-organized, meaningful chunks. As new information is presented to be memorized, it should be linked to previously learned, meaningful information. For example, to teach subtraction, the teacher would demonstrate the relationship to addition. Students should also be encouraged to rehearse new information and be given many opportunities for practice. These and other effective learning strategies are presented in Figure 3.4.

THE SECONDARY LEVEL

Academic and language deficits, social and emotional problems, and differences in cognitive and metacognitive functioning continue to plague many adolescents with learning disabilities. With the focus on content classes in junior and high school, **remediation** of basic skills often is minimal.

However, the accommodation described in the next section and the learning strategies described in the previous section can also be used with secondary students to facilitate basic skill acquisition and to make learning and performance more effective and efficient (Deshler, Ellis, & Lenz, 1996). For example, instead of trying to bring basic skills to a level high enough to read a chapter in a content area textbook written on grade level, a teacher might assist students in comprehension by reading the heading and one or two sentences in each paragraph in a chapter. Figure 3.5 shows how the PASS method can be used as a reading comprehension strategy.

The teacher can also make an impact on student learning and performance by accounting for individual differences when developing lesson plans. Schumm, Vaughn, and Leavell (1994) suggest the following questions to guide teachers:

1. Will a concept be difficult for a student because of language differences?
2. Will difficulties in reading comprehension make it difficult for a student to learn concepts independently from the text?
3. Will concentration be a problem for students with attention and behaviour problems?
4. Will the vocabulary need to be taught in order for students to understand the concepts?
5. Do students have prior knowledge of the concept to facilitate understanding?
6. Can the cultural and linguistic backgrounds of the students be tied in to the concept in some way?

A major problem for secondary students with learning disabilities is a negative self-image regarding school which often stems from years of school failure. One study found that the dropout rate for students with learning disabilities was 36 percent, compared to 13 percent for students without disabilities (de Bettencourt, Zigmond, & Thornton, 1989). To help ameliorate unhappiness, school environments must be structured to create successful experiences. One

CONSIDER THIS
Review the strategies described in Figure 3.4. Discuss situations in which each one would be helpful for students.

SELF-QUESTIONING

Students quietly ask themselves questions about the material. This process is also referred to as verbal mediation. The internal language, or covert speech, helps organize material and behavior. Camp and Bash (1981) suggest the following types of questions:

What is the problem? (or) What am I supposed to do?

What is my plan? (or) How can I do it?

Am I using my plan?

How did I do?

VERBAL REHEARSAL AND REVIEW

Students practice and review what they have learned. This self-rehearsal helps students remember. People forget when the brain trace, which is a physical record of memory, fades away. Recitation and review of material to be learned help the student remember.

Students observe the instructor's modeling of verbalization of a problem.

Students instruct themselves by verbalizing aloud or in a whisper.

Students verbalize silently.

ORGANIZATION

To aid in recall, students figure out the main idea of the lesson and the supporting facts. The organization of the material has a great deal to do with how fast we can learn it and how well we can remember it. Already-existing memory units are called chunks, and through *chunking,* new material is reorganized into already-existing memory units. The more students can relate to what they already know, the better they will remember the new material.

USING PRIOR KNOWLEDGE

New material is linked to already-existing memory units. The more students can relate what they are learning to what they already know, the better they will remember.

MEMORY STRATEGIES

If new material is anchored to old knowledge, students are more likely to remember it. For example, one student re-membered the word *look* because it had two eyes in the middle. Some pupils can alphabetize only if they sing the "ABC" song. Some adults can remember people's names by using a mnemonic device that associates the name with a particular attribute of that individual, for example "blond Bill" or "green-sweater Gertrude."

PREDICTING AND MONITORING

Students guess about what they will learn in the lesson and then check on whether their guesses were correct.

ADVANCE ORGANIZERS

This technique establishes a mindset for the learner, relating new material to previously learned material. Students are told in advance about what they are going to learn. This sets the stage for learning and improves comprehension and the ability to recall what has been learned.

COGNITIVE BEHAVIOR MODIFICATION

This behavioral approach teaches students self-instruction, self-monitoring, and self-evaluation techniques (Meichenbaum, 1977). There are several steps:

The teacher models a behavior while giving an explanation.

The student performs the task while the teacher describes it.

The student talks the task through out loud.

The student whispers it to himself or herself.

The student performs the task with nonverbal self-cues.

MODELING

The teacher provides an example of appropriate cognitive behavior and problem-solving strategies. The teacher can talk through the cognitive processes being used.

SELF-MONITORING

Students learn to monitor their own mistakes. They learn to check their own responses and become conscious of errors or answers that do not make sense. To reach this stage requires active involvement in the learning process to recognize incongruities.

FIGURE 3.4
Learning Strategies

From *Learning Disabilities: Theories, Diagnosis, and Teaching Strategies* (6th ed.) (pp. 207–208), by J. W. Lerner, 1993, by Houghton Mifflin Company. Used by permission.

method involves students more actively designing their educational experiences and monitoring their own success. Students should be active members in IEP meetings, especially when they are deciding whether to take postsec-

PREVIEW, REVIEW, AND PREDICT

Preview by reading the heading and one or two sentences.

Review what you know already about this topic.

Predict what you think the text will be about.

ASK AND ANSWER QUESTIONS

Content-Focused Questions

Who? What? When? Where? Why? How?

How does this relate to what I already know?

Monitoring Questions

Is my prediction correct?

How is this different from what I thought it was going to be about?

Does this make sense?

Problem-Solving Questions

Is it important that it make sense?

Do I need to reread part of it?

Can I visualize the information?

Do I need to read it more slowly?

Does it have too many unknown words?

Do I need to pay more attention?

Should I get help?

SUMMARIZE

Say what the short passage was about.

SYNTHESIZE

Say how the short passage fits in with the whole passage.

Say how what you learned fits with what you knew.

FIGURE 3.5
PASS Reading Comprehension Strategy

From *Teaching Strategies and Methods* (2nd ed.) (p. 29), by D. Deshler, E. S. Ellis, and B. K. Lenz, 1996, Denver, CO: Love Publishing. Reprinted by permission.

TEACHING TIP

When teaching the PASS strategy to other students, model use of the strategy as you "think out loud" while applying the strategy to a chapter they might have to read. This demonstration will make the process more concrete for students.

ondary education or to obtain employment after high school (Lovitt, Cushing, & Stump, 1994).

Motivation is also a key ingredient to successful high school programming. Fulk and Montgomery-Grymes (1994) suggest the following techniques for increasing motivation:

- Involve students in decision making.
  1. Provide a menu from which students can select assignments to demonstrate knowledge.
  2. Allow flexible due dates.
  3. Involve students in scoring and evaluating their own work.
  4. Vary the length of assignments for differing student abilities.
  5. Set goals with the students.
- Create and maintain interest.
  1. Challenge each student at the optimal level.
  2. Show your enthusiasm as you introduce lessons.

Adolescents with learning disabilities experience problems in academic, language, social, and emotional areas.

3. Give clear, simple directions.
4. Set specific expectations.
5. Explain the relevance of each lesson.
6. Vary your teaching style.
- Address affective variables.
   1. Maintain a positive classroom environment.
   2. Give frequent feedback on performance.
   3. Acknowledge all levels of achievement.

High school students with learning disabilities especially need to acquire transition skills (e.g., abilities that will help students be successful after high school in employment and independent living). For students in inclusive settings, teachers can find ways to integrate transition topics into the regular curriculum. For example, when an English teacher assigns letter writing or term papers, students might focus their work on exploring different career opportunities. Math teachers can bring in income tax and budget forms to connect them to a variety of math skills. When planning any lesson, ask yourself, "Is there any way I can make this meaningful to my students' lives after high school?" See Table 3.1 for more ideas.

ADULTS

The instruction provided in high school classes can have a powerful impact on the outcome for adults with learning disabilities. The life skills applications of various school activities and lessons are described in Chapter 13. Relevant lessons in the general education curriculum can help adults be more successful in many aspects of independent living. Individuals with learning disabilities are deficient in choosing and carrying out strategies and they do not automatically generalize previously learned information to new challenges. Other cognitive difficulties include organizing thoughts and ideas, integrating and remembering information from a variety of sources, and solving problems

TABLE 3.1

Examples of Study Skill Functions in and out of the Classroom

Study Skill	School Examples	Life Skills Applications
READING RATE	Reviewing an assigned reading for a test	Reviewing an automobile insurance policy
	Looking for an explanation of a concept discussed in class	Reading the newspaper
LISTENING	Understanding instructions about a field trip	Understanding how a newly purchased appliance works
	Attending to morning announcements	Comprehending a radio traffic report
NOTE TAKING/ OUTLINING	Capturing information given by a teacher on how to dissect a frog	Writing directions to a party
	Framing the structure of a paper	Planning a summer vacation
REPORT WRITING	Developing a book report	Completing the personal goals section on a job application
	Completing a science project on a specific marine organism	Writing a complaint letter
ORAL PRESENTATION	Delivering a personal opinion on a current issue for a social studies class	Describing car problems to a mechanic
	Describing the results of a lab experiment	Asking a supervisor/boss for time off work
GRAPHIC AIDS	Setting up the equipment of a chemistry experiment based on a diagram	Utilizing the weather map in the newspaper
	Locating the most densely populated regions of the world on a map	Deciphering the store map in a mall
TEST TAKING	Developing tactics for retrieving information for a closed-book test	Preparing for a driver's license renewal test
	Comparing notes with textbook content	Participating in television self-tests
LIBRARY MATERIALS	Using picture files	Obtaining travel resources (books, videos)
	Searching a computerized catalogue	Viewing current periodicals
REFERENCE MATERIALS	Accessing CD-ROM encyclopedias	Using the yellow pages to locate a repair service
	Using a thesaurus to write a paper	Ordering from a mail-order catalog
TIME MANAGEMENT	Allocating a set time for homework	Maintaining a daily "to do" list
	Organizing a file system for writing a paper	Keeping organized records for tax purposes
SELF-MANAGEMENT	Ensuring that homework is signed by parents	Regulating a daily exercise program
	Rewarding oneself for controlling temper	Evaluating the quality of a home repair

From *Teaching Students with Learning Problems to Use Study Skills: A Teacher's Guide* (p. 7), by J. J. Hoover & J. R. Patton, 1995, TX: Pro-Ed. Reprinted by permission.

(Ryan & Price, 1992). Intervention in these areas must often be implemented for adults if the high school curriculum is not based on future needs and challenges (Dowdy & Smith, 1991).

An important study by Ginsberg, Gerber, and Reiff (1994) identified important characteristics of highly successful adults with learning disabilities.

Development of many of these factors can be encouraged by teachers and other individuals; however, some factors seem to be innate personality traits of the individuals themselves. One of the strongest predictors for success was the desire and willingness to persist and work extremely hard. Identifying appropriate goals and working to meet them were also important. The successful adults developed a plan and then worked hard to accomplish their goals.

Unfortunately, many adults leave high school without the skills and confidence necessary to find employment to help them realize their maximum potential and to live independently. A sample of 21-year-olds with learning disabilities studied by Haring, Lovitt, and Smith (1990) revealed that 79 percent were living with their parents. According to Ryan and Price (1992), problems in work settings can include the following:

- Identifying appropriate goals
- Getting started on tasks
- Maintaining attention to task
- Organizing and budgeting time
- Completing tasks
- Checking for errors
- Requesting support when appropriate
- Using self-advocacy skills to obtain resources

These skills can be taught and should be addressed in a secondary curriculum. For adults with learning disabilities, the Learning Disabilities Association of Canada (LDAC) offers a number of resources as well as access to a specific group of adults with learning disabilities that advises the Association. (See Resources at the end of the chapter.)

Controversial Approaches

Some interventions, often presented to the public through television or newsstand magazines, are controversial and have not been validated as effective for students with learning disabilities. Educators may be asked for an opinion on these therapies by parents who are attempting to find solutions to their children's frustrating problems. A brief overview of these nontraditional approaches follows. More extensive reviews are provided by Rooney (1991) and Silver (1995).

A recent controversial therapy involves the prescription of **tinted glasses** as a cure for dyslexia. In this approach, scotopic sensitivity, proposed to interfere with learning, is treated by identifying a coloured lens to reduce sensitivity. Rooney (1991) notes that the studies that support this treatment do not meet acceptable scientific standards and should be viewed with caution.

An older treatment theory is **orthomolecular therapy**, which focuses on vitamins, minerals, and diet. Proponents of this treatment claim that large doses of vitamins and minerals straighten out the biochemistry of the brain to reduce hyperactivity and to increase learning. Hair analysis and blood studies are used to determine the doses needed.

Feingold's Diet is another dietary treatment frequently cited. Feingold (1975) proposes that negative behaviours such as hyperactivity and limited learning are due to the body's reaction to unnatural substances such as food colourings, preservatives, and artificial dyes. His patients are asked to keep a comprehensive diary of their diet and to avoid harmful chemical substances. Other diets have focused on avoiding sugar and caffeine.

Another proponent of orthomolecular therapy suggests that negative behaviours result from allergies to food and environmental substances (Silver, 1995). The research on the efficacy of these diet-related interventions usually consists of clinical studies without control groups. When control groups are used, the diets do not substantiate the claims made for them. Only a small percentage of children benefit from them.

Vision therapy or training is another controversial treatment for individuals with a learning disability. It is based on the theory that learning disabilities are the result of visual defects that occur when the eyes do not work together and that these deficits can be cured by visual training. This widespread practice has been supported primarily by groups of optometrists. The American Academy of Ophthalmology (1984) has issued a statement clearly stating that "no credible evidence exists to show that visual training, muscle exercises, perceptual, or hand/eye coordination exercises significantly affect a child's Specific Learning Disabilities" (p. 3).

Silver (1995) reviewed another controversial therapy involving the use of **vestibular dysfunction medication** to cure dyslexia. He notes that the relationship between dyslexia, the vestibular system, and the medication was not supported by research. Silver also warns that physicians often do not diagnose dyslexia consistently and are prescribing doses of medication that are not recommended by pharmaceutical companies.

Silver is also concerned about the widespread use of other medications such as Ritalin for learning and attention problems. He warns that prescriptions are often given based on the recommendations of parents or teachers alone, without a comprehensive evaluation. Rooney (1991) states that the actual effectiveness of the medication is less an issue than the concerns that (1) the medication is prescribed without a thorough evaluation, (2) educational and behavioural treatments are not implemented in conjunction with the medication, and (3) there is insufficient monitoring of the effects of the medication. Monitoring these effects is a very important part of the role of classroom teachers. Use of medication is discussed further in Chapter 4.

CLASSROOM ACCOMMODATIONS

When developing classroom accommodations, remember the wide range of behaviours identified earlier that might characterize individuals with learning disabilities. The heterogeneity in this population is sometimes baffling. No child with a learning disability is going to be exactly like any other, so teachers must provide a wide range of accommodations to meet individual needs. In the following sections, accommodations are discussed for each of the areas described earlier: academic and language deficits, social-emotional problems, and other differences such as attention, memory, cognition, metacognition, perception, and motor skills.

Academic and Language Deficits

Students with learning disabilities may manifest deficits in the academic areas of reading skill, reading comprehension, math calculation, math applications, listening, speaking, and written language. Chapters 12 and 13 provide extensive modifications for students with learning disabilities at the elementary and secondary levels. Some general guidelines proposed by Chalmers (1991) include these:

FURTHER READING

Reading and understanding textbooks can be an overwhelming challenge for students with learning disabilities. R. Meese provides excellent strategies for modifying texts and teaching students how to understand content in her article "Adapting Textbooks for Children in Mainstreamed Classrooms," published in 1992 in volume 24, issue 3, of *Teaching Exceptional Children* (pp. 49–51)

- Preteach vocabulary, and assess the prior knowledge of students before you introduce new concepts.
- Establish a purpose for reading that gives students a specific goal for comprehension.
- Provide multiple opportunities to learn content: cooperative learning activities, study guides, choral responses, and hands-on participation.
- Provide oral and written directions that are clear and simple.
- Have students rephrase directions to make sure they understand them.
- Reduce time pressure by adjusting requirements: give more time to complete a challenging project, or shorten the assignment. Ask students to work every other problem or every third problem so they won't be overwhelmed.
- Provide frequent feedback, and gradually allow students to evaluate their own work.
- Have students use an assignment notebook to record important information and daily assignments.
- Provide options for students to demonstrate their knowledge or skill (e.g., videotape presentation, artwork, oral or written report).
- Use demonstrations and manipulatives frequently to make learning more concrete.
- Modify textbooks as shown in Figure 3.6.
- When using worksheets, avoid crowding too much material on a single page.
- Provide a listening guide or a partial outline to assist students in note taking.
- Use a buddy system for studying or for note taking. Allow a good note taker to work with the student with the learning disability, sharing notes duplicated on carbon paper or NCR paper.
- Allow students to tape-record lectures if necessary.
- Reduce the homework load, or allow the parent to write the student's dictated answers.

TEACHING TIP

Each word-processing program has unique features. Try to have several programs available so students can experiment and find the one that works best for them.

For students with learning difficulties in writing, a word processor can be invaluable. It allows students to see their work in a more legible format and simplifies proofreading and revising.

A variety of software programs meet the needs of students with learning disabilities. In addition to those that help students to work around or to accommodate their difficulties, there are programs that provide fun and interesting drill and skill-building activities for younger children. The programs that provide accommodations for students with learning disabilities include the common spell-checkers, grammar checkers, thesaurus options, and the less common voice word processors. The voice word processors allow students with learning disabilities to dictate their written work and then listen to the computer read it back to them. As a student dictates, the words appear on the screen where they can be read. The drill and skill-building programs consist of a variety of game-format drills in areas such as basic math facts, word attack, other reading skills, and spelling. Other skill-building programs that are appropriate for both younger and older students teach geography, history, science, and problem solving. A few of the best established, award-winning programs are listed below; however, because new innovations occur constantly

FIGURE 3.6
Guidelines for Adapting
Content Area Textbooks
Adapted from "Guidelines for
Adapting Content Area
Textbooks: Keeping Teachers
and Students Content," by J. S.
Schumm and K. Strickler, 1991,
Intervention in School and Clinic,
27 (2), pp. 79–84.

Determine "goodness of fit" by comparing the readability level of the text and the student's reading ability. If accommodations are needed, consider the following:

1. **SUBSTITUTE TEXTBOOK READING BY**
   - supplying an audiotape of the text.
   - pairing students to learn text material together.
   - substituting the text with direct experiences or videos.
   - holding tutorial sessions to teach content to a small group.

2. **SIMPLIFY TEXT BY**
   - developing abridged versions (volunteers may be helpful).
   - developing chapter outlines or summaries.
   - finding a text with similar content written at a lower level.

3. **HIGHLIGHT KEY CONCEPTS BY**
   - establishing the purpose for reading.
   - overviewing the assignment before reading.
   - reviewing charts, graphs, vocabulary, and key concepts before reading.
   - reducing amount of work by targeting the most important information or slowing down pace of assignments.

in the field, contact your local computer software outlet to obtain information on the newest software to fit your needs.

- Magic School Bus series by Microsoft: Software programs explore a variety of science activities in an interactive manner. Ages 6 to 10.
- Early Learning House series by Edmark Corporation: The series teaches a variety of math, reading, and science concepts. It includes Sammy's Science House, Millie's Math House, and Bailey's Book House. Ages 3 to 6.
- Reader Rabbits by the Learning Company: This program builds basic reading skills. Ages 3 to 8.
- Blaster series by Knowledge Adventure: Reading Blaster, Math Blaster, and Spelling Blaster software programs build basic skills through fun drills. Ages 5 and up.
- Carmen Sandiego series by the Learning Company: Where in the world is Carmen Sandiego? and Where in time is Carmen Sandiego? teach geography and history, respectively, using an interactive game format. Ages 8 and up.

In summary, software distributors that have consistently earned high ratings by educators are Knowledge Adventure ((310) 793-0600), the Learning Company (1-(800) 852-2255/(510) 792-2101), and Edmark ((206) 556-8484). Children and adolescents with learning disabilities benefit enormously from computer software where they can control their own learning.

Social-Emotional Problems

As discussed earlier, the social and emotional problems of individuals with learning disabilities may be closely tied to academic failure. Many of the academic accommodations already described will encourage success in the classroom,

FURTHER READING

Students with learning disabilities face many challenges, both at home and at school. It is important to identify these challenges and determine where the student will have trouble meeting the demands. J. E. Ysseldyke, S. Christenson, and J. F. Kovaleski (1994) provide a practical example in their article "Identifying Students' Instructional Needs in the Context of Classroom and Home Environments, published in volume 26, issue 3, of *Teaching Exceptional Students* (pp. 37–41).

FURTHER READING

Tips for accommodating a variety of behaviours associated with learning disabilities and attention deficit can be found in a text by C. A. Dowdy, J. R. Patton, E. A. Polloway, and T. E. C. Smith, *Attention-Deficit/Hyperactivity Disorder in the Classroom: A Practical Guide for Teachers*, published in 1997 by Pro-Ed.

which ultimately leads to increased emotional stability and greater confidence in approaching new academic tasks. A student who has deficits in social skills may need previously described training. However, some accommodations may still be needed even when the training begins to show results. All students need to work in an isolated setting in the classroom during particularly challenging times. Distractions caused by peers may interfere with meeting academic challenges successfully. However, if teachers make the student with learning disabilities sit in a segregated portion of the room all the time, it sends a bad message to others. Be sure to include students with disabilities in group activities such as cooperative learning to provide them with models of appropriate interactions and social skills. Identify the students in the classroom who seem to work best with individuals with a learning disability, and give them opportunities to interact. When conflicts arise, provide good modelling for the student by verbalizing the bad choices that were made and the good choices that could have been made.

Students with learning disabilities may have difficulty responding appropriately to verbal and nonverbal cues, so avoid sarcasm and use simple concrete language when giving directions and when teaching. If a student has difficulty accepting new tasks without complaint, consider providing a written assignment that the student can refer to for direction. When a student frequently upsets or irritates others in the classroom, you might agree on a contract to reduce the inappropriate behaviour and reinforce positive peer interaction. Periodically review the rules for the classroom, and keep them posted as a quick reference. To assist students who have difficulty making and keeping friends, you can subtly point out their strengths to encourage the other students to want to be their friends. Allowing a student to demonstrate his or her expertise in an area or to share a hobby may stimulate conversations that can eventually lead to friendships.

Because many students with learning disabilities cannot predict the consequences of negative behaviour, teachers need to explain the consequences of rule breaking and other inappropriate actions. Though you can implement many behaviour management techniques to reinforce positive behaviour, it is important to train the student in methods of self-monitoring and self-regulation. The ultimate goal is for the student to be able to identify socially inappropriate behaviour and get back on track.

Cognitive Differences

Cognitive problems described earlier include deficits in attention, perception, motor abilities, problem solving, and metacognition. Accommodations for individuals exhibiting problems in attention will be described more fully in Chapter 4. Accommodations can also help individuals with difficulties or preferences in the area of perception. For some students, presenting information visually through the overhead projector, reading material, videos, and graphics will be most effective. Other individuals will respond better by hearing the information. Teachers can accommodate these individual differences by identifying the preferred style of learning and either providing instruction and directions in the preferred style or teaching in a multisensory fashion that stimulates both auditory and visual perception. Combining seeing, saying, writing, and doing provides multiple opportunities for presenting new information. It also helps children remember important information.

Difficulties in the area of motor abilities might be manifested as poor handwriting skills or as struggles with other fine motor activities. Accommodations might include overlooking the difficulties in handwriting and providing a grade based not on the appearance of the handwriting but on the content of the material. You might allow students with such difficulties to provide other evidence of their learning, such as oral reports or special projects. Let them select physical fitness activities that focus on their areas of strength, rather than their deficits.

Students with difficulties in problem solving require careful direction and programming. Their deficits in reasoning skills make them especially prone to academic failures. The instructional strategies described earlier will remedy problems in this area; also frequent modelling of problem-solving strategies will strengthen developing skills.

Students with problems in the area of metacognition need to keep an assignment notebook or a monthly calendar to project the time needed to complete tasks or to prepare for tests. Students should be taught to organize their notebooks and their desks so that materials can be retrieved efficiently. If students have difficulty following or developing a plan, assist them in setting long-range goals and breaking down those goals into realistic steps. Prompt them with questions such as "What do you need to be able to do this?" Help students set clear time frames in which to accomplish each step. Assist them in prioritizing activities and assignments, and provide them with models that they can refer to often.

Encourage students to ask for help when needed and to use self-checking methods to evaluate their work on an ongoing basis. Reinforce all signs of appropriate self-monitoring and self-regulation in the classroom. These behaviours will facilitate success after high school.

Accommodations for attention deficits and hyperactivity are addressed in Chapter 4.

PROMOTING A SENSE OF COMMUNITY AND SOCIAL ACCEPTANCE

After identifying an appropriate educational plan for individuals with learning disabilities and determining the accommodations that should lead to a successful educational program, the next challenge is to ensure that the children in the general education classroom and the child with the learning disability understand the disability and the need for special education. Primarily, children should be made aware that all people are different.

Teaching tips for general educators are offered in Chapters 12 and 13, which focus on behaviour management and accommodations for elementary and secondary classrooms. The following list of recommended guidelines for teaching children and adolescents with learning disabilities has been compiled from work by Mercer (1997), Deiner (1993), and Bender (1995):

1. Be consistent in class rules and daily schedule of activities.
2. State rules and expectations clearly. Tell children what to do—not what *not* to do. For example, instead of saying, "Don't run in the halls," say, "Walk in the halls."

CONSIDER THIS

What are your personal strengths and challenges? How are you alike and different from your family members and your peers? We are all different—can we learn to celebrate our differences?

PERSONAL SPOTLIGHT

Special Education Specialist ■ LYNN HEATH

Teacher at EAST Alternative School, Toronto

Lynn Heath has been a special education/regular education teacher for 20 years in Quebec and Ontario. She has taught from Grade 4 to Grade 13 in both the public and private systems. During that time she has dealt extensively with all aspects of special education, primarily focusing on students with learning disabilities and those designated as gifted. She has worked in segregated classrooms for students with learning disabilities, as well as in the integrated models. She has also always worked privately as an educational consultant and tutor for students with learning disabilities. She is currently teaching Grades 7 and 8 at an alternative school within the Toronto District School Board, where her students exhibit a wide range of challenges and abilities.

Lynn feels strongly that the accepted definition of the student with a learning disability as a person with average or above-average intelligence who faces one or more specific areas of learning challenges needs to be emphasized within the schools, and to the students themselves. She has worked extensively with students, parents, and teachers who do not seem to understand this basic fact about students with learning disabilities. She has seen such students become discouraged and often turn away from academics. Having closely followed some students with learning disabilities from the very early grades to their university graduation, Lynn has witnessed the frustration and the real pain experienced by students with learning disabilities as the academic world mislabels them and underestimates their abilities. She has also seen educators who assume that, because the difficulties are invisible, students are simply "lazy" or "not working up to potential." These misconceptions are equally damaging.

Lynn has listened to student after student express doubt about his or her own ability, after a well-meaning guidance counsellor or teacher has suggested that maybe the student shouldn't consider university—it would be too hard. And she has seen such students feel terribly guilty about asking for any kind of special consideration as that would be "unfair." No one else gets extra time . . .

Lynn speaks out at parent teacher association meetings to parents, teachers, and especially to her own students about the need to recognize the issues that arise around students with learning disabilities as equity issues. In education, we do not talk about equality, everyone getting the same thing, but equity—each student getting what she or he needs to succeed.

Much of Lynn's work with students with learning disabilities is focused on training them to be their own advocates: to recognize that just as blind students have the right to Braille, they have the right to the accommodations that will allow them to receive an education. Many schools and universities have recognized the enormous potential of students with learning disabilities, and accommodations have been legislated but, far too often, the students still have to fight for them.

Lynn has been consistently impressed and moved by the response of her students with learning disabilities to the challenges facing them. To one who asked, in a particularly bleak time in his academic life, was he just "tilting at windmills," Lynn responded that there was no windmill he couldn't defeat given his intelligence, persistence, and incredible courage. She believes this is true, but also recognizes that such a student needs aware and informed educators to make it possible.

3. Give advance organizers to prepare children for any changes in the day's events and to highlight the important points to be covered during instructional time.
4. Eliminate or reduce visual and auditory distractions when children need to concentrate. Help children focus on the important aspects of the task.

5. Give directions in clear, simple words. A long series of directions may need to be broken down and given one at time. Reinforcement may be needed as each step is completed.

6. Begin with simple activities focused on a single concept and build to more abstract ideas as the child appears ready. If problems occur, check for the presence of the prerequisite skills or knowledge of the vocabulary being used.

7. Use concrete objects or demonstrations when teaching a new concept. Relate new information to previously known concepts.

8. Teach the children strategies for remembering.

9. Present information visually, auditorially, and through demonstration to address each child's preferred learning style.

10. Use a variety of activities and experiences to teach or reinforce the same concept. Repetition can be provided without inducing boredom.

11. Use activities that are short or that encourage movement. Some children may need to work standing up!

12. Incorporate problem-solving activities or other projects that involve the children. Use both higher-level and lower-level questions.

13. Always gain the student's attention before presenting important information.

14. Use cooperative instructional groupings and peer tutoring to vary modes of instruction.

15. Plan for success!

SUMMARY

- A learning disability is frequently misunderstood because it is hidden. It may be mistaken for purposely uncooperative behaviour.

- Learning disabilities is a relatively young field, and basic definitions, etiology, and criteria for special education eligibility remain controversial.

- The most widely used criterion for identifying a learning disability is a severe discrepancy between ability and achievement that cannot be explained by another handicapping condition or lack of learning opportunity.

- Characteristics of learning disabilities are manifested across the lifespan.

- Learning disabilities are manifested in seven areas of academics and language: reading skills, reading comprehension, mathematical calculations, mathematical reasoning, written expression, oral expression, and listening comprehension.

- Other common characteristics of learning disabilities include social-emotional problems and difficulties with attention and hyperactivity, memory, cognition, metacognition, motor skills, and perceptual abilities.

- Interventions for elementary children with learning disabilities address academic and language deficits, social-emotional problems, and cognitive and metacognitive problems.

- Secondary students with learning disabilities continue to need remediation of basic skills, but they also benefit from strategies that will make them more efficient learners.

- A secondary curriculum that includes application of life skills can produce successful outcomes for adults with learning disabilities.

- Successful adults with learning disabilities are goal directed, work hard to accomplish their goals, understand and accept their strengths and limitations, and advocate for themselves.

- Accommodations in the general education classroom can address the academic, social-emotional, and cognitive, metacognition, and attentional differences of students with learning disabilities.

- The role of the classroom teacher includes using effective teaching strategies and accommodations to address the challenges of students with LD, as well as helping a child with a learning disability and other children in the general class understand and accept a learning disability.

RESOURCES

Books

Learning Disabilities Association of Canada. *The Learning Disabilities Association of Canada (LDAC) Resource Directory.* (1999). Ottawa: Author.

The LDAC Directory is the only comprehensive up-to-date listing of services throughout Canada for children, youth, and adults with learning disabilities. It, like the title below, is available from the Association (see National Association below).

Learning Disabilities Association of Canada. (1998). *Advocating for Your Child with Learning Disabilities: A Guide Developed for Parents by the Learning Disabilities Association of Canada.* Ottawa: Author.

This practical guide for parents provides straightforward information on how to advocate for your child with LD as he or she moves through the school system.

Winebrenner, Susan. (1996). *Teaching Kids with Learning Difficulties in the Regular Classroom: Strategies and Techniques Every Teacher Can Use to Challenge and Motivate Struggling Students.* Minneapolis, MN: Free Spirit Publishing.

A valuable collection of easy-to-use strategies is backed up by scenarios that illustrate each technique. Winebrenner, a skilled classroom teacher, presents techniques for dealing with diverse learning styles, language literacy, science, math, social studies, behaviour problems, and more.

Special "Question and Answer" sections address specific issues and concerns. There are more than 50 reproducible pages to use with students.

Videos

A Mind of Your Own. National Film Board.

This 37-minute video, excellent viewing for students in elementary and secondary classes, will heighten awareness about the experience of having a learning disability. Students with learning disabilities tell about their experiences in school.

How difficult can this be? Understanding Learning Disabilities: The F.A.T. City Workshop by Richard Lavoie. (1989). Etobicoke, ON: PBS and Visual Educational Centre.

This video provides a simulation of having a learning disability while teaching the viewer about learning disabilities. Teachers remember it for years and seek to view it again and again. Many school boards and most local chapters of learning disabilities associations have a copy of the video for loan.

National Association

Learning Disabilities Association of Canada
323 Chapel Street, Suite 200, Ottawa, ON K1N 7Z2
Phone: (613) 238-5721; Fax: (613) 235-5391
E-mail: ldactaac@fox.nstn.ca
Web site: **educ.queensu.ca/~lda**

WEBLINKS

Learning Disabilities Association of Ontario (LDAO)
www.ldao.on.ca/
LDAO's site, one of the few specifically Canadian sites on learning disabilities, provides a number of resources and suggested books and videos, as well as other related links.

Learning Disabilities Online
www.ldonline.org/index.html
This site provides information on research, links, articles, and more. It is recommended by the Learning Disabilities Association of Canada.

Division for Learning Disabilities (DLD)
www.dldcec.org/
One of 17 divisions of the Council for Exceptional Children, DLD provides mainly American links, but there is information that is applicable to all individuals with LD.

Council for Learning Disabilities (CLD)
www.cldinternational.org/
The CLD site provides services to professionals who work with individuals with learning disabilities. Information focuses on interventions for teachers working with individuals with LD. Journal and conference information are available.

National Centre for Learning Disabilities (NCLD)
www.ncld.org
As this site reflects, the NCLD develops training and educational materials for parents and practitioners.

Learning Disabilities Association of America (LDA)
www.ldanatl.org
Visit this Web site to see the range of resources available through the Association. The LDA national office has a resource centre of more than 500 publications for sale; it also operates a film rental service.

CHAPTER FOUR

Teaching Students with Attention Deficit/Hyperactivity Disorder

Jenny is 20 years old and is a successful student at university. For many years Jenny and her parents did not think she would be able to attend university. She was raised in a rural part of Alberta; her parents had not gone to university, but they had high hopes for their child, who was obviously very bright. However, when Jenny entered school, she was soon labelled a failure. She did not seem to listen to the teacher, she didn't follow instructions, she would leave unfinished work and begin a new project, she seldom had appropriate school supplies, and she rarely turned in homework. Her mother said she knew Jenny did her homework because she helped her, and she also purchased the necessary school supplies. She couldn't understand what was going on between home and school.

The teachers called Jenny's mom frequently to complain that Jenny wasn't trying and to urge her to get Jenny to straighten up! Her mother tried to get help at school, but Jenny didn't qualify for special education services. She wasn't intellectually disabled or seriously emotionally disturbed, and her academic skills were not low enough to qualify her for a learning disabilities class. Jenny's mother tried to help with lessons, but by high school, the demands were beyond the abilities of the family members, and school had become so painful for Jenny that she started skipping classes. She was befriended by a group of students who were also skipping school, but they were into drugs. Jenny was really heading for trouble when her mother heard about attention deficit/hyperactivity disorder on a radio show. Recognizing her own daughter in the descriptions and personal stories, Jenny's mother made an appointment with Jenny's pediatrician.

Through a collaboration between her physician and the school and home, Jenny was diagnosed as having an attention deficit/hyperactivity disorder (AD/HD). With specific accommodations and support from the school Jenny was able to finish high school. She learned that universities had special services for students with AD/HD, so she applied and was admitted. At the university, she takes her tests in a distraction-free environment and is allowed to use 2 1/2 times the normal testing period. Another student takes notes for Jenny in classes, and a tutor is available if she has special problems in class. It looks as if Jenny will finish university and lead a productive life. Still very bitter about her treatment in school, she says that if she is a success in life, it will be in spite of her school experiences—not because of them! She attributes her current success to the effort and support of her mom.

1. How could Jenny's teacher have made a difference in her early school years?

2. How could Jenny's school years have been more positive?

INTRODUCTION

Attention deficit/hyperactivity disorder (AD/HD) is a complex condition that has been a major concern in public education for several years. It is a complicated but intriguing topic and a real challenge for classroom teachers. This condition remains controversial because professional perspectives and personal opinions vary regarding the nature of AD/HD and effective intervention techniques. In the past few years awareness of this disability has significantly increased, along with successful intervention plans for students who struggle with it.

In the United States students with attention-deficit disorder who need special education or related services can qualify for those services under existing special education categories. The category of **other health impaired (OHI)** is recommended as the appropriate classification for students whose primary disability is AD/HD. This category includes "any chronic and acute condition that results in limited alertness and adversely affects educational performance" (U.S. Department of Education, 1991). To date, there is little evidence that the category of OHI is used on a widespread basis for students identified as having AD/HD (Reid, Maag, Vasa, & Wright, 1994).

CONSIDER THIS

Do the results of the study by Reid and his colleagues surprise you? Although you have not yet studied behavioural disorders or intellectual disabilities, can you predict how they differ from learning disabilities? How would AD/HD overlap with these other disabilities?

In the event that a student with AD/HD does not qualify for services using the special education categories, services might be made available under a civil rights law (Section 504 of the Rehabilitation Act of 1973) which protects any individual with a disability. If the student is found to be disabled under the law, the school must develop a plan for delivery of services (Council of Administrators of Special Education, 1992). Thus, in the United States students with AD/HD are eligible for services through both educational and civil legislation.

However, in a school-based study of students with AD/HD, Reid et al. (1994) found that only 50 percent of these students were receiving special services under the legal and educational provisions noted above. Nearly 52 percent of students with AD/HD were identified as behaviourally disordered, 29 percent were identified as learning disabled, and 9 percent were identified as "mentally retarded." These findings serve to illustrate the difficulty in identifying and serving students with AD/HD.

In Canada, provincial educational jurisdictions do not list AD/HD as a distinct category of exceptionality (Friend, Bursuck, & Hutchinson, 1998). However, for example, British Columbia's special education policy manual (1995) suggests that the category of learning disability may include AD/HD. In general, the policy in Canada is that children with AD/HD may qualify for services under other categories such as behavioural disorders and learning disabilities. The identification of a student with an AD/HD requires a physician's input; it is not primarily an educational diagnosis.

Teachers must understand AD/HD in order to recognize the characteristics of AD/HD and, most important, to implement effective intervention strategies and accommodations to facilitate success for these children in their classrooms.

BASIC CONCEPTS

A ttention deficit/hyperactivity disorder is an invisible, hidden disability in that no unique physical characteristics differentiate these children from others. However, AD/HD is not hard to spot in the classroom.

> Just look with your eyes and listen with your ears as you walk through the places where children are—particularly those places where children are expected to behave in a quiet, orderly, productive fashion. In such places, children with AD/HD will identify themselves quite readily. They will be doing or not doing something which frequently results in their receiving a barrage of comments and criticisms such as, "Why don't you ever listen?" "Think before you act." "Pay attention." (Fowler, 1992, p. 3)

The condition can be recognized only through specific behavioural manifestations that may occur during the learning process. As a **developmental disability**, AD/HD becomes apparent before the age of seven; however, in as many as two thirds of the cases, it continues to cause problems in adulthood. During the school years AD/HD may have an impact on success in both academic and nonacademic areas. It occurs across all cultural, racial, and socioeconomic groups. It can affect children and adults with all levels of intelligence (Fowler, 1992).

Definition

Although a variety of terms have been used over the years to describe this disorder, currently the term *attention deficit/hyperactivity disorder* is most common. The terminology stems from the ***Diagnostic and Statistical Manual of Mental Disorders*** (4th ed.; *DSM-IV*; American Psychiatric Association, 1994). On a global level, the *International Classification of Diseases* (10th ed.; *ICD-10*, 1992) is used to describe these children. This classification system uses the term **hyperkinetic disorders** to describe conditions related to problems in attention and hyperactivity.

AD/HD primarily refers to deficits in attention and behaviours characterized by impulsivity and hyperactivity. The *DSM-IV* (American Psychiatric Association, 1994) classifies AD/HD as a disruptive disorder expressed in persistent patterns of inappropriate degrees of attention or hyperactivity-impulsivity. A distinction must be made between AD/HD and other disorders such as conduct disorder (e.g., physical fighting) and oppositional defiant disorder (e.g., recurrent patterns of disobedience). The *DSM-IV* has been widely adopted as a guide to the diagnosis of AD/HD. According to this document, AD/HD encompasses four types of disabilities. The diagnostic criteria for AD/HD are presented in Figure 4.1. The identification of the specific type of AD/HD depends on the number of symptoms in Sections 1 and 2 that can be ascribed to the child. For example, a combination of attention deficit and hyperactivity is designated if six or more symptoms are identified from each section. A diagnosis of attention deficit/hyperactivity with predominant problems with attention is indicated if six or more symptoms are identified from Section 1 only. A third

FURTHER READING
The *DSM-IV* is a diagnostic guide and classification system for mental disorders. Survey a copy to see the range of disorders included. Select a disorder, such as conduct disorder or oppositional defiant disorder, and compare the criteria for identification to that of AD/HD.

A. Either (1) or (2):
   (1) **Inattention:** At least six of the following symptoms of inattention have persisted for at least 6 months to a degree that is maladaptive and inconsistent with developmental level:
      (a) Often fails to give close attention to details or makes careless mistakes in schoolwork, work, or other activities
      (b) Often has difficulty sustaining attention in tasks or play activities
      (c) Often does not seem to listen to what is being said to him or her
      (d) Often does not follow through on instructions and fails to finish schoolwork, chores, or duties in the workplace (not due to oppositional behaviour or failure to understand instructions)
      (e) Often has difficulties organizing tasks and activities
      (f) Often avoids and strongly dislikes tasks that require sustained mental effort (such as schoolwork and homework)
      (g) Often loses things necessary for tasks and activities (e.g., school assignments, pencils, books, tools, or toys)
      (h) Often is easily distracted by extraneous stimuli
      (i) Often is forgetful in daily activities
   (2) **Hyperactivity-impulsivity:** At least six of the following symptoms of hyperactivity-impulsivity have persisted for at least six months to a degree that is maladaptive and inconsistent with developmental level:
      Hyperactivity:
      (a) Often fidgets with hands or feet or squirms in seat
      (b) Often leaves seat in classroom or in other situations in which remaining in seat is expected
      (c) Often runs about or climbs excessively in situations where it is inappropriate (in adolescents and adults, may be limited to subjective feelings or restlessness)
      (d) Often has difficulty playing or engaging in leisure activities quietly
      (e) Always is "on the go" or acts as if "driven by a motor"
      (f) Often talks excessively
      Impulsivity:
      (g) Often bursts out answers to questions before the questions have been completed
      (h) Often has difficulty waiting in lines or awaiting turn in games or group situations
      (i) Often interrupts or intrudes on others (e.g., butts into others' conversations or games)

B. Some symptoms that caused impairment were present before age 7.

C. Some symptoms that cause impairment are present in two or more settings (e.g., at school, work, and at home).

D. There must be clear evidence of clinically significant impairment in social, academic, or occupational functioning.

E. Does not occur exclusively during the course of a pervasive developmental disorder, schizophrenia or other psychotic disorder, and is not better accounted for by mood disorder, anxiety disorder, dissociative disorder, or a personality disorder.

FIGURE 4.1
Criteria for Attention Deficit/Hyperactivity Disorder

From *Diagnostic and Statistical Manual of Mental Disorders* (4th ed.) (pp. 83–85), by the American Psychiatric Association, 1994, Washington, DC: Author. Used by permission.

type of attention deficit/hyperactivity disorder has a predominant number of hyperactivity-impulsivity behaviours. Last, a category called "attention deficit/hyperactivity disorder not otherwise specified" is typically used for students who do not meet the criteria for AD/HD but have significant symptoms related to the condition.

There are many different theories regarding the cause of AD/HD.

Identification of the characteristics associated with AD/HD is critical in the diagnosis. They are listed in Figure 4.1. The teacher often brings the AD/HD-like behaviours to the attention of the parents. When parents initiate contact with the school to find help, as Jenny's parents did, they will be served best by teachers who are already well informed about this condition and the special education assessment process.

Prevalence and Causes

According to the Canadian Pediatric Society (1998), estimates of the prevalence of attention deficit/hyperactivity disorder in school-age children vary from 1.0 percent to 14.0 percent, with evidence that at any given time 9.0 percent of boys and 3.3 percent of girls will meet criteria for diagnosis. Only about half that number continue to show evidence of AD/HD over a longer term. In the United States the prevalence rates have ranged widely, from a conservative 2 percent to a high of 30 percent of school-age children (American Psychiatric Association, 1994). Regardless of the exact prevalence figure, a number of students with this condition attend general education classrooms.

Several theories have been developed to explain the primary causes of AD/HD. Most professionals agree that AD/HD is a neurologically based condition. The cause might be

- neuroanatomical—related to brain structure;
- neurochemical—related to a chemical imbalance in the brain or a deficiency in chemicals that regulate behaviour;
- neurophysiological—related to brain function;
- some combination of these causes.

CONSIDER THIS
Review the characteristics and criteria in Figure 4.1. Can you think of examples of situations in which these characteristics might be observed in a school setting? at home? at work?

Some data suggest that genetics plays a significant role in AD/HD. Studies have shown that parents and siblings of children with this disorder have higher rates of AD/HD than expected in the general population. This finding suggests a familial association with various features of AD/HD. It is possible for neurological conditions to be transmitted genetically, predisposing an individual to hyperactivity or attention problems. Little or no evidence points to physical environment, social factors, diet, or poor parental management as causes of AD/HD (Barkley, 1991).

For most students, the precise cause of the problem may never be understood. Riccio, Hynd, Cohen, and Gonzales (1993) report that neurological evidence that precisely explains AD/HD is not yet available. Although many parents want to understand why their children have a developmental disability such as AD/HD, its cause is really not relevant to educational strategies or medical treatment. These can succeed without pinpointing the root of the problem.

Characteristics

CROSS-REFERENCE

Refer to the opening vignette in this chapter. Identify which of Jenny's characteristics would lead a teacher or parent to suspect AD/HD.

The characteristics of AD/HD manifest themselves in many different ways in the classroom. Recognizing them and identifying accommodations or strategies to lessen the impact in the classroom constitute a significant challenge for teachers. The characteristics listed in the *DSM-IV* criteria highlight the observable behaviours. Barkley (1991) groups these characteristics into the following five features:

1. *Limited sustained attention or persistence of attention to tasks:* Particularly during tedious, long-term tasks, the students become rapidly bored and frequently shift from one uncompleted activity to another. They may lose concentration during long work periods and fail to complete routine work unless closely supervised.

2. *Reduced impulse control or limited delay of gratification:* This feature is often observed in an individual's difficulty in waiting for his or her turn while talking to others or playing. Students may not stop and think before acting or speaking. They may have difficulty working toward long-term goals and long-term rewards, preferring to work on shorter tasks that promise immediate reinforcement.

3. *Excessive task-irrelevant activity or activity poorly regulated to match situational demands:* Individuals with AD/HD are often extremely fidgety and restless. Their movement seems excessive and often not directly related to the task—for example, tapping pencils, rocking, or shifting positions frequently. They also have trouble sitting still and inhibiting their movements when the situation demands it.

4. *Deficient rule following:* Individuals with AD/HD frequently have difficulty following through on assignments and instructions. The problem is not due to inability to comprehend the instructions, memory impairment, or defiance. The instructions simply do not regulate behaviour or stimulate the desired response.

5. *Greater than normal variability during task performance:* Individuals with AD/HD demonstrate considerable variation in the accuracy, quality, and speed of their performance of assigned tasks. Their relatively high performance on some occasions, coupled with low levels of accuracy on other occasions, can be baffling. Low levels of performance often occur with repetitive or tedious tasks.

Barkley (1991) points out that many of these characteristics are prevalent in normal individuals, particularly young children; however, the behaviours occur to a far greater degree and at a higher frequency in individuals with AD/HD. Figure 4.2 cites specific behaviours from the previous categories that are reported during preschool and later periods by parents and teachers, showing how the behaviours can be manifested in different environments.

The characteristics of AD/HD may also be present in adulthood. For some individuals the condition continues to cause problems and limitations in the world of work, as well as in other life activities. Barkley (1991) reports that between 35 percent and 65 percent of individuals with AD/HD will have trouble with tendencies toward aggressiveness, inappropriate conduct, and violation of social norms or legal mandates during adolescence. As many as 25 percent may be antisocial as adults.

Goldstein and Goldstein (1990) suggest that the characteristics of AD/HD affect ultimate success of many aspects of adult adjustment: intelligence, socioeconomic status, socialization, activity level, ability to delay rewards, limiting aggression, and family mental health. For some adults the effects of AD/HD

TEACHING TIP

As another technique for recording a student's behaviour, observe a child for 3–5 minutes every hour during a school day, and document whether the child is on or off task. Record what the child is supposed to be doing, what he or she is actually doing, and the consequences of that behaviour (e.g., praise, ignoring). Figure the percentage of on- and off-task behaviour.

PRESCHOOL AGE

Parents' Reports

excessive busyness

accidents related to independence

resistance to routines, e.g., brushing teeth, getting dressed

shifts frequently across play activities

talks too much

easily upset or frustrated

disruptiveness

noncompliance

aggressive in play

Teachers' Reports

more activity

more talking

less time spent on any single activity

noncompliance

SCHOOL AGE

Parents' Reports

fidgeting, talking especially during homework

greater dependence on adults

noisiness

interrupting

bossiness

less sharing; rough play

poor peer relations

immature social interactions; few friends

self-centered

easily bored

Teachers' Reports

fidgeting

out of seat

requiring more supervision

more talking

interrupting

off task, especially visual off task (looks about)

bossiness

erratic productivity

intrudes on others' activities

poor persistence of effort

FIGURE 4.2

Characteristics of Children with AD/HD During Preschool and School-Age Periods as Reported by Parents and Teachers

From the *Ch.A.D.D. Manual* (pp. 11–12), by Mary Fowler, 1992, Fairfax, VA: CASET Association. Used by permission.

linger, but change somewhat—for example, hyperactivity may evolve into a general feeling of restlessness. Other symptoms may also be felt or observed to a lesser degree. In any case, AD/HD can have significant effects on adult outcomes. Teachers who can identify and plan meaningful interventions for students with AD/HD can have a powerful impact on their success during the school years as well as their quality of life as adults.

Identification, Assessment, and Eligibility

Although in the United States the assessment of an AD/HD is the responsibility of public education personnel (Cantu, 1993), in Canada the identification of an AD/HD ultimately requires the involvement of a physician or psychiatrist. As Weber and Bennett (1999) indicate in their book, *Special Education in Ontario*, while educational jurisdictions acknowledge AD/HD, similar to how they acknowledge conditions like Tourette's syndrome, AD/HD is not an exceptionality category in the education systems across Canada. However, the identification of an AD/HD in a student frequently begins in the school through a teacher or parent referral to the school psychologist or school team. Because of the large overlap between attention deficits and other recognized exceptionalities, such as learning disabilities and behavioural disorders, the school assessment of the student with suspected AD/HD is essential. Therefore, teachers should be familiar with the specific behaviours and the commonly used assessment techniques associated with attention-deficit disorders. Formal assessment for AD/HD should require the teacher to complete measures assessing the student's behaviour at school, documenting behaviour over a period of time and in different settings, and to conduct ongoing monitoring of the child's behaviour in response to medication (Schwean, Parkinson, Francis, & Lee, 1993).

Atkins and Pelham (1991) support the participation of teachers as an important source of information in AD/HD assessment. They note that teachers spend a significant amount of time with students in a variety of academic and social tasks, are considered more objective than parents, and have a better sense of normal behaviours for the comparison group. Their research has demonstrated that teachers can differentiate well between students with and without symptoms of AD/HD.

Burnley (1993) proposes a four-part plan that could be implemented to structure the assessment process for schools. A modified version of Burnley's process is depicted in Figure 4.3.

STEPS IN THE ASSESSMENT PROCESS

Step 1: Preliminary Assessment and Initial School Team Meeting   Initially, a teacher who has been trained in identifying the symptoms of attention deficit/hyperactivity disorder may begin to observe that a particular student manifests these behaviours in the classroom to a greater degree than peers do. At this point, the teacher should begin to keep a log to document the child's AD/HD-like behaviours, noting the times at which behaviours appear to be more intense, more frequent, or of a longer duration. Figure 4.4 provides a simple format for this observational log.

If the teacher's anecdotal records confirm the continuing presence of these behaviours, the referral process should be initiated and the observational log

FURTHER READING

Vicki Schwean and colleagues at the University of Saskatchewan write about the key role that teachers can and should play in the identification of and intervention for children who have AD/HD. For more information, read the 1993 article, "Educating the AD/HD Child: Debunking the Myths," by Schwean, Parkinson, Francis, and Lee, volume 9, issue 1, of the *Canadian Journal of School Psychology* (pp. 37–52).

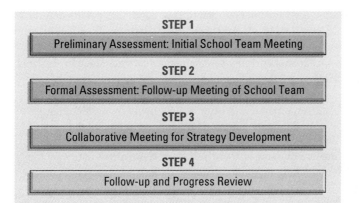

FIGURE 4.3
AD/HD Process for Identification and Intervention

Modified from "A Team Approach for Identification of an Attention Deficit/Hyperactivity Disorder Child," by C. D. Burnley, 1993, *The School Counselor, 40,* pp. 228–230. Adapted by permission.

turned in as documentation. At that point a less biased observer should come into the classroom to provide comparative information (Schaughency & Rothlind, 1991). Schaughency and Rothlind (1991) caution that this form of data collection is costly in terms of professional time; however, if the observation period is not long enough, behaviour that occurs infrequently may be missed. The assessment team should realize that direct observation is just one source of information to be considered in the identification process.

As soon as the school suspects that a child is experiencing attention problems, the parents should be notified and invited to meet with the school team. Often, the parents, the teacher, the principal, and the school psychologist will come together for the initial meeting. During this meeting parents should be asked to respond to the observations of the school personnel and describe their own experiences with attention problems outside of the school setting. If the team agrees that additional testing is needed, the school psychologist will direct the assessment process. This person must understand the impact of AD/HD on the family; the bias that might occur during the assessment process because of cultural, socioeconomic, language, and ethnic factors; and other conditions that may mimic AD/HD and prevent an accurate diagnosis.

Teacher: _____	School: _____	
Child: _____	Grade: _____	Age: _____

Class Activity	Child's Behaviour	Date/Time

FIGURE 4.4
Sample Form for Documenting Classroom Manifestations of AD/HD-like Behaviours

Step 2: Formal Assessment Process: Follow-up Meeting of the School Team   Schools typically use the *DSM-IV* criteria described earlier to identify attention deficit/hyperactivity disorder (McBurnett, Lahey, & Pfiffner, 1993). The following questions, recommended by Schaughency and Rothlind (1991), need to be addressed during the formal assessment process:

FURTHER READING
Another method of obtaining information to determine the match between a student's ability and classroom demands is through an ecological assessment. For an example, see the article "Classroom Ecological Inventory," by D. Fuchs, P. Fernstrom, S. Scott, L. Fuchs, and L. Vandermeer, published in 1994 in volume 26, issue 3, of *Teaching Exceptional Children* (pp. 14–15).

1. Is there an alternative educational diagnosis or medical condition that accounts for the attention difficulties?
2. Are the behaviours demonstrated by the child developmentally appropriate? (For example, children with intellectual disabilities may be diagnosed correctly as having AD/HD, but only if their attention problems are significantly different from those of the children at comparable developmental levels.)
3. Does the child meet the *DSM-IV* criteria?
4. Do the AD/HD-like behaviours affect the child's functioning in several settings, such as home, school, and other social situations?

A variety of methods and assessment procedures will be needed to answer these questions. The school system will most likely interview parents and teachers, obtain a developmental history, evaluate intellectual and academic performance, administer rating scales to multiple informants, and document the impact of the behaviour through direct observation.

Atkins and Pelham (1991) suggest the following as the most typical components of a comprehensive assessment battery for identifying AD/HD-like behaviours:

- Observation
- Interviews with the child, parents, and teachers
- Review of intellectual and academic achievement testing
- Review of school records
- Rating scales completed by the teachers, parents, and possibly peers
- Medical examination

After the necessary observations have been made, the interview process can begin. According to Woodrich (1994), an interview with parents might include the following topics:

- The student's health, psychiatric, and developmental history
- Family history
- Details of referral concern
- The student's behaviour at home
- School history and previous testing
- Interpersonal and social development

Woodrich (1994) recommends that the following areas be addressed during the teacher interview:

- Class work habits and productivity
- Skill levels in academic subjects
- Length of time attention can be sustained for novel tasks and for monotonous tasks
- Degree of activity during class and on the playground
- Class structure and standards for self-control

- Degree of compliance with class rules
- Manifestation of more serious conduct problems
- Onset, frequency, and duration of inappropriate behaviour in the antecedent events
- Peer acceptance and social skills
- Previous intervention techniques and special services now considered appropriate

An interview with the child is appropriate in many cases, to determine the child's perception of the reports by the teacher, attitude toward school and family, and perception of relationships with peers. Although the child's responses will be slanted by personal feelings, it still is an important source of information.

The assessment of achievement and intelligence is not required in the identification of AD/HD but is essential to determine if the child can qualify for services in categories of learning disabilities or intellectual disabilities. Also, knowing the levels of intelligence and achievement will help eventually in developing an intervention plan.

Rating scales that measure the presence of AD/HD symptoms are widely used to quantify the severity of the behaviours. They offer a way to objectively measure the extent of the problem. Rating scales should be completed by several informants who know the child in a variety of settings. The results should be compared to responses from interviews and the results of observations. Some rating scales are limited to an assessment of the primary symptoms contained in the *DSM-IV* criteria; other assessment instruments are multidimensional and might address emotional-social status, communication, memory, reasoning and problem solving, and cognitive skills such as planning and self-evaluation. Figure 4.5 contains an excerpt from the "Strengths and Limitations Inventory: School Version" (Dowdy et al., 1997).

When the school team reconvenes to review all of the data, the following *DSM-IV* (1994) criteria should be considered:

- Six or more of the nine characteristics of inattention and/or six or more of the nine symptoms of hyperactivity-impulsivity should be demonstrated as present for longer than six months.
- The behaviours observed should be considered maladaptive and developmentally inconsistent.
- The symptoms should have been observed since or before age seven.
- The limitations that stem from the characteristics should be observed in two or more settings (e.g., home, school, work).
- The characteristics are not considered solely the result of schizophrenia, pervasive developmental disorder, or other psychiatric disorder, and they are not better attributed to the presence of another mental disorder such as anxiety disorder or mood disorder.

The school team should look for consistency across reports from the assessment instruments and the informants to validate the existence of AD/HD. If it is confirmed, the team must determine if it has caused an adverse effect on school performance and if a special educational plan is needed. Montague, McKinney, and Hocutt (1994) cite the following questions developed by the Professional Group on Attention and Related Disorders (PGARD) to guide the team in determining educational needs:

	Never Observed	Sometimes Observed	Often Observed	Very Often Observed
ATTENTION/IMPULSIVITY/HYPERACTIVITY				
Exhibits excessive nonpurposeful movement (can't sit still, stay in seat).				
Does not stay on task for appropriate periods of time.				
Verbally or physically interrupts conversations or activities.				
Does not pay attention to most important stimuli.				
REASONING/PROCESSING				
Makes poor decisions.				
Makes frequent errors.				
Has difficulty getting started.				
MEMORY				
Has difficulty repeating information recently heard.				
Has difficulty following multiple directions.				
Memory deficits impact daily activities.				
EXECUTIVE FUNCTION				
Has difficulty planning/organizing activities.				
Has difficulty attending to several stimuli at once.				
Has difficulty monitoring own performance throughout activity (self-monitoring).				
Has difficulty independently adjusting behaviour (self-regulation).				
INTERPERSONAL SKILLS				
Has difficulty accepting constructive criticism.				
Exhibits signs of poor self-confidence.				
EMOTIONAL MATURITY				
Inappropriate emotion for situation.				
Displays temper outbursts.				
Does not follow classroom or workplace "rules."				

FIGURE 4.5

Sample Test Items from "Strengths and Limitations Inventory: School Version"

From *Attention-Deficit/Hyperactivity Disorder in the Classroom: A Practical Guide for Teachers,* by C. A. Dowdy, J. R. Patton, T. E. C. Smith and E. A. Polloway, 1997, Austin, TX: Pro-Ed. Reprinted by permission.

1. Do the AD/HD symptoms negatively affect learning to the extent that there is a discrepancy between the child's productivity with respect to listening, following directions, planning, organizing, or completing academic tasks requiring reading, math, writing, or spelling skills?
2. Are inattentive behaviours the result of cultural or language differences, socioeconomic disadvantage, or lack of exposure to education?
3. Are the inattentive behaviours evidence of stressful family functioning (e.g., death or divorce), frustration related to having unattainable educational goals, abuse, or physical or emotional disorders (e.g., epilepsy or depression)?

If question 1 is answered positively and questions 2 and 3 are answered negatively, the team can conclude that there is an educational need that requires special services. At that point, a planning meeting should address the educational program.

Step 3: Collaborative Meeting for Strategy Development   This meeting might be very emotional and overwhelming for parents, or it might generate relief and hope that the services can truly assist the child. The team must be sensitive to the feelings of the parents and take adequate time to describe the results of the testing. If the parents are emotionally upset, it may help to wait a week before developing the intervention plan for school services.

Step 4: Follow-up and Progress Review   After the educational plan has been developed, the parents and school personnel should monitor the child's progress closely to ensure success. Adjustments may be needed occasionally to maintain progress. For example, a reinforcement for good behaviour may eventually lose its novelty and need to be changed. The ultimate goal is to remove accommodations and support as the child becomes capable of regulating his or her behaviour. As the setting and school personnel change each year, re-evaluating the need for special services will yield benefits. As the student becomes more efficient in learning and demonstrates better social skills under one plan, a new, less restrictive plan must be designed to complement this growth.

Cultural and Linguistic Diversity

When AD/HD coexists with cultural and linguistic diversity, it presents a special set of challenges to the educator. Failure to address the special needs of these children can be detrimental to their academic success. Issues related to assessment and cultural diversity have been discussed previously; the same concerns exist in the identification and treatment of students with AD/HD. To address the needs of multicultural students with AD/HD, teachers must become familiar with their unique values, views, customs, interests, and behaviours and their relation to instructional strategies (Wright, 1995). *DSM-IV* (American Psychiatric Association, 1994) simply states that the behaviours cannot be the result of cultural differences. More research is needed to explore the multicultural issues related to AD/HD.

Teachers must learn to recognize the cultural differences of each child in the classroom. The majority of teachers (both in special and general education) in Canada are Caucasian; generally, they lack training related to meeting the individual needs of culturally diverse children. During the identification process, the team must recognize cultural differences and influences for what they

> **TEACHING TIP**
> Begin a parent conference by relating the strengths of the student! Give parents time to respond to the limitations observed in the school setting by reporting examples of behaviour from home and other environments.

are, rather than labelling them as a symptom of attention deficit/hyperactivity disorder.

Barkley (1990) raises the issue that a chaotic home environment exacerbates the problems of children with AD/HD. Although the homes of many children with AD/HD may seem disorganized and the parenting characterized by inconsistencies or lack of structure, teachers and schools should seriously question such judgments. The Canadian Pediatric Society (1998) emphasizes the importance of understanding the "transactional approach" when dealing with children with school problems, particularly with children with AD/HD. The **transactional approach** acknowledges that over time the child's difficulty will affect all aspects of his or her environment which, in turn, will affect the child. In other words, to understand the parenting or home environment we must recognize the cumulative effect of the child's difficulties on the parenting. We are left with a "chicken or the egg" question about poor parenting and children with AD/HD. When teachers use carefully organized and structured instruction, students with AD/HD benefit. Wright (1995) suggests that, first and foremost, teachers should treat students with respect, attempt to establish good rapport with them, and only then impose instructional demands.

Sleeter and Grant (1993) encourage teachers to make educational experiences more meaningful to students by developing activities and homework that acknowledge cultural differences and build on the specific experiences of the student. Teachers can integrate personal and community experiences into teaching an academic concept to help make it relevant to students.

THE ROLE OF MEDICATION

Since many students with AD/HD will be prescribed medication by their physicians, teachers need to understand the types of medications used, their side effects, and the way they work. Medication therapy can be defined as treatment by chemical substances that prevent or reduce inappropriate behaviours, thus promoting academic and social gains for children with learning and behaviour problems (Dowdy et al., 1997). Although medication therapy has been used to treat children with AD/HD since the 1940s, it is still not exactly understood why or how some chemicals affect attention, learning, and hyperactivity. Studies have shown that different outcomes occur for different children. In 70 percent to 80 percent of the cases, children with AD/HD respond in a positive manner to psychostimulant medication (Fowler, 1992). The desired outcomes include increased attention, more on-task behaviour, completion of assigned tasks, improved social relations with peers and teachers, increased appropriate behaviours, and reduction of inappropriate, disruptive behaviours such as talking out, getting out of seat, and breaking rules. These changes frequently lead to improved academic and social achievement. Virginia Douglas at McGill University has been one of the central researchers in the field of AD/HD in children. She and her colleagues at the Montreal Children's Hospital have documented an improvement in flexible thinking as a result of psychostimulant medication in children with AD/HD (Douglas, Barr, Desilets, & Sherman, 1995). In addition, at Dalhousie University in Halifax, Bawden and colleagues examined the effects of stimulants on preschoolers with attention-

Most children with AD/HD are in general education classrooms.

deficit disorders and found significant improvements on a variety of attentional tasks (Byrne, Bawden, DeWolfe, & Beattie, 1998).

For some children, the desired effects do not occur. In these situations the medication has no negative effect, but simply does not lead to the hoped-for results. However, parents and teachers often give up too soon, prematurely concluding that the medication did not help. It is important to contact the physician when no effect is noticed, because the dosage may need to be adjusted or a different type of medication may be called for.

A third possible response to medication is side effects. Side effects are changes that are not desired. Figure 4.6 lists the most common side effects of the medications used for AD/HD. This checklist may be used by parents and teachers when communicating with physicians. Teachers should constantly be on the lookout for signs of side effects and report any concerns to parents or the child's physician.

The most commonly prescribed medications for AD/HD are **psychostimulants** such as Dexedrine (dextroamphetamine), Ritalin (methylphenidate), and Cylert (pemoline). Studies have shown that 84 percent to 93 percent of medical professionals prescribing medicine for children with AD/HD select methylphenidate (Safer & Krager, 1988). This medication is considered a "mild central nervous system stimulant, available as tablets of 5, 10, and 20 mg for oral administration" (*Physician's Desk Reference,* 1994, p. 835). A typical dosage of Ritalin for an initial trial is 5 mg, two to three times daily. Students who are described as anxious or tense, have tics, or have a family history or diagnosis of **Tourette's syndrome** are generally not given Ritalin (*Physician's Desk Reference,* 1994). The specific dose of medicine must be determined individually for each child. Generally, greater side effects come from higher dosages, but some students may need a high dosage to experience the positive effects of the medication. No clear guidelines exist as to how long a child should take medication; both adolescents and adults respond positively to these stimulants.

CONSIDER THIS

Teens often refuse to take medication prescribed for AD/HD. Reflect on the period of adolescence; what happens during this developmental period that might account for this behaviour?

FIGURE 4.6
Stimulant Side Effects
Checklist

From *ADHD Project Facilitate: An In-Service Education Program for Educators and Parents* (p. 55), by R. Elliott, L. A. Worthington, and D. Patterson, Tuscaloosa, AL: University of Alabama. Used by permission.

Side Effects Checklist: Stimulants

Child _____ Date Checked _____

Person Completing Form: _____ Relationship to Child _____

I. SIDE EFFECTS

Directions: Please check any of the behaviors which this child exhibits while receiving his or her stimulant medication. If a child exhibits one or more of the behaviors below, please rate the extent to which you perceive the behavior to be a problem using the scale below (1=Mild to 7=Severe).

	Mild						Severe
1. Loss of appetite	1	2	3	4	5	6	7
2. Stomachaches	1	2	3	4	5	6	7
3. Headaches	1	2	3	4	5	6	7
4. Tics (vocal or motor)	1	2	3	4	5	6	7
5. Extreme mood changes	1	2	3	4	5	6	7
6. Cognitively sluggish/disoriented	1	2	3	4	5	6	7
7. Excessive irritability	1	2	3	4	5	6	7
8. Excessive nervousness	1	2	3	4	5	6	7
9. Decreased social interactions	1	2	3	4	5	6	7
10. Unusual or bizarre behavior	1	2	3	4	5	6	7
11. Excessive activity level	1	2	3	4	5	6	7
12. Light picking of fingertips	1	2	3	4	5	6	7
13. Lip licking	1	2	3	4	5	6	7

II. PSYCHOSOCIAL CONCERNS

Please address any concerns you have about this child's adjustment to medication (e.g., physical, social, emotional changes; attitudes toward the medication, etc.).

III. OTHER CONCERNS

If you have any other concerns about this child's medication (e.g., administration problems, dosage concerns), please comment below.

IV. PARENT CONCERNS (FOR PARENTS ONLY)

Using the same scale above, please check any behaviors which this child exhibits while at home.

	Mild						Severe
1. Insomnia; sleeplessness	1	2	3	4	5	6	7
2. Possible rebound effects (excessive hyperactivity, impulsivity, inattention)	1	2	3	4	5	6	7

FURTHER READING

For more information of the role of medication in the treatment of AD/HD, read the Canadian Pediatric Society's position paper in the 1990 *Canadian Medical Association Journal*, issue 142 (8), pages 817 and 818.

Constant monitoring, preferably through behavioural rating scales completed by parents and teachers, is essential.

Antidepressants are also used to manage AD/HD. They are prescribed less frequently than psychostimulants and might include Tofranil (imipramine), Norpramin (desipramine), and Elavil (amytriptyline). These medications are generally used when negative side effects have occurred with stimulants or when the stimulants have not been effective. The long-term use of antidepressants has not been well studied. Again, frequent monitoring is necessary for responsible management. Tofranil is the most commonly administered antidepressant; however, individuals with a history of cardiac problems should not use it. The initial dosage of Tofranil is generally 10 mg twice daily, but this might be increased to 20 to 100 mg in later stages of treatment (Herskowitz & Rosman, 1982). Other medications that are used much less frequently include antipsychotics such as Mellaril (thioridazine), Thorazine (chlorpromazine), Catapres (clonidine), Eskalith (lithium), and Tegretol (carbamazepine). Whatever medication is prescribed by the child's physician, teachers should ask the physician for a thorough description of the possible positive and negative outcomes for that medication. Table 4.1 contains a list of common myths associated with medication treatment for AD/HD.

Fowler (1992) suggests the following considerations when using medication:

- Handle the dispensing of medication discreetly. Don't make announcements in front of the class that it's time for a child to take his or her pill. Students, especially teens, are often very embarrassed by the necessity to "take a pill" during school. If it is not given in private, they may refuse the medication.
- Make sure the medication is given as prescribed. Although the child should not be pulled away from an important event, the dosage should be given as close as possible to the designated time.

TABLE 4.1

Common Myths Associated with AD/HD Medications

Myth	Fact
Medication should be stopped when a child reaches teen years.	Research clearly shows there is continued benefit to medication for those teens who meet criteria for diagnosis of AD/HD.
Children tend to build up tolerance for medication.	Although the dose of medication may need adjusting from time to time, there is no evidence that children build up a tolerance to medication.
Taking medicine for AD/HD leads to greater likelihood of later drug addiction.	There is no evidence to indicate that AD/HD medication leads to an increased likelihood of later drug addiction.
Positive response to medication is confirmation of a diagnosis of AD/HD.	The fact that a child shows improvement of attention span or a reduction of activity while taking AD/HD medication does not substantiate the diagnosis of AD/HD. Even some normal children will show a marked improvement in attentiveness when they take AD/HD medication.
Medication stunts growth.	AD/HD medications may cause an initial and mild slowing of growth, but over time the growth suppression effect is minimal if not nonexistent in most cases.
Taking AD/HD medications as a child makes you more reliant on drugs as an adult.	There is no evidence of increased medication taking when medicated AD/HD children become adults, nor is there evidence that AD/HD children become addicted to their medications.
AD/HD children who take medication attribute their success only to medication.	When self-esteem is encouraged, children taking medication attribute their success not only to the medication but to themselves as well.

Adapted from *The Ch. A.D.D. Manual (p. 75)*, by M. C. Fowler, 1992, Fairfax, VA: CASET Association.

- Avoid placing too much blame or credit for the child's behaviour on the medication. *All* children will have good and bad days. When problems arise, teachers should avoid comments such as "Did you take your pill this morning?"
- Monitor the behaviour of the child, looking for any side effects.
- Communicate with the school nurse, the parents, and the physician.

Remember, not all children diagnosed with attention deficit/hyperactivity disorder need medication. The decision to intervene medically should come only after a great deal of thought about the possibility of a variety of interventions. Children whose impairments are minimal are certainly less likely to need medication than those whose severe impairments result in major disruptions.

Although teachers and other school personnel are important members of a therapeutic team engaged in exploring, implementing, and evaluating diverse treatment methods (Reiff, 1993), the decision to try medication is primarily the responsibility of the parents and the physician. This fact often puts educators in a dilemma when they feel strongly that medication is needed to address the symptoms of the AD/HD. In any case, students with AD/HD will benefit from the classroom accommodations discussed in the following section.

STRATEGIES FOR INSTRUCTION AND CLASSROOM ACCOMMODATIONS

Since no two children with attention deficit/hyperactivity disorder are exactly alike, a wide variety of interventions and service options must be used to meet their needs. One practice that has not been reported as a solution for children with AD/HD is retention (Fowler, 1992). Often, the idea that holding these children back gives them a chance to mature is used as an excuse. However, the symptoms of AD/HD will not go away simply by allowing more time to pass. Success for these students depends on the qualifications of the teacher, effective strategies for instruction, and classroom accommodations.

Classroom Accommodations

Since attention deficit/hyperactivity disorder describes a set of characteristics that affect learning, most interventions take place in the school setting. Any approach to addressing the needs of students with AD/HD must be comprehensive. Figure 4.7 depicts a model of educational intervention built on four intervention areas: environmental management, instructional accommodations, student-regulated strategies, and medical management (Dowdy et al., 1997). Medical management was described previously. This section identifies specific strategies for addressing the challenges of AD/HD in the classroom.

MANAGING THE CLASSROOM ENVIRONMENT
A classroom with even one or two students with AD/HD can be difficult to control if the teacher is not skilled in classroom management. Rather than reacting spontaneously—and often inconsistently—to disruptive situations, teachers should have a management system to help avoid crises. Dowdy et al.

PERSONAL SPOTLIGHT

Teacher with an Attention Deficit/Hyperactivity Disorder

■ KATIE BOISVERT, Elementary Teacher

Katie teaches in an elementary French immersion program in an English language school in Montreal, Quebec. Now in her third year of teaching, she loves her work. Katie has students with different abilities and challenges in her class, and she is known for her empathy and warmth for all of them. Katie also has an attention-deficit disorder.

Katie describes how school was for her and how she came to be a teacher.

"A teacher once told me that my work was too disorganized and since she could not make sense of it, no one ever would. That was three years ago and I was just about to finish my teaching degree! When I was a child, my grades were never exceptional and I could not focus in class no matter how interesting it was. But worst of all, I was always getting in trouble. I was very agitated and could never get along with the other children. I had no friends and basically no self-esteem. My work was messy, often late, half done or not done at all. It seemed like I could never get the instructions right. I desperately wanted to belong, but somehow knew I was different.

"I made my way through high school and college having the impression that no matter how long I studied, I was set for failure. Still I kept going and somehow found myself in university trying to pursue a degree in education. Maybe I was drawn to education because my own school experience was so bad. It was when I was studying to be a teacher that I discovered that I had AD/HD. To me, in light of my past experiences, the diagnosis made a lot of sense. The "label" was a relief: it made me understand what had been going on all those years. What didn't make sense to me is, why didn't anyone ever realize there was something wrong and that I needed help? I didn't get help so I had to help myself. All these years I have worked to develop my own strategies to deal with my disability. I am still working to find my own way and continuing to develop more strategies, but now I have support and understanding.

"I have now been teaching for two years and I have a great class. Every day is an amazing experience. I enter the class in the morning with the belief that all of the children can learn and progress. We work together to achieve this goal. They help me be more organized and they challenge my creativity. In return, I help them find ways and strategies to facilitate their learning. We try to respect everyone's differences!"

(1997) define *classroom management* as a combination of techniques that results in an orderly classroom environment where social growth and learning can occur. Good classroom management is beneficial for all students, including those with AD/HD. Techniques include group management, physical management, and behaviour management.

Group Management Though they benefit all members of a class, group management techniques are critical in managing the behaviour of individual students with AD/HD. One of the most basic and effective techniques is to establish classroom rules and consequences for breaking those rules. Children with AD/HD need to understand the classroom rules and school procedures in order to be successful. Jones and Jones (1995) suggest that students feel more committed to following rules when they have contributed to developing them. The rules should be displayed prominently in the room and reviewed periodically, if students with AD/HD are to retain and follow them. It is important for teachers to apply the rules consistently, even though students can sometimes frustrate teachers

CROSS-REFERENCE
Teachers should develop a list of procedures to make the classroom run smoothly. For example, how should students request help? How should they respond during a fire drill? For more tips in this area, refer to Chapter 5.

FIGURE 4.7
Model for AD/HD
Intervention

From *Attention-Deficit/Hyperactivity Disorder in the Classroom: A Practical Guide for Teachers,* by C. A. Dowdy, J. R. Patton, E. A. Polloway, & T. E. C. Smith, 1997, Austin, TX: Pro-Ed.

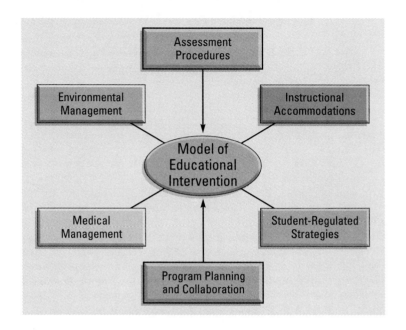

and make them want to "give in." Teachers may start the process of rule development by offering one or two rules of their own and then letting the children pick up with their own ideas. The following is a list of recommendations for developing rules (Dowdy et al., 1997).

- State rules positively, if possible. For example, a rule requiring students to raise their hands to talk is more effective than a rule that says "Do not talk out loud."
- Rules should be stated in simple terms so students can easily understand them. For young students, rules can be depicted with drawings and figures.
- The number of rules should be no more than five or six.
- Rules should be displayed conspicuously in the room.
- Rules should be practised and discussed at the beginning of the year and periodically throughout the year.
- For students with AD/HD, role-playing how to carry out the rules is an effective technique.
- Adopt rules and consequences that you are willing to enforce.
- Positively reinforce students who abide by the rules. It is more effective to reinforce the students who abide by the rules than to punish those who break them.
- To avoid misunderstandings, communicate rules and consequences to parents. It is helpful to have parents and students sign a contract documenting their understanding of the rules.

Time management is also important in effective classroom management. Students with AD/HD thrive in an organized, structured classroom. Many of the acting-out and inappropriate behaviours occur during unscheduled, unstructured free time, when the number of choices of activities may become overwhelming. If free time is scheduled, limit the choices and provide positive reinforcement for appropriate behaviour during free time. Encourage students to investigate topics that interest them and to complete projects that bring their strengths into play.

Polloway and Patton (1993) suggest that teachers begin each day with a similar routine. The particular activity is not as important as the consistency. For example, some teachers like to start the day with quiet reading, whereas others might begin with singing, recognizing birthdays, or talking about special events that are coming up. This routine will set the stage for a calm orderly day, and students will know what to expect from the teacher. Secondary teachers need to advise students of scheduling changes (e.g., assembly, pep rally) and provide a brief overview of the topics and activities to be expected during the class period. Gallagher (1979) gives these useful techniques to consider in developing daily schedules for both elementary and secondary students:

CONSIDER THIS
What are some appropriate activities to begin and end the day or class period for elementary and secondary students?

- Discuss the daily schedule with students.
- Alternate tasks that have high activity with tasks that require low activity.
- Schedule work that can be completed in the specified time.
- Require students to complete one task before beginning another.
- Challenge students to continue on tasks and reinforce their persistence.
- Do not assign additional work when students finish before the allotted time.
- Provide clear expectations for students in advance, and do not change the expectations after the activity has begun.
- Provide feedback to students frequently.
- Provide positive feedback to students as often as possible.
- When changes in the schedule are necessary, be sure to discuss these changes thoroughly and well in advance for students with AD/HD.

Like the beginning of the day, closure on the day's or the class period's activities is important for secondary students. Reviewing the important events of the day and describing the next day's activities help students with AD/HD. Take the time to provide rewards for students who have maintained appropriate behaviour during the day. If parents are involved in a contract, discuss the transmitted notes and review homework that might have been assigned during the day.

To work successfully with students with AD/HD, group students to create the most effective learning environment. They may be taught more effectively in small groups of four to seven students and may complete work more successfully as a team. Perhaps two or three students may need to receive more individualized instruction. The teacher should plan the makeup of the groups to combine AD/HD students with students who will be supportive, positive role models. The resulting peer pressure to abide by the rules is often more effective than teacher-directed behaviour management. Also, students with AD/HD may become friends with students without AD/HD if they work together in cooperative learning groups.

Teachers may want to offer incentives to individual students and groups to reward outstanding work. You might place a marble in a jar each time students are "caught being good." When the jar is filled the class receives an award such as a picnic or a skating party. Another technique involves adding a piece to a puzzle whenever the teacher recognizes that the class is working especially hard. When the puzzle is complete, the class is rewarded. These group incentives can be very effective; however, some students will need an individual contract or behaviour management plan to help direct their behaviour.

Physical Management   The physical environment of a classroom can also have an impact on the behaviours of students with AD/HD. The arrangement of the room is most important. The classroom needs to be large enough for students to have space between themselves and others, so they will be less likely to impose themselves on one another. Each student needs some personal space.

Desk arrangement is also important. The student with AD/HD should be near the teacher in order to focus attention on the information being presented in the classroom. But students should never be placed near the teacher as a punitive measure. There should also be various places in the room where quiet activities can take place, where small groups can work together, where sustained attention for difficult tasks can be maintained, and where a relaxed and comfortable environment can be enjoyed for a change of pace. At one time, classrooms with lots of visual stimulation were considered inappropriate for students with AD/HD, leading to the creation of sterile environments with colorless walls and no bulletin boards. This spartan setting is no longer considered necessary; however, order is needed in the classroom; materials should be located consistently in the same place, and bulletin boards should be well organized. Set aside places where students can work in a carrel or other private space with minimal visual and auditory stimuli.

Behaviour Management   Behaviour management techniques can enhance the education of students with AD/HD, especially those that reward desired behaviour. For example, when students with AD/HD are attending to their tasks, following classroom rules, or participating appropriately in a cooperative learning activity, their behaviours should be positively reinforced. Unfortunately, teachers often ignore appropriate behaviour and call attention only to what is inappropriate. When students receive attention for actions that are disruptive or inconsiderate, the negative behaviours can be reinforced and may thus increase in frequency.

CONSIDER THIS
These ideas are effective with elementary-age students. Generate some reinforcers that would be more effective in secondary settings.

Positive reinforcement tends to increase appropriate behaviour (Smith, Finn, & Dowdy, 1993). The idea that individuals do things that result in rewards can work with adults as well as with students in the classroom. Consider which rewards appeal most to the individuals who will receive them. Common ones include small toys, free time, time to listen to music, time in the gym, opportunities to do things for the teacher, having lunch with the teacher, and praise. Because a reward that acts as a reinforcer for one student may not work for another, teachers might generate a menu of rewards and allow students to select their own. Rewards do not have to be expensive; in fact, simply allowing students to take a break, get a drink of water, or sharpen a pencil may be just as effective as providing expensive toys and games.

CONSIDER THIS
What is an example of how the Premack principle can be applied for elementary, junior, and high school students?

Another helpful idea in working with children with AD/HD is called the Premack principle. Also known as "grandma's law," it is based on the traditional comment "If you eat your vegetables, then you can have your dessert" (Polloway & Patton, 1993, p. 102). The teacher announces that a reward or highly desired activity will be awarded to students after they complete a required or desired activity. For example, students might be required to sit in their seats and complete work for 15 minutes; then a snack or free time will follow. This simple technique can be very effective for students with AD/HD.

Often students will need an individual contract that focuses on their particular needs. Together, student and teacher develop goals to improve behaviour and then put these goals in writing. They also stipulate consequences for not following the contract and reinforcement for completing the contract (Westling & Koorland, 1988). This instrument provides structure and forms an explicit way to communicate with children with AD/HD and their parents. Westling and Koorland (1988) offer the following guidelines for making and using such contracts:

- Determine the target behaviour or activity.
- Identify desired reinforcement.
- Specify the length of time for the contract.
- Use clear, simple language.
- See that both teacher and student sign the contract (and the parents, when appropriate).
- Keep a record of the student's behaviour.
- Provide the agreed-upon consequences or reinforcements in a timely fashion.
- Rewrite a new contract when one has been completed.

A sample contract is provided in Figure 4.8.

Another behaviour management technique is cueing or signalling AD/HD students when they are on the verge of inappropriate behaviour. First, student and teacher sit down privately and discuss the inappropriate behaviour that has been creating problems in the classroom. The teacher offers to provide a cue when the behaviour begins to be noticed. Teachers and students can have fun working together on the signal, which might involve flipping the light switch, tapping the desk lightly, or making simple eye contact (Wood, 1984). These cueing techniques help establish a collegial relationship between the

FIGURE 4.8
Sample of Contingency Contract

From *Attention-Deficit/ Hyperactivity Disorder in the Classroom: A Practical Guide for Teachers,* by C. A. Dowdy, J. R. Patton, E. A. Polloway, and T. E. C. Smith, 1997, Austin, TX: Pro-Ed.

Contract

This agreement is between _____ and _____ .
                                    (student)   (teacher)
The contract begins on _____ and continues until
_____ . The terms of this contract include the following:

The student will:

_____

_____

_____

_____

When these things are completed, the teacher will:

_____

_____

_____

_____

Student's Signature: _____ Date_____
Teacher's Signature: _____ Date_____

Cueing or signalling students is one method that teachers can use to help get their attention.

teacher and the student that says, "We are working on this together; we have a problem, but we also have a plan."

Making Instructional Accommodations

Barkley (1990) says, "Knowing what to do is a strategy problem. Doing what you know is a motivational problem." His research suggests that AD/HD may be caused by neurological differences in the motivational centre of the brain; however, children with AD/HD are often misunderstood and labelled lazy or unmotivated, as if they are choosing not to perform at their maximum potential. Instead, teachers need to find ways to cope with the frustration and stress that are sometimes involved in working with the students, while modifying their teaching style, their curriculum, and possibly their expectations in order to engineer academic success for the students. Goldstein and Goldstein (1992) state that it is essential for schools to succeed with children with AD/HD; otherwise, these students will carry the emotional burden of 30 or more hours per week filled with frustration and academic and social failure. Teachers need to be patient, empathetic, and understanding as they work with this challenging group of students, viewing the characteristics of AD/HD as "variability, not disability" (Roller, 1996).

MODIFYING TEACHER BEHAVIOUR

Since students with AD/HD are not easily stimulated, they need novelty and excitement in their learning environment. Although structure and consistency are extremely important, students need challenging, novel activities to keep them focused and learning. Fowler (1992) reports that the incidence of inappropriate behaviour increases during nonstimulating, repetitive activities. She suggests that teachers allow and encourage movement that is purposeful and not disruptive, give frequent breaks, and even let students stand as they listen, take notes, or perform other academic tasks. Here are some more recommendations:

- Use active, responsive instruction, such as talking, moving, and asking frequent questions.
- Use multiple, small periods of practice for rote tasks, rather than mass practice.
- Allow students to work with partners in cooperative learning groups.
- Alternate high- and low-interest tasks.
- Use videos, an overhead projector, and other visual aids when lecturing.
- Use instructional games to provide practice for learning specific skills and for practice of skills.
- Allow limited choices of tasks.
- Bring the child's areas of interest into assignments.
- Provide both verbal and written directions.
- Ask the students to repeat directions to ensure that they understand them.

CONSIDER THIS
If you are currently teaching, complete the Time-on-Task Self-Assessment; if not, rewrite the questions and use them as an observation tool to evaluate a teacher who is willing to be observed. Analyze the results, and identify changes that could be made to improve learning in the classroom.

Templeton (1995) suggests that teachers speak clearly and loudly enough for students to hear, but not too fast. She points out that enthusiasm and humour will help engage students and excite those who might become easily bored and distracted. She also recommends helping students see the value in what they learn and the importance of the material. During a long lecture period, teachers might list main ideas or important questions on the chalkboard or by using the overhead projector, to help students focus on the most important information. When a student's attention does wander, a small, unobtrusive signal such as a gentle pat on the student's shoulder can cue the student to return to the task. To perk up tiring students, try a quick game of Simon Says or purposeful physical activities such as taking a note to the office, feeding the animals in the classroom, or returning books to the library. Prater (1992) provides a self-assessment for teachers to determine if they are doing everything they can to increase each student's attention to task during instructional time. This strategy for improving instruction for all students is included in the nearby Inclusion Strategies feature.

MODIFYING THE CURRICULUM

Although students with AD/HD are typically taught in the general education classroom, using the regular curriculum, they need a curriculum adapted to focusing on "doing" and one that avoids long periods of sitting and listening. These adaptations can benefit all students. For example, experience-based learning, in which students might develop their own projects, perform experiments, or take field trips, can help all students grow as active learners. Cronin (1993) suggests that teachers modify curriculum by using activities that closely resemble challenges and experiences in the real world. They can use story problems within traditional textbooks, curriculum-based experiments and projects, or lesson extensions such as writing letters to environmental groups to obtain more information than is offered in a textbook.

Describing a related curriculum model, Stephien and Gallagher (1993) suggest that problem-based learning provides authentic experiences in the classroom. In this model, students are asked to solve an "ill-structured problem"

INCLUSION STRATEGIES

Time-on-Task Self-Assessment for Teachers

Read the following statements and rate yourslf according to the following scale:

N	**R**	**S**	**U**	**A**
never	**rarely**	**sometimes**	**usually**	**always**

DURING GROUP INSTRUCTION:

1. Students are attending to me before I start the lesson. _____

2. Students use choral group responses to answer questions. _____

3. Individual students answer questions or orally read when called in a random order. _____

4. I ask a question, then call on a student to answer. _____

5. Students answer correctly most of the questions I ask. _____

6. I have all my materials and supplies ready before class begins. _____

7. If possible, I write all the necessary material on the board, an overhead, or poster before instructing. _____

8. I use some type of signal with group responses. _____

9. Students are involved in reading directions, practice items, or the answers. _____

10. Students are involved in housekeeping procedures such as passing out papers. _____

DURING SEATWORK:

11. I move around the classroom checking students' work. _____

12. I can make eye contact with all of my students. _____

13. I allow students to work together and to talk about their seatwork. _____

14. Immediately after instruction my students can work on their seatwork without any questions. _____

15. Students need not wait for my assistance if they have questions about their seatwork. _____

16. I spend little time answering questions about what the students are to do next. _____

17. Most of my students finish their work about the same time. _____

DURING INSTRUCTION OR SEATWORK:

18. I spend little time reprimanding students for misbehavior. _____

19. My students are not restless. _____

20. My students follow a routine for transition times (i.e., getting materials ready, collecting papers, lining up for lunch). _____

21. My students respond quickly during transition times. _____

22. I have well-defined rules for appropriate behavior in my classroom. _____

23. I consistently provide appropriate consequences for students who are and remain on-task. _____

24. I teach my students self-management procedures (e.g., self-monitoring, self-instruction). _____

From "Increasing Time-on-Task in the Classroom," by M. A. Prater, 1992, *Intervention in School and Clinic*, 28 (1), pp. 22–27.

before they receive any instruction. Teachers act as coaches and tutors, questioning the student's hypotheses and conclusions and sharing their own thoughts when needed during "time out" discussions. Students act as doctors, historians, or scientists, or assume other roles of individuals who have a real stake in solving the proposed problem. When students "take ownership" of the problem, motivation soars. Teachers can model problem-solving strategies by thinking out loud and questioning their own conclusions and recommendations. This model increases self-directed learning and improves motivation. The nearby Technology Today feature describes how technology can be used to complement a variety of learning techniques commonly used in a general education classroom.

Developing Student-Regulated Strategies

The previous sections on classroom environment and instructional accommodations focused on activities that the teacher directs and implements to increase the success of children with AD/HD. This section will describe student-regulated strategies. Dowdy et al. (1997) define *student-regulated strategies* as interventions, initially taught by the teacher, that the student will eventually implement independently. These interventions developed from the study of cognitive behaviour modification, an exciting new field combining behavioural strategies with cognitive intervention techniques.

Fiore, Becker, and Nerro (1993) note that these cognitive approaches directly address core problems of children with AD/HD, including impulse control, higher-order problem solving, and self-regulation. Because student-regulated strategies are new, teachers are encouraged to validate their effectiveness in their classrooms (Abikoff, 1991). Fiore et al. (1993) argue that teachers should try implementing these approaches, bearing in mind that they do need further study.

The benefits of implementing self-regulation strategies for children with AD/HD include the following:

- Modifying impulsive responses
- Increasing selective attention and focus
- Providing verbal mediators to facilitate academic and social problem-solving challenges (e.g., self-talk to calm down during an argument)
- Teaching self-instructional statements to assist students in "talking through" problems and tasks
- Providing strategies that may develop prosocial behaviours and lead to improved peer relations (Rooney, 1993)

The following discussion addresses four types of student-regulated strategies: study and organizational tactics, self-management, learning strategies, and social skills.

STUDY AND ORGANIZATIONAL TACTICS

Children with AD/HD have difficulty organizing their work and implementing effective study skills in general education classrooms. Many strategies have been developed to assist them; for example, the editing and writing strategies described in Chapter 3 can help promote independence for students with AD/HD.

TEACHING TIP

Practise what you teach! Identify an activity or task that you need to accomplish by a date in the future (e.g., develop a unit on ecology). Break down the steps to completion, including target dates. Model your planning skills by "thinking out loud" for your students. Doing this will make the concept of planning and organizing more concrete for them.

Summary of Major Instructional Principles and Guidelines for Using the Computer

Principle	Summary	Guidelines
DIRECT INSTRUCTION	If teachers describe objectives and demonstrate exact steps, students can master specific skills more efficiently.	1. Use programs that specify exact steps and teach them clearly and specifically. 2. Show the relationship of computer programs to steps in the direct teaching process.
MASTERY LEARNING	Given enough time, nearly all learners can master objectives.	1. Use programs that provide extra help and practice toward reaching objectives. 2. Use programs to stimulate and enrich students who reach objectives early. 3. Use record-keeping programs to keep track of student performance.
OVERLEARNING AND AUTOMATICITY	To become automatic, skills must be practiced and reinforced beyond the point of initial mastery.	1. Use computer programs to provide self-paced individualized practice. 2. Use computer programs that provide gamelike practice for skills that require much repeated practice. 3. Use computer programs that provide varied approaches to practicing the same activity.
MEMORIZATION SKILLS	Recall of factual information is a useful skill that enhances learning at all levels.	1. Use computer programs to provide repeated practice and facilitate memorization. 2. Use programs designed to develop memory skills.
PEER TUTORING	Both tutor and pupil can benefit from properly structured peer tutoring.	1. Have students work in groups at computers. 2. Use programs that are structured to help tutors provide instruction, prompts, and feedback. 3. Teach students to give feedback, prompts, and instruction at computers.
COOPERATIVE LEARNING	Helping one another is often more productive than competing for score rewards.	1. Have students work in groups at computers. 2. Use programs that promote cooperation. 3. Provide guidelines for cooperative roles at computers.
MONITORING STUDENT PROGRESS	Close monitoring of student progress enables students, teachers, and parents to identify strengths and weaknesses of learners.	1. Use programs that have management systems to monitor student progress. 2. Use record-keeping programs. 3. Use computers to communicate feedback.
STUDENT MISCONCEPTIONS	Identifying misconceptions helps develop an understanding of topics.	1. Use programs to diagnose misconceptions. 2. Use programs to teach correct understanding of misunderstood concepts.
PREREQUISITE KNOWLEDGE AND SKILLS	Knowledge is usually hierarchical; lower-level skills must be learned before higher-level skills can be mastered.	1. Use programs to assess prerequisite knowledge and skills. 2. Use programs to teach prerequisite skills.
IMMEDIATE FEEDBACK	Feedback usually works best if it comes quickly after a response.	1. Use programs that provide immediate feedback. 2. Use programs that provide clear corrective feedback.
PARENTAL INVOLVEMENT	Parents should be informed about their children's progress and assist in helping them learn.	1. Use computers to communicate with parents about educational activities and progress. 2. Exploit home computers.

▼

Principle	Summary	Guidelines
LEARNING STYLES	Learners vary in preference for modes and styles of learning.	1. Use programs that appeal to students' preferred learning styles. 2. Use programs that supplement the teachers' weaker teaching style. 3. Use programs that call upon students to employ a variety of learning styles.
CLASSROOM MANAGEMENT	Effective classroom management provides more time for instruction.	1. Use the computer as a tool to improve classroom management. 2. Use programs that have a management component.
TEACHER QUESTIONS	If teachers ask higher-order questions and wait for students to answer, higher-level learning is likely to occur.	1. Select programs that ask higher-level questions. 2. Use programs that individualize the pace of instruction, since wait time is likely to be better than with traditional instruction.
STUDY SKILLS	Effective study skills can be taught, and these almost always enhance learning.	1. Teach students to use the computer as a tool to manage and assist learning. 2. Use programs that teach thinking skills. 3. Teach generalization of thinking and study skills across subject areas.
HOMEWORK	When homework is well planned by teachers, completed by students, and related to class, learning improves.	1. Assign homework for home computers. 2. Have students do preparatory work off the computer as homework.
WRITING INSTRUCTION	Writing should be taught as a recursive process of brainstorming, composing, revising, and editing.	1. Use word processors for composition. 2. Use programs that prompt writing skills. 3. Teach students to use grammar and spelling checkers effectively.
EARLY WRITING	Even very young children should be encouraged to write stories.	1. Use simple word-processing programs. 2. Use programs that combine graphics with writing. 3. Use graphics programs to stimulate creativity.
LEARNING MATHEMATICS	Concrete experience helps students understand and master abstract principles.	1. Match programs to children's level of cognitive development. 2. Use programs that provide concrete demonstrations with clear graphics.
PHONICS	Instruction in phonics helps students to "break the code" and develop generalized word attack skills.	1. Use programs that combine sound with visual graphics to teach the sight/sound relationships of reading.
READING COMPREHENSION	Students often learn better if reading lessons are preceded by preparatory materials and followed by questions and activities.	1. Use programs that have pre- and postactivities to accompany them 2. Use computer programs before or after traditional reading materials.
SCIENCE EXPERIMENTS	Students learn science best if they can do concrete experiments to see science in action.	1. Use computer simulations. 2. Use tutorial and drill programs with concrete graphics. 3. Use database and word processing programs to manage and report noncomputerized science experiments. 4. Use science interface equipment to manage and analyze science experiments.

From "Principles behind Computerized Instruction for Students with Exceptionalities," by E. Vockell and T. Mihail, 1993, *Teaching Exceptional Children*, Spring, pp. 39–43.

Hoover and Patton (1995) suggest teaching 11 study skills: increasing and/or adjusting reading rate according to the purpose for reading, listening, note taking, writing reports, giving oral presentations, using graphic aids, taking tests, using the library, using reference material, time management, and self-management. Students should practise planning as an organizational strategy. For an assignment such as a term paper, deciding how to break the task into small parts and how to complete each part should be practised before such an assignment is made. Students should also practise estimating how much time will be needed for various activities so they can establish appropriate and realistic goals. Outlining skills can also help with organization and planning. Students may want to use a word processor to order their ideas and to help organize their work.

SELF-MANAGEMENT

The primary goal of programs that teach self-management or self-control is to "make children more consciously aware of their own thinking processes and task approach strategies, and to give them responsibility for their own reinforcement" (Reeve, 1990, p. 76). Here are some advantages of teaching self-control:

- It saves the teacher's time by decreasing the demand for direct instruction.
- It increases the effectiveness of an intervention.
- It increases the maintenance of skills over time.
- It increases student's ability to use the skill in a variety of settings. (Lloyd, Landrum, & Hallahan, 1991, p. 201)

Polloway and Patton (1993) cite four types of self-regulation. In *self-assessment,* the individual determines the need for change and also monitors personal behaviour. In *self-monitoring,* the student attends to specific aspects of his or her own behaviour. In *self-instruction,* the student cues himself or herself to inhibit inappropriate behaviours or to express appropriate ones. In *self-reinforcement,* the student administers self-selected reinforcement for an appropriate behaviour that has been previously specified. Figure 4.9 demonstrates a self-management planning form that was completed to help a high school student control his talking out in class.

LEARNING STRATEGIES

FURTHER READING

This alternative approach to educating adolescents with learning disabilities is presented in a text by D. Deshler, E. Ellis, and B. K. Lenz, *Teaching Adolescents with Learning Disabilities; Strategies and Methods* (2nd ed.), published in 1996 by Love Publishing.

Deshler and Lenz (1989) define a learning strategy as an individual approach to a task. It includes how an individual thinks and acts when planning, executing, or evaluating performance. The learning strategies approach combines what is going on in an individual's head (cognition) with what a person actually does (behaviour) to guide the performance and evaluation of a specific task. All individuals use strategies; however, not all strategies are effective. The strategies intervention model proposed by Deshler and Lenz (1989) suggests that teachers promote learning strategies that

- contain steps leading to specific and successful outcomes.
- contain steps that are sequenced in an efficient manner.
- contain steps to cue students to use specific cognitive strategies.

To motivate students, they recommend using self-affirmation statements, setting goals, and monitoring progress toward those goals. To help students take

FIGURE 4.9
Self-Management Planning Form

Adapted from "Self-Management: Education's Ultimate Goal," by J. Carter, 1993, *Teaching Exceptional Children, 25* (3), pp. 28–32.

Student _____ *Geoff* _____   Teacher _____ *Mr. Sherman* _____

School _____ *Royalcrest High* _____   Date _____ *15–10–99* _____

STEP 1: SELECT A TARGET BEHAVIOUR

(a) Identify the target behaviour.
Geoff talks without raising his hand and does not wait to be recognized by the teacher during structured class time. Geoff talks to himself and to peers in a voice loud enough to be heard by the teacher standing half a metre or more away from Geoff.

(b) Identify the replacement behaviour.
During structured class times, Geoff will raise his hand without talking and wait to be recognized by the teacher before talking.

STEP 2: DEFINE THE TARGET BEHAVIOUR

Write a clear description of the behaviour (include conditions under which it is acceptable and unacceptable).
Given a structured class setting with teacher-directed instructional activity, Geoff will raise his hand and wait to be called on before talking 9 out of 10 times. Geoff may talk without raising his hand during unstructured, noninstructional times and during class discussion.

STEP 3: DESIGN THE DATA-RECORDING PROCEDURES

(a) Identify the type of data to be recorded.
Geoff will make a plus mark (+) on his data sheet if he raises his hand and waits to be called on before talking during each 5-minute interval for 9 intervals. If he talks without raising his hand, Geoff will mark a minus (–).

(b) Identify when the data will be recorded.
Geoff will self-record his third-period English class.

(c) Describe the data recording form.
Geoff will use 5 x 8 index cards with 5 rows of 9 squares each, one row for each day of the week. At the end of each row will be a box marked "Total" in which Geoff will record the total number of pluses earned that day.

STEP 4: TEACH THE STUDENT TO USE THE RECORDING FORM

Briefly describe the instruction and practice.
The teacher will review the data recording form with Geoff, showing him where and how to self-record. The teacher will role play with Geoff the use of a timer and will model examples and nonexamples of appropriate hand raising.

STEP 5: CHOOSE A STRATEGY FOR ENSURING ACCURACY

Geoff will match his self-recording form with the teacher's record at the end of each English period.

STEP 6: ESTABLISH GOAL AND CONTINGENCIES

(a) Determine how the student will be involved in setting the goal.
Geoff will meet with the teacher and discuss his goal and then share the goal with his parents.

(b) Determine whether or not the goal will be made public.
No, it will not.

(c) Determine the reinforcement for meeting the goal.
Each day that Geoff meets his performance goal, the teacher will buy Geoff a soda from the soda machine.

▼

STEP 7: REVIEW GOAL AND STUDENT PERFORMANCE
(a) Determine how often the student and teacher will review performance.

Geoff and the teacher will meet one time per week before school to review the progress and make new goals.

(b) Identify when and how the plan will be modified if the goal is met or is not met.

If Geoff has not met his performance goal for 3 consecutive days, the teacher will schedule an extra meeting with Geoff. If Geoff meets his goal for 3 consecutive days, the teacher and Geoff will modify his goal at their next meeting.

STEP 8: PLAN FOR REDUCING SELF-RECORDING PROCEDURES

Geoff will match with teacher's record daily, then 3 days per week, and eventually 1 day per week (picked randomly).

STEP 9: PLAN FOR GENERALIZATION AND MAINTENANCE

Geoff will self-record initially in English only. When he can successfully self-record, accurately match the teacher's record, and has met his performance goal in English for 2 weeks, he will begin self-recording in math and then social studies. When Geoff has met his performance goal for 3 weeks, self-recording will be eliminated and Geoff will earn the reinforcer for maintaining his performance goals.

in new information, they recommend activating prior knowledge on the subject, predicting the content of the material to be learned, self-questioning during reading and listening, visualizing the content being presented, paraphrasing and summarizing new information, prioritizing new information, and comparing or linking new information to existing information.

An example of an efficient reading strategy is the RAP strategy. RAP stands for

R **R**ead a paragraph: As you are reading the paragraph, look for topic sentences or clue words that signal the main ideas and details.
A **A**sk yourself, "What are the main ideas and details in this paragraph?" Ask yourself, "What was this paragraph about, and what should I remember about it?"
P **P**ut the main idea and details into your own words. Say to yourself, "This paragraph is about _____."

The Council for Exceptional Children (1992) recommends using these instructional steps when teaching a strategy:

- Isolate the techniques necessary for a certain task.
- Model or demonstrate them for the student.
- Have the student rehearse the strategy.
- Provide the student with feedback.
- Encourage and monitor the student for several practice sessions until the student can implement the strategy.

SOCIAL SKILLS

Because students with attention deficit/hyperactivity disorder often do not exhibit good problem-solving skills and are unable to predict the consequences of their inappropriate behaviour, specific and direct instruction in social skills may be necessary. Although it is better for students to be able to assess their own inappropriate behaviour and adjust it to acceptable standards, many students may need social skills training first. Goldstein and Goldstein (1990) propose a social skills training program that is taught during six training sessions. This curriculum is reviewed in Chapter 12.

PROMOTING A SENSE OF COMMUNITY AND SOCIAL ACCEPTANCE

The Professional Group for Attention and Related Disorders (PGARD) proposes that most children with AD/HD can be served in the general education program by trained teachers providing appropriate instruction and modifications. One of the most important aspects of promoting success for children with AD/HD is the the teacher. Fowler (1992) suggests that success for children with AD/HD might vary from year to year, class to class, teacher to teacher. She reports that the most commonly cited reason for a positive or negative school experience is the teacher. She cites the following 17 characteristics of teachers as likely indicators of positive learning outcomes for students with AD/HD:

1. Positive academic expectations
2. Frequent review of student work
3. Clarity of teaching (e.g., explicit directions, rules)
4. Flexibility
5. Fairness
6. Active interaction with the students
7. Responsiveness
8. Warmth
9. Patience
10. Humour
11. Structured and predictable approach
12. Consistency
13. Firmness
14. Positive attitude toward inclusion
15. Knowledge of and willingness to work with students with exceptional needs
16. Knowledge of different types of effective interventions
17. Willingness to work collaboratively with other teachers (e.g., sharing information, requesting assistance as needed, participating in conferences involving students)

> **CONSIDER THIS**
> Use these characteristics of an effective teacher as a tool for self-assessment. Identify your strengths, and determine goals for improving your teaching skills.

Teachers with these traits will provide a positive role model for students in how to understand and accept children with AD/HD for the whole class. Teachers should confer with parents and the child with AD/HD to obtain advice on explaining AD/HD to other children in the classroom. The child with AD/HD may wish to be present during the explanation or even to participate in informing his or her classmates.

The following books may help introduce this topic to children.

Shelley, the Hyperactive Turtle
  Deborah Moss, Author
  Woodbine House
  5616 Fishers Lane
  Rockville, MD 20852
  (800) 843-7323

Sometimes I Drive My Mom Crazy, but I Know She's Crazy about Me!
Childworks
Center for Applied Psychology, Inc.
P.O. 61586
King of Prussia, PA 19406
(800) 962-1141

Zipper: The Kid with ADHD
Caroline Janover, Author
Woodbine House
5616 Fishers Lane
Rockville, MD 20852
(800) 843-7323

SUMMARY

- AD/HD is a complex condition that offers a real challenge to classroom teachers.

- In Canada AD/HD is not a separate category of exceptionality in provincial educational jurisdictions.

- AD/HD is a hidden disability with no unique physical characteristics to differentiate children who have it from others in the classroom.

- The diagnosis of AD/HD is primarily based on the criteria in the *Diagnostic and Statistical Manual of Mental Disorders (DSM-IV)*.

- Many theories explain the cause of AD/HD; however, AD/HD is considered primarily a neurologically based condition.

- AD/HD manifests itself across the lifespan; characteristics include limited sustained attention, reduced impulse control, excessive task-irrelevant activity, deficient rule following, and greater than normal variability during task performance.

- The process of identifying AD/HD must be done in collaboration with a psychiatrist or a physician and at the school level. It includes a preliminary assessment, an initial meeting of the school team, a formal assessment and follow-up meeting of the school team, a collaborative meeting to develop an intervention plan, and follow-up and progress reviews.

- Cultural and linguistic diversity complicates issues related to assessment and treatment for children with AD/HD.

- The majority of students with AD/HD spend all or most of the school day in general education classes.

- An individual accommodation plan is written collaboratively with parents, professionals, and when possible, the student, to identify interventions that will create success in the general education classroom.

- Medication is frequently used to enhance the educational experience of students with AD/HD.

- The most commonly prescribed medication is a psychostimulant such as Dexedrine, Ritalin, or Cylert.

- Both positive outcomes and negative side effects should be monitored for individual children taking medication for AD/HD.

- Classroom accommodations include environmental management techniques, instructional accommodations, and student-regulated strategies.

- Techniques used to manage the classroom environment include strategies for group management, physical arrangement of the room, and individual behaviour management techniques.

- Through instructional accommodations, teachers modify their behaviour to include novel and stimulating activity, to provide structure and consistency, to allow physical movement as frequently as possible, to include cooperative learning activities, and to give both spoken and written direction.

- The curriculum for students with AD/HD should be stimulating and should include experience-based learning and problem-solving activities.

- Student-regulated strategies include study and organizational tactics, self-management techniques, learning strategies, and social skills training.

- Effective teachers for students with AD/HD provide positive classroom environments, review student work frequently, and are flexible, fair, responsive, warm, patient, consistent, firm, and humorous. They develop a knowledge of the strengths and needs of their students with AD/HD and know about different intervention strategies. They are also willing to work collaboratively with other teachers, parents, and professionals.

RESOURCES

Books

Rief, Sandra F. (1993). *How to Reach and Teach ADD/ADHD Children: Practical Techniques and Strategies for Grades K–8*. Paramus, NJ: The Center for Applied Research in Education.

This complete resource provides information on how to teach organizational and study skills and also offers detailed, multisensory strategies for teaching reading, writing, and math.

McCarney, S. B. (1989). *The Attention Deficit Disorders Intervention Manual*. Columbia, MO: Hawthorne Educational Services.

Recommended and reviewed by the National Attention Deficit Disorder Association, this manual provides a wealth of practical guidelines and suggestions for school-based accommodations, for both learning and behavioural problems. It should be required reading for anyone attending an IEP conference for a child with AD/HD.

Pfiffner, L. J. (1996). *All about ADHD: The Complete Practical Guide for Classroom Teachers*. Jefferson City, MO: Scholastic Professional Books.

A leading researcher in the area of classroom management and family-based interventions for AD/HD offers very practical information in this excellent comprehensive manual on identifying and managing AD/HD behaviours.

Associations

Children and Adults with Attention Deficit/Hyperactivity Disorder, Canadian Office
P.O. Box 361019, Richmond, British Columbia
V7E 3E5
Phone: (604) 271-9285; Fax: (604) 272-6651
Canadian CHADD will provide you with a variety of resources and can direct you to the CHADD chapter closest to you.

Children and Adults with Attention Deficit/Hyperactivity Disorder, U.S. Office
8181 Professional Place, Suite 201, Landover, MD 20785
Phone: 1 (800) 233-4050/(301) 306-7070
Web site: **www.chadd.org**
American CHADD has a wealth of resources and materials that pertain to individuals with AD/HD. It also has a very detailed and helpful Web site that is constantly updated.

WEBLINKS

Children and Adults with Attention-Deficit Hyperactivity Disorder (CHADD)
www.chadd.org/
This comprehensive Web site provides basic facts about AD/HD, current research, helpful strategies, up-to-date resources, and related links. The focus is on education, advocacy, and support for people with AD/HD, their parents, and educators.

CHADD Canada
www.members.tripod.com/~chaddcanada/ index.html/
This Web site describes the mission of CHADD in Canada and provides links to local chapters across the country.

The National Attention Deficit Disorder Association (ADDA)
www.add.org/
The Association's Web site is especially focused on the needs of adults and young adults with ADD, but is also relevant for parents of children with ADD. It provides specific sites focused on family issues, school, and ADD, as well as a kids' area. An excellent aspect of this Web site is a bookstore for which the Association has selected and reviewed books and categorized them by topic (e.g., for parents, for children, for educators).

About.com
add.miningco.com/health/add/
Fascinating to browse, this Web site provides a guide to a huge array of information related to AD/HD. It covers parenting, educating, medication, comorbid disorders, career issues, and more, and offers book lists, video lists, and chat rooms.

CHAPTER FIVE

Teaching Students with Emotional and Behavioural Disorders

Frank is a six-year-old Kindergarten student who always seems to be in trouble. On the very first day of school, he stole some crayons from one of his new classmates. When confronted with the fact that the crayons in his desk belonged to another student, Frank adamantly denied stealing them. Frank's behaviour became more difficult over the first six months of the school year. Ms. Walters, Frank's Kindergarten teacher, uses a classroom management system that rewards students with checkmarks for appropriate behaviours. Students can redeem their checkmarks at the end of the week for various toys. Frank has never earned enough checkmarks to get a toy. Now he openly states that he doesn't care if he ever receives any checkmarks.

Frank's primary behaviour difficulty is his inability to leave his classmates alone. He is constantly pinching, pulling hair, or taking things from other students. Ms. Walters has placed Frank's chair away from those of the other students in an attempt to prevent him from bothering them. Still, he gets out of his chair and manages to create disturbances regularly. Ms. Walters has sent Frank to the principal's office on numerous occasions. Each time he returns, his behaviour improves, but only for about half of the day. Then he returns to his old ways of causing problems for other students and Ms. Walters. Frank's schoolwork has begun to suffer as a result of his behaviour. Whereas many of his classmates are beginning to read and can write their names, Frank still has difficulties associating sounds with letters and can print his name only in a very rudimentary form.

Ms. Walters has had four parent conferences about Frank. On each occasion, only Frank's mother took part—there is no father figure in the home. She indicates to Ms. Walters that she does not know what to do with Frank. Ms. Walters and Frank's mother are both concerned that Frank's behaviour will continue to worsen unless some solution is found. They are currently discussing whether to retain him in Kindergarten for the next school year.

1. Why did the behaviour management system used by Ms. Walters not work with Frank?

2. What are some strategies that Ms. Walters can use to promote an improvement in Frank's behaviour?

3. Would retention likely benefit Frank? Why or why not?

INTRODUCTION

Although most children and youth are disruptive from time to time, the majority do not display negative behaviours sufficient to create serious problems in school. Most comply with classroom and school rules without needing extensive interventions. However, some students' behaviours and emotions result in significant problems. This may be due to the way school personnel deal with various student behaviours. The behaviour may continue even after several interventions have been tried. Students whose behaviours and emotions result in significant school problems, such as Frank in the preceding vignette, may require identification and intervention. At a minimum, they require that classroom teachers try different methods in an effort to enhance their school success and reduce the problem behaviour.

Although emotional and behaviour problems may result in serious actions such as suicides and depression, they have long been associated with acting out and disruptive behaviours in classrooms—in general, discipline problems. The primary problem faced by most teachers when dealing with students with emotional and behaviour problems is classroom discipline.

Behaviour problems are a major concern for professional educators (Elam, Rose, & Gallup, 1996). In a survey of general education classroom teachers, the behaviour of students was cited as a primary reason for deciding to leave the teaching profession (Smith, 1990). Teachers noted that they spent too much time on student behaviour problems and not enough on instruction. In an American study by Knitzer, Steinberg, and Fleisch (1990), it was found that 80 percent of all students identified as having emotional and behaviour problems are educated in regular schools. Nearly 50 percent of these students spend some or all of their school day in general education classrooms with general education classroom teachers, not special education teachers. Similarly, all of Canada is committed to the inclusion of children with emotional and behavioural disorders in the regular classroom. Usually, though, there are pull-out services available for these students too. In 1990 Dworet and Rathgeber, in a review of existing services across Canada, reported that services available in each of the provinces generally conformed to a range of educational services model. Schwean and colleagues also note that from province to province the services vary somewhat but generally range from full inclusion to a hospital setting (Schwean, Saklofske, Shatz, & Falk, 1996).

CONSIDER THIS

What kinds of children do you think of when you hear the term *emotionally disturbed?* Can this term have an impact on teachers' expectations of children?

Students who experience emotional and behavioural disorders receive a variety of labels. The Council for Children with Behavior Disorders (CCBD) of the Council for Exceptional Children refers to the group as emotionally disturbed and behaviourally disordered (E/BD) because it believes the term better describes the students served in special education programs (Huntze, 1985). *E/BD* is the term that will be used throughout this chapter.

Numerous problems exist in providing services to students with emotional and behaviour problems. These problems include difficulties in defining **emotional and behavioural disorders (E/BDs)**, difficulties in measuring behaviour and emotions, diversity of behaviours among "normal" individuals, diversity of individuals with behaviour and emotional problems, and difficulties identifying children with behavioural and emotional disorders (Wicks-Nelson & Israel, 1991). Despite the problems, these children must be identified and provided with appropriate interventions or they will continually disrupt the classroom environment.

BASIC CONCEPTS

This section provides basic information about emotional disturbance and behavioural disorders. Understanding children with these problems will aid teachers and other educators in developing appropriate intervention programs.

Definition

In Canada no single definition of emotional and behavioural disorders is in use in schools, but practitioners have established certain commonalities in their understanding of what constitutes an emotional or behavioural disorder (Hallahan & Kauffman, 1997; Weber, 1994). These commonalities include the following:

- behaviour that goes to an extreme, that is significantly different from what is normally expected
- a behaviour problem that is chronic and does not quickly disappear
- behaviour that is unacceptable because of social or cultural expectations
- behaviour that affects the student's academic performance
- behaviour that cannot be explained by health, sensory, or social difficulties

In most cases, in identifying a student as having an emotional/ behavioural disorder, the school assessment team will use criteria aimed at establishing these general assumptions. However, exactly how to apply the definition remains vague: when the definition is interpreted broadly, many more children are served than when it is interpreted narrowly. This fact may explain the variability in prevalence estimates from province to province (Weber, 1994). In addition, Dworet and Rathgeber (1998) have noted that in the 10 jurisdictions across Canada that use definitions of E/BD, 8 different definitions are in use. They found significant variability across Canada—and even within provinces—in exact definitions of E/BD.

Creating another problem, most agencies other than schools that provide services to children and adolescents with emotional problems use the definition and classification system found in the ***Diagnostic and Statistical Manual of Mental Disorders (DSM–IV)***. This manual, published by the American Psychiatric Association (1994), uses a definition and classification system totally different from the one used in public schools. The discrepancy adds to confusion and results in fragmented services; some children are considered E/BD according to one system but not according to the other.

Classification

Children who experience emotional and behavioural disorders make up an extremely heterogeneous population. Professionals have subcategorized the

CONSIDER THIS

How would you, as a teacher, decide which behaviours are "significantly different" from behaviour normally expected? How would teachers' evaluation differ as a function of experience, personality, and school setting?

FURTHER READING

For more information on extreme variability across the country in definitions of behavioural disorders, read Dworet and Rathgeber's 1998 article, "Confusion Reigns: Definitions of Behavior Exceptionality in Canada," in volume 8, pages 3–19, of *Exceptionality Education Canada.*

group into smaller, more homogeneous subgroups so that these students can be studied, understood, and served better (Wicks-Nelson & Israel, 1991). Several different classification systems are used to group individuals with emotional and behavioural disorders.

One classification system focuses on the clinical elements found in the field of emotional and behaviour problems. This system is detailed in the *DSM-IV* (American Psychiatric Association, 1994), a manual widely used by medical and psychological professionals in both Canada and the United States, though infrequently used by educators. It categorizes emotional and behaviour problems according to several different clinical subtypes, such as developmental disorders, organic mental disorders, and schizophrenia. Educators need to be aware of the *DSM-IV* classification system, because of the occasional need to interact with professionals from the field of mental health.

The classification schemes used by teachers and other educators are usually associated with functional behaviours and related interventions. For example, one classification system that can be useful in schools was developed by Quay and Peterson (1987). They described six major subgroups of children with emotional and behavioural disorders:

1. Individuals are classified as having a **conduct disorder** if they seek attention, are disruptive, and act out. This category includes behaving aggressively toward others.

2. Students who exhibit **socialized aggression** are likely to join a "subcultural group," a group of peers who are openly disrespectful to their peers, teachers, and parents. Delinquency, truancy, and other "gang" behaviours are common among this group.

3. Individuals with **attention problems–immaturity** can be characterized as having attention deficits, being easily distractible, and having poor concentration. Many students in this group are impulsive and may act without thinking about the consequences.

4. Students classified in the **anxiety/withdrawal** group are self-conscious, reticent, and unsure of themselves. Their self-concepts are generally very low, causing them to simply "retreat" from immediate activities. They are also anxious and frequently depressed.

5. The subgroup of students who display **psychotic behaviour** may hallucinate, deal in a fantasy world, talk in gibberish, and display other bizarre behaviour.

6. Students with **motor excess** are hyperactive. They have difficulties sitting still, listening to another individual, and keeping their attention focused. Often these students are also hypertalkative. (See Chapter 4 for more information on hyperactivity.)

It is important for the teacher to know that students can demonstrate behaviour from a number of different dimensions or categories; in other words, the categories are not mutually exclusive. For example, Ryan, a Grade 8 student who is constantly disruptive and threatens both his peers and his teachers (conduct disorder), may also suffer from depression (anxiety/withdrawal).

Classification becomes less important when school personnel utilize a functional assessment/intervention model. This approach, which will be described in more detail later, emphasizes finding out which environmental stimuli result in inappropriate behaviours. Once these stimuli are identified and altered,

FURTHER READING

For more information on the American Psychiatric Association's classification of students with intellectual disabilities, review the *Diagnostic and Statistical Manual (DSM-IV)*, published in 1994.

CONSIDER THIS

Do students without disabilities ever exhibit these characteristics? What differentiates nondisabled students from those classified as E/BD?

the inappropriate behaviours may decrease or disappear (Foster-Johnson & Dunlap, 1993). In such instances, the process of classifying a student's problem is unnecessary.

Prevalence and Causes

Compared to children classified as having learning disabilities and intellectual disabilities, the category of E/BD represents a much smaller number of children.

Although prevalence rates vary by province or territory in Canada, all estimates place prevalence of E/BD well below prevalence of learning disabilities. Estimates range from 0.0002 percent in Saskatchewan to 1.0 percent in Alberta, New Brunswick, and Newfoundland, with the Northwest Territories, Prince Edward Island, Ontario, and British Columbia falling somewhere between. Nova Scotia, Quebec, and the Yukon failed to provide prevalence rates, while Manitoba had a highly variable within-province prevalence of 0.5 percent to 2.0 percent depending on the specific definition used within regions (Dworet & Rathgeber, 1998). Thus, Dworet and Rathgeber report an average across-Canada prevalence of 0.49 percent based on their survey. Weber (1994) reports marginally different prevalence rates in *Special Education in Canadian Schools*. Using 1980s data he concludes that 0.78 percent of the school population in Canada were identified as having an E/BD (Canada Council of Ministers of Education, 1983, as cited in Weber, 1994) with a range by province from 0.26 percent in Saskatchewan to 1.45 percent in Quebec (Council for Exceptional Children, 1989). In summary, the differences between these two frequently cited Canadian sources are small—notably less than the 6–10 percent prevalence estimates of E/BD in school-age children (Kauffman, 1997; Kazdin, 1989).

The discrepancy between identified and actual rates of children with E/BD is probably due to students with E/BD being identified as having other

CONSIDER THIS
What factors will likely lead to larger or smaller numbers of children being identified as having emotional and behavioural disorders?

Depression is a characteristic of students with emotional and behavioural disorders.

TABLE 5.1	
Causes of Serious Emotional and Behavioural Disorders	
Theoretical Framework	**Etiologies/Causal Factors**
BIOLOGICAL	Genetic inheritance Biochemical abnormalities Neurological abnormalities Injury to the central nervous system
PSYCHOANALYTICAL	Psychological processes Functioning of the mind: id, ego, and superego Inherited predispositions (instinctual process) Traumatic early-childhood experiences
BEHAVIORAL	Environmental events 1. Failure to learn adaptive behaviors 2. Learning of maladaptive behaviors 3. Developing maladaptive behaviors as a result of stressful environmental circumstances
PHENOMENOLOGICAL	Faulty learning about oneself Misuse of defense mechanisms Feelings, thoughts, and events emanating from the self
SOCIOLOGICAL/ECOLOGICAL	Role assignment (labeling) Cultural transmission Social disorganization Distorted communication Differential association Negative interactions and transactions with others

From *Human Exceptionality* (p. 148), by M. L. Hardman, C. J. Drew, M. W. Egan, and B. Wolf, 1993, Boston: Allyn & Bacon. Used by permission.

exceptionalities such as a learning disability. Or, if the students are showing more anxious or withdrawn behaviours, they may be overlooked altogether. Heath, a researcher at McGill University, has observed that teachers have difficulty identifying a student with depression if the student is simultaneously acting out (Heath, Vella, & Miezitis, 1992).

Among students classified as having emotional and behavioural disorders, the majority are males. Some studies have revealed that as many as 10 times more boys than girls are found in special classes for students with behavioural disorders (Rosenberg, Wilson, Maheady, & Sindelar, 1992; Smith, Price, & Marsh, 1986).

Furthermore, prevalence of E/BD is low in the early elementary grades and highest in late elementary and early high school; it then decreases in later high school years (Hallahan & Kauffman, 1997).

Many different factors can cause students to display emotional and behavioural disorders. These can be found in five different theoretical frameworks, including biological, psychoanalytical, behavioural, phenomenological, and sociological/ecological. Within each framework are numerous specific causal factors. Table 5.1 summarizes some of these variables by theoretical framework.

Characteristics

Students with emotional and behaviour problems exhibit a wide range of characteristics that differ in type as well as intensity. The wide range of behaviours and emotions experienced by all individuals reflects the broad variety of characteristics associated with individuals with emotional and behaviour problems (Bullock, Zagar, Donahue, & Pelton, 1985).

Problems typically associated with children with emotional and behavioural disorders include the following:

- Aggressive/acting-out behaviours (Grosenick, George, George, & Lewis, 1991; Kauffman, Lloyd, Baker, & Riedel, 1995)
- Social deficits (Smith & Luckasson, 1995)
- Irresponsibility (Smith et al., 1993)
- Inadequate peer relationships (Searcy & Meadows, 1994)
- Hyperactivity/distractibility
- Lying, cheating, and stealing (Rosenberg et al., 1992)
- Academic deficits (Bullock, 1992)
- Depression (Kauffman et al., 1995; Wicks-Nelson & Israel, 1991)
- Anxiety (Kauffman et al., 1995; Wicks-Nelson & Israel, 1991)

All children classified as having emotional and behavioural disorders do not exhibit all of these characteristics. The ones exhibited by a particular child will depend on the nature of the emotional or behaviour problem.

CONSIDER THIS
Do students without disabilities ever exhibit these characteristics? What differentiates nondisabled students from those classified as E/BD?

Identification, Assessment, and Eligibility

Students with emotional and behavioural disorders are evaluated for several purposes, including identification, assessment to determine appropriate intervention strategies, and determination of eligibility for special education services. The first step is for students to be identified as potentially having emotional and behavioural problems. Teachers' awareness of the characteristics of students with these problems is critical in the identification process. Behavioural checklists can be used to identify students for possible referral.

Once students are identified as possibly having emotional and behavioural problems, they are referred for formal assessment to determine their eligibility for special education programs and to ascertain appropriate intervention strategies. Kaplan (1996) lists clinical interviews, observations, rating scales, personality tests, and neurological examinations as methods for obtaining information for assessment. Table 5.2 summarizes each of these procedures.

When determining appropriate intervention strategies, **functional assessment**, which focuses on abilities to succeed in daily activities, provides extensive information for teachers. A functional assessment helps teachers better understand disruptive behaviours, which can lead to an insightful intervention approach. Foster-Johnson and Dunlap (1993) list the following variables that influence behaviours:

TEACHING TIP
When you suspect a student of having an emotional or behavioural disorder, develop a systematic method of collecting information during observations of the student.

1. Physiological factors
   - Sickness or allergies
   - Side effects of medication

TABLE 5.2	Assessment Procedures Used for Students with Emotional and Behavioural Disorders
CLINICAL INTERVIEW	• The clinical interview is the most common tool for assessment. • Questions are directed to the child and others regarding behaviors and any relevant relationships. • Some questions are planned; some are developed as the interview progresses. • The interview can be highly structured, using questions generated from the *DSM-IV* criteria.
OBSERVATION	• The observation can be structured with time limitations, or unstructured. • Observations should occur in a variety of different settings and at different times.
RATING SCALES	• A rating scale contains a listing of behaviors to note. • It provides for much more structure than simple observation. • It ensures that certain behaviors are observed or asked about.
PERSONALITY TESTS	• The two kinds of personality test include self-completed inventories and projective tests. • Both kinds of personality test can provide insightful information. • Interpretation of personality tests is subjective and needs to be done by a trained professional.

From *Pathways for Exceptional Children: School, Home, and Culture*, by P. Kaplan, 1996, St. Paul, MN: West Publishing.

- Fatigue
- Hunger or thirst
- Increased arousal due to a fight, missing the bus, a disrupted routine
2. Classroom environment
   - High noise level
   - Uncomfortable temperature
   - Over- or understimulation
   - Poor seating arrangement
   - Frequent disruptions
3. Curriculum and instruction
   - Few opportunities for making choices
   - Lack of predictability in the schedule
   - Inadequate level of assistance provided to the student
   - Unclear directions provided for activity completion
   - Few opportunities for the student to communicate
   - Activities that are too difficult
   - Activities that take a long time to complete
   - Activities that the student dislikes
   - Activities for which the completion criterion is unclear
   - Activities that might not be perceived as being relevant or useful by the student

After reviewing these variables with a particular child in mind, teachers can devise interventions that target a specific variable to alter a particular behaviour (Foster-Johnson & Dunlap, 1993).

STRATEGIES FOR CURRICULUM AND INSTRUCTION

Students with emotional and behavioural disorders often present significant problems for teachers, especially in general education settings. Unlike students with other types of disabilities, those with emotional and behavioural problems may act out and create disruptions. Their behaviour affects not only their own learning, but often the learning of others.

Despite these difficulties, all of the Canadian provinces and territories are committed to the inclusion of children with E/BD in the regular classroom. Although placement options for these students range from the regular classroom to a hospital setting, the majority of students with E/BD will remain in the regular classroom for most of the time (Schwean, Saklofske, Shatz, & Falk, 1996). Dworet and Rathgeber (1998) argue that, since the services for students with E/BD across Canada are so variable largely because of the lack of a clear definition, eligibility for services is hard to determine.

CONSIDER THIS
What role should mental health professionals play in serving students with E/BD? how can schools involve mental health professionals more?

Continuum of Placement Options

Because many students with emotional and behaviour problems are included in general education classrooms, teachers and special education teachers need to collaborate in developing and implementing intervention programs. Without this collaboration, appropriate interventions will be very difficult to provide. Consistency in behaviour management and other strategies among teachers and family members is critical. If students receive feedback from the special education teacher that significantly differs from the feedback received from the classroom teacher, confusion often results.

As more students with disabilities are included in general education classrooms, many students with serious emotional disturbance and behavioural disorders are being reintegrated into general classrooms from more restrictive settings. The ability of students and teachers to effectively deal with behaviour problems is critical for successful reintegration (Carpenter & McKee-Higgins, 1996). Rock, Rosenberg, and Carran (1995) studied the variables that affected this reintegration. Their findings indicate that success can be predicted when reintegration orientation, demographic characteristics of restrictive programs, and particular experiences and training of special educators are features of the reintegration process. Programs that were more likely to have better success at reintegration include those with a more positive reintegration orientation; those with certain demographic characteristics, such as being located in a wing of the general classroom building; and particular training experiences of teachers, such as having reintegration training in several sites. Administrators might want to take these variables into consideration when planning the reintegration of students with emotional and behavioural disorders into general education programs.

FURTHER READING
For more information on methods to reintegrate students with E/BD into general education classrooms, read "Variables Affecting the Reintegration Rate ..." by E. E. Rock, M. S. Rosenberg, and D. T. Carran, published in 1995 in volume 61 of *Exceptional Children.*

PERSONAL SPOTLIGHT

Parent of a Student with Asperger's Syndrome

■ LOUISE KOWALENKO, Burnaby, British Columbia

"I am the mother of a now 14-year-old son who has Asperger's.

"Kevin was not diagnosed until he was 10 years old. He taught himself to read and had a voracious appetite for books. He was a happy and affectionate child. The teachers always said he was such a gifted student. In Grade 1 we noticed he was having problems socially. In Grade 3 he found a best friend, but late in Grade 4 his grandfather died and then early in Grade 5 his best friend moved away. Alone and vulnerable, he found the teasing he faced unbearable and one day at school he attempted to suffocate himself with a plastic bag. Ten years old and he wanted to die! He was treated for depression, and when the depression lifted they diagnosed Kevin as having Asperger's. Returning to school in Grade 6 brought on outbursts of uncontrollable anger which eventually led to his being isolated to a small room, where he was assigned a morning aide and I acted as his afternoon aide.

"Kevin was finally assigned a full-time aide in Grade 7 and we began to integrate him back into the regular classroom. The aide was a most intuitive, calm, and understanding woman who not only taught curriculum, but helped Kevin and myself to develop a better understanding of Kevin's strengths and his weaknesses and how to cope. It was amazing how successful the team-work between Kevin, his aide, his teachers, and home was that year. Kevin excelled socially and was on the honour roll. This serves as an example of how, with collaboration, needed supports, and teamwork, inclusion can work.

"In Grade 8 Kevin moved to a large high school (2000 students) and had new aides. He managed Grade 8 well, finding a friend who he also socialized with on weekends but now, in Grade 9, the old anger and frustration are evident. His outbursts have led to suspensions and his depression makes it hard for him to concentrate on schoolwork. A C+ average has been devastating to his self-worth because his self-worth is based on intelligence, not a circle of friends. We continue to struggle to make it all work for Kevin.

"My greatest frustration is having to teach his new aides *repeatedly* how to deal with Kevin. They know so little about Asperger's and don't understand how important it is not to keep talking or nagging at him, to be quiet so he can process information. When he is raging, he needs quiet so that he can compose himself and think 'logically.' They need this information and they need to be sensitive to Kevin and his style, instead of reacting to it. I can teach anyone about Asperger's, but I cannot teach them caring and sensitivity."

FUNDAMENTALS OF CLASSROOM ORGANIZATION AND MANAGEMENT

CONSIDER THIS

Why would students with E/BD particularly benefit from good classroom organization?

The importance of good classroom organization and management techniques has been affirmed numerous times by many professionals in the field of education. Yet although much attention is given to curricular and instructional aspects of students' educational programs, organizational and management dimensions are typically underemphasized, despite their importance as prerequisites to instruction. They represent the one area that first-year teachers consistently identify as most problematic. Further, while classroom management benefits all students, for students with E/BD it is particularly important. Basic management will serve to prevent many behavioural difficulties as well as providing a predictable and accepting atmosphere for students with E/BD. Therefore, although the following approach to **classroom management** applies to all students, it appears in this chapter as the core of working with students with E/BD.

Model of Classroom Management

Every classroom environment involves a number of elements that have a profound impact on the effectiveness of instruction and learning (Doyle, 1986). Six of these are described briefly here:

- *Multidimensionality* refers to the vast number and variety of activities that occur in a classroom within the course of an instructional day.
- *Simultaneity* refers to the fact that many different events occur at the same time.
- *Immediacy* refers to the rapid pace at which events occur in classrooms.
- *Unpredictability* refers to the reality that some events occur unexpectedly, cannot be anticipated, but require attention nonetheless.
- *Publicness* refers to the fact that classroom events are witnessed by a significant number of students who are very likely to take note of how teachers deal with these ongoing events.
- *History* refers to the reality that, over the course of the school year, various events (experiences, routines, rules) will shape the dynamics of classroom behaviour.

FURTHER READING
For more information on models of classroom management, read *Applied Behavior Analysis for Teachers,* fourth edition, by P. A. Alberto and A. C. Troutman, published in 1995 by Merrill.

Considering these elements reaffirms the complexity of teaching large numbers of students who have diverse learning needs. To address these classroom dynamics, teachers need to identify ways to organize and manage their classrooms to maximize the potential opportunities for learning. Figure 5.1 depicts the multifaceted dimensions of **classroom organization** and management. This model of organization and management evolved from one designed by Polloway and Patton (1997). It reflects an adaptation of what they identify as "precursors to teaching."

The effective and efficient management of a classroom is based on numerous considerations. To create an environment conducive to learning, teachers must pay attention to psychosocial, procedural, physical, behavioural, instructional, and organizational variables that have a critical impact on learning and behaviour. Much of what is contained in the dimensional model (Figure 5.1) and discussed in this chapter needs to be considered before the beginning of the school year, to prevent problems from developing. Prevention is frequently more effective than powerful behaviour management strategies.

Guiding Principles

A number of overarching principles guide the development and implementation of appropriate classroom organization and management procedures:

- Good classroom organization and management must be planned.
- Successful management derives from a positive classroom climate.

FIGURE 5.1
Dimensions of Classroom
Organization and
Management

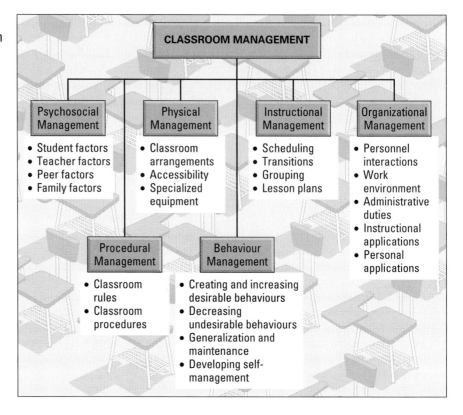

- Proactive management is preferable to reactive approaches.
- Consistency is the key to establishing an effective management program.
- Two characteristics enhance a teacher's ability to manage classrooms effectively (Kounin, 1970):
  1. *With-it-ness:* Overall awareness of what is happening in the classroom.
  2. *Overlap:* The ability to deal with more than one event simultaneously.

Although sound classroom management practices are useful in working with all students, the recommendations provided in this chapter are particularly helpful for students who have special needs and require individualized consideration. Often, they struggle to learn in an environment that is not well managed.

COMPONENTS OF EFFECTIVE CLASSROOM ORGANIZATION AND MANAGEMENT

This section of the chapter discusses the major elements and subcomponents of classroom management highlighted in the model in Figure 5.1.

Psychosocial Management

This dimension refers to the psychological and social dynamics of the classroom. It includes consideration of **classroom climate**, the classroom atmosphere in which students must function.

The dynamics of classrooms are influenced by certain *student factors.* Their attitudes about school, authority figures, and other classmates can have a remarkable impact on how they behave and react to organizational and management demands. Other factors that shape student attitudes include the nature of previous educational experiences, the way they feel about themselves, and their own expectations (i.e., potential for success or failure).

The psychological atmosphere of any classroom depends in great part on certain *teacher factors,* including disposition, competencies and skills, and actions. A teacher's attitudes toward students with special needs can dramatically affect the quality of education that a student will receive during the time he or she is in the classroom. Personal philosophies about education, discipline, and curriculum weigh heavily. The type of expectations a teacher holds for students can significantly influence learning outcomes.

Peers are also key players in forming the psychological and social atmosphere of a classroom, especially among older students. Peer values and pressures must be understood by teachers and used to benefit students with special needs. Valuable cooperative learning can result from successful peer involvement.

The final component involves a variety of *family-generated factors.* Three major issues include family attitudes toward education, level of family support and involvement in the student's education, and amount of pressure placed on a child by the family. Extremes can be problematic—for example, burdening a child with overwhelming pressure to succeed can cause as many difficulties as taking no interest at all in a child's education.

The behaviours of teachers can have a great impact on effective behaviour management.

The dynamics of a classroom are determined by many different student factors.

These recommendations should help create a positive, nurturing environment that contributes to positive outcomes for all students:

- Let students know that you are sensitive to their needs and concerns.
- Convey enthusiasm about learning and the school experience.
- Create a supportive, safe setting in which students who are different can learn without fear of being ridiculed or threatened.
- Treat all students with fairness.
- Acknowledge all students in some personal way each day to affirm that they are valued within the room.
- Create a learning environment that is built on success, avoiding the failure common to the learning patterns of students with disabilities.
- Understand the family and cultural contexts from which students come.
- Make yourself available to students if they need to talk.
- Establish that each student in the classroom has rights (e.g., not to be interrupted when working or responding to a teacher inquiry) and that you expect everyone to respect those rights.
- Instill in students the understanding that they are responsible for their own behaviour.
- Convey to students that every student's thoughts and ideas are important.
- Encourage risk taking and nurture students to take on scholastic challenges.

Procedural Management

As noted in Figure 5.1, this dimension refers to the rules and procedures that are part of the operating procedures of a classroom. The guidelines discussed here provide direction to school staff and students as to what is expected of all. All rules, procedures, and regulations must be identified before the school year begins, and plans should be in place to teach them to students during the first days of the school year.

Equally important is preparation for dealing with violations of rules. Immediate and consistent consequences are needed. Various disciplinary techniques can be implemented to ensure that inappropriate behaviour is handled effectively. (These will be covered in a subsequent section of the chapter.)

Students with exceptional needs will benefit from being taught systematically the administrative and social rules operative in a classroom. The suggestions provided in this section focus on classroom rules and in-class procedures.

Most individuals respond best when they know what is expected of them. *Classroom rules* provide a general sense of what is expected of students. The rules that are chosen should be essential to classroom functioning and help create a positive learning environment (Christenson, Ysseldyke, & Thurlow, 1989; Smith & Rivera, 1995; Evertson et al., 1989; Salend, 1994). Reasonable classroom rules, presented appropriately, will be particularly beneficial to students with special needs who are in general education settings because this process assists in clarifying expectations. Some specific suggestions are presented in Table 5.3.

An often overlooked area of classroom management is the development of logical *classroom procedures,* the specific way in which certain activities will be performed or the way certain situations will be handled. For example, procedures need to be established for using the pencil sharpener, using the rest room, and entering and leaving the classroom. Again, clear procedures are of particular importance especially for some students with special needs who may have difficulty attending to details or following instructions.

This area can cause much distress for teachers if not attended to prior to the beginning of the school year. Teachers are often surprised by the complexity and detail associated with many seemingly trivial areas (Evertson et al., 1989). The procedures for these areas combine to form the mosaic of one's management system. Here are some suggestions:

- Identify all situations for which a procedure will be needed. Develop the procedures.
- Explain each procedure thoroughly.

CONSIDER THIS
Why are classroom rules such an important component of classroom management? Describe classrooms with effective rules and those without effective rules.

TABLE 5.3

Recommendations for Classroom Rules

- Develop no more than seven rules for the classroom.
- Keep the rules brief, and state them clearly.
- Explain the rules thoroughly, and discuss the specific consequences if they are violated.
- State the rules in a positive way—avoid statements that are worded in a negative way, such as "not allowed."
- Post the rules in a location that all students can see.
- Discuss exceptions in advance so that students understand them.
- Teach the rules through modelling and practice.
- Review the rules on a regular basis and when new students are placed in the class.
- Use reminders of rules as a preventive measure for times when possible disruption is anticipated.
- Involve students in rule setting.

- Teach each procedure through modelling, guided practice, and independent practice, letting every student have an opportunity to practise the procedure.
- Introduce classroom procedures during the first week of school, scheduling priority procedures for the first day and covering other ones on subsequent days.
- Avoid introducing too many procedures at once (Doyle, 1986).
- Incorporate any school regulation of importance and relevance into classroom procedures (e.g., using the rest rooms).

Physical Management

FURTHER READING

For more information on physical management of classrooms, read *Applied Behavior Analysis in the Classroom*, by P. Schloss and M. Smith, published by Allyn & Bacon in 1994.

This dimension includes the aspects of the physical environment that teachers can manipulate to enhance the conditions for learning. For students with disabilities, some features of the physical setting may need to be especially arranged to ensure that individual needs are met.

Classroom arrangements refer to physical facets of the classroom, including layout, storage, wall space, and signage. Figure 5.2 addresses seating arrangement. Teachers are encouraged to think carefully about where to seat students who have problems with controlling their behaviours and students with sensory impairments. The judicious use of seating arrangements can minimize problems as well as create better learning opportunities for students.

Other suggestions for classroom arrangement are listed here:

- Consider establishing areas of the classroom for certain types of activities (e.g., discovery, independent reading).
- Clearly establish which areas of the classroom, such as the teacher's desk, are off limits.
- Begin the year with a structured environment, moving to more flexibility after rules and procedures have been established.
- Notify students with visual impairments of changes made to the physical environment.

FIGURE 5.2
Seating Arrangements

- Seat students with behaviour problems first so that they are in close proximity to the teacher for as much of the time as possible.

- After more self-control is demonstrated, more distant seating arrangements are possible and desirable.

- Locate students for whom visual distractions can interfere with attention to tasks (e.g., learning and attentional problems, hearing impairments, behaviour problems) so that these distractions are minimized.

- Establish clear lines of vision (a) for students so that they can attend to instruction and (b) for the teacher so that students can be monitored throughout the class period (Rosenberg et al., 1991).

- Ensure that students with sensory impairments are seated so that they can maximize their residual vision and hearing.

- Consider alternative arrangements of desks (e.g., table clusters) as options to traditional rows.

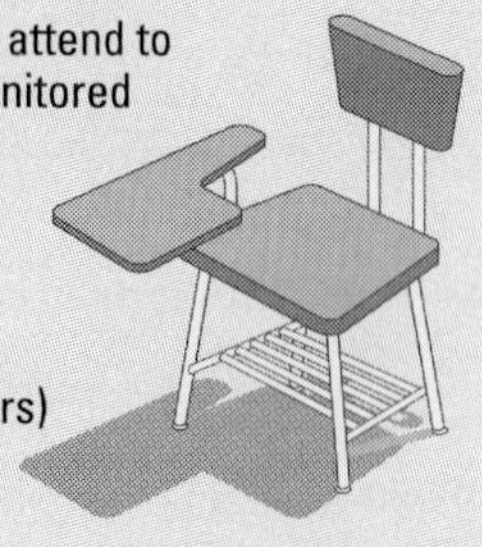

- Furniture should be arranged so that the teacher and students can move easily around the classroom.
- Direct students' attention to the information to be learned from bulletin boards, if they are used for instructional purposes.
- Establish patterns that students can use in moving around the class that minimize disruption.
- Secure materials and equipment that are potentially harmful if used without proper supervision, such as certain art supplies, chemicals, and science equipment.
- Avoid creating open spaces that have no clear purpose, as they often can become staging areas for problem behaviours (Rosenberg et al., 1991).
- Provide labels and signs for areas of the room to assist students in better understanding what and where things are.

The accessibility of the classroom warrants special attention. The concept of **accessibility** extends beyond physical accessibility, touching on overall program accessibility for students with special needs. This means that students with disabilities must be able to utilize the classroom like other students and that the room must be free of potential hazards. For students with E/BD accessibility is an issue when social isolation or time out is used for substantial periods of time. This type of treatment limits the student's access to the classroom and is therefore problematic.

Behaviour Management

An important component of classroom management involves the management of those specific behaviours that disrupt the learning environment. Yet the ability to control inappropriate behaviours represents only a part of a comprehensive behaviour management program. Such a plan should also include techniques for creating new behaviours or increasing desirable behaviours that are minimally existent. Moreover, a sound program must ensure that behaviours learned or changed will be maintained over time and demonstrated in different contexts; it must also teach self-control mechanisms. The nearby Inclusion Strategies feature describes the components of a behaviour management plan.

It is not possible to cover in sufficient detail all facets of behaviour management. However, this section provides recommendations that should guide practice in increasing desirable behaviours, decreasing undesirable behaviours, promoting generalization and maintenance, and enhancing self-management.

CREATING AND INCREASING DESIRABLE BEHAVIOURS

TEACHING TIP
Students should take part in selecting positive reinforcers to make sure that the reinforcers are indeed attractive to the student.

The acquisition of desired new behaviours, whether scholastic, personal, social, or vocational, is a classroom goal. A new desired behaviour can be affirmed with a reinforcer, any event that rewards, and thus strengthens, the behaviour it follows. **Positive reinforcement** presents a pleasant consequence for performance of an appropriate behaviour. Positive reinforcers can take different forms; what serves as reinforcement for one individual may not work for another. Reinforcers can consist of praise, physical contact, tangible items, activities, or privileges. The use of reinforcement is the most socially acceptable and instructionally sound tactic for increasing desired behaviours.

Three basic principles must be followed for positive reinforcement to be effective. It must be meaningful to the student, contingent upon the proper performance of a desired behaviour, and presented immediately. In other words, for positive reinforcement to work, students must find the reinforcement pleasurable in some fashion, understand that it is being given as a result of the behaviour demonstrated, and receive it soon after they do what was asked. Principles for the use of positive reinforcement are presented in Figure 5.3.

FIGURE 5.3
Implementing
Positive
Reinforcement
Techniques

- Determine what reinforcements will work for particular students:
  1. Ask the child by using direct formal or informal questioning or by administering an interest inventory or reinforcement survey.
  2. Ask those knowledgeable about the student (e.g., parents, friends, or past teachers).
  3. Observe the student in the natural environment as well as in structured observation such as arranging reinforcement alternatives from which the student may select.
- Select meaningful reinforcers that are easy and practical to deliver in classroom settings (Idol, 1993).
- "Catch" students behaving appropriately, and provide them with the subsequent appropriate reinforcement (referred to as the differential reinforcement of behaviour *incompatible* with problem behaviour). Begin this technique early so that students experience the effects of positive reinforcement.
- Use the Premack (1959) principle ("Grandma's law": "eat your vegetables and then you can have dessert") regularly.
- Use reinforcement techniques as the student makes gradual progress in developing a desired behaviour that requires the mastery of numerous substeps (reinforce each successive approximation). This concept is called *shaping.*
- Demonstrate to a student that certain behaviours will result in positive outcomes by reinforcing nearby peers.

Contract

_____ will demonstrate the following
(Student's name)
appropriate behaviors in the classroom:

1. Come to school on time.

2. Come to school with homework completed.

3. Complete all assigned work in school without prompting.

4. Ask for help when necessary by raising hand and getting teacher's attention.

_____ will provide the following reinforcement:
(Teacher's name)

1. Ten tokens for the completion of each of the above four objectives. Tokens for the first two objectives will be provided at the beginning of class after all homework assignments have been checked. Tokens for objectives 3 and 4 will be provided at the end of the school day.

2. Tokens may be exchanged for activities on the Classroom Reinforcement Menu at noon on Fridays.

_____   _____
Student's signature   Teacher's signature

                                                    _____
                                                    Date

FIGURE 5.4
Sample Contract between Student and Teacher

From _Behavior Management: Applications for Teachers and Parents_ (p. 189), by T. Zirpoli and G. Melloy, 1993, Columbus, OH: Merrill. Used by permission.

The first illustrative application of the principle of positive reinforcement is **contingency contracting**, a concept first introduced by Homme (1969). With this methodology, the teacher develops contracts with students that state (1) what behaviours (e.g., academic work, social behaviours) students are to complete or perform and (2) what consequences (e.g., reinforcement) the instructor will provide. These contracts are presented as binding agreements between student and teacher. To be most effective, contracts should (1) initially reward imperfect approximations of the behaviour, (2) provide frequent rewards, (3) reward accomplishment rather than obedience, and (4) be fair, clear, and positive. Figure 5.4 shows an example of a contract for a secondary school student.

Group contingencies, in which contingencies are set up for groups rather than individuals, provide excellent alternatives for managing behaviour and actively including students with special needs in the general education classroom. There are three types:

■ _Dependent contingencies:_ All group members share in the reinforcement if one individual achieves a goal.

CONSIDER THIS
Some people say that contracts, as well as other forms of positive reinforcement, amount to little more than bribery. Do you agree or disagree, and why?

■ *Interdependent contingencies:*   All group members are reinforced if all collectively (or all individually) achieve the stated goal.

■ *Independent contingencies:*   Individuals within the group are reinforced for individual achievement toward a goal.

Whereas independent contingencies are commonly used, the other two forms are less widely seen in the classroom. The dependent strategy is sometimes referred to as a "hero approach" because it singles out one student's performance for attention. Although it can be abused, such an approach may be particularly attractive for a student who responds well to peer attention. A student with special needs may feel more meaningfully included in class when his or her talents are recognized in this way.

Others may feel reinforced and accepted as part of a group when interdependent contingencies are employed. The most common use of an interdependent strategy is the "good behaviour game." Because it is most often used as a behavioural reduction intervention, it is discussed later in the chapter.

FURTHER READING
For more information on group-oriented contingencies, read P. A. Alberto and A. C. Troutman's book *Applied Behavior Analysis for Teachers*, fourth edition, published in 1995 by Merrill.

The benefits of group-oriented contingencies (or peer-mediated strategies, as they are often called) include the involvement of peers, the ability of teachers to enhance motivation, and increased efficiency for the teacher. In some instances, students will raise questions of fairness concerning group contingency programs. Those who typically behave appropriately may feel that they are being penalized for the actions of others if reinforcement occurs only when the whole group evidences a desired behaviour. You can assure them that, ultimately, they and everyone else will benefit from group compliance with particular guidelines or goals.

DECREASING UNDESIRABLE BEHAVIOURS

Every teacher will face situations involving undesired behaviours, resulting in the need for behaviour reduction techniques. Teachers can select from a range of techniques; however, it is usually best to begin with the least intrusive interventions (Smith & Rivera, 1995). A recommended sequence of reduction strategies is depicted in Figure 5.5. As teachers consider reductive strategies, they are cautioned to keep records, develop plans of action, and follow provincial/territorial and local guidelines.

The use of *natural* and *logical consequences* can help children and adolescents learn to be more responsible for their behaviours (West, 1986, 1994). In **natural consequences**, the situation itself provides the contingencies for a certain behaviour. For example, if a student forgets to return a permission slip to attend an off-campus event, the natural consequence is that the student is not allowed to go and must remain at school. Thus, rather than intervening in a given situation, the teacher allows the situation to teach the students. Natural consequences are an effective means to teach common sense and responsibility (West, 1994).

In **logical consequences**, there is a logical connection between inappropriate behaviour and the consequences that follow. If a student forgets lunch money, a logical consequence might be that money must be borrowed from someone else. The uncomfortable consequence is the hassle or embarrassment of requesting financial assistance. These tactics can help students recognize that their own behaviour has created the discomfort and not something the teacher has done to them. When using this approach, teachers should clarify to students that they are responsible for their own behaviours.

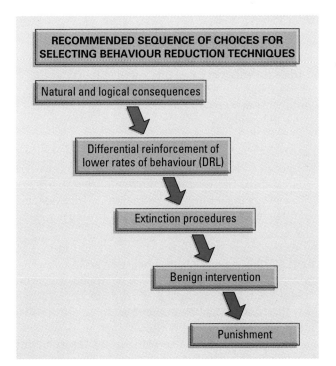

FIGURE 5.5
Recommended Sequence of Behaviour Reduction Techniques

Logical consequences relate the disciplinary response directly to the inappropriate behaviour.

The next option on the continuum is the use of **differential reinforcement of lower (DRL) rates of behaviour**. This technique uses positive reinforcement strategies as a behaviour reduction tool. A teacher using this procedure provides appropriate reinforcement to students for displaying lower rates of a certain behaviour that has been targeted for reduction. It is important to remember that the goal should be to decrease the frequency or duration of the unwanted behaviour.

An example of this technique used with groups of students is the "good behaviour game" (originally developed by Barrish, Saunders, & Wolf, 1969), in which student teams receive reinforcement if the number of occurrences of inappropriate behaviours remains under a preset criterion. Tankersley (1995) provides a good overview of the use of the good behaviour game:

> First, teachers should define target behaviors that they would like to see improved and determine when these behaviors are most problematic in their classrooms. Criteria for winning must be set and reinforcers established; the students should be taught the rules for playing. Next, the classroom is divided into teams and team names are written on the chalkboard. If any student breaks a rule when the game is in effect, the teacher makes a mark by the name of the team of which the disruptive student is a member. At the end of the time in which the game is played, any team that has fewer marks than the preestablished criterion wins. Members of the winning team(s) receive reinforcers daily. In addition, teams that meet weekly criterion receive reinforcers at the end of the week. (p. 20)

CONSIDER THIS
What are some advantages of using a DRL approach when working on a complex behaviour, rather than simply reinforcing the student only after a targeted behaviour has completely disappeared?

Here are additional considerations:

- Understand that undesirable behaviours will still occur and must be tolerated until target levels are reached.
- Reduce the criterion level after students have demonstrated stability at the present level.
- Avoid making too great a jump between criterion levels to ensure that students are able to meet the new demands.

Tankersley (1995, p. 23) stresses the value of this strategy in noting that it "can be very effective in changing students' behaviors, can lead to improved levels of academic skills . . . , can reduce the teacher's burden of incorporating several individual contingency systems for managing behavior, . . . [makes] use of natural supports available in the classroom, [and] can help promote generalization" (p. 26).

The next option involves **extinction** procedures. In this technique, the teacher withholds reinforcement of a behaviour. Over time, such action, in combination with the positive reinforcement of related desirable behaviours, should extinguish the inappropriate behaviour. One example is for the teacher to cease responding (i.e., reinforcement) to student misbehaviour. For some situations, it will be necessary to involve a student's peers in the extinction process to eliminate a behaviour because the peers' actions are controlling the relevant reinforcers. The following are additional suggestions:

- Be sure to analyze what is reinforcing the undesirable behaviour, and isolate the reinforcer(s) before initiating this procedure.
- Understand that the extinction technique is desirable because it does not involve punishment, but it will take time to be effective.
- Do not use this technique with behaviours that require immediate intervention (e.g., fighting).
- Recognize that the withholding of reinforcement (1) is likely to induce a "spiking" effect in the occurrence of the undesirable behaviour, as students intensify their efforts to receive the reinforcement they are used to getting, and (2) may produce an aggressive response.
- Provide reinforcement to students who demonstrate appropriate incompatible behaviours (e.g., taking turns vs. interrupting).

The fourth option is the use of techniques that border on being punishment but are so unobtrusive that they can be considered *benign tactics*. Most of the suggestions come from a concept developed by Cummings (1983) called the "law of least intervention." Her idea is to eliminate disruptive behaviours quickly with a minimum of disruption to the classroom or instructional routine. The following suggestions can be organized into physical, gestural, visual, and verbal prompts:

- Position yourself physically near students who are likely to create problems.
- Touch a student's shoulder gently to convey your awareness that the student is behaving in some inappropriate way.
- Use subtle and not-so-subtle gestures to stop undesirable behaviours (e.g., pointing, head-shaking).
- Establish eye contact and maintain it for a while with a student who is behaving inappropriately. This results in no disruption to the instructional routine.
- Stop talking for a noticeable length of time to redirect student attention.

TEACHING TIP

When attempting to reduce an inappropriate behaviour by ignoring it, teachers must remember to positively reinforce behaviours that are desired.

TEACHING TIP

Being physically close to students who often display behaviour problems is a powerful method of reducing inappropriate behaviours.

Positioning yourself by a student who is disruptive is often a powerful management technique.

■ Call on students who are not attending, but ask them questions that they can answer successfully.
■ Use humour to redirect inappropriate behaviour.

The last option in this reduction hierarchy and the one that is most intrusive is the use of **punishment**. It is the least preferable option because it involves the presentation of something unpleasant or the removal of something pleasant as a consequence of the performance of an undesirable behaviour. However, situations arise in which punishment becomes necessary as a more immediate cessation of undesirable behaviours. Because of their potency, punishment strategies should be weighed carefully; they can interfere with the learning process if not used sparingly and appropriately.

Three punishment techniques are commonly used in classrooms. These include **reprimands**, **time out**, and **response cost**. For these forms of punishment to work, it is critical that they be applied immediately after the occurrence of the undesirable behaviour and that students understand why they are being applied. A useful overview of these techniques is provided in Table 5.4.

A reprimand represents a type of punishment in which an unpleasant condition (verbal reprimand from the teacher) is presented to the student. The following are some specific suggestions:

■ Do not let this type of interchange dominate your interactions with students.
■ Look at the student and talk in a composed way.
■ Do not verbally reprimand a student from across the room. Get close to the student and maintain a degree of privacy.
■ Let the student know exactly why you are concerned.
■ Convey to the student that it is the behaviour that is the problem and not the person.

Time out is a technique whereby a student is removed from a situation in which he or she typically receives positive reinforcement, thus being prevented from enjoying something pleasurable. There are different ways to remove a

TABLE 5.4			
Three Commonly Used Punishment Techniques			
Type	**Definition**	**Advantages**	**Disadvantages**
REPRIMAND	A verbal statement or nonverbal gesture that expresses disapproval	Easily applied with little or no preparation required No physical discomfort to students	Sometimes not effective Can serve as positive reinforcement if this is a major source of attention
RESPONSE COST	A formal system of penalties in which a reinforcer is removed contingent upon the occurrence of an inappropriate behaviour	Easily applied with quick results Does not disrupt class activities No physical discomfort to students	Not effective once student has "lost" all reinforcers Can initially result in some students being more disruptive
TIME OUT	Limited or complete loss of access to positive reinforcers for a set amount of time	Fast-acting and powerful No physical discomfort to students	Difficult to find secluded areas where students would not be reinforced inadvertently May require physical assistance to the time-out area Overuse can interfere with educational and prosocial efforts

Reprinted with permission of Macmillan College Publishing Company from *Student Teacher to Master Teacher*, by Michael S. Rosenberg, Lawrence O'Shea, and Dorothy J. O'Shea. Copyright © 1991 by Macmillan College Publishing Company, Inc.

student from a reinforcing setting: (1) students are allowed to observe the situation from which they have been removed (contingent observation); (2) students are excluded from the ongoing proceedings entirely (exclusion time out); and (3) students are secluded in a separate room (seclusion time out). The first two versions are most likely to be used in general education classrooms. The following suggestions are extremely important if time out is to succeed:

- Confirm that the ongoing situation from which a student is going to be removed is indeed reinforcing; if not, this technique will not serve as a punisher and may be a form of positive reinforcement.
- Ensure that the time-out area is devoid of reinforcing elements. If it is not a neutral setting, this procedure will fail.
- Do not keep students in time out for long periods of time (i.e., more than 10 minutes) or use it frequently (e.g., daily), as students will miss significant amounts of instructional time.
- As a rule of thumb with younger children, never allow time-out periods to extend beyond 1 minute for every year of the child's age (up to a maximum of 10 minutes).
- Use a timer to ensure accuracy in the length of time out.
- Incorporate this procedure as one of the classroom procedures explained and taught at the beginning of the school year.
- Consider using a time-out system in which students are given one warning before being removed.

TEACHING TIP

To ensure proper compliance, teachers must always be aware of the appropriate provincial/territorial or local guidelines when using time out for reducing student behaviour.

- Signal to the student when it is appropriate to return.
- As they return to the ongoing activities, ask students if they know why they were removed. If they do not know, explain the reasons to them at a time when instructional routine will not be interrupted. Older students can complete a form with this information on it.
- Do not use this technique with certain sensitive students.
- Keep records on frequency, reason for using, and amount of time spent in seclusion time out.

Response cost involves the loss of something the student values, such as privileges or points. It is a system in which a penalty or fine is levied for occurrences of inappropriate behaviour. The following are some specific suggestions:

- Explain clearly to students how the system works and how much one will be fined for a given offence.
- Tie this procedure in with positive reinforcement.
- Make sure all penalties are presented in a nonpersonal manner.
- Confirm that privileges that are lost are indeed reinforcing to students.
- Make sure that all privileges are not lost quickly, resulting in a situation in which a student may have little or no incentive to behave appropriately.

GENERALIZATION AND MAINTENANCE

After behaviours have been established at acceptable levels, the next stages involve transferring what has been learned to new contexts and maintaining established levels of performance. Teachers often succeed in teaching students certain behaviours but fail to help them apply the skills to new situations or to retain them over time. Teaching appropriate behaviours and then hoping that students will be able to use various skills at some later time is detrimental to many students with special needs.

Teachers need to program for generalization, the wider application of a behaviour skill, by giving students opportunities to use new skills in different settings, with different people, and at different times. Students often need help in identifying the cues that should trigger the performance of an acquired behaviour, action, or skill.

Students also need to practise what they have learned previously, to maintain their skills. Instructional planning should allow time for students to determine how well they have retained what they have learned. This review usually can be done during seatwork activities.

Suggestions for generalization and maintenance of skills include the following:

- Create opportunities for students to practise in different situations what they have learned.
- Work with other teachers to provide additional opportunities.
- Place students in situations that simulate those that they will encounter in the near and distant future, both within school and in other areas of life.
- Show students how these skills or behaviours will be useful to them in the future.
- Prompt students to use recently acquired skills in a variety of contexts.
- Maintain previously taught skills by providing ongoing practice or review.

FURTHER READING

For more information on generalization and transferring newly learned behaviours, read *Educational Psychology*, by R. P. McGowan, published in 1996 by Allyn & Bacon.

SELF-MANAGEMENT

Ultimately, we want students to be able to manage their own behaviours without any external assistance because this ability is a requirement of functioning independently in life. Special attention needs to be given to those who do not display independent behavioural control and thus must develop *student-regulated strategies*—interventions that, though initially taught by the teacher, are intended to be implemented independently by the student. The concept is an outgrowth of cognitive behaviour modification, a popular and exciting emphasis for educational interventions for students with disabilities since the 1980s, that stresses active thinking about behaviour.

CONSIDER THIS

Why is it so important to teach students to manage their own behaviours without external guidance from teachers? How can self-management assist students with disabilities in their inclusion in the community?

Fiore, Becker, and Nerro (1993) state the rationale for such interventions: "Cognitive-behavioral [intervention] is the most intuitively appealing because it combines behavioral techniques with cognitive strategies designed to directly address core problems of impulse control, higher order problem solving, and self-regulation" (p. 166). Whereas traditional behavioural interventions most often stress the importance of teacher-monitoring of student behaviour, extrinsic reinforcement, and teacher-directed learning, cognitive interventions instead focus on teaching students to monitor their own behaviour, to engage in self-reinforcement, and to direct their own learning in strategic fashion (Dowdy, Patton, Smith, & Polloway, 1997).

Such approaches have become particularly popular with students with learning and attentional difficulties because they offer the promise of

- increasing selective attention;
- modifying impulsive responding;
- providing verbal mediators to assist in academic and social problem-solving situations;
- teaching effective self-instructional statements to enable students to "talk through" tasks and problems;
- providing strategies that may lead to improvement in peer relations. (Rooney, 1993)

Student-regulated strategies form the essence of self-management. Although variations exist in how these are defined and described, the components listed in Figure 5.6 represent the most central aspects of self-management.

CONSIDER THIS

Do you engage in any self-monitoring techniques? If so, how do you use them, and how effective are they?

Two components with particular utility for general education teachers are self-monitoring and self-instruction. **Self-monitoring**, a technique in which students observe and record their own behaviour, has been commonly employed with students with learning problems. Lloyd, Landrum, and Hallahan (1991) note that self-monitoring was initially seen as an assessment technique, but as clients observed their own behaviour, the process also resulted in a change in behaviour. Self-monitoring of behaviour, such as attention, is a relatively simple technique that has been validated with children who have learning disabilities, intellectual disabilities, multiple disabilities, attention deficits, and behavioural disorders; it has also been profitable for nondisabled students (Lloyd et al., 1991; Prater, Joy, Chilman, Temple, & Miller, 1991). Increased attention, beneficial to academic achievement, has been reported as a result.

A common mechanism for self-monitoring has been developed by Hallahan, Lloyd, and Stoller (1982). It involves using a tape-recorded tone, which sounds at random intervals (e.g., every 45 seconds), and a self-recording sheet. Each time the tone sounds, children ask themselves whether they are paying attention and then to mark the *yes* or the *no* box on the sheet.

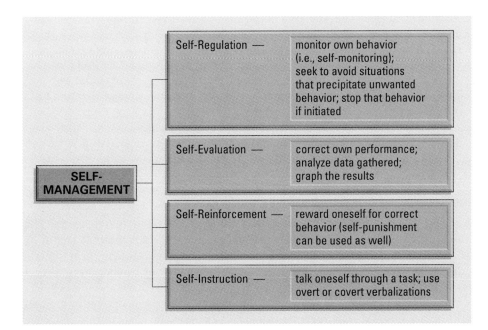

FIGURE 5.6
Components of
Self-Management
From *Attention-Deficit/Hyperactivity Disorder: A Practical Guide for Teachers,* by C. A. Dowdy, J. R. Patton, E. A. Polloway, and T. E. C. Smith, 1997, Austin, TX: Pro-Ed. Used by permission.

Self-instruction represents another useful intervention. Pfiffner and Barkley (1991) describe possible components of a self-instruction program as follows:

> Self-instructions include defining and understanding the task or problem, planning a general strategy to approach the problem, focusing attention on the task, selecting an answer or solution, and evaluating performance. In the case of successful performance, self-reinforcement (usually in the form of a positive self-statement, such as "I really did a good job") is provided. In the case of an unsuccessful performance, a coping statement is made (e.g., "Next time I'll do better if I slow down") and errors are corrected. At first, an adult trainer typically models the self-instructions while performing a task. The child then performs the same task while the trainer provides the self-instructions. Next, the child performs the task while self-instructing aloud. These overt verbalizations are then faded to covert self-instructions. (p. 525)

Clear, simple self-instruction strategies form an appropriate beginning for interventions with students with learning or attentional difficulties in the general education classroom. Such approaches are likely to enhance success. Pfiffner and Barkley (1991, p. 529) recommend the STAR program, in which "children learn to *Stop, Think* ahead about what they have to do, *Act* or do the requested task while talking to themselves about the task, and *Review* their results."

Detailed and systematic procedures have been developed for implementing self-management strategies. Some basic recommendations follow:

- Allocate sufficient instructional time to teach self-management to students who need it.
- Establish a sequence of activities that move by degrees from teacher direction to student direction and self-control.

CROSS-REFERENCE
Review Chapter 3 on learning disabilities to see how self-monitoring and self-instructional techniques are used with students with learning disabilities.

- Provide strategies and assistive materials (e.g., self-recording forms) for students to use.
- Model how effective self-managers operate. Point out actual applications of the elements of self-management (as highlighted in Figure 5.6), and give students opportunities to practise these techniques with your guidance.
- Provide for the maintenance of learned strategies and for generalization to other settings.

This section has outlined management strategies to use with a variety of students. Table 5.5 highlights strategies especially helpful to older students.

Instructional Management

All of the dimensions discussed in this chapter relate to instructional outcomes. However, certain aspects of instruction are closely related to sound organizational and management practices, such as scheduling, transitions, grouping, and lesson planning, and can have a significant impact on quality of instruction.

Scheduling involves the general temporal arrangement of events for both (1) the entire day (i.e., master schedule) and (2) a specific class period. This section focuses on the latter. The importance of a carefully planned schedule, especially for classrooms that include students with disabilities, cannot be overemphasized.

The thoughtful scheduling of a class period can contribute greatly to the amount of time that students can spend actively engaged in learning. It can also add to the quality of what is learned. For instance, a science lesson might include the following components:

- Transitional activities
- Attention-getting and motivating techniques
- Data-gathering techniques
- Data-processing techniques
- Closure activities
- Transitional activities

FURTHER READING

For more information on scheduling and instructional management, read E. A. Polloway and J. R. Patton's *Strategies for Teaching Learners with Special Needs,* sixth edition, published in 1997 by Merrill.

TABLE 5.5

Considerations for Working with Adolescents

- Anticipate the likely consequences of any intervention strategy being considered.
- Emphasize self-management strategies.
- Stress the application of natural and logical consequences.
- Use group-oriented contingencies to involve peers in a comprehensive plan for change.
- Select only age-appropriate reinforcers.
- Avoid response cost procedures that are likely to result in confrontations.
- Collaborate with other professionals and parents in designing effective programs.
- Select strategies that will not exacerbate problem situations.

Lesson planning helps teachers prepare for instruction and aids in managing classrooms.

All components support the instructional goal for the day. Reminders or cues from the teacher can augment such a system. The following are some specific suggestions:

■ Provide time reminders (visual and audible) for students during the class period so that they know how much time is available.
■ Plan for transitions (see next section).
■ Require students to complete one activity or task before moving on to the next.
■ Vary the nature of class activities to keep students engaged and to create a stimulating instructional tempo and pace.

Scheduling involves planning for class period *transitions*. Efficient transitions can minimize disruptions, maximize the amount of time allocated to instructional tasks, and maintain desired conditions of learning. Structured approaches to transitions will be particularly helpful to students with special needs. Several ways to ease transitions follow:

■ Model appropriate ways to make transitions between activities (Rosenberg et al., 1991).
■ Let students practise appropriate transition skills.
■ Use specific cues (e.g., light blinking, a buzzer, teacher signal) and associated activities to signal to students that it is time to change instructional routine. Several other examples of strategies for transitions are listed in Table 5.6.

Grouping refers to how students are organized for instructional purposes. The need to place students into smaller group arrangements depends on the nature of the curricular area or the goal of a specific lesson. For students with special needs, the main concern within a group setting is attention to individual needs. The use of innovative grouping arrangements and different cooperative

TABLE 5.6	
Potential Transition Problems and Suggested Solutions	
Transition Problem	**Suggested Solution**
Students talk loudly at the beginning of the day. The teacher is interrupted while checking attendance, and the start of content activities is delayed.	Establish a beginning-of-day routine, and clearly state your expectations for student behavior at the beginning of the day.
Students talk too much during transitions, especially after a seatwork assignment has been given but before they have begun working on it. Many students do not start their seatwork activity for several minutes.	Be sure students know what the assignment is; post it where they can easily see it. Work as a whole class on the first several seatwork exercises so that all students begin the lesson successfully and at the same time. Watch what students do during the transition, and urge them along when needed.
Students who go for supplemental instruction stop work early and leave the room noisily while rest of the class is working. When these students return to the room, they disturb others as they come in and take their seats. They interrupt others by asking for directions for assignments.	Have a designated signal that tells these students when they are to get ready to leave, such as a special time on the clock. Have them practice leaving and returning to the room quietly. Reward appropriate behavior. Leave special instructions for what they are to do, when they return, in a folder, on the chalkboard, or on a special sheet at their desks. Or for younger students, establish a special place and activity (e.g., the reading rug) for returning students to wait until you can give them personal attention.
During the last afternoon activity students quit working well before the end; they then begin playing around and leave the room in a mess.	Establish an end-of-day routine so that students continue their work until the teacher gives a signal to begin preparations to leave; then instruct students to help straighten up the room.
Whenever the teacher attempts to move the students from one activity into another, a number of students don't make the transition, but continue working on the preceding activity. This delays the start of the next activity or results in confusion.	Give students a few minutes' notice before an activity is scheduled to end. At the end of the activity students should put all the materials from it away and get out any needed materials for the next activity. Monitor the transition to make sure that all students complete it; do not start the next activity until students are ready.

From *Classroom Management for Elementary Teachers* (2nd ed.) (pp. 127–128), by C. M. Evertson, E. T. Emmer, B. J. Clements, J. P. Sanford, and M. E. Worsham, 1989, Englewood Cliffs, NJ: Prentice-Hall. Used by permission.

learning opportunities allow for variety in the instructional routine for students with special needs. Some specific suggestions follow:

CROSS-REFERENCE
See Chapter 12 for more information on using grouping strategies for students with disabilities.

- Give careful consideration to the makeup of groups.
- Make sure that group composition is not constant. Vary membership as a function of having different reasons for grouping students.
- Use different grouping arrangements that are based on interest or for research purposes (Wood, 1996).
- Use cooperative learning arrangements on a regular basis, as this approach, if structured properly, facilitates successful learning and socialization.
- Determine the size of groups based on ability levels: the lower the ability, the smaller the size of the group (Rosenberg et al., 1991).

Lesson plans help teachers prepare for instruction. Many teachers start out writing very detailed lesson plans and eventually move to less comprehensive formats. However, many teachers continue to use detailed plans throughout their teaching careers, as they find the detail helpful in providing effective instruction. Detailed planning is a requirement for lessons that must be modified for gifted students or students with disabilities. Typical components include objectives, anticipatory set, materials, guided practice, independent practice, closure, options for early finishers, specific accommodations, and evaluation. Suggestions in developing lesson plans follow:

- Create interest in and clarify the purpose of lessons. Doing this is particularly important for students with special needs.
- Consider providing direct instruction on some topics to help students acquire an initial grasp of new material.
- Assign independent practice, some of which can be accomplished in class and some of which should be done as homework.
- Plan activities for students who finish early. This might be particularly useful for gifted students.
- Anticipate problems that might arise during the course of the lesson, and identify techniques for dealing with them.

Organizational Management

The increased diversity in today's general education classrooms has created numerous new challenges for the teacher. Some have likened the current classroom to a "one-room schoolhouse," in which the classroom teacher must respond to the unique needs of many students. This section acknowledges how time management in the areas of personnel interactions, the work environment, administrative duties, instructional applications, and personal applications can promote success.

In the current general education classroom, teachers will perhaps regularly interact with special education teachers, other classroom teachers, professional support staff (e.g., speech-language pathologists, psychologists), para-educators, teacher trainees, volunteers, and peer tutors. To enhance *personal interactions,* teachers should consider these recommendations:

- Establish good initial working relationships with support personnel.
- Clarify the supports professional personnel are providing to students in your class. See the nearby Inclusion Strategies feature for more ideas.
- Clarify the roles of these persons and the classroom teachers as collaborators for instructional and behavioural interventions.
- Establish the roles and responsibilities of aides, volunteers, and trainees.
- Determine the level of expertise of para-educators and discuss with them specific activities that they can perform and supports they can provide to students.
- Delegate noninstructional (and, as appropriate, instructional) duties to classroom aides when these assistants are available.
- In cases in which a para-educator accompanies a child with a disability in the general education classroom, develop a comprehensive plan with the special education teacher for involving this person appropriately.

The *work environment* refers to the immediate work area used by teachers—usually the desk and files. Teachers must consider how to utilize work areas and how to organize them. For instance, a teacher's desk may be designated as

CONSIDER THIS
How has the inclusion of students with disabilities and other special needs affected classroom management? Is teaching more difficult or about the same as a result of inclusion?

INCLUSION STRATEGIES

Collaboration: Ways to Involve Other Personnel in Management

1. The school principal or administrator can
   - Supply any necessary equipment or materials
   - Provide flexibility in staffing patterns
   - Show support for the teacher's actions
2. The school guidance counsellor can
   - Provide individual counselling sessions
   - Work with other students who may be reinforcing the inappropriate behaviour of the disruptive student
   - Offer the teacher information about what may be upsetting to the student
3. The school nurse can
   - Review the student's medical history for possible causes
   - Recommend the possibility and practicality of medical or dietary intervention
   - Explain the effects and side effects of any medication the student is taking or may take in the future
4. The school psychologist can
   - Review the teacher's behaviour management plan and make recommendations for changes
   - Observe the student in the classroom and in other settings to collect behavioural data and note possible environmental instigators
   - Provide any useful data on the student that may have been recently collected, e.g., test scores, behavioural observations, etc.
5. The social worker can
   - Provide additional information about the home environment
   - Schedule regular visits to the home
   - Identify other public agencies that may be of assistance
6. Other teachers can
   - Provide curricular and behaviour management suggestions that work for them
   - Offer material resources
   - Provide carryover and consistency for the tactics used

Adapted from *The Special Educator's Handbook* (p. 119), by D. L. Westling and M. A. Koorland, 1989, Boston: Allyn & Bacon. Used by permission.

---

off-limits to all students or may be used for storage only or as a work area. Suggestions for establishing a work environment are listed here:

- Keep the teacher's desk organized and free of stacks of papers.
- Organize files so that documents and information can be retrieved easily and quickly. Use colour-coded systems if possible.
- Handle most paperwork only once.

Along with instructional duties, teaching includes numerous *administrative duties*. Two of the most time-demanding activities are participating in meetings and handling paperwork, including various forms of correspondence. The presence of students with special needs will increase such demands. The following are some strategies for handling paperwork:

- Prepare form letters for all necessary events (e.g., permissions, notifications, status reports, memo formats, reimbursement requests).
- Prepare master copies of various forms that are used regularly (e.g., certificates and awards, record sheets, phone conversation sheets).
- Keep notes of all school-related phone conversations with parents, teachers, support staff, administrators, or any other person.

■ Make the most of meetings—request an agenda and ask that meetings be scheduled at times that are convenient.

Some additional *instructional applications* of time-management techniques are provided here, focusing on materials and technology that can make the job of teaching easier. The most attractive piece of equipment available to teachers is the microcomputer. With the appropriate software, teachers can greatly reduce the amount of time spent on test generation, graphic organizers, IEP development, and so on. The following are some specific suggestions:

TEACHING TIP
Teachers must develop their own time management strategies; adopting strategies that are effective for other teachers may or may not be effective for you.

■ Use self-correcting materials with students to reduce the amount of time required to correct student work.
■ Use software programs for recording student scores and determining grades.
■ Use computers to generate a variety of instructionally related materials (tests, graphic organizers, puzzles).
■ Give students computer-generated calendars that include important dates.

Since it is impossible to completely divorce the management of one's personal time from management of professional time, it is worthwhile considering various time management tactics that have a more *personal application* but can affect one's efficiency and effectiveness in the classroom as well. Some basic recommendations are provided here:

■ Use a daily to-do list.
■ Break down major tasks into smaller pieces and work on them.
■ Avoid getting overcommitted.
■ Work during work time. This might mean avoiding situations at school in which long social conversations will cut into on-task time.
■ Avoid dealing with trivial activities if important ones must be addressed.
■ Use idle time (e.g., waiting in lines) well. Always be prepared for these situations by having reading material or other portable work available.

The efficient management of one's professional and personal time can pay off in making day-to-day demands less overwhelming. Thus, the efforts to become a better time manager are certainly worthwhile.

Multicultural Considerations

Educators must always remember the multicultural issues related to classroom management. Different cultural groups expect different behaviours from their children. Methods used for disciplining children vary significantly from group to group. Expectations of the school, regarding discipline and management principles, also vary from culture to culture. The nearby Diversity Forum feature discusses discipline and behaviours in families with Asian roots.

As schools become increasingly more diverse, teachers and other school personnel must take the time to learn about the different cultures represented in the school district. Having a better understanding of parents' expectations of the school as well as of their children can facilitate communication between parents and school personnel and lead to more effective behaviour management programs.

FURTHER READING
For additional information on managing students from diverse cultural groups, read *Developing Cross-Cultural Competence*, edited by E. W. Lynch & M. J. Hanson and published by Brookes in 1992.

Uses of Videotaping in Classrooms Serving Youth with Behavioural Disorders

1. To provide a permanent antecedent-behavior-consequence (ABC) analysis.

2. To self-monitor one's behavioral strengths and weaknesses.

3. To evaluate peer behavioral strengths and weaknesses.

4. To provide reality replay on facial expressions, body language, expressions of feelings, tone of voice, and other hard-to-define performance criteria.

5. To provide motivation and enthusiasm for group sessions.

6. To add vitality to simulations and role-playing.

7. To reinforce shared experience.

8. To "catch" unobserved misbehavior or adaptive behaviors.

9. To provide a less intrusive consequence for misbehavior.

10. To give parents and other agencies a realistic perspective on child misbehavior and classroom interventions.

11. To build cooperation and trust.

12. To plan for inclusion.

From "The Many Uses of Videotape in Classrooms Serving Youth with Behavioral Disorders," by S. A. Broome and R. B. White, 1995, *Teaching Exceptional Children, 27*, pp. 10–13.

When Techniques Are Ineffective

Regardless of efforts, at times preventive methods will be simply ineffective. Teachers have to act quickly to defuse situations in which students are out of control, engage in open defiance, refuse to do what they are told, and get into fights; teachers must be prepared to react appropriately to these situations. Westling and Koorland (1989) provide the following suggestions for teachers when dealing with students who are fighting:

- In a firm, strong voice, order (don't ask) the students to stop at once.
- If they don't respond, try again and send for or call another adult.
- If they stop, send them in separate directions, i.e., one to one corner of a room, the other to another corner. In some cases one can be sent to one classroom and the second to another, provided that the procedure is approved by the other personnel involved.
- Direct the students to start working on a task. What they work on is not as important as being engaged in something other than fighting.
- After things have settled down, talk to the students individually and apply the appropriate school rules.
- You may want to have the students involved write an essay about how each could have avoided the fight and what to do about similar situations in the future. (p. 147)

Behaviours and Punishments in Asian North American Families

Observance of specific roles, relationships, and codes of conduct results in a persistent awareness of the effects of one's behavior on others. In contrast to the more egocentric individualistic orientation, Asian children are socialized to think and act in proper relation to others and must learn to transcend their personal concerns. They are obliged to be sensitive to the social environment. The parent thus effectively controls the child by modeling appropriate behaviors by appealing to the child's sense of duty or obligation. Parents may thus periodically evoke fear of personal ridicule or the prospect of family shame as a consequence of misbehaviour.

Behaviors that are punished include disobedience, aggression (particularly sibling directed), and failure to fulfill one's primary responsibilities. Typical forms of discipline include the use of verbal reprimands such as scolding and shaming, which result in disgrace. The child is reminded that his or her negative behaviors reflect poorly on the entire family and family name. The child can absolve him- or herself of this "loss of face" by actively displaying changes in behavior. It is not sufficient for children to ask for forgiveness and verbally promise to do better. Actions speak louder than words. Parents may respond to more serious transgressions by either threatening or actually engaging in temporary removal of the child from the family household and/or isolating the child from the family social life. On occasion, the use of physical punishment (e.g., spanking or paddling with a stick on the buttocks) is considered acceptable. While assuming primary responsibility for teaching the child to behave properly, the mother serves as the main disciplinarian for daily problems. The father assumes the role of implementing harsher punishment for more serious misbehavior. . . .

In general, Asian parents who adhere to more traditional childrearing values and practices are relatively controlling, restrictive, and protective of their children. Children are taught to suppress aggressive behavior, overt expressions of negative emotions, and personal grievances; they must inhibit strong feelings and exercise self-control in order to maintain family harmony. There is a typical avoidance of frank discussion or highly verbal communication between parent and child—particularly in the area of sexuality, which is suppressed in cultures where physical contact between members of the opposite sex is minimized and public displays of affection are rare and embarrassing. The communication pattern is also one way: parent to child (the parent speaks, and the child listens).

From "Families with Asian Roots," by S. Chang. In *Developing Cross-Cultural Competence,* edited by E. W. Lynch and M. J. Hanson, 1992, p. 219. Baltimore, MD: Brookes. Used by permission.

ENHANCING INCLUSIVE CLASSROOMS FOR STUDENTS WITH EMOTIONAL AND BEHAVIOURAL DISORDERS

Classroom teachers usually make the initial referral for students with emotional and behavioural problems (Polloway & Smith, 1992). Unless the problem exhibited by the student is severe, it has usually gone unnoticed until the school years. In addition to referring students, classroom teachers must be directly involved in implementing the student's individualized education program (IEP) because the majority of students in this category receive at least a portion of their educational program in general education classrooms. General education classroom teachers must deal with behaviour problems much of the

Videotaping can be used as an effective management tool by teachers.

CONSIDER THIS

Can general classroom teachers effectively deal with students with emotional and behavioural disorders in their classrooms? What factors will enhance the likelihood of success?

time since in addition to E/BD students there are a large number of students who from time to time display inappropriate behaviours, although they have not been identified as having emotional and behavioural problems.

Kauffman and Wong (1991) point out that "effective teaching of behaviorally disordered students may require skills, attitudes, and beliefs different from those of teachers who work effectively with more ordinary students" (p. 226). However, no single characteristic will guarantee success for teachers dealing with students who are experiencing emotional and behavioural problems.

SUPPORTS FOR GENERAL EDUCATION TEACHERS

Since most students with emotional and behavioural disorders are educated in general classrooms, classroom teachers are the key to the success of these students. Too often, if these students do not achieve success, the entire classroom will be disrupted and all students will suffer. Therefore, appropriate supports must be available to teachers. They include special education personnel, psychologists and counsellors, and mental health service providers.

The level of collaboration among professionals who provide services to this group of students is critical. Mental health professionals should be involved with services to these students, and in some cases, personnel from the juvenile justice system, child welfare system, and social work agencies should also collaborate. Without a close working relationship among the many groups who serve children and adolescents with E/BD, services will be fragmented and disorganized.

Special educators should consult with teachers regarding behaviour management as well as instructional support. These teachers may provide this support in the classroom or confer with teachers in a different setting. A particularly helpful way to assist classroom teachers involves modelling methods of dealing with behaviour problems. Dr. Ingrid Sladeczek of McGill University continues to study various methods of school psychologist and parent/teacher conjoint consultation to manage behavioural disorders in the regular classroom. She is the first in Canada to study empirically the effectiveness of conjoint behavioural consultation (Sladeczek, Heath, 1997; Wayland & Sladeczek, 1999).

At times, it is best for students with emotional and behavioural problems to leave the general education setting and receive instruction from special educators. School psychologists and counsellors can provide intensive counselling to students with emotional and behavioural disorders; they may also consult with teachers on how to implement specific programs, such as a student's individual behaviour management plan.

Finally, mental health personnel can provide helpful supports for teachers. Too often, mental health services are not available in schools; however, some schools are beginning to develop school-based mental health programs that serve students with emotional and behavioural disorders. These programs, jointly staffed by school personnel and mental health staff, provide supports for teachers as well as direct interventions for students. If mental health services are not available in a particular school, teachers should work with school administrators to involve mental health specialists with students who display emotional and behavioural problems.

Presently, in Montreal, an innovative program that works to include students with moderate to severe E/BD in the regular classroom is under way. At the heart of the program is a partnership between hospital personnel, school personnel, and community agencies. The Family School Support and Treatment Team aims to bring the needed expertise and support into the classroom, rather than removing the student. Although still under examination this model has been very efficient in increasing teachers' willingness to have students with E/BD in their classes (Grinberg, Heath, & McLean-Heywood, 1998; Heath & McLean-Heywood, 1999).

SUMMARY

- Most children and youth are disruptive from time to time, but most do not require interventions. Some students' emotional or behavioural problems are severe enough to warrant interventions.

- Many problems complicate serving students with emotional and behavioural disorders, including inconsistent definitions of the disorder, numerous agencies involved in defining and treating it, and limited ways to objectively measure the extent and precise parameters of the problem.

- Despite general agreement about key elements in the educational definition of E/BD, there is great variability across provinces and territories in both definitions and prevalence estimates.

- Emotional problems can be caused by biological or environmental factors.

- The majority of students with E/BD are served in general education classrooms.

- Classroom management strategies benefit all students with exceptionalities but are essential for students with E/BD.

- Key elements of the classroom environment that have a significant effect on instruction and learning are multidimensionality, simultaneity, immediacy, unpredictability, publicness, and history.

- Key principles of successful classroom management are careful planning, proactive strategies, consistency, awareness, and overlap.

- A significant aspect of successful management is a teacher's attitude toward students with special needs.

- Classroom rules provide a general sense of what is expected of students. The rules chosen should be essential for classroom functioning and for the development of a positive learning environment.

- Classroom procedures should include the specific ways in which certain activities or situations will be performed.

- Effective physical management includes classroom arrangement, accessibility, seating, and the use of specialized equipment.

- Desirable behaviours are increased through the use of positive reinforcement.

- Undesirable behaviours can be reduced through a variety of reduction strategies. A hierarchy of options would include (from least to most restrictive) natural and logical consequences, differential reinforcement, extinction, benign tactics, reprimands, response costs, and time out.

- Successful educational programs help students develop self-management.

- Instructional management includes careful attention to scheduling, transitions, grouping, and lesson plans.

- Successful teachers are organized and engage in the careful management of time.

- Teachers need to take the student's culture into consideration when dealing with management issues.

RESOURCES

Handbooks/Documents

British Columbia Ministry of Education, Special Education Branch. (1996). *Teaching Students with Learning and Behavioural Differences: A Resource Guide for Teachers*. Victoria: Author.

This resource guide provides an array of strategies for classroom management as well as suggested resources related to behavioural and learning difficulties.

DeBruyn, R., & Larson, J. (1984). *You Can Handle Them All*. Manahattan, KS: The Master Teacher Inc.

This practical manual for managing even the most difficult student comes recommended by the B.C. Ministry of Education, Special Education Branch.

Dreikurs, R., Grunwald, B, & Pepper, F. (1982). *Maintaining Sanity in the Classroom: Classroom Management Techniques*. New York: Harper and Row.

Dreikurs's positive approach to discipline is both helpful to teachers and beneficial to students' self-worth. It goes beyond simple behaviour modification.

Rockwell, Sylvia (1995). *Back Off, Cool Down, Try Again: Teaching Students How to Control Aggressive Behavior*. Reston, VA: Council for Exceptional Children.

Rockwell, Sylvia. (1993). Tough to Reach, *Tough to Teach: Students with Behavior Problems*. Reston, VA: Council for Exceptional Children.

Sylvia Rockwell's two guides that provide a practical approach to dealing with students with behaviour problems are very successful with teachers and have been recommended by the Council for Exceptional Children.

Videos

Webster-Stratton, C. (1998). The Teacher Video Tape Series. Eugene, OR: Castalia.

Webster-Stratton, C. (1987). The Parent and Children Video Tape Series. Eugene, OR: Castalia.

These videotape series, which come with a handbook, provide suggestions for managing a variety of behaviour problems of children ages 3 to 10 and show actual demonstrations. The use of these videotapes to improve parent and teacher ability to better manage behaviour is being studied by Dr. Webster-Stratton and by McGill University's Dr. Sladeczek.

Laser Disk

ACCESS, The Education Station.(1992). Improving Classroom Behavior: A Preventive Approach. Edmonton, AB: ACCESS, The Education Station, Media Resource Centre.

This laser disk, which comes with a workbook, helps teachers develop strategies to prevent behaviour problems from occurring or escalating for children in elementary and early childhood programs.

Associations

Council for Children with Behavior Disorders (CCBD)
As a division of the Council for Exceptional Children, CCBD is an international professional organization committed to promoting and facilitating the education and general welfare of children and youth with behavioural and emotional disorders. CCBD, whose members include educators, parents, and a variety of professionals, actively pursues quality educational services and program alternatives for persons with behavioural disorders; advocates for the needs of such children and youth; emphasizes research and professional growth as vehicles for better understanding behavioural disorders; and provides professional support for persons who are involved with and serve children and youth with behavioural disorders. CCBD currently includes 37 active subdivisions throughout the United States and Canada. For information about the Canadian CCBD, contact the Canadian member-at-large, Joyce Mounsteven, at 60 Cliffwood Road, Willowdale, ON M2H 3J7 (Phone: (416) 397-3591; E-mail: joyce.mounsteven@tdsb.on.ca)

WEBLINKS

Council for Children with Behavior Disorders (CCBD)
www.ccbd.net/index.htm
The Council for Children with Behavior Disorders (CCBD) is a division of the Council for Exceptional Children. This site has a number of recent relevant publications, suggested resources, and a list of upcoming relevant events/conferences. (See Associations for more information.)

B.C. Ministry of Education
www.bced.gov.bc.ca/specialed/landbdif/toc.htm
The ministry's resource guide on learning and behavioural difficulties appears online. In addition to

providing specific classroom strategies, this Web site also lists related resources.

National Depressive and Manic-Depressive Association
www.ndmda.org/
The Association's Web site provides information about adolescent depression, including a screening list of symptoms specifically for adolescents, a list of symptoms for the use of others in the student's life, and a suicide prevention plan.

CHAPTER SIX

CHAPTER OBJECTIVES

- To describe the concept of intellectual disability

- To summarize key definitional and classification considerations

- To identify the instructional implications of common characteristics of students with mild intellectual disabilities

- To highlight the transitional needs of students with mild intellectual disabilities

- To apply considerations of the needs of students with intellectual disabilities to curriculum design

- To present ways of enhancing the inclusion of students with intellectual disabilities

Teaching Students with Intellectual Disabilities

Clare, a Grade 2 teacher, tells about a student in her class. "Shari is a student with an intellectual disability who is integrated into my Grade 2 class. She is filled with energy, is healthy and cheerful, but can be a real handful! Shari's speech is really delayed: she speaks in one to six word statements, for example, "Want lunch now." Her academic skills are not great. She knows eight letters of the alphabet, but she cannot print her name. She can copy shapes at her table, but cannot copy from the blackboard. And she can count to six, but not reliably. Shari's fine motor skills are poor, giving her difficulty with printing, colouring, and scissors work. Also because of her fine motor difficulties, it takes her a long time to get herself into her outdoor clothes which leads to delays for the whole class.

"Maybe the biggest difficulty I am having with Shari is her short attention span. She often wants things right away and will sometimes use physical force or aggression to get it. This leads to lots of fights and disruptions in class and at play. The rest of the class is frustrated with Shari, and many complain that they do not want to work or play with her. I have an integration aide for half of every day and lunch, and she will work with Shari for that time, but I am wondering, how will I meet Shari's needs when I don't have the aide and how will I still have time for the rest of my students?"

1. How do you think Clare feels about having Shari in her class? Based on what you have read so far, do you feel that Shari is included? Why or why not?

2. If you were going to work with this teacher to help her include Shari, what might you suggest?

3. What goals would you set for Shari in the individualized education program?

INTRODUCTION

The Canadian Association for Community Living (CACL) is an association that works to promote the full participation of people with intellectual disabilities in all aspects of community life. The membership includes both individuals with intellectual disabilities and advocates for them.

The CACL defines an intellectual disability as an impaired ability to learn which sometimes causes difficulty in coping with the demands of daily life, noting that the disability is usually present from birth and differs from mental or psychiatric illness. An intellectual disability is sometimes referred to as "mental retardation," although the CACL (1999) states, "We have been informed by people who have an intellectual disability that they resent being labeled by this term . . . preferred terms are: people who have an intellectual disability, people who have a mental handicap, and people who have a developmental disability."

However, the largest North American organization in the field continues to use the term *mental retardation*. The American Association of Mental Retardation (AAMR) is an international multidisciplinary association of professionals responsible for defining mental retardation. In the schools even more variation is seen in terminology and may occasionally lead to confusion about the "correct" descriptor.

For the purposes of our discussion we will respect the CACL position and use the term "intellectual disability," although in the formal definition specified by the AAMR, the less preferred term mental retardation is used. As teachers bear in mind that the actual terminology is less important than respecting the preferences of students and parents regarding terminology.

In the field of intellectual disabilities, the past decade or so has seen momentous changes. Shifts in public attitudes toward persons with intellectual disabilities and the resulting development and provision of services and supports for them have been truly phenomenal. Consequently, the first decade of the new millennium is an exciting time to be participating in the changing perspectives on intellectual disabilities (Polloway, Smith, Patton, & Smith, 1996).

BASIC CONCEPTS

The concept of intellectual disability is a broad one. It includes a wide range of functioning levels, from mild disabilities to more severe limitations. The discussion in this chapter initially will address the global concept of intellectual disability. Then the remainder of the chapter will focus on the educational implications of mild intellectual disabilities.

Definitions

It has been difficult for professionals to formulate definitions of intellectual disabilities that could then be used to govern practices such as assessment and placement. Intellectual disability has been most often characterized by two dimensions: limited intellectual ability and difficulty in coping with the social demands of the environment. Thus, all individuals with intellectual disabilities must, by definition, demonstrate some degree of impaired mental abilities, most often reflected in an intelligence quotient (IQ) significantly below average, which necessarily relates to a **mental age (MA)** appreciably lower than the individual's chronological age (CA). In addition, these individuals would necessarily demonstrate less mature adaptive skills, such as social behaviour or functional academic skills, when compared to their same-age peers. For individuals with mild disabilities, this discrepancy can be relatively subtle and may not be readily apparent in a casual interaction outside of school. These individuals may be challenged most dramatically by the school setting, and thus between the ages of 6 and 21 their inability to cope may be most evident—for example, in problems with peer relationships, difficulty in compliance with adult-initiated directions, or academic challenges. Although discussed as a comprehensive disability, intellectual disability has been typically defined, and diagnosed, as reflecting limitations in two dimensions: intellectual functioning and adaptive skills.

In 1992, the American Association on Mental Retardation revised its definition in order to bring it into line with recent developments and thus reflect changes in current thinking about persons with intellectual disabilities. According to Luckasson et al., and as shown in Table 6.1 (1992),

> Mental retardation refers to substantial limitations in present functioning. It is manifested by significantly subaverage intellectual functioning, existing concurrently with related limitations in two or more of the following applicable adaptive skill areas: communication, self-care, home living, social skills, community use, self-direction, health and safety, functional academics, leisure, and work. Mental retardation begins before age 18.

Luckasson et al. (1992) provide a further context for the definition. The appropriate application of the definition requires consideration of four key assumptions. These are detailed in Figure 6.1. Note that these elements are deemed essential to the use of the 1992 AAMR definition.

The 1992 definition retains the focus of earlier AAMR definitions on the two key dimensions of intelligence and adaptation as well as the modifier of

CONSIDER THIS

What are some dangers of relating the concept of intellectual disability to a numerical index, such as IQ?

TABLE 6.1

Key Adaptive Skill Areas

Communication	Community use	Functional academics
Self-care	Self-direction	Leisure
Home living	Health and safety	Work
Social skills		

From *Mental Retardation: Definition, Classification, and Systems of Supports* (p. 1), by R. Luckasson, E. L. Coulter, E. A. Polloway, S. Reiss, R. L. Schalock, M. E. Snell, D. M. Spitalnik, and J. A. Stark, 1992, Washington, DC: American Association on Mental Retardation. Used by permission.

FIGURE 6.1

Four Assumptions Essential to the Application of the AAMR Definition of Mental Retardation

From *Mental Retardation: Definition, Classification, and Systems of Supports* (p. 1), by R. Luckasson, D. L. Coulter, E. A. Polloway, S. Reiss, R. L. Schalock, M. E. Snell, D. M. Spitalnik, and J. A. Stark, 1992, Washington, DC: American Association on Mental Retardation. Used by permission.

The following four assumptions are *essential* to the application of the definition.

1. Valid assessment considers cultural and linguistic diversity, as well as differences in communication and behavioral factors.
2. The existence of limitations in adaptive skills occurs within the context of community environments typical of the individual's age peers and is indexed to the person's individualized needs for supports.
3. Specific adaptive limitations often coexist with strengths in other adaptive skills or other personal capabilities.
4. With appropriate supports over a sustained period, the life-functioning of the person with mental retardation will generally improve.

FURTHER READING

For more information on the 1992 AAMR definition, read the article by Polloway et al., published in 1997 in volume 32 of *Education and Training in Mental Retardation and Developmental Disabilities.*

age of onset. However, the conceptual basis varies from those earlier efforts. The 1992 definition reflects a more *functional approach,* thus shifting focus to the individual's functioning within the community rather than giving weight mainly to the psychometric and clinical aspects of the person (e.g., IQ scores, limited adaptive behaviour evaluations). In Canada, the 1992 AAMR definition is used as the basis for most provincial criteria for intellectual disability (Weber, 1994).

Classification

Historically, classification in this field has been done by both etiology (i.e., causes) and level of severity. Whereas the former has limited application to nonmedical practice, the latter has been used by a range of disciplines, including education and psychology. The classification system cited most often in the professional literature is one reported by Grossman (1983). This system uses the terms **mild**, **moderate**, **severe**, and **profound mental retardation**, which are summative judgments based on both intelligence and adaptive behaviour assessment. Often, however, the emphasis has been on the former only, so IQ scores have unfortunately been equated with level of functioning.

Terms such as **educable** and **trainable** reflect an alternative system that has been used in some school environments. These terms remain in use today in many places; it is not uncommon to hear students referred to as EMR (educable mentally retarded) and TMR (trainable mentally retarded). However, they are inherently stereotypical and prejudicial; consequently (and appropriately) they have often been criticized, thus leading to decreased use.

One alternative has been to classify intellectual disabilities according to only two levels of functioning (i.e., mild and severe) and to avoid reliance on IQ scores in considerations of level of severity. Consideration of level of adaptive skills would thus be used as a yardstick for determining level of intellectual disability, resulting in a more meaningful, broad-based system of classification.

Finally, an emerging alternative is the classification system of Luckasson et al. (1992), which has particular merit for use in inclusive settings. According to this system, classification is not derived from levels of disability, but rather from needed **levels of support**. Thus, this system would classify the *needs,* rather than the *deficits,* of the individual. Individuals would be designated as needing limited, extensive, or pervasive levels of support as related

TABLE 6.2

Levels of Supports × Intensity Grid

	Intermittent	Limited	Extensive	Pervasive
TIME: Duration	As needed	Time limited, occasionally ongoing	Usually ongoing	Possibly lifelong
TIME: Frequency	Infrequent, low occurrence	Regular, anticipated, could be high frequency		High rate, continuous, constant
SETTINGS: Living, Work, Recreation, Leisure, Health, Community, etc.	Few settings, typically one or two settings	Across several settings, typically not all settings		All or nearly all settings
RESOURCES: Professional/ Technological Assistance	Occasional consultation or discussion, ordinary appointment schedule, occasional monitoring	Occasional contact or time limited but frequent regular contact	Regular, ongoing contact or monitoring by professionals typically at least weekly	Constant contact and monitoring by professionals
INTRUSIVENESS	Predominantly all natural supports, high degree of choice and autonomy	Mixture of natural and service-based supports, lesser degree of choice and autonomy		Predominantly service-based supports, controlled by others

From "The 1992 AAMR Definition and Preschool Children: Response from the Committee on Terminology and Classification," by R. Luckasson, R. Schalock, M. Snell, and D. Spitalnik, 1996, *Mental Retardation, 34*, p. 250.

to each of the adaptive skills areas (see Table 6.1). Of course, in a given area, an individual may also not need any support to function successfully. These levels of support are defined as follows:

Intermittent: Supports on an "as needed" basis, episodic in nature. Short-term supports may be needed during lifespan transitions (e.g., job loss or an acute medical crisis).

Limited: Supports are consistent over time, are time-limited but not intermittent, and may require fewer staff and less cost than more intense levels of support (e.g., employment training or transitional supports during the school-to-adult period).

Extensive: Supports characterized by regular involvement (e.g., daily) in at least some environments (e.g., long-term support and long-term home living support).

Pervasive: Supports characterized by their constancy and high intensity; provided across environments, potentially life-sustaining in nature. Pervasive supports typically involve more staff and intrusiveness than extensive or limited supports. (Adapted from Luckasson et al., 1992, p. 26)

CONSIDER THIS
What are some advantages to using a classification system based on levels of support rather than levels of severity?

Terms such as educable *and* trainable *have often been used to categorize students with intellectual disabilities, but are no longer acceptable.*

The supports classification system of the AAMR manual (Luckasson et al., 1992) has been further explicated in another publication by Luckasson, Schalock, Snell, and Spitalnik (1996). Table 6.2 presents a grid showing different levels of intensity of supports to illustrate the way that this classification system can be put into practice.

Prevalence and Causes

CROSS-REFERENCE

Review the causes of other disabilities (see Chapters 3–9) to determine the overlap of etiological factors.

There are hundreds of known causes of intellectual disabilities, and at the same time, numerous cases exist for which the cause is unknown. Table 6.3 outlines some causes to show the complexity of this area of concern. When all of these different causes of intellectual disability are considered, it is estimated that about 899 000 Canadians, or 3 percent of the population, have an intellectual disability (CACL, 2000).

Characteristics

Since the mid-1970s, substantial changes have occurred in terms of the nature and number of students identified and served as having an intellectual disability. Traditional assumptions, particularly about the characteristics of individuals with mild intellectual disabilities (MacMillan & Borthwick, 1980; Polloway & Smith, 1988), have been significantly altered. Definitional changes and sociopolitical factors (e.g., concerns over minority overrepresentation) have

TABLE 6.3

Selected Causes of Intellectual Disabilities

Cause	Nature of Problem	Considerations
DOWN'S SYNDROME	Trisomy 21 (three chromosomes on this pair)	IQ range from severe intellectual disability to no intellectual disability Wide variance in learning characteristics Classic physical signs
ENVIRONMENTAL DISADVANTAGE	Elements of poverty environment	Can result in mild intellectual disability Commonly associated with school failure
FETAL ALCOHOL SYNDROME	Caused by drinking during pregnancy Toxic effects of alcohol	Associated with varying degrees of disability Often accompanied by facial and other malformations
FRAGILE X SYNDROME	Related to a "fragile site" on the X chromosome Typically transmitted from mother to son	Associated with intellectual disabilities in males and learning disabilities in females (in some instances) May be accompanied by variant patterns of behaviour, social skills, language
HYDROCEPHALUS	Multiple causes Disruption in appropriate flow of cerebrospinal fluid on the brain	Previously associated with enlarged head and brain damage Controlled by a shunt
PHENYLKETONURIA	Autosomal recessive genetic disorder	Associated with metabolic problems in processing proteins Can be controlled via restrictive diets
PRADER-WILLI SYNDROME	Chromosomal error of the autosomal type	Associated with biological compulsion to overeat Obesity as a common secondary trait to intellectual disability
TAY-SACHS DISEASE	Autosomal recessive genetic disorder	Highest risk for Ashkenazic Jewish persons Associated with severe disabilities and early death No known cure

brought about an overall enrollment decline in programs for individuals with intellectual disabilities.

In the United States, data provided by the federal government show the magnitude of the numerical decreases in students served in programs for students with intellectual disabilities. For example, between the school years 1976–1977 and 1993–1994, virtually all states and territories showed a decline in the number of children served in such school programs; the overall national decrease exceeded 37 percent (U.S. Department of Education, 1996). This numerical "cure" (Reschly, 1988) reflects both the declassification of many students previously described as most "adaptive" in programs for students with

CONSIDER THIS

Why do you think the prevalence of students identified as having an intellectual disability has declined so much over the past 20 years?

mild intellectual disabilities and the restrictiveness in eligibility procedures for subsequently referred children who might have been considered borderline cases (MacMillan, 1989; Mascari & Forgnone, 1982; Polloway, 1984). Thus, programs showing significant reductions have likely been refocused to serve a population that MacMillan and Borthwick (1980) describe as "a more patently disabled group" (p. 155) that is more likely to include individuals with multiple disabilities (Forness & Polloway, 1987). Students with milder intellectual disabilities have been increasingly served in general education classrooms. Although there are no recorded similar Canadian statistics, the observed trend in the schools is the same in Canada.

Intellectual disabilities are associated with a number of challenges to learning. Table 6.4 identifies the most significant learning domains, lists representative problem areas, and notes certain instructional implications. In addition, the table focuses on related concerns for cognitive, language, and sociobehavioural development.

Identification, Assessment, and Eligibility

Procedures for the identification of intellectual disability proceed directly from the specific AAMR scheme that is followed. For the 1992 manual, the diagnostic process, and hence the eligibility for services, is based on the model presented in Table 6.5.

TRANSITION CONSIDERATIONS

TEACHING TIP
Students with intellectual disabilities should be taught functional skills that will prepare them for success as adults.

Occupational success and community living skills are among the critical life adjustment variables that ensure successful transition into adulthood. At the Centre for Research and Education in Human Services in Ontario, Lord (1991) identified another crucial aspect: the empowerment of individuals with disabilities through their involvement in the community, However, the research on these variables does not inspire overconfidence regarding students with mild intellectual disabilities.

Polloway, Patton, Smith, and Roderique (1991) pose the question: "What happens when students who are mildly retarded get older?" They considered in particular the data that Edgar (1987, 1988, 1990) and Affleck, Edgar, Levine, and Kortering (1990) reported, indicating that students who went through special education programs have not fared well. Less than one half were either working or involved in training programs. Although few dropped out of school, this additional time in school had not been productive in terms of employment outcomes (Edgar, 1987). Only 21 percent were living independently 30 months after completion of secondary school, a figure that compares poorly to data on individuals without disabilities. The transition period can be seen as a time of "floundering" (Edgar, 1988); it is clearly more so for students who have mild intellectual disabilities. Unfortunately, "productive adulthood" has been an elusive goal for these students (Edgar, 1990). In *Disability Community and Society*, the Roeher Institute of Canada (1996, p. 42) notes that people with intellectual disabilities are generally poor: that is because of the difficulties encountered in finding paid employment outside the sheltered workshop setting.

TABLE 6.4	Characteristics and Implications of Intellectual Disabilities	
Domain	**Representative Problem Areas**	**Instructional Implications**
ATTENTION	Attention span (length of time on task) Focus (inhibition of distracting stimuli) Selective attention (discrimination of important stimulus characteristics)	Teach students to be aware of the importance of attention. Teach students how to actively monitor their attention (i.e., self-monitoring). Highlight salient cues.
USE OF MEDIATIONAL STRATEGIES	Production of strategies to assist learning Organizing new information	Teach specific strategies (rehearsal, labelling, chunking). Involve students in active learning process (practise, apply, review). Stress meaningful content.
MEMORY	Short-term memory (i.e., over seconds, minutes)—common deficit area Long-term memory—usually more similar to that of persons who are nondisabled (once information has been learned)	Because strategy production is difficult, students need to be shown how to use specific strategies in order to proceed in an organized, well-planned manner. Stress meaningful content.
GENERALIZED LEARNING	Applying knowledge or skills to new tasks, problems, or situations Using previous experience to formulate rules that will help solve problems of a similar nature	Teach in multiple contexts. Reinforce generalization. Remind students to apply what they have learned.
MOTIVATIONAL CONSIDERATIONS	External locus of control Outerdirectedness Lack of encouragement to achieve Failure set (expectancy of failure)	Create environment focused on success opportunities. Emphasize self-reliance. Promote self-management strategies. Encourage problem-solving strategies (vs. only correct responses).
COGNITIVE DEVELOPMENT	Ability to engage in abstract thinking Symbolic thought, as exemplified by introspection and hypothesizing	Provide concrete examples in instruction. Encourage interaction between students and the environment, being responsive to their needs so that they may learn about themselves as they relate to the people and objects around them.
LANGUAGE DEVELOPMENT	Delayed acquisition of vocabulary and language rules Possible interaction with cultural variance and language dialects Speech disorders (more common than in general population)	Create environment that facilitates development and encourages verbal communication. Provide opportunities for students to interact with language. Provide opportunities for students to use language for a variety of purposes and with different audiences. Encourage student speech and active participation.
SOCIOBEHAVIOURAL CONSIDERATIONS	Social adjustment Problems in "everyday intelligence" (Greenspan, 1996) Self-concept Social acceptance Classroom behavioural difficulties (e.g., disruptions)	Promote social competence through direct instruction in social skills. Reinforce appropriate behaviours. Seek an understanding of reasons for inappropriate behaviour. Involve peers as classroom role models. Program for social acceptance. Use peers in reinforcing.

TABLE 6.5

Diagnostic System for Mental Retardation

Dimensions	Steps
DIMENSION I: Intellectual Functioning and Adaptive Skills	**STEP 1. Diagnosis of Mental Retardation** ***Determines Eligibility for Supports*** Mental retardation is diagnosed if: 1. The individual's intellectual functioning is approximately 70 to 75 or below. 2. There are significant disabilities in two or more adaptive skill areas. 3. The age of onset is below 18.
DIMENSION II: Psychological/Emotional Considerations **DIMENSION III:** Physical/Health/Etiology Considerations **DIMENSION IV:** Environmental Considerations	**STEP 2. Classification and Description** ***Identifies Strengths and Weaknesses and the Need for Supports*** 1. Describe the individual's strengths and weaknesses in reference to psychological/emotional considerations. 2. Describe the individual's overall physical health and indicate the condition's etiology. 3. Describe the individual's current environmental placement and the optimal environment that would facilitate his/her continued growth and development.
	STEP 3. Profile and Intensities of Needed Supports ***Identifies Needed Supports*** Identify the kind and intensities of supports needed for each of the four dimensions. 1. Dimension I: Intellectual Functioning and Adaptive Skills 2. Dimension II: Psychological/Emotional Considerations 3. Dimension III: Physical Health/Etiology Considerations 4. Dimension IV: Environmental Considerations

From *Mental Retardation: Definition, Classification, and Systems of Supports* (p. 24), by R. Luckasson, D. L. Coulter, E. A. Polloway, S. Reiss, R. L. Schalock, M. E. Snell, D. M. Spitalnik, and J. A. Stark, 1992, Washington, DC: American Association on Mental Retardation. Used by permission.

FURTHER READING

For more information on students with intellectual disabilities and educational demands at the secondary level, read T. E. C. Smith and I. K. Puccini's article "Secondary Programming Issues," published in 1996 in volume 31 of *Education and Training in Mental Retardation and Developmental Disabilities* (pp. 320–327).

The Institute cites that "only 31% of people with intellectual disabilities have jobs; 61% of people with intellectual disabilities with jobs work in sheltered settings." The challenge of productive adulthood is clearly demonstrated by Table 6.6, which identifies adult domains and relates them to Knowles's (1984) life problems areas.

In general, the vast majority of adults with intellectual disabilities can obtain and maintain gainful employment. Two critical factors, however, influence their success. First, postschool adjustment hinges on their ability to demonstrate personal and social behaviours appropriate to the workplace. Second, the quality of the transition programming provided will predict subsequent success. Such programs recognize that programming must reflect a top-down perspective (i.e., from community considerations to school curriculum) that bases curriculum on the demands of the next environment in which the individual will live, work, socialize, and recreate.

TABLE 6.6		
Demands of Adulthood		
Adult Domains	**Knowles' Domains**	**Examples**
VOCATIONAL AND EDUCATION	Vocation and career	Being interviewed Getting along at work Changing jobs
HOME AND FAMILY	Home and family living	Dating Family planning Raising children Solving marital problems Financial planning
RECREATION AND LEISURE	Enjoyment of leisure	Choosing hobbies Buying equipment Planning recreational outings
COMMUNITY INVOLVEMENT	Community living	Using community resources Voting Getting assistance
EMOTIONAL AND PHYSICAL HEALTH	Health	Exercising Treating medical emergencies Understanding children's diseases
PERSONAL DEVELOPMENT	Personal development	Making decisions Dealing with conflict Establishing intimate relationships Understanding oneself

From "Curricular Considerations: A Life Skills Orientation," by J. R. Patton, M. E. Cronin, E. A. Polloway, D. Hutchinson, and G. A. Robinson. In *Best Practices in Mild Mental Retardation*, edited by G. A. Robinson, J. R. Patton, E. A. Polloway, and L. Sargent, 1989, p. 27. Reston, VA: CEC-MR. Used by permission.

STRATEGIES FOR CURRICULUM AND INSTRUCTION

Teaching students with mild intellectual disabilities in inclusive settings is a challenge. Without question, however, educators must deliver quality programs, or else the prognosis for young adults with mild intellectual disabilities, as noted in the studies discussed earlier, will not be positive.

Demands on General Education

The pessimistic data on postschool outcomes point out areas that teachers who work with students with mild intellectual disabilities in inclusive settings must attend to. These areas should be kept in mind as curricula and instructional plans are developed and implemented in conjunction with special education teachers. Patton et al. (1996) identify four primary goals for individuals who have mild intellectual disabilities: productive employment, independence and

FURTHER READING
For more information on a step-by-step approach to including a student with intellectual disabilities in the regular classroom, read "Everyone Belongs with the MAPS Action Planning System," a 1990 article by the Canadian authors Forest and Lusthaus, in volume 22 of *Teaching Exceptional Children*.

PERSONAL SPOTLIGHT

Best Friends ■ HANNAH LUSTHAUS and TINA LEMIEUX

Graduates of Integrated Classrooms

When asked what the best thing was about school, Hannah quips, "Graduation!"

At 22 Hannah and Tina, best friends for 19 years, are enjoying the freedom of having their own apartments. "I like being able to see my boyfriend whenever I want," says Hannah. "Yeah, all the time, all the time!" adds Tina, laughing. "No, no, I always make time for my best friend Tina!" "Not so much as for Tim," insists Tina. "I do, I do!" "Okay, Hahn . . . we both like to be with each other and our boyfriends."

Hannah and Tina both have an intellectual disability.

Dorothy, Tina's mother, tells how, as Tina grew up and they moved into different school board districts, the family's desire to have Tina included in the local community school and regular classroom was received with varying degrees of acceptance. "It was so different place to place. In high school, it was difficult but finally they tried something creative—they had Tina in the high achieving class and that worked very well. The kids were very accepting and Tina modelled her behaviour on theirs. It was great." Tina tells what she liked about school: "Being with other people I like, that is the best to me— a good reason for school."

Hannah's mother, Evy, tells about the struggle to have Hannah accepted into the regular class at the neighbourhood school during a time when other children with Hannah's disability were being sent to segregated schools. "It was difficult to achieve but once Hannah was allowed to attend, I found that most teachers were very successful by making down-to-earth common-sense adaptations that enabled Hannah to be a part of the class and to learn at her own level."

Both Tina and Hannah have moved on from being integrated in their neighbourhood schools for the majority of their schooling. They attended the John Abbott College work-study program after high school, and now both have jobs and live in their own apartments within a supportive apartment building. Tina works at a large pet store looking after the animals which she loves (even the iguanas!), and Hannah works at Concordia University, cataloguing CDs at the radio station and assisting with the Concordia basketball team. Hannah tells how, after her older sister and brother moved away from home, it was her turn to do it. Now that her brother is getting married, she and Tim are talking about it too. It is clear that she has every expectation that she will follow in the footsteps of her siblings—and she has!

However, it has not always been easy for Tina and Hannah. They are reluctant to talk about the difficulties they have had. Instead, they move on to what they liked. Hannah tells of one inclusion experience that meant a lot to her: "I had a bad experience. A bad time—one's enough. Usually, I liked the teachers and the classes and especially when I got good grades. But I remember this one guy, he was big and . . . uh . . . big and, not really a bully ("He was bossy," says Tina.) No! Not bossy, but mean. Tough and mean, mean, mean. ("That's a bully," says Tina.) No, no, not a bully, just big and tough and mean. Anyway, uh . . . my teacher uh she was being mean, really mean to me," Hannah says, "and this big tough guy he did something about it. The big tough guy he went and told her off! It was the one person . . . I can't believe this big tough guy and he did that . . . stuck up for me!" (Says Tina, "Yeah, yeah, that's good.")

Tina adds, "I had wonderful teachers. They gave me a lot of good skills. Remember with Linda, we learned to read and you know, Hannah, what was it?" "Reading," says Hannah. "No, no, with Linda the other . . . you know, not read . . ." "Count?" asks Hannah. "Yes, yes, thank you, Miss Hannah!" replies Tina. "Numbers. That was good. But some bad was . . . kids criticizing me, like 'What is *she* doing here?!' You know people being mean, calling me names . . . I had a lot of good experiences."

If you were to talk to Tina and Hannah, you would be amazed at their resilience, their focus on the positive. You would also be filled with a good feeling about what is possible for students with an intellectual disability.

self-sufficiency, life skills competence, and opportunity to participate successfully within the schools and the community. These goals should guide the educational program for these students.

In terms of *employment,* teachers should build students' career awareness and help them see how academic content relates to applied situations; at the secondary level, this thrust should include training in specific job skills. This concern should be the primary focus of vocational educators who work with these students.

In terms of *independence* and *self-sufficiency,* young adults with mild intellectual disabilities need to become as responsible as possible for themselves. As Miller (1995) states, the educational goal "is to develop self-directed learners who can address their own wants and concerns and can advocate for their goals and aspirations" (p. 12). Thus, successful inclusion of students who have intellectual disabilities depends on the ability of teachers, peers, and the curriculum to create a climate of empowerment. Empowerment involves self-efficacy, a sense of personal control, self-esteem, and a sense of belonging to a group. One essential element of empowerment is self-determination (Wehmeyer, 1994). As Wehmeyer (1993, p. 16) notes:

> Self-determination refers to the attitudes and abilities necessary to act as the primary causal agent in one's life, and to make choices and decisions regarding one's quality of life free from undue external influence or interference.

Empowerment is by no means an automatic byproduct of inclusive classrooms. However, when students become members of the group while retaining the right to make decisions for themselves, they are becoming prepared for the challenges and rewards of life.

A third key consideration is the inclusion of *life skills* in the curriculum, focusing on the importance of competence in everyday activities. This area includes, but is not limited to, use of community resources, home and family activities, social and interpersonal skills, health and safety skills, use of leisure time, and participation in the community as a citizen (e.g., compliance with legal and cultural standards).

A critical concern relative to school and community inclusion and to life adjustment is the acquisition of social skills. A useful model has been developed by Sargent (1991). It embraces three processes: development of *social affect* (appearance to others), *social skills* (specific behaviours that are central to interactions), and *social cognition* (understanding and being able to respond appropriately to various social situations). Specific aspects of these three areas follow:

- Social affect
  1. Cheerfulness
  2. Enthusiasm
  3. Confidence
  4. Optimism
  5. Risk taking
  6. Independence
  7. Good posture

TEACHING TIP

Instructional activities for students with intellectual disabilities should focus on development of self-determination skills.

FURTHER READING

For more information on teaching social skills to persons with intellectual disabilities, read *Social Skills in School and Community,* by L. Sargent, published in 1991 by a Council for Exceptional Children division, Mental Retardation and Developmental Disabilities.

   8. Good grooming
   9. Sense of humour
   10. Affection
   11. Assertiveness
- Social skills
   1. Interaction initiative (e.g., starting a conversation)
   2. Interaction responses (e.g., responding to a complaint)
   3. Personal social behaviours (e.g., dealing with embarrassment)
   4. Setting specific skills and behaviours:
      a. School behaviour
      b. Workplace behaviour
      c. Public setting behaviour
      d. Family setting behaviour
- Social cognition
   1. Role taking and empathy
   2. Social discrimination and inference
   3. Social understanding
   4. Understanding motives of others
   5. Moral and ethical judgments
   6. Referential communication
   7. Social problem solving

An area with significant implications for social adjustment is sex education. The purposes of sex education for students with intellectual disabilities are as follows:

1. Understand and appreciate his or her own sexuality.
2. Know basic male and female anatomy and male and female roles in the reproductive process.
3. Understand that no one has the right to do something sexual to anyone else without permission.
4. Understand the responsibilities of parenting.
5. Understand that birth control methods should be used unless children can be provided for and are wanted.
6. Understand his or her role in protecting personal health and the health of others.
7. Know the resources available for persons who have been sexually abused or have contracted a sexually transmitted disease.
8. Understand the social and sexual values of society (Sparks & Caster, 1989).

Finally, successful *community involvement* requires that students experience inclusive environments. Students with mild intellectual disabilities can learn to participate in school and community by being included in general education classrooms. Although school inclusion is viewed by some as an end in itself, in reality it is only a condition that can provide instruction and training for success in subsequent life activities. As a necessary step toward this goal, individuals with mild intellectual disabilities should be included within school programs to the maximum extent possible while there still is assurance that such placement facilitates their learning and ultimately their preparation for adulthood (Patton et al., 1996).

A key to successful inclusion for students with intellectual disabilities is provision of appropriate supports.

General Considerations for Inclusion

The key to including students with mild intellectual disabilities in the general education classroom is providing necessary and appropriate supports, such as personal supports, natural supports (e.g., parents, friends), support services, and technical supports. This model, called *supported education,* assumes that individuals should be maintained in inclusive classroom settings to the maximum degree possible and supported in those locations in order to ensure successful learning (Polloway et al., 1996).

Strains have occurred during the transition to the supports model, both for students and for the inclusion movement itself. An unfortunate tendency is simply to place the student physically in the classroom and call it full inclusion, rather than achieve the more appropriate goal of *supported education.* The terminology has caused some confusion. Inclusion calls for supported education and focuses on welcoming and involving persons with intellectual disabilities. Mere physical integration does not ensure involvement or participation. Merely placing students in general education without social integration and active classroom participation is not the intent of inclusion and will not result in positive gains for students. Likewise, adults with intellectual disabilities who live in the community but do not participate in community activities do not fulfill the true spirit of inclusion (Gardner & O'Brien, 1990; Storey, 1993).

TEACHING TIP

The supports model emphasizes providing whatever supports are necessary to enable a student with intellectual disabilities to succeed in a general education setting.

CROSS-REFERENCE

See Chapter 1 to review the purposes of including students with disabilities in general education settings.

CLASSROOM ACCOMMODATIONS

Table 6.4 presented an outline of the common characteristics associated with intellectual disabilities, along with their implications for instruction. When

TABLE 6.7

Typical and Modified Curriculum Outcomes for Students with Intellectual Disabilities

Grade Level	Typical Outcomes	Modified Outcomes
GRADE 2: LANGUAGE ARTS	Learn 10 spelling words per week and be able to use them correctly in sentences.	Identify 15 safety words (e.g., *stop, poison*) and functional words (e.g., *men, women*).
GRADE 4: LANGUAGE ARTS	Read a book and write a two-page report, using correct grammar, punctuation, and spelling.	Listen to a taped book, tape a personal reaction to the story, and illustrate the story.
GRADE 6: SOCIAL STUDIES	Locate all 10 provinces and 3 territories on a map, and name their capitals.	Locate own province/territory and those immediately adjacent to it, and name the capitals.
GRADE 8: SOCIAL STUDIES	Name and explain the functions of the government in power, the Opposition, and the Senate.	Describe the jobs of the prime minister, the leader of the Opposition, and a member of the Senate.
GRADE 10: SCIENCE	Describe the body systems of three different mammals, and identify the major components and functions of each system.	Label diagrams of the human body, identifying each body system and its purpose and naming major body organs.

Adapted from *Exceptional Individuals in School, Community, and Work* (p. 131), by P. Wehman, 1997, Austin, TX: Pro-Ed. Used by permission.

they are considered collectively, certain instructional themes emerge. Teachers should focus on accommodations that

■ ensure attention to relevant task demands.
■ teach ways to learn content while teaching content itself.
■ focus on content that is meaningful to the students, to promote learning as well as to facilitate application.
■ provide training that crosses multiple contexts.
■ offer—and this is the most important focus—opportunities for active involvement in the learning process.

FURTHER READING

For more information on how a person's future should drive the curriculum, read the article "Future-Based Assessment for Persons with Mental Retardation," by T. E. C. Smith and C. A. Dowdy, published in 1992 in volume 27 of *Education and Training in Mental Retardation and Developmental Disabilities* (pp. 255–260).

One promising approach that has merit for all students and can particularly benefit students with mild intellectual disabilities is the use of cognitively oriented instructional methods. Based on the premise that learning problems experienced by low-achieving students are due more to a lack of knowledge regarding the processes involved in independent learning than of any underlying deficits, these approaches incorporate learning strategies, metacognition, and cognitive behaviour modification (e.g., self-monitoring) as exciting alternatives to traditional instructional practices. The use of such approaches is discussed at length in Chapter 5. Their potential for students with mild intellectual disabilities is clear (see Polloway, Patton, Smith, & Buck, 1997).

Curricular accommodations are likewise important to consider. In general, the key focus should be on relevant and meaningful curricular content that students can master and apply to their current and future lives. Polloway et al. (1991) stress the importance of focusing on the subsequent environments that students will live in (in terms of learning, working, residing) as a basis for curriculum design.

To make the curriculum appropriate for students with intellectual disabilities, specific accommodations can enhance learning and increase relevance. One useful format, developed by Wehman (1997) (see Table 6.7), offers useful ideas for curriculum modification.

Technological Considerations

Technology can enhance instructional and curricular accommodations. Although students with intellectual disabilities can benefit from a variety of technological applications, the key concern is that technology be used in a way that effectively enhances learning. Hasselbring and Goin (1993) note that technology can be used to facilitate the acquisition of new skills, the development of fluency and proficiency, maintenance of skills over time, and generalization to new situations. Conscious attention to each of these four stages of learning is a necessity for teaching students with intellectual disabilities in general, as well as for using technological approaches in particular. A nearby Technology Today feature outlines some principles for selecting drill-and-practice programs to enhance fluence and proficiency and to maintain learning.

Assistive technology is a particularly important classroom accommodation. The nearby Technology Today feature on assistive technology introduces and briefly describes these devices.

ENHANCING INCLUSIVE CLASSROOMS

Several considerations are central to the successful inclusion of students with intellectual disabilities. The first concern is the creation of a sense of community in the school in general and in the classroom in particular. As noted earlier, successful inclusion represents supported education—an environment

Teachers need to promote an environment where social relationships can be developed.

Features of Effective Drill-and-Practice Software

What to Look for	What to Avoid	Rationale
Programs that provide high rates of response relevant to the skill to be learned	Programs that take too much time to load and run or that contain too many unrelated activities	The more time students spend on task, the more they learn.
Programs in which graphics and animation support the skill or concept being practiced	Programs with graphics or animation that are unrelated to the instructional objective	While graphics and animation may facilitate student interest in an activity, they may also distract students, interfere with skill mastery, and reduce practice time.
Programs in which reinforcement is used sparingly and approximates the type of reinforcement schedule students encounter in the classroom	Programs that provide a reinforcing graphic or activity after every correct response	If students are reinforced too frequently, they may no longer exhibit those responses when fewer reinforcers are offered. Furthermore, excessive time spent engaging in the reinforcing activities detracts from time to learn and interferes with the development of automaticity.
Programs in which reinforcement is clearly related to task completion or mastery	Programs in which events that occur when students are incorrect (e.g., an explosion) are more reinforcing than events that occur when the student is correct (e.g., a smiling face)	Some programs may actually encourage students to practice the incorrect response in order to view the event that they find more reinforcing.
Programs in which feedback helps students locate and correct their mistakes	Programs in which students are merely told if they are right or wrong or are told to "try again"	Without feedback that informs them of the correct answer after a reasonable number of attempts, students may become frustrated and make random guesses.
Programs that store information about student performance or progress that can be accessed by the teacher at a later time	Programs without record-keeping features	Students may encounter difficulties with the skills covered by a program that requires teacher intervention. Access to records of student performance enables the teacher to determine if a program is benefiting a student and whether the student needs assistance.
Programs with options for controlling features such as speed of problem presentation, type of feedback, problem difficulty, and number of practice trials	Programs that must be used in the same way with every student	Options enable the same program to be used with a broad range of students and permit teachers to provide more appropriately individualized instruction.

From "Computers and Individuals with Mild Disabilities," by C. M. Okolo. In *Computers and Exceptional Individuals*, edited by J. D. Lindsay, 1993, p. 117. Austin, TX: Pro-Ed. Used by permission.

Assistive Technology

Assistive technology can be low- or high-tech devices designed to remove barriers or provide practical solutions to common everyday problems. . . . [Such] devices can be applied in the classroom to assist a student with learning curriculum content or in a community setting to promote skill development and participation.

Assistive technology can include such complex devices as (1) an environmental control unit to allow an individual with little or no mobility to control his or her environment (e.g., turn on the lights), (2) a voice-activated computer to allow an individual with mobility or sensory impairments to input data on a computer and receive output information, (3) augmentative communication systems to allow an individual with poor speech to be able to communicate with others (e.g., electronic communication aids), and (4) microswitches to allow an individual to perform a more complex task by reducing the number of steps to complete it to one press on the switch or to allow someone with poor motor skills to access something by touching a very large switch pad as opposed to a small button or lever. In addition, switches can be activated by a number of means, such as sound, air, light, or movement, and are very versatile as to the functions they can perform.

Assistive technology can also include low-tech devices or modifications that can be very inexpensive and easy to apply, such as (1) a reach device to assist an individual with picking things off the floor or taking something off a high shelf, (2) a precoded push button phone to allow an individual with poor memory to complete a call to an important or frequently used number by lightly touching a large color-coded button, (3) audiotape instruction to allow an individual with cognitive or sensory impairments to have access to the instructions, directions, or classroom materials in a format that can be repeated as often as necessary to either learn or perform a task, and (4) a holder made out of wood with suction cups on the bottom that will keep a bowl or pan in place to allow an individual to mix ingredients using only one hand.

The range of high- and low-tech devices to assist with completing an activity or just to make the task easier is virtually endless. Many of these devices are commercially available while others can oftentimes be developed by any interested persons. The major ingredients for developing useful assistive technology devices are creativity, open-mindedness, and resourcefulness.

Adapted from "Severe Mental Retardation," by P. Wehman and W. Parent. In *Exceptional Individuals in School, Community, and Work*, edited by P. Wehman, 1997, pp. 170–171. Austin: Pro-Ed. Used by permission.

where students succeed because they are welcomed, encouraged, involved, and supported in their learning.

A helpful strategy for promoting social acceptance for students with intellectual disabilities involves "circles of support," or "circles of friends." The nearby Inclusion Strategies feature discusses an example of such a program.

The challenge for teachers seeking to successfully include students with intellectual disabilities reaches beyond the students' acquisition of, for example, specific academic skills. Rather, it requires finding ways to provide a "belonging place" for them in the general education classroom. Such a place is created through friendships. Despite the broad support for inclusion—in fact, parents of students with intellectual disabilities have, in general, been its primary proponents (see Arc, 1993)—inclusion does bring with it the potential loss of friendships present in traditional, self-contained classes. For example, Stainback, Stainback, East, and Sapon-Shevin (1994) note the concern of adolescents (and their parents) over finding dating partners in general education classes. Teachers should be sensitive to this consideration and promote an environment in which the benefits of friendships can be realized. The nearby inclusion feature, "Why Friends Are Important," underscores the importance of this point.

INCLUSION STRATEGIES

Circles of Friends in Schools

Marsha Forest came away from her Joshua Committee experiences as if she had put on a better pair of glasses. Her position as a professor of special education suddenly seemed less important to her. She spent long hours on the road helping school boards, principals, and teachers to see how everybody can experience richness when someone with a disability is placed in a regular classroom and the so-called regular students are encouraged to form a circle of friends around that person.

Forest always believed in getting teachers down to meticulous detail when it came to educating persons with disabilities. Now, however, she saw that some of the most valuable educational steps can come *naturally* from regular classmates, if the right conditions exist in the classroom.

She also knew that parents and teachers fear peer group pressure. After all, when kids get together these days, they can give themselves quite an education—one that often shapes lives more powerfully than adults can shape them. But peer group education doesn't always lead to belligerence and destruction and drugs. It can lead to caring and nurturing and helping others do healthy things they had never done before.

This twist, however, generated fears in some teachers when it dawned on them that a circle of friends might foster better growth and development in a student than they were capable of teaching.

And so Forest moved into regular schools and worked hard at

1. helping boards and principals understand the circles-of-friends process.

2. finding a teacher and class willing to include a person with a disability.

3. helping the regular teacher handle any initial fears about the venture.

4. letting the teacher and class call the shots as much as possible.

5. providing strong support persons who would assist only when they really were needed.

6. then finding a handful of kids willing to work at being friends with their classmate with the disability.

"The first placement in a school is the toughest," she said. "After that, it's usually easy to include others."

Forest sees building a circle of friends as a person-by-person process, not an all-encompassing program. So she focuses on students with disabilities one at a time, and sets up a framework that enables a circle to surround that person.

Because no two settings are alike, she watches as the circle, the regular teacher, and the rest of the students develop and coordinate their own routines for helping. Then, never predicting an outcome, she waits. And when new learning takes place in the person with the disability, Forest moves in and makes all the students, the teacher, the principal—even the board members—feel simply great.

According to her, the average school can handle up to twelve of these arrangements. After that, the efficiency of the process may diminish.

She doubts that circles of friends will work in every school. "If a school is all screwed up," she said, "and if it has lost its zest and commitment for really helping kids learn—forget it. On the other hand, I'm sure that circles of friends can help make a good school—and especially the kids—better. Then coming to school takes on fresh values and meaning. Some enjoy coming to school as they never did before."

Adapted from *Circles of Friends: People with Disabilities and Their Friends Enrich the Lives of One Another* (pp. 39–40), by R. Perske, 1988, Nashville, TN: Abingdon Press.

Another concern relates to policy issues and procedures pertaining to inclusion. Polloway et al. (1996) pose questions valid for students who have mild intellectual disabilities and other students as well:

■ Is inclusion achieved via teacher and parental involvement or solely via administrative decision?

INCLUSION STRATEGIES

Why Friends Are Important

Friendships are such an everyday thing, we just take them for granted. They are like electricity, telephone, clothing, and three meals a day—we languish only when we are deprived of them.

And yet we have just begun to sense the pain experienced by people with disabilities when they are deprived of mutually satisfying friendships with ordinary people. We suddenly see that family support, regular schooling, and community living programs are not enough. Those people need friends just as we do. Consider these facts:

- *Friendship is a familiar but elusive term.* Researchers reduce their focus to specific *relationships* or *social interactions*, classifying, counting, and analyzing them. But the rest of us need to view a good friendship the way we look at a sunrise, seeing it in all its radiance.

- *Friends help us stretch beyond our families.* In *Just Friends,* social scientist Lillian Rubin illustrates vividly that young people turn more to friends than to family when they seek to be affirmed as adults.

- *Friends help us move beyond human-service goals.* Friends provide us with myriad options that never could be programmed.

- *Friends help us rehearse adult roles.* You and I are the way we are largely because we rehearse our actions and attitudes with friends—things we wouldn't think of saying or doing with family or human-service workers.

- *Friends serve as fresh role models.* We often choose certain friends because we see something in them that we wish for ourselves.

- *Good friendships are a mystery.* There's no ritual or program for starting them. Sometimes they thrive and sometimes they fade.

- *Good friendships are attractive.* Others watch interactions between friends with great interest.

- *Friendships generate their own energy.* Quite often, when two people do things together, their zest and success equal much more than the sum of two people's efforts.

- *Friendships become a haven from stress.* When things get tough, many of us have good friends "on call."

- *Friendships are reciprocal.* Both parties receive enrichment from the relationship.

- *Friends can demystify strange behaviours.* While I visited two friends in a print shop, one friend—during a moment of boredom—began to move his arms and fingers in patterns professionals call "autistic." When I asked the other friend what he thought about such movements, he replied, "Hey man, if you think that's weird, you should come with me to my favourite tavern on Friday nights."

- *Every friendship is unique and unrepeatable.* Each relationship is as vivid as a fingerprint.

- *One can learn much from good friendships.* A good friendship can become a *living document.* With great interest, we can study the remarkable things friends do with each other. And it doesn't matter whether society has imaged us as a so-called normal or as a person with a disability, good friendships can inspire us to try refreshing new interpersonal activities in our own lives—things we've never done before.

Adapted from *Circles of Friends: People with Disabilities and Their Friends Enrich the Lives of One Another* (pp. 12–13), by R. Perske, 1988, Nashville, TN: Abingdon Press.

- Is it selected because it is considered a cheaper form of intervention or chosen for its value in spite of potentially being more costly?
- Are sufficient numbers of properly trained paraprofessionals available to assist special education teachers in providing supports within general education?

- Has training been provided to all staff regarding collaborative relationships?
- Has training been provided to general educators regarding meeting the needs of students with diverse abilities?
- Is there attention to appropriate adaptations in instructional practices?

FINAL THOUGHTS

As special and general education teachers jointly develop and implement educational programs for students with intellectual disabilities, they should keep in mind that these students require a comprehensive, broad-based curriculum to meet their needs. The most effective programs will provide appropriate academic instruction, adapted to facilitate learning. However, the curriculum cannot solely be academic in orientation, but rather should focus on developing social skills and transition skills to facilitate the students' success in general education classrooms and subsequent integration into community settings.

TEACHING TIP

Curricular decisions for students with intellectual disabilities should always be made with the student's future needs in mind.

In making curriculum choices, teachers will have to consider how responsive the general education classroom can be to the needs of students with intellectual disabilities. The ultimate goal is not simply school inclusion but rather community or "life" inclusion; whichever curriculum achieves that purpose most effectively is the most appropriate one (Polloway et al., 1991). As Cassidy and Stanton (1959) suggested nearly four decades ago, the key question in evaluating the effectiveness of programs is *effective for what?* What is it that the schools are to impart to the students? Affleck et al. (1990) argue that although general education class placement is consistent with current philosophical and legal trends, educators must design programs that provide the instructional intensity to meet skill needs while addressing the long-term needs of students. The challenge of inclusion for students with intellectual disabilities is to ensure that the curriculum they pursue prepares them for their future.

SUMMARY

- The concept of intellectual disability has variant meanings to professionals and the lay public.
- The three central dimensions of the definition are lower intellectual functioning, deficits or limitations in adaptive skills, and an onset prior to age 18.
- The 1992 AAMR definition retains the three dimensions but also stresses the importance of four assumptions: cultural and linguistic diversity, an environmental context for adaptive

skills, the strengths of individuals as well as their limitations, and the promise of improvement over time.

- Common practice in the field has been to speak of two general levels of intellectual disability, mild and severe, but emerging efforts in classification stress levels of needed supports rather than levels of disability.
- Attention difficulties can be addressed by modifying instruction to highlight relevant stimuli

and by teaching students to monitor their own attention.

■ Teachers should teach not only content but also mediation strategies that facilitate learning. Examples include rehearsal, classification, and visual imagery.

■ Memory problems respond to mediation strategies (as above) and to an emphasis on content that is meaningful and relevant.

■ Many students with a history of failure have an external locus of control, which can be enhanced by an emphasis on successful experiences and by reinforcement for independent work.

■ Cognitive development for students with intellectual disabilities can be enhanced by emphasizing active interaction with the environment and concrete experiences.

■ To enhance language development, teachers should provide a facilitative environment, structure opportunities for communication, and encourage speech.

■ Social competence is a critical component of instructional programs for students with intellectual disabilities. Teaching social skills can have a positive effect on successful inclusion both in school and in the community.

■ Educational programs must be outcomes-oriented and attend to transitional concerns so that students receive the appropriate training to prepare them for subsequent environments. The curriculum should thus have a top-down orientation.

■ Opportunities for inclusion are essential and should focus on social benefits such as friendship while not neglecting curricular needs.

RESOURCES

Hileman, Camilla. (1997). *Point! Click! & Learn!!!* Arlington, TX: Future Horizons Publishers.

Here is a user-friendly guide to educational software programs for individuals with developmental disabilities.

British Columbia Ministry of Education, Special Programs Branch. (1996). *Students with Intellectual Disabilities: A Resource Guide for Teachers.* Victoria: Author.

Teachers will find this very practical resource guide excellent for working with students with intellectual disabilities. The guide also suggests additional resources and materials.

WEBLINKS

Canadian Association for Community Living (CACL)
www.cacl.ca/
The CACL advocates the full inclusion of individuals with intellectual disabilities in the community. The Association's Web site provides information, supports, and leads on other Web sites focused on inclusion. Checking it out is essential if you have questions regarding Canadian law about inclusion of individuals with disabilities and transition to the

workplace or want to reach a provincial or territorial association.

Roeher Institute
www.roeher.ca/roeher/
As Canada's leading organization to promote the equality, participation, and self-determination of people with intellectual and other disabilities, the Institute examines the causes of marginalization and provides research, information, and social develop-

ment opportunities. It states, "If you are looking for a contact person, an organization, articles or books on a particular topic in the disability field, lists of resources, examples of innovative inclusionary practices, annotated bibliographies—in other words, information of any kind to support the inclusion of people with disabilities—we have it, or we can help locate it." The Web site is a must visit for all individuals working with people with disabilities.

TASH: Disability Advocacy Worldwide
www.tash.org/
Here is an excellent site for learning about the disability rights movement and finding links to other Web sites relevant to a variety of exceptionalities. "TASH" used to stand for The Association for the Severely Handicapped. Although the Association no longer uses the title, it has retained the acronym. TASH is an international association of people with disabilities, their family members, other advocates, and professionals. TASH's mission and commitment is to achieving full inclusion and participation of persons with disabilities in all aspects of life. Its Web site provides a wealth of information relevant to achieving that goal.

American Association of Mental Retardation
www.aamr.org/
The Web site of this Association, which has chapters in both Canada and the United States, provides information, resources, related links, and a bookstore of current books in the area of intellectual disability.

CHAPTER SEVEN

CHAPTER OBJECTIVES

- To explain the nature of low-incidence disabilities

- To define hearing impairment and visual impairment

- To describe educationally relevant characteristics of students with hearing impairments and visual impairments

- To describe accommodations and modifications for students with hearing impairments and visual impairments

Teaching Students with Sensory Impairments

It was only the end of September, but Ana was already beginning to fall behind most of her peers in the second grade. Although she was promoted at the end of the first grade, she did not acquire most of the skills necessary for success in the second grade.

For the first half of Grade 1, Ana had tried very hard. She wanted to learn to read like her classmates, but seemed always to miss out on sounding letters and words correctly. According to her teacher, Ms. Pryor, Ana also appeared to daydream a lot. The teacher frequently had to go to Ana's desk to get her attention when giving directions and assignments. By the middle of the first grade, Ana seemed to be giving up. Her efforts always fell short. Her spelling was poor, and her reading skills were not improving. She began having behaviour problems, which Ms. Pryor attributed to the influence of her older brother, who was always getting into trouble. Ana's parents were interested but did not have any answers. They said that Ana was in her own world at home and often did not respond to what was happening around her. In addition to Ana's poor academic skills and behaviour problems, she also had difficulties with her peers. She was not very popular, and some of the other students made fun of her poor articulation of certain words.

Ms. James, Ana's new second-grade teacher, decided to refer Ana for vision and hearing screening. Sure enough, Ana was found to have a hearing loss in both ears. Although the loss was not significant enough to warrant specialized placement, it did suggest that a hearing aid might be useful.

Thanks to the awareness of Ms. James, Ana's hearing loss was detected before she experienced more failure. Unfortunately, she had missed much of what she should have learned during Grade 1 and Kindergarten, probably because of the hearing impairment.

1. Should schools routinely screen Kindergarten and Grade 1 students for hearing and vision problems? Why or why not?

2. What can Ana's Grade 2 teacher do to help her overcome the problems created by the late identification of her hearing impairment?

INTRODUCTION

Although there is some debate regarding the best setting in which to provide services to students with **sensory impairments**, many students with these conditions are placed in general education settings. Most are capable of handling the academic and social demands of these settings. However, for these students to receive an appropriate education, a variety of accommodations may be needed, ranging from minor seating adjustments to the use of sophisticated equipment for communicating or listening. Students with these impairments may also need the support of additional personnel (e.g., an *interpreter* or *Braille instructor*).

To provide appropriate accommodations, teachers must have accurate information about how to modify their classrooms and adapt instruction to meet student needs. In addition, they need to understand the psychosocial aspects of having these types of disabilities. Ultimately, teachers must feel comfortable and confident that they can address the range of needs these students present.

Sensory impairments are considered *low-incidence* disabilities, since there are not large numbers of these students in the school population. Weber (1994) cites data suggesting that 0.06 percent of the school population are identified as having a visual impairment and 0.14 percent as having a hearing impairment. These groups represent a very small percentage of all students who have a disability.

CONSIDER THIS

Should students whose only disability is hearing or visual impairment be segregated in residential schools, often many miles away from their families?

However, having only one of these students in a classroom may seem overwhelming. He or she may require a variety of modifications in the way a classroom is managed and in the way certain instructional practices are implemented. Students with both vision and hearing losses present significant challenges for educators; *multisensory impairments* will be covered in Chapter 8.

HEARING IMPAIRMENT

Hearing impairment is a hidden disability—an unknowing observer typically cannot tell from looking at physical features alone that a person's hearing is impaired. However, in any context where communicative skills are needed, hearing limitations become evident.

Students with a hearing disability pose a variety of challenges to the general classroom teacher. Although their numbers are increasing, relatively few students with profound hearing loss (deafness) are educated in general education settings. However, when these students are placed in general education classes, they need major accommodations (e.g., an interpreter).

The number of students who have some degree of hearing loss (i.e., mild to severe) is more noteworthy, because these students can function in general education settings more easily when certain accommodations are provided. For this to happen, it is critical for teachers to understand the nature of hearing impairments and to know how to address the needs associated with these conditions.

The importance of language acquisition and usage to the development of cognitive abilities and achievement in academic subject areas is unassailable (Polloway & Smith, 1992). Hearing loss, even in milder forms, greatly affects language ability. This leads to problems in academic areas, particularly in language-related subjects such as reading and written expression.

Basic Concepts

This section provides basic information on hearing impairments. Teachers who build a solid working knowledge in this area can teach more effectively and communicate more clearly with other professionals and with families.

DEFINITION

A number of different terms are associated with hearing loss, which often causes confusion. Three terms frequently encountered in print and in professional conversation are *hearing impairment, deafness,* and *hard of hearing.*

- *Hearing impairment* is the generic term used to describe any level of hearing loss, ranging from mild to profound.
- *Deafness* describes a hearing loss that is so profound, the auditory channel (the ear) cannot function as the primary mode for perceiving and monitoring speech or acquiring language.
- *Hard of hearing* describes individuals who have a hearing loss, but are able to use the auditory channel as their primary mode for perceiving and monitoring speech or acquiring language. (Diefendorf, 1996)

Hearing loss is often measured in decibel loss (dB). Individuals with losses from 25 to 90 dB are considered hard of hearing, whereas those with losses greater than 90 dB are classified as deaf.

CLASSIFICATION

Hearing loss can be categorized in several different ways. Diefendorf (1996) organized hearing loss into four different groups: **conductive hearing loss** (mild loss in both ears), unilateral hearing loss (loss only in one ear), mild bilateral **sensorineural hearing loss** (caused by sound not being transmitted to the brain), and moderate-to-severe bilateral sensorineural hearing loss (more severe loss in both ears). Table 7.1 summarizes the audiological, communicational, and educational implications for each type of loss. Each specific type and degree of loss poses challenges in learning and communicating.

PREVALENCE AND CAUSES

Only about 0.14 percent of school-age children are served in special education programs for students with hearing impairments in Canada. Since hearing impairments become more prevalent as individuals get older, the number of people experiencing hearing loss in the total population is higher than the number found in schools. It is estimated that between 2 percent and 5 percent of the total population has some degree of hearing loss.

Many different factors can lead to hearing impairments. These include genetic causes (Arnos, Israel, Devlin, & Wilson, 1996); developmental anomalies (Clark & Jaindl, 1996); and toxic reaction to drugs, infections, trauma, premature birth, anoxia (lack of oxygen for a period of time), and birth trauma (Chase, Hall, & Werkhaven, 1996). Knowing the specific cause of a hearing impairment

FURTHER READING
For additional information regarding definitions and terminology in the area of hearing impairments, read *Hearing Care for Children,* by F. N. Martin and J. G. Clark, published by Allyn & Bacon in 1996.

CONSIDER THIS
Is it important for teachers to know the type of hearing loss experienced by a student? Why or why not?

CROSS-REFERENCE
Review the etiological sections of Chapters 3 through 9, and compare the causes of hearing impairments and other disabilities. There are many common factors.

TABLE 7.1

Symptoms Associated with Conductive Hearing Loss; Unilateral Hearing Loss; Mild, Bilateral Sensorineural Hearing Loss; and Moderate-to-Severe Bilateral Sensorineural Hearing Loss

	Audiological	Communicative	Educational
CONDUCTIVE HEARING LOSS	• Hearing loss 30 dB (range 10–50 dB) • Poor auditory reception • Degraded and inconsistent speech signal • Difficulty understanding under adverse listening conditions • Impaired speech discrimination • HL overlays developmental requirement for greater stimulus intensity before infants can respond to and discriminate between speech • Inability to organize auditory information consistently	• Difficulty forming linguistic categories (plurals, tense) • Difficulty in differentiating word boundaries, phoneme boundaries • Receptive language delay • Expressive language delay • Cognitive delay	• Lower achievement test scores • Lower verbal IQ • Poorer reading and spelling performance • Higher frequency of enrollment in special support classes in school • Lower measures of social maturity
UNILATERAL HEARING LOSS	• Hearing loss moderate to profound • Impaired auditory localization • Difficulty understanding speech in presence of competing noise • Loss of binaural advantage: binaural summation, binaural release from masking	• Tasks involving language concepts may be depressed	• Lags in academic achievement: reading, spelling, arithmetic • Verbally based learning difficulties • High rate of grade repetition • Self-described: embarrassment, annoyance, confusion, helplessness • Less independence in the classroom
MILD BILATERAL SENSORINEURAL HEARING LOSS	• Hearing loss 15–20 dB • Speech recognition depressed • Auditory discrimination depressed • Amplification considered: FM systems, classroom amplification	• Potential problems in articulation • Problems in auditory attention • Problems in auditory memory • Problems in auditory comprehension • Possible delays in expressive oral language • Impact on syntax and semantics • Impact on vocabulary development	• Lowered academic achievement: arithmetic problem solving, math concepts, vocabulary, reading comprehension • Educational delays progress systematically with age
MODERATE-TO-SEVERE BILATERAL SENSORINEURAL HEARING LOSS	• Hearing loss 41 dB–90 dB • Noise and reverberation significantly affect listening and understanding • Audiologic management: essentials, amplification recommendations, monitor hearing for: – otitis media – sudden changes in hearing – progressive hearing loss	• Deficits in speech perception • Deficits in speech production (mild-to-moderate articulation problems) • Language deficits from slight to significant: syntax, morphology, semantics, pragmatics • Vocabulary deficits	• Slight to significant deficits in literacy (reading and writing) • Deficits in academic achievement • High rate of academic failure • Immaturity • Feelings of isolation and exclusion • Special education supports needed

From "Hearing Loss and Its Effect," by A. O. Diefendorf. In *Hearing Care for Children*, edited by F. N. Martin and J. G. Clark, 1996, p. 5. Boston: Allyn & Bacon. Used by permission.

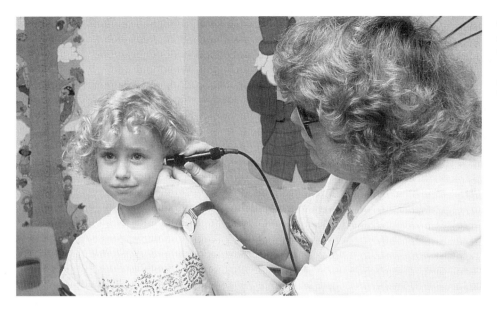

Some children may require an audiological evaluation to determine the nature of their hearing loss.

is usually not important for school personnel, since the cause rarely affects interventions needed by students.

CHARACTERISTICS

The characteristics of students with hearing impairment vary greatly. Four categories of characteristics are especially meaningful to the classroom setting: psychological, communicational, academic, and social-emotional. Specific characteristics that fall into each of these general categories are listed in Table 7.2. (Table 7.1 listed characteristics associated with types and degrees of hearing losses.)

IDENTIFICATION, ASSESSMENT, AND ELIGIBILITY

The ease of identifying students with hearing impairment is related to the degree of hearing loss. Students with severe losses are more easily recognized, whereas those with mild losses may go unrecognized for many years. Teachers should be aware of certain indicators of possible hearing loss and refer students who show these signs for a comprehensive assessment (Kuster, 1993). Teachers should consider referring a student for a comprehensive audiological evaluation if any of these behaviours are present:

- Turns head to position an ear in the direction of the speaker
- Asks for information to be repeated frequently
- Uses a loud voice when speaking
- Does not respond when spoken to
- Gives incorrect answers to questions
- Has frequent colds, earaches, or infections
- Appears inattentive and daydreams
- Has difficulty following directions
- Is distracted easily by visual or auditory stimuli
- Misarticulates certain speech sounds or omits certain consonant sounds
- Withdraws from classroom activities that involve listening
- Has a confused expression on face
- Has a restricted vocabulary

TEACHING TIP
Teachers should keep records of students who display these types of behaviours to determine if there is a pattern that might call for a referral.

TABLE 7.2	

Possible Characteristics of Students with Hearing Impairments

Area of Functioning	Possible Effects
PSYCHOLOGICAL	• Intellectual ability range similar to hearing peers • Problems with certain conceptualizations
COMMUNICATIONAL	• Poor speech production (e.g., unintelligibility) • Tested vocabulary limited • Problems with language usage and comprehension, particularly abstract topics • Voice quality problems
SOCIAL–EMOTIONAL	• Less socially mature • Difficulty making friends • Withdrawn behaviour—feelings of being an outsider • Possible maladjustment problems • May resent having to wear a hearing aid or use other amplification devices • May be dependent on teacher assistance
ACADEMIC	• Achievement levels significantly below those of their hearing peers • Reading ability most significantly affected • Spelling problems • Limited written language production • Discrepancy between capabilities and performance in many academic areas

A teacher's careful observations and referral can spare a student months or years of struggle and frustration.

Formal Assessment   The assessment of hearing ability requires the use of various audiological techniques. The most common method of evaluating hearing is the use of **pure-tone audiometry**, in which sounds of different frequencies are presented at increasing levels of intensity. Bone conduction hearing (related to the outer and middle ear) can also be assessed to determine if there are problems in the sensorineural portion of the hearing mechanism (occurring in the inner ear).

FURTHER READING

For more information on audiological assessment, read *Hearing Care for Children*, by F. N. Martin and J. G. Clark, published by Allyn & Bacon in 1996.

Informal Assessment   In addition to the formal assessment conducted by audiologists, teachers and other school personnel should engage in informal assessment of students, especially those suspected of having a hearing impairment. Informal assessment focuses on observing students for signs that might indicate a hearing loss. Tables 7.1 and 7.2 list indicators that, if recorded over a period of time, show that a student may need formal assessment.

Eligibility   The eligibility of students for special education and related services is determined by provincial and territorial guidelines, which are based on certain levels of decibel loss. Teachers should not be concerned about specific eligibility criteria, but should refer students who display characteristics suggesting the presence of a hearing loss.

Strategies for Curriculum and Instruction

Students with hearing impairment may present a significant challenge for general education teachers. Language is such an important component of instruction that students who have problems processing language because of hearing losses make it difficult for teachers to use standard instructional methods effectively. Teachers have to rely on the supports provided by special education staff and specialists in hearing impairments to assist them in meeting the needs of these students.

REALITIES OF THE GENERAL EDUCATION CLASSROOM

Students with hearing impairments vary greatly in their need for supports in the general education classroom. Students with mild losses, generally classified as hard of hearing, need minimal supports. In fact, these students resemble their nondisabled peers in most ways. If amplification assistance can enable these students to hear clearly, they will need little specialized instruction (Dagenais, Critz-Crosby, Fletcher, & McCutcheon, 1994).

Students with severe hearing impairments, those classified as deaf, present unique challenges to teachers. Specialized instructional techniques usually involve alternative communication methods; the use of interpreters is typically a necessity for these students. (See Figure 7.1.)

CONTINUUM OF PLACEMENT OPTIONS

Students with hearing impairments are educated in the complete continuum of placement options, depending on their individual needs. These range from general education classrooms to residential schools for the deaf. "The topic of educational placement has generated more controversy in the education of children who are hard of hearing and deaf than any issue in curriculum" (Edwards, 1996, p. 403). No single educational setting is best for all students with hearing impairments. Often the choice of where the deaf student is placed is a result

CONSIDER THIS
How do educational needs differ for these two students: one with a mild hearing loss who can effectively use a hearing aid and one who is not disabled?

CROSS-REFERENCE
Review the continuum of placement options for students with all disabilities, including those with hearing impairments, listed in Chapter 1.

FIGURE 7.1
Interpreters in Educational Settings

GENERAL GUIDELINES	■ Include the interpreter as a member of the IEP team to help determine the communication needs of the student.
	■ Request an interpreter (i.e., do not let parents interpret for their children) for certain important situations (e.g., transition planning meetings).
	■ Supervise the interpreter if this person has additional classroom tasks.
	■ Meet with the interpreter regularly to discuss the needs of the student and to review ongoing communication patterns.
	■ Evaluate the effectiveness of interpreters.
SPECIFIC SUGGESTIONS	■ Allow the interpreter to be positioned so that the student can easily see both the teacher (or media) and the interpreter.
	■ Prepare the interpreter for the topic(s) that will be covered and the class format that will be followed.
	■ Provide copies of all visual materials (e.g., overhead transparencies) before class begins.
	■ Be sensitive to the "time-lag" factor associated with interpreting—the few-word delay that the interpreter lags behind the spoken message.
	■ Program breaks in lecturing if at all possible.
	■ Limit movement so that the student can see the interpreter and teacher without difficulty.
	■ Check student understanding regularly—ensure that the student does not fake understanding.

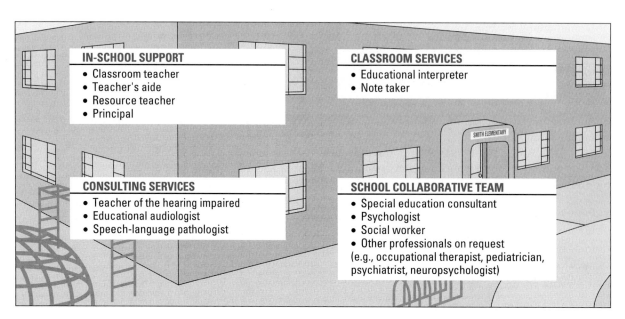

FIGURE 7.2

Types of Supports for Students with Hearing Impairments in Inclusive Settings

From "Educational Management of Children with Hearing Loss," by C. Edwards. In *Hearing Care for Childen*, edited by F. N. Martin and J. G. Clark, 1996, p. 306. Boston: Allyn & Bacon. Used by permission.

CONSIDER THIS

What are some obvious advantages and disadvantages to the different placement options for students with hearing impairments?

of the parents' feelings rather than educational reasons. One view holds that deaf students should be integrated in the hearing school and learn oral language; the other view states that deaf students should be placed in a school for the deaf and learn sign language to maximize their development. Still, the trend continues toward educating more students with hearing impairments in the general education classroom. Figure 7.2 describes the types of supports that students with hearing impairments will need in inclusive settings. They resemble those needed by students with other disabilities, except for a few services specific to students with hearing problems.

CLASSROOM ACCOMMODATIONS FOR STUDENTS WITH HEARING IMPAIRMENTS

FURTHER READING

For further information on the development of education for the deaf, read *Deaf Heritage in Canada: A Distinctive, Diverse and Enduring Culture* by Clifton F. Carbin, published in 1995 by McGraw-Hill Ryerson in Whitby, Ontario.

As mentioned before, the general education setting is appropriate for most students who are hard of hearing and for many students who are deaf. However, this statement is true only if the specific needs of these students are taken into consideration.

The following sections provide recommendations for accommodating these students in general education classrooms. Specific suggestions are also given. Both general recommendations and specific suggestions are clustered under three major areas: management considerations, curricular and instructional accommodations, and social-emotional interventions.

Management Considerations

The effective management of a classroom is critical to maximizing the potential for learning. Attention to classroom management can help include students with various degrees of hearing impairment in general education settings.

STANDARD OPERATING PROCEDURES

This dimension refers to the rules, regulations, and procedures that operate in a classroom. Students who have hearing impairments must be subject to the same requirements as other students. Some procedures may have to be modified to accommodate special needs. For instance, students may be allowed to leave their seats to get the attention of a student who cannot hear a spoken communication.

Teachers should always confirm that students understand the rules and procedures developed for the classroom. Teachers may also want to establish a buddy system (i.e., a peer support system). With such a system, a student with normal hearing is assigned to assist the student with a hearing impairment in, for example, following procedures for a fire drill or helping the student take notes during a class lecture.

CROSS-REFERENCE
Review Chapter 5 for information on rules and procedures appropriate for *all* students with disabilities—and even students without disabilities.

PHYSICAL CONSIDERATIONS

Seating is the major consideration related to the physical setup of the classroom. Teachers need to ensure that students are seated to maximize the use of their residual hearing or to have an unobstructed view of an interpreter. Since information presented visually is extremely helpful to these students, they need to be positioned to take advantage of all visual cues (Berry, 1995). Below are some specific suggestions:

- Seat students near the teacher or source of orally presented information.
- Seat students so they can take advantage of their residual hearing, avoid being distracted either visually or auditorily, and follow different speakers during class discussions.
- Seat students who use interpreters so that they can easily see the interpreter, the teacher, and any visual aids that are used.

FURTHER READING
For additional information on maximizing the auditory environment of classrooms, read "Communication Strategies for Fully Inclusive Classrooms," by V. S. Berry in B. Rittenhouse and J. Dancer's *The Full Inclusion of Persons with Disabilities in American Society,* published in 1995 by Levin Publishing Co.

Students with hearing impairments should be seated near the front of the class.

PERSONAL SPOTLIGHT

Mother of a Child with a Hearing Impairment ■ GAEL COLE

Gael Cole is the mother of three children ages 13, 10, and 7. She works part-time as a book-keeper, chairs an organization called VOICE for hearing impaired children, and serves as a stay-at-home mother. Her oldest child, Brianne, was born with a cleft lip and palate and then diagnosed as being deaf after a severe bout of meningitis at age two. "I will find a way for her to hear again" was Gael's immediate response. After a year of various obstacles Brianne received a cochlear implant. The implant is an electronic hearing aid which allows Brianne to hear by stimulating the hearing nerve with electrodes surgically implanted and triggered by an external processor.

Ten years later Brianne is in Grade 8, mainstreamed in the regular public school system. Although she is very comfortable and functions independently now, it was not always an easy road. Brianne experienced numerous frustrations and much teasing by some children. Also, learning to listen and to speak with the implant required many hours of practice. Little by little, though, Brianne began to blossom. She had a one-on-one teacher's aide until Grade 2, although she was integrated in the regular class. The full-time teacher's aide was a critical factor in her success.

Those initial years were the most difficult due to her lack of communication. However, most of her teachers were very supportive and an itinerant monitored her progress within the school system. Gael also played a very active role by coming into the school, working with the itinerant, teacher's aide, and teacher on a regular basis. There was also lots of work with Brianne at home. As Brianne's speech and listening became more sophisticated, she developed a strong sense of independence, self-confidence, and some social life. Each year was better than the last. Academically, she excelled. Now, she is a happy well-adjusted teenager who loves the implant. She has a good circle of friends and a bright future.

"I have always been sure of our decision to mainstream Brianne," says Gael, "but the crème de la crème for me was when she was in Grade 5 and Brianne won not only the school finals but the division finals and runner-up in the regional finals for public speaking amongst her hearing peers. There were times in those early years when none of us could imagine that day happening! But we all worked so hard to get there, as parents, teachers, aides, itinerants, and, most of all, Brianne herself. It is *not* easy, but it can be done."

PREINSTRUCTIONAL CONSIDERATIONS

Teachers must also carefully plan ahead to deliver instruction in a way that will benefit students with hearing impairments. The following list gives many practical suggestions:

- Allow students to move about the classroom to position themselves for participation in ongoing events.
- Let students use swivel chairs.
- Reduce distracting and competing noise by modifying the classroom environment (e.g., carpeting on floor, corkboard on walls).
- Ensure that lighting is adequate.
- Provide visual reminders indicating the amount of time left for an activity or until the end of class.
- Use cooperative learning arrangements to facilitate student involvement with hearing peers.
- Include a section of the lesson plan for special provisions for students with hearing impairments.

- Acquire or develop visually oriented materials to augment orally presented topics—use overhead projection systems when appropriate.
- Use homework assignment books, and make sure that students understand their assignments.

Specific suggestions related to grouping, lesson planning, materials acquisition and adaptation, and homework systems can be found in Chapter 12.

Curricular and Instructional Considerations

All basic elements of effective instructional practice will benefit students with hearing impairment. However, certain specific ideas will enhance their learning experiences.

COMMUNICATION

Perhaps the most challenging aspect of teaching students whose hearing is impaired is making sure that (1) they participate in the communicational activities (i.e., teacher to student, student to teacher, student to student) that are occurring in the classroom and (2) they are able to handle the reading and writing demands of the class.

Students who have profound hearing loss must rely on alternative methods of communication such as sign language or speech reading. Because these students typically do not become facile with standard forms of English, they can have significant problems in the areas of reading and writing. Sign language does not follow the grammatical conventions of English.

When students using some form of manual communication, usually **American Sign Language (ASL)**, are in general education classrooms, teachers are not required to learn this language. However, teachers should make an effort to know some of the more common signs and to be able to finger-spell the letters of the alphabet as well as the numbers 1 to 10.

If students can communicate only by using sign language, an interpreter will most likely need to be present. Teachers should know basic information about the role and functions of an interpreter.

Teachers should be conscious of how well they are communicating with their students. The teacher's speech, location, and movement in the classroom can affect the facility with which a student with a hearing impairment can follow a discussion or lecture. The proper use of assistive equipment (e.g., amplification devices) can also make a difference. This topic is covered in a subsequent section.

FURTHER READING

For more information on sign language and different forms of sign language, read *Educating the Deaf: Psychology, Principles, and Practices,* by D. Moore, published in 1995 by Houghton-Mifflin.

DELIVERY OF INSTRUCTION

Teachers need to utilize a host of practices that allow students to learn more effectively and efficiently. One suggestion already mentioned, the use of visually oriented material, is especially valuable for students with hearing problems. The following are additional suggestions:

- Make sure students are attending.
- Provide short, clear instructions.
- Speak clearly and normally—do not exaggerate the pronunciation of words.
- Keep your face visible to students.
- Avoid frequent movement around the classroom, turning your back on students while talking, and standing in front of a bright light source.

- Use gestures and facial expressions.
- If the student reads speech and you have a mustache and beard, make sure that your facial hair is trimmed to maximize visibility.
- Maintain eye contact with the student, not the interpreter.
- Check with students to confirm that they are understanding what is being discussed or presented.
- Encourage students to request clarification and to ask questions.
- Identify other speakers by name so that students can more easily follow a discussion among more than one speaker.
- Repeat the comments of other students who speak.
- Paraphrase or summarize discussions at the end of a class session.
- Write information when necessary.
- Have students take responsibility for making themselves understood.
- Provide students with advance organizers such as outlines of lectures and copies of overhead transparencies.
- Preview new vocabulary and concepts prior to their presentation during a lecture.
- Use the demonstration-guided practice–independent practice paradigm as often as possible (see Polloway & Patton, 1993, for a comprehensive discussion of this paradigm).
- Utilize a variety of instructional formats, including demonstrations, experiments, and other visually oriented activities.
- Emphasize the main points covered in a lecture both verbally and visually.
- Use lots of visual aids (e.g., overhead transparencies, slides, diagrams, charts, multimedia) to explain material.
- Provide summaries, outlines, or scripts of videotapes, videodiscs, or films.
- Let students use microcomputers for word processing and for checking their spelling and grammar.

Teaching secondary-level content classes to students with hearing impairments is uniquely challenging. The nearby Inclusion Strategies feature provides suggestions for teaching science to students who are hearing impaired.

Social-Emotional Considerations

Classrooms constitute complex social systems. In addition to development of scholastic abilities and academic support skills, personal development is also occurring. Students need to learn how to get along with their peers and authority figures while they learn how to deal with their beliefs and emotions. Teachers should help students develop a realistic sense of their abilities (i.e., strengths and weaknesses), become more responsible and independent, interact appropriately with their peers, and enhance their self-concept and sense of belonging (Luckner, 1994). The following are some specific suggestions:

- Create a positive, supportive, and nurturing classroom environment.
- Encourage class involvement through active participation in classroom activities and interaction in small groups.
- Let students know that you are available if they are experiencing problems and need to talk.
- Help the students with normal hearing understand the nature of hearing impairment and the ways in which they can assist.
- Practise appropriate interactive skills.

FURTHER READING
For additional material on teaching science to students with hearing impairments, see the article, "Teaching Science to Deaf Students," written by F. R. Mangrubang and published in 1993 in *The Good Newsletter,* by R. DeBuck, in Boulder, Colorado.

INCLUSION STRATEGIES

Teaching Science to Students Who Are Hearing Impaired

The following are several suggestions on how to give better individual attention in teaching science to students who are hearing impaired:

1. Individualize assignments so that students progress at their own rate and at the end of the period hand in what they have accomplished. This may be a laboratory or written assignment.

2. Extend special recognition to a student who goes beyond minimum acceptance level for doing and formulating laboratory investigation.

3. Use multiple resources, including texts in class. If a student has difficulty reading one text, endeavour to find another or attempt to help him or her learn the material in ways other than through books.

4. Offer special activities for the academically talented. Let them assist you in preparing solutions and materials for laboratory work.

They should gain experiences that are educationally desirable.

5. Encourage students to do research. They should consult with a scientist or engineer in the community on their research problem. Local industries, museums, zoos, botanical gardens, and hospitals have resource people who will often help.

6. Have students from the upper grades go to some of the lower grades and demonstrate a scientific principle or explain a science project. This approach has the advantage of giving recognition to the younger students and motivating them to greater achievement.

7. Encourage parents to obtain books and to take trips advantageous to science students. Parents often welcome a suggestion from the teacher about books and type of trips to help enrich their children's science education.

- Encourage and assist students to get involved in extracurricular activities.
- Help them develop problem-solving abilities.
- Help students develop realistic expectations.
- Prepare students for dealing with the demands of life and adulthood.

Technology

Students with hearing impairments placed in general education classrooms often use devices to help them to maximize their communicational abilities (Pratt, Heintzelman, & Deming, 1993). Teachers need a working knowledge of these devices so that they can ensure that the student benefits from the equipment.

ASSISTIVE LISTENING DEVICES

Assistive listening devices (ALDs) include hearing aids and other devices that "amplify voices and sounds, communicate messages visually, or alert users to environmental sounds" (Bloom, 1996). Hearing aids, which are battery-powered electronic devices, are the predominant ALDs found in schools. These devices pick up sound with a microphone, amplify and filter it, and then convey that sound into the ear canal through a loudspeaker, also called a receiver (Shimon, 1992, p. 96). The nearby Technology Today feature describes hearing aids and other ALDs that can be used in school programs.

TEACHING TIP
When students in your classroom use assistive listening devices, learn as much about the devices as possible so that you will be able to maximize their use.

ALDs at a Glance

Assistive devices, whether used as stand-alone systems or in conjunction with hearing aids, amplify voices and sounds, communicate messages visually, or alert users to environmental sounds. Subcategories within the major classifications address a variety of hearing needs in different situations.

The ability of a device to perform in a specific setting can be determined by studying the specifications of the individual product in conjunction with a patient's case history.

In general, dispensers interested in expanding their scope of practice to include assistive technology, or those who want to broaden their involvement in this area, can use the following overview as a guide to the kinds of technology available in the field:

AMPLIFICATION

In some settings, hearing aids alone are less effective than ALDs in discerning voices in the presence of background noise or picking up speech clearly from a distance. Large-area amplification systems as well as portable personal devices improve the signal-to-noise ratio at the listener's ear, making it easier for users to hear and understand speech, whether watching television at home or listening to a lecture in a public auditorium.

Amplification devices can be further divided into hard-wired or wireless systems.

- In hard-wire devices, the user is connected to the sound source by a wire and, consequently, limited in movement by the length of the cord connected to an earphone headset, hearing aid, or neck loop. Hard-wired systems are more appropriate for television watching and small-group business or social settings than for listening in large public areas.

- Wireless systems, in which sound is transmitted from the source to the listener's ear by means of electromagnetic energy, invisible light waves, or on radio bands, are more practical in large public areas, like theaters and lecture halls. Typically, users access the system from a telecoil circuit built into their hearing aids or from a receiver attached to a headset.

  1. An induction loop wireless system transmits sound in the form of electromagnetic energy. A loop of wire that encircles a room receives the signal from an amplifier

▼

To assist students in maximizing the use of their ALDs, teachers should

- know what type of ALD a student uses;
- understand how the device works: on/off switch, battery function (e.g., selection, lifespan, insertion), volume controls;
- be able to determine whether a hearing aid is working properly;
- help students keep their hearing aids functioning properly (e.g., daily cleaning, appropriate storage);
- make sure students avoid getting their aids wet, dropping or jarring them, spraying hairspray on them, and exposing them to extreme heat (Shimon, 1992);
- keep spare batteries on hand;
- ensure that the system is functioning properly;
- be sure that students turn the transmitter off when not engaged in instructional activities;
- perform daily troubleshooting of all components of the system (Brackett, 1990);
- make sure background noises are minimized.

connected to a lecturer's microphone or, in small settings, to a tape recorder or television.

2. An infrared wireless system transmits sound via light waves. A photo detector diode picks up infrared light and changes the information into sound, which users hear with a hearing aid, telecoil feature, or earphones.

3. In an FM wireless system, sound is transmitted and received via radio waves.

COMMUNICATIONS

Assistive technology facilitates communication by telephone for deaf and hard-of-hearing people. Cost and the degree of hearing loss determine appropriateness of products, which are available in a number of forms. Consult manufacturers for advantages and limitations of individual products.

- *Amplified replacement handsets* are available for most telephone models, for use at home and at work.

- *In-line telephone amplifiers* splice an existing handset and telephone base to a device that amplifies a voice. Portable, strap-on amplifiers can be attached directly to the handset.

- *TDD (telecommunications devices for the deaf),* also known as *TTs (text telephones),* supply a visual medium for communication. A TDD user types a message that is trans-

lated into electrical pulses and sent over a telephone line to the receiving TDD or to an intercept operator. Some TDDs can be used in conjunction with personal computers.

- *Decoders* provide closed captioning subtitles for television and VCR viewing.

ALERTING

Alerting devices signal users to sound by means of visual, auditory, or vibrotactile stimuli. In general, alerting devices detect sound (e.g., a telephone, doorbell, or smoke alarm) and either amplify the sound or convert it to another signal, such as a flashing light, to make the person aware of the sound.

- *Visual* alerting devices connected to lamps flash different patterns to differentiate among sounds. One pattern can be programmed to signal that the telephone is ringing, while another indicates the doorbell.

- *Auditory* alerting devices amplify the sound or convert it to a lower pitch, which is more easily audible than high-frequency sound.

- *Vibrotactile* devices respond to sound with a gentle shaking motion. The ringing of an alarm clock or smoke detector, for instance, makes the mattress vibrate. Body-worn vibrotactile devices are available also.

From "ALDs at a Glance," 1996, *The Hearing Journal, 49*, p. 21. Used by permission.

This information should provide teachers with a beginning understanding of how to meet the needs of students with hearing loss. We strongly recommend that teachers consult with a hearing specialist to determine the best possible accommodations to provide an appropriate educational environment for students with hearing problems.

ENHANCING INCLUSIVE CLASSROOMS FOR STUDENTS WITH HEARING IMPAIRMENTS

Promoting a Sense of Community and Social Acceptance

Being an integral part of the inclusive school community is important for students with hearing impairments who receive their educational programs in

CROSS-REFERENCE
Review Chapter 2 for additional considerations to help teachers enhance the student's acceptance in the general education setting.

CONSIDER THIS
Do you think that students with hearing impairments can be included and accepted in the classroom by their peers in spite of their lack of language skills? Should students with hearing impairments be isolated in institutions with other students who have hearing losses? Why or why not?

public schools, especially for those placed in general education classrooms. Physically situating students in classrooms does not automatically result in their being included members of the class. Therefore, teachers must ensure that these students become part of the community of the school and class and are socially accepted by their peers.

Teachers may have to orchestrate opportunities for interaction between students with hearing impairments and their nondisabled peers. Making opportunities could include grouping, pairing students for specific tasks, assigning buddies, and establishing a circle of friends. Kluwin (1996) suggests using dialogue journals to facilitate this interaction. Students are paired (one hearing and one nonhearing) to make journal entries and then exchange them. Rather than assign deadlines, allow students to exchange journal entries whenever they want to. You may need to give them ideas appropriate for sharing, to get them started. Reinforce students for making and exchanging journal entries. This approach encourages interactions between students with hearing impairments and their nondisabled peers without using a rigidly structured activity or assignment.

Supports for the General Education Teacher

Students with hearing impairments often create major challenges for general classroom teachers, primarily because of the language barrier that hearing loss often creates. Therefore, teachers must rely on support personnel such as educational consultants who specialize in the area of hearing impairment, interpreters, audiologists, and medical personnel to assist them in their efforts to provide appropriate educational programs.

VISUAL IMPAIRMENTS

TEACHING TIP
Try using an idea from a children's game to work with children with visual impairments. Just as you would ask a blindfolded child what information he or she needs to make progress in the game, ask the children what assistance or information they need in order to benefit from your teaching.

Students with visual impairments also pose unique challenges to teachers in general education classrooms. Although the number of students whose vision creates learning-related problems is not large, having one such student in a classroom may require a host of accommodations.

Vision plays a critical role in the development of concepts, the understanding of spatial relations, and the use of printed material. Thus children with visual problems have unique educational needs. "Learning the necessary compensatory skills and adaptive techniques—such as using braille or *optical devices* for written communication—requires specialized instruction from teachers and parents who have expertise in addressing disability-specific needs" (Corn et al., 1995, p. 1). Teachers may be able to use their usual instructional techniques with some modifications with students who have some functional vision. But for students who have very little or no vision, teachers will need to implement alternative techniques to provide effective educational programs.

General education classes are appropriate settings for many students with visual impairments. However, teachers working with these students need to understand the nature of a particular student's vision problem to be able to choose appropriate accommodative tactics. They need basic information related to four categories: (1) fundamental concepts of vision and visual impairment, (2) signs of possible visual problems, (3) typical characteristics of students with visual problems, and (4) specific accommodative techniques for meeting student needs.

Basic Concepts

This section will define the terminology used to describe vision and visual problems, identify different types of vision problems, discuss how vision is assessed, and highlight the major educationally relevant characteristics associated with vision problems.

DEFINITION

Because a number of different terms are associated with this concept, confusion regarding the exact meaning of visual terminology is often a problem. These are the most frequently used terms and their definitions:

- *Visual impairment* is a generic term that includes a wide range of visual problems.
- *Blindness* has different meanings depending upon context, resulting in some confusion. *Legal blindness* refers to a person's visual acuity and field of vision. It is defined as a visual acuity of 20/200 or less in the person's better eye after correction, or a field of vision of 20° or less. An educational definition of *blindness* implies that a student must use Braille (a system of raised dots that the student reads tactilely) or aural methods in order to receive instruction (Hallahan & Kauffman, 1994).
- *Low vision* indicates that some functional vision exists to be used for gaining information through written means with or without the assistance of optical, nonoptical, or electronic devices.

Students with **low vision** are capable of handling the demands of most classroom settings. However, they will need some modifications to perform successfully. Students who are blind (i.e., have very little or no vision) will need major accommodations to be successful in general education settings.

CLASSIFICATION

Visual problems can be categorized in a number of ways. One typical method organizes visual problems as refractive errors (e.g., farsightedness, nearsightedness, and astigmatism); retinal disorders; disorders of the cornea, iris, and lens; and optic nerve problems. In addition to common refractive problems, which usually can be improved with corrective lenses, other visual problems include the following:

- *Strabismus*—improper alignment of the eyes
- *Nystagmus*—rapid involuntary movements of the eye
- *Glaucoma*—fluid pressure buildup in the eye
- *Cataract*—cloudy film over the lens of the eye
- *Diabetic retinopathy*—changes in the blood vessels of the eye caused by diabetes
- *Macular degeneration*—damage to the central portion of the retina, causing central vision loss
- *Retinitis pigmentosa*—genetic eye disease leading to total blindness (Smith & Luckasson, 1995)

CONSIDER THIS
Some students who are classified as blind are actually able to read print and do not need to use Braille. Are there descriptors other than *blind* and *low vision* that would better describe students with visual impairments for educational purposes?

Tunnel vision denotes a condition caused by deterioration of parts of the retina, which leaves the person with central vision only. Individuals who have tunnel vision can see as if they are looking through a long tube; they have little or no peripheral vision.

Regardless of the cause of the visual problem, educators primarily have to deal with its functional result. Whether or not the student has usable residual vision is an important issue, as is the time at which the vision problem developed. Students who are born with significant visual loss have a much more difficult time understanding some concepts and developing basic skills than students who lose their vision after they have established certain concepts (Warren, 1994).

PREVALENCE AND CAUSES

Vision problems are common in our society. Fortunately, corrective lenses allow most individuals to see very efficiently. However, many individuals have vision problems that cannot be corrected in this way. Like persons with hearing impairments, the number of individuals who have visual impairments increases with age as a result of the aging process. In the school-age population, approximately 0.06 percent of students are classified as visually impaired. However, according to the Canadian National Institute for the Blind (1999), the prevalence rates vary by region. The Institute notes that First Nations peoples are at increased risk of visual impairments both in youth and with age due to premature birth, trauma, and diabetes. Dr. Farrell, a member of the board of directors of CNIB, states, "The risk of vision loss is three to four times greater in First Nations Peoples than it is in the general population."

Etiological factors associated with visual impairments include genetic causes, physical trauma, infections, premature birth, anoxia, and retinal degeneration. *Retrolental fibroplasia (RLF)* was a common cause of blindness in the early 1950s, when premature infants were exposed to too much oxygen in incubators. Once the cause of this problem was understood, it became nearly nonexistent. However, it is reasserting itself as medical science faces the challenge of providing care to infants born more and more prematurely. Blindness sometimes accompanies very early premature birth.

CHARACTERISTICS

FURTHER READING
For additional information about characteristics of individuals with visual impairments, read *Visual Handicaps and Learning,* third edition, by N. C. Barraga and J. N. Erin, published in 1992 by Pro-Ed.

The most educationally relevant characteristic of students who have visual impairments is the extent of their visual efficiency. More specific characteristics can be categorized as psychological, communicational, academic, and social-emotional. These areas are listed in Table 7.3.

IDENTIFICATION, ASSESSMENT, AND ELIGIBILITY

Students with visual impairments can be easily identified if their visual loss is severe. However, many students have milder losses that are much more difficult to identify and may go several years without being recognized. Teachers must be aware of behaviours that could indicate a vision problem. Figure 7.3 summarizes possible symptoms of vision problems.

Formal Assessment   Students are screened for vision problems in schools, and when problems are suspected, a more in-depth evaluation is conducted. The typical eye examination assesses two dimensions: visual acuity and field of vision. Visual acuity is most often evaluated by the use of a **Snellen chart**.

TABLE 7.3

Possible Characteristics of Students with Visual Impairments

Area of Functioning	Possible Effects
PSYCHOLOGICAL	• Intellectual abilities similar to those of sighted peers • Concept development can depend on tactile experiences (i.e., synthetic and analytic touch) • Unable to use sight to assist in the development of integrated concepts • Unable to use visual imagery
COMMUNICATIONAL SOCIAL-EMOTIONAL/ BEHAVIOURAL	• Relatively unimpaired in language abilities • May display repetitive, stereotyped movements (e.g., rocking or rubbing eyes) • Socially immature • Withdrawn • Dependent • Unable to use nonverbal cues
MOBILITY	• Distinct disadvantage in using spatial information • Visual imagery and memory problems with functional implications
ACADEMIC	• Generally behind sighted peers

As Smith and Luckasson (1995) note, two versions of this chart are available: the traditional version using alphabetic letters of different sizes, and the other version using the letter *E* presented in different spatial arrangements and sizes. Regardless of the assessment used, the person conducting it should have expertise in the area of visual impairment (Corn et al., 1995).

Once students are identified as having possible vision problems, they should be referred for more extensive evaluations. **Ophthalmologists**, medical doctors, and **optometrists** (who specialize in evaluating vision and prescribing glasses) are typically involved in this more extensive evaluation. These specialists determine the specific nature and extent of any vision problem.

TEACHING TIP
For students who are not doing well in their academic work and who display some of these symptoms, conduct a functional visual screening to determine if the child should be referred for more formal screening.

BEHAVIOR	■ Rubs eyes excessively ■ Shuts or covers one eye, tilts head, or thrusts head forward ■ Has difficulty in reading or in other work requiring close use of the eyes ■ Blinks more than usual or is irritable when doing close work ■ Holds books close to eyes ■ Is unable to see distant things clearly ■ Squints eyelids together or frowns
APPEARANCE	■ Crossed eyes ■ Red-rimmed, encrusted, or swollen eyelids ■ Inflamed or watery eyes ■ Recurring styes
COMPLAINTS	■ Eyes that itch, burn, or feel scratchy ■ Cannot see well ■ Dizziness, headaches, or nausea following close eye work ■ Blurred or double vision

FIGURE 7.3
Symptoms of Possible Vision Problems

From *Exceptional Learners: Introduction to Special Education* (7th ed.) (p. 358), by D. P. Hallahan and J. M. Kauffman, 1997, Boston: Allyn & Bacon. Used by permission.

Informal Assessment   A great deal of informal assessment should be completed by school personnel. Like that of students with hearing impairments, the informal assessment of students with visual impairments focuses on observation. Teachers and other school personnel note behaviours that might indicate a vision loss or change in the vision of the child. Once students are identified as having a problem, school personnel must be alert to any changes in the student's visual abilities.

Eligibility   In Canada, students with a 20/200 acuity or worse in the better eye with best correction are identified as blind, whereas those with a visual acuity of 20/70 to 20/200 are considered as having low vision.

STRATEGIES FOR CURRICULUM AND INSTRUCTION

Students with visual impairments need specific curricular and instructional modifications. For students with low vision, these modifications may simply mean enlarging printed materials to sufficient size so that the student can see them. For students with little or no vision, modifications must be more extensive.

Realities of the General Education Classroom

Students with visual impairments present a range of needs. Those who are capable of reading print, with modifications, often require minimal curricular changes; those who must read using Braille require significant changes. Teachers should remember that even students who are capable of reading print may need modifications in many day-to-day activities. These may be as simple as ensuring appropriate contrast in printed materials and having students sit in a place that will optimize their vision.

Continuum of Placement Options

Like students with hearing impairments, students with visual problems may be placed anywhere on the full continuum of placement options, ranging from general education classrooms to residential schools for students with visual impairments. Students must be evaluated individually to determine the appropriate educational placement. Although some blind students function very well in general education settings, many are placed in residential schools where they receive more extensive services.

CLASSROOM ACCOMMODATIONS FOR STUDENTS WITH VISUAL IMPAIRMENTS

Certain classroom accommodations will enhance the quality of programs for students with visual problems. This section recommends ways to address the needs of these students, organized according to four categories: general considerations, management considerations, curricular and instructional accommodations, and social-emotional interventions.

General Considerations

When educating students with visual impairments, the unique needs of each student must be considered. However, some general practices apply for most, if not all, students with these problems. These practices include the following:

- Ask the student if assistance is needed.
- Do not assume that certain tasks and activities cannot be accomplished without accommodations or modifications.
- Include students with visual impairments in all activities that occur in the class.
- Use seating arrangements to take advantage of any vision the child can use.
- Encourage the use of residual vision.
- Remember that many characteristics of students with visual impairment (e.g., intelligence, health) may not be negatively affected by the vision problem.

Management Considerations

A variety of classroom management tactics can be helpful to students who have vision problems. Classroom management is discussed in detail in Chapter 5. When students with vision problems are present, attention needs to be given to standard operating procedures, physical considerations, and preinstructional considerations.

STANDARD OPERATING PROCEDURES

The same standards of expected behaviour should be applied to all students, including those who have visual problems. However, students with visual limitations may need special freedom to move around the classroom, to find the place where they can best see demonstrations or participate in activities.

PHYSICAL CONSIDERATIONS

Students with visual problems need to know the physical layout of the classroom so that they can navigate through it without harming themselves. Meeting this need requires orienting them to the classroom. This can be accomplished by taking students around the classroom and noting certain features, such as the location of desks, tables, and materials. Use a clock orientation approach, such as the front of the class is 12 o'clock, at 3 o'clock is the teacher's desk, at 6 o'clock is the reading table, and at 9 o'clock is the area for students' coats and backpacks. Appropriate seating is extremely important for students who are able to use their existing vision. Placement of the student's desk, lighting, glare, and distractions should be considered when situating such students in the classroom. Guarantee that the classroom is free of hazards (e.g., low-hanging mobiles or plants) that could injure students who have a visual impairment. Label storage areas and other parts of the classroom for students with visual impairment by using raised lettering or Braille.

Some students with disabilities require the use of *specialized equipment,* such as wheelchairs, hearing aids, and other types of amplification systems, communication devices, adaptive desks and trays, prone standers (i.e., stand-up desks), and medical equipment. Teachers need to understand how the equipment works, how it should be used, and what adaptations will need to be made to the classroom environment to accommodate the student using it. The other students in the classroom should be introduced to the special equipment as well. Instructional lessons on specific pieces of equipment will not only be helpful in creating an inclusive environment, but may also provide a basis for science and health curricular tie-ins. Suggestions include the following:

- Identify what special equipment will be needed in the classroom well ahead of the arrival of the student who needs it.
- Learn how special equipment and devices work and how they can be repaired—this task usually can be accomplished by talking with parents.
- Learn how to identify problems or malfunctions in medical equipment.
- Find out how long students need to use time-specified equipment or devices.
- Let students who are hearing impaired sit on swivel chairs with casters so they can move about to follow a discussion involving many participants. (Salend, 1994)

PREINSTRUCTIONAL CONSIDERATIONS

Teachers should plan ahead to adapt instruction to the needs of students with visual impairments. Class schedules must allow extra time for students who use large-print or Braille materials, as it takes longer to use these materials.

Test-taking procedures may need to be modified, for example, by preparing an enlarged version of the test, allowing extra time, or arranging for someone to read the test to the student.

Some students may need special instruction in study skills such as note taking, organizational skills, time management, and keyboarding. These become increasingly important as students move to middle school and high school.

The following are some specific accommodation suggestions:

- Assign a classmate to assist students who may need help with mobility in emergency situations.
- Teach all students in the class the proper techniques of being a sighted guide.
- In advance, inform staff members at field-trip sites that a student with a visual problem will be part of the visiting group.
- Tell students with visual problems that you are entering or leaving a room so that they are aware of your presence or absence.
- Have all students practise movement patterns that you expect of them, to maintain an orderly classroom.
- Orient students to the physical layout and other distinguishing features of the classroom.
- Maintain consistency in the placement of furniture, equipment, and instructional materials—remove all dangerous obstacles.
- Keep doors to cabinets, carts, and closets closed.
- Assist students in getting into unfamiliar desks, chairs, or other furniture.
- Eliminate auditory distractions.

TEACHING TIP

Have vision specialists, such as an orientation and mobility specialist, come into your class and demonstrate sighted guide techniques and other strategies that provide supports for students with visual impairments.

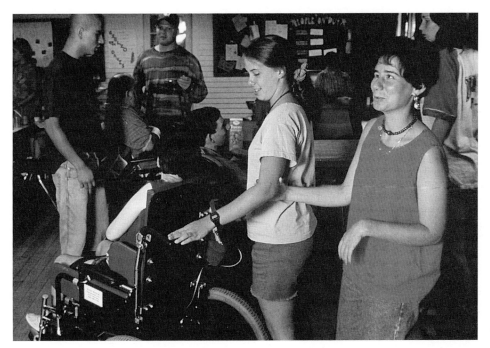

Classmates can assist students with visual problems in areas such as mobility.

- Seat students to maximize their usable vision and listening skills—often a position in the front and centre part of the room is advantageous.
- Seat students so that they are not looking into a source of light or bothered by glare from reflected surfaces.
- Ensure that proper lighting is available.
- Create extra space for students who must use and store a piece of equipment (e.g., brailler, notebook computer).
- As a special section of the lesson plan, include notes for accommodating students with visual problems.

Curricular and Instructional Considerations

TEACHER-RELATED ACTIVITIES

As the principal agents in delivering instruction, teachers should use techniques that will ensure success for students who have visual problems. A special challenge involves conveying primarily visual material to those who cannot see well. For example, it will require some creativity on the part of the teacher to make a graphic depiction of the circulatory system in a life science book (a two-dimensional illustration) accessible to a student who can see little or not at all. Three-dimensional models or illustrations with raised features might address this need.

MATERIALS AND EQUIPMENT

Special materials and equipment can enhance the education of students who have visual impairments. Some materials (e.g., large-print materials) are not appropriate for all and must be considered in light of individual needs. Vision specialists can help teachers select appropriate materials and equipment.

TEACHING TIP

Make sure that students with visual impairments have ample storage area near their desks for materials such as large-print or Braille books and other equipment.

Many materials found in general education classrooms may pose problems for students who have problems with their vision. For instance, low-contrast materials (in which information does not stand out well on a page) and books that are printed on glossy paper can be difficult for some students to use. The *size* and *contrast* of print materials have a real effect on students with visual problems. Print size can generally be taken care of with magnification devices; however, little can be done to enhance the poor contrast often found on ditto worksheets and photocopies. Consider these points when using dittos and photocopies:

■ Avoid using both sides of the paper (ink often bleeds through, making it difficult to see either side).
■ Avoid old or light worksheet masters.
■ Avoid worksheet masters with missing parts or creases.
■ Give the darkest copies of handouts to students with visual problems.
■ Do not give a student with a visual impairment a poor copy and say, "Do the best you can with this."
■ Copy over lines that are light with a dark marker.
■ Use photocopies rather than dittos, whenever possible.
■ Make new originals when dittos and photocopies become difficult to read.
■ Avoid the use of coloured inks that may produce limited contrast.
■ Do not use coloured paper—it limits contrast.

FURTHER READING

For additional information regarding the appropriate media for students with visual impairments, read *Learning Media Assessment*, by C. Holbrook and A. Koening, published in 1994 by the Texas School for the Blind in Austin.

Although large-print materials seem like a good idea, they may be used inappropriately. Barraga and Erin (1992) recommend that these materials be used only as a last resort, since they may not be readily available. They believe that large-print materials should be utilized only after other techniques (e.g., optical devices or reduction of the reading distance) have been tried.

Teachers also may want to use concrete materials (i.e., realia—realistic representations of actual items). However, concrete representations of large real-life objects may not be helpful for young students, who may not understand the abstract notion of one thing representing another. Teachers must carefully ensure that all instructional materials for students with visual impairments are presented in the appropriate medium for the particular student (Corn et al., 1995).

Various optical, nonoptical, and electronic devices are also available for classroom use. These devices help students by enlarging existing printed images. If these devices are recommended for certain students, teachers will need to learn about them to ensure that they are used properly and to recognize when there is a problem. Teachers should practise the use of optical and electronic devices with students after consultation with a vision specialist.

TEACHING TIP

Have a student who uses a Braille writer demonstrate the Braille code and methods of writing Braille to members of the class so they can understand the learning medium used by students with visual impairments.

Some students with more severe visual limitations may use Braille as the primary means of working with written material. They may use instructional materials that are printed in Braille and may also take notes using it. Through the use of computers, a student can write in Braille and have the text converted to standard print. The reverse process is available as well. If a student uses this system of communication, the teacher should consult with a vision specialist to understand how it works.

Below are some specific accommodation suggestions:

■ Call students by name, and speak directly to them.
■ Take breaks at regular intervals to minimize fatigue in listening or using a brailler or optic device.

- Ensure that students are seated properly so that they can see you (if they have vision) and hear you clearly.
- Vary the type of instruction used, and include lessons that incorporate hands-on activities, cooperative learning, or the use of real-life materials.
- Use high-contrast materials, whether on paper or on the chalkboard—dry-erase boards may be preferable.
- Avoid using materials with glossy surfaces and, if possible, dittoed material.
- Use large-print materials only after other methods have been attempted and proved unsuccessful.
- Use environmental connectors (e.g., ropes or railing) and other adaptations for students with visual problems for physical education or recreational activities (Barraga & Erin, 1992).
- Avoid using written materials with pages that are too crowded.

Social-Emotional Considerations

Although the literature is mixed on whether students with visual impairments are less well adjusted than their sighted peers (Hallahan & Kauffman, 1995), many students with visual problems will benefit from attention to their social and emotional development. Social skill instruction may be particularly useful. However, because social skills are typically learned through observing others and imitating their behaviours, it is difficult to teach these skills to students who are not able to see.

Concern about emotional development is warranted for all students, including those with visual problems. Teachers should make sure that students know that they are available to talk about a student's concerns. A system can be developed whereby a student who has a visual impairment can signal the need to chat with the teacher. Being accessible and letting students know that someone is concerned about their social and emotional needs are extremely important.

The following are some specific accommodation suggestions:

- Encourage students with visual problems to become independent learners and to manage their own behaviours.
- Create opportunities for students to manipulate their own environment (Mangold & Roessing, 1982).
- Reinforce students for their efforts.
- Help students develop a healthy self-concept.
- Provide special instruction to help students acquire social skills needed to perform appropriately in classroom and social situations.
- Teach students how to communicate nonverbally (e.g., use of hands, etc.).
- Work with students to eliminate inappropriate mannerisms that some students with visual impairments display.

Technology

Like students with hearing impairments, those with visual problems often use technological devices to assist them in their academic work and daily living skills. Low-vision aids include magnifiers, closed-circuit televisions, and monoculars. These devices enlarge print and other materials for individuals with visual impairments. The nearby Technology Today feature describes some basic

FURTHER READING

For more information on technological devices that are used by students with visual impairments, read *Visual Handicaps and Learning,* third edition, by N. C. Barraga and J. N. Erin, published in 1992 by Pro-Ed.

TECHNOLOGY TODAY

Using a Monocular

1. A monocular severely restricts the visual field. Students will be taught by the vision teacher to scan to pick up all visual information and increase their visual memory so they can copy more quickly and efficiently.

2. A monocular is typically used for distance tasks only.

3. Copying while using a monocular is laborious, and it will take the student with low vision longer to copy from the board or chart. You can adapt the assignment by providing a copy of the material to be copied or by modifying its length. Some ways of doing this include
   a. assigning even or odd numbers of items.
   b. allowing the student to write only the answers to questions rather than recopy entire sentences, questions, and/or paragraphs.

4. When a student is using a monocular, walking up to the board or chart should be discouraged. This annoys other students and severely hinders speed, continuity of thought, and proficiency when reading or completing an assignment.

5. Singling out the desk of a student with low vision (to place him or her closer to the board) is discouraged for social reasons. A monocular will enable the child to sit within the group at all times.

6. Monoculars break easily and should be worn around the neck when in use and stored in a case at other times. Encourage students to keep their monoculars out of sight when the room is empty.

7. Encourage the student to take the monocular to other school events, such as assemblies, film presentations, and so on.

8. Do not allow other students to handle the monocular.

9. Do not allow the monocular to be taken home with younger students unless arrangements have been made with the itinerant vision teacher.

10. A student who is using the monocular should be seated facing the board or chart to allow straight-on viewing. This arrangement also enables the student to rest the elbow on the desk while looking through the monocular.

considerations for educators when working with a child using a *monocular,* a small telescope that enables a student to see print, pictures, diagrams, maps, and people.

Many other technological devices are used by students with visual impairments. The following list notes some of them:

Talking calculator:	A hand-held calculator that provides voice output of information put into the calculator and the solution
Optacom:	A machine that scans printed material and transforms it into raised dot configurations that can be read with the fingertips
Speech synthesizers:	An adaptation to a computer that provides voice output of material presented on the computer
Braille embossers:	Computer printers that produce material from the computer in Braille
Software programs:	Numerous software programs for both DOS and Apple computers that produce voice output, large print, or both (Torres & Corn, 1990)

ENHANCING INCLUSIVE CLASSROOMS FOR STUDENTS WITH VISUAL IMPAIRMENTS

Promoting a Sense of Community and Social Acceptance

Students with visual impairments, like those with hearing impairments, need to be part of the school community. Many can be included without special supports. However, for others, teachers may need to consider the following:

1. Remember that the student with a visual impairment is but one of many students in the classroom with individual needs and characteristics.
2. Use words such as *see*, *look*, and *watch* naturally.
3. Introduce students with visual impairments the same way you would introduce any other student.
4. Include students with visual impairments in all classroom activities, including physical education, home economics, and so on.
5. Encourage students with visual problems to seek leadership and high-profile roles in the classroom.
6. Use the same disciplinary procedures for all students.
7. Encourage students with visual problems to move about the room just like other students.
8. Use verbal cues as often as necessary to cue the student with a visual impairment about something that is happening.
9. Provide additional space for students with visual impairments to store materials.
10. Allow students with visual impairments to learn about and discuss with other classmates special topics related to visual loss.
11. Model acceptance of visually impaired students as an example to other students.
12. Encourage students with visual impairments to use their specialized equipment, such as a braille writer.
13. Discuss special needs of the child with a visual impairment with specialists, as necessary.
14. Always tell a person with a visual impairment who you are as you approach.
15. Help students avoid inappropriate mannerisms associated with visual impairments.
16. Expect the same level of work from students with visual impairments as you do from other students.
17. Encourage students with visual impairments to be as independent as possible.
18. Treat children with visual impairments as you treat other students in the classroom (Torres & Corn, 1990).

In your efforts to promote a sense of community, consider that some students with visual impairments may have different cultural backgrounds than the majority of students in the school. School personnel must be sensitive to different cultural patterns. To communicate clearly with a family that speaks a different language, you may need to use a language interpreter. Lynch and Hansen (1992) offer guidelines to use when working with a language inter-

CONSIDER THIS
Students with visual impairments may not be able to monitor visual cues from peers regarding social behaviours. In what ways can understanding these visual cues be taught to students with visual impairments?

Suggestions for Working with Language Interpreters

- Introduce yourself and the interpreter, describe your respective roles, and clarify mutual expectations and the purpose of the encounter.

- Learn basic words and sentences in the family's language and become familiar with special terminology they may use so you can selectively attend to them during interpreter-family exchanges.

- During the interaction, address your remarks and questions directly to the family (not the interpreter); look at and listen to family members as they speak and observe their nonverbal communication.

- Avoid body language or gestures that may be offensive or misunderstood.

- Use a positive tone of voice and facial expressions that sincerely convey respect and your interest in the family, and address them in a calm, unhurried manner.

- Speak clearly and somewhat more slowly, but not more loudly.

- Limit your remarks and questions to a few sentences between translations and avoid giving too much information or long complex discussions of several topics in a single session.

- Avoid technical jargon, colloquialisms, idioms, slang, and abstractions.

- Avoid oversimplification and condensing important explanations.

- Give instructions in a clear, logical sequence; emphasize key words or points; and offer reasons for specific recommendations.

- Periodically check on the family's understanding and the accuracy of the translation by asking the family to repeat instructions or whatever has been communicated in their own words, with the interpreter facilitating. But avoid literally asking, "Do you understand?"

- When possible, reinforce verbal information with materials written in the family's language and visual aids or behavioral modeling if appropriate. Before introducing written materials, tactfully determine the client's literacy level through the interpreter.

- Be patient and prepared for the additional time that will inevitably be required for careful interpretation.

- Learn proper protocols and forms of address (including a few greetings and social phrases) in the family's primary language, the name they wish to be called, and the correct pronunciation.

From "From Culture Shock to Cultural Learning," by E. W. Lynch In *Developing Cross-Cultural Competence,* edited by W. E. Lynch and M. J. Hanson, 1992, p. 56. Baltimore, MD: Brookes. Used by permission.

preter; they are summarized in the nearby Diversity Forum feature. Being sensitive to the culture and family background of students with visual impairments will facilitate the delivery of appropriate services.

Supports for the General Education Teacher

As noted earlier, general education teachers can effectively instruct most students with visual impairments, with appropriate supports. A vision specialist may need to work with students on specific skills, such as Braille; an orientation and mobility instructor can teach students how to travel independently; an adaptive physical education instructor can help modify physical activities for the student with visual impairment. Counsellors, school health personnel, and vocational specialists may also provide support services for general education teachers. Other ways to enhance the education of students with visual impairments are, as follows:

■ Get help from others. Teach other students to assist in social as well as academic settings. Call parents and ask questions when you don't understand terminology, equipment, or reasons for prescribed practices.

■ Learn how to adapt and modify materials and instruction.

■ Learn as much as you can, and encourage the professionals you work with to do the same. Find out about training that may be available and ask to go.

■ Suggest that others, especiall students, become informed. Use your local library and bookstores to find print material that you can read and share.

SUMMARY

■ Many students with sensory deficits are educated in general education classrooms.

■ For students with sensory impairments to receive an appropriate education, various accommodations must be made.

■ Students with hearing and visual problems represent a very heterogeneous group.

■ Most students with hearing problems have some residual hearing ability.

■ The term *hearing impairment* includes individuals with deafness and those who are hard of hearing.

■ The effect of a hearing loss on a student's ability to understand speech is a primary concern of teachers.

■ An audiometric evaluation helps understand the extent of a hearing disorder.

■ Several factors should alert teachers to a possible hearing loss in a particular student.

■ Teachers in general education classrooms must implement a variety of accommodations for students with hearing impairments.

■ The seating location of a student with hearing loss is critical for effective instruction.

■ The most challenging aspect of teaching students with hearing problems is making sure that they participate in the communicational activities that occur in the classroom.

■ Specialized equipment, such as hearing aids, may be necessary to ensure the success of students with hearing losses.

■ Vision plays a critical role in the development of concepts such as understanding the spatial relations of the environment.

■ Teachers must use a variety of accommodations for students with visual disabilities.

■ Most students with visual disabilities have residual or low vision.

■ Refractive errors are the most common form of visual disability.

■ Visual problems may be congenital or occur later in life.

■ The most educationally relevant characteristic of students who have visual impairments is the extent of their visual efficiency.

■ It is critical that students with visual impairments be socially accepted in their general education classrooms.

■ Academic tests may need to be adapted when evaluating students with visual disabilities.

■ Special materials may be needed when working with students with visual problems.

■ Using large-print and nonglare materials may be sufficient accommodation for many students with visual disabilities.

■ A very small number of students require instruction in Braille.

■ Specialists to teach Braille and develop Braille materials may be needed in order to successfully place students with visual disabilities in general education classrooms.

RESOURCES

Resource Guides and Other Print Materials

Alberta Education, Special Education Branch. (1995). *Teaching Students Who Are Deaf or Hard of Hearing*. Edmonton: Author.

Alberta Education, Special Education Branch. (1996). *Teaching Students with Visual Impairments*. Edmonton: Author.

These resource guides from Alberta Education, Special Education Branch, are excellent sources of information about teaching students with visual and hearing impairments in the classroom. Teachers new to teaching such students in their classrooms will find the books invaluable. Additional teaching resources are suggested.

British Columbia Ministry of Education, Special Programs Branch. (1995). *Students with Visual Impairments: A Resource Guide to Support Classroom Teachers*. Victoria: Author.

British Columbia Ministry of Education, Special Programs Branch. (1995). *Hard of Hearing and Deaf Students: A Resource Guide to Support Classroom Teachers*. Victoria: Author.

Teachers will find these very practical teacher resource guides good for working with students with visual or hearing impairments. A number of simple tips and suggestions are included.

Quigley, Stephen, and King, Cynthia. (1989). *Reading Milestones*. Bellevue, WA: Dormac Inc.

These readers and workbooks are linguistically controlled and specifically designed for children who are hearing impaired.

Rikhe, C. H., et al. (1989). "A Classroom Environment Checklist for Students with Dual Sensory Impairments." *Teaching Exceptional Children*, 22(1), 44–46.

A good summative check of the classroom for teachers of students with dual sensory impairments, this checklist helps teachers be aware of what aspects of their classroom need to be adapted.

Metropolitan Toronto School Board. (1993). *Vision Video: Integrating the Visually Impaired Student in the 90s*. Toronto: Author.

This video demonstrates specific teaching methods and adaptations necessary for the integration of students with visual impairments (K–12) as well as current technology which can assist students with such impairments.

Associations

The following national organizations offer a variety of positions on the education of students with hearing impairments. Many have provincial/territorial offices.

The Canadian Hearing Society
271 Spadina Road, Toronto, ON M5R 2V3
Voice: (416) 964-9595
TTY: (416) 964-0023
Fax: (416) 928-2525
Web site: **www.chs.ca/**

Canadian Association of the Deaf
Suite 203, 251 Bank Street, Ottawa, ON K2P 1X3
Phone/TTY: (613) 565-2882; Fax: (613) 565-1207
E-mail: cad@cad.ca
Web site: **www.cad.ca/**

Canadian Hard of Hearing Association (CHHA)
2435 Holly Lane, Suite 205, Ottawa, ON K1V 7P2
Voice: 1 (800) 263-8068; (613) 526-1584
TTY: (613) 526-2692
Fax: (613) 526-4718
E-mail: chhanational@chha.ca
Web site: **www.cyberus.ca/~chhanational/**

Canadian Association of Educators of the Deaf and Hard of Hearing
Kiki Papaconstantinou, National Director
Mackay Center, 3500 Decarie Blvd., Montreal, PQ H4A 3J5
Phone: (514) 482-0500 ext. 278; Fax: (514) 482-4536
E-mail: kiki@mackayctr.org

CAEDHH Journal

c/o Department of Educational Psychology
6-102 Education North, University of Alberta, Edmonton, AB T6G 2G5
Web site: **www.education.ualberta.ca/educ/journals/caedhh.html**

Canadian National Institute for the Blind (CNIB)

1929 Bayview Avenue, Toronto, ON M4G 3E8
Phone: (416) 486-2500
Web site: **www.cnib.ca/**
The Institute provides a variety of resources, services, and related Web sites. Its library is a huge resource of books, magazines, newspapers, and information, all of which are available to anyone who is blind or print disabled (including individuals with learning disabilities). The Institute has a Web site specifically for children (CNIB Library: For kids) which includes a newsletter on audiocassette, summer reading clubs, creative writing and Braille accuracy competitions, pen pals, and lists of good Web sites for children who are blind, visually impaired, or print disabled. Finally, the CNIB Library: VISUNET: CANADA provides materials to individuals and school libraries through mail or over the Internet.

WEBLINKS

The Canadian Hearing Society
www.chs.ca/
An excellent Web site to first learn about individuals who are hard of hearing or deaf, this site provides information, resources, and links related to both manual/sign approaches to education, oral approaches, and deaf culture. A must visit for anyone working with students who are deaf or hard of hearing.

The Canadian Association of the Deaf
www.cad.ca/
A variety of information relevant to people interested in learning about the deaf community and deaf education appears here. There is a fair and good introduction to the area of the deaf and hard of hearing.

DeafCanadaOnline
www.deafcanada.com/
An online site maintained by individuals who are part of the deaf community in Canada, this site lists Canadian, American, and international Web sites related to education of the deaf, social and political issues, business, religion, resources, sports, recreation, social services, and interpreters. In addition, contributors provide current events and news as well as humour and resources on their own site. Content is constantly updated and expanding.

Deaf World Web
dww.deafworldweb.org/
The most comprehensive deaf-related Web site, this multiple award-winning international site lists resources and information by country and provides a link worldwide. The excellent resources include a Deaf Kids link for sites relevant to children and adolescents who are deaf.

Canadian Hard of Hearing Association (CHHA)
www.cyberus.ca/~chhanational/
Here is a good site for those who are interested in learning more about the integration of people who are hard of hearing into the mainstream. The site provides resources and links committed to the goal of integration.

Canadian Association for the Education of the Deaf and Hard of Hearing (CAEDHH)
www.education.ualberta.ca/educ/journals/caedhh.html
The CAEDHH Journal site serves teachers of students who are deaf or hard of hearing.

Canadian National Institute for the Blind
www.cnib.ca/
This excellent Web site provides a huge source of information, resources, and activities relevant to individuals with varying degrees of visual impairment.

CHAPTER EIGHT

CHAPTER OBJECTIVES

- To define and describe students with autism
- To define and describe students with traumatic brain injury
- To define and describe students with health and physical disabilities
- To describe various intervention strategies for students with autism, traumatic brain injury, health problems, and physical disabilities

Teaching Students with Autism, Traumatic Brain Injury, and Other Low-Incidence Disabilities

Our second child, Brea, was born three years ago with a muscle weakness. She had a club foot, a dislocated hip, and some joint stiffness. She has a tracheostomy due to chronic respiratory problems and is fed via a G-button because of swallowing difficulties. At night, while Brea sleeps, we put her on a CPAP (continuous positive airway pressure) machine to put positive pressure into her lungs.

Brea says a few words and seems to understand almost everything. She can sit up when put in a sitting position, plays with her toys, and loves books. She can scoot backwards on her bottom a little bit, but tires easily. . . . She is happy and cheerful when healthy and entertained. She tends to get bored and irritable in the evening and it can be frustrating finally getting her to sleep. (She is very normal that way!)

. . . For the last three years, Brea has had a nurse who arrives when I go to work and leaves when I get home. In addition to the normal household and family chores waiting for me when I get home, there are breathing treatments, lung suctioning, chest therapy, and blended food therapy. There is always physical therapy to be done, not to mention cuddling and playing with Brea as well as our five-year-old, Ross, and our dog, Willie. . . . Needless to say, our stress level is high.

It is very hard to successfully deal with the stress and heartbreak of having a child like Brea. You have to be "thick-skinned" (not my strong point) and you have to be able to "transcend" the pain. . . . Taking Brea anywhere can be very painful for me, especially when I notice people's reactions to her or watch other little girls. But not taking her places is equally painful. . . .

Ever since Brea was born, I have been hoping to write a miracle story—the kind where the child beats all the odds, surprises all the doctors, and lives a normal life. Although that miracle has not taken place, I can see other miracles at work here—the miracle of Brea who is happy and living in spite of all her hardships. The miracle that my husband and I—basically immature and unprepared for the crisis—are handling it (sometimes ineptly and other times well). And the miracle of my little boy, Ross—happy, healthy, and telling his playmate on the way home from school, "Wait till you see my sister!"

(Adapted from "The Miracles of Brea," by C. Howatt, 1993, *Exceptional Parents, 23*, 22–23.)

1. In what ways does a child like Brea have an impact on families?

2. Should schools provide programs for children like Brea?

INTRODUCTION

The previous chapter dealt with students with sensory impairments, typically considered low-incidence disabilities because they do not occur in many children. In addition to these two categories of disabilities, many other conditions that occur relatively rarely in children can result in significant challenges for these students, their families, school personnel, and other professionals. These conditions include autism, traumatic brain injury (TBI), and a host of physical and health problems that may be present in school-age children, such as cerebral palsy, spina bifida, AIDS, cystic fibrosis, and diabetes.

Many general education classroom teachers will teach their entire careers without encountering children with these problems. However, because children with these kinds of conditions might be included in their future classrooms, teachers need to generally understand the conditions and how to support these students in the classroom. This chapter will provide substantial information on autism and traumatic brain injury; other conditions will be presented more briefly. Often, schools provide support personnel for teachers and students with these types of problems. Therefore, teachers should not have to "go it alone" when working with students with these disabilities. Behavioural specialists, psychologists, physical therapists, occupational therapists, and other health personnel are often available to provide services to students and supports to their teachers. The fact that many different professionals provide services for some of these children may have repercussions for students of certain cultural backgrounds. Individuals from some cultures, for example, prefer to interact with only one person at a time, rather than a team of individuals. Professionals providing services must be sensitive to the cultural traits that characterize different families. They should consider the unique characteristics of each student's cultural background.

It is impossible to describe every single condition experienced by children with autism, TBI, and other low-incidence disabilities. Though this chapter will discuss the more well-known conditions and some that are unique and interesting, the conditions described here do not form an exhaustive list. Rather, they cover only a small range of the problems experienced within these groups.

CONSIDER THIS

What are some problems that may be encountered by general classroom teachers with which specialists could provide assistance?

AUTISM

CONSIDER THIS

How can movies that depict persons with disabilities help, as well as hurt, the cause of providing appropriate educational opportunities to students with disabilities?

Autism is a pervasive developmental disorder that primarily affects social interactions, language, and behaviour. Although autism has been glamorized by several movies, such as *Rain Man*, it still has a significant impact on individuals and their families. The characteristics displayed by individuals with autism vary significantly; some individuals are able to assimilate into community settings and activities, whereas others have major difficulties achieving such *normalcy*.

The field of autism has had a confusing and controversial history since the condition was first described less than 50 years ago by Dr. Leo Kanner (Eaves,

1992). Some of the early controversy centred on attempts to relate the cause of autism to poor mother-child bonding. Until this hypothesis was disproved, it caused a great deal of misunderstanding. In most jurisdictions in Canada autism is not a separate category of exceptionality. Instead, students with autism are served under such categories as intellectual disability, communication disorder, or learning disability, depending on the severity of the condition.

One of the early leaders in the field of autism, Kanner described 11 children with similar characteristics in the late 1930s and early 1940s who did not speak and who were very aloof. Kanner believed that the condition was present at birth, or soon after birth, and hence used the term **early infantile autism** to label these children. Until the 1960s, many professionals thought that children with autism made a conscious decision to withdraw from their environment because of its hostile nature. During the past two decades, autism has been found to be an organic disorder, laying to rest much of this speculation (Eaves, 1992).

Autism is a relatively rare condition, occurring in only about 1 per 2 000 children. In the United States during the 1993–1994 school year, 18 903 children were classified as having autism, which accounted for only 0.3 percent of children in special education programs, making it one of the smallest disability categories recognized in the schools (U.S. Department of Education, 1995). No figures are available for Canada largely due to the lack of a separate category. Eaves (1992) notes that the prevalence rate is 6 to 10 per 10 000 individuals. Compared to the 300 per 10 000 prevalence rate of intellectual disabilities (Beirne-Smith, Patton, & Ittenbach, 1994), autism represents a very low-incidence disability. Some children have a higher risk for autism than others. For example, children who are born with rubella and those classified as having fragile X syndrome are more likely to develop autism than other children (Blackman, 1990). In general, however, autism strikes randomly in all segments of society.

Definition

Although many definitions of autism have been developed, no single definition has been universally accepted. However, it is important to be familiar with two definitions: the one in the U.S. Individuals with Disabilities Act (IDEA), primarily used by educators, and the one found in the *Diagnostic and Statistical Manual of Mental Disorders* (*DSM-IV* fourth edition), used by psychologists and medical professionals. IDEA defines autism as "a developmental disability that primarily results in significant deficits in verbal and non-verbal communication and social interactions." The condition generally presents itself before the age of three years and adversely affects the child's educational performance once school age is reached. Knoblock (1982) describes autism as a lifelong, severely disabling condition. It is typically marked by significant impairments in intellectual, social, and emotional functioning (McEachlin, Smith, & Lovaas, 1993). This definition differs substantially from the one found in the *DSM-IV,* which uses a multitude of criteria. Figure 8.1 provides the *DSM-IV* definition and diagnostic criteria.

Just as autism is hard to define, children with autism are difficult to identify. Problems related to the identification of these children include the following:

FURTHER READING

Read sections in the *Diagnostic and Statistical Manual* (1994) *(DSM-IV)* of the American Psychiatric Association that deal with autism and pervasive developmental disorder (PDD). Compare PDD with autism.

FURTHER READING

For more information on identifying children with autism, read the chapter on autism by R. C. Eaves in P. J. McLaughlin & P. Wehman's book, *Developmental Disabilities*, published in 1997 by Andover Press in Boston.

■ Children with autism display many characteristics exhibited by individuals with other disabilities, such as speech and language disorders.

■ Many children with autism, because they exhibit disorders across multiple domains, are mistakenly classified as multihandicapped.

■ No stable classification system is used among educators and other professionals who encounter children with autism. (Eaves, 1992)

Still another problem in identifying children with autism is the large, diverse group of professionals responsible for the evaluation and diagnosis. In diagnosing some disabilities, educators function as the lead professionals; in the area of autism, pediatricians, speech-language pathologists, psychologists, au-

FIGURE 8.1
Definition of Autism
Using *DSM-IV*

From *Diagnostic and Statistical Manual of Mental Disorders* (4th ed.) (p. 32), American Psychiatric Association, 1994, Washington, DC: Author. Used by permission.

A. A total of six (or more) items from (1), (2), and (3), with at least two from (1), and one each from (2) and (3):

   (1) qualitative impairment in social interaction, as manifested by at least two of the following:

      (a) marked impairment in the use of multiple nonverbal behaviors such as eye-to-eye gaze, facial expression, body postures, and gestures to regulate social interaction

      (b) failure to develop peer relationships appropriate to developmental level

      (c) a lack of spontaneous seeking to share enjoyment, interests, or achievements with other people (e.g., by a lack of showing, bringing, or pointing out objects of interest)

      (d) lack of social or emotional reciprocity

   (2) qualitative impairments in communication as manifested by at least one of the following:

      (a) delay in, or total lack of, the development of spoken language (not accompanied by an attempt to compensate through alternative modes of communication such as gesture or mime)

      (b) in individuals with adequate speech, marked impairment in the ability to initiate or sustain a conversation with others

      (c) stereotyped and repetitive use of language or idiosyncratic language

      (d) lack of varied, spontaneous make-believe play or social imitative play appropriate to developmental level

   (3) restricted repetitive and stereotyped patterns of behavior, interests, and activities, as manifested by at least one of the following:

      (a) encompassing preoccupation with one or more stereotyped and restricted patterns of interest that is abnormal either in intensity or focus

      (b) apparently inflexible adherence to specific, nonfunctional routines or rituals

      (c) stereotyped and repetitive motor mannerisms (e.g., hand or finger flapping or twisting, or complex whole-body movements)

      (d) persistent preoccupation with parts of objects

B. Delays or abnormal functioning in at least one of the following areas, with onset prior to age 3 years: (1) social interaction, (2) language as used in social communication, or (3) symbolic or imaginative play.

C. The disturbance is not better accounted for by Rett's Disorder or Childhood Disintegrative Disorder (two pervasive developmental disorders characterized by impairment in the development of reciprocal social interaction).

PERSONAL SPOTLIGHT

The *Real* Rain Man ■ KIM PEEK

(Interviewed by Marcy Mezzano)

For all appearances, Kim Peek seems to be just an overgrown kid. With a perpetual pouty lip, a cranky attitude when he's tired, and a reliance on his father, Fran, to help him with the little things in life, he is just like any other kid. His dad helps him get dressed, brush his teeth, and communicate with others. He wants to answer every question he is asked in order to show off what he knows, and he becomes excited when he has given you information. Kim, however, is not a kid. Rather, he is a 45-year-old man whose innocent, honest, and vibrant personality belies the cynicism that too often is associated with his age.

Kim is a megasavant and perhaps the only *mega*savant in the world. His IQ is estimated at over 180 (Einstein's was measured at 149). Despite having almost total recall of everything he reads, Kim is challenged to think in abstract terms. He has difficulties in problem solving, motor control, and social relationships. However, he does have some remarkable skills. He can read "faster than a speeding bullet," with his left eye reading the left page of a book while his right eye is reading the right side. Kim read Tom Clancy's *Hunt for Red October* in about one hour and twenty minutes. He can quote passages from it

if you give him the page number. (If you tell Kim your birthdate, for example, July 19, 1974, he will tell you that you were born on a Friday, the years the date falls on Saturday, and that you will retire on Tuesday in the year 2039.)

Although Kim Peek's name may not be familiar, many people know about him. Kim was the inspiration for the Oscar-winning best picture of 1988, *Rain Man*. Unlike the character in the movie, Kim does not have autism. Rather, he has deficiencies in social and motor skill areas. He easily talks to whomever he meets and is not shy about telling people exactly what he is thinking. Kim and his father travel around the country in an effort to educate people, not merely about his disability, but about a universal problem—intolerance. While he always knew his son was special, it wasn't until the movie *Rain Man* that Fran knew exactly how bright his son was.

Kim is truly a remarkable individual. He is a great example about how being different, significantly different, does not mean that you are incapable of doing incredible things. All educators should remember Kim Peek when they are dealing with students with special needs. Accepting people for whom they are and what they can do is a quality we all need to enhance.

diologists, and social workers are typically involved as well (Powers, 1989). Working with such a large group of individuals can cause difficult logistical problems. Diverse definitions and eligibility criteria, different funding agencies, and varying services complicate the process of identifying and serving these children and adults.

Causes

There is no single specific cause of autism, but a variety of factors that can result in this disability. Organic factors such as brain damage, genetic links, and complications during pregnancy may cause this condition, though in most cases, no cause can be confirmed (Kaplan, 1996).

Characteristics

The Autism Treatment Services of Canada (ATSC, 1999) notes that children with autism have difficulty relating to other people, avoid eye contact, and have significant impairments in communication although it adds, "If a person were to walk into a room full of people with autism, they would likely be struck more by the differences than the similarities" (pg. 1). Nevertheless, autism carries numerous distinct characteristics. Eaves (1992) notes that these characteristics fall into five major groups. These groups and conditions associated with each one are, as follows:

1. Affective and cognitive indifference
   - Avoids eye contact
   - Presents a blank expression
   - Does not like to be hugged
   - Displays self-stimulating behaviour, such as finger flicking, hand shaking, rocking, head banging, and staring at hands
   - Likes to spin jars, lids, tops, and other objects
   - Has a fascination for crinkly sounds
   - Enjoys dangling objects
   - Mouths objects
2. Expressive affect
   - Cries on happy occasions
   - Hits, bites, or scratches others
   - Cries and screams when desires are not met
   - Smiles or laughs for no apparent reason
   - Hallucinates
   - Masturbates
   - Is overly sensitive to certain smells and odours

CROSS-REFERENCE

Review the section in Chapter 5 on children with serious emotional disturbance (SED). Compare the characteristics of children with autism and those with SED. How are these children similar and different?

3. Passive affect
   - Collects and hoards things of no apparent value
   - Is compulsive about cleanliness and orderliness
   - Walks on tiptoes, twirls, and overreacts to any environmental changes
4. Anxiety and fears
   - Is fearful of nonfrightening things
   - Has excessive fear of loud sounds or noises
   - Fears water
   - Fears crowds
5. Cognition
   - Displays savant behaviours in some areas, such as number counting, memorizing, spelling
   - Exhibits unique speech patterns, such as flat and monotonal in quality
   - Has uneven skill development
   - Has recorded low intellectual levels

Although most of these characteristics are negative, some children with autism present some positive, as well as unexpected, characteristics. For example, Tirosh and Canby (1993) describe children with autism who also have hyperlexia, which is defined as "an advance of at least one standard deviation (SD) in the reading over the verbal IQ level" (p. 86). For these children, spelling and contextual reading also appeared to be advanced.

CONSIDER THIS

How might splinter skills confuse family members about the abilities and capabilities of a child with autism?

In some cases, children with autism display unique **splinter skills**. Some are incredible spellers and some, artists. Some have calendar skills that allow them to always know what day of the week a certain date will fall on. These types of skills are found in only a small number of children with autism, but they do add interest to studying children with this disability.

Interventions

Until recently, the prognosis for individuals with autism was pessimistic; most children with autism would grow into adulthood with severe impairments. However, recently, intensive intervention programs have been somewhat effective with this group. No single method is effective with all children with autism, partly because these children display widely variable characteristics (Cartwright, Cartwright, & Ward, 1995). However, several different techniques have shown positive results (Kaplan, 1996). Table 8.1 summarizes some of these techniques.

Growing evidence shows that placing children with autism with their nondisabled peers in general education settings, with appropriate supports, can make a significant difference in their behaviours. Appropriate role models appear to be very important. Recent research also indicates that behavioural treatment of children with autism, especially young children, may result in significant long-term gains in intellectual and adaptive behaviour areas (McEachlin et al., 1993). Also, social skills training has been shown to be effective for this group of children (Kamps et al., 1992).

When determining appropriate intervention for children with autism, consider the underlying cause of various behaviours. For example, if a child is

TEACHING TIP

Peer buddies can be very useful to a student with autism in a general education classroom. Peers can serve as excellent role models and provide supports for these students.

TABLE 8.1

Classroom Tips for Teaching Children with Autism

Tip	Reason
1. Teaching a child with autism should be seen as a team approach with many professionals helping the classroom teacher.	The child with autism being educated in a regular class has probably been treated by many professionals who have extensive experience with the child. Their experiences and suggestions are of great help to the teacher. Regular consultations should be scheduled.
2. Learn everything possible about the child's development, behavior, and what services the child has received.	Understanding the nature of the child's difficulties and what has been accomplished previously can serve as a beginning for designing a program that will enable the child to learn.
3. Try to foster an atmosphere of shared decision making with other professionals responsible for the child's progress.	Successful models for integration of children with autism into regular classes show that shared decision making among all professionals leads to superior results.
4. Do not assume that children with autism have mental retardation.	The serious behavioral and linguistic difficulties of these children may lead to the assumption that they have mental retardation. The meaning of intelligence tests for children with autism is subject to question.
5. Beware of even suggesting that parents have caused their children's difficulties.	Blaming parents is counterproductive since parental help is so often required. However, in the case of autism, old discredited theories did suggest such a connection. Even though these ideas have been proven false, parental guilt may be present.
6. Prepare the class for the child with autism.	Discussing the nature of autism and some behaviors, such as rocking, may help allay the concerns of other children in the class.

From *Pathways for Exceptional Children* (p. 595), by P. S. Kaplan, 1996, St. Paul, MN: West Publishing. Used by permission.

self-injurious, it is important to find out what stimulates the abusive behaviour. Determining what causes or reinforces the behaviour helps in developing an appropriate intervention approach. If the behaviour has an organic cause, certain drugs may be effective. On the other hand, removing positive reinforcement for the behaviour may be effective by itself (Eaves, 1992).

Regardless of the specific intervention used, some general principles should be considered when teaching new skills to children with autism. Bruey (1989) suggests the following steps:

TEACHING TIP

Always remember that students with autism present a wide range of characteristics, strengths, and weaknesses. Treat each child as a unique individual, and do not expect them all to need the same kinds of services.

1. *Make instructions clear and simple.* For children with autism, doing this is critical, especially since many do not attend to instructions and therefore do not understand what is expected.
2. *Prompt as needed.* Many students do not respond to instructions, regardless of their clarity and simplicity. In these situations, prompts may be necessary. Prompts can be environmental, gestural, verbal, or physical.
3. *Provide corrective feedback.* All children need corrections when they perform a task incorrectly, or they may continue to perform the task incorrectly. Corrective feedback provides an opportunity to help the students respond correctly.
4. *Reinforce appropriate behaviour.* When appropriate behaviours are exhibited, effective reinforcement must be used. Without reinforcement, the appropriate behaviours may diminish and be replaced by other behaviours that are less appropriate.

Just as no single set of techniques is effective with all children with autism, no single curriculum is appropriate for each child in this group. Rather, several curricular areas should be considered when developing programs for them. These include the following:

CONS'DER THIS

How should the curriculum for students with autism be balanced between academic skills and functional life skills?

1. Cognitive skills
2. Social skills
3. Communication skills
4. Self-help skills
5. Motor skills
6. Vocational skills (Egel, 1989)

Although all children with autism will not need special attention in all of these areas, the areas should all be considered when developing individual programs.

Egel (1989) has emphasized two important principles that should inform educational programs for children with autism: the use of functional activities and an effort to make programs appropriate for the student's developmental level and chronological age. Children with autism grow up to be adults with autism; the condition cannot be cured. As a result, educational programs should help them deal with the daily needs that will extend throughout their lives. To help educators focus more on the functionality of curriculum choices, they should ask themselves the following questions:

CROSS-REFERENCE

Review in Chapter 6 program recommendations for students with intellectual disabilities. How are programs for these two groups of students similar and different?

1. Does the program teach skills that are immediately useful?
2. Will the materials used be available in the student's daily environment?
3. Will learning certain skills make it less likely that someone will not have to do the task for the student in the future?

If the answer to any of these questions is no, then the instructional program should be changed.

Self-management is a promising intervention strategy for children with autism.

Programs for students with autism should also be age appropriate and **developmentally appropriate**. The individual's chronological age and developmental status must be considered together. Sometimes a real incongruency exists between these two realms, making program planning a challenge (McDonnell, Hardman, McDonnell, & Kiefer-O'Donnell, 1995). In this case, developmentally appropriate materials must be modified to make them as age appropriate as possible.

A promising intervention strategy for children and adults with autism is **self-management**—implementing a variety of techniques that assist in self-control. Although total self-management is not possible for many students with autism, most can be taught to improve their skills in this area (Alberto & Troutman, 1995). Koegel, Koegel, Hurley, and Frea (1992) studied four children with autism who displayed a variety of inappropriate behaviours, including **self-injurious behaviours** (or self-abusive behaviours), running away from school personnel, delayed echolalic speech (repeating what is said to them), hitting objects, and stereotypical twirling of hair. After several sessions in which the children were taught how to use self-management strategies, such as **self-recording** (documenting their own behaviour) and **self-reinforcement** (giving themselves reinforcers), marked improvement occurred. The results indicate that "the lack of social responsivity that is so characteristic in autism can be successfully treated with self-management procedures, requiring minimal presence of a treatment provider in the children's natural environments" (p. 350). This particular study focused on self-management related to social skills, yet hints at the possibility that such interventions could be successful in other areas.

Over the past several years, a major controversy has erupted in the education of children with autism over the use of **facilitated communication**, a process in which a *facilitator* helps the person with autism (or some other disability related to expressive language) type or use a keyboard for communication purposes. The process is described by Biklen, Morton, Gold, Berrigan, and Swaminathan (1992) as follows:

FURTHER READING

For more information on teaching self-management skills to students with autism, read *Applied Behavior Analysis for Teachers*, by P. A. Alberto and A. C. Troutman, published by Merrill in 1995; and "Improving Social Skills and Disruptive Behavior in Children with Autism through Self-management" in volume 25 of the *Journal of Applied Behavior Analysis* by L. K. Koegel, R. L. Koegel, C. Hurley, and W. D. Frea.

Facilitated communication involves a series of steps. The communicator types with one index finger, first with hand over hand or hand-at-the-wrist support and then later independently or with just a touch to the elbow or shoulder. Over time, the communicator progresses from structured work such as fill-in-the-blanks/cloze exercises and multiple-choice activities to open-ended, typed, conversational text. (p. 5)

CONSIDER THIS

How can the use of invalidated procedures harm students? Why do some ideas become popular with some educators and family members before they are proved effective?

Although this method was once touted as the key to establishing communication with children with autism, recent studies have cast doubt on its authenticity. The heart of the controversy concerns how to validate the technique. Advocates of the method offer numerous qualitative research studies as proof of success, yet recent quantitative research raises significant questions about the program. After reviewing much of the empirical research related to facilitated communication, Kaplan (1996) reported that evidence often shows that the facilitator influences the person with autism, though the facilitator may be unaware of it.

Autism is a very significant disability. Characterized by language and social deficiencies, the condition results in lifelong problems for the person with autism and the person's family. As more research into autism is completed, better methods of managing and teaching these children will be developed.

TRAUMATIC BRAIN INJURY

FURTHER READING

For more information on traumatic brain injury, read *A Handbook for Educators for Traumatic Brain Injury* by R. C. Savage, published in 1992 by Pro-Ed. Also, see *Traumatic Brain Injury in Children and Adolescents: A Sourcebook for Teachers and Other School Personnel,* by M. P. Miran, B. F. Tucker, and J. S. Tyler, published in 1992 by Pro-Ed.

Traumatic brain injury (TBI) is caused by an external insult to the brain, resulting in "brain contusion, laceration, or compression or damage to the cerebral blood vessels" (Tver & Tver, 1991, p. 230). It can affect psychological and cognitive abilities, speech and language, physical functioning, and personal and social behaviours.

Traumatic brain injury can be caused by any number of events. The primary causes of head injury in children are motor vehicle accidents and physical abuse (Mira, Tucker, & Tyler, 1992). Bicycle accidents, sports injuries, and assaults account for some cases of TBI.

Information about the severity of a traumatic brain injury is important for teachers to know, as it can provide a sense of the expected long-term outcomes for a student. Although no standardized system has been developed to describe levels of severity, Mira et al. (1992) offer the following one, which is derived from a variety of sources:

Mild: Signs of concussion or a blow resulting in some aftereffects, such as dizziness or loss of consciousness, for less than an hour; no skull fracture; majority of brain injuries are mild.

Moderate: Loss of consciousness for from 1 to 24 hours or evidence of a skull fracture; may develop secondary neurological problems such as swelling within the brain and subsequent complications; neurosurgery may be required.

Severe: Loss of consciousness for more than 24 hours, or evidence of contusion (actual bruising of brain tissue) or intracranial hematoma (bleeding within the brain); long-term medical care is likely; typical sequelae (consequences) include motor, language, and cognitive problems.

The social-emotional and cognitive deficits caused by the injury may persist long after physical capabilities recover. Students with TBI can experience a host of confusing and frustrating symptoms. "There is an inability to concentrate; short-term memory is affected; one's self-confidence is undermined; self-esteem is diminished; the personality changes; . . . the family and friends are affected" (Infusini, 1994, pp. 4–5). Teachers must guard against minimizing an injury because it presents no visible evidence. Many teachers doubt the severity of the cognitive deficits of a student who has experienced mild TBI because the child seems normal. Table 8.2 lists possible lingering effects of TBI that can have an impact on a student's education.

The prognosis for recovery depends on many variables. Initially, it is "influenced by the type of injury and the rapidity and quality of medical and surgical care" (Bigge, 1991, p. 197). Later, it will be influenced by the nature of rehabilitative and educational intervention.

The reentry of students with TBI to school settings needs to be coordinated among a number of people. Intervention involves the efforts of professionals

TABLE 8.2

Persisting Features of Traumatic Brain Injury

Area of Functioning	Possible Effects
PHYSICAL/MEDICAL	• Reduced stamina and fatigue • Seizures (5%) • Headaches • Problems with regulation of various functions (e.g., growth, eating, body temperature)
SENSORY	• Hearing problems (e.g., conductive and/or sensorineural loss) • Vision problems (e.g., blurred vision, visual field defects)
COGNITIVE	• Memory problems (e.g., storage and retrieval) • Attentional difficulties • Intellectual deficits • Reasoning and problem-solving difficulties
LANGUAGE-RELATED	• Word retrieval difficulties • Motor-speech problems (e.g., dysarthria) • Language comprehension deficits (e.g., difficulty listening) • Difficulty acquiring new vocabulary and learning new concepts • Socially inappropriate verbal behavior
BEHAVIORAL/ EMOTIONAL	• Problems in planning, organizing, and problem solving • Disinhibition • Overactivity • Impulsivity • Lack of self-direction • Helplessness or apathy • Inability to recognize one's injury

From *Traumatic Brain Injury in Children and Adolescents: A Sourcebook for Teachers and Other School Personnel* (pp. 71–72), by M. P. Mira, B. F. Tucker, and J. S. Tyler, 1992, Austin, TX: Pro-Ed. Used by permission.

CONSIDER THIS

What can school personnel do to facilitate the transition of children with TBI from hospital and residential settings to the public school? What kind of relationship should school personnel and hospital personnel maintain with each other after the transition is completed?

from many different disciplines, including teachers (Bergland & Hoffbauer, 1996). In addition to the injury itself and its implications on functioning and potential learning, students probably will have missed a significant amount of schooling. All of these factors can have a significant impact on educational performance. An effective educational program creates a positive attitude about the student's prognosis which reaches beyond just speaking positively. A positive attitude is communicated by the type of programming presentation and by the level of expectations that are established. Remember to "keep expectations for students' performance high. Often, this means providing students with mild TBI with multiple opportunities for practice that do not carry penalties for inaccuracy" (Hux & Hackley, 1996). This will show the student that programs and instruction are designed to support them and not just to give them a grade. They will respond better when programs do not seem punitive.

A well-planned program of instruction should focus on "retaining impaired cognitive processes, developing new skills or procedures to compensate for residual deficits, creating an environment that permits effective performance, identifying effective instructional procedures, and improving metacognitive awareness" (Ylvisaker, Szekeres, Hartwick, & Tworek, 1994, p. 17). The impact of the injury may require that the student learn compensatory strategies to make up for deficits. Such strategies can address problems with attending, language comprehension, memory, sequencing, and thought organization.

The following suggestions will help provide a positive learning program and environment for students with TBI:

TEACHING TIP

Develop and implement intervention programs based on the student's specific needs. TBI results in a wide variety of deficits, producing a great diversity of needs.

- Prepare classmates for the reentry of a fellow student who has sustained a traumatic brain injury—it is important to discuss changes in physical functioning and personality.
- Modify the classroom to ensure safety and to address any specific needs of the student.
- Minimize visual and auditory distractions that may interfere with attention to task.
- Be familiar with any special equipment that might be needed (e.g., augmentative communication devices).
- Be familiar with the effects and administration procedures of prescribed medications.
- Consider special seating, depending on needs.
- Ensure that students are attending to instructional activities—teach students to monitor their own attention behaviour.
- Help students with memory problems by teaching them mnemonic strategies.
- Assist students who are having difficulty with organization.
- Break down learning tasks into substeps.
- Create many opportunities for the student to use problem-solving skills.
- Allow extra time for students to respond to questions, take tests, complete assignments, and move from one setting to another.
- Teach students social skills appropriate for their age and needs.
- Implement behaviour reduction techniques to eliminate inappropriate and undesirable behaviours.
- Help students to understand the nature of their injury.
- Provide information about academic, social, and psychomotor progress to families on a regular basis. Describe the nature of the educational program to them.

TABLE 8.3

Suggestions for Teaching Students with Traumatic Brain Injury

Area of Functioning	Suggestion
RECEPTIVE LANGUAGE	• Limit the amount of information presented at one time. • Provide simple instructions for only one activity at a time. • Have the student repeat instructions. • Use concrete language.
EXPRESSIVE LANGUAGE	• Teach the student to rehearse silently before verbally replying. • Teach the student to look for cues from listeners to ascertain that the student is being understood • Teach the student to directly ask if he or she is being understood.
MAINTAINING ATTENTION	• Provide a study carrel or preferential seating. • After giving instructions, check for proper attention and understanding by having the student repeat them. • Teach the student to use self-regulating techniques to maintain attention (e.g., asking "Am I paying attention?" "What is the required task?").
IMPULSIVENESS	• Teach the student to mentally rehearse steps before beginning an activity. • Reduce potential distractions. • Frequently restate and reinforce rules.
MEMORY	• Teach the student to use external aids such as notes, memos, daily schedule sheets, and assignment sheets. • Use visual imagery, when possible, to supplement oral content. • Teach visual imaging techniques for information presented. • Provide repetition and frequent review of instruction materials. • Provide immediate and frequent feedback to enable the student to interpret success or failure.
FOLLOWING DIRECTIONS	• Provide the student with both visual and auditory directions. • Model tasks, whenever possible. • Break multistep directions into small parts and list them so that the student can refer back when needed.
MOTOR SKILLS	• Allow the student to complete a project rather than turn in a written assignment. • Have the student use a word processor or typewriter to complete assignments. • Allow extra time for completing tasks requiring fine-motor skills. • Assign someone to take notes for the student during lectures.

Adapted from *Traumatic Brain Injury: A Sourcebook for Teachers and Other School Personnel* (pp. 71–72), by M. P. Mira, B. F. Tucker, J. S. Tyler, 1992, Austin, TX: Pro-Ed. Used by permission.

LOW-INCIDENCE HEALTH PROBLEMS AND PHYSICAL DISABILITIES

As noted in the beginning of this chapter, many health and **physical disabilities** may be present in children that result in a need for special education and related services. The remainder of this chapter will provide a quick guide to some of these disabilities and some considerations for educators. Teachers who work with children with one of these conditions should refer to a more thorough reference work to learn more about it. Margin notes suggest such sources of information.

Asthma

FURTHER READING

For more information on asthma, read *Understanding Physical, Sensory, and Health Impairments*, by K. W. Heller, P. A. Alberto, P. E. Forney, and M. N. Schwartzman, published in 1996 by Brooks/Cole.

In Canada, 5 to 10 percent of Canadians, and as many as 20 percent of children, have asthma. According to the Asthma Society of Canada (2000), asthma is the most common chronic childhood disease, the number one cause of emergency room visits in pediatric centres and the number one cause of school absenteeism.

It is characterized by repetitive episodes of coughing, shortness of breath, and wheezing. These characteristics result from the narrowing of small air passages, caused by irritation of the bronchial tubes by allergic reactions to various substances, such as animal dander, air pollutants, and pollens. Asthma attacks can be very dangerous and should be taken seriously by school personnel. Specific suggestions for teachers include the following:

- Know the signs and symptoms of respiratory distress.
- Ensure that students have proper medications and that they are taken at the appropriate times.
- Allow students to rest when needed, as they often tire easily.
- Eliminate any known **allergens** from the classroom.
- Determine what types of physical limitations might have to be set (e.g., restriction of a certain physical activity that can induce attacks), but otherwise encourage students to play games and participate in activities.
- Recognize the side effects of prescribed medication.
- Remain calm if an attack occurs.
- Allow the student to participate in nonstressful activity until an episode subsides.
- Introduce a vaporizer or dehumidifier to the classroom when recommended by the student's physician.
- Work on building up the student's self-image.
- Sensitize other students in the class to the nature of allergic reactions.
- Develop an effective system for helping the student keep up with schoolwork, as frequent absences may occur.

Childhood Cancer

CONSIDER THIS

What are some ways that teachers can maintain contact with students with cancer during their extended absences from the classroom? How can the teacher facilitate contact between other students and the student with cancer?

Childhood cancer occurs in only about 1 in 600 children prior to the age of 15 years (Stehbens, 1988) but is devastating for those with the condition. Childhood cancer can take several different forms, including **leukemia**, lymphoma, tumours of the central nervous system, bone tumours, tumours affecting the eyes, and tumours affecting various organs (Heller, Alberto, Forney, & Schwartzman, 1996). Treatment of cancer includes chemotherapy, radiation, surgery, and bone marrow transplantation. Suggestions for teachers who have children with cancer include the following:

- Express your concern about a student's condition to the parents and family.
- Learn about a student's illness from hospital personnel and parents.
- Inquire about the type of treatment and anticipated side effects.
- Refer the student for any needed special education services.
- Prepare for a student's terminal illness and possible death.
- Encourage discussion and consideration of future events.
- Allow for exceptions to classroom rules and procedures when indicated (e.g., wearing a baseball cap to disguise hair loss from chemotherapy).

INCLUSION STRATEGIES

How to Handle the Issue of Death

Almost all students will want to know, but be afraid to ask, whether their classmate can die from the cancer. If a classmate asks, respond honestly with something like "Nobody knows. Some children as sick as _____ have died, some other children have gotten better and are just fine. We don't know what will happen to _____, but [she/he] and [her/his] doctors are working very hard to make [her/him] well." If the class does not raise the issue of death, you *should* bring it up. Ask a question such as "Have any of you known anyone who has died from cancer?" (You will get nods.) Once you have raised the question, you can address it. "Cancer is a very serious disease and people do die from it." Then proceed with, "Nobody knows . . ."

Remember that elementary school children do not have the philosophical understanding of death that teenagers and adults do. Until children are capable of formal operational thought, they cannot truly conceptualize the finality of death. As educators we know that it is futile to try to teach history with concepts of past and future generations until children are 11 or 12 years old. Most elementary school students have had some experience with a pet or older relative who has died. They do understand that it means that the person does not come back. Be careful of the language you use. One child thought he was going to die when he was told he would be "put to sleep" for his operation. He knew his dog had been "put to sleep" and never came back. By having a discussion, you may be able to clarify such misconceptions. Generally, children are much more concerned with the concrete and immediate consequences to themselves and their friend. The classmates and friends of the ill student will understand that their friend is worried about physical pain, needles, and bodily harm. Some children will view their friend as a hero for having conquered forces they all fear. Children of this age are able to feel for another's pain. Most children have had flu, viruses, mouth sores, nausea, and even hospital experiences from which they are able to relate personal pain to that of another. The more you emphasize things children understand, the more you will tap into their altruism in helping their ill classmate.

Older children (and sometimes teachers) may be worried that their friend might die suddenly while they are together. The basic fear is that they would not know what to do or how to handle the situation. Assure them that children do not die suddenly. They get much sicker first. Their doctors and parents would be taking care of them, and they would not be in school.

From "Children with Cancer in the Classroom," by V. C. Peckham, 1993, *Teaching Exceptional Children, 26,* p. 31. Used by permission.

- Be available to talk with a student when the need arises.
- Share information about the student's condition and ongoing status with teachers of the student's siblings.
- Be prepared to deal with issues concerning death and dying with students. See the nearby Inclusion Strategies feature for ideas.

Cerebral Palsy

Cerebral palsy is a disorder of movement or posture that is caused by brain damage. It affects the voluntary muscles and often leads to major problems in communication and mobility. Cerebral palsy is neither progressive nor communicable (Gersh, 1991; Schleichkorn, 1993). It is also not "curable" in the usual sense of the word although education, therapy, and applied technology can help persons with cerebral palsy lead productive lives.

Teachers who have students with cancer should learn about the child's illness from medical personnel.

Between 6 and 10 individuals for every 10 000 in the population have cerebral palsy (Eaves, 1992). There are three primary methods for classifying individuals with cerebral palsy: by type (physiological), by distribution (topological) (Inge, 1992), and by degree of severity (Bigge, 1991). Table 8.4 describes the different types of cerebral palsy according to two classification systems. The primary intervention approach for children with cerebral palsy focuses on their

TABLE 8.4	
Classification of Cerebral Palsy	
Topographical Classification System	**Classification System by Motor Symptoms (Physiological)**
A. *Monoplegia:* one limb	A. Spastic
B. *Paraplegia:* legs only	B. Athetoid
C. *Hemiplegia:* one-half of body	1. Tension
D. *Triplegia:* three limbs (usually two legs and one arm)	2. Nontension
E. *Quadriplegia:* all four limbs	3. Dystonic
F. *Diplegia:* more affected in the legs than the arms	4. Tremor
G. *Double hemiplegia:* arms more involved than the legs	C. Rigidity
	D. Ataxia
	E. Tremor
	F. Atonic (rare)
	G. Mixed
	H. Unclassified

From *Understanding Physical, Sensory, and Health Impairments* (p. 95), by K. W. Heller, P. A. Alberto, P. E. Forney, and M. N. Schwartzman, 1996, Pacific Grove, CA: Brooks/Cole. Used by permission.

physical needs. Physical therapy, occupational therapy, and even surgery often play a part. Specific suggestions for teachers include the following:

- Create a supportive classroom environment that encourages participation in every facet of the school day.
- Allow extra time for students to move from one location to another.
- Ask students to repeat verbalizations that may be hard to understand because of their speech patterns.
- Provide many real-life activities.
- Learn the correct way for the student to sit upright in a chair or wheelchair and the methods of using adaptive equipment (e.g., prone standers).
- Understand the functions and components of a wheelchair and any special adaptive pieces that may accompany it.
- Consider the use of various augmentative communication techniques with students who have severe cerebral palsy (Musselwhite, 1987).
- Encourage students to use computers that are equipped with expanded keyboards if necessary or other portable writing aids for taking notes or generating written products.
- Consult physical and occupational therapists to understand correct positioning, posture, and other motor function areas.

TEACHING TIP

Develop some simulation activities for nondisabled students that will help them understand mobility problems. Trying out wheelchairs and restricting the use of arms or hands will help them understand the problems experienced by some students with cerebral palsy.

Cystic Fibrosis

Cystic fibrosis is an inherited, fatal disease that results in an abnormal amount of mucus throughout the body, most often affecting the lungs and digestive tract. On the average, children will live to their midteens. Teachers must make sure that children with cystic fibrosis take special medication before they eat. As the disease progresses, it greatly affects stamina and the student's physical condition. Here are some specific suggestions for dealing with students with this disease.

- Prepare students in class for the realities of this disease (e.g., coughing, noncontagious sputum, gas).
- Learn how to clear a student's lungs and air passages, as such assistance may be needed after certain activities.
- Know the medications a student must take and be able to administer them (e.g., enzymes, vitamins).
- Consider restricting certain physical activities.
- Inquire about the therapies being used with the student.
- Support the implementation of special diets if needed.
- Provide opportunities for students to talk about their concerns, fears, and feelings.
- Ensure that the student is included in all class activities to whatever extent is possible.

FURTHER READING

For more information on cystic fibrosis, read *Understanding Physical, Sensory, and Health Impairments*, by K. W. Heller, P. A. Alberto, P. E. Forney, and M. N. Schwartzman, published in 1996 by Brooks/Cole.

Multisensory Impairments

Students who have visual impairments or auditory impairments create unique problems for educators. Since most instruction emphasizes vision and hearing, students who have deficits in these areas may have incredible difficulties with school activities. When students present deficits in both sensory areas, their needs become extremely complex.

Students who have multisensory impairments may be blind or deaf, or they may have degrees of visual and auditory impairments that do not classify as blindness or deafness. "The Helen Keller National Center estimates that about 94% of such individuals have residual hearing or residual sight that can facilitate their educational programs" (Marchant, 1992, p. 114). Obviously, these individuals present a variety of characteristics. While these characteristics represent those exhibited by students who have visual and hearing impairments, the overlap of the two disabilities results in significant educational needs.

Wolfe (1997) suggests the following educational techniques for teachers to use when working with students with multisensory impairments:

■ Use an ecological approach to assessment and skill selection to emphasize functional needs of students.
■ Use a variety of prompts, cues, and reinforcement strategies in a systematic instructional pattern.
■ Use time delay prompting, where time between prompts is increased.
■ Use groups and cooperative learning strategies.
■ Implement environmental adaptations, such as enlarging materials, using contrasting materials, altering seating arrangements, and reducing extraneous noises to maximize residual hearing and vision of the student.

Diabetes (Juvenile Diabetes)

Diabetes is a metabolic disorder in which the pancreas cannot produce sufficient insulin to process food. Teachers should be alert to possible symptoms of diabetes. (See Table 8.5.) Children with type I (insulin-dependent) diabetes must take daily injections of insulin. School personnel must have knowledge of the special dietary needs of these children and understand their need for a daily activity regimen. Below are some specific suggestions on dealing with diabetic students:

■ Communicate regularly with the family to determine any special needs the student may have.
■ Schedule snacks and lunch at the same time every day.
■ Be prepared for hypoglycemia—a situation in which the student needs to have sugar.
■ Help the student deal with the disease.
■ Teachers and other school personnel must understand the distinction between having too much insulin in the body and not having enough. Table 8.6 describes both of these conditions and actions to address them.

Epilepsy

Epilepsy is a seizure disorder resulting in *recurrent* seizures. A seizure can be described as a "brief, sudden malfunction of the brain that is attributable to a massive abnormal electrical discharge" (Jan, Ziegler, & Erba, 1991, p. 16). Several different types of seizures are related to epilepsy (Baroff, 1991). Table 8.7 details four types. In Canada, up to 2 percent of the population have been diagnosed with epilepsy (Epilepsy Ontario, 1999). The Epilepsy Foundation of America (1992) notes the following significant signs of the disorder: (1) staring spells, (2) tic-like movements, (3) rhythmic movements of the head, (4) pur-

---

TEACHING TIP

Before an emergency develops, be prepared to deal with students with diabetes in your classroom. Keep a list of symptoms to watch for and things to do if a student has too much or too little insulin.

TABLE 8.5

Indicators of Diabetes

Increased thirst

Increased appetite

Weight loss

Fatigue

Irritability

Increased urination

TABLE 8.6

Hyperglycemia and Hypoglycemia

Category	Possible Symptoms	Cause	Treatment
Ketoacidosis; hyperglycemia (too much sugar)	Symptoms occur gradually (over hours or days): polyuria; polyphagia; polydipsia; fatigue; abdominal pain; nausea; vomiting; fruity odor on breath; rapid, deep breathing; unconsciousness	Did not take insulin; did not comply with diet	Give insulin; follow plan of action
Insulin reaction; hypoglycemia (too little sugar)	Symptoms occur quickly (in minutes): headache; dullness; irritability; shaking; sweating; lightheadedness; behavior change; paleness; weakness; moist skin; slurred speech; confusion; shallow breathing; unconsciousness	Delayed eating; participated in strenuous exercise; took too much insulin	Give sugar; follow plan of action

From *Understanding Physical, Sensory, and Health Impairments* (p. 302), by K. W. Heller, P. A. Alberto, P. E. Forney, and M. N. Schwartzman, 1996, Pacific Grove, CA: Brooks/Cole. Used by permission.

poseless sounds and body movements, (5) head drooping, (6) lack of response, (7) eyes rolling upward, and (8) chewing and swallowing movements. Medical intervention is the primary recourse for individuals with epilepsy. Most people with epilepsy are able to control their seizures with the proper regimen of medical therapy (Baroff, 1991).

Even persons who respond very well to medication have occasional seizures. Therefore teachers and other school personnel must know what actions to take

TABLE 8.7

Types of Seizures

Type of Seizure	Description
GENERALIZED SEIZURE	A seizure involving a large part of the brain.
PARTIAL SEIZURE	A seizure beginning in a localized area and involving only a small part of the brain.
TONIC-CLONIC SEIZURE	Loss of consciousness (usually for 2 to 5 minutes) followed by repeated tonic and clonic contractions of muscles of the limbs, trunk, and head (i.e., convulsions); also called grand mal seizure.
ABSENCE SEIZURE	Brief, generalized seizures manifested by a brief "absence" or lapse of consciousness lasting up to 30 seconds; the individual suddenly stops any activity in which he or she is engaged and then resumes the activity following the seizure; also called petit mal seizures.

From *Exceptional Children* (6th ed.) (p. 94), by D. Hallahan and J. Kauffman, 1994, Boston: Allyn & Bacon. Used by permission.

should a person experience a grand mal seizure. Figure 8.2 summarizes the steps that should be taken when a child has a seizure. Teachers, parents, or others need to record behaviours that occur before, during, and after the seizure because they may be important to treatment of the disorder. Figure 8.3 provides a sample form to assist in observing and documenting seizures.

CONSIDER THIS
Students with HIV and AIDS should not be allowed to attend school because of their potential ability to infect other students. Do you agree or disagree with this statement? Why or why not?

HIV and AIDS

Human immunodeficiency virus (HIV) infection occurs when the virus attacks the body's immune system, leaving an individual vulnerable to infections or cancers. In its later stages, HIV infection becomes **acquired immunodeficiency syndrome (AIDS)**. Two of the fastest-growing groups contracting HIV are infants and teenagers. HIV is transmitted only through the exchange of blood or semen. Students with HIV will likely display a variety of academic, behavioural, and social-emotional problems. Teachers need to take precautions when dealing

FIGURE 8.2
Steps to Take When Dealing with a Seizure

From *Seizure Recognition and Observation: A Guide for Allied Health Professionals* (p. 2), Epilepsy Foundation of America, 1992, Landover, MD: Author. Used by permission.

In a generalized tonic-clonic seizure, the person suddenly falls to the ground and has a convulsive seizure. It is essential to protect him or her from injury. Cradle the head or place something soft under it—a towel or your hand, for example. Remove all dangerous objects. A bystander can do nothing to prevent or terminate an attack. At the end of the episode, make sure the mouth is cleared of food and saliva by turning the person on his or her side to provide the best airway and allow secretions to drain. The person may be incontinent during a seizure. If the assisting person remains calm, the person will be reassured when he or she regains consciousness.

Breathing almost always resumes spontaneously after a convulsive seizure. Failure to resume breathing signals a complication of the seizure such as an aspiration of food, heart attack, or severe head or neck injury. In these unusual circumstances, cardiopulmonary resuscitation must start immediately. If repeated seizures occur, or if a single seizure lasts longer than five minutes, the person should be taken to a medical facility immediately. Prolonged or repeated seizures may suggest *status epilepticus* (nonstop seizures), which requires emergency medical treatment. In summary, *first aid for generalized tonic-clonic seizures is similar to that for other convulsive seizures.*

TEACHING TIP
Turn a student's seizure into an educational opportunity for other students. Ensure that students know that they cannot "catch" epilepsy from someone.

- Prevent further injury. Place something soft under the head, loosen tight clothing, and clear the area of sharp or hard objects.
- Force no objects into the person's mouth.
- Do not restrain the person's movements unless they place him or her in danger.
- Turn the person on his or her side to open the airway and allow secretions to drain.
- Stay with the person until the seizure ends.
- Do not pour any liquids into the person's mouth or offer any food, drink, or medication until he or she is fully awake.
- Start cardiopulmonary resuscitation if the person does not resume breathing after the seizure.
- Let the person rest until he or she is fully awake.
- Be reassuring and supportive when consciousness returns.
- A convulsive seizure is not a medical emergency unless it lasts longer than five minutes or a second seizure occurs soon after the first. In this situation, the person should be taken to an emergency medical facility.

Student's Name _____ John _____

Date of Seizure _____ 3/13/90 _____

Time of
Seizure _____ about 9:00 A.M. _____

Approximate
Duration
of Seizure _____ 2 minutes _____

BEHAVIOUR BEFORE SEIZURE
John appeared to be tired and complained of a headache. He was resting at his desk, putting his head down on his arms.

INITIAL SEIZURE BEHAVIOUR
He let out a short cry. His whole body appeared to stiffen.

BEHAVIOUR DURING SEIZURE
John fell to the floor. His whole body, including his arms and legs, began to jerk violently. His eyes rolled upward and his eyelids were fluttering. John had lost consciousness and fallen to the floor. His facial skin was very pale and his lips were bluish. The seizure lasted about 2 minutes.

BEHAVIOUR AFTER SEIZURE
John was very tired and wanted to rest. He complained that he had a severe headache.

STUDENT REACTION TO SEIZURE
John was quite upset and confused. He didn't seem to understand what had happened.

PEER REACTION TO SEIZURE
At the time of the seizure, other children were not in the room. However, the children in the room should be made aware of the seizure, given an understanding of the behaviour, and taught basic safety procedures. It was recommended that I call Epilepsy Canada (toll-free 1-877-734-0873) for additional assistance and referral to local chapter.

TEACHER COMMENTS
John was not injured. The school nurse assisted with the incident and the parents were notified. John's fears and concerns need to be addressed. I will begin by obtaining help from the local epilepsy chapter. The parents, school nurse, and guidance counsellor will assist me in helping John address his concerns.

FIGURE 8.3
Seizure Observation Form
Adapted from "Seizures: Teacher Observations and Record Keeping," by R. J. Michael, 1992, *Interventions in School and Clinic, 27,* p. 212. Used by permission.

with children with HIV/AIDS, hepatitis B, or any other blood borne pathogen. See Figure 8.4 for specific precautions. Some specific suggestions for teachers include the following:

- Follow the guidelines (universal precautions) developed by the Centers for Disease Control and the U.S. Food and Drug Administration for working with HIV-infected individuals (see Figure 8.4).
- Ask the student's parents or physician if there are any special procedures that must be followed.
- Discuss HIV infection with the entire class, providing accurate information, dispelling myths, and answering questions.
- Discuss with students in the class that a student's skills and abilities will change over time if he is infected with HIV.

FURTHER READING

For more information about HIV and AIDS, read "Special Educators' Knowledge of HIV Transmission: Implications for Teacher Education Programs," by R. M. Foley and M. J. Kittleson, published in 1993 in volume 16 of *Teacher Education and Special Education.*

FIGURE 8.4
Universal Precautions for Prevention of HIV, Hepatitis B, and Other Blood-Borne Pathogens

From *AIDS Surveillance Report* (p. 7), Centers for Disease Control, 1988, Atlanta, GA: Author. Used by permission.

The Centers for Disease Control and the Food and Drug Administration (1988) published guidelines designed to protect health care workers and to ensure the confidentiality of patients with HIV infection. These guidelines include the following information that is useful for classroom teachers.

■ Blood should always be handled with latex or nonpermeable disposable gloves. The use of gloves is not necessary for feces, nasal secretions, sputum, sweat, saliva, tears, urine, and vomitus unless they are visibly tinged with blood. Handwashing is sufficient after handling material not containing blood.

■ In all settings in which blood or bloody material is handled, gloves and a suitable receptacle that closes tightly and is child-proof should be available. Although HIV does not survive well outside the body, all spillage of secretions should be cleaned up immediately with disinfectants. This is particularly important for cleaning up after a bloody nose or a large cut. Household bleach at a dilution of 1:10 should be used. Only objects that have come into contact with blood need to be cleaned with bleach.

■ When intact skin is exposed to contaminated fluids, particularly blood, it should be washed with soap and water. Handwashing is sufficient for such activities as diaper change; toilet training; and clean-up of nasal secretions, stool, saliva, tears, or vomitus. If an open lesion or a mucous membrane appears to have been contaminated, AZT therapy should be considered.

■ Prepare for the fact that the student will die, especially if AIDS is present.
■ Ensure that the student with HIV is included in all aspects of classroom activities.
■ Be sensitive to the stress that the student's family is undergoing.

Muscular Dystrophy

Muscular dystrophy is an umbrella term used to describe several different inherited disorders that result in progressive muscular weakness (Tver & Tver, 1991). The most common and most serious form of muscular dystrophy is **Duchenne dystrophy**. In this type of muscular dystrophy, fat cells and connective tissue replace muscle tissue. Individuals with Duchenne dystrophy ultimately lose their ability to walk, typically by age 12. Functional use of arms and hands will also be affected. Muscle weakness will also result in respiratory complications. Teachers must adapt their classrooms to accommodate the physical needs of students. Most individuals with this form of muscular dystrophy die during young adulthood. Specific suggestions for teachers include the following:

CONSIDER THIS
Should students who require extensive physical accommodations be placed in the same school, so that all schools and classrooms do not have to be accessible? Defend your response.

■ Be prepared to help the student deal with the loss of various functions.
■ Involve the student in as many classroom activities as possible.
■ Using assistive techniques that do not hurt the individual, help the student as needed in climbing stairs or in getting up from the floor.
■ Understand the functions and components of wheelchairs.
■ Monitor the administration of required medications.
■ Monitor the amount of time the student is allowed to stand during the day.

Children in wheelchairs need opportunities for social interactions.

- Be familiar with different types of braces (short leg, molded ankle-foot) students might use.
- Prepare other students in class for the realities of the disease.

Prader-Willi Syndrome

Prader-Willi syndrome is a condition characterized by compulsive eating, obesity, and intellectual disability (Silverthorn, & Hornak, 1993). Other characteristics include hypotonia (deficient muscle tone), slow metabolic rate, small or underdeveloped testes and penis, excessive sleeping, round face with almond-shaped eyes, nervous picking of skin, and stubbornness (Davies & Joughin, 1993; Silverthorn & Hornak, 1993; Smith & Hendricks, 1995). The only effective treatment for persons with Prader-Willi syndrome is weight management through diet and exercise.

Spina Bifida

Spina bifida is a "congenital condition characterized by a malformation of the vertebrae and spinal cord" (Gearheart, Weishahn, & Gearheart, 1996). It affects about 1 in 2,000 births (Bigge, 1991). There are three different types of spina bifida: spina bifida occulta, meningocele, and myelomeningocele (Gearheart et al., 1996; Robertson et al., 1992).

The least serious form of spina bifida is spina bifida occulta. In this type, the vertebral column fails to close properly, leaving a hole in the bony vertebrae that protect the delicate spinal column. With this form of spina bifida, surgically closing the opening to protect the spinal column is generally all that is required and does not result in any problems. **Meningocele** is similar to spina bifida occulta in that the vertebral column fails to close properly, leaving a hole in the bony vertebrae. Skin pouches out in the area where the vertebral column is not closed. In meningocele, the outpouching does not contain any nerve

TEACHING TIP

Get in a wheelchair and try to move about your classroom to see if it is fully accessible; often, areas look accessible but are not.

CROSS-REFERENCE

Review intervention approaches for students with intellectual disabilities, found in Chapter 6, and determine which ones would be appropriate for a student with intellectual disability and Prader-Willi syndrome.

FURTHER READING

For more information on spina bifida, read *Understanding Physical, Sensory, and Health Impairments,* by K. W. Heller, P. A. Alberto, P. E. Forney, and M. N. Schwartzman, published in 1996 by Brooks/Cole.

Pushing a Wheelchair

1. Over rough terrain or a raised area:
   a. Tilt the wheelchair by stepping down on tipping lever with foot as you pull down and back on hand grips.
   b. Continue to tilt chair back until it requires little or no effort to stabilize it.
   c. When the wheelchair is at the balance point, it can then be pushed over obstacles or terrain.
   d. Reverse the procedure and lower slowly. Make sure the wheelchair does not slam down or drop the last few inches.

2. Over curbs and steps:
   a. As you approach the curb or step, pause and tilt the wheelchair back to the balance point.
   b. When the wheelchair is stabilized, move toward curb until casters are on curb, and rear wheels come in contact with the curb.
   c. Move in close to the chair and lift the chair up by the handles. Roll the wheelchair up over the curb and push it forward.
   d. To go down, reverse the steps—back the wheelchair down off the curb without allowing it to drop down. Once rear wheels are down, step down on tipping lever and slowly lower casters.

3. Down a steep incline:
   a. Take the wheelchair down backward.
   b. The wheelchair can pick up speed too easily, and you can lose control if the wheelchair goes down first.
   c. Turn the chair around until your back is in the direction you plan to go.
   d. Walk backward, and move slowly down the ramp.
   e. Look backward occasionally to make sure you are staying on track and to avoid collisions.

tissue. Surgically removing the outpouching and closing the opening usually result in a positive prognosis without any problems. **Myelomeningocele** is the most common and most severe form of spina bifida. Similar to meningocele, it has one major difference: nerve tissue is present in the outpouching. Because of the nerve tissue, this form of spina bifida generally results in permanent paralysis and loss of sensation. Incontinence is also a possible result of this condition (Bigge, 1991; Robertson et al., 1992). School personnel must ensure appropriate use of wheelchairs (see the nearby Technology Today feature) and accommodations for limited use of arms and hands. Teachers should do the following when accommodating a child with spina bifida:

- Inquire about any acute medical needs the student may have.
- Learn about the various adaptive equipment a student may be using (see Baker & Rogosky-Grassi, 1993).
- Maintain an environment that assists the student who is using crutches by keeping floors from getting wet and removing loose floor coverings.
- Understand the use of a wheelchair as well as its major parts.
- Learn how to position these students to develop strength and to avoid sores from developing in parts of their bodies that bear their weight, or that receive pressure from orthotic devices they are using. Because they do not have sensation, they may not notice the sores themselves. Healing is complicated by poor circulation.

■ Understand the process of **clean intermittent bladder catheterization (CIC)**, as some students will be performing this process to become continent and avoid urinary tract infections—the process involves insertion of a clean catheter through the urethra and into the bladder four times a day and can be done independently by most children by age six.

■ Be ready to deal with the occasional incontinence of students. Assure the student with spina bifida that this is not a problem and discuss this situation with other class members.

■ Learn how to deal with the special circumstances associated with students who use wheelchairs and have seizures.

■ Ensure the full participation of the student in all classroom activities.

■ Help the student with spina bifida develop a healthy, positive self-concept.

■ Notify parents if there are unusual changes in the student's behaviour or personality or if the student has various physical complaints such as headaches or double vision—this may indicate a problem with increased pressure on the brain (Deiner, 1993).

Tourette's Syndrome

Tourette's syndrome is a neuropsychiatric disorder that occurs in males three times as often as in females, resulting in a prevalence rate for males as high as 1 in 1 000 individuals (Hansen, 1992). The syndrome is "characterized by multiple motor and one or more vocal tics, which occur many times a day, nearly every day or intermittently, throughout a period of more than one year" (Crews et al., 1993, p. 25). Characteristics include various motor tics; inappropriate laughing; rapid eye movements; winks and grimaces; aggressive behaviours; in infrequent cases, intellectual disabilities; mild to moderate incoordination; and peculiar verbalizations. Most important, school personnel should be understanding with children who have Tourette's syndrome. Monitoring medication and participating as a member of the interdisciplinary team are important roles for teachers and other school personnel.

CONSIDER THIS
How should students with Tourette's syndrome be dealt with when they shout obscenities and display other inappropriate behaviours that disrupt the classroom?

SUMMARY

■ Children with physical and health needs are entitled to an appropriate educational program according to the Canadian Charter of Rights and Freedoms.

■ Physical and health impairments constitute low-incidence disabilities.

■ The severity, visibility, and age of acquisition affect the needs of children with physical and health impairments.

■ Students with physical and health problems display a wide array of characteristics and needs..

■ Autism is a pervasive developmental disability that primarily affects social interactions, language, and behaviour.

■ Although originally thought to be caused by environmental factors, autism is now considered to be caused by organic factors, including brain damage and complications during pregnancy.

■ Growing evidence suggests that placing students with autism in general education classrooms with their nondisabled peers results in positive gains for them.

■ Children with traumatic brain injury (TBI) exhibit a wide variety of characteristics, including emotional, learning, and behaviour problems.

■ Asthma affects many children; teachers primarily need to be aware of medications to control asthma, side effects of medication, and the limitations of students with asthma.

- The survival rates for children with cancer have increased dramatically over the past 20 years. Teachers need to be prepared to deal with the emotional issues surrounding childhood cancer, including death issues. Children with cancer may miss a good deal of school; the school should make appropriate arrangements in these situations.

- Cerebral palsy is a condition that affects muscles and posture; it can be described by the way it affects movement or which limb is involved.

- Physical therapy is a critical component of treatment for children with cerebral palsy. Accessibility, communication, and social-emotional concerns are the primary areas that general educators must attend to.

- Cystic fibrosis is a terminal condition that affects the mucous membranes of the lungs.

- Juvenile diabetes results in children having to take insulin injections daily. Diet and exercise can help children manage their diabetes.

- Epilepsy is caused by abnormal activity in the brain that is the result of some brain damage or insult. Teachers must know specific steps to take in case children have a generalized tonic-clonic seizure in their classrooms.

- Infants and teenagers are two of the fastest-growing groups to contract HIV. Teachers need to keep up to date with developments in HIV/AIDS prevention and treatment approaches.

- Muscular dystrophy is a term used to describe several different inherited disorders that result in progressive muscular weakness and may cause death.

- Prader-Willi syndrome, a condition caused by a defect in the number 15 chromosome pair, is characterized by excessive overeating and mild intellectual disabilities.

- Spina bifida is caused by a failure of the spinal column to close properly; this condition may result in paralysis of the lower extremities.

- Tourette's syndrome is a neuropsychiatric disorder that is characterized by multiple motor tics, inappropriate laughter, rapid eye movements, winks and grimaces, and aggressive behaviours.

RESOURCES

British Columbia Ministry of Education, Special Programs Branch. (1995). *Awareness of Chronic Health Problems: What the Teacher Needs to Know*. Victoria: Author.

This practical information guide with specific classroom strategies for teachers covers 14 different health problems, including allergies, asthma, autism, cerebral palsy, Crohn's disease, diabetes, epilepsy, fetal alcohol syndrome, muscular dystrophy, and spina bifida.

Parent/Family Resource: A Resource Package Developed Based on a Parent Survey and Parent Focus Groups Conducted by Alberta Health, the Alberta Community Health Nurses Association and the AIDS Network of Edmonton Society.

Parents indicated a need for more strategies and skills on how to discuss sexual issues, age-appropriate materials and background information on sexual development, HIV/AIDs, and sexually transmitted diseases (STDs). The resource contains directories, brochures, posters, and contact information on videos. Age-appropriate materials are included, with consideration given to literacy and language challenges. Topics include sex, maturation, pregnancy, STDs, and HIV/AIDS prevention.

Jones, Melissa M. (1998). *Within Our Reach: Behavior Prevention and Intervention Strategies for Learners with Mental Retardation and Autism.* (Available through the Council for Exceptional Children)

This book is designed for teachers, parents, teacher trainees, and other service providers. It provides practical ways to resolve behavioural concerns about students with intellectual disabilities, autism, and other developmental disabilities. It focuses on responding to the communicative intent of various behaviour problems.

WEBLINKS

Autism Treatment Services of Canada
www.autism.ca/atsc.html
Autism Treatment Services of Canada, a national affiliation of organizations, provides treatment, educational, management, and consultative services to people with autism and related disorders across Canada. Their Web site provides excellent information about all aspects of autism as well as related resources.

Asthma Society of Canada
www.asthma.ca
This Web site will help teachers work with students with asthma. It has a whole section on managing asthma at school for teachers, who often misunderstand the problem. In a class of 30 students, an average of 4 will have asthma. Thus, asthma is one of the most common health impairments in the classroom. The Asthma Society of Canada, a national organization, is devoted to enhancing the quality of life of people living with asthma.

Epilepsy International
www.epilepsy-international.com/
At this Web site there are forums where teachers can pose questions about epilepsy and receive informed answers. Any teacher of a student with epilepsy should find this site a useful resource.

Spina Bifida and Hydrocephalus Association of Canada
www.sbhac.ca/
This Web site is an excellent starting point for any parent/teacher of a child with spina bifida (SB). In addition to providing a fact sheet, it provides links to related sites and educational information on students with SB, especially about common learning disabilities associated with the problem.

Canadian Brain Injury Coalition
www.cbic.ca/english
The Coalition is a national non-profit, charitable organization founded by provincial brain injury organizations in 1990. Its Web site provides important information on resources and supports available to persons with brain injuries and their families.

Muscular Dystrophy Association of Canada
www.mdac.ca/
The Association provides information on all types of muscular dystrophy and related resources as well as a forum where you can pose questions to a qualified expert. This Web site is very useful for teachers who may be working with a student with muscular dystrophy.

CHAPTER NINE

Teaching Students with Communication Disorders

BY KATHLEEN FAD

Don Ayers, now an adult, remembers his childhood days in speech therapy. "I got help for my speech from the time I was in Kindergarten until third or fourth grade. Now my speech is as normal as anyone else's. When I get excited, I still stutter and mispronounce words as anyone does.

"A lot of what has happened to me is reflected in the way I am today. I have never been one to make a lot of friends. I have a lot of associates, but only one or two close friends. It was the same in Kindergarten. It might be a habit from not having lots of friends then. I had one or two, maybe three friends who could understand me and who took the time to listen to me. They were what you'd call good active listeners who would try to understand me.

"That time ties into today and the way I make speeches. Once you know how to do something, you enjoy doing it. I know people who were called dyslexic and now love to read. I will give a presentation in front of a crowd—no problem. I like to talk in public.

"I can't remember any bad things about special ed or speech therapy. I thought I was the cream of the crop. I didn't feel bad at all. There were a lot of good, positive things. My teachers did things in an encouraging way. They really made the kids feel comfortable. I think they got better results that way. I liked my resource time and looked forward to it. I think that my experiences have helped me make some positive relationships. I am a lot more self-reliant."

1. In what ways did the special services provided to Don have an impact on his life as an adult?

2. Why is it important to be concerned with a student's self-concept? What kind of atmosphere helped Don have such a positive view of himself?

INTRODUCTION

For most of us, the ability to communicate is a skill we take for granted. Our communication is effortless and frequent. In one day, we might share a story with family members, discuss problems with our co-workers, ask directions from a stranger on the street, and telephone an old friend. When we are able to communicate easily and effectively, it is natural to participate in both the commonplace activities of daily living and the more enjoyable experiences that enrich our lives.

CONSIDER THIS

How would your life be different if you could not talk, or if you could not write, or if you could not hear?

However, when communication is impaired, absent, or qualitatively different, the simplest interactions may become difficult or even impossible. Moreover, because the communication skills that most of us use so fluently and easily almost always involve personal interactions with others, disorders in speech or language may also result in social problems. For children, these social problems are most likely to occur in school. School is a place not only for academic learning, but also for building positive relationships with teachers and enduring friendships with peers. When a student's communication disorder, however mild, limits these experiences, makes him or her feel different and inadequate, or undermines confidence and self-esteem, the overall impact can be devastating.

Communication problems are often complex. There are many types of communication disorders, related to both speech and language. This chapter describes strategies that teachers can use with students who have such disorders. Suggestions will address specific communication disorders as well as associated problems in socialization and adjustment.

BASIC CONCEPTS

Definitions

Speech and **language** are interrelated skills, tools that we use for communication. Heward (1995) defines the related terms this way:

> *Communication* is the exchange of information and ideas. Communication involves encoding, transmitting, and decoding messages. It is an interactive process requiring at least two parties to play the roles of both sender and receiver. . . . *Language* is a system used by a group of people for giving meaning to sounds, words, gestures, and other symbols to enable communication with one another. . . . *Speech* is the actual behavior of producing a language code by making appropriate vocal sound patterns. Although it is not the only possible vehicle for expressing language (gestures, manual signing, pictures, and written symbols can also be used to convey ideas and intentions), speech is a most effective and efficient method. Speech is also one of the most complex and difficult human endeavors. (pp. 234–236)

Various cultures develop and use language differently, and the study of language is a complex topic. The **American Speech-Language-Hearing**

Association (ASHA) (1982) includes the following important considerations in its discussion of language: (1) language evolves within specific historical, social, and cultural contexts; (2) language is rule-governed behaviour; (3) language learning and use are determined by the interaction of biological, cognitive, psychosocial, and environmental factors; and (4) effective use of language for communication requires a broad understanding of human interactions, including associated factors such as nonverbal cues, motivation, and sociocultural roles (p. 949).

Because language development and use are such complicated topics, determining what is *normal* and what is *disordered* communication is also difficult. According to Emerick and Haynes (1986), a communication difference is considered a disability in any of the following situations:

- The transmission or perception of messages is faulty.
- The person is placed at an economic disadvantage.
- The person is placed at a learning disadvantage.
- The person is placed at a social disadvantage.
- There is a negative impact upon the person's emotional growth.
- The problem causes physical damage or endangers the health of the person. (pp. 6–7)

In order to better understand communication disorders, it is helpful to be familiar with the dimensions of language and the terms used to describe related disorders.

Dimensions of Language

In its definition of communicative disorders, ASHA (1982) describes both speech disorders and language disorders. **Speech disorders** include impairments of *voice, articulation,* and *fluency.* **Language disorders** are impairments of *comprehension* or *use of language*, regardless of the symbol system used. A language disorder may involve the *form* of language, the *content* of language, or the *function* of language. Specific disorders of language form include **phonologic** and **morphologic impairments. Semantics** refers to the content of language, and **pragmatics** is the system controlling language function. Figure 9.1 contains the definitions of communication disorders as described by ASHA. The terms in this figure will be discussed in more detail later in the chapter. The category of communication disorders is broad in scope and includes a wide variety of problems, some of which may overlap. It is not surprising that this group of disorders includes a large proportion of all students with disabilities.

Prevalence and Causes

After learning disabilities, speech and language impairments are the most common disability seen in the schools. It is estimated that 8–10 percent of school-age children have some type of speech or language impairment (Winzer, 1999). These students have impairments in their ability to send or receive a message, to articulate clearly or fluently, or to comprehend the pragmatics of social interactions. The majority of them also have other disabilities such as learning disabilities, autism, or traumatic brain injury, so they are served under a variety

CONSIDER THIS
Can you think of instances in which you have been involved wherein communication between two or more persons was so poor that problems resulted?

CROSS-REFERENCE
See Chapter 3 on learning disabilities, and reflect on how communication disorders are similar to learning disabilities.

FIGURE 9.1
Definitions of Communication Disorders from ASHA

From "Definitions: Communicative Disorders and Variations," by the American Speech-Language-Hearing Association, 1982, *ASHA, 24,* pp. 949–950. Reprinted by permission of the American Speech-Language-Hearing Association.

COMMUNICATION DISORDERS

A. A *speech disorder* is an impairment of voice, articulation of speech sounds, and/or fluency. These impairments are observed in the transmission and use of the oral symbol system.

   1. A *voice disorder* is defined as the absence or abnormal production of voice quality, pitch, loudness, resonance, and/or duration.

   2. An *articulation disorder* is defined as the abnormal production of speech sounds.

   3. A *fluency disorder* is defined as the abnormal flow of verbal expression, characterized by impaired rate and rhythm, which may be accompanied by struggle behavior.

B. A *language disorder* is the impairment or deviant development of comprehension and/or use of a spoken, written, and/or other symbol system. The disorder may involve (1) the form of language (phonologic, morphologic, and syntactic systems), (2) the content of language (semantic system), and/or (3) the function of language in communication (pragmatic system) in any combination.

   1. Form of language

      a. *Phonology* is the sound system of a language and the linguistic rules that govern the sound combinations.

      b. *Morphology* is the linguistic rule system that governs the structure of words and the construction of word forms from the basic elements of meaning.

      c. *Syntax* is the linguistic rule governing the order and combination of words to form sentences, and the relationships among the elements within a sentence.

   2. Content of language

      a. *Semantics* is the psycholinguistic system that patterns the content of an utterance, intent, and meanings of words and sentences.

   3. Function of language

      a. *Pragmatics* is the sociolinguistic system that patterns the use of language in communication, which may be expressed motorically, vocally, or verbally.

COMMUNICATION VARIATIONS

A. *Communicative difference/dialect* is a variation of a symbol system used by a group of individuals that reflects and is determined by shared regional, social, or cultural/ethnic factors. Variations or alterations in use of a symbol system may be indicative of primary language interferences. A regional, social, or cultural/ethnic variation of a symbol system should not be considered a disorder of speech or language.

B. *Augmentative communication* is a system used to supplement the communicative skills of individuals for whom speech is temporarily or permanently inadequate to meet communicative needs. Both prosthetic devices and/or nonprosthetic techniques may be designed for individual use as an augmentative communication system.

of categories. In Canada, students with communication disorders constitute about 17 percent of all students with disabilities (Nessner, 1990). Almost all students with speech or language impairments are 6 to 12 years of age (Winzer, 1999). For this reason, most of the suggestions in this chapter focus on that age group, although many of the language development activities would also be useful for older students.

Identification and Assessment

Students with speech or language impairments receive services under a variety of categories depending on the appropriate provincial or territorial guidelines. The categories used in the Yukon, Saskatchewan, and Alberta indicate the range. In the Yukon, learning disabilities and speech and language impairments are combined under the heading of "communication exceptionality" (Yukon Education, Special Programs Services, 1995). In Saskatchewan, a student with a speech impairment is served under the category of "low cost disabled," a catch-all category for students who require specialized services (Saskatchewan Education Special Education Policy Manual, 1989). And in Alberta, a specific communication exceptionality category specifies the severity of a student's communication disorder (Alberta Education Special Education, Special Education Data Definitions, 1998). Regardless of the category, the focus across the country remains on providing services to these children in the regular classroom wherever possible. The traditional model of pullout services for speech therapy occurs only in cases where intensive specific intervention is required.

> **CONSIDER THIS**
> What are the advantages of serving most of the students with communication disorders in general education classrooms? When would pullout services be appropriate?

SPEECH DISORDERS

This section of the chapter discusses speech disorders that include problems in *articulation, voice,* and *fluency.* The discussion includes (1) a description and definition, (2) a brief explanation of causes, and (3) information related to identifying problems serious enough to require a referral for possible assessment or remediation. Next, suggestions for classroom teachers will be presented.

Articulation Disorders

Articulation disorders are the most common speech disorder (McReynolds, 1990). The ability to articulate clearly and correctly is a function of many variables, including a student's age and culture. Although some articulation errors are normal and acceptable at young ages, when students are older these same errors may be viewed as unacceptable and problematic. McReynolds (1990) has described the most common types of articulation errors: **distortions, substitutions, omissions,** and **additions**. (See Table 9.1.)

> **CONSIDER THIS**
> Think of all the young children you have encountered who have had articulation problems. Have most of the problems improved over time without intervention, or has intervention been required?

CAUSES OF PROBLEMS IN ARTICULATION

Speech impairments can be either *organic* (i.e., having a physical cause) or *functional* (i.e., having no identifiable organic cause). When you encounter a child with articulation disorders, consider the child's environment. Many functional disorders may be related to the student's opportunities to learn appropriate and inappropriate speech patterns, including opportunities to practise appropriate speech and the absence or presence of good speech models. Many functional articulation problems have causes that may be related to complex neurological or neuromuscular activities and might never be understood. Differences in speech can also be related to culture. These differences often do not constitute a speech disorder and will be discussed later in the chapter.

TABLE 9.1		
The Four Kinds of Articulation Errors		
Error Type	**Definition**	**Example**
SUBSTITUTION	Replace one sound with another sound.	Standard: The ball is red. Substitution: The ball is wed.
DISTORTION	A sound is produced in an unfamiliar manner.	Standard: Give the pencil to Sally. Distortion: Give the pencil to Sally. (the /p/ is nasalized)
OMISSION	A sound is omitted in a word.	Standard: Play the piano. Omission: P_ay the piano.
ADDITION	An extra sound is inserted within a word.	Standard: I have a black horse. Addition: I have a balack horse.

Reprinted with the permission of Macmillan Publishing Company from *Human Communication Disorders*, Third Edition, by George H. Shames and Elisabeth H. Wiig. Copyright © 1990 by Macmillan Publishing Company.

CROSS-REFERENCE
Review Chapter 7 on sensory impairments to see the impact of a hearing loss on articulation skills.

Organic articulation disorders are related to the physical abilities required in the process of producing speech sounds, which is a highly complex activity involving numerous neurological and muscular interactions. According to Oyer, Crowe, and Haas (1987), organic causes of speech impairments may include cleft palate, dental malformations, or tumours. Hearing loss, brain damage, or related neurological problems may also result in disorders of speech. The severity of articulation disorders can vary widely, depending in part on the causes of the disorders.

WHEN ARTICULATION ERRORS ARE A SERIOUS PROBLEM

Because we know the developmental patterns for normal sound production, we can recognize those children who are significantly different from the norm. According to Sander (1972), the normal pattern of consonant sound production falls within relatively well-defined age limits. For example, children usually master the consonant *p* sound by age three, but may not produce a correct *s* sound consistently until age eight. Although young children between ages two and six often make articulation errors as their speech develops, similar errors in older students would indicate an articulation problem. At age three it might be normal for a child to say *wabbit* instead of *rabbit*. If a 12-year-old made the same error, it would be considered a problem, and the teacher might want to refer the student to a **speech-language pathologist** for evaluation. Figure 9.2 presents this pattern of normal development.

CONSIDER THIS
How could cultural differences have an impact on a child's development of the specific sounds listed in Figure 9.2?

For a general education teacher, evaluating a student's articulation errors requires looking at the big picture, that is, how well the student is doing in class and whether the articulation disorder is interfering with either overall academic performance or social adjustment. A few common-sense considerations may give some insight into whether the student has a serious problem and what, if anything, should be done about it:

- *Take note of how intelligible the student's speech is.*
  This factor may vary over time. Sometimes, the context of the student's speech will make it easier for listeners to understand her or him. Also, some

FIGURE 9.2
Ages at Which 90 percent of All Children Typically Produce a Specific Sound Correctly

Note: Average estimates and upper age limits of customary consonant production. The solid bar corresponding to each sound starts at the median age of customary articulation; it stops at an age level at which 90 percent of all children are customarily producing the sound. The q symbol stands for the breathed "th" sound, as in *bathroom,* and the ∂ symbol stands for the voiced "th" sound, as in feather (Smith and Luckasson, 1992, p. 168).

From "When Are Speech Sounds Learned?" by E. K. Sander, 1972, *Journal of Speech and Hearing Disorders, 37,* p. 62. Reprinted by permission of the American Speech-Language-Hearing Association.

errors are easier to understand than others. For example, omissions are usually more difficult to understand than distortions or substitutions.

■ *Consider how many different errors the student makes.*
If the errors are consistent, that is, if the student repeats the same error rather than numerous different errors, he or she will be easier to understand. Peers and teachers will become familiar with these speech problems, and the student will have less of a problem relating to others. However, the problem should still be addressed so that the student's speech is intelligible to strangers.

■ *Observe whether the articulation errors cause the student problems in socialization or adjustment.*
If a student with articulation problems is ridiculed, excluded, or singled out because of a speech problem, then the teacher may want to refer the student

TEACHING TIP
General classroom teachers should screen all students in their classes, especially during the early elementary grades, to determine which students have articulation problems that might require intervention.

Articulation problems can result in problems in socialization or adjustment.

for a speech-language evaluation. Likewise, if a student is reluctant to speak in class, or seems self-conscious or embarrassed by articulation errors, the general education teacher should seek an evaluation.

■ *Consider whether the problems are due to physical problems.*
If they are, be sure that the student is referred to a physician. Some articulation problems are due to malformations of the mouth, jaw, or teeth. When the problems are structural, such as cleft lip or palate, they can often be corrected surgically. Likewise, dental malocclusions (abnormal closures and fit of the teeth) can be corrected with orthodontic treatment.

Voice Disorders

Voice disorders are abnormalities of speech related to volume, quality, or pitch. Voice problems are not very common in children, and it is difficult to distinguish an unpleasant voice from one that would be considered disordered. People generally tolerate a wide range of voices. Because our voices are related to our identities and are an integral part of who we are and how we are recognized, we usually allow for individual differences in voice. Voice disorders are not commonly thought of as either prevalent or serious.

According to Heward (1995), there are two basic types of voice disorders, **phonation** and **resonance**. Phonation refers to the production of sounds by the vocal folds. Humans have two vocal folds, which are located in the larynx and lie side by side. When we speak, healthy vocal folds vibrate, coming together smoothly along the length of their surfaces, separating, and then coming together again. These movements are usually very rapid and are controlled by the air pressure coming from the lungs. The rate of vibration controls the pitch of our voices (slow movements result in a low pitch, and a faster rate results in a high pitch). If the vocal folds do not meet and close together smoothly, the voice is likely to sound breathy, hoarse, husky, or strained.

Disorders of resonance involve either too many sounds coming out through the air passages of the nose (hypernasality) or the opposite, too little resonance of the nasal passages (hyponasality). Hypernasality sounds like talking through one's nose or with a "twang," and hyponasality sounds like one has a cold or a stuffy nose. Because resonance is related to what happens to air that travels from the vocal folds into the throat, mouth, and nasal cavity, when there are abnormalities in any of these structures, resonance problems can result.

CAUSES OF VOICE DISORDERS

Voice disorders can result from vocal abuse and misuse, trauma to the larynx from accidents or medical procedures, or congenital malformations of the larynx, nodules, or tumours. Sometimes, voice disorders are related to other medical conditions, so that when students evidence a voice disorder, the speech-language pathologist will often refer them to an otolaryngologist (ear, nose, and throat doctor). Some examples of organic problems related to voice disorders include congenital anomalies of the larynx, Reye's syndrome, juvenile arthritis, psychiatric problems, or Tourette's syndrome. Because most of these conditions are relatively rare, it may be more likely that the student's voice disorder is a functional problem, perhaps resulting from learned speech patterns (Oyer et al., 1987).

FURTHER READING
For more information on voice disorders, read *Human Communication Disorders* (third edition), by G. H. Shames and E. H. Wiig, published in 1990 by Macmillan.

WHEN VOICE DISORDERS ARE A SERIOUS PROBLEM

A student who has a voice disorder should be observed over the course of several weeks, since many symptoms of voice disorders are similar to other temporary conditions such as colds, seasonal allergies, or minor respiratory infections (Oyer et al., 1987). One way to get a meaningful measure of the student's speech during this time is to tape-record him or her several times during the observation period. The tape recordings will be helpful to the speech-language pathologist and will provide a basis for comparison. Again, our voices are part of our identity, and, quite often, differences in voice quality, volume, or pitch may be considered to be part of who we are, rather than a problem that requires correction. Teachers might ask themselves the following questions before referring a student for evaluation of a voice disorder:

CONSIDER THIS
How can a student's voice quality affect classroom and peer acceptance? What are some things that teachers can do to influence what the response is?

- Is the student's voice having such an unpleasant effect on others that the student is excluded from activities?
- Is there a possibility that the voice disorder is related to another medical condition?
- Might the voice quality be related to a hearing loss?

Fluency Disorders

Fluency refers to the pattern of the rate and flow of a person's speech. Normal speech has a rhythm and timing that is regular and steady; however, normal speech patterns also include some interruptions in speech flow. We all sometimes stumble over sounds, repeat syllables or words, mix up speech sounds in words, speak too fast, or fill in pauses with "uh" or "you know." Often dysfluencies of speech are related to stressful or demanding situations. When the interruptions in speech flow are so frequent or pervasive that a speaker cannot be understood, when efforts at speech are so intense that they are uncomfortable, or when they draw undue attention, then the dysfluencies are considered a problem (Hallahan & Kauffman, 1995).

Many young children, especially those between ages three and five, demonstrate dysfluencies in the course of normal speech development. Parents and teachers may become concerned about young children's fluency problems, but most of these dysfluencies of early childhood begin to disappear by age five. The most frequent type of fluency disorder is **stuttering**, which affects about 2 percent of school-age children, more often boys than girls (Smith & Luckasson, 1992).

Fluency problems usually consist of blocking, repeating, or prolonging sounds, syllables, words, or phrases. In *stuttering,* these interruptions are frequently obvious to both the speaker and the listener. Often, they are very disruptive to the act of speaking, much more so than disorders of articulation or voice. When the speech dysfluencies occur, listeners may become uncomfortable and try to finish the speaker's words, phrases, or sentences. This discomfort is exacerbated when a speaker's stuttering is accompanied by gestures, facial contortions, or physical movements. Because stuttering is such a pronounced interruption of normal speech and also has a profound impact on listeners, the disorder receives a lot of attention, even though it is not as prevalent as other communication disorders (Hardman, Drew, Egan, & Wolf, 1993).

CAUSES OF STUTTERING

Although many causes of stuttering have been suggested over the years, the current thinking among professionals in the field of communication disorders is that there may be many different causes of the disorder. According to Van Riper and Emerick (1984), these theories include (1) the view that stuttering is related to emotional problems, (2) the idea that stuttering is the result of a person's biological makeup or of some neurological problem, and (3) the view that stuttering is a learned behaviour. The most persistent theory is that stuttering is a learned behaviour resulting from normal dysfluencies evident in early speech development. Also, the role that heredity plays in the development of stuttering remains interesting, in light of the fact that male stutterers outnumber females by a ratio of four to one (Hardman et al., 1990).

There seems to be no doubt that the children who stutter are very vulnerable to the attitudes, responses, and comments of their teachers and peers. When considerable attention is focused on normal dysfluencies or when students begin to have negative feelings about themselves because of their stuttering, they may become even more anxious and their stuttering may get worse. Most students who stutter beyond the age of five years will require therapy by a speech-language clinician.

WHEN FLUENCY DISORDERS ARE A SERIOUS PROBLEM

We know that many children outgrow their speech dysfluencies. However, classroom teachers should be sensitive to students' problems and be sure to refer children who stutter so that they receive speech therapy. Teachers may wish to consider the following questions when deciding whether speech dysfluencies are serious:

■ *Is there a pattern to situations in which the student stutters?*
    Collect information about the student related to his stuttering. With careful observation, teachers may be able to determine if a student's stuttering occurs

---

TEACHING TIP

Teachers who have students who stutter should attempt to reduce the stress on these students and create an accepting atmosphere.

TEACHING TIP

Teachers should keep a log to record instances of stuttering and the activities occurring with the student and rest of the class when stuttering occurs. They should also note circumstances in which it does not occur.

under specific conditions, that is, with certain individuals, in particular settings, or when in stressful situations.

■ *Is the student experiencing social problems?*
Carefully monitor unstructured situations to determine the level of the student's acceptance by peers. Much of the socialization that occurs in school takes place in the cafeteria, on the playground, in the halls, on the bus, and in other nonacademic settings. When students are not successfully relating to peers in these environments because of a stuttering problem, then the problem is likely to grow worse.

■ *Is the student confident?*
Talk to the student to ascertain his or her level of confidence and self-esteem. One of the biggest problems facing children who stutter is the interactive effect of the disorder. The more they stutter, the more anxious, fearful, or nervous they become when they speak, thereby increasing the likelihood of stuttering. Children caught in this cycle of behaviour may be so self-conscious that they avoid situations in which they are required to speak and thus become isolated from friends and teachers.

Classroom Accommodations for Students with Speech Disorders

BUILD A POSITIVE CLASSROOM CLIMATE

Regardless of the type of speech disorder that students in general education classes demonstrate, it is crucial that teachers make every effort to create a positive, accepting, and safe climate. The following points are helpful to remember when dealing with children who have speech disorders:

■ Don't think of or refer to students with speech disorders in terms of their behaviours ("students," not "stutterers").
■ Work closely with the speech-language pathologist, following suggestions and trying to reinforce specific skills.
■ Encourage the student.
■ Be positive.
■ Accept the child just as you would any other student in the class.
■ Provide lots of opportunities for students to participate in oral group activities.
■ Give students lots of chances to model and practise appropriate speech.
■ Maintain eye contact when the student speaks.
■ Be a good listener.
■ Don't interrupt or finish the student's sentence for him or her.
■ When appropriate, educate other students in the class about speech disorders and about acceptance and understanding.
■ Reward the child just as you would reward any student.

HELP STUDENTS LEARN TO MONITOR THEIR OWN SPEECH

By using simple contract formats, teachers can help students focus on using the skills they learn in speech therapy. When students are aware of how to make sounds correctly, they can then practise, monitor their own performance, and earn reinforcement from the teacher or parents whenever specific criteria are met.

PAIR STUDENTS FOR PRACTICE

If students are to master articulation skills, they will need to practise the skills taught by the speech-language pathologist. One way for students to practise

FURTHER READING
For more information on working with speech-language pathologists, read the article "Collaboration: Working with the Speech-Language Pathologist" by R. G. Kerrin, published in 1996 in volume 21 of *Intervention in School and Clinic* (pp. 56–59).

TEACHING TIP
Self-monitoring strategies, such as record keeping, can facilitate a student's attempts to monitor his or her own speech.

specific sounds is to use practice exercises like those in *Hall's Articulation Remediation Training Sheets (HARTS)* (Butler-Hall, 1987). (See Figure 9.3.) With a partner, students can use short periods of downtime such as those between or before classes to work on their articulation. First, the student is trained in the speech therapy setting on a specific phoneme in a key word, for example, the *ch* sound in *hatch*. After the student has reached 90 percent mastery of the sound in the key word, she or he then reads the key word and every other word on the skill sheet, in alternating sequence (*hatch, catch, hatch, witch, hatch, sandwich,* etc.). Each practice session should take no more than five minutes and will provide students with practice that is simple and fun. Both partners

FIGURE 9.3
Sample Form for Articulation Practice

From *Hall's Articulation Remediation Training Sheets (HARTS)* (p. 3), by B. Butler-Hall, 1987, Henderson, TX: Creations Publications. Used by permission.

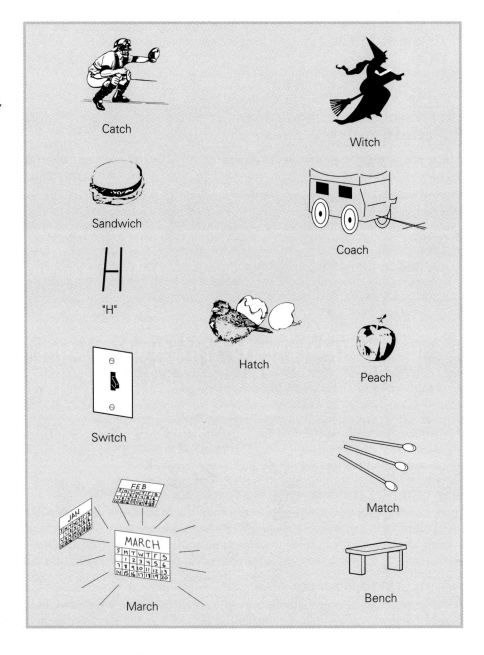

should be reinforced for their participation. This practice format can also be used at home with parents.

MODIFY INSTRUCTION AND MATERIALS

The Pre-Referral Intervention Manual (PRIM) (McCarney & Wunderlich, 1988) presents numerous ways of intervening with students who demonstrate speech errors. Some of the suggestions include the following:

- Set up a system of motivators to encourage students' efforts.
- Highlight material to identify key syllables and words in a passage.
- Give students practice listening so that they can learn to discriminate sounds.
- Tape-record the students' reading so that they can evaluate their speech for omissions, additions, distortions, substitutions, or reversals (saying words backwards).
- Reduce the emphasis on competition. Competitive activities may increase students' stress and result in even more speech errors.

ENCOURAGE PARENTS TO WORK WITH THEIR CHILDREN

There are many ways to structure practice activities so that students can work at home with their parents. One program is described in the book *Weekday Speech Activities to Promote Carryover* (Fehling, 1993; see Figure 9.4). This series of activities is designed for the carryover phase of an articulation program. There are 36 worksheets for summer activities. They are designed to be an enjoyable approach to maintenance and generalization of sounds into everyday conversation. By completing the activities, students assume responsibility for correct production of sounds in environments other than the speech therapy room. It is suggested that students complete one activity per day and then have their parents discuss it with them and provide feedback and guidance.

TEACH STUDENTS THEIR OWN STRATEGIES

Many of the speech problems that students demonstrate while young can be corrected and modified with therapy. While the therapy is going on, the

FURTHER READING
For more information on this program, read R. H. Fehling's *Weekday Speech Activities to Promote Carryover,* published by Pro-Ed in 1993.

Students with speech disorders can learn "tricks" and "strategies" that will help them to maximize their social strengths.

Sample Worksheet #1 (front)   **Sample Worksheet #1 (back)**

Sample Worksheet #1 (front)

Student's Name _____ *Eric* _____   Date *Oct. 7*

Sound ___ *52* _____

Mon. —Look for two street or road signs that have your sound.
1. Countryway Street
2. STOP Sign

Tues. —What letters of the alphabet have your sound as you
pronounce the names of those letters?
Write them down here.
C, S, X, Z

Wed. —Who are two relatives or neighbors with your sound in
their names?
1. Elizabeth
2. Robyn Pearse

Thurs. —Tell how you get over the hiccups. Be sure to use at
least one word with your sound.
drink a glass of water

Fri. —On the back of this paper draw something with your
sound that is COLD.

Comments:
Eric seems to be doing better
making his sound at home.

Please return ___ *Mon., Oct. 14* _____

Susan Garrison
Parent Signature

Ice Cream Cone

FIGURE 9.4
Speech Activities
That Parents Can
Use

From *Weekday Speech
Activities to Promote
Carryover* (p. 117), by R. H.
Fehling, 1993, Austin, TX:
Pro-Ed. Used by
permission.

teacher should focus on giving students strategies for successful learning. The strategies are little "tricks of the trade" that students can use to maximize their academic and social strengths. Some of these strategies also require accommodations on the part of the teacher in structuring situations and requirements.

- Teach them to relax with breathing exercises or mental imagery.
- Encourage them to participate in groups in which responses do not have to be individually generated.
- Teach them to reinforce themselves by recognizing when they are doing well and by appreciating themselves.
- Let them practise skills with a friend in real situations so that they are not afraid or nervous when it's the "real thing."
- Let them tape-record their own speech and listen carefully for errors so that they can discriminate between correct and incorrect sounds.
- Help them come up with strategies for dealing with specific people or situations that make them nervous (walking away, counting to 10 before they speak, deep breathing, etc.).

LANGUAGE DISORDERS

Language is the system we use to communicate our thoughts and ideas to others. According to Lahey (1988), language is a code "whereby ideas about the world are expressed through a conventional system of arbitrary signals for communication" (p. 2). The interrelationships of what we hear, speak, read, and write become our format for sharing information.

For most of us, spoken language is the tool we use to communicate our ideas, but even the most articulate, fluent, pleasant speech would be useless without a language system that enables us to understand and be understood. Language is an integral component of students' abilities in reading, writing, and listening. Disorders of language may have a serious impact on academic performance. In recent years, the emphasis in the field of communication disorders has shifted away from remediation of speech problems to an increased focus on language disorders. Estimates today are that 50 percent to 80 percent of the children seen by speech-language pathologists have language disorders (Wiig, 1986).

CONSIDER THIS
Try to go through a social situation without using oral language. Did you become frustrated when attempting to make your needs or ideas known to other people? How did you deal with the frustrations?

More important for classroom teachers, however, is the fact that remediation of language disorders will often be as much their responsibility as it is the speech-language pathologist's. Although remediation of speech problems is provided primarily in a therapeutic setting and then supported and reinforced by the classroom teacher, teachers will often direct and manage overall language development.

We know that humans can communicate in several ways. Heward (1995) describes a child's process for learning language this way: "A child may learn to identify a familiar object, for example, by hearing the spoken word *tree,* by seeing the printed word *tree,* by viewing the sign language gesture for *tree,* or by encountering a combination of these signals" (p. 235). We generally describe modes of communication as either **receptive language**, which involves receiving and decoding or interpreting language, or **expressive language**, which is the encoding or production of a message. Reading and listening are examples of receptive language; writing and speaking are forms of expressive language.

As with speech disorders, knowing the normal sequence of language development is important in working with students with language disorders. Some children may be delayed in their development of language but still acquire skills in the same sequence as other children. Other children may acquire some age-appropriate language skills but have deficits in other specific areas. Table 9.2 shows the normal patterns of language development for children with language disorders and children without language disorders. Although they may refer to these general patterns of language development to judge students' overall progress, teachers should not expect every child to follow this precise sequence on these exact timelines.

CONSIDER THIS
Remember when some children with whom you are familiar began to talk. What were some of their first words? What factors influence a child's early oral language development?

Dimensions of language

Earlier in the chapter, some terminology related to language disorders was introduced. In addition, we refer to the dimensions of language and their related impairments in terms of form, content, and function (or use). Students can demonstrate impairments in any or all of these areas.

TABLE 9.2

Language Development for Children with Language Disorders and without Language Disorders

	LANGUAGE-DISORDERED CHILD		NORMALLY DEVELOPING CHILD		
Age	Attainment	Example	Age	Attainment	Example
27 MONTHS	First words	*this, mama, bye bye, doggie*	13 MONTHS	First words	*here, mama, bye bye, kitty*
38 MONTHS	50-word vocabulary		17 MONTHS	50-word vocabulary	
40 MONTHS	First two-word combinations	*this doggie more apple this mama more play*	18 MONTHS	First two-word combinations	*more juice here ball more TV here kitty*
48 MONTHS	Later two-word combinations	*Mimi purse Daddy coat block chair dolly table*	22 MONTHS	Later two-word combinations	*Andy shoe Mommy ring cup floor keys chair*
52 MONTHS	First sentence length of 2.00 words		24 MONTHS	Mean sentence length of 2.00 words	
55 MONTHS	First appearance length of *-ing*	*Mommy eating*	24 MONTHS	First appearance of *-ing*	*Andy sleeping*
63 MONTHS	Mean sentence length of 3.10 words		30 MONTHS	Mean sentence length of 3.10 words	
66 MONTHS	First appearance of *is*	*The doggie's mad*	30 MONTHS	First appearance of *is*	*My car's gone!*
73 MONTHS	Mean sentence length of 4.10 words		37 MONTHS	First appearance length of 4.10 words	
79 MONTHS	Mean sentence length of 4.50 words		37 MONTHS	First appearance of indirect requests	*Can I have some cookies?*
79 MONTHS	First appearance of indirect requests	*Can I get the ball?*	40 MONTHS	Mean sentence length of 4.50 words	

From "Language Disorders in Preschool Children," by L. Leonard. In *Human Communication Disorders: An Introduction* (2nd ed.), edited by G. H. Shames and E. H. Wiig, 1990, p. 242. New York: Macmillan. Reprinted with permission of Merrill, an imprint of Macmillan Publishing Company.

FORM

Form describes the rule systems used in oral language. Three different rule systems are included when we discuss form: **phonology**, **morphology**, and **syntax**.

Phonology is the rule system that governs the individual and combined sounds of a language. Phonological rules vary from one language to another. For example, some of the guttural sounds heard in German are not used in English.

Morphology refers to the rule system controlling the structure of words. Because the structures of words govern their meanings, comparative suffixes such as *-er* or *-est* and plural forms such as the *s* that changes *book* to *books* are important. Oyer et al. (1987) provide an example of how morphemes (units of meaning) can change a basic word into similar words with many different meanings:

> The word "friend" is composed of one free morpheme that has meaning. One or more bound morphemes may be added, making "friend*ly*," "*un*friendly," "friend*less*," "friend*liness*," "friend*ship*," and "friend*lier*." There are rules for combining morphemes into words that must be followed (e.g., "*dis*friend" is not an allowable word and thus has no meaning). (p. 61)

Syntax is the ordering of words in such a way that they can be understood. Syntax rules determine where words are placed in a sentence. Just like phonology, syntax rules vary from one language to another. Rules governing negatives, questions, tenses, and compound or simple sentences determine the meanings of word combinations. For example, the same words used in different combinations can mean very different things: *The boy hit the ball* is not the same as *The ball hit the boy.*

All of these rule systems affect how we use and understand language. Children's abilities to understand and correctly use all of these rules related to form develop sequentially as their language skill develops. Form is important not only in spoken language, but in written language and in sign language systems, too.

CONTENT

Content refers to the intent and meaning of language and its rule system; *semantics* deals with the meaning of words and word combinations. Without specific words to label and describe objects or ideas, our language would have no meaning. When students fail to comprehend concrete and abstract meanings of words, inferences, or figurative phrases, it is difficult for them to understand more subtle uses of language such as jokes, puns, smiles, proverbs, or sarcasm. As children mature, they are better able to differentiate meanings of similar words, classify them by similarities, and understand abstract meanings of words.

USE

When we use language in various social contexts, we follow another set of rules, *pragmatics.* The purpose and setting of our communication as well as the people with whom we are communicating determine the language we use. If children are to build and maintain successful relationships with others, it is important that they understand and effectively use skills appropriate to the context. For example, when children speak to adults, it is helpful if they use polite, respectful language; when they speak to their friends, they will most likely use less formal spoken language, demonstrate more relaxed body language, and take turns while talking (Owens, 1984).

TEACHING TIP

Teaching students appropriate social skills has a link to pragmatics and helps them understand how to tailor language to different social situations.

Types and Causes

Hallahan and Kauffman (1991) have described four basic categories of language disorders: absence of verbal language, qualitatively different language,

TABLE 9.3	
Types of Language Disorders and Their Causes	
Type	**Commonly Suspected Causative Factors or Related Conditions**
NO VERBAL LANGUAGE Child does not show indications of understanding or spontaneously using language by age 3.	• Congenital or early acquired deafness • Gross brain damage or severe intellectual disability/developmental disabilities • Severe emotional disturbance
QUALITATIVELY DIFFERENT LANGUAGE Child's language is different from that of nondisabled children at any stage of development—meaning and usefulness for communication are greatly lessened or lost.	• Inability to understand auditory stimuli • Severe emotional disturbance • Learning disability • Intellectual disability/developmental disabilities • Hearing loss
DELAYED LANGUAGE DEVELOPMENT Language follows normal course of development, but lags seriously behind that of most children who are the same chronological age.	• Intellectual disability • Experiential deprivation • Lack of language stimulation • Hearing loss
INTERRUPTED LANGUAGE DEVELOPMENT Normal language development begins but is interrupted by illness, accident, or other trauma; language disorder is acquired.	• Acquired hearing loss • Brain injury due to oxygen deprivation, physical trauma, or infection

Adapted from "Language Disorders in Children," by R. C. Naremore. In *Introduction to Communication Disorders*, edited by T. J. Hixon, L. D. Shriberg, and J. H. Saxman, 1980, p. 224. Englewood Cliffs, NJ: Prentice-Hall. Used by permission.

delayed language development, and interrupted language development. Table 9.3 from Naremore (1980) summarizes these four categories and includes some suspected causes of each. For children who are not deaf, a complete absence of language would likely indicate severe emotional disturbance or a severe developmental disorder. Qualitatively different language is also associated with developmental disorders and emotional disturbance. A good example of this type of problem is the echolalic speech of children with autism, who may repeat speech they hear in a singsong voice and fail to use their spoken language in a meaningful way. Delayed language occurs when a child develops language in the same sequence as other children, but at a slower rate. Causes of delayed language include intellectual disability, hearing loss, or lack of stimulation or appropriate experiences. Sometimes language development is interrupted by illness or physical trauma. This type of language problem is increasingly common among children as a result of traumatic brain injury (TBI). In general education classrooms, teachers may encounter any or all of these types of language disorders at ranges from very mild to severe.

Indicators of Language Impairments

Some teachers may have an overall sense that a student is demonstrating language problems; others may not notice anything amiss. Wiig and Semel (1984) have identified some indicators of language problems by grade levels:

- Primary grades:
  — Problems in following verbal directions
  — Difficulty with preacademic skills (recognizing sound differences)
  — Phonics problems
  — Poor word-attack skills
  — Difficulties with structural analysis
  — Problems learning new material
- Intermediate grades:
  — Word substitutions
  — Inadequate language processing and production that affects reading comprehension and academic achievement
- Middle and high school:
  — Inability to understand abstract concepts
  — Problems understanding multiple word meanings
  — Difficulties connecting previously learned information to new material that must be learned independently
  — Widening gap in achievement when compared to peers

In addition, Figure 9.5 presents a checklist of behaviours that may indicate either speech or language problems. Children who have language disorders sometimes develop patterns of interaction with peers, teachers, and family members that may result in behaviour problems. The behaviour problems might seem to have nothing to do with language problems but may in fact have developed in response to inabilities to read, spell, talk, or write effectively.

Classroom Accommodations for Students with Language Disorders

Numerous strategies can be used in general education classrooms to improve students' language skills and remedy language deficits. The following section presents some ways of structuring learning situations and presenting information to enhance communication.

TEACH SOME PREREQUISITE IMITATION SKILLS

Nowacek and McShane (1993) recommend the following activities:

- Show a picture (of a girl running) and say, "The girl is running."
- Ask the student to repeat a target phrase.
- Positively reinforce correct responses.
- Present a variety of subject-verb combinations until the student correctly and consistently imitates them.

INCREASE RECEPTIVE LANGUAGE IN THE CLASSROOM

Clary and Edwards (1992) suggest some specific activities to improve students' receptive language skills:

- *Give students practice in following directions.*
  Begin with one simple direction, and then increase the length of the list of directions. Have the student perform a simple task in the classroom such as closing the door, turning around, and so on.
- *Have students pair up and practise descriptions.*
  Place two students at a table separated by a screen. Place groups of identical objects in front of both students. Have one describe one of the objects; the

TEACHING TIP

If you suspect a child of having language problems, keep a record of the problems to better determine if a referral for services is warranted.

CROSS-REFERENCE

When reading Chapters 12 and 13, consider specific activities that could be used to teach listening skills to elementary students and secondary students.

FIGURE 9.5
Teacher's Checklist
of Behaviours That *May*
Indicate Communication
Disorders

SPEECH

☑ Poor articulation

☑ Different voice quality

☑ Dysfluencies

☑ Slurred conversational speech

LANGUAGE

☑ Has problems following oral directions

☑ Speech rambles; isn't able to express ideas concisely

☑ Appears shy, withdrawn, never seems to talk or interact with others

☑ Asks questions that are off-topic

☑ Has a poor sense of humour

☑ Has poor comprehension of material read

☑ Doesn't plan ahead in pencil/paper activities

☑ Takes things literally

☑ Is not organized; appears messy

☑ Doesn't manage time well; has to be prodded to complete assignments

other must determine which object is being described. Reverse roles with new sets of objects.

■ *Let students work on categorizing.*
Orally present a list of three words. Two should be related in some way. Ask a student to tell which two are related and why (e.g., horse, tree, dog).

The nearby Inclusion Strategies feature provides some additional suggestions for teaching listening skills.

GIVE STUDENTS OPPORTUNITIES FOR FACILITATIVE PLAY
This type of interaction provides modelling for the students so that they can imitate and expand their own use of language. The following is an abbreviated sequence for facilitative play:

■ The teacher models self-talk in a play activity. ("I'm making the cars go.")
■ The teacher elicits comments from the student and then expands on them. ("Yes, the cars are going *fast*.")

INCLUSION STRATEGIES

Teaching Listening Skills for Class Discussions

ENCOURAGE ACTIVE LISTENING DURING DIRECTIONS

You can do this in several ways:

1. Restate the directions in question form. ("How many problems are you supposed to do?")
2. Ask a student to rephrase the direction. ("Tell the class what page we need to read.")
3. Write the key words from the direction on the board (not the entire direction; it discourages listening).

USE LISTENING BUDDIES

Students can rephrase information for each other in a cooperative structure. ("Turn to your partner and explain what the first step is.") Students could also quiz each other at regular intervals, either for test reviews or less formal checks for understanding.

ENCOURAGE LISTENING DURING LECTURES

After stating the objectives for the lesson, one way to encourage good active listening is to make use of students' prior knowledge. Let students begin discussion of a topic with a brainstorming session. Brainstorming ideas is fun for students. Students can generate ideas and share information; teachers can acknowledge students' input and remind them of how much they already know.

AROUSE STUDENT CURIOSITY

There are numerous questioning strategies that arouse students' interest in various topics. At the beginning of a lesson, let students generate a list of questions about the topic. As the lesson progresses, return to the students' questions. Point out the ones that have been answered, and, if there are still some questions unanswered at the end of the lesson, allow students to work independently or in cooperative groups to locate the information. Always try to encourage some higher-level *thinking questions* that call for creative, open-ended responses.

From *Listen to Learn* (p. 10), by L. K. Pruden, 1992, Bedford, TX: GG Publishing. Used by permission.

■ The teacher uses "buildups" and "breakdowns" by expanding on a student's ideas, breaking them down, and then repeating them. ("Red car go? Yes, look at the red car. It's going fast on the road. It's going to win the race.") (Nowacek & McShane, 1993)

USE NATURALISTIC TECHNIQUES AND SIMULATED REAL-LIFE ACTIVITIES TO INCREASE LANGUAGE USE

Often, the most effective techniques to instill language acquisition and use are those that will be easy for teachers to use and easy for students to generalize to everyday situations. Teachers can encourage generalization by using naturalistic and situational strategies and real-life activities.

■ Naturalistic Techniques
   — Try cloze activities. ("What do you need? Oh, you need paint and a _____. That's right, you need paint and a brush.")
   — Emphasize problem solving. ("You can't find your backpack? What should you do? Let's look on the hook. Is your coat there? What did we do to find your coat? That's right, we looked on the hook.")
   — Use questioning techniques. ("Where are you going? That's right, you are going to lunch.")

CONSIDER THIS
When using some of these strategies to encourage students to speak, what can you do that will make it more likely that the student will continue to speak without these strategies?

- Simulated Real-Life Activities
  — Let students simulate a newscast or commercial.
  — Have students write and follow their own written directions to locations in and around the school.
  — Play "social charades" by having students act out social situations and decide on appropriate responses.
  — Have one student teach an everyday skill to another (e.g., how to shoot a basket).
  — Using real telephones, give students opportunities to call each other, and to give, receive, and record messages.

ENCOURAGE STUDENTS' CONVERSATIONS THROUGH STORY READING

McNeill and Fowler (1996) give some excellent suggestions for helping students with delayed language development. Since students with language development problems often do not get the results they want through their ordinary conversations, they need more practice. What better way to practise effective language skills than through story reading! Students of all ages enjoy being read to, whether individually or in small groups while students are young, or in larger classes when they are in intermediate or secondary grades.

These authors suggest four specific strategies for teachers to use when reading stories aloud:

- Praise the students' talk.
- Expand on their words.
- Ask open-ended questions.
- Pause long enough to allow students to initiate speaking.

FURTHER READING

For more information on this technique, read the article "Using Story Reading to Encourage Children's Conversations," by J. H. McNeill and S. A. Fowler, published in 1996 in volume 28 of *Teaching Exceptional Children* (pp. 43–47).

In addition, they emphasize taking turns, so that students have an opportunity to clarify their messages, hear appropriate language models, and practise the unspoken rules of communication. McNeill and Fowler (1996) also recommend coaching parents in how to give their children opportunities to talk and how to respond when their children *do* talk. When parents pause, expand on answers, and ask open-ended questions that require more than just "yes" or "no" responses, they can become their children's best teachers.

USE MUSIC AND PLAY GAMES TO IMPROVE LANGUAGE

Teachers should always try to have some fun with students. Using music and playing games are two ways language can be incorporated into enjoyable activities.

- Music
  — Use songs that require students to request items (e.g., rhythm sticks or tambourines passed around a circle).
  — Have picture symbols for common songs so that students can request the ones they like.
  — Use props to raise interest and allow students to act out the story (e.g., during "Humpty Dumpty" the student falls off a large ball).
  — Use common chants such as "When You're Happy and You Know It," and let students choose the action (e.g., clap your hands).
- Games That Require Receptive or Expressive Language
  — Do "Simon Says."
  — Play "Musical Chairs" with words. (Pass a ball around a circle. When the teacher says a magic word, the student with the ball is out.)

— Use key words to identify and organize students. ("All of the boys with red hair stand up. Everyone who has a sister sit down.")
— Play "Twenty Questions." ("I'm thinking of a person." Students ask yes-or-no questions.)

ARRANGE YOUR CLASSROOM FOR EFFECTIVE INTERACTIONS

For students who have either speech or language problems, the physical arrangement of the classroom can contribute to success. The following guidelines may improve students' language development:

■ Give instructions and important information when distractions are at their lowest.
■ Use consistent attention-getting devices, either verbal, visual, or physical cues.
■ Be specific when giving directions.
■ Write directions on the chalkboard, flipchart, or overhead so that students can refer to them.
■ Use students' names frequently when talking to them.
■ Emphasize what you're saying by using gestures and facial expressions.
■ Pair students up with buddies for modelling and support.
■ Allow for conversation time in the classroom so that students can share information and ideas.
■ Encourage students to use calendars to organize themselves and manage their time. (Breeding, Stone, & Riley, n.d.)

USE CHALLENGING GAMES WITH OLDER STUDENTS

Older students may require continued intervention to improve language skills. However, the activities chosen must be appropriate and not seem like "baby" games. Thomas and Carmack (1993) have collected ideas to involve older students in enjoyable, interactive tasks:

■ Read fables or stories with morals. Discuss outcomes, and focus on the endings.
■ Do "Explain That." Discuss common idiomatic phrases, and help students discover the connection between the literal and figurative meanings (e.g., *She was on pins and needles*).
■ "Riddlemania" presents riddles to students and has them explain what makes them humorous.
■ Have "Sense-Able Lessons." Bring objects to see, taste, hear, and smell, and compile a list of students' verbal comments. (p. 155)

MODIFY STRATEGIES TO DEVELOP STUDENTS' LEARNING TOOLS

When facilitating language development for older students, help them develop their own strategies to use in challenging situations (Thomas & Carmack, 1993). Requiring them to use higher-order thinking skills will both require and stimulate higher-level language.

■ Pair students to find word meanings. Use partners when working on categories such as synonyms or antonyms. Let students work together to master using a thesaurus.
■ Teach students to categorize. Begin with concrete objects that they relate to easily, such as types of cars or names of foods, and then move to more abstract concepts such as feelings or ideas.
■ Play reverse quiz games like "Jeopardy!" in which students have to work backward to think of questions for answers. (pp. 155–163)

FURTHER READING
For more information on fun activities that can facilitate the use of language, read *The Developmentally Appropriate Inclusive Classroom in Early Education,* written by R. Miller and published in 1996 by Delmar.

WORK COLLABORATIVELY WITH THE SPEECH-LANGUAGE PATHOLOGIST

LINC (Language IN the Classroom) is a program adapted for use in schools (Breeding et al., n.d.). The program philosophy holds that language learning should occur in the child's most natural environment and in conjunction with other content being learned. The development of students' language should relate to their world and should be a learning experience, not a teaching experience.

The purpose of the program is to strengthen the language system of those students in general education classrooms who need to develop coping and compensatory skills to survive academically. Another goal is to transfer language learned from the therapy setting to the classroom, thereby allowing children to learn to *communicate,* rather than merely *talk.* The teacher and the speech-language pathologist must both be present for the approach to be successful. The two professionals work together to plan unit lessons that develop language skills in students.

Hiller (1990) presents an example of how LINC works. His elementary school implemented classroom-based language instruction. At the beginning of the program, the speech-language pathologist visited each classroom for a specified amount of time each week (90 minutes) during the language arts period. The first 45 minutes were used for an oral language activity, often a cooking activity from the *Blooming Recipes* workbook (Tavzel, 1987). During the second 45 minutes, students did paragraph writing. For example, after preparing peanut butter on celery ("Bumps on a Log"), students responded to these questions:

What was the name of the recipe we made?
Where did we do our preparing?
Who brought the peanut butter, celery, and raisins?
How did we make "Bumps on a Log"?
When did we eat "Bumps on a Log"?
Why do you think this recipe was called "Bumps on a Log"?

Responses were written on the board or on an overhead transparency. Students copied the responses in paragraph format.

Teachers and speech-language pathologists later extended the activities to teaching language lessons on current topics, team-teaching critical thinking activities during science experiments, and team planning and teaching social studies units. Reports from Hiller's and other schools using LINC programs described better collaboration among professionals, more accurate language referrals, and increased interest in speech-language activities among the entire staff.

USE STORYTELLING AND PROCESS WRITING

When children listen to and retell a story, they incorporate it into their oral language repertoire. McKamey (1991) has described a structure for allowing students to retell stories they had heard, to tell stories from their own experience, and to write down and illustrate their oral presentations. In process writing, students are instructed based on what they can already do. This and other whole language experiences often allow students who have had negative language experiences to begin to succeed, to link written and spoken language, and to grow as communicators.

LANGUAGE DIFFERENCES RELATED TO CULTURE

Children's patterns of speech and use of language reflect their culture and may be different from that of some of their peers. It is important not to mistake a language *difference* for a language *disorder,* but also a disorder must not be overlooked in a student with language differences. Cultural variations in family structure, child-rearing practices, family perceptions and attitudes, and language and communication styles can all influence students' communication (Wayman, Lynch, & Hanson, 1990).

Relationship between Communication Style and Culture

Culture has a strong influence on the *style* of communication. Many areas of communication style can be affected, including gender, status, and age roles; rules governing interruptions and turn taking; use of humour; and how to greet or leave someone (Erickson, 1992). Teachers must be aware of the many manifestations of culture in nonverbal communication, as well. Differences in rules governing eye contact, the physical space between speakers, use of gestures and facial expression, and use of silence can cause dissonance between teachers and students of differing cultures. Walker (1993) has described how differences such as directness of a conversation, volume of voices, and reliance on verbal (low-context) versus nonverbal (high-context) parts of communication affect attitudes toward the speaker. Teachers can respond to cultural differences in several ways. These suggestions are adapted from Walker (1993) and should be helpful for teachers who want to enhance both overall achievement and communication skills with students who are culturally or linguistically different:

- Try to involve community resources, including churches and neighbourhood organizations, in school activities.
- Make home visits.
- Allow flexible hours for conferences.
- Question your own assumptions about human behaviour, values, biases, personal limitations, and so on.
- Try to understand the world from the student's perspective.
- Ask yourself questions about an individual student's behaviour in light of cultural values, motivation, and world views, and how these relate to his or her learning experiences.

Considerations in Assessment

Assessment in the area of communication disorders is often complicated, just as it is for students with other disabilities. Linguistic differences are a contributing factor. For example, one Canadian secondary school enrolled students with 54 languages other than English (Housego, 1990). Because of the increasing numbers of students who are linguistically different and who require services in ESL (English as a second language) or who are limited English proficient (LEP), teachers should consult with personnel in special education, ESL, speech and language services, and bilingual education to obtain appropriate evaluation and programming services. Observation is an important form of as-

FURTHER READING

For a detailed discussion of bilingual education and special education, see a book written by Margaret Winzer and Kasper Mazurek of the University of Lethbridge: *Special Education in Multicultural Contexts*, published in 1998 by Prentice-Hall.

TEACHING TIP

Remember the basic tenets of nondiscriminatory assessment when evaluating students with diverse cultural backgrounds or when reviewing assessment data that have already been collected.

Considerations for Observing Linguistically Different Students

1. Identify exactly what is to be observed. Be specific and know what you are watching as a part of the ongoing behavior stream in classroom settings.

2. Record the time, date, and duration of your observation.

3. Number your observations of the same children across days. Important here is a systematic context and an easy, readily available reminder that this is, for example, the third observation of Juan, Tom, Hector, and Zoraida.

4. Make notes of what you are observing in a descriptive, specific form that tells exactly what occurred. Also, jot down any unexpected events that happened during your observation. However, when taking notes of these occurrences, it is helpful to note that they were "unexpected."

5. Keep notes of your interpretations of what happened.

From *Assessment and Instruction of Culturally and Linguistically Diverse Students* (p. 105), by V. Gonzalez, R. Brusca-Vega, and T. Yawkey (1997), Boston: Allyn & Bacon. Used by permission.

sessment, particularly when assessing students who are linguistically different. The nearby Diversity Forum feature provides some suggestions for observing these children.

There are many considerations for assessment personnel who work with students having cultural and linguistic differences. The following suggestions have been adapted from Toliver-Weddington and Erickson (1992) and may be useful for classroom teachers who suspect that students may have communication disorders.

■ When screening with tests, always select tests that have the most valid items for the skills to be assessed.
■ Consider procedural modifications such as lengthening the time limit.

The cultural background of a child will have a profound impact on the style of communication that is used.

- Try to assess whether the minority child has had access to the information.
- Consider scoring the test in two ways, first as the manual indicates, then allowing credit for items that may be considered correct in the child's language system and/or experiences. (Record and report both ways and indicate the adjustments.)
- Focus on what the child does well rather than what he or she cannot do.

Because of the increasing number of students in public schools from cultural and/or linguistic minority groups, teachers are recognizing the need for information related to learning and communication styles as well as modifications to curriculum and instruction. Although many of these children will never be identified as having a communication disorder, teachers in general education must be aware that differences in language and culture may often impact a student's apparent proficiency in both oral and written communication.

AUGMENTATIVE AND ALTERNATIVE COMMUNICATION

The term **augmentative communication** denotes techniques that supplement or enhance communication by complementing whatever vocal skills the individual already has (Harris & Vanderheiden, 1980). Other individuals (e.g., those who are severely neurologically impaired and cannot speak) must employ techniques that serve in place of speech—in other words, **alternative communication**. According to Shane and Sauer (1986), the term *alternative communication* applies when "the production of speech for communication purposes has been ruled out" (p. 2).

Communication techniques can be *aided* or *unaided*. Unaided techniques do not require any physical object or entity in order to express information (e.g., speech, manual signs or gestures, facial communication). Aided communication techniques require a physical object or device to enable the individual to communicate (e.g., communication boards, charts, and mechanical or electrical devices). Because substantial numbers of individuals lack speech because of intellectual disabilities, traumatic brain injury, deafness, neurological disorders, or other causes, there has been increased demand for augmentative and alternative communication. The nearby Technology Today feature lists the types of computer applications suitable for students with speech and language disorders.

Students without spoken language may use a basic nonautomated **communication board** with no electronic parts. Typically, the board will contain common words, phrases, or numbers. The communication board can be arranged in either an alphabetic or nonalphabetic format (see Figure 9.6). Because they are easy to construct and can be modified to fit the student's vocabulary, nonautomated communication boards are very useful in communicating with teachers, family members, and peers. There are some commercially available sets of symbols, including *The Picture Communication Symbols* (Mayer-Johnson, 1986) and *The Oakland Picture Dictionary* (Kirsten, 1981).

Electronic communication aids encompass a wide variety of capabilities, from simple to complex. Often, a voice synthesizer is used to produce speech output, and written output is produced on printers or displays. Software, which

FURTHER READING

For more information on how to select appropriate technology, read the article "Selection of Appropriate Technology for Children with Disabilities" by P. Parette, M. Hourcade, and R. VanBiervliet, published in the spring 1993 edition of *Teaching Exceptional Children.*

Speech and Language Disorders and Types of Computer Applications

Disorder	Types of Applications
ARTICULATION	Phonologic analysis, intelligibility analysis, drill and practice, and games
VOICE	Biofeedback programs and client information
FLUENCY	Biofeedback and relaxation programs
SYNTACTIC	Language sample analysis, drill and practice, games, and tutorials
SEMANTIC	Language sample analysis and cognitive rehabilitation
PRAGMATIC	Problem solving and simulations
HEARING IMPAIRMENT	Visual feedback, sign language instruction with CAI, and telecommunication applications

From "Computers and Individuals with Speech and Language Disorders," by P. S. Cochran and G. L. Bull. In *Computers and Exceptional Individuals*, edited by J. D. Lindsey, 1993, p. 146. Austin, TX: Pro-Ed. Used by permission.

is becoming increasingly sophisticated, can accommodate the many different needs of individuals who cannot produce spoken language. The following are some examples of communication aids and their key features:

- All Talk:
  - A portable, battery-powered speech output communication device
  - Voice output selection is made with an adaptable, touch-sensitive overlay
  - Human voice quality output; completely reprogrammable
  - Standard memory capacity is 600 words with option for 1200 words by special order
  - Expanded memory permits the user to sequence pictures and store different vocabularies on four levels
  - Additional vocabularies may be stored using a tape recorder
- Help U Key and Speak:
  - For people who have difficulty using the computer keyboard and are non-speaking or speech impaired
  - Has one-finger operation, Repeat Key Defeat, Word Prediction, user-defined dictionaries and macros
  - Provides complete keyboard control and the ability to speak sentences via Text to Speech Converter
- EvalPAC:
  - A portable, battery-powered communication aid with human quality and diphone-based voice synthesizer available with a male or female voice
  - Mounts on the Epson keyboard and can be accessed through light pointer, scanning, joystick, Morse code and Memkey Board
  - Software provides for relocating letter, function, and picture/symbol/phrase placement, rearranging the QWERTY keyboard
  - Has built-in text-to-speech features
  - Has an abbreviation expansion program and memory up to 27 000 characters
  - Voice output can be assigned to single picture selection or sequencing

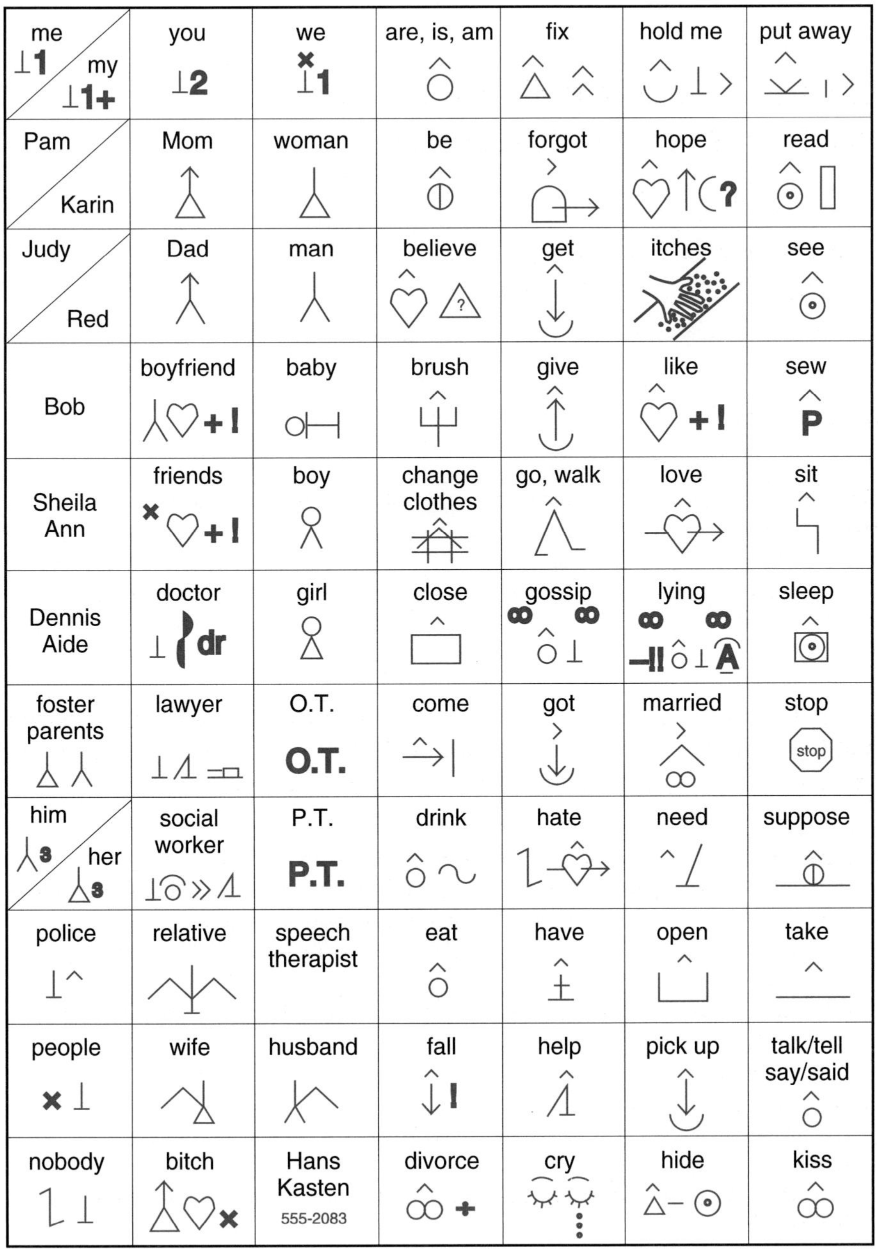

FIGURE 9.6
Communication Board in Alphabetic and Nonalphabetic Formats

From *Augmentative and Alternative Communication* (p. 58), by H. C. Shane and M. Sauer, 1986, Austin, TX: Pro-Ed. Used by permission.

me / my / 1+	you	we	are, is, am	fix	hold me	put away
Pam / Karin	Mom	woman	be	forgot	hope	read
Judy / Red	Dad	man	believe	get	itches	see
Bob	boyfriend	baby	brush	give	like	sew
Sheila Ann	friends	boy	change clothes	go, walk	love	sit
Dennis Aide	doctor	girl	close	gossip	lying	sleep
foster parents	lawyer	O.T.	come	got	married	stop
him / her	social worker	P.T.	drink	hate	need	suppose
police	relative	speech therapist	eat	have	open	take
people	wife	husband	fall	help	pick up	talk/tell say/said
nobody	bitch	Hans Kasten 555-2083	divorce	cry	hide	kiss

Facilitated Communication

Facilitated communication is a process that has recently been used with individuals who have developmental disabilities, including autism. First introduced by Rosemary Crossley in Australia, facilitated communication usually involves having someone support the arm or wrist of the person with autism, who then points to letters on a keyboard. The keyboard is often connected to a computer so that the individual's words can be displayed or printed (Kirk, Gallagher, & Anastasiow, 1993). The facilitator's support is seen as the key to enabling the individual to type out words and phrases.

Dr. Mary Parker, a school psychologist, has been employed by a Vancouver school board for more than 20 years. During that time Dr. Parker has seen vast changes in the school system and in her practice of which three stand out particularly.

First, her clientele has changed, a reflection of the changed demographic composition of society. Canada is today a country of ethnic and linguistic differences; the number and origins of immigrants who have come to Canada in the past 20 years have dramatically changed the composition of the country. Montreal, Toronto, and Vancouver, the three largest cities, accept 60 percent of all immigrants. Today, the United Nations recognizes Toronto as the most culturally and ethnically diverse city in the world (Lewington & Orpwood, 1993). Vancouver is the fastest-growing city in Canada. One in nine residents of British Columbia is of Asian origin, and the once overwhelmingly white Anglo-Saxon and Protestant school body has become largely Asian.

In Canadian urban school systems, the number of students whose home language is different from that in the schools has increased dramatically. By 1987, close to half the students in the major school boards in Toronto had learned English as a second language (Cummins, 1987). In Vancouver, where 79 different nationalities are registered for school, one-quarter of the student population does not have English as a first language (McLaren, 1988). Diversity only begins with language. Some of the students come from modern industrialized nations such as Hong Kong and Korea, others from vastly depressed areas such as Honduras and Mexico.

Second, the nature of the work has changed. When Dr. Parker first began as a school psychologist the greatest part of her time was spent administering tests of mental ability, such as the WISC and the Stanford-Binet. Recently her role has expanded. Now when a student is referred, the teacher hopes for valid evidence to guide decisions about curriculum and instruction and to evaluate the outcomes of instruction. As well as reviewing and assessing the cognitive, emotional, and sociobehavioral needs of children, Dr. Parker consults with centers and schools, counsels about behavior management, and provides support for parents and teachers. More and more teachers want assistance with behavior and emotional problems followed by assistance with problems related to home and family.

Third, the daily adjustments made by all assessors in procedures and interpretations have increased dramatically. The students referred to

Much of the work done in facilitated communication has been carried out by Biklen (1990), who has reported great success with the procedure. At this time, results of research on the effectiveness of facilitated communication are mixed; some individuals have shown great promise, and others have not done as well.

ENHANCING INCLUSIVE CLASSROOMS FOR STUDENTS WITH COMMUNICATION DISORDERS

The traditional service delivery model for speech therapy used to include a twice weekly, 30 minutes per session, pullout model in which speech-language pathologists worked with students in a separate setting. Even though this model may still be appropriate in clinical settings, there may be more effective ap-

Dr. Parker include new arrivals to the country, at-risk students, and those suspected of having disabilities. This means that Dr. Parker is constantly grappling with three major concerns: the instruments to use for appropriate assessments, the best way to present unbiased testing to students from minority groups and those with limited English, and the assessment of abilities of students with disabilities. When a student who is limited English proficient is suspected of having a speech or language delay or disability, the problem of assessment becomes even more complex for Dr. Parker and challenges her ingenuity.

For a number of reasons, Dr. Parker worries about assessing these students. First, she is frequently faced with assessing ethnic and minority-group children using standardized tests that have been normed on a representative sample of the general population. Not only does she hold concerns about the instruments themselves, but she often feels that she does not have the training to interpret and apply test results properly.

Another assessment problem is the assumption that a student has acquired full language competence when actually the student has only conversational English. Unless Dr. Parker can clearly distinguish between superficial and substantial competency, she may administer English language tests of intelligence and achievement and interpret the findings as she would for children whose first language is English. Dr. Parker is always cautious not to make a hasty reclassification as fluent English proficient. As well, dialectical differences in a language can result in misinterpretation, even when the examiner is proficient in that language (Bracken & Bartana, 1991). Immigrants from Caribbean countries such as Jamaica and Bermuda, for example, speak dialects of English that Dr. Parker finds difficult.

Finally, Dr. Parker is always aware of the need for cultural and gender sensitivity. She knows that if she is unaware of the behavior of a particular culture, she may perceive the behavior differently from trained observers and produce biased results.

Dr. Parker uses a wide variety of assessment techniques and tools so that no single one is advantageous to certain ethnic groups. For students whose primary language is not English, she uses a crosscultural battery. For example, if the child is Cantonese-speaking from Hong Kong, all assessment will be conducted in both English and Cantonese. After assessing aptitude, a crosscultural achievement battery will cover the following areas: language development in Cantonese and English, mathematical reasoning in both languages, cultural knowledge in Cantonese and English, spatial perception, visual motor coordination, and adaptive behavior in school and community (after Mercer, 1989).

From *Special Education in Multicultural Contexts* (pp. 174–175), by M. Winzer and K. Mazurek, 1994, Upper Saddle River, NJ: Merrill.

---

proaches for public schools. Moreover, just as academic services to students with disabilities have become more and more integrated into general education programs, speech-language services are following a more inclusive model. This collaboration might involve bringing the speech-language pathologists into the classroom to work with individual students, the teacher and speech-language pathologists teaching alternate lessons, or professionals co-teaching the same lesson at the same time.

As schools try to maximize the positive impact of professional collaboration, it is important to recognize and overcome the barriers inherent in the process. According to Kerrin (1996), the barriers to greater collaboration among speech-language professionals and teachers can include the following:

- Territorial obstacles (*"This is my job; that is your job."*)
- Time concerns (*"When are general ed teachers supposed to find the time to meet, plan, and modify?"*)
- Terror (*"I'm afraid this new way won't work."*)

CONSIDER THIS

What are some of the advantages and disadvantages, to both the child and general classroom teacher, for pull-out speech therapy services?

Fortunately, Kerrin has also offered some good ideas for overcoming these obstacles. She suggests that team members act on the following tips:

- Try to be flexible and creative when scheduling conferences.
- Encourage everyone involved to ask questions.
- Invite speech-language professionals into the classroom.
- Ask for assistance in planning.
- Maintain open, regular communication.
- Keep an open mind, a cooperative spirit, and a sense of humour.

FUTURE TRENDS

Several forces are changing the field of communication disorders. First, general education teachers are likely to see more students with moderate to severe disabilities in their classrooms. The movement toward more inclusive environments for students will require classroom teachers to provide more instruction for these students. The caseloads of speech-language pathologists are continuing to grow, and there is an ever-increasing demand for services, especially in the area of language disorders. Although pullout speech-language remediation will still be offered, many of the services will be delivered in an increasingly collaborative framework, with teachers and pathologists cooperating and sharing resources.

Another area of change is the expected continuation of technological advances. Some of the improved technology has already been described here; however, it is virtually impossible to keep up with the rapid improvements in this area. With continued improvements in technology, students with more severe communication disorders will have opportunities to interact with family members, teachers, and peers, perhaps participating in activities that would have seemed impossible ten years ago.

Author's note: The author would like to express her appreciation to Janice Maxwell, B.A., M.S. (SLP), for her assistance in providing much of the practical information that was presented in this chapter. Janice is an exemplary speech pathologist and a wonderful friend to teachers in general education.

SUMMARY

- Most people take the ability to communicate for granted.
- Communication problems result in difficulties in even simple interactions.
- Speech and language are interrelated skills that we use for communication.
- Speech disorders include impairments of voice, articulation, and fluency.

- Language disorders are impairments of comprehension or use of language.
- It is estimated that 8–10 percent of school-age children have some type of speech or language impairment.
- Most students with speech and language problems are placed in general education classrooms.

- Articulation disorders are the most common speech disorders.

- Significant problems with articulation require interventions.

- Voice disorders are related to volume, quality, or pitch.

- Building a positive classroom environment is an important accommodation for students with speech and language problems.

- Language disorders can affect receptive as well as expressive language skills.

- Form includes phonology, morphology, and syntax.

- Teachers can make numerous accommodations and modifications for students with language disorders.

- Some language problems may be due to the cultural diversity of students.

- Technology, through augmentative and alternative communication, can greatly facilitate the language use of persons with speech and language problems.

RESOURCES

Ontario Ministry of Education, Ministry of Training. (1992). *Hearing and Communication Resource Guide.* Toronto: Queens Printer of Ontario.

This resource guide covers hearing loss and communication with a detailed section on language development and ways to foster language. The 56-page document is also available on the Internet to download at **www.edu.gov.on.ca/eng/document/resource/resource.html**

Alberta Education, Special Education Branch. (1996). *Teaching Students with Learning Disabilities.* Edmonton: Author.

A whole section on the communication and language domain appears within this resource. There are specific classroom strategies for dealing with articulation difficulties, fluency difficulties, word retrieval difficulties and other problems.

WEBLINKS

Ontario Association for Families of Children with Communication Disorders (OAFCCD)
www.cyberus.ca/oafccd/
The Association's Web site has a wonderful array of resources, related links, personal stories, supports, and information on children with communication disorders as well as children's activities.

Ontario Association for Families of Children with Communication Disorders, Lanark, Leeds, & Grenville Chapter
www.cyberus.ca/oafccd/lanark/
Here is a particularly effective Web site with resources, information, chat rooms, inspirational poems, stories, quotes, excellent related links for

education and families, and superb kid links. The site has won numerous awards and is a must visit.

Net Connections for Communication Disorders and Sciences: An Internet Guide by Judith Maginnis Kuster
www.mankato.msus.edu/dept/comdis/kuster2/welcome.html
This Web site has an excellent list of Internet sources related to all different types of communication disorders. A teacher will be able to find information and strategies on all communication disorders from stuttering or fluency disorders to ESL or voice disorders.

CHAPTER TEN

CHAPTER OBJECTIVES

- To define giftedness
- To describe the characteristics of gifted students
- To describe ways to identify and evaluate gifted students
- To describe appropriate instructional methods for gifted students
- To discuss the curricular needs of gifted students

Teaching Students Who Are Gifted

Adam is a lively, talkative young boy. His vocabulary and the way he lectures on his main interests, science and ecology, have resulted in the teachers laughingly referring to him as the "little professor." Despite his excellent verbal abilities, though, he does not excel in language arts—his spelling is poor and his handwriting messy. Adam loves math and science, and enjoys all sports.

Adam's Grade 3 teacher, Mr. Garner, has recommended Adam for the enrichment program at their school. Adam will attend a resource room with two or three other children to work on a special enrichment project which will be related to the classroom curriculum. The students will then present their project to their classmates.

However, Adam's Grade 2 teacher, Mrs. Petrakos, argues with Mr. Garner that the boy's time would be better spent improving his spelling and handwriting skills. A heated discussion in the staff room ensues. Mr. Garner is convinced that Adam is gifted and should be provided with opportunities to excel in his areas of strength. Mrs. Petrakos insists that, while Adam has good verbal skills, his average to below-average written work would suggest that he needs remediation more than enrichment. Although the two teachers finish by agreeing to disagree, Mr. Garner is happy when he learns that Adam's parents have made the decision to have him independently tested by a psychologist. They are considering a small private school that requires academic tests for entrance, and they want to know if Adam would be successful. Mr. Garner is sure the results of the psychologist's tests will prove him right.

When the results are finally shared with Mr. Garner, he realizes they don't tell him anything he did not know. Adam does exceptionally well on the verbal subtests of the intelligence testing and overall scores in the "Superior" range. In the achievement tests he is above average in reading and arithmetic, but slightly below average in spelling and written language.

Mr. Garner is still convinced that Adam is gifted, but he knows that even if he could share these results with Mrs. Petrakos, it wouldn't change her mind; she would remain convinced that Adam is not gifted.

1. Is Adam gifted? Why or why not?

2. What kind of programming would you put in place for Adam?

3. In Adam's school, formal identification as gifted is not available and is not required for enrichment activities. What are the advantages and disadvantages of this system?

INTRODUCTION

Children and youth such as Adam, who perform or have the potential to perform at levels significantly above those of other students, have special needs as great as those of students whose disabilities demonstrably limit their performance. Also, since these students will probably spend most of the school day in general education settings, classroom teachers should have basic information about giftedness and know some useful techniques for maximizing the students' educational experiences.

Although there is no general agreement on the best way to educate students who are gifted, many professionals argue that such students benefit from a curricular focus different from that provided in general education. Yet the vast majority spend a considerable amount of time in the general education classroom, offering teachers the challenges and rewards of working with them.

The purpose of the chapter is twofold: (1) to provide basic information about giftedness in children and youth and (2) to suggest practices for working with these students in inclusive settings. This chapter is a primer only; confidence and competence in teaching students who are gifted come with study and experience.

BASIC CONCEPTS

CONSIDER THIS

Should there be provincial/territorial legislation to provide appropriate educational programs for students who are gifted and talented?

Students with exceptional abilities continue to be an underidentified, underserved, and often inappropriately served group. In some provinces/territories special services are available, but others do not identify or provide services for gifted students. Moreover, local school boards vary greatly in the type and quality of services provided—if indeed they are provided at all. McGill University's Bruce Shore, a leader in the gifted field, and colleagues make a compelling argument for the need for increased funding for gifted programs both in Canada and the United States (Shore, Cornell, Robinson, & Ward, 1991).

Students who could benefit from special programming are often not identified because of several factors. Teachers in general education may not be aware of the characteristics that suggest giftedness, particularly those associated with students who are culturally different. Historically, ineffective assessment practices have not identified gifted students coming from diverse backgrounds.

For students who are identified as gifted, a common problem is a mismatch between their academic, social, and emotional needs and the programming they receive. In many schools, a limited amount of instructional time is devoted to special activities. Furthermore, much of the gifted programming that exists today is geared for students who are gifted in the linguistic and mathematical areas. In too many instances, gifted students do not receive the education they need in the general education classroom.

Services to gifted students remain controversial, partly because the general public and many school personnel hold misconceptions about these students. Hallahan and Kauffman (1991) highlight some of these misguided beliefs:

- Gifted students are physically weak, socially inept, narrow in interests, and prone to emotional instability. *Fact:* In general, these students are quite the opposite.
- Gifted students do everything well. *Fact:* Some students show exceptional abilities in a broad range of areas; others show highly specialized abilities.
- Giftedness is a stable trait, always consistently evident in all periods of a person's life. *Fact:* Some students show indications of special abilities early on, whereas others will not demonstrate their unique and special abilities until later in life. Some individuals who show exceptional abilities at a young age will not do so later in their lives.
- Gifted students will excel without special education, needing only the incentives and instruction that are appropriate for all students. *Fact:* Most students with exceptional abilities will need a different educational program to meet their needs. (p. 399)

Many professionals in the field of gifted education find current services unacceptable and are frustrated by the lack of specialized programming for these students. Undoubtedly, the programming provided in inclusive settings to students who are gifted should be improved. VanTassel-Baska (1989) suggests that these students cannot be served appropriately unless their learning is accelerated, they are grouped in ways that promote appropriate levels of activities, and they have the opportunity to socialize with other students who also possess exceptional abilities.

Definition

Our understanding of giftedness has changed over time, and the terminology used to describe it has also varied. The term **gifted** is often used to refer to the heterogeneous spectrum of students with exceptional abilities, although in Canada the term *developmentally advanced* is also recognized (Keating, 1990). Other terms such as **talented** and **creative** are used to differentiate subgroups of gifted people.

Across Canada definitions of giftedness vary. In British Columbia (1995) the definition is, as follows:

> A student is considered gifted when she/he possesses demonstrated or potential abilities that give evidence of exceptionally high capability with respect to intellect, creativity, or the skills associated with specific disciplines. Students who are gifted often demonstrate outstanding abilities in more than one area. They may demonstrate extraordinary intensity of focus in their particular areas of talent or interest. However, they may also have accompanying disabilities and should not be expected to have strengths in all areas of intellectual functioning. (p. 17)

In contrast, the Yukon (1995) defines intellectual exceptionality in this way: "intellectual abilities are two or more standard deviations above the mean on a standardized, individually administered test of cognitive abilities in conjunction with superior performance in one or more academic subjects as measured by standardized achievement tests or classroom performance." (p. 19)

CONSIDER THIS
Why do you think these misconceptions developed about children and adults who are gifted and talented?

FURTHER READING
For more information on the history of services to children who are gifted and talented, read Chapter 1 in the *Handbook of Gifted Education,* edited by N. Colangelo and G. A. Davis, published in 1997 by Allyn & Bacon.

CROSS-REFERENCE
Review the definitions of other categories of disabilities discussed in previous chapters to compare components of definitions.

These two definitions illustrate two different approaches. While the Yukon's emphasis on standardized test scores significantly above the mean is the more traditional approach to giftedness, the broader definition offered by British Columbia is more illustrative of current thought in the field of giftedness. Of special interest in this type of definition is the reference to "potential abilities"—students do not have to have already produced significant accomplishments to be considered gifted. Also, the statement that the students should not be expected to have strengths in all areas should be noted, since many teachers believe that a gifted student must perform extremely well in all aspects of school. The majority of definitions used by provinces and territories adhere more to the model alluded to by British Columbia, which is based on Gardner's Theory of Multiple Intelligences, and Renzulli's three-ring conception of giftedness (British Columbia, 1995).

Renzulli (1979) promotes a model of giftedness depicted by three interlocking clusters of traits: above-average ability, task commitment, and creativity (see Figure 10.1). He stresses that it is the "interaction among the three clusters that research has shown to be the essential ingredient for creative/productive accomplishments" (p. 9).

Gardner and Hatch (Gardner, 1983; Gardner & Hatch, 1989) have developed a very popular model that proposes the idea of **multiple intelligences**. It comprises seven areas of ability, which are presented in Table 10.1, along with examples of roles that might be characteristic of a person with a high degree of a given intelligence. The table also briefly describes the features of each type of intelligence.

If Gardner's ideas were followed closely, students would be assessed in all areas of intelligence. If found to have strengths in an area, students would be provided opportunities to expand their interests, skills, and abilities accordingly. The attractiveness of this conceptualization is that (1) it acknowledges some ability areas that are frequently overlooked and (2) it recognizes the importance of different types of intelligences and gives them all equal footing.

FURTHER READING

For more information on multiple intelligences, read Chapter 5 in the *Handbook of Gifted Education*, edited by N. Colangelo and G. A. Davis, published in 1997 by Allyn & Bacon.

FIGURE 10.1
Renzulli's Three-Ring Conception of Giftedness

From *What Makes Giftedness?* (Brief #6, p. 10), by J. Renzulli, 1979, Los Angeles: National/State Leadership Training Institute. Reprinted by permission.

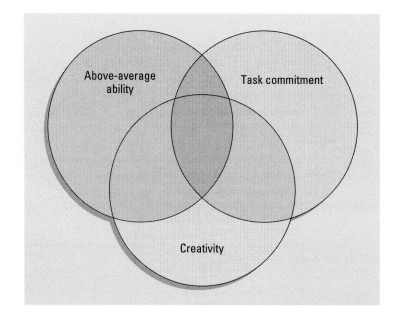

TABLE 10.1

Multiple Intelligences

Intelligence	End States	Core Components
LOGICAL–MATHEMATICAL	Scientist Mathematician	Sensitivity to, and capacity to discern, logical or numerical patterns; ability to handle long chains of reasoning
LINGUISTIC	Poet Journalist	Sensitivity to the sounds, rhythms, and meanings of words; sensitivity to the different functions of language
MUSICAL	Composer Violinist	Abilities to produce and appreciate rhythm, pitch, and timbre; appreciation of the forms of musical expressiveness
SPATIAL	Navigator Sculptor	Capacities to perceive the visual-spatial world accurately and to transform one's initial perceptions
BODILY-KINESTHETIC	Dancer Athlete	Abilities to control one's body movements and to handle objects skillfully
INTERPERSONAL	Therapist Salesperson	Capacities to discern and respond appropriately to the moods, temperaments, motivations, and desires of other people
INTRAPERSONAL	Person with detailed, accurate self-knowledge	Access to one's own feelings and the ability to discriminate among them and draw upon them to guide behavior; knowledge of one's own strengths, weaknesses, desires, and intelligences

From "Multiple Intelligences Go to School: Educational Implications of the Theory of Multiple Intelligences," by H. Gardner and T. Hatch, 1989, *Educational Researcher, 18* (8), p. 6. Copyright © 1989 by the American Educational Research Association. Reprinted by permission of the publisher.

Prevalence and Causes

The number of students who display exceptional abilities is uncertain. It is, of course, influenced by how giftedness is defined and how it is measured. A figure of 2 percent is cited to reflect the extent of giftedness in the school population (B.C. Ministry of Education, 1995).

Much professional discussion has focused on what causes giftedness in a person. Most researchers suggest that giftedness results from the interaction between biology and environment. Research has shown that behaviour is greatly affected by genetics. Although this notion is sometimes overemphasized, genetic factors do play a role in giftedness. Other biological factors, such as nutrition, also have an impact on an individual's development.

The environment in which a child is raised also affects later performance and intellectual abilities. Homes in which there is much stimulation and opportunity to explore and interact with the environment, accompanied by high expectations, tend to produce children more likely to be successful scholastically and socially.

CONSIDER THIS

How can the way in which "gifted" and "talented" are defined influence the prevalence of children classified?

Characteristics

Students who are gifted demonstrate a wide range of specific aptitudes, abilities, and skills. Though they should not be overgeneralized or considered stereotypical, certain characteristics distinguish students who are gifted or talented.

An interesting phenomenon is the paradoxical negative effect of certain positive behaviours displayed by gifted students. For instance, their sincere, excited curiosity about a topic being covered in class can sometimes be interpreted as annoying or disruptive by a teacher or fellow students. Their quick answers or certainty that they are right may be misconstrued as well. Such desirable behaviour can be misperceived as problem behaviour.

A comprehensive listing of characteristics of gifted children has been developed by Clark (1992); a summary is presented in Table 10.2. Her study also highlights the needs and possible problems that may surface in working with these individuals.

An interesting characteristic that has important classroom implications is the gifted student's expenditure of minimum effort while still earning high grades (Reis & Schack, 1993). Many gifted students are able to handle the general education curriculum with ease. But the long-term effect of being able to excel without working hard may be a lack of the work habits needed for challenging university programs.

Identification, Assessment, and Eligibility

General education teachers need to know about the assessment process used to confirm the existence of exceptional abilities. Teachers play a crucial role in the initial stages of the process, for they are typically the first to recognize that a student might be gifted.

The assessment process includes a sequence of steps, beginning with an initial referral (i.e., nomination) and culminating with the validation of the decision. General education teachers are largely responsible for identifying gifted students. Although many children displaying exceptional abilities may be spotted very early (i.e., preschool years), many are not recognized until they are in school. For this reason, teachers need to be aware of classroom behaviours that gifted students typically display. A listing of such behaviours is provided in Table 10.3.

Teachers who recognize such behaviours should determine whether a student should be evaluated more comprehensively. This usually involves nominating the student for gifted services. Teachers can take part in the next step in the assessment process as well. After a student has been nominated or referred, they can assemble information to help determine whether the student should receive special services. The following sources of information can contribute to understanding a student's demonstrated or potential ability: formal tests; informal assessments; interviews with teachers, parents, and peers; and actual student products.

A helpful technique used in many school systems to determine the performance capabilities of students is **portfolio assessment**. Portfolios contain a collection of student-generated products, reflecting the quality of a student's work. They may also contain permanent products such as artwork, poetry, or videotapes of student performance (e.g., theatrical production, music recital).

As VanTassel-Baska, Patton, and Prillaman (1989) point out, students who are culturally different and those who come from socially and economically disadvantaged backgrounds are typically overlooked in the process of identifying

TEACHING TIP
Classroom teachers need to be alert to students who may be gifted and talented and refer these students to appropriate professionals for testing and services.

TABLE 10.2

Differentiating Characteristics of the Gifted

Domain	Characteristic
THE COGNITIVE DOMAIN	• Extraordinary quantity of information; unusual retentiveness • Advanced comprehension • High level of language development • High level of verbal ability • Unusual capacity for processing information • Accelerated pace of thought processes • Flexible thought processes • Comprehensive synthesis • Early ability to delay closure • Heightened capacity for seeing unusual and diverse relationships, integration of ideas, and disciplines • Ability to generate original ideas and solutions • Early differential patterns for thought processing (e.g., thinking in alternatives; abstract terms; sensing consequences; making generalizations; visual thinking; use of metaphors and analogies) • Early ability to use and form conceptual frameworks • An evaluative approach toward oneself and others • Unusual intensity; persistent goal-directed behavior
THE AFFECTIVE DOMAIN	• Large accumulation of information about emotions that have not been brought to awareness • Unusual sensitivity to the expectations and feelings of others • Keen sense of humor—may be gentle or hostile • Heightened self-awareness, accompanied by feelings of being different • Idealism and a sense of justice, which appear at an early age • Earlier development of an inner locus of control and satisfaction • Unusual emotional depth and intensity • High expectations of self and others, often leading to high levels of frustration with self, others, and situations; perfectionism • Strong need for consistency between abstract values and personal actions • Advanced levels of moral judgment • Strongly motivated by self-actualization needs • Advanced cognitive and affective capacity for conceptualizing and solving societal problems • Leadership • Solutions to social and environmental problems • Involvement with the metaneeds of society (e.g., injustice, beauty, truth)
THE PHYSICAL/SENSING DOMAIN	• Unusual quantity of input from the environment through a heightened sensory awareness • Unusual discrepancy between physical and intellectual development • Low tolerance for the lag between their standards and their athletic skills • Cartesian split—can include neglect of physical well-being and avoidance of physical activity
THE INTUITIVE DOMAIN	• Early involvement and concern for intuitive knowing, and metaphysical ideas and phenomena • Open to experiences in this area; will experiment with psychic and metaphysical phenomenon • Creativity apparent in all areas of endeavor • Ability to predict; interest in future

From *Growing Up Gifted*, fourth edition, by Barbara Clark. Copyright 1992 by Merrill/Prentice Hall. Reprinted by permission.

TABLE 10.3

Observed Classroom Behaviours of Gifted Children

IN THE CLASSROOM, DOES THE CHILD:

- Ask a lot of questions?
- Show a lot of interest in progress?
- Have lots of information on many things?
- Want to know why or how something is so?
- Become unusually upset at injustices?
- Seem interested and concerned about social or political problems?
- Often have a better reason than you do for not doing what you want done?
- Refuse to drill on spelling, math facts, flash cards, or handwriting?
- Criticize others for dumb ideas?
- Become impatient if work is not "perfect"?
- Seem to be a loner?
- Seem bored and often have nothing to do?
- Complete only part of an assignment or project and then take off in a new direction?
- Stick to a subject long after the class has gone on to other things?
- Seem restless, out of seat often?
- Daydream?
- Seem to understand easily?
- Like solving puzzles and problems?
- Have his or her own idea about how something should be done? And stay with it?
- Talk a lot?
- Love metaphors and abstract ideas?
- Love debating issues?

This child may be showing giftedness cognitively.

DOES THE CHILD:

- Show unusual ability in some area? Maybe reading or math?
- Show fascination with one field of interest? And manage to include this interest in all discussion topics?
- Enjoy meeting or talking with experts in this field?

- Get math answers correctly, but find it difficult to tell you how?
- Enjoy graphing everything? Seem obsessed with probabilities?
- Invent new obscure systems and codes?

This child may be showing giftedness academically.

DOES THE CHILD:

- Try to do things in different, unusual, imaginative ways?
- Have a really zany sense of humor?
- Enjoy new routines or spontaneous activities?
- Love variety and novelty?
- Create problems with no apparent solutions? And enjoy asking you to solve them?
- Love controversial and unusual questions?
- Have a vivid imagination?
- Seem never to proceed sequentially?

This child may be showing giftedness creatively.

DOES THE CHILD:

- Organize and lead group activities? Sometimes take over?
- Enjoy taking risks?
- Seem cocky, self-assured?
- Enjoy decision making? Stay with that decision?
- Synthesize ideas and information from a lot of different sources?

This child may be showing giftedness through leadership ability.

DOES THE CHILD:

- Seem to pick up skills in the arts—music, dance, drama, painting, etc.—without instruction?
- Invent new techniques? Experiment?
- See minute detail in products or performances?
- Have high sensory sensitivity?

This child may be showing giftedness through visual or performing arts ability.

From *Growing Up Gifted*, fourth edition, by Barbara Clark. Copyright 1992 by Merrill/Prentice Hall. Reprinted by permission.

Too few students from minority cultural groups are identified as gifted and talented.

students for gifted programs. For the most part, this problem results from entry requirements that stress performance on standardized tests. When students obtain low test scores on standardized instruments that may be biased against them, exclusion results.

It has also been difficult to identify and serve students who are gifted and who also have disabilities. For instance, the problems that characterize a learning disability (e.g., problems in language-related areas) often mask high levels of accomplishment in other areas such as drama, art, or music. Special services or activities are warranted for these students.

After the student has been identified as gifted and begins to participate in special activities, ongoing assessment should become part of the student's educational program. Practical and personal needs should be monitored regularly (Del Prete, 1996). Practical concerns, such as progress in academic areas and realization of potential, can be evaluated. On the other hand, the personal needs of students who are gifted (e.g., feeling accepted and developing confidence) need to be addressed as well.

FURTHER READING
For more information on students with learning disabilities who are gifted and talented, read Chapter 12 in *Children and Adults with Learning Disabilities*, by T. E. C. Smith, C. A. Dowdy, E. A. Polloway, and G. E. Blalock, published in 1997 by Allyn & Bacon.

Multicultural Issues

As pointed out earlier, cultural diversity remains an area of concern in the education of gifted students. Too few students who are culturally different from mainstream students are identified and served through programs for gifted students. "Culturally diverse children have much talent, creativity, and intelligence. Manifestations of these characteristics may be different and thus require not only different tools for measuring these strengths, but also different eyes from which to see them" (Plummer, 1995, p. 290).

Observational Checklist for Identifying Strengths of Culturally Diverse Children

1. Ability to express feeling and emotions

2. Ability to improvise with commonplace materials and objects

3. Articulateness in role-playing, sociodrama, and storytelling

4. Enjoyment of and ability in visual arts, such as drawing, painting, and sculpture

5. Enjoyment of and ability in creative movement, dance, drama, etc.

6. Enjoyment of and ability in music and rhythm

7. Use of expressive speech

8. Fluency and flexibility in figural media

9. Enjoyment of and skills in group or team activities

10. Responsiveness to the concrete

11. Responsiveness to the kinesthetic

12. Expressiveness of gestures, body language, etc., and ability to interpret body language

13. Humor

14. Richness of imagery in informal language

15. Originality of ideas in problem solving

16. Problem-centeredness or persistence in problem solving

17. Emotional responsiveness

18. Quickness of warmup

From "Identifying and Capitalizing on the Strengths of Culturally Different Children," by E. P. Torrance. In *The Handbook of School Psychology*, edited by C. R. Reynolds and J. B. Gulkin, 1982, pp. 451–500. New York: Wiley. Copyright 1982 by John Wiley & Sons. Reprinted by permission.

VanTassel et al. (1989), in summarizing the literature related to culturally different gifted students, note four major needs:

- Nontraditional measures for identification
- Recognition of cultural attributes and factors in deciding on identification procedures
- A focus on strengths in nonacademic areas
- Programs that capitalize on noncognitive skills that enhance motivation

CONSIDER THIS

How can teachers take into consideration multicultural issues when identifying children who are gifted?

Teachers should look for certain behaviours associated with giftedness in children who are culturally different. An example of an observational checklist for accomplishing this task is presented in the nearby Diversity Forum feature.

Even when culturally diverse students have been identified as gifted, programming often has not been sensitive to their needs. As Plummer (1995) notes, few programs have the resources (i.e., personnel, materials) available to tap the interests and strengths of these students. Often, the general education teacher needs such supports to address these students' educational needs in inclusive settings. The twofold challenge for teachers is (1) to respect racial, ethnic, and cultural differences of students from diverse backgrounds and (2) to integrate diverse cultural topics into the curriculum (Plummer, 1995).

STRATEGIES FOR CURRICULUM AND INSTRUCTION

The literature on providing effective services for students with exceptional abilities consistently stresses the need for **differentiated programming**. This means that learning opportunities provided to these students must differ according to a student's needs and abilities. Differentiation includes the content of what students learn, the processes used in learning situations, and the final products that students develop. Furthermore, as Lopez and MacKenzie (1993) note, "Difference lies in the depth, scope, pace, and self-directedness of the expectations" (p. 288).

VanTassel-Baska (1989) notes some of the mistaken beliefs that some educators have about educating students with exceptional abilities:

- A "differentiated" curriculum for the gifted means "anything that is different from what is provided for all learners." *Fact:* A "differentiated" curriculum implies a coherently planned scope and sequence of instruction that matches the needs of students and that typically does differ from the regular education curriculum.
- All experiences provided for gifted learners must be creative and focused on process. *Fact:* Core content areas are important areas of instructional focus.
- One curriculum package will provide what is needed for the entire gifted population. *Fact:* Students need a variety of materials, resources, and courses.
- **Acceleration**, moving through the curriculum at a more rapid pace, can be harmful because it pushes children socially and leaves gaps in their knowledge. *Fact:* This approach to meeting the needs of students with exceptional abilities is the intervention technique best supported by research. (pp. 13–14)

Many professionals in the field of gifted education argue that the preferred setting for these students is not general education; they recommend differentiated programs delivered in separate classes for the greater part, if not all, of the school day. However, gifted students are more likely to spend nearly all day in general education classrooms, possibly receiving some differentiated opportunities in a pullout program.

Realities of the General Education Classroom

In general education settings, students who are gifted or talented are sometimes subject to conditions that indeed hinder the possibility for having their individual needs met. In the United States, the U.S. Department of Education (1993) has noted the following concerns related to educating gifted students in general education settings:

- Elementary level
    - The general education curriculum does not challenge gifted students.
    - Most academically talented students have already mastered up to one half of the required curriculum offered to them in elementary school.
    - Classroom teachers do little to accommodate the different learning needs of gifted children.
    - Most specialized programs are available for only a few hours a week.
    - Students talented in the arts are offered few challenging opportunities.

FURTHER READING
For further information and suggestions, read Shore, Cornell, Robinson and Ward's 1991 book, *Recommended Practices in Gifted Education*, published by Teachers College Press in New York.

CROSS-REFERENCE
Review Chapters 3–9, and compare curriculum and instruction modifications suggested for students with other special needs.

- Secondary level
  — Appropriate opportunities in junior high schools are scattered and uncoordinated.
  — High school schedules do not meet the needs of talented students (i.e., pacing of coverage of content).
  — The university preparatory curriculum in the United States generally does not require hard work from able students.
  — Small-town and rural schools often have limited resources and are unable to offer advanced classes and special learning opportunities.
  — Specialized schools, magnet schools, and intensive summer programs serve only a fraction of the secondary students who might benefit from them.
  — Dual enrollment in secondary school and university is uncommon.

CONSIDER THIS

Do you think many, or all, of these concerns about educating gifted students would also apply to Canadian schools?

Other more specific practices that can be problematic for gifted students include the following:

- When involved in group activities, gifted students may end up doing all of the work (Clinkenbeard, 1991).
- They are often subjected to more stringent grading criteria (Clinkenbeard, 1991).
- When they finish assignments early, they are given more of the same type of work or assigned more of the same types of tasks at the outset (Shaner, 1991).
- They are overused as co-teachers to help students who need more assistance.
- Vocabulary use in the average classroom is inappropriate for advanced learners (Clark, 1996).
- Advanced levels of critical thinking are not typically incorporated into lessons (Clark, 1996).
- Instructional materials in general education classrooms are frequently limited in range and complexity (Clark, 1996).

Unfortunately, most general education teachers are not provided with the necessary understanding, skills, and resources to deal appropriately with this population. This situation is exacerbated by the fact that teachers have to deal with a wide range of abilities and needs in their classrooms. The composition of the general education classroom in many of today's public schools requires an array of accommodative knowledge and skills.

In addition, some teachers feel uncomfortable working with students who have exceptional abilities. Figure 10.2 highlights this situation by way of a personal experience. Shaner (1991) remarks that teachers who are working with gifted students can be "intimidated by him or her, paralyzed with a fear of not being able to keep up, or threatened by the student's challenges to authority" (pp. 14–15). Teachers are also concerned about being asked questions they are unprepared to answer or challenged on points they may not know well. These are reasonable fears; however, they can be minimized by using these opportunities as a way of increasing everyone's knowledge and by understanding how to address gifted students' needs within the general classroom setting.

Differentiated programming for students with exceptional abilities, wherever it occurs, must address individual needs and interests in the context of preparing the students for a world characterized by change and complexity. Reis (1989) suggests that we reassess how we look at gifted education and

FIGURE 10.2
A Personal Experience
From *Exceptional Children in Focus* (p. 216), by J. R. Patton, J. Blackbourn, and K. Fad, 1996, Columbus, OH: Merrill. Used by permission.

Not long ago, I was invited to go on a "reef walk" with a class of gifted third- and fourth-graders. It was a very educational experience.

While we were wading in shallow water, we came upon a familiar marine organism commonly called a feather duster (tube worm). Forgetting that these students had vocabularies well advanced of their nongifted age peers, I was ready to say something like, "Look how that thing hangs on the rock."

Before I could get my highly descriptive statement out, Eddie, who always amazes us with his comments, offered the following: "Notice how securely anchored the organism is to the stationary coral?"

All I could reply was "Yes. I did."

move away from the content-based nature of most current curriculums to an orientation based on a realistic view of future education.

Continuum of Placement Options

A variety of ways exist for providing educational programs to students who are gifted and talented. The value of a particular option reflects the extent to which it meets an individual's needs. A continuum of potential settings for providing programs to gifted students is shown in Figure 10.3. As Clark (1992) points out, all of the options have some advantages; none address the needs of all students with exceptional abilities. For this reason, she feels that school systems should provide a range of programmatic alternatives.

Gifted students who are in general education classrooms for the entire instructional day can have their needs met through a variety of special provisions such as **enrichment**, acceleration, or special grouping and clustering. The challenge for teachers is to coordinate these provisions with those required for other students in the classroom.

In some schools, students who have been identified as gifted are pulled out for a specified period of time each day to attend a special class for gifted students. When they are in the general education setting, it may be possible for them to participate in an individualized program of study, apart from the regular curriculum.

Gifted students may also participate in various adjunct programs such as mentorships, internships, special tutorials, independent study, and resource rooms—many of which will occur outside the regular classroom. For students at the secondary level, spending time in special programming for part of the day, in addition to attending heterogeneous classes, is another possibility.

These programmatic options affect the role and responsibilities of the general education teacher. In some situations, the general education teacher will be the primary source of instruction for these students. In others, the general

FURTHER READING
For more information on placement options for students who are gifted and talented, read Chapter 4 in *Educating Exceptional Children*, by S. A. Kirk and J. J. Gallagher, published by Houghton Mifflin.

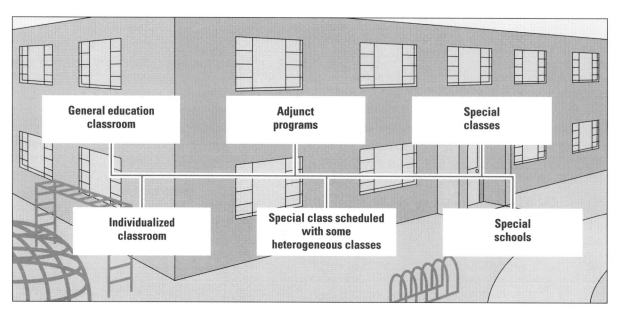

FIGURE 10.3

Options for Providing Services to Gifted Students

Text reprinted with permission of Macmillan College Publishing Company from *Growing Up Gifted*, fourth edition, by Barbara Clark. Copyright © 1992 by Macmillan College Publishing Company, Inc.

education teacher may serve as a manager, coordinating the services provided by others. However, it is probable that most teachers will be responsible for providing some level of instruction to gifted students.

Approaches

Three general practices are used in designing programs for students who have exceptional abilities: acceleration, enrichment, and special grouping. All three have merit and can be used in general education settings.

Acceleration refers to practices that introduce content, concepts, and educational experiences to gifted students sooner than for other students. It presents gifted students with more advanced materials appropriate to their ability and interests. There are many types of accelerative practices, as reflected in the array of options provided in the nearby Inclusion Strategies feature.

All of the accelerative options described by Southern and Jones (1991) have relevance for gifted students in general education classrooms. The techniques that have the most direct application in the general education classroom are **continuous progress**, **self-paced instruction**, **subject-matter acceleration**, **combined classes, curriculum compacting**, and **curriculum telescoping**. If these practices are to be used, teachers must plan and implement instructional activities.

Other accelerative practices have a more indirect impact on ongoing activities in the general education classroom. Nevertheless, teachers should be aware of them. They include early entrance to school, grade skipping, mentorships, extracurricular programs, concurrent enrollment, advanced placement, and credit by examination.

INCLUSION STRATEGIES

Range and Types of Accelerative Options

1. Early entrance to kindergarten or first grade

   The student is admitted to school prior to the age specified by the district for normal entry to first grade.

2. Grade skipping

   The student is moved ahead of normal grade placement. This may be done during an academic year (placing a third-grader directly into fourth grade), or at year end (promoting a third-grader to fifth grade).

3. Continuous

   The student is given material deemed appropriate for current achievement progress as the student becomes ready.

4. Self-paced instruction

   The student is presented with materials that allow him or her to proceed at a self-selected pace. Responsibility for selection of pacing is the student's.

5. Subject matter acceleration

   The student is placed for a part of a day with students at more advanced grade levels for one or more subjects without being assigned to a higher grade (e.g., a fifth-grader going to sixth grade for science instruction).

6. Combined classes

   The student is placed in classes where two or more grade levels are combined (e.g., third- and fourth-grade split rooms). The arrangement can be used to allow younger children to interact with older ones academically and socially.

7. Curriculum compacting

   The student is given reduced amounts of introductory activities, drill review, and so on. The time saved may be used to move faster through the curriculum.

8. Telescoping curriculum

   The student spends less time than normal in a course of study (e.g., completing a one-year course in one semester, or finishing junior high school in two years rather than three).

9. Mentorships

   The student is exposed to a mentor who provides advanced training and experiences in a content area.

10. Extracurricular programs

    The student is enrolled in course work or summer programs that confer advanced instruction and/or credit for study (e.g., fast-paced language or math courses offered by universities).

11. Concurrent enrollment

    The student is taking a course at one level and receiving credit for successful completion of a parallel course at a higher level (e.g., taking algebra at the junior high level and receiving credit for high school algebra as well as junior high math credits upon successful completion).

12. Advanced placement

    The student takes a course in high school that prepares him or her for taking an examination that can confer [university] credit for satisfactory performances.

13. Credit by examination

    The student receives credit (at high school or [university] level) upon successful completion of an examination.

14. Correspondence cently,

    The student takes high school or college courses by mail (or, more recoursesthrough video and audio presentations).

15. Early entrance into junior high, high school, or [university]

    The student is admitted with full standing to an advanced level of instruction (at least one year early).

According to Gallagher and Gallagher (1994), the most common acceleration practices are (1) primary level—early admittance to school, ungraded primary, (2) upper elementary—ungraded classes, grade skipping, (3) junior high school—three years in two, senior high classes for credit, and (4) high school—extra load (early graduation), advanced placement (AP). Interestingly, some professionals (Davis, 1996) advocate separate advanced placement classes for gifted students because their needs differ from those of nongifted students enrolled in AP classes. Matthews (1993), from the University of Toronto, has argued that advanced programming needs to be done on a subject-specific basis since gifted students are likely to be advanced in specific areas.

Enrichment refers to techniques that provide topics, skill development, materials, or experiences that extend the depth of coverage beyond the typical curriculum. This practice is commonly used in general education classes to address the needs of students who move through content quickly. Many teachers' manuals and guides provide ideas on how to deliver enriching activities to students who finish their work quickly.

As Southern and Jones (1991) note, some enrichment activities ultimately involve acceleration. For instance, whenever topics of an advanced nature are introduced, a form of acceleration is actually being employed. There is, however, a distinction between materials or activities that are accelerated and possess a dimension of difficulty or conceptual complexity and materials or activities that provide variety but do not require advanced skills or understanding.

Special grouping refers to the practice whereby gifted students of similar ability levels or interests are grouped together for at least part of the instructional day (VanTassel-Baska, 1989). One commonly cited technique is the use of cluster grouping. This practice allows for interaction with peers who share a similar enthusiasm, bring different perspectives to topics, and stimulate the cognitive and creative thinking of others in the group.

FURTHER READING

For more information on schoolwide enrichment, read Chapter 11 in the *Handbook of Gifted Education,* edited by N. Colangelo and G. A. Davis, published in 1997 by Allyn & Bacon.

CLASSROOM ACCOMMODATIONS

This section highlights techniques for addressing the needs of students with exceptional abilities. Teachers who will be working closely with these students are encouraged to consult resources that thoroughly discuss teaching gifted students in general education settings—see Maker (1993), Parke (1989), or Winebrenner (1992).

First and foremost, teachers should strive to create classroom settings that foster conditions in which gifted students feel comfortable and are able to realize their potential. They need a comprehensive long-term plan of education and must enjoy learning experiences that reflect this plan (Kitano, 1993).

Although special opportunities for enrichment, acceleration, and the use of higher-level skills are particularly beneficial to gifted students, these opportunities can also be extended to other students when appropriate (Roberts, Ingram, & Harris, 1992). Many students in general education settings will find practices such as integrated programming (combining different subject matter) to be exciting, motivating, and meaningful.

CONSIDER THIS

How can special opportunities for gifted and talented children benefit other students, including those with other special needs?

Teachers must create a psychological classroom climate that is conducive to a variety of ideas and viewpoints.

Management Considerations

It is essential to organize and systematically manage the classroom environment. Teachers must create a psychosocial climate that is open to a "variety of ideas, materials, problems, people, viewpoints, and resources" (Schiever, 1993, p. 209). The learning environment should be safe, accepting, and supportive.

Grouping gifted students is useful and can be done in a variety of ways, for example, cooperative cluster grouping on the basis of similar abilities or interests dyads, or seminar-type formats. Gifted students should be afforded an opportunity to spend time with other gifted students, just as competitive tennis players must play opponents with similar or more advanced ability in order to maintain their skills.

Even though the merits of cooperative learning in classroom settings have been established, heterogeneous cooperative learning arrangements involving gifted students must be managed carefully. Teachers must guarantee that most of the work does not always fall on gifted students in such arrangements. Cooperative learning arrangements should be encouraged but continually monitored to ensure effectiveness and fairness.

Teachers should develop comprehensive record-keeping systems that monitor the progress of all students, including gifted students who may be taking part in a mix of enrichment and accelerated activities. A differentiated report card may be useful for conveying to parents more information about a gifted student's performance. An example of such a report is shown in Figure 10.4. Much qualitative information about student performance can be communicated through this document.

TEACHING TIP
Pairing a gifted student with students who are not gifted can make an excellent cooperative learning situation for all students, but should not be used to exclusion of similar ability grouping.

The following are some specific suggestions on dealing with gifted students:

- Require gifted students to follow classroom rules and procedures while allowing them to explore and pursue their curiosity when appropriate (Feldhusen, 1993a and b).
- Include gifted students in the development of class procedures that emerge during the course of a school year (e.g., introduction of animals in the room).
- Explain the logic and rationale for certain rules and procedures.
- Use cluster seating arrangements rather than strict rows (Feldhusen, 1993a).
- Identify a portion of the room where special events and activities take place and where stimulating materials are kept.
- Develop lesson plan formats that include instructional ideas for gifted students.
- Consult teacher guides of textbook series for ideas for enrichment activities.
- Let students who are working in independent arrangements plan their own learning activities (Feldhusen, 1993a).
- Use contracts with students who are involved in elaborate independent study projects to maximize communication between teacher and students (Rosselli, 1993).
- Involve students in their own record keeping, thus assisting the teacher and developing responsibility.
- Use periodic progress reports, daily logs, and teacher conferences to monitor and evaluate students who are in independent study arrangements (Conroy, 1993), as described in Figure 10.4.

Curricular and Instructional Considerations

CONSIDER THIS

How can differentiated programming be used effectively with students with a variety of different learning needs?

Many professionals interested in gifted education promote the use of differentiated programming. With this in mind, general education teachers should develop instructional lessons that consider a range of abilities and interests. For gifted students, instructional activities should be qualitatively different from those assigned to the class in general—or completely different if certain accelerative options are being used.

When designing instructional activities for the entire class, teachers can use the following series of questions offered by Kitano (1993) to guide planning for gifted students:

- Do the activities include provisions for several ability levels?
- Do the activities include ways to accommodate a variety of interest areas?
- Does the design of activities encourage development of sophisticated products?
- Do the activities provide for the integration of thinking processes with concept development?
- Are the concepts consistent with the comprehensive curriculum plan? (p. 280)

Another technique that can be used effectively with gifted students in general education classes is curriculum compacting. This practice allows students to cover assigned material in ways that are faster or different. As Renzulli, Reis, and Smith (1981) point out, this process has three phases: the assessment of what students know and the skills they possess, identification of ways

Differentiated–Integrated Curriculum Report

Student: _____
Teacher: _____
Semester/Year: _____

CONTENT

DISCIPLINES

| Area of Study | Broad-Based Theme | Language Arts Enrichment/Acceleration | | | | Math/Science Enrichment | | Social Science | Arts | Individual Extension Activities |
		Reading	Written Expression	Oral Expression	Spelling	Math	Science	Social Studies/Social Issues	Music/Visual Arts/Performance Arts	

PROCESSES

Basic Skills

Research Skills
- Reading for general information
- Creating hypotheses
- Taking notes
- Making an outline
- Reading for supportive evidence
- Writing the thesis
- Using various sources
- Writing bibliography
- Making appendices

- Brainstorm
- Observe
- Classify
- Interpret
- Analyze
- Evaluate
- Judge

Productive Thinking/Critical Thinking Skills
- Compare
- Categorize
- Synthesize
- Exhibit fluency
- Display flexibility
- Demonstrate originality
- Problem solve

- Elaborate
- Hypothesize
- Exhibit awareness
- Appreciate
- Create
- Redesign
- Prove

PRODUCTS

a variety of ways to communicate and express selves ◄ the opportunity to share information with an audience

☐ Proposed } in-depth study of
☐ Completed } student's choice:

FIGURE 10.4
Differentiated–Integrated Curriculum Report
Adapted from Sandra N. Kaplan by Joy Kataoka, revised 1990. Copyright © ASSETS 1986.

of covering the curriculum, and suggestions for enrichment and accelerative options. Renzulli et al. have developed a form, presented in Figure 10.5, to assist teachers in compacting curriculum.

Many viable ways exist to address the needs of gifted students within the context of a general education lesson. Two examples of such practices are provided here:

1. Enrichment: Literature. Figure 10.6 illustrates how the play *Romeo and Juliet* can be taught, keeping in mind the needs of the regular and gifted students. This example developed by Shanley (1993) shows how the content of the play and the activities used by the teacher can be adapted for gifted students.
2. Cluster/Grouping: Mathematics. Conroy (1993) offers a one-week schedule of activities related to the topic of two-digit multiplication (see Figure 10.7). She recommends that cluster grouping of gifted students be used to accomplish the instructional goals.

FIGURE 10.5
Curriculum
Compacting Form

From *The Revolving Door Identification Model* (p. 79), by J. Renzulli, S. Reis, and L. Smith, 1981, Mansfield Center, CT: Creative Learning Press. Reprinted with permission from Creative Learning Press, copyright © 1981.

Individual Educational Programming Guide
The Compactor

Name _____   Age _____   Teacher(s) _____   Individual conference dates and persons participating in planning of IEP

School _____   Grade ____   Parent(s) _____

Curriculum areas to be considered for compacting. Provide a brief description of basic material to be covered during this marking period and the assessment information or evidence that suggests the need for compacting.	*Procedures for compacting basic material.* Describe activities that will be used to guarantee proficiency in basic curricular areas.	*Acceleration and/or enrichment activities.* Describe activities that will be used to provide advanced-level learning experiences in each of the regular curricula.

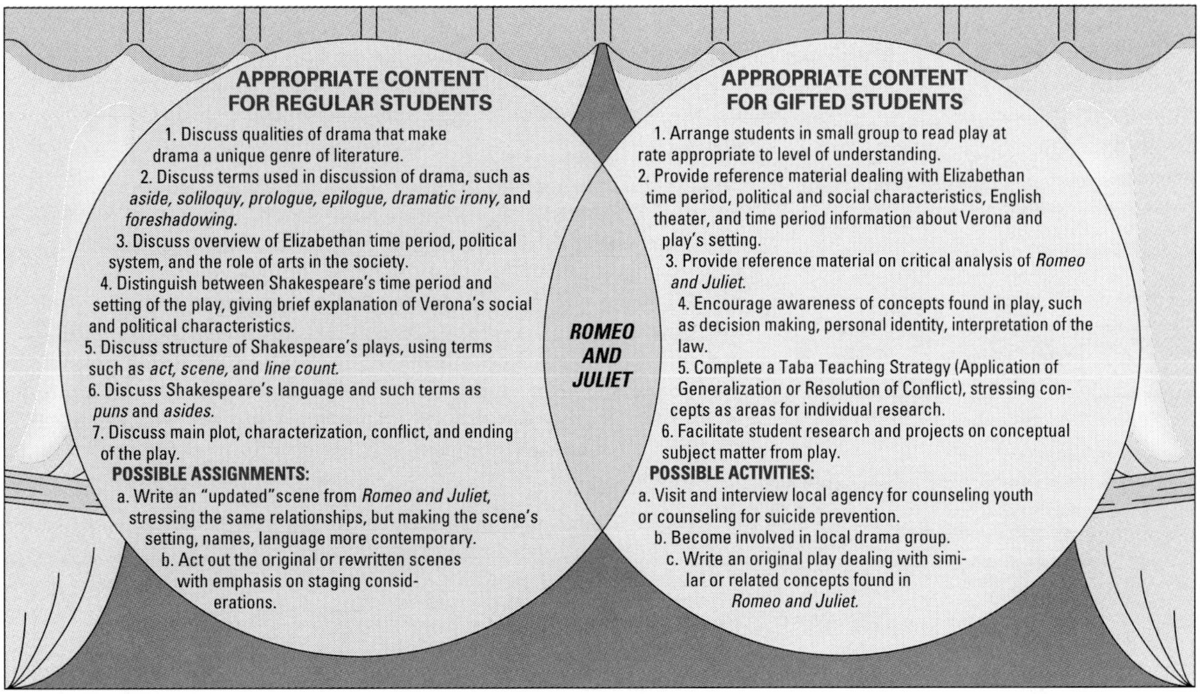

FIGURE 10.6

Adapting Curricular Content for Teaching *Romeo and Juliet*

From "Becoming Content with Content," by R. Shanley. In *Critical Issues in Gifted Education: Vol. 1. Defensible Programs for the Gifted*, edited by C. J. Maker, 1993, pp. 43–89. Austin, TX: Pro-Ed. Used by permission.

The following are more specific suggestions related to areas such as questioning strategies and product differentiation:

- Balance coverage of basic disciplines and the arts (Feldhusen, 1993a).
- Acquire an array of different learning-related materials for use with gifted students—these can include textbooks, magazines, artifacts, software, CD-ROM disks, and other media.
- Include time for independent study.
- Teach research skills (data-gathering and investigative techniques) to gifted students to develop their independent study abilities (Reis & Schack, 1993).
- Use integrated themes for interrelating ideas within and across domains of inquiry (VanTassel-Baska, 1989). This type of curricular orientation can be used for all students in the general education setting, with special activities designed for gifted students. An example of an integrated unit on the topic of change is provided in Figure 10.8.
- Include higher-order thinking skills in lessons.
- Allocate time for students to have contact with adults who can provide special experiences and information to gifted students (e.g., mentors).
- Avoid assigning regular class work missed when gifted students spend time in special programs.
- Manage classroom discussions so that all students have an equal opportunity to contribute, feel comfortable doing so, and understand the nature of the discussion.

FIGURE 10.7
Schedule of
Activities to Teach
Two-Digit
Multiplication

From "Classroom
Management: An Expected
View," by J. Conroy. In
*Critical Issues in Gifted
Education: Vol. 1. Programs
for the Gifted in Regular
Classrooms,* edited by C. J.
Maker, 1993, pp. 227–257.
Austin, TX: Pro-Ed. Used
by permission.

MONDAY	Regular students—introduce two-digit multiplication. Gifted students—same. Teacher gives all members of class an outline of the entire week of math seatwork and homework assignments, ending with a test on Friday.
TUESDAY	Regular students—review concepts presented Monday, guided practice. Gifted students—introduce some enrichment material, including math logic problems. Gifted students work on these as soon as they have mastered the concepts of the other problems. Teacher assigns their group to come up with some story problems and logic problems related to the week's concepts. Teacher then assigns regular students in doing seatwork. Although gifted students are responsible for the Friday test and for specific portions of the homework throughout the week, such as every third problem, they choose to use class working on the enrichment or a group project.
WEDNESDAY	Regular students—introduce three-digit multiplication. Gifted students—listen to explanation of concepts, demonstrate that they can do three problems correctly, and continue with enrichment project. Teacher moves between both groups.
THURSDAY	Regular students—review and guided practice in seatwork, with introduction of story problems. Gifted students—do three of six story problems and continue enrichment activities.
FRIDAY	Regular and gifted students—take unit test on two- and three-digit multiplication. Test has application story problems. One challenge problem is more difficult. It is designed for the gifted students, but others may try it.

- Use standard textbooks and materials carefully, as gifted students will typically be able to move through them rapidly and may find them boring.
- Include questions that are open-ended and of varying conceptual levels in class discussions.
- Make sure gifted students have access to the latest developments in microcomputers, including simulation software, interactive technologies, CD-ROM databases, and telecommunications (Internet access).

Gifted and talented students need to learn about possible career choices that await them. They may need to do so at an earlier time than other students because they may participate in accelerated programs that necessitate early decisions about career direction. Students should learn about various career options, the dynamics of different disciplines, and the training required to work in a given discipline.

Teachers can select different ways to address the career needs of students. One way is to ensure that gifted students have access to mentor programs, spending time with adults who are engaged in professional activities that interest them. Another method is to integrate the study of careers into the existing curriculum by discussing various careers when appropriate and by requiring students to engage in some activities associated with different careers. Students can become acquainted with a number of different careers while covering traditional subject areas.

TEACHING TIP

Arrange a career day for students, at which community members discuss various careers with students.

DISCIPLINES

Area of Study	Terminal Objective Broad-Based Issue/Problem/Theme	Language Arts Enrichment/Acceleration				Math Enrichment		Social Science	Arts
		Reading	Written Expression	Oral Expression	Spelling	Math	Science	Social Studies/Social Issues	Music/Visual Arts/Performance Arts
Geological Evolution / Civil Rights	Change	Research to locate answers in various sources; Teacher-made handouts specific to area of study/issue; Poetry and/or short stories related to issues; Literature; Jr. great books	Reports; Essays; Poetry cinquains acrostics narrative poems; Short stories; Creation legends; Personal reaction papers	Oral presentation of each procedure outlined under written expression; Discussions; Inquiry discussions	Functional spelling; Dictionary skills; New vocabulary words; Word search; Crosswork puzzles	Graphing reading designing; Problem solving; Logic	Geology (elements of change in geology); Metamorphosis; Archaeology; Astronomy beliefs seasons/tides	Historical and contemporary issues that have influenced change in our society; Civil rights	Redesigned lyrics; Team skits; 3-D posters; Illustrations; Improvisation; Role-playing/role reversals simulations
Evolution of Humanity's Beliefs / Mythology → Scientific Fact → Literature	Change	Research to gain/locate information on individual topics; Mythology; Literature (poetry on topic)	Note taking; Outlining; Referencing; Writing/editing; Final draft of integrated paper	Oral reports; Oral discussions; Demonstration of scientific project	Functional spelling; Dictionary/thesaurus skills; New vocabulary words; Word search	Graphs; Charts; Diagrams; Time lines where applicable	Research on scientific facts; Process diagram; Working model; Demonstration	How humanity's beliefs/ideas and knowledge evolved; Progress or dissension?; Compare/contrast with contemporary issues	Process diagram; Illustrations; 3-D diagram; Simulations
Hawaiiana	Change	Research to locate information from various sources; Teacher-made handouts specific to discussion topics; Legends of old Hawaii	Legends; Creation myth; Migration letter; Evolution of plantlife, birds, insects; Lava poetry; Reports on selected topics; Script for skit	Daily oral discussions; Oral presentations; Skits	Functional spelling; Dictionary/thesaurus skills; New vocabulary words; Vocabulary board; Word search	Averaging age of islands; Graphing; Problem solving; Logic	Geology and geography; Volcanism; Continental drift; Revegetation after eruption; How plants/animals got to Hawaii; Evolution of plant life, birds, insects	Study of ancient Hawaiian civilization and factors that influenced change. *Migration:* reasons for beginning a new society. *Social Issues:* compare and contrast problems in ancient Hawaii to contemporary Hawaiian/world issues	Skit; Vocabulary board; Illustrations; Role-playing/role reversals simulations; Creative dramatics

CONTENTS

FIGURE 10.8
A Differentiated-Integrated Curriculum

Gifted and Talented Individuals and Computer Applications

Individual	Computer Applications
ACADEMICALLY GIFTED	Programming (e.g., BASIC, LOGO, Pascal)
	Computer-assisted instruction
	Word processing, databases, spreadsheets, and graphics
	Telecommunications
CREATIVE/TALENTED	Computer-assisted design (CAD) and other art activities (e.g., using color graphics with the Amiga system)
	Music synthesis and Music Instrument Digital Interface (MIDI)
	Analysis and cataloging of athletics, dance, acting, and other physical activities

Note: Many gifted and talented individuals are academically and creatively strong, and would therefore use computer applications from both areas.

From "Computers and Gifted/Talented Individuals," by E. J. Dale. In *Computers and Exceptional Individuals*, edited by J. D. Lindsay, 1993, p. 203. Austin, TX: Pro-Ed. Used by permission.

Career counselling and guidance are also recommended. As Hardman, Drew, Egan, and Wolf (1993) point out, because of their multiple exceptional abilities and wide range of interests, some gifted students have a difficult time making career choices or narrowing down mentorship possibilities. These students should spend some time with counsellors or teachers who can help them make these choices and other important postsecondary decisions.

Students who are gifted should have access to technology to facilitate their instructional needs. Numerous programs are appropriate for gifted students; encourage them to think of their own ways of using the computer to gather and analyze information, to organize their work, and to exercise their creativity. The nearby Technology Today feature describes some computer applications appropriate for gifted students.

Social-Emotional Considerations

Gifted students have the same physiological and psychological needs as their peers. However, they may also be dealing with perplexing concepts that are well ahead of the concerns of their peers. For instance, a gifted fourth-grade girl asked her teacher questions related to abortion—a topic with which she was already dealing conceptually.

Perhaps the most important recommendation is for teachers to develop relationships with students that make them feel comfortable discussing their concerns and questions. Teachers can become important resources to gifted students, not only for advice, but also for information. Regularly scheduled individual time with a teacher can have important paybacks for the student.

PERSONAL SPOTLIGHT

Gifted Students ■ KAEGAN AND CONAL SHEPHERD

Kaegan and Conal, two brothers, have both been identified as gifted and are in inclusive settings. As with many gifted students, they feel the need to be with children at their developmental or ability level, which is unlikely to be their chronological age because of developmental differences.

Their mother, Lesley, states, "Scheduling appropriate groupings and pacing for gifted students in ability clusters rather than totally age-based inclusion is often essential to provide them with opportunities for learning and social support."

"It's lonely being gifted in a regular class," says 11-year-old Kaegan. "It's hard when teachers think I should fit in with my own age group. Kids my age aren't interested in the things I like. They don't read the same books or talk about stuff that interests me. I want to know about chemistry and marine biology. I work on those subjects at home, but I wish I could work on them now with someone else." Lesley notes that both her children feel lonely in the regular classroom and are subject to bullying for being different.

Conal, 15 years of age, finds his interests often lead him to a different outlook than that of his classmates. He says, "To fit in socially I find I have to politely fake an interest in things I feel remote from: popular TV shows, sports, clothes." This circumstance often makes it hard for him to take part in discussion when topics are chosen to fit the interests of most students his age. He really enjoys multi-age elective classes where he can be with students who share similar approaches despite their different ages.

Conal comments that he feels teachers misunderstand the concept of being gifted. "Most of the time I can't explain how or why I do things. My brain is always working in the background, like a bunch of windows open on a computer. I see different answers, different ways to do things. Being gifted doesn't mean I always answer questions the way my teachers expect or want," he notes. "Sometimes, I know material way beyond what is being taught and that gets in the way of answering questions about the lesson."

Kaegan agrees with his brother. "I can't explain what being gifted means. It doesn't mean I get all good marks. It means I think differently from other kids, but they don't really understand that. Everyone always expects me to know the answer and I don't like that. Like other gifted kids, I worry about things more. I can put myself in someone else's shoes and that gives me nightmares a lot of times. It upsets me when the teacher is angry at another student or when we talk about wars or poverty. The other kids think I'm weird, but they like it when I help them."

When Kaegan and Conal are asked what teachers should do to accommodate them, they express strong opinions. "Give me credit for what I already know and let me use the extra time to work on my own projects. Don't always make me do more when I show you I can already do the normal assignment. If I repeat things too many times, I start to change them around, embellish them so I don't get bored. I end up getting the information mixed up if there are too many repetitions. Usually repeating something once is enough," says Conal. Kaegan adds, "I need quiet time to work and concentrate because I like really getting into things. If I am reading a book, the teacher has to touch me on the shoulder to bring me back because I concentrate so hard I block out sounds. I don't like it when we change subjects before I am finished. It breaks my concentration and I hate having to start all over again some other time. If I know we only have a little time, I just don't bother to start on stuff. I like teachers who let me work at my own speed. I like long projects that don't get broken up into small parts. I hate repeating things. I wish there was a fullness gauge on my back that showed teachers how much I know, so they wouldn't keep testing me on the same stuff."

Kaegan and Conal, like many gifted students, know how they can learn best. They just need our support in letting them do it.

Teachers may also find it beneficial to schedule weekly room meetings (Feldhusen, 1993b) or class councils (Kataoka, 1987) to identify and address social, procedural, or learning-related problems that arise in the classroom. The group discussion includes articulation of a problem, brainstorming and discussion of possible solutions, selection of a plan of action, and implementation, evaluation, and reintroduction of the problem if the plan of action is not effective.

The following are specific suggestions for dealing with the social-emotional needs of gifted students:

- Know when to refer students to professionals trained to deal with certain types of emotional problems.
- Create a classroom atmosphere that encourages students to take academic risks and allows them to make mistakes without fear of ridicule or harsh negative critique.
- Provide time on a weekly basis, if at all possible, for individual sessions with students so that they can share their interests, ongoing events in their lives, or concerns.
- Encourage the involvement of volunteers (e.g., parents, college practicum students) to assist in addressing the needs of gifted students (Feldhusen, 1993a).
- Provide opinions for developing differentiated products as outcomes of various projects or lessons—see Figure 10.9 for a list of examples.
- Have students consider intended audiences when selecting potential final products of their endeavours.
- Maintain regular, ongoing communication with the families of gifted students, notifying them of the goals, activities, products, and expectations you have for their children.
- Require, and teach if necessary, appropriate social skills (e.g., appropriate interactions) to students who display problems in these areas.
- Work with parents on the personal development of students.
- Use different types of activities (e.g., social issues) to develop self-understanding and decision-making and problem-solving skills. Rosselli (1993) recommends the use of bibliotherapy (literature that focuses on children with disabilities).

FURTHER READING
For more information on social-emotional considerations, read Chapter 30 in the *Handbook of Gifted Education*, edited by N. Colangelo and G. A. Davis, published in 1997 by Allyn & Bacon.

Methods that are effective with gifted students are also useful for nongifted students.

LITERARY

Literary magazine (prose or poetry)
Newspaper for school or class
Class reporter for school newspaper
Collections of local folklore (*Foxfire*)
Book reviews of childrens' books for children,
  by children
Storytelling
Puppeteers
Student editorials on a
  series of topics
Kids' page in a city newspaper
Series of books or stories
Classbook or yearbook
Calendar book
Greeting cards (including original poetry)
Original play and production
Poetry readings
Study of foreign languages
Organizer of story hour in local or school library
Comic book or comic book series
Organization of debate society
Monologue, sound track, or script

MATHEMATICAL

Contributor of math puzzles, quizzes, games for
  children's sections in newspapers, magazines
Editor/founder of computer magazine or newsletter
Math consultant for school
Editor of math magazine, newsletter
Organizer of metrics conversion
  movement
Original computer programming
Programming book
Graphics (original use of) films

MEDIA

Children's television show
Children's radio show
Children's reviews (books, movie)
  on local news shows
Photo exhibit (talking)
Pictorial tour
Photo essay
Designing advertisement (literary magazine)
Slide/tape show on self-selected topic

ARTISTIC

Displays, exhibits
Greeting cards
Sculpture
Illustrated books
Animation
Cartooning

MUSICAL, DANCE

Books on life of famous composer
Original music, lyrics
Electronic music (original)
Musical instrument construction
Historical investigation of folk songs
Movement—history of dance, costumes

HISTORICAL AND SOCIAL SCIENCES

Roving historian series in newspaper
"Remember when" column in newspaper
Establishment of historical society
Establishment of an oral history tape library
Published collection of local folklore and historical
  highlight stories
Published history (written, taped, pictorial)
Historical walking tour of a city
Film on historical topic
Historical monologue
Historical play based on theme
Historical board game
Presentation of historical research topic
  (World War II, etc.)
Slide/tape presentation of historical research
Starting your own business
Investigation of local elections
Electronic light board explaining historical battle, etc.
Talking time line of a decade (specific time period)
Tour of local historical homes
Investigate a vacant lot
Create a "hall" of local historical figures
Archaeological dig
Anthropological study (comparison of/within groups)

SCIENTIFIC

Science journal
Daily meteorologist posting weather conditions
Science column in newspaper
Science 'slot' in kids television show
Organizer at a natural museum
Science consultant for school
"Science Wizard" (experimenters)
Science fair
Establishment of a nature walk
Animal behavior study
Any prolonged experimentation involving
  manipulation of variables
Microscopic study involving slides
Classification guide to natural habitats
Acid rain study
Future study of natural conditions
Book on pond life
Aquarium study/study of different ecosystems
Science article submitted to national magazines
Plan a trip to national parks (travelogue)
Working model of a heart
Working model of a solar home
Working model of a windmill

FIGURE 10.9   Outlet Vehicles for Differentiated Student Products

From "Differentiating Products for the Gifted and Talented: The Encouragement of Independent Learning," by
S. M. Reis and G. D. Schack. In *Critical Issues in Gifted Education: Vol. 3. Programs for the Gifted in Regular
Classrooms,* edited by C. J. Maker, 1993, pp. 161–186. Austin, TX: Pro-Ed. Used by permission.

- Teach gifted students how to deal with their "uniqueness."
- Recognize that gifted students may experience higher levels of social pressure and anxiety—for example, peer pressure not to achieve at a high level or lofty expectations originating internally or from others (Del Prete, 1996).

ENHANCING INCLUSIVE CLASSROOMS FOR STUDENTS WHO ARE GIFTED

CROSS-REFERENCE

Review Chapters 3–9 to determine if methods of enhancing an inclusive classroom for students with other special needs will be effective with students who are gifted and talented.

Addressing the needs of students with exceptional abilities in the context of the general education classroom is a monumental challenge. Current realities and probable trends in programming for gifted students suggest that general education will continue to be the typical setting in which they receive instruction. Thus it is important that we do all that we can to enrich the educational experiences of this population in these settings. To do so requires (1) creating classrooms where gifted students feel wanted and supported, in addition to having their instructional needs met by appropriate programming, and (2) providing the necessary supports to general education teachers to achieve desired outcomes for this group of students.

Promoting a Sense of Community and Social Acceptance

TEACHING TIP

Assigning students who are gifted and talented to be peer tutors can both enhance their acceptance in the classroom and give them opportunities for leadership. However, do so in moderation.

The climate of any classroom is determined by the interaction between the teacher and the students in the class; in particular, the teacher plays a leading role in establishing the parameters by which a classroom operates and the foundation for classroom dynamics. The degree to which a classroom becomes a community in which students care for one another and strive to improve the daily experience for everyone will depend on each class's unique dynamics. When a healthy and nurturing classroom context is established, students who are gifted can be important members of the classroom community. In such an environment, their abilities are recognized as assets to the class rather than something to be jealous of, envied, or despised.

To promote acceptance of gifted students, teachers should strive to dispel prevailing stereotypes. Discuss the uniqueness of these students in terms of the diversity of the classroom, implying that everyone is different. The notion that we all have strengths and weaknesses is also useful. It is particularly important to support gifted students who come from underserved groups, such as students with disabilities, those who are economically disadvantaged, and those from different racial or ethnic groups. Special attention should also be given to the needs of gifted females. Some suggestions for nurturing giftedness in females are listed in Figure 10.10.

Instructionally, many of the strategies suggested for gifted students can also be used successfully with nongifted students (Del Prete, 1996). By doing this, teachers can accommodate the needs of gifted students without drawing undue attention to the special programming they are receiving.

To be a successful general education teacher of gifted students, a wide range of competencies are needed. Maker (1993) highlighted the following competen-

- Believe in girls' logicomathematical abilities, and provide many opportunities for them to practise mathematical reasoning within other subject areas.
- Accelerate girls through the science and mathematics curriculum whenever possible.
- Have special clubs in mathematics for girls who are high-achieving.
- Design coeducational career development classes in which both girls and boys learn about career potentialities for women.
- Expose boys and girls to role models of women in various careers.
- Discuss nontraditional careers for women, including salaries for men and women and schooling requirements.
- Help girls set long-term goals.
- Discuss underachievement among females who are gifted, and ask how they can combat it in themselves and others.
- Have girls read biographies of famous women.
- Arrange opportunities for girls to "shadow" female professionals for a few days to see what their work entails.
- Discourage sexist remarks and attitudes in the classroom.
- Boycott sexist classroom materials, and write to the publishers for their immediate correction.
- Discuss sexist messages in the media.
- Advocate special classes and afterschool enrichment opportunities for students who are gifted.
- Form support groups for girls with similar interests.

FIGURE 10.10

Suggestions for Teachers and Counsellors in Fostering Giftedness in Girls

Adapted from "What Happens to the Gifted Girl?" by L. K. Silverman. In *Critical Issues in Gifted Education: Vol. 1. Defensible Programs for the Gifted,* edited by C. J. Maker, 1986, pp. 43–89. Austin, TX: Pro-Ed. (Copyright owned by author.) Used by permission.

cies as important in teaching gifted students: commitment, belief that people learn differently, high expectations, organization, enthusiasm, willingness to talk less/listen more, facilitative abilities, creativity, and the ability to juggle.

SUPPORTS FOR THE GENERAL EDUCATION TEACHER

The responsibility to deliver a quality education to gifted students in general education settings rests on the shoulders of the instructional staff, especially general education teachers. As discussed earlier in this book, for an inclusion model to work successfully, these features must be in place:

- Classroom teachers need to be well trained in dealing with the many and varied needs of gifted students.
- Teachers need to be provided with resource personnel (specialists who assist the general education teacher by helping in the classroom or providing classroom teachers with strategies and materials).
- Teachers need adequate planning time. (Goree, 1996, p.22)

Using school-based supports such as teacher assistance teams (Chalfant & Van Dusen Pysh, 1993) can also assist with addressing the needs of gifted students. When staffed properly, these teams become a rich resource of experience and ideas for dealing with a myriad of student needs.

CONSIDER THIS

What kind of supports would be ideal to help general education teachers meet the needs of gifted and talented students in their classes?

If appropriate training and supports are provided to general education teachers, we will do a great service to students with exceptional abilities. It is only when these conditions are met that teachers will be able to "stimulate the imagination, awaken the desire to learn, and imbue the students with a sense of curiosity and an urge to reach beyond themselves" (Mirman, 1991, p. 59).

SUMMARY

- Definitions of giftedness and services to gifted students vary across Canada.

- Professionals do not agree on the best way to provide educational programs for children who are gifted.

- Children with exceptional abilities continue to be an underidentified, underserved, and often inappropriately served group.

- Controversy and confusion characterize the delivery of services to gifted students.

- There are many misconceptions about gifted students.

- The understanding of giftedness has changed over time.

- Remarkable potential to achieve is a key component of many definitions of giftedness.

- The concept of multiple intelligences suggests that there are different kinds of intelligence.

- The generally accepted prevalence rate of giftedness is 2 percent in the schools.

- Students who are gifted demonstrate a wide range of aptitudes, abilities, and skills.

- Identification of gifted students is a complex and multifaceted process.

- Gifted students with diverse cultural backgrounds and with disabilities are underidentified.

- Differentiated programming is necessary to meet the needs of gifted students.

- Enrichment, acceleration, and grouping are ways to address the educational programs of gifted students.

- Many general educators are not provided with the necessary understanding, skills, and resources to deal effectively with gifted students.

- There are numerous ways to accelerate programs for gifted students.

- Special methods used for gifted students are often very effective for other students.

- Gifted students should be encouraged to develop career interests early in their educational programs.

- Teachers need to address the social-emotional needs of gifted students.

- Teachers can do a great deal to promote a sense of community and social acceptance in their classrooms.

- General classroom teachers need to have a variety of supports in order to effectively meet the needs of gifted students.

- Comprehensive gifted programs must be committed to identify and serve underrepresented groups of gifted students. These include students who are female, culturally and ethnically different, economically disadvantaged, or disabled.

RESOURCES

Winebrenner, Susan. (1998). *Excellence in Educating Gifted and Talented Learners*, 3rd ed. Denver, CO: Love Publishing Co.

This resources provides techniques and strategies to motivate and challenge gifted students in your class.

VanTassel-Baska, Joyce. (1992). *Planning Effective Curriculum for Gifted Learners.* (Available through the Council for Exceptional Children)

This resource focuses on curriculum for gifted students and provides a variety of checklists,

forms, differentiated activities, and practical ideas for planning curriculum K–12. Sample units provide practical applications for all students, including disadvantaged and learning disabled populations.

British Columbia Ministry of Education, Special Programs Branch. (1996). *Gifted Education: A Resource Guide for Teachers.* Victoria: Author.

This very practical teacher's resource guide is a good starting point for understanding and working with gifted students.

WEBLINKS

Gifted Canada
www.edu.gov.on.ca/eng/document/resource/resource.html
Gifted Canada provides a variety of resources, information, and related links in the area of giftedness and lists provincial and territorial chapters. It covers organizations, research, and teaching strategies, useful for teachers and parents. There is an excellent collection of teaching resources on a teaching resource and manuals page.

Eskimo North
www.eskimo.com/%7euser/kids.html
This Web site, called the "gifted resources" home page, serves as a central locator of all sites pertaining to gifted education. It is an excellent jumping off point to explore all that is available for gifted education.

The Association for the Gifted (TAG)
education.idbsu.edu/tag/
The U.S.-based association is a division of the Council for Exceptional Children. Its Web site provides a number of publications that are relevant for teachers of gifted students.

National Association of Gifted Children (NAGC)
www.nagc.org/
The U.S.-based association's Web site provides excellent resources relevant to all teachers of gifted students. Look especially for NAGC publications for teachers: these are useful, practical, and very affordable even with exchange.

CHAPTER ELEVEN

CHAPTER OBJECTIVES

- To define students who are considered to be at risk

- To describe the different types of children who are considered at risk for developing learning and behaviour problems

- To discuss general considerations for teaching at-risk students

- To describe specific methods for teaching at-risk students effectively

Teaching Students Who Are at Risk

with SHARON R. MORGAN

Mary is a thin, eight-year-old girl with blonde hair and blue eyes. She is finishing first grade; she was kept back once in Kindergarten. Ms. Skates, her teacher, does not know how to help her. She referred Mary for special education, but the assessment revealed that she was ineligible. Although her intelligence is in the low-average range, she does not have an intellectual disability or any other qualifying disability. Mary is shy and very insecure. She frequently cries if Ms. Skates leaves the classroom; she is very dependent on her teacher. Mary does not have any close friends, but a few of the other girls in the classroom will play with her from time to time. Mary is reading at the preprimer level and does not recognize all letters and sounds. She can count to 10, but does not understand any math facts.

Mary lives with her mother and three younger brothers in a three-room apartment. Her mother has been divorced twice and works as a waitress at a local coffee shop. Her mother's income barely pays the rent, buys groceries, and provides day care for her brothers. Occasionally, when Mary's mother gets the chance to work extra at nights, when tips are better, she leaves all four children with Mary in charge. Although Mary's mother appears interested in her schoolwork, Ms. Skates has been unable to get her to a teacher's meeting, even though several have been scheduled. Ms. Skates is not sure if she should refer Mary for special education and retain her in first grade, or promote her so that she does not fall farther behind her age peers.

One thing that can be done for Mary is prereferral interventions, actions that teachers can take that may improve student performance. If prereferral interventions are successful, further consideration for special education may not be necessary.

1. Should Mary be provided special education services to prevent her from experiencing more failure? What services would you recommend?

2. What can teachers do with Mary and students like her to help prevent failure?

INTRODUCTION

The movement to include students with special needs in general education has made substantial progress over the past several years. One beneficial result has been the recognition that many students who are not officially eligible for special education services still need them. Although they do not manifest problems severe enough to result in a disability classification, these students are **at risk** of developing achievement and behaviour problems that could limit their success in school and as young adults.

Mary, the student in the vignette, is a good example of a child who is at risk of developing major academic and behaviour problems. In the current system, children like Mary cannot be provided with special education and related services from provincial/territorial programs. The result, too often, is that Mary and children like her drop out of school and experience major problems as adults.

The term *at risk* can be defined in many different ways. It is often used to describe children who have personal characteristics, or who live in families that display characteristics, that are associated with problems in school (Bowman, 1994). Students identified as being at risk generally have difficulty learning basic academic skills, exhibit unacceptable social behaviours, and cannot keep up with their peers (Pierce, 1994). They represent a very heterogeneous group (Davis, 1995).

CONSIDER THIS

Should students at risk of failure be identified as disabled and served in special education programs? Why or why not?

Unlike students with disabilities, who have historically been segregated full-time or part-time from their age peers, students who are considered at risk have been fully included in educational programs. Unfortunately, rather than receiving appropriate interventions, they have been neglected in the classroom and consigned to failure. Although not eligible for special education and related services, students who are at risk need special interventions. Without them, many will be retained year after year, become behaviour problems, develop drug and alcohol abuse problems, drop out of school, and fail as adults. School personnel need to recognize students who are at risk of failure and develop appropriate programs to facilitate their success in school and in society. Not doing so will result in losing many of these children, and "to lose today's at-risk students implies [that] society is more than a little out of control itself" (Greer, 1991, p. 390).

TYPES OF STUDENTS WHO ARE AT RISK

Many factors place students at risk of developing school problems. These include poverty, homelessness, single-parent homes, abusive parents, substance abuse, and unrecognized disabilities. Although the presence of these factors often makes failure more likely for students, it is important not to label every child who is poor or who lives with a single parent as an at-risk student.

Although overly simplistic conclusions should not be drawn about students at risk, research identifies certain factors as having a clear correlation with school problems. Using only a few factors, "schools can predict with better than

80% accuracy students in the third grade who will later drop out of school" (Barr & Parrett, 1995, p. 9). For example, McPartland and Slavin (1990) reported that third-graders who (1) read one year below grade level, (2) have been retained in one grade, (3) come from low socioeconomic backgrounds, and (4) attend school with many other poor children have almost no chance of graduating from high school. Figure 11.1 depicts the relationship between these four factors that are such strong predictors of school failure.

Poverty compounded by cultural differences can deepen the risks of students failing school or dropping out. The 1996 Canadian census data showed that more than half (54 percent) of First Nations peoples did not have a high school diploma, versus 35 percent of other Canadians (Statistics Canada, 1996). However, the relative effects of poverty in these figures are hard to determine.

Even when children are strongly indicated as being at risk, school personnel must be cautious about predicting their actual abilities and potential for achievement. Similarly, before teachers refer students who appear to be at risk and who represent culturally different backgrounds, they should consider the characteristics included in the nearby Diversity Forum feature. Addressing these issues will decrease the likelihood of referring students for special education programs when in-class interventions might be effective.

FURTHER READING

For more information on predicting failure in children, read *Hope at Last for At-Risk Youth,* by R. D. Barr and W. H. Parrett, published in 1995 by Allyn & Bacon.

Students Who Grow Up in Poverty

Poverty is a social condition associated with many different kinds of problems. It has been related to crime, physical abuse, learning problems, behaviour problems, and emotional problems. Davis (1993) notes that poverty is the number one factor that places children at risk of academic failure. In 1995 Statistics Canada reported an increase in the percentage of children living in low-income families: the prevalence rose to 21 percent in 1995 from the 1989 rate of 15.3

CROSS-REFERENCE

To read more about how poverty relates to incidence of intellectual disabilities and learning disabilities, review Chapters 3 and 6.

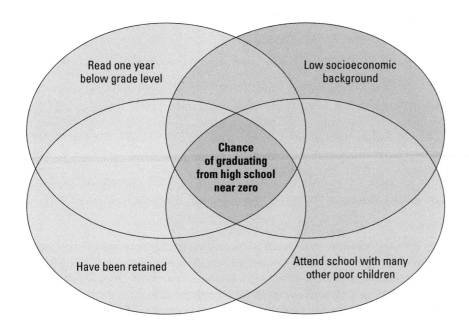

FIGURE 11.1
Research on Third-Grade Students

From *Policy Perspectives Increasing Achievement of At-Risk Students at Each Grade Level,* by J. M. McPartland and R. E. Slavin, 1990, Washington, DC: U.S. Department of Education. Cited in *Hope at Last for At-Risk Youth* (p. 10), by R. D. Barr and W. H. Parrett, 1995, Boston: Allyn & Bacon. Used by permission.

Issues to Consider before Referring Students from Culturally Diverse Backgrounds for Special Education Programs

- *Stage of language development:* At what stage of language proficiency, oral and written, is the student in L1 (student's first language) and L2 (student's second language)? What impact have past educational experiences had on language development? Will the environment facilitate further development?

- *Language skills:* What are the particular strengths and weaknesses of the student in oral and written L1 and L2 skills? What curriculum materials and instructional expertise are available to meet the student's needs? What skills are the parents able to work on at home?

- *Disability/at-risk status:* What impact does the student's specific disability or at-risk circumstances have on the acquisition of language skills in L1 and L2 and on other academic skills? Does the teacher have an adequate knowledge base to provide effective services? Does the school have access to community supports?

- *Age:* What impact does the student's age have on the ability to acquire L1 and L2

and to achieve in content areas? Is there a discrepancy between a child's age and emotional maturity? Is the curriculum developmentally appropriate?

- *Needs of the student:* What are the short-term and long-term needs of the student in academic, vocational, and community life? What are the needs of the student in relation to other students in the environment?

- *Amount of integration:* How much time will be spent in L1 and L2 environments? Will the student be able to interact with students who have various levels of ability?

- *Personal qualities:* How might the student's personality, learning style, and interests influence the acquisition of L1 and L2, achievement in content areas, and social-emotional growth? How might personal qualities of the student's peers and teacher influence learning?

From *Assessment and Instruction of Culturally and Linguistically Diverse Students with or at Risk of Learning Problems* (pp. 221–222), by V. Gonzalez, R. Brusca-Vega, and T. Yawkey, 1997, Boston: Allyn & Bacon. Used by permission.

percent. Statistics Canada notes that over the last 20 years fewer elderly people are represented in the low-income category and more lone-parent families headed by women are in this category. Thus, in 1995 one in five Canadian children was in a low-income family (Statistics Canada, 1995, 1999).

Poverty is associated with different kinds of disabilities (Smith & Luckasson, 1992), including intellectual disabilities (Beirne-Smith, Patton & Ittenbach, 1994), learning disabilities (Smith, Dowdy, Polloway, & Blalock, 1997), and various health problems. Poverty is also associated with poor prenatal care, poor parenting, hunger, limited health care, single-parent households, and poor housing conditions.

CONSIDER THIS

What kinds of actions can our society take to reduce poverty? What are some barriers to doing these things?

HUNGER

Although many people in this country have a difficult time believing it, thousands of children go to bed hungry every night. Children who are hungry have a difficult time concentrating on schoolwork and frequently display behaviour problems in the classroom. Although free school breakfast programs have been instituted over the past years as a result of nutrition budgets from ministries of education, hunger among schoolchildren remains a significant problem. Now that education budgets have been cut, many of the nutrition programs have been decreased. Frequently, the local home and school association has worked in the school to provide this essential service. This parent-run organization is prominent in many Canadian schools.

SCHOOL PERSONNEL AND POVERTY

Unfortunately, there is not a great deal teachers and other school personnel can do to alleviate the poverty experienced by students. However, teachers can reduce the impact of poverty on achievement and behaviour in some ways:

1. Recognize the impact that poverty has on students.
2. Make all students in the classroom feel important.
3. Avoid placing students in situations in which limited family finances become obvious to other students.
4. Coordinate with school social workers or other school personnel who can work with family members to secure social services.
5. Realize that students may not have supplies and other equipment required for certain class activities. Contingency funds or other means to help pay for these items should be available.

Homeless Students

The growing number of homeless people in society represents a tragedy. The problems of homeless people have only recently become commonly known. Whereas "the homeless" historically were aging adults, often with mental illness or alcohol abuse, today as many as 25 percent of all homeless persons are children (Davis, 1993).

Poverty is directly associated with homelessness, so the problems of poverty affect this group of children. The added impact of not having a home greatly compounds problems of poverty. Homeless children are usually very embarrassed by the fact that they do not have a place to live. Although some are lucky enough to stay in a shelter, many live on the streets or in cars with their parents.

Of course, school personnel can do little to find homes for these children. Probably the best advice is to avoid putting students in situations in which their homelessness will result in embarrassment. For example, going around the room after Christmas and having everyone tell what Santa Claus brought them would be very uncomfortable for students who do not even have a home to go to after school. Also, if you insist on a home visit, families may avoid interaction with you to escape an embarrassing situation.

In order to work with parents who are homeless, teachers and other school personnel should consider the following:

1. Arrange to meet parents at their place of work or at school.
2. Offer to assist family members in securing services from available social service agencies.
3. Do not require excessive school supplies that many families cannot afford.
4. Do not expect homework of the same quality as that of children who have homes.

TEACHING TIP

For students who are homeless, reduce the amount of homework and do not lower the students' grade if the work lacks neatness.

Students in Single-parent Homes

Of the 1 137 510 lone-parent families in Canada in 1996, 83 percent were headed by mothers (Statistics Canada, 1996). In these situations, the absence of a father generally has a more negative impact on boys than on girls. The academic achievement of both boys and girls has been shown to be affected, with lower achievement correlating with limited presence of the father.

Although not nearly as prevalent as single-parent homes headed by mothers, the number of single-parent homes headed by fathers has increased significantly over the past decade. The effects of growing up in a single-parent home headed by a father varies a great deal from child to child. Some study findings indicate that single-parent fathers are more likely to use other adults in their support networks than single-parent mothers, and children seem to fare better with a large adult support network than with a limited one (Santrock & Warshak, 1979).

ROLE OF SCHOOLS WITH CHILDREN IN SINGLE-PARENT FAMILIES

Children who find themselves in single-parent families, due to divorce or death, require much support. For many of these children, the school may be their most stable environment. School personnel must develop supports to prevent negative outcomes, such as school failure, manifestation of emotional problems, or the development of behaviour problems. An interview conducted with children residing in single-parent homes resulted in the following conclusions on the positive role schools can play:

1. Schools are a place of security and safety for students from single-parent homes.
2. Students who lose parents due to death are often treated differently by school personnel than when the loss is from divorce. Unfortunately, the child's needs are similar in both situations.
3. Teachers are the most important people in the school for children who are in single-parent homes because of their tremendous influence on self-esteem.

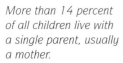

More than 14 percent of all children live with a single parent, usually a mother.

4. Students want to be considered just as they were before they were from a single-parent home.
5. Trust with peers and teachers is the most important factor for students from single-parent homes.
6. School personnel often seem oblivious to the new financial situation of families with only one parent.
7. Keeping a log or diary is considered an excellent method to explore feelings and create opportunities for meaningful discussions. (Lewis, 1992)

There are many things schools should and should not do when dealing with students who are from single-parent homes (Wanat, 1992). Figure 11.2 summarizes some of these "do's" and "don'ts."

For children whose parents are divorced, schools must consider the involvement of the noncustodial parent. Unfortunately, many schools do not even include spaces for information on forms for students' noncustodial parents (Austin, 1992). In order to ensure that noncustodial parents are afforded their rights regarding their children, and to actively solicit their involvement, school personnel should

1. establish policies that encourage the involvement of noncustodial parents;
2. maintain records of information about the noncustodial parent;
3. distribute information about school activities to noncustodial parents;
4. insist that noncustodial parents be involved in teacher conferences;
5. structure parent conferences to facilitate the development of a shared relationship between the custodial and noncustodial parent;
6. conduct surveys to determine the level of involvement desired by noncustodial parents. (Austin, 1992)

Some Do's

- Collect information about students' families.
- Analyze information about students' families to determine specific needs.
- Create programs and practices that address areas of need unique to particular schools.
- Include curricular areas that help students achieve success, such as study skills.
- Provide nonacademic programs such as child care and family counselling.
- Involve parents in determining appropriate roles for school and family.
- Take the initiative early in the year to establish a communication link with parents.
- Enlist the support of both parents, when possible.
- Provide a stable, consistent environment for children during the school day.

Some Don'ts

- Don't treat single parents differently than other parents.
- Don't call attention to the fact that a child lives with only one parent.
- Don't have "room mothers"; have "room parents."
- Don't overlook the limitations of single-parent homes in areas such as helping with projects, helping with homework, and so forth.

FIGURE 11.2
Some Do's and Don'ts When Working with Children with Single Parents

Adapted from "Meeting the Needs of Single-Parent Children: School and Parent Views Differ," by C. L. Wanat, 1992, *NAASP Bulletin, 76,* pp. 43–48. Used by permission.

Students Who Experience Significant Losses

Although the continued absence of one or both parents through separation or divorce is considered a loss, the loss created by the death of a parent can result in significantly more problems for children. Unlike children living in the early part of this century, when extended families often lived together and children observed death close at hand, often in the home environment with grandparents, children of today are generally insulated from death. Therefore, when death does occur, especially that of a significant person in a child's life, the result can be devastating, often resulting in major problems in school.

DEATH OF A PARENT

When a child's parent dies, external events impinge on the child's personality in three main ways (Felner, Ginter, Boike, & Cowan, 1981; Moriarty, 1967; Tennant, Bebbington, & Hurry, 1980):

1. The child must deal with the reality of the death itself.
2. The child must adapt to the resulting changes in the family.
3. The child must contend with the perpetual absence of the lost parent.

Children respond in many different ways to a parent's death. Some responses are guilt, regression, denial, bodily distress, hostile reactions to the deceased, eating disorders, enuresis (incontinence), sleep disturbances, withdrawal, anxiety, panic, learning difficulties, and aggression (Anthony, 1972; Elizer & Kauffman, 1983; Van Eerdewegh, Bieri, Parrilla, & Clayton, 1982). It is also not unusual for sibling rivalry to become very intense and disruptive. Often, extreme family turmoil results from the death of a parent, especially when the parent who dies was the controlling person in the family (Van Eerdewegh et al., 1982).

DEATH OF A SIBLING

A sibling plays an important and significant part in family dynamics, so the death of a sibling can initiate a psychological crisis for a child. Sometimes the grief of the parents renders them unable to maintain a healthy parental relationship with the remaining child or children, significantly changing a child's life situation.

When experiencing the death of a sibling, children frequently fear that they will die. When an older sibling dies, the younger child may revert to childish behaviours in hopes of not getting older, thereby averting dying. Older children often react with extreme fear and anxiety if they are ignored by parents during the grieving period. Often these children become preoccupied with the horrifying question about their own future: "Will it happen to me tomorrow, or next week, or next year?" (McKeever, 1983). Children often react with severe depression when a sibling dies (McKeever, 1983).

Students Who Are Abused

Growing up in an abusive family places children at significant risk of problems. Child abuse occurs in families from every socioeconomic status, race, religion, and ethnic background in society. Family members, acquaintances, or strangers may be the source of the abuse. Although there is no single cause, several factors may make a person more likely to commit abuse:

- Experience of abuse as a child (Litty, Kowalski, & Minor, 1996)
- Being an adolescent parent (Buchholz & Korn-Bursztyn, 1993)
- Poverty
- Having low self-esteem as a parent (Goldman & Gargiulo, 1990)
- Substance abuse (Goldman & Gargiulo, 1990)
- Emotional problems (Litty et al., 1996)

Children can be abused in several different ways that place them at risk of problems in school. There are two major types of abuse (1) **emotional abuse** and (2) **physical abuse**, which includes sexual abuse. Emotional abuse involves unreasonable demands placed on children by parents, siblings, peers, or teachers, that cannot possibly be met. Although difficult to identify, several characteristics may be exhibited by children who are being emotionally abused. These include the following:

- Absence of a positive self-image
- Behavioural extremes
- Depression
- Psychosomatic complaints
- Attempted suicide
- Impulsive, defiant, and antisocial behaviour
- Age-inappropriate behaviours
- Inappropriate habits and tics
- Enuresis
- Inhibited intellectual or emotional development
- Difficulty in establishing and maintaining peer relationships
- Extreme fear, vigilance
- Sleep and eating disorders
- Self-destructive tendencies
- Rigidly compulsive behaviours (Gargiulo, 1990, p. 22)

Physical abuse is more easily identified than emotional abuse. Physical abuse includes beating, strangulation, burns to the body, and other forms of physical brutalization. It is defined as "any physical injury that has been caused by other than accidental means, including any injury which appears to be at variance with the explanation of the injury" (*At Risk Youth in Crisis*, 1991, p. 9). In 1996, 3500 cases of physical or sexual abuse were investigated in Toronto (Gadd, 1997). There are no national statistics for child abuse in Canada as it is under provincial/territorial jurisdiction; however, in the United States in 1991 there were more than 2.7 million cases of reported child abuse; 1400 children were abused every day; and more than 1300 reported cases of child abuse and neglect resulted in death (Davis, 1993). Most authorities believe that only one in five cases is reported, meaning that the actual numbers are significantly greater. Between 1976 and 1985, the number of reported cases of child abuse increased from 669 000 to 1.9 million (National Center on Child Abuse and Neglect, 1986).

Children who are physically abused are two to three times more likely than nonabused children to experience failing grades and to become discipline problems. They have difficulty with peer relationships, show physically aggressive behaviours, and are frequent substance abusers (Emery, 1989). Studies also show that children who suffer from physical abuse are likely to exhibit social

CONSIDER THIS
Think about how being abused would affect you at this point in your life. Then consider these feelings from the perspective of a young child and how they would affect a child's school activities.

FURTHER READING
For more information on long-term effects of abuse, read the article "The Long-Term Sequelae of Children and Adolescent Abuse: A Longitudinal Community Study," by R. B. Silverman, H. Z. Reinherz, and R. M. Giaconia, published in 1996 in volume 20 of *Child Abuse & Neglect* (pp. 709–723).

skill deficits, including shyness, inhibited social interactions, and limited problem-solving skills. Deficits in cognitive functioning are also found in greater numbers in students who are abused than in their nonabused peers (Weston, Ludolph, Misle, Ruffins, & Block, 1990).

Sexual abuse is another form of physical abuse that puts children at risk for school failure. Children may be sexually abused by their own families as well as by strangers. Sexual abuse can include actual physical activities, such as touching a child's genital areas, attempted and completed sexual intercourse, and the use of children in pornography. Exposing children to sexual acts by adults with the intention of shocking or arousing them is another form of sexual abuse (Jones, 1982; Williamson, Borduin, & Howe, 1991). Children who are sexually abused are not only at risk of developing problems during their school years, but will typically manifest problems throughout their adulthood (Silverman, Reinherz, & Giaconia, 1996).

School personnel should be aware of typical physical and behavioural symptoms of sexual abuse:

- Physical injuries to the genital area
- Sexually transmitted diseases
- Difficulty in urinating
- Discharges from the penis or vagina
- Pregnancy
- Fear of aggressive behaviour toward adults, especially a child's own parents
- Sexual self-consciousness
- Sexual promiscuity and acting out
- Inability to establish appropriate relationships with peers
- Running away, stealing, and abusing substances
- Using the school as a sanctuary, coming early, and not wanting to go home

CROSS-REFERENCE
Review Chapter 5 for more information on emotional and behavioural disorders, and consider the impact of child abuse on emotional and behavioural functioning.

The first thing that school personnel should be prepared to do when dealing with children who might be abused is to report any incident to the appropriate agencies (Pearson, 1996). School personnel have a moral and legal obligation to report suspected child abuse. If you suspect a student is being abused, you should follow your school district's procedures for reporting the problem. If you are uncertain about those procedures, contact your principal. School personnel need to understand their responsibility in reporting suspected abuse and know the specific procedures to follow when making such a report.

Students Who Abuse Substances

Substance abuse among children and adolescents results in major problems and places students significantly more at risk for school failure (Eggert & Herting, 1993). Students who are abusing substances have a much more difficult time succeeding in school than their peers.

Although there were indicators that drug use among youth was declining (*The Condition of Education*, 1990), more recent data suggest that substance abuse among children and adolescents is once again on the increase (Teen drug use is on the rise again, 1996). A survey of students in junior high and high schools revealed that drug use was higher in all categories, including alcohol, cocaine, marijuana, hallucinogens, and inhalants. Twenty-eight percent of eighth-graders surveyed indicated that they had used marijuana at least once—almost double the number reporting use in 1991. More than 48 percent of all high school seniors in the class of 1995 reported that they had tried some type of illegal drug (Teen drug use, 1996). Nagel et al. (1996) report that boys have a tendency to use illegal drugs slightly more than girls, but that girls use more over-the-counter drugs inappropriately than boys do.

While no factors are always associated with drug use in children, some appear to increase the likelihood of such use. Parental factors, such as (1) drug use by parents, (2) parents' attitudes about drug use, (3) family management styles, and (4) parent-child communication patterns, have an impact on children's drug use (Young, Kersten, & Werch, 1996). Additional cross-pressures such as the perception of friends' approval or disapproval of drug use, peer pressure to use drugs, and the assessment of individual risk also play a role (Robin & Johnson, 1996).

Although a great deal of attention has been paid to the impact of marijuana, cocaine, and alcohol abuse on children and youth, only recently has attention been focused on **inhalants**. Inhalant use increased for every grade level from the 1990–1991 school year to the 1991–1992 school year (Drug use increasing, 1992). One of the problems with inhalants is the wide number of readily available ones that can be used by students. Examples include cleaning solvents, gasoline, room deodorizers, glue, perfume, wax, and spray paint.

School personnel must be alert to the symptoms of substance abuse, whether the substance is alcohol, marijuana, inhalants, or something else. The following characteristics might indicate possible substance abuse:

- Inability to concentrate
- Chronic absenteeism
- Poor grades or neglect of homework
- Poor scores on standardized tests not related to IQ or learning disabilities
- Uncooperative and quarrelsome behaviour
- Sudden behaviour changes
- Shy and withdrawn behaviour
- Compulsive behaviours
- Chronic health problems
- Signs of neglect and abuse
- Low self-esteem
- Anger, anxiety, and depression
- Poor coping skills
- Unreasonable fears
- Difficulty adjusting to changes

Once a student is identified as having a substance abuse problem and the student has been referred to the appropriate agency, a supportive classroom environment must be provided. This includes a structured program to build self-esteem and create opportunities for students to be successful.

Students Who Become Pregnant

There are many unfortunate outcomes from teenage pregnancies, and one of the most significant is the increased risk that young girls, and boys, who find themselves involved in a pregnancy will drop out of school. In an era of extensive sex education and fear of AIDS, the continued high levels of teenage

FURTHER READING
For more information on current drug use among children, read the article "Students' Self-Reported Substance Use by Grade Level and Gender" by L. Nagel, D. McDougall, and C. Granby, published in 1996 in volume 26 of the *Journal of Drug Education* (pp. 49–56).

pregnancy are surprising. Despite all of the information available for adolescents about sex and AIDS, it appears that many adolescents continue to engage in unprotected sexual activity (Weinbender & Rossignol, 1996).

School personnel should deal with teenage pregnancy issues before pregnancy occurs. Sex education, information about AIDS, and the consequences of unprotected sex should be a focus. Unfortunately, sex education and practices such as distributing free condoms are very controversial, and many schools refuse to enter the fray of such emotion-laden issues.

In addition to having a pregnancy prevention program, school personnel can do the following to intervene in teenage pregnancy situations:

1. Provide counselling for girls who become pregnant.
2. Develop programs that encourage girls who are pregnant to remain in school.
3. Provide parenting classes for all students.
4. Do not discriminate against girls who become pregnant, or boys who are married, in extracurricular activities.
5. Consider establishing a school-based child care program for girls who have babies and wish to remain in school.
6. Work with families of girls who are pregnant to ensure that family support is present.

Students Who Are Delinquents

Students who get into trouble with legal authorities are frequently labelled juvenile delinquents. Morrison (1997) defines *delinquency* as "behavior that violates the rules and regulations of the society" (p. 189). **Juvenile delinquency** often results in school failure; students who take part in illegal activities often do not focus on school activities. Juvenile delinquency must be considered in light of other factors related to at-risk students, though the relationship of these factors may be difficult to discern. Juvenile delinquency is highly corre-

Teen empowerment can help at-risk students overcome the dangers of drugs and gangs.

lated with substance abuse and may be found in higher rates among poor children than among children who are raised in adequate income environments. It is also more prevalent in single-parent homes (Morgan, 1994).

Juvenile delinquency is frequently related to gang activity. Although gangs are relatively new, they currently represent a major problem for adolescents, especially in large urban areas. Morgan (1994) cites numerous studies showing that adolescents raised in single-parent homes or homes that sustain a great deal of conflict often join gangs and exhibit other delinquent behaviours. Again, although no single factor leads children to delinquent behaviours, certain factors can indicate high risk. Delinquent behaviours often disrupt school success. School personnel need to work with legal and social service agencies to reduce delinquency and academic failure.

PROGRAMS FOR STUDENTS WHO ARE AT RISK

There are four primary approaches to dealing with students who are at risk of failure in schools: compensatory education, prevention programs, intervention programs, and transition programs. Figure 11.3 depicts these approaches. Compensatory education programs "are designed to compensate or make up for existing or past risk factors and their effects in students' lives" (Morrison, 1997, p. 192). Reading recovery, a program currently gaining popularity in Canada, has been shown to effectively improve the reading skills of at-risk students (Dorn & Allen, 1995; Ross, Smith, Casey, & Slavin, 1995).

Prevention programs focus on keeping certain negative factors from having an impact on students. Drug prevention programs, antismoking educational efforts, and sex education programs are examples of efforts designed to

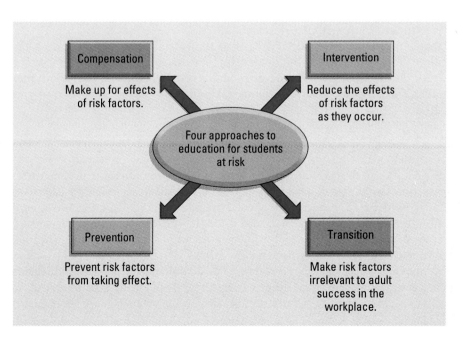

FIGURE 11.3
Four Approaches to Education for Students at Risk

From *Teaching in America* (p. 193), by G. S. Morrison, 1997, Boston: Allyn & Bacon. Used by permission.

Using Technology with Multicultural and Bilingual Students Who May Be at Risk

MICROCOMPUTERS

As computerized language translators begin to develop, there may be a significant impact for special education students with a primary language other than English. Imagine if the student could use a computer to write an assignment in his or her primary language, check the spelling and punctuation, then press a button to translate the work into English and transmit it to the teacher. Or perhaps the student wrote the assignment in a dialect, and then the computer was able to translate it into the standard form of that language. Such technology is possible.

One successful use of the microcomputer has been for the students to write their journals and for the teacher to respond via computer (Goldman and Rueda, 1988). Multicultural bilingual special education students were successful in developing their writing skills and their interaction skills with their teacher.

George Earl (1984) created a Spanish-to-English as well as an English-to-Spanish computerized version of the word game "hangman." Hangman is one of the many instructional games used by special education teachers to help improve language skills. Although the program had some difficulty (Zemke, 1985) with dialects (it translates standard Spanish), it demonstrates how technology can be applied to the learning needs of children who are multicultural and bilingual.

From *Introduction to Special Education* (p. 63), by D. D. Smith and R. Luckasson, 1995, second edition, Boston: Allyn & Bacon. Used by permission.

keep students from developing problem behaviours. Intervention programs focus on eliminating risk factors. They include teaching teenagers how to be good parents and helping at-risk preschool children (Sexton et al., 1996). Finally, transition programs are designed to help students see the relationship between what they learn in school and how it will be used in the real world. School-to-work programs, which help students move from school to work, are effective transition programs (Morrison, 1997).

Schools must use a variety of programs to prevent problems from developing and to address problems that do develop. The use of technology often proves beneficial. The Technology Today feature above provides information about how computers can be used with multicultural and bilingual groups, two at-risk populations.

FURTHER READING

For more information on classroom climate and at-risk students, read the article "Implications of Classroom Climate for At-Risk Learners," by C. Pierce, published in 1994 in volume 88 of the *Journal of Educational Research* (pp. 37–44).

Characteristics of Effective Programs

Several factors are associated with schools that provide effective programs for students who are at risk. These include (1) a clear academic mission, (2) an orderly environment, (3) a high rate of time on academic tasks, and (4) frequent student monitoring (Teddlie & Stringfield, 1993). Figure 11.4 summarizes characteristics associated with schools that are effective and those that are ineffective in working with students who are at risk.

The movement to include students with disabilities in general education classrooms provides an opportunity to meet the needs of at-risk students. In an inclusive classroom, students should be educated based on their needs

EFFECTIVE
LOW SOCIOECONOMIC STATUS SCHOOLS

1. Although principals and teachers had modest long-term expectations for their students' achievement, particularly in regard to higher education, they held firm present academic expectations for their students.

2. Teachers reported spending more time on reading and math and assigning more homework rather than the other two low socioeconomic status groups [in the study].

3. Students perceived teachers as pushing them academically. They also reported receiving more teacher help than did students in less successful low socioeconomic status schools.

4. Students perceived their teachers as having high present expectations for them.

5. Teachers reported that principals visited their classrooms frequently.

6. The teachers in this group [effective low socioeconomic status schools] were the youngest and least experienced of the low socioeconomic status group.

7. The teachers in this group were the most likely of all the teachers to have teacher's aides.

8. Principals in these schools were the most likely to say that they had major input in hiring teachers. Twenty-three percent of the principals in the effective low socioeconomic status schools said that they hired their teachers. No other group of schools had more than 9% of its principals report this power.

INEFFECTIVE
LOW SOCIOECONOMIC STATUS SCHOOLS

1. An overall negative academic climate in these schools appears to have contributed to the low student achievement. Of all the groups [studied], teachers had the lowest expectations for students and rated them the lowest academically; the teachers accepted little responsibility for and perceived having little influence on student outcomes; they also appeared less satisfied with teaching and perceived themselves as unsuccessful in helping students attain goals.

2. When compared with students in low socioeconomic status groups, students perceived their teachers as less praising, less caring, less helpful, and more critical. More than in the other groups, these students reported that their teachers did not consider learning important.

3. Principals, teachers, and pupils all perceived the lack of achievement within the schools.

4. Compared with the other groups [studied], a higher percentage (21%) of teachers in these schools would rather teach in another school. By contrast, only 2% of the teachers in the typical middle socioeconomic status schools wanted to teach elsewhere. Teachers in the low socioeconomic status, ineffective schools were absent an average of 3.51 days in the fall semester, whereas teachers in effective low socioeconomic status schools were absent only an average of 2.03 days. (Teddlie & Stringfield, 1993, pp. 34–35)

FIGURE 11.4
Effective and Ineffective Low Socioeconomic Status Schools
From *Hope at Last for At-Risk Youth* (p. 56), by R. D. Barr and W. H. Parrett, 1995, Boston: Allyn & Bacon. Used by permission.

rather than on their clinical labels. In fact, inclusion, rather than separate programming, is supported by the lack of evidence that different teaching techniques are required by students in different disability groups. Techniques developed for a specific population often benefit everyone. By removing labels from students and providing programs based on individual needs, students who are at risk can benefit from the strategies and activities supplied for students with various disabilities (Wang, Reynolds, & Walberg, 1994–1995).

School personnel should be proactive in efforts to prevent school drop-outs.

Specific Strategies for Students at Risk

In addition to the general principles cited earlier, specific programs can prove effective with these students. These include an emphasis on teaching every child to read, **accelerated schools**, **alternative schools**, one-on-one tutoring, extended day programs, cooperative learning activities, **magnet schools**, teen parent programs, vocational-technical programs, mentoring, and school-to-work programs (Barr & Parrett, 1995). Table 11.1 provides a brief description of each of these approaches.

One program described in Table 11.1 has been used effectively in many schools: a **mentor program** (Slicker & Palmer, 1993). Elementary, middle, and high schools design such programs to provide students with a positive personal relationship with an adult—something that many children and youth lack (Barr & Parrett, 1995). A mentor can be any person of any background who is committed to serve as a support person for a child or youth.

Mentor programs range in scope from national programs such as Big Brothers/Big Sisters to programs developed by and for specific schools, such as a program wherein adults employed in the community have lunch with students (Friedman & Scaduto, 1995). Programs large and small proved effective for many children. It is important to ensure that a positive match is made between the mentor and the child. Other features of successful mentor programs are listed in the nearby Inclusion Strategy feature.

The population of at-risk children is incredibly diverse. Many different professionals need to get involved in developing and implementing programs for this group of students. For more information on the topic, as well as a comprehensive list of available support services, see the book *Hope at Last for At-Risk Youth*, by R. D. Barr and W. H. Parrett, published in 1995 by Allyn & Bacon.

CROSS-REFERENCE

Review some of the teaching strategies included in Chapters 3–9, and determine whether any of these methods would be effective with children who are at risk.

TABLE 11.1	

Strategies for Teaching Students at Risk

Strategy	Description
READING EMPHASIS	• Recognizes the importance of reading • Emphasizes teaching reading early to each child
ACCELERATED SCHOOLS	• Utilize the same approaches used with gifted and talented children • Use an extended school day with emphasis on language and problem solving • Stress acceleration rather than remediation
ALTERNATIVE SCHOOLS	• Have a separate focus that may meet the needs of at-risk students better than regular schools • Example: Montessori schools, back-to-basics schools, nongraded schools, and open schools
ONE-ON-ONE TUTORING	• Provides concentrated time for direct instruction • Uses volunteers from the community, peers, or older students as tutors • Example: Reading Recovery, a one-on-one program (using a certified teacher) showing major success
EXTENDED SCHOOL DAY	• Provides after-school programs as an opportunity for extra tutoring time • Is staffed with regular teachers or volunteers
COOPERATIVE LEARNING	• Provides opportunities for learning from other students in small groups • Shown by research to be a very successful model for at-risk students
MAGNET SCHOOLS	• Focus on specific areas, such as the arts or international studies • Give students an opportunity to focus on their strengths and interests
TEEN PARENT PROGRAMS	• Provide opportunities for students to learn parenting techniques • Help students with young children stay in school
VOCATIONAL-TECHNICAL PROGRAMS	• Enable students to develop skills that are specific to jobs • Help with transition from school to postschool environments • Enable students who do poorly in academic areas to perform well in other areas
MENTORING	• Provides role models for students • Creates opportunities for tutoring and social skills development
SCHOOL-TO-WORK PROGRAMS	• Give students the opportunity to begin work early • Provide training for students in real jobs

Adapted from *Hope at Last for At-Risk Youth*, by R. D. Barr and W. H. Parrett, 1995, Boston: Allyn & Bacon.

PERSONAL SPOTLIGHT

Inclusion Teacher ■ LING-SHU KAO

Elementary Teacher

Ling-shu Kao completed Grades 1–11 in Taipei, Taiwan, and came to Canada at the age of 17. She took Grade 12 at a private boarding school in Montebello, Quebec, then attended Centennial and Vanier colleges in Montreal before completing a bachelor of education degree in Elementary at McGill University. She has taught for three years as a Chinese Language teacher at the Montreal Metropolitan Chinese School and has also tutored students with special needs. She is presently leading a second-year professional seminar for teachers in training at McGill University; she is also working with the McGill Student Teaching Office, where she supervises second-year students in their field experience focused on working with children with individual differences.

Ling-shu feels strongly that she has something to share with her teachers in training. As a new teacher, she felt unprepared to deal with students with special needs. She has learned from those experiences. Although she is committed to inclusion, she believes there are both positives and negatives to an inclusive approach.

"I feel that different adaptations and strategies used for 'inclusion' are actually just good teaching—they are beneficial to everyone, not just students with special needs! For me, a big plus about inclusion is that everyone learns to accept individual differences. Not just exceptionalities, but race and cultural differences—multiculturalism is a part of inclusion too, and if no one is treated as an outsider, outcast, or 'freak,' but as a part of the community, that is so important."

For Ling-shu the negative side of the inclusive approach focuses on teachers' views and concerns.

"Teachers may be scared about working with students with exceptionalities because they feel they do not have sufficient knowledge or skills to do it. And if teachers aren't given the supports and resources they need to include the students, they may feel overwhelmed and angry at the system and even take it out on the student. I have seen and heard of this happening. If a teacher gets burnt out, everyone suffers! But I know that, with the right resources and a willingness to learn, it can work."

Asked to say why she is committed to inclusion when she sees the difficulties so clearly, Ling-shu replies: "The most influential individual with exceptionalities in my life so far is my niece, Ming. She is two years older than I am, and she has Down's syndrome. Even though her mother, my cousin, and my family are close, I have seen my niece only twice in my life, and I remember that I was a little bit scared of her because she was different. So how can she be influential? You have to understand how important cultural diversity is in approach to people with exceptionalities. Chinese people are very private. We do not talk to outsiders about anything 'shameful' in the family—even to relatives. Having an individual with exceptional needs at home is such a taboo in Taiwan. People with special needs are sent to special education schools or institutions, and they are usually hidden from the public and even family members. My cousin also saw her daughter's exceptionality as a taboo and burden, and she was ashamed of her—she never brought Ming to family gatherings. Since Grade 1, Ming was sent to a special education school, where she stayed until the end of high school, completely segregated. Then Ming stayed with her grandmother, who had Alzheimer's and took care of her until her death just a few years ago. Now, Ming cleans and helps her mother around the home without complaints, while her brothers and sister offer no help. Only now, when Ming is at home with her mom and working with her cheerfully has her mom really gotten to know her and come to realize that Ming is not a burden, but a blessing! Only now, after 28 years does my cousin appreciate her daughter as a person and a member of the family.

"Ming has overcome many obstacles, and most important of all, she singlehandedly changed her own mother's attitude toward her. Ming is not only a person with special needs, but also an extraordinary individual. She managed against the odds, but when I hear stories like those of Tina and Hannah (see Chapter 6's Personal Spotlight) and think what might have been for Ming if the society were more accepting, I feel sad and determined to work toward that acceptance for all students with exceptionalities."

INCLUSION STRATEGIES

Components of Effective Mentoring Programs for At-Risk Students

- *Program compatibility:* The program should be compatible with the policies and goals of the organization. In a program for students in a community group, for example, program organizers should work closely with school personnel to ensure that the mentoring they provide complements the student's education.

- *Administrative commitment:* The program must be supported from the top as well as on a grassroots level. In a school-based program, all school and district administrators, teachers, and staff must provide input and assistance. For a sponsoring business, the president or chief executive officer must view the program as important and worthy of the time and attention of the employees.

- *Proactive:* Ideally the programs should be proactive; that is, not a quick-fix reaction to a crisis. Successful mentoring programs for youth work because they are well thought out, they have specific goals and objectives, and they exist within a larger realm of programs and policies that function together.

- *Participant oriented:* The program should be based on the goals and needs of the participants. These goals will determine the program's focus, recruitment, and training. For example, if the primary aim of a mentoring program is career awareness, students should be matched with successful businesspeople in the youth's area of interest. Activities and workshops should be job related.

- *Pilot program:* The first step should be a pilot program of 6 to 12 months, with 10 to 40 participants, in order to work out any problems before expanding to a larger audience. Trying to start out with a large-scale plan that includes more than this number can prove unwieldy and disastrous. In the words of Oregon's guide to mentorship programs, "Think big but start small."

- *Orientation:* An orientation should be provided for prospective participants. It will help determine interest and enthusiasm, as well as give prospective mentors and students an idea of what to expect. In addition, it will provide them with opportunities to help design the program.

- *Selection and matching:* Mentors and their protégés should be carefully selected and matched. Questionnaires are helpful in determining needs, areas of interest, and strengths.

- *Training:* Training must be provided for all participants, including support people, throughout the program. Assuming that because a person is knowledgeable, caring, and enthusiastic he or she will make a good mentor is a mistake. Training must be geared to the specific problems experienced by at-risk youth as well as different styles of communication.

- *Monitoring progress:* The program should be periodically monitored for progress and results to resolve emerging conflicts and problems.

- *Evaluation and revision:* The program should be evaluated with respect to how well goals and objectives are achieved. This can be done using questionnaires, interviews, etc.

From *Mentoring Programs for At-Risk Youth* (pp. 5–6), by National Dropout Prevention Center, 1990, Clemson, SC: Clemson University.

SUMMARY

- Students who are at risk may not be eligible for special education programs.

- At-risk students include those who are in danger of developing significant learning and behaviour problems.

- Poverty is a leading cause of academic failure.

- Poverty among children is increasing in this country.

- Poverty is associated with homelessness, poor health care, hunger, and single-parent households.

- Hunger is a major problem in our country.

- Students in single-parent homes face major problems in school.

- About 14.5 percent of all children live in single-parent homes.

- Schools must take into consideration the rights of the noncustodial parent.

- The death of a parent, sibling, or friend can have a major impact on a child and school success.

- National statistics on child abuse in Canada are not available, but there are high prevalence rates in major urban centres.

- Child abuse is a major problem in this country and causes children to experience much emotional trauma.

- School personnel are required by law to report suspected child abuse.

- Drug use among students is on the increase.

- Teenage pregnancy continues to be a problem, despite the fear of AIDS and the presence of sex education programs.

- Numerous programs and interventions have proved effective in working with at-risk students.

RESOURCES

Levin, Diane E. (1994). *Teaching Young Children in Violent Times: Building a Peaceful Classroom Environment*. Gabriola, BC: New Society Publishers.

Levin promotes ways of fostering a peaceful environment in the classroom, especially through teaching conflict resolution and acceptance of diversity.

Sprick, R., Sprick, M., and Garrison, M. (1993). *Interventions: Collaborative Planning for Students at Risk*. Longmont, CO: Sopris.

Interventions is a comprehensive resource designed to assist education professionals as they plan and implement strategies to meet the needs of at-risk students. It includes information on how to manage physically dangerous and severely disruptive behaviour, provide academic assistance and mentoring, and intervene in other ways to help students at risk.

Vaughn, Sharon, et al. (1996). *Teaching Mainstreamed, Diverse, and At-Risk Students in the General Education Classroom*. Needham Heights, MA: Allyn & Bacon.

This textbook resource provides more background information and many practical suggestions for teaching students at risk.

WEBLINKS

Canadian Centre on Substance Abuse
www.ccsa.ca/
As part of the Centre's work to minimize the harm associated with the use of alcohol, tobacco, and other drugs, this site provides information and resources on a variety of issues related to at-risk youth, including prevention and education.

Substance Abuse Prevention Tool Kit
substanceabuse.region.halton.on.ca
This Halton Region of Ontario Web site is dedicated to the prevention of youth substance abuse. The Substance Abuse Prevention Tool Kit is full of interesting ideas, including a student video club, a youth support league, a peer leader training program, and a parent support group. It also offers definitions of substance abuse terms, useful survey results, a list of protective and risk factors, and a list of information resources available from the Halton Regional Health Department.

The Internet Public Library on Substance Abuse
www.ipl.org
As an Internet library, this site provides a catalogue of Web sites that pertain to teen substance abuse, including information, clubs, and support groups.

National Clearinghouse on Child Abuse and Neglect Information
www.calib.com/nccanch/
This Web site provides online information about the prevention of child abuse and neglect and outlines how educators can help both prevent and treat the problem. It lists the different levels of prevention, the individuals at risk, the ways to evaluate risk, and how to work together with the community for prevention. A lot of information and some related resources are offered, but the funding information is not relevant because this site is American based; no equivalent Canadian site was found.

CHAPTER TWELVE

CHAPTER OBJECTIVES

- To describe the impact of the inclusion movement on the placement of elementary students with disabilities

- To define the concept of comprehensive curriculum for students at the elementary level

- To identify curricular content considerations for academic, social skills, and transitional instruction

- To identify appropriate instructional modifications and accommodations for students with disabilities in elementary schools

Teaching Students with Special Needs in Elementary Schools

Julie Bennington was told by one of her university professors that elementary classrooms were becoming increasingly similar to the old "one-room school houses," encompassing a diversity of learning needs that had never been greater. Julie was excited by this challenge and, in her first year of teaching, often reflected on this comment.

Julie is teaching a class of third-graders in a self-contained arrangement. She has full responsibility for 25 eager students for all subjects except art, music, and physical education. She has found their diversity to be both exciting and somewhat overwhelming.

Naturally, one of her greatest concerns has been in the area of language arts. After doing some informal evaluation and after reading the records of her students, she realized during the second week of the academic year that the ability levels of her students ranged greatly; two students were virtual nonreaders, whereas five pupils were significantly above grade level.

It has become apparent to Julie that these students do not all learn in the same way, but she continues to struggle to find approaches that will meet the needs of her diverse classroom. She is fortunate to be working two hours a day during her language arts block with Alisa Rinaldi, a special education teacher who is certified in learning disabilities.

1. How can Julie and Alisa develop effective cooperative teaching strategies that will take advantage of their own talents and meet the needs of their students?

2. How can they resolve the ongoing questions about the effectiveness of holistic versus decoding approaches for beginning reading instruction for those with learning difficulties?

3. What adaptations in the curriculum can be made to more effectively meet the needs of students with special needs in this classroom?

INTRODUCTION

As the opening vignette illustrates, elementary school presents both unique challenges and unique opportunities for young students with disabilities and other special needs to be included in general education. Although the learning needs of the students are frequently quite diverse and challenging, the degree of curricular differentiation (i.e., the need for alternative curricular focuses) tends to be more limited than it is at the secondary level. In elementary school, the necessity for similarity of educational content for all students is at its greatest. Thus, there is an excellent opportunity for students with special needs to prosper in general education with the support of special education professionals.

Elementary school also offers an important beginning point for students with disabilities to profit from positive interactions with their nondisabled peers. Preparation for successful lives beyond the school setting requires the ability to learn, live, and work with a diversity of individuals. Thus, inclusion offers benefits both to students who are disabled and those who are not. There is clearly no better time for this to take place than in early childhood and throughout the primary and elementary grades.

CONSIDER THIS

Inclusive classrooms are more common at the elementary than secondary level. Why do you think this is the case?

The advent of the inclusion movement has increased the likelihood that many students with disabilities will receive a significant portion, or all, of their instruction in the general education classroom. Thus, beginning at the elementary level, careful attention must be given to these students' educational needs.

This chapter provides an overview of curricular and instructional accommodations for elementary-age students with special needs in inclusive settings. The initial section outlines core curriculum considerations. The discussion that follows emphasizes instructional accommodations and modifications that provide the means for achieving curricular goals.

GENERAL CURRICULAR CONSIDERATIONS

Curriculum has been defined in varied ways. Hoover (1988) describes it as the planned learning experiences that have intended educational outcomes. Armstrong (1990) refers to it as a "master plan for selecting content and organizing learning experiences for the purpose of changing and developing learners' behaviors and insights" (p. 4). For all students, any consideration of curriculum should include an outcomes orientation; our working definition of curriculum thus embraces the preparation of students for life after school.

Although curriculum design often is preordained in some general education programs, it is nevertheless important to consider the concept of *comprehensive curriculum*. It takes into account the reality that students are enrolled in school on a time-limited basis. Educators must consider what will happen to their students in the future and take into account the environments that students will need to adapt to in order to function successfully. Then curriculum design can be influenced by a focus on these subsequent environments (e.g., high school, college, community) (Polloway, Patton, Smith, & Roderique, 1992). The degree to which this **subsequent environments attitude** permeates general education will significantly affect the ultimate success of students with disabilities taught in such settings.

An elementary-level comprehensive curriculum has the following characteristics:

- Responsive to the needs of the individual at the current time
- Reflective of the need to balance maximum interaction with peers against critical curricular needs
- Derived from a realistic appraisal of potential long-term outcomes for individual students
- Consistent with relevant forthcoming transitional needs (e.g., transition from elementary to high school) (adapted from Polloway, Patton, Epstein, & Smith, 1989)

As mentioned before, the curricular needs of the vast majority of students at the elementary level, both those with and without special needs, are quite consistent. Thus, with appropriate modification in instruction and with collaborative arrangements, most students' needs can be met to a significant extent in the general education classroom.

CURRICULAR CONTENT

Academic Instruction

Elementary students in general, and certainly most students with disabilities, primarily need sound instruction in reading, writing, and mathematics to maximize their academic achievement. These needs can typically be met by a developmental approach to instruction, supplemented as needed by a remedial focus. In both resource rooms and general education classrooms, the general modes of instruction tend to be very similar (Wesson & Deno, 1989).

READING INSTRUCTION

There are three common approaches in elementary-level reading and language arts programs: **basal series**, **direct instruction**, and **whole language**.

Basal Series Basal series, graded class-reading texts, are the most traditional means of teaching reading—and, for that matter, other curricular domains including spelling and math—in the elementary school. Most reading basals are intended to meet developmental needs in reading. Although they are routinely criticized, they still remain a common approach to reading instruction. Polloway and Smith (1992) indicate that such series have both advantages and disadvantages:

On the positive side, they contain inherent structure and sequence, controlled vocabulary, a wide variety of teaching activities, and preparation for the teacher. Weaknesses, on the other hand, include inappropriate

CONSIDER THIS

Although general educators can rarely offer a truly "comprehensive curriculum," collaborative efforts with special educators can effect a more broad-based program. How does this work?

CONSIDER THIS

Basal programs vary significantly in terms of emphasis. How does this affect students with special needs?

pacing for an individual child, overconcern for certain skills to the exclusion of others, and encouragement of group instructional orientation. (pp. 307–308)

Direct Instruction

Direct instruction, that is, the directive teaching of reading skills, has often been associated with a remedial perspective, although it clearly has played a significant preventive role as well. Often it has been tied to a focus on basic skills, which has typically constituted the core of most elementary special education curricula. In the area of reading, direct instruction programs are often associated with an emphasis on skills-based decoding (i.e., phonetic analysis).

FURTHER READING
The principles of direct instruction are based on the classic work in the mid-1960s by Carl Bereiter and Siegfried Engelmann with at-risk children. See *Teaching Disadvantaged Children in the Preschool,* published in 1966 by Prentice-Hall.

Basic skills programs typically have a long-term orientation based on the assumption that such skills ultimately will increase students' academic achievement and enable all to reach at least a minimal level of functional literacy. Not all basic skills programs are equally effective; those that incorporate effective instructional practice (e.g., Stevens & Rosenshine, 1981) have most often empirically demonstrated substantial gains in achievement. The characteristic features of successful direct instruction include high levels of academic engaged time, signals for attention, ongoing feedback to learners, group-based instruction, fast pacing, and error-free learning.

Whole Language

Whole language approaches at the primary and elementary levels dramatically increased in popularity in the 1990s. Emphasizing meaning in the beginning of the reading process, they embrace a more holistic view of learning than direct instruction, which tends to be oriented to specific skills. Whole language programs attempt to break down artificial barriers between reading, writing, and speaking, as well as barriers between reading and other curricular areas. Some recent research supports the efficacy of such approaches with learners of diverse abilities (see Mather, 1992, for a review). Schewel (1993) provides a clear picture of whole language "in action":

> Core activities that characterize the whole language approach include orally sharing stories by the teacher; sharing book experiences through material such as "Big Books"; sustained silent reading; silent reading time segments in which students write responses to what they are reading and share this with other students or with the teacher in individual conferences; language experience activities in which children write stories in a group or individually to be used for future reading experiences; time set aside for large group writing instruction followed by students' writing, revising, editing, and sharing their own writing; and finally reading and writing activities that involve a content area theme such as science or social studies. (p. 241)

Whole language programs rely on literature as the main source of content for reading opportunities. Literature (e.g., novels, stories, magazine articles) has the following advantages: it is authentic and varied; it is current, since it reaches the market quickly; it provides a basis for meeting diverse student needs and interests; and it offers alternative views on topics and issues as well as opportunities to study them in depth. In addition, students can be given more opportunity to select their own reading material (Mandlebaum, Lightbourne, & VardenBrock, 1994).

Reading Perspectives These three methods can each enhance the inclusion of students with disabilities in general academic programs. However, teachers must review progress on a regular basis and make modifications as needed, because it is unlikely that a single program can meet all of a student's needs. Mather (1992) presents an excellent review of issues surrounding both whole language and the decoding emphasis of direct instruction programs. Her review of the literature argues persuasively that students who are not good readers need specific skill instruction to achieve satisfactory progress. The challenge for classroom teachers is to balance the needs of able readers (for whom explicit instruction in phonics may prove unnecessary and for whom meaning-based instruction is clearly most appropriate) with the needs of students who require more systematic instruction to unlock the alphabetic relationships within our written language.

The arguments parried between these two general approaches reflect the concerns revised by Durden (1995) about the absence of a "middle ground" in education in the 1990s. As he notes,

> Dualistic, mutually exclusive thinking permeates education in this country. A pervasive set of educational either/ors (e.g., ability grouping vs. cooperative learning, phonics vs. whole language, "exclusion" vs. full inclusion, and homogeneous grouping vs. heterogeneous grouping) is involved, and the potential harm both to educators and students is immense.
>
> Teachers are asked daily by theoreticians and their supporters in professional associations and the public at large to make choices between polar opposites. They are deprived of a reflective professionalism. Each pole of their choice range is championed as a solution for an astonishing and dissimilar array of education problems. (p. 47)

Inclusion presents a complex challenge in the area of curriculum design. Teachers who rigidly adhere to one position in the controversy about reading instruction may inadvertently neglect the learning needs of individual children who experience difficulties in school. Outstanding teachers draw eclectically from a variety of approaches to design reading programs (Pressley & Rankin, 1994).

MATHEMATICS

Mathematics represents another challenging area for students with disabilities. Development of both computational skills and problem-solving abilities forms the foundation of successful math instruction and learning.

Computation In the area of computation, teachers should focus first on the students' conceptual understanding of a particular skill and then on the achievement of automaticity with the skill. Cawley's (1984) interactive unit and Miller, Mercer, and Dillon's (1992) concrete/semiconcrete/abstract systems afford excellent options to the teacher (see Figure 12.1). The interactive unit gives teachers 16 options for teaching math skills, based on four teacher input variables and four student output variables. The resulting 4×4 matrix provides a variety of instructional approaches that can be customized to assist learners who experience difficulties. It also reflects a logical process that begins with the important emphasis on the concrete (do/do) to build concepts, moves to a semiconcrete focus (see/see) to enhance concept development, and

CONSIDER THIS
The emphasis on meaning and the integration of the language arts make whole language approaches particularly attractive for use with students with special needs. Why do you think this is effective?

FURTHER READING
John Cawley's research in mathematics over the past 30 years has been very influential in the development of effective programs for students with disabilities.

Group A: Geometry (8 students)	Group B: Fractions (10 students)	Group C: Addition (5 students)
Manipulate/Manipulate* *Input:* Teacher walks the perimeter of a geometric shape. *Output:* Learner does the same.	**Display/Write** *Input:* Write the fraction that names the shaded part. 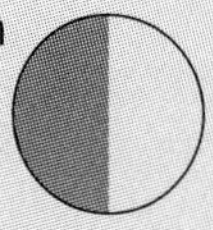 *Output:* Learner writes $\frac{1}{2}$	**Write/Write** *Input:* $\begin{array}{r} 3 \\ +\ 2 \\ \hline \end{array}$ Write the answer. *Output:* Learner writes 5
Display/Identify *Input:* 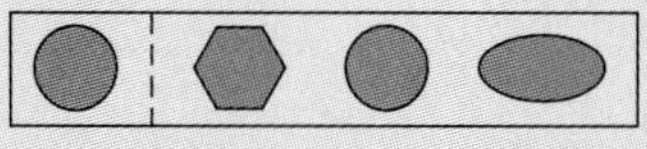 From the choices, mark the shape that is the same as the first shape. *Output:* Learner marks 	**Manipulate/Say*** *Input:* 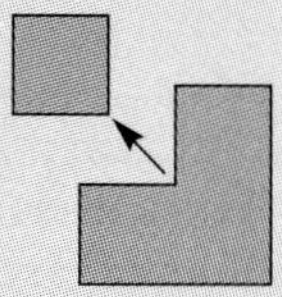 Teacher removes portion of shape and asks learner to name the part. *Output:* Learner says, "One fourth"	**Display/Write** *Input:* 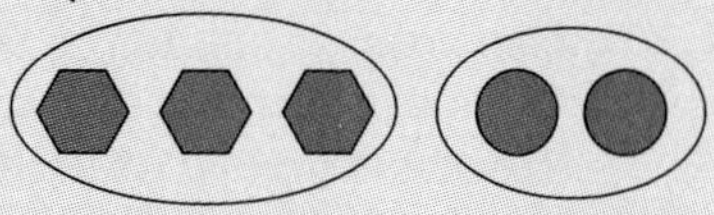 Write the number there is in all. *Output:* Learner writes 5
Write/Identify *Input:* 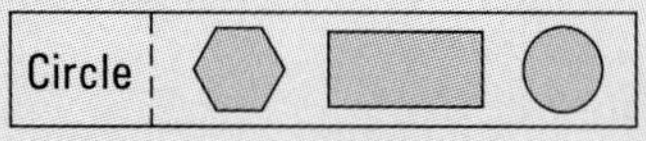 Circle Mark the shape that shows the word. *Output:* Learner marks 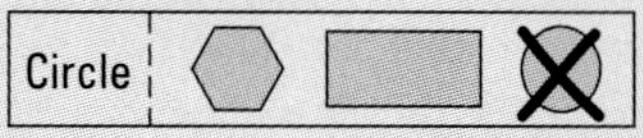 Circle	**Write/Write** *Input:* one half Write this word statement as a numeral. *Output:* Learner writes $\frac{1}{2}$	**Say/Say*** *Input:* Teacher says, "I am going to say some addition items. Six plus six. Tell me the answer." *Output:* Learner says, "Twelve"

Row labels (left margin): 15 minutes / 15 minutes / 15 minutes

FIGURE 12.1 Interactive Unit Model

*Teacher present in group

From *Developmental Teaching of Mathematics for the Learning Disabled* (p. 246), by J. F. Cawley (Ed.), 1984, Austin, TX: Pro-Ed. Copyright 1984 by Pro-Ed, Inc. Reprinted by permission.

at last arrives at the abstract (say/say, write/write), leading to automaticity (automatic responses to math facts). These emphases offer two proven benefits in the general education classroom: they have been used successfully with students with disabilities, and they offer alternative teaching strategies for nondisabled learners—a particularly significant advantage, given that math is the most common area of failure in schools.

Problem Solving Problem solving can be particularly difficult for students with disabilities and thus warrants special attention. For learners with special needs, and for many other students as well, instruction in specific problem solving strategies can greatly enhance math understanding. A given strategy's steps should be taught and followed systematically so that students learn to reason through problems and understand problem-solving processes. One such example is the SOLVE-IT strategy (see Figure 12.2). The use of learning strategies and their value for students with and without disabilities are discussed further in Chapter 13.

The potential benefits of including students with special needs in general education classrooms to study core academic areas (i.e., basic skills) also extend to other academic areas. Subjects such as science, social studies, health and family life, and the arts offer excellent opportunities for social integration. **Cooperative teaching** presents an excellent instructional alternative in these areas because it combines the expertise and resources of the classroom teacher with the special talents of the special education teacher, rather than requiring them each to develop separate curricula in these areas. These subjects also lend themselves well to integrated curricular approaches (discussed later in the chapter).

Social Skills Instruction

Virtually all students identified as having an intellectual disability or an emotional and behavioural disorder, and many with learning disabilities, need instruction in the area of **social skills** (Cullinan & Epstein, 1985). The challenge for classroom teachers will be to find ways to incorporate this focus in their

S	SAY	the problem to yourself (repeat).
O	OMIT	any unnecessary information from the problem.
L	LISTEN	for key vocabulary indicators.
V	VOCABULARY	Change vocabulary to math concepts.
E	EQUATION	Translate problem into a math equation.
I	INDICATE	the answer.
T	TRANSLATE	the answer back into the context of the word problem.

FIGURE 12.2
Problem-Solving Strategy for Mathematics

From *Strategies for Teaching Learners with Special Needs* (6th ed.) (p. 183), by E. A. Polloway and J. R. Patton, 1997, Columbus, OH: Merrill. Reprinted by permission.

classes. Seeking assistance from a special education teacher, a counsellor, or a school psychologist is a good idea. Because performance in the social domain is often predictive of success or failure in inclusive settings, the development of social skills should not be neglected. Gresham (1984) notes that students with disabilities interact infrequently and, to a large extent, negatively with their peers because many lack the social skills that would enable them to gain acceptance by their peers.

Polloway and Patton (1997) identify four approaches to educating students about appropriate social behaviour: direct social skills training, behavioural change, affective education, and cognitive interventions. *Direct social skills training* focuses on attaining skills that help students overcome situations in classrooms and elsewhere that prevent assimilation. A *behavioural change* strategy typically targets a behaviour that needs modification and creates a re-inforcement system that will lead to a behaviour change. Steps in such programs typically include (1) selecting the target behaviour, (2) collecting baseline data, (3) identifying reinforcers, (4) implementing a procedure for reinforcing appropriate behaviours, and (5) evaluating the intervention (see Chapter 5). *Affective education* typically emphasizes self-control and the relationship between self and others in the environment. The emotional, rather than only the behavioural, aspects of social adjustment figure prominently in this approach. Finally, *cognitive interventions* have proved fruitful in effecting behavioural change and social skills acquisition; they involve teaching students to monitor their own behaviour, engage in self-instruction, and design and implement their own reinforcement programs. All four programs offer significant promise for social adjustment programming in the future.

FURTHER READING

The social skills program developed by Sargent is in the book *Social Skills for School and Community* by L. R. Sargent, published in 1991 by CEC-MR.

Korinek and Polloway (1993) note two key considerations related to social skills instruction for students who have difficulties in this area. First, priority should be given to skills most needed for immediate interactions in the classroom, thus enhancing the likelihood of a student's successful inclusion. Teachers can begin by teaching behaviours that will "naturally elicit desired responses from peers and adults" (Nelson, 1988, p. 21), such as sharing, smiling, asking for help, attending, taking turns, following directions, and solving problems (McConnell, 1987). These skills will promote social acceptance and can be applied across many settings.

A second consideration involves selecting a social adjustment program that promotes both social skills and *social competence*. Whereas social skills facilitate individual interpersonal interactions, social competence involves the broader ability to use skills at the right times and places, showing social perception, cognition, and judgment of how to act in different situations (Sargent, 1989, 1991). A focus limited to specific skill training may make it difficult for the child to maintain the specific social skills or transfer them to various settings. Table 12.1 outlines a typical sequence within a social skills curriculum.

The increasing placement of students with more severe disabilities in inclusive classes has significant implications for the social environment; there is little reason to believe that the social skills of these students will develop just because they are physically located in such classes. McEnvoy, Shores, Wehby, Johnson, and Fox's (1990) review of the literature on inclusion reveals that the more that teachers provide specific instruction, physical prompts, modelling, and praise, the more successfully students learn social interaction skills.

TABLE 12.1

Sample Social Skills Curriculum Sequence

SESSION I

Listening
Meeting people—introducing self,
    introducing others
Beginning a conversation
Listening during a conversation
Ending a conversation
Joining an ongoing activity

SESSION II

Asking questions appropriately
Asking favors appropriately
Seeking help from peers and adults
Following directions

SESSION III

Sharing
Interpreting body language
Playing a game successfully

SESSION IV

Suggesting an activity to others
Working cooperatively
Offering help

SESSION V

Saying thank you
Giving and accepting a compliment
Rewarding self

SESSION VI

Apologizing
Understanding the impact your behavior has
    on others
Understanding others' behavior

From *Managing Attention Disorders in Children: A Guide for Practitioners* (pp. 342–343), by S. Goldstein and M. Goldstein, 1990, New York: John Wiley. Used by permission.

Transitional Needs

In addition to the academic and social components of the curriculum, career education and transition form an important emphasis. For all elementary students, career awareness and a focus on facilitating movement between levels of schooling (i.e., vertical transitions) are curricular essentials.

TRANSITION FROM PRESCHOOL TO PRIMARY SCHOOL

Research on students moving from preschool programs into school settings has identified variables that predict success in school. Four such variables include academic readiness skills, social skills, responsiveness to instructional style, and responsiveness to the structure of the school environment (Polloway et al., 1991). Analyzing the new school environment can help a teacher determine the skills a student will need to make this crucial adjustment.

Academic readiness skills have traditionally been cited as good predictors of success at the primary school level. Examples include the ability to recognize numbers and letters, grasp a writing utensil, count to ten, and write letters and numbers. Yet a clear delineation between academic readiness and academic skills is not warranted. Rather, to use reading as an example, it is much more productive to consider readiness as inclusive of examples of early reading skills, or what has been termed emergent literacy. Programming in this area should focus on academic activities that advance the processes of learning to read, write, or calculate.

TABLE 12.2

Life Skills in the Elementary School Curriculum

	Consumer Economics	Occupational Knowledge	Health	Community Resources	Government and Law
READING	Look for ads in the newspaper for toys.	Read books from library on various occupations.	Read the school lunch menu.	Find television listing in the *TV Guide*.	Read road signs and understand what they mean.
WRITING	Write prices of items to be purchased.	Write the specific tasks involved in performing one of the classroom jobs.	Keep a diary of food you eat in each food group each day.	Complete an application to play on a Little League team.	Write a letter to the mayor inviting him/her to visit your school.
SPEAKING, WRITING, VIEWING	Listen to bank official talk about savings accounts.	Call newspaper in town to inquire about delivering papers in your neighborhood.	View a film on brushing teeth.	Practice the use of the 911 emergency number.	Discuss park playground improvements with the mayor.
PROBLEM SOLVING	Decide if you have enough coins to make a purchase from a vending machine.	Decide which job in the classroom you do best.	Role-play what you should do if you have a stomachache.	Role-play the times you would use the 911 emergency number.	Find the city hall on the map. Decide whether you will walk or drive to it.
INTERPERSONAL RELATIONS	Ask for help finding items in a grocery store.	Ask a student in the class to assist you with a classroom job.	Ask the school nurse how to take care of mosquito bites.	Call the movie theater and ask the show times of a movie.	Role-play being lost and asking a police officer for help.
COMPUTATION	Compute the cost of a box of cereal with a discount coupon.	Calculate how much you would make on a paper route at $3 per hour for 5 hours per week.	Compute the price of one tube of toothpaste if they are on sale at 3 for $1.	Compute the complete cost of going to the movie (admission, food, transportation).	Compute tax on a candy bar.

From "Curricular Considerations: A Life Skills Orientation," by J. R. Patton, M. E. Cronin, E. A. Polloway, D. R. Hutchison, and G. A. Robinson. In *Best Practices in Mild Mental Retardation*, edited by G. A. Robinson, J. R. Patton, E. A. Polloway, and L. Sargent, 1989, p. 31. Reston, VA: CEC-MR. Used by permission.

Social skills consistent with the developmental attributes of other five- and six-year-olds are clearly important to success in the elementary school. It is particularly critical that students be able to function in a group. Thus, introducing small group instructional activities in preschool programs prepares students to function in future school situations.

Developing responsiveness to a new instructional style is another challenge for the young child. Since the instructional arrangement in the preschool program may vary significantly from that of the school program, providing instructional experiences that the student can generalize to the new school setting will be helpful; some learning activities in the preschool class should approximate those of Kindergarten. If the child is entering an immersion program, the preschool should introduce basic terms and phrases in the future language of instruction.

Responsiveness to the environment is a fourth concern. Changes may include new transportation arrangements, extended instructional time, increased expectations of individual independence, and increased class size resulting in a reduction in individual attention. Teachers may set up opportunities for the preschoolers to visit Kindergarten classes to familiarize them with the future environment.

ELEMENTARY CURRICULAR CONSIDERATIONS

Career education in general, and **life skills** education in particular, have become major emphases among secondary school teachers, especially those who work with students who have disabilities. Yet life skills concepts should also be incorporated into elementary and middle school programs. The Adult Performance Level (APL) model of functional competency (LaQuey, 1981) offers a good example. Based on an adult education program, it since has been used as a model for developing a secondary-level special education curriculum as well as an elementary-level program (Cronin, 1988; Patton & Cronin, 1993). The APL model's content focuses on career and life skills that prepare students for subsequent environments. Table 12.3 provides a matrix of topics that may be incorporated into an elementary-level life skills curriculum. Even programs for young children should be designed to encourage positive long-term outcomes for all students.

Concepts and topics related to life skills should be integrated into existing subject areas, thus broadening the curriculum without creating a "new subject." This can be done in three ways. The first approach, *augmentation*, uses career education–oriented materials to supplement the existing curriculum. The second approach *infuses* relevant career education topics into the lessons laid out in the existing curriculum. A third approach employs an *integrated curriculum*, similar to the unit approach traditionally used in many education programs (Kataoka & Patton, 1989). An integrated curriculum addresses a topic by drawing together content related to it from various academic areas, enabling students to apply academic skills across these areas. Life skills related to the broad topic can be woven into the curriculum. Using a matrix format (see Table 12.3), reading, math, and language skills, as well as career topics and life skills, can be tied together. This curriculum can also help primary- and elementary-age students understand that different academic subjects have important interrelationships.

TEACHING TIP
Teachers should accept responsibility to prepare students for their next school-life challenge or transition (e.g., preschool to elementary school, elementary school to secondary school).

FURTHER READING
The APL adaptation project began in Austin, Texas, as a way to train students with disabilities for adulthood. See the book *Life Skills Instruction for All Students with Disabilities,* published in 1993 by Pro-Ed.

TEACHING TIP
Integrated curricular approaches also can enable gifted students to extend their learning beyond the curriculum.

TABLE 12.3			
Integrated Curriculum			
Science Subtopics	Science Activities	Math	Social Studies
INTRODUCTORY LESSON	• Attraction of ants • Collection • Observation • Research ant anatomy	• Measurement of distance traveled as a function of time	• Relationship of population demographics for ants and humans
ANT FARMS	• Individual set-ups • Daily observation • Development of collection procedures	• Linear measurement • Frequency counts	• Roles in the community • Relationship to human situations
FOOD PREFERENCES CHART	• Research and predict • Construct apparatus for determining preference • Design data collection procedures • Collect/record data • Experiment with food substance positions	• Frequency counts • Graphs of daily results	• Discussion of human food preferences • Cultural differences
ANT RACES	• Conduct races with and without food • Data collection • Predictive activities	• Temporal measurement • Averages	• History of racing • Sports and competition
CLOSING	• Analyze information	• Tabulate data	

From Kataoka, J. C., & Patton, J. R. (1989). Integrated curriculum. *Science and Children*, *16*, 52–58. Reprinted with permission from NSTA Publications, copyright 1989, from *Science and Children*, National Science Teachers Association, 1840 Wilson Boulevard, Arlington, VA 22201-3000.

TRANSITION TO MIDDLE SCHOOL

Students with disabilities in the elementary school need to be prepared for movement to junior high school. To make this vertical transition successfully, students need an organized approach to their work, time management and study skills, note-taking strategies, homework strategies, and the ability to use lockers. Robinson, Braxdale, and Colson (1988) observe that the new behaviour demands faced by students in junior high school fall into three categories: academic skills, self-management and study skills, and social-adaptive skills. Problems in any of these three areas may cause difficulties for students.

A variety of instructional strategies may assist in the transition process: having junior high school faculty visit elementary classes to discuss programs and expectations, viewing videotaped junior high school classes, and taking field trips to the middle school to get a sense of the physical layout, the chang-

RELATED SUBJECT/SKILL AREAS

Arts	Computer Application	Life Skills	Language Arts
• Drawings of ant anatomy • Ant mobiles • Creative exploration	• Graphic drawings of ants	• Picnic planning • Food storage and protection	• Oral sharing of observations
• Diagram of farm • Diorama • Ant models • Role-playing of ant behavior	• Spreadsheets for calculations • Graphing • Database storing observations	• Relate to engineers, architects, sociologists, geographers	• Library skills • Creative writing • Spelling • Research involving note taking, outlining, and reading • Vocabulary development • Oral reports
• Design data collection forms • Role-play ant eating behaviour		• Graphic designer • Food services • Researchers	
• Film making • Rewrite lyrics to "The Ants Go Marching In" based on activities	• Graphic animation	• Athletics • Coaches	
• Finalize visual aids	• Printout	• Guest speakers	• Presentation

ing of classes, and environmental and pedagogical factors (Jaquish & Stella, 1986). Cooperative planning and follow-up between both general and special education teachers at the two school levels will smooth the transition.

COMMUNITY-BASED INSTRUCTION

In developing life skills and facilitating transition, community-based instruction can benefit all students but is particularly effective for students with disabilities, as it addresses common problems in applying academic learning to life outside the classroom. Field trips to stores to make purchases, to observe work patterns, and to learn about advertising and marketing techniques can be supplemented by bringing community members into the classroom to speak about careers or demonstrate life skills. Curriculum guides can assist teachers in integrating community resources into instructional programming.

Science class offers an excellent opportunity for social integration of students with special needs.

Diversity Considerations

Considerations of linguistic and cultural diversity must inform all aspects of curriculum design. In the past, multicultural education was frequently presented as special units or as "heritage days" that celebrated different cultures. Winzer and Mazurek (1998) from Alberta note that this approach still prevails in many elementary schools. They criticize what they see as a "tourist curriculum," deeming it neither effective nor sufficient, and call for an infusion approach to multicultural education.

Infusion, another approach, requires that the multicultural perspective is "infused" into all aspects of the curriculum on a day-to-day basis. It spans the perspectives, histories, traditions, and contributions of all groups, calling for culturally appropriate and relevant curriculum materials. McGill University's Ratna Ghosh, an international leader in the area of multicultural education, makes the point that multicultural education should neither showcase different cultures nor ignore the differences (Ghosh, 1996). She writes eloquently about the need to include all cultures, including that of the dominant group, in the multiculturalism in the schools: "multicultural education is not only for minority groups . . . whiteness cannot remain invisible and outside the framework of multiculturalism" (p. 2).

The regular classroom teacher may recognize the need to have a multicultural curriculum, but may be at a loss about how to realize this goal. Gollnick and Chinn (1994) suggest a starting point when they state, "If students seldom see representations of themselves, their families, or their communities, it becomes difficult to believe that the academic content has any meaning or usefulness for them" (p. 300). Teachers need to incorporate material that is relevant to the cultures of students in the classroom.

In Canada, there will never be prepackaged relevant curriculum due to the enormous diversity across the country. In Northern Quebec, a classroom will have a large proportion of First Nations peoples; in Vancouver, a significant number of students are of Asian heritage; in many rural areas across Canada,

PERSONAL SPOTLIGHT

Role Model ■ MARLA BELLIN

Elementary Teacher, Special Needs Tutor

Marla Bellin received her professional teaching certificate from the University of British Columbia, Vancouver, in 1992. She taught three years in Chilliwack, B.C.: one year team-teaching Grade 1 and French as a second language to Kindergarten through Grade 3 classes and two years teaching her own Grade 3 class. She then chose to go overseas and taught for three years at the American School of Bucharest in Romania. Subsequently, she returned to Canada to obtain a master's degree in integrated education from McGill University; at the same time, she worked as a special needs tutor with a variety of children integrated into the regular schools.

In her eight years of teaching primary grades, Marla has worked with gifted students; a number of students with severe reading disabilities, behaviour problems, and attention-deficit disorder; a young girl diagnosed with Asperger's syndrome; many students having general difficulties learning; and some children needing enrichment.

Marla is known for her creative approach to teaching basic skills. "She always works to find a fun way to teach some of the most boring materials! She finds a way to make a game out of so many things and then the kids really learn. We call her the game queen!" says one colleague.

"I have always taught in integrated classrooms, assuming this was the norm. In my second year I utilized a school's pullout program for intensive teaching of reading for two students because I felt I did not have the knowledge or time to properly teach the skills they required. I found that the resource program interrupted the flow of my lessons and stigmatized the students.

To change this, I sought high-interest and engaging systematic phonics programs to implement *in* my class for the benefit of *all* students. I continue to integrate the programs I learned into my daily language lessons. They now take less time to explain, and they have proven useful for decoding and spelling for all my students. Having children understand that not everyone learns in the same way or at the same pace and teaching them tolerance of and patience with others are lifelong lessons that they gain in inclusive environments.

"One year I set up a special spelling individualized program for my students with spelling problems. After all my planning I discovered my most needy student struggling with a very challenging list made for the most advanced students. Out of frustration at seeing him fail, and trying to send a message that this was not the appropriate work for him (and looking upon this as a waste of all my individualizing effort!), I took his paper and threw it in the garbage. After school I received a phone call from his mother. I learned that he was doing this harder list to try to impress me! I know the personal apology I gave him the following day did not erase the bad feelings that both he and I felt. Since then, I take the extra time needed to find out the reason behind students' actions before explaining my perspective to the student.

"Teachers' frustration, oftentimes not justified, only does harm. Being a good role model by taking the time to use polite communication to immediately clarify problems has been my most treasured lesson. Our children deserve it!"

students of European and East European descent may predominate, although, in this instance, diversity will be less apparent—families may have been here for three or more generations. Therefore, the responsibility almost always remains with individual teachers to adapt their curricula to reflect the diversity in their classrooms.

For specific suggestions on how to adapt existing curriculum, read Carl Grant and Christine Sleeter's 1989 book, *Turning on Learning: Five Approaches for Multicultural Teaching Plans for Race, Class, Gender, and Disability*.

INSTRUCTIONAL MODIFICATIONS AND ACCOMMODATIONS

Modifications and accommodations made to instructional programs in the general education classroom form the keys to successful inclusion (see Figure 12.3, in which multilevel instruction is identified as one of several effective inclusive practices). As the traditional adage goes, special education is not necessarily special, it is just *good teaching*. "Good teaching" often means making appropriate modifications and accommodations. Assuming the curricular content is appropriate for individual students who have disabilities, the challenge is to adapt it to facilitate learning.

In inclusive programs, instruction must be modified to ensure that all students learn successfully. As Fuchs, Fuchs, Hamlett, Phillips, and Karns (1995) note:

> General education's capacity to incorporate meaningful adaptation has become a critical issue during the past decade, as the rhetoric of the regular education initiative and the inclusive schools movement has increased pressure to provide educational programs to students with disabilities in general education classrooms. (p. 440)

Thus, a key component of successful inclusion is the treatment acceptability of specific interventions to accommodate the needs of students with dis-

FIGURE 12.3

Effective Inclusive Practices

Adapted from "National Survey Identifies Inclusive Educational Practices," Appalachian Educational Laboratory, 1995, *The Link, 14* (1), p. 8.

The following practices have been identified by the National Center on Educational Restructuring and Inclusion as supporting inclusive education:

■ **Multilevel instruction** allows for different kinds of learning within the same curriculum. Here the focus is on key concepts to be taught, alternatives in presentation methods, acceptance of varying types of student activities and multiple outcomes, different ways in which students can express their learning, and diverse evaluation procedures.

■ **Cooperative learning** involves heterogeneous groupings of students, allowing for students with a wide variety of skills and traits to work together. Models of cooperative learning differ in the amount of emphasis given to the process of the group's work and to the assessment of outcomes for individual members as well as for the team as a whole.

■ **Activity-based learning** emphasizes learning in natural settings, the production of actual work products, and performance assessment. It moves learning from being solely classroom-based to preparing students to learn in community settings.

■ **Mastery learning** specifies what a student needs to learn and then provides sufficient practice opportunities to gain mastery.

■ **Technology** is often mentioned as being a support for students and teachers. Uses include record keeping, assistive devices such as reading machines and braille-to-print typewriters, and drill and instructional programs.

■ **Peer support and tutoring programs** have multiple advantages. Placing students in instructional roles enhances the teaching resources of the school. It recognizes that some students learn by teaching others.

abilities. The term *treatment acceptability* has been used in a variety of ways. Polloway, Bursuck, Jayanthi, Epstein, and Nelson (1996) use the term in a broad sense to refer to the likelihood that certain specific classroom interventions will be acceptable to the general education teacher. Thus it may include, for example, the helpfulness, desirability, feasibility, and fairness of the intervention, as well as how other students will perceive it in a particular setting. As Witt and Elliott (1985) note, the "attractiveness" of an intervention is important: if the treatment is not deemed acceptable, it is unlikely to be implemented.

FURTHER READING
Polloway et al. (1996) provide a full discussion of treatment acceptability and efforts to research the concept.

Cheney (1989) suggests that curricular modifications should address three matches: the level of achievement of the student and the level of the instructional material, the characteristics of the learner and the response modes required by the material or technique, and the motivational aspects of the learner and of the material. To "make the match," teachers should informally assess the instructional program to ensure that students in general, and those with disabilities in particular, are learning at a satisfactory level.

In a related vein, Cohen (1990) states that modifications address content, environment, or instruction through approaches that are teacher-, peer-, and self-mediated (see Figure 12.4). This model provides nine categories of adaptations, and the teacher should use several in any given program. For example, a peer-mediated instructional adaptation would include the use of a peer tutoring program (discussed in a subsequent section). A teacher-mediated content adaptation would include modifications in reading or writing tasks (discussed later in the chapter).

FURTHER READING
In the article "Curriculum Adaptation: A Five-Step Process for Classroom Implementation," published in 1990 in volume 25 of *Academic Therapy* (pp. 407–416), J. J. Hoover provides a useful model for curriculum modification.

Finally, technology can assist teachers in modifying the curriculum, providing additional supports for the student, and increasing instructional effectiveness. The nearby Technology Today feature provides specific examples.

Specific modifications and accommodations for students with disabilities in elementary classes are discussed next. They vary in nature and in terms of treatment acceptability. The authors do not intend to suggest that all suggestions will be appropriate or desirable in a given situation. Teachers should determine how far to go in making specific adaptations. Many of the suggested modifications will prove beneficial to all students, not only those with special needs.

	Content	Environment	Instruction
Teacher-Mediated			
Peer-Mediated			
Self-Mediated			

FIGURE 12.4
Curricular Modification: Teacher Decision Making
From "A Modification Perspective of Special Education Curriculum: Introduction," by S. B. Cohen, 1990, *Academic Therapy, 25,* p. 393. Used by permission.

Computer Applications Facilitating Teacher's Productivity

Stage	Description	Related Topics and Strategies
PLANNING	Assist in the outlining of instructional interventions and strategies.	Assess student abilities and difficulties; identify software that enhances instructional objectives; use computer lesson plans.
PREPARING	Facilitate the production of print and electronic instructional materials.	Use utilities that create worksheets, certificates, flash cards; use authoring systems to create online lessons.
MANAGING	Conduct and manage instruction; facilitate and manage student behaviour and interests during computer-based learning activities.	Implement time management of classroom-based and lab-based computers; monitor students' computer performance.
EXTENDING	Use existing technology creatively and effectively for additional instructional impact.	Review and maintain skills; remain current with teaching/practice-oriented literature on technology.

Adapted from "Teaching Applications with Exceptional Individuals," by J. E. Gardner and D. L. Edyburn. In *Computers and Exceptional Individuals*, edited by J. D. Lindsey, 1993, p. 247. Austin, TX: Pro-Ed. Used by permission.

Enhancing Content Learning through Listening

Wallace, Cohen, and Polloway (1987) argue that children will not necessarily listen simply because they are told to do so. Rather, they often need oral presentations provided in ways that promote successful listening. Students who struggle with *selective attention* (i.e., focus) or *sustained attention* (i.e., maintained over a period of time) respond more easily to speaking that supports the listener. Wallace et al. (1987, p. 75) note that listeners attend more when

TEACHING TIP
For many students with disabilities, the skill of listening must be directly targeted if academic success is to occur in inclusive settings.

- the salience of content is increased through repetition, vocal emphasis, and cueing;
- the message is meaningful, logical, and well organized;
- messages are given in short units;
- the speaker can be clearly heard and understood;
- the speaker allows for listener participation in the form of clarification, feedback, or responding;
- the speaker has focused attention by stating how the message will be of importance to the listener;
- reinforcement for attending is given in the form of participation, praise, or increased ability to perform;
- oral presentations are accompanied by visual aids that emphasize important points;
- the listener knows there will be an opportunity to reflect upon and integrate the message before having to formulate a response.

To complement this approach, strategies to build listening skills can also be taught. A variety of techniques can enhance listening. Mandlebaum and

Wilson (1989, pp. 451–452) suggest that teachers select from the following techniques:

1. Provide students with direct instruction in listening strategies.
2. Establish a goal for the lesson so that students will know what is expected.
3. Plan listening lessons so that students are actively involved with the information they have learned.
4. Plan purposeful listening activities that relate to other curriculum areas.
5. Make messages logical and well organized, repeating important information.
6. Give information in short segments.
7. Following a listening activity, ask questions that require more than simply recalling facts.
8. Act as a model of listening behaviour, use peer models, and have students self-monitor their listening behaviour.
9. Involve students in rehearsing, summarizing, and taking notes of the information to be learned.
10. Before a lesson begins, use verbal, pictorial, or written advance organizers to cue students about important information.
11. Provide prompts to notify students that the information about to be presented is important to remember or to write down.
12. Before beginning a listening activity, review the rules for good listening behaviour (e.g., sitting quietly, not getting up and moving around, paying close attention).
13. Involve students in a wide variety of listening activities that relate to the skills that they will need outside the school environment.
14. Use teacher questions and prompts to cue students to respond (e.g., "Tell me more").
15. Teach students to use a self-questioning technique while listening.

GUIDED LISTENING

One way to develop good listening skills is through guided listening. As Wallace et al. (1987) note, this procedure aims to increase long-term retention. It can be used every few weeks. Accompanying a 10- to 15-minute presentation (e.g., tape, lecture), the teacher leads the class through the following steps:

1. The teacher sets the major purpose (e.g., "Listen to remember everything").
2. The teacher lists what students remember on the board. During this stage, the teacher accepts and writes everything the students contribute. She makes no corrections and asks no questions.
3. The teacher reads everything listed on the board, directing the students to look for incorrect or missing information.
4. The students listen again to the tape or reading to correct wrong information and obtain missing information.
5. The information on the board is amended and added to as needed.
6. The teacher asks the students which ideas seem to be the main ideas and marks them.
7. Now that the students have mastered the literal level of the selections, the teacher raises inferential questions vital to complete understanding.
8. The teacher erases the board and tests short-term memory with a test not dependent on reading or writing skills.
9. Long-term memory should then be assessed with a similar test containing different items several weeks later. (Adapted from Manzo, 1975, pp. 302–303.)

Modifying Oral Presentations

To facilitate learning, teachers must consider effective vehicles for the presentation of content. Accommodations in this area typically prove beneficial to all students. Some specific considerations follow:

TEACHING TIP

Few students at the elementary level, disabled or not, can attend to a lengthy lecture. Although learning to focus for 20 minutes is a useful skill to acquire for upper elementary students, teachers should plan for variety within a given period.

- When mastery of prior content is uncertain, use concrete concepts before teaching abstractions (e.g., teach the concept of human rights by discussing specific rights that the students are entitled to).
- Relate information to students' prior experiences.
- Provide students with an overview before beginning.
- Reduce the number of concepts introduced at a given time.
- Encourage children to detect errors in messages and report what they could not understand.
- Monitor and adapt presentation language to make sure that students understand you. Adjust vocabulary level and complexity of sentence structures accordingly. Avoid puns, idiomatic speech, and metaphors unless clear explanations are provided.
- Review lessons before additional content is introduced.
- Lessen distractions, such as visual and auditory ones, within the environment.
- Adjust pace as needed.
- Keep oral directions short and direct, and supplement them with written directions as needed.
- Provide repetition, review, and additional examples.
- Provide further guided practice by requiring more responses, lengthening practice sessions, or scheduling extra sessions.
- Clarify directions for follow-up activities so that tasks can be completed successfully. (Adapted from Chalmers, 1991; Cheney, 1989; Dowdy, 1990; McDevitt, 1990.)

FACILITATING NOTE TAKING

Learning from classroom presentations is obviously critical to academic achievement. For students in the primary grades, instruction is generally not delivered through lengthy oral presentation. However, as lecturing begins to become more common in the upper elementary grades and in junior high school, students will need to develop note-taking skills. The teaching of note taking may be undertaken by special education teachers; how content is presented by the teacher is an important factor to focus on. The following pointers are adapted from Beirne-Smith (1989); they overlap somewhat with ideas for listening and modifying presentations discussed earlier.

1. Organize your lecture.
2. Use key words and phrases, such as "first," or "the main theme."
3. Summarize ideas.
4. Repeat important statements to emphasize the importance of the statement.
5. Pause occasionally to allow students time to fill in blank spaces or catch up to the previous statement.
6. Provide advance organizers (e.g., topic outlines, partially completed notes) to assist the student in organizing and recording information.
7. Write important points on the board.
8. Simplify overhead transparencies. Too much information is confusing and less likely to be recorded.

9. Encourage students to record all visually presented material exactly as displayed and to leave space between main sections for questions about the material.
10. Use humour or anecdotes to illustrate important points.
11. Model note-taking skills (e.g., with the overhead projector).

Adapting Reading Tasks

In many instances, instructional tasks, assignments, or materials may be relevant and appropriate for students with disabilities, but may present problematic reading demands. Teachers should consider options for modifying the task or the materials. The following suggestions address problems that may arise in processing reading content:

- Clearly establish a given assignment's purpose and importance.
- Highlight key words, phrases and concepts. Ways of doing this include colour-coding text and providing outlines and study guides.
- Encourage periodic feedback from students to check their understanding.
- Preview reading material with students to assist them in establishing purpose, activating prior knowledge, budgeting time, and focusing attention.
- Create vocabulary lists, and teach these words to ensure that students can use them rather than simply recognize them.
- Provide page numbers where specific answers can be found in a reading comprehension or content assignment.
- Use brief individual conferences with students to verify their comprehension.
- Locate lower-level content material on the same topic to adapt tasks for students with reading difficulties.
- Tape a reading of a text, or have it read orally to a student. Consider using peers, volunteers, and paraprofessionals in this process.
- Rewrite material (or solicit volunteers to do so) to simplify its reading level, or provide chapter outlines or summaries.
- Utilize visual aids (e.g., charts, graphs) to supplement reading tasks.
- Demonstrate how new content relates to content previously learned.
- Promote comprehension by raising questions about a text's content.
- Teach students to consider K-W-L as a technique to focus attention. "K" represents prior knowledge, "W" what the student wants to know, and "L" what has been learned as a result.
- Use reciprocal teaching. Have students take turns leading discussions that raise questions about the content read, summarize the most important information, clarify concepts that are unclear, and predict what will occur next. (Adapted from Chalmers, 1991; Cheney, 1989; Dowdy, 1990; Gartland, 1994; Hoover, 1990; Reynolds & Salend, 1990; Schumm & Strickler, 1991.)

CROSS-REFERENCE
Ultimately, students will need to learn to adapt reading tasks themselves, through the use of learning strategies, in order to become independent learners. See Chapter 13 for how this plays out at the secondary level.

Enhancing Written Responses

The modifications noted here may assist students who may have difficulty with responding in written form. These adaptations relate not to the presentation of material but rather to the responses implicit in the task or assignment.

- Avoid assigning excessive amounts of written classwork and homework.
- When appropriate, allow children to select the most comfortable method of writing, whether it be cursive, manuscript, or typing.

- Change the response mode to oral when appropriate.
- Set realistic, mutually agreed upon expectations for neatness.
- Allow children to circle or underline responses.
- Let students tape-record answers instead of giving them in writing.
- Fasten materials to the desk to alleviate coordination problems.
- Provide the student with a copy of lecture notes produced by the teacher or a peer.
- Reduce amounts of board copying or text copying; provide the written information itself or an outline of the main content.
- Allow sufficient space for answering problems.
- Allow group-written responses (via projects or reports) (see the section on involving peers later in the chapter). (Adapted from Chalmers, 1991; Cheney, 1989; Dowdy, 1990.)

FURTHER READING
The key consideration for all students is the provision of frequent opportunities to write. The work of Donald Graves has been particularly influential in encouraging teachers to increase chances for true writing.

In addition to enhancing written responses, teachers should work to improve students' writing ability. Provide sufficient opportunities to write relative to meaningful tasks (e.g., for an authentic audience, or on a topic important or interesting to the student). Graham (1992, p. 137) suggests the following ideas for providing frequent and meaningful writing opportunities:

- Assist students in thinking about what they will write.
- Ask students to establish goals for what they hope to achieve.
- Arrange the writing environment so that the teacher is not the sole audience for students' writing.
- Provide opportunities for students to work on the same project across days or even weeks.
- Incorporate writing as part of a larger, interesting activity.

Portfolios also represent a positive approach to enhancing writing development. Portfolios involve students in the evaluation of their own writing samples by selecting samples to be kept and by comparing changes in their writing over time.

Involving Peers

COOPERATIVE LEARNING

FURTHER READING
For more information on cooperative learning, see *What Research Says to the Teacher on Cooperative Learning: Student Teams* (second edition) by R. E. Slavin, published in 1987 by the National Education Association.

Cooperative learning has been promoted as a means of facilitating the inclusion of students with disabilities in general education classrooms. It is categorized by classroom techniques that involve students in group learning activities, in which recognition and reinforcement are based on group, rather than individual, performance. Heterogeneous small groups work together to achieve a group goal, and an individual student's success directly affects the success of other students (Slavin, 1987).

A variety of formats can be used to implement cooperative learning. These include peer tutoring, group projects, the jigsaw technique, and student-team achievement divisions.

PEER TUTORING

Peer teaching, or **peer tutoring**, is a relatively easy-to-manage system of cooperative learning. It can benefit both the student being tutored and the tutor. Specific activities that lend themselves to peer tutoring include reviewing task directions, doing drill and practice, recording material dictated by a peer, modelling acceptable or appropriate responses, and providing pretest practice (such as in spelling). Cooke, Heron, and Heward (1983) summarize the advantages of peer tutoring:

> First, [students] can be highly effective tutors. Research clearly indicates that children can effectively teach each other skills. These gains are optimized when the peer tutoring program is highly structured, when there is an emphasis on repetition, when learning reaches mastery levels before the tutee advances, when a review system is incorporated, and when tutors are trained. Second, tutors benefit academically from teaching skills to a peer. Third, with a peer tutoring program, both the content and pairs can be individualized to meet each student's needs. Fourth, peer tutoring allows for intensive one-to-one instruction without requiring the rest of the class to work on "independent seat work." Fifth, one-to-one instruction can substantially increase the number of opportunities a child has to give correct responses and receive immediate feedback on those responses. Sixth, peer tutoring is an excellent tool for successfully [including] students [with special needs] into the regular classroom for academic instruction. Finally, . . . students can be taught valuable social skills through a structured and positive peer tutoring program. (p. 2)

One effective tutoring program is *classwide peer tutoring* (CWPT). As summarized by Seeley (1995), this system involves the following arrangements:

- Classes are divided into two teams, which engage in competitions of 1–2 weeks' duration.
- Students work in pairs, both tutoring and being tutored on the same material in a given instructional session.
- Partners reverse roles after 15 minutes.
- Typical subjects tutored include math, spelling, vocabulary, science, and social studies.
- The teacher breaks down the curriculum into manageable subunits.
- Students accumulate points for their team by giving correct answers and by using correct procedures, and they receive partial credit for corrected answers.
- Individual scores on master tests are then added to the team's total.

CWPT is a promising approach to use in inclusive settings. It has been positively evaluated in terms of enhancing content learning, promoting diversity and integration, and freeing teachers to prepare for other instructional activities (King-Sears & Bradley, 1995; Simmons, Fuchs, Hodge, & Mathes, 1994).

COOPERATIVE PROJECTS

Group projects allow students to pool their knowledge and skills to complete an assignment. The task is assigned to the entire group, and the goal is to develop a single product reflecting the contributions of all members. For example, in art, creating a collage is a good example of a group project. In social studies, a report on one of the provinces or territories might involve making individual students responsible for particular tasks: drawing a map, sketching an outline of province/territory history, collecting photos of scenic attractions, and developing a display of products from that province/territory. Groups that include high, average, and low achievers together can be effective (Peck, 1989).

THE JIGSAW TECHNIQUE

The jigsaw format involves giving all students in a group individual tasks to be completed before the group can reach its goal. Each individual studies a portion of the material and then shares it with other members of the team. For example, Salend (1990) discussed an assignment related to the life of Dr. Martin Luther King, Jr., in which each student was given a segment of his life to research. The students then had to teach others in their group the information from the segment they had mastered.

STUDENT-TEAM ACHIEVEMENT DIVISIONS

The concept of student-team achievement divisions (STAD) involves assigning students to diversely constituted teams (typically four to a group), which then meet together to review specific teacher-generated lessons. This technique typically focuses on learning objectives that relate to one correct answer (e.g., facts). The teams work together toward content mastery, comparing answers, discussing differences, and questioning one another. Subsequently all students take individual quizzes, without assisting one another. The combined scores of the group determine how well the team succeeds. As Slavin (1987) notes, STAD embraces three concepts central to successful team learning methods: team rewards, individual accountability, and equal opportunities for success. Team rewards derive from content learning by members, who are then assessed by team scores produced by pooled individual scores. Individual accountability is essential because all must learn the content for the team to be successful. Equal opportunities for success come by focusing on degree of individual improvement.

Cooperative learning strategies offer much promise as inclusive practices. The various approaches can be used successfully with low, average, and high achievers to promote academic and social skills and to enhance independence. Cooperative learning also can enhance the social adjustment of students with special needs and help create natural support networks of which nondisabled peers are a part. However, cooperative learning strategies should be used only for part of the curriculum, not exclusively.

Modifying the Temporal Environment

Time is a critical element in the implementation of classroom modifications. For many students with disabilities, modifying deadlines and other time constraints can help promote success. When handled properly, these modifications need not impinge on the integrity of the assignments nor place undue burdens on the classroom teacher. Some suggestions follow:

- Develop schedules that balance routines (to establish predictability) with novelty (to sustain excitement).
- Review class schedules with students to reinforce routines.
- Provide each student with a copy of the schedule.
- Increase the amount of time allowed to complete assignments or tests.
- Contract with students concerning time allotment, and tie reinforcement to a reasonable schedule of completion.

- Consider reducing the amount of work or the length of tests rather than allow more time for completion (e.g., complete every other math problem).
- Allow extra practice time for students who understand content but need additional time to achieve mastery.
- Adjust homework assignments (e.g., the number of math problems, total length of a reading assignment) to produce equity in engaged time.
- Teach time-management skills (use of time lines and checklists, and prioritization of time and assignments).
- Space short work periods with breaks or changes of task (thus using the Premack principle for scheduling: making desirable events contingent on completion of less desirable events). (Adapted from Chalmers, 1991; Dowdy, 1990; Guernsey, 1989.)

Modifying the Classroom Arrangement

Changes in the classroom arrangement can also help in accommodating students with special needs. Some specific examples are listed here:

- Establish a climate that fosters positive social interactions between students.
- Balance structure, organization, and regimentation with opportunities for freedom and exploration.
- Use study carrels.
- Locate student seats and learning activities in areas free from distractions.
- Allow students to select their own seats based on where it is best for them to work and study.
- Help students keep their work spaces free of unnecessary materials.
- Arrange materials in the class based on frequency of use.
- Provide opportunities for approved movement within the class.
- Establish high- and low-frequency areas for class work (thus using the Premack principle—allow students to move to "fun" areas contingent on work completion in more academically rigorous areas).
- Set aside space for group work, individual seatwork, and free-time activities. (Adapted from Cheney, 1989; Dowdy, 1990; Guernsey, 1989; Hoover, 1990; Minner & Prater, 1989.)

CROSS-REFERENCE
See also the discussion on classroom arrangement in Chapter 5.

Enhancing Motivation

For many students with special needs, school activities may appear irrelevant or uninteresting. Given the failure often experienced by students with disabilities—as well as the boredom experienced by gifted students—motivational problems can seriously undermine the learning process. Although this typically becomes more problematic at the secondary level, young students must be taught in a way that prevents subsequent motivational problems. Attention to both the motivational qualities of the material and the characteristics of the student can enhance motivation. The following suggestions, which are particularly apt for students with special needs, can help spark motivation:

- Have students set personal goals and graph their progress.
- Use contingency contracts in which a certain amount of work at a specified degree of accuracy earns the student a desired activity or privilege.
- Allow students to choose where to work, what tools to use, and what to do first, as long as their work is being completed.

Teachers should avoid assigning excessive amounts of written classroom and homework to some students with special needs.

- Make drill-and-practice exercises into a game.
- Provide immediate feedback (e.g., through teacher monitoring or self-correcting materials) on the correctness of work.
- Give extra credit for bonus work.
- For certain students with special needs, camouflage instructional materials at a lower instructional level (using folders, covers).
- Use high-status materials for instructional activities (magazines, catalogues, newspapers, chequebooks, drivers' manuals).
- Allow students to earn points or tokens to exchange for a valued activity or privilege.
- Provide experiences that ensure success, and offer positive feedback when students are successful. (Adapted from Cheney, 1989, p. 29.)

Developing Effective Homework Programs

Homework has always been an essential element of education, but recently its use by teachers in elementary education has increased. Research on the effectiveness of homework as an instructional tool suggests that it leads to increased school achievement for students in general, with particular benefits in the area of habit formation for elementary students (Cooper, 1989; Walberg, 1991). But without question, students with disabilities experience significant problems in this area because of difficulties in attention, independence, organization, and motivation (Epstein, Polloway, Foley, & Patton, 1993; Gajria & Salend, 1995).

Homework for students with disabilities presents several dilemmas for general education teachers. In a recent study, Epstein et al. (1996) recognized that communication concerning homework is often negatively affected by the inadequate knowledge base of general education teachers. Figure 12.5 presents typical problems (ordered from most to least serious by teachers) in this area.

CONSIDER THIS

The importance of homework adaptations to the successful inclusion of students with special needs has been confirmed in numerous recent research studies. How important do you think it is?

1. Do not know enough about the abilities of students with disabilities who are mainstreamed in their classes.

2. Do not know how to use special education support services or teachers to assist students with disabilities about homework.

3. Lack knowledge about the adaptations that can be made to homework.

4. Are not clear about their responsibility to communicate with special education teachers about the homework of students with disabilities.

5. Are not aware of their responsibility to communicate with parents of students with disabilities about homework.

FIGURE 12.5
Homework Communication Problems Noted by Elementary Teachers

Note: Items were ranked by general education teachers from *most* to *least* serious.

From "Homework Communication Problems: Perspectives of General Education Teachers," by M. H. Epstein, E. A. Polloway, G. H. Buck, W. D. Bursuck, L. M. Wissinger, F. Whitehause, & M. Jayanthi. In *Learning Disabilities Research and Practice* (in press). Used by permission.

Epstein et al. (1993) suggest the following homework interventions:

- Assess possible problem areas as a basis for designing individualized programming.
- Provide assistance in study and organizational skills.
- Increase the relevance of the assignment by relating it to student interests and life skills.
- Assign homework that can be completed on an independent basis.
- Provide sufficient initial guidance when assignments are made.
- Control the time that assignments may take so that successful completion is realistic.
- Provide feedback to students on specific assignments.

CROSS-REFERENCE
Parental involvement in homework is discussed at length in Chapter 14.

Finally, Polloway, Epstein, Bursuck, Jayanthi, and Cumblad (1994) asked teachers to rate specific strategies that were most helpful to students with disabilities. Table 12.4 summarizes these responses; each column reflects teachers' ratings from most to least helpful.

Developing Responsive Grading Practices

The assignment of grades is an integral aspect of education. As Hess, Miller, Reese, and Robinson (1987) indicate, "Grading is an important aspect of documenting the educational experience of students, [and thus] assignment of grades has created and will continue to create debate within the educational community" (p. 1). Thus, grading practices have been subject to frequent evaluation and review, generating a number of problematic issues.

Grading received little attention prior to the increased inclusion of students with disabilities in general education. A series of research papers has addressed various aspects of grading. In a study of school district policies, Polloway, Epstein, Bursuck, Roderique, McConeghy, and Jayanthi (1994) reported that over 60 percent of districts with grading policies had one related to students with disabilities; most common was the inclusion of stated accommodations within the IEP. In one study, Bursuck, Polloway, Plante, Epstein, Jayanthi, and McConeghy (1996) found that approximately 40 percent of general educators shared responsibilities for grading with special education teachers. Thus, there is some evidence that the trend toward collaboration may be having an impact on this important area.

TABLE 12.4

Teachers' Ratings of Helpfulness of Homework Adaptations and Practices

Types of Homework	Consequences: Teacher-Directed Activities	Consequences: Failure to Complete	Complete Assignments	Adaptations
PRACTICE OF SKILLS ALREADY TAUGHT	Communicate clear consequences about successfully completing homework.	Assist students in completing the assignment.	Give praise for completion.	Provide additional teacher assistance.
PREPARATION FOR TESTS	Begin assignment in class, and check for understanding.	Make adaptations in assignment.	Provide corrective feedback in class.	Check more frequently with student about assignments and expectations.
UNFINISHED CLASS WORK	Communicate clear expectations about the quality of homework completion.	Talk to them about why the assignment was not completed.	Give rewards for completion.	Allow alternative response formats (e.g., oral or other than written).
MAKEUP WORK DUE TO ABSENCES	Use a homework assignment sheet or notebook.	Require corrections and resubmission.	Monitor students by charting performance.	Adjust length of assignment.
ENRICHMENT ACTIVITIES	Communicate clear consequences about failure to complete homework.	Call students' parents.	Record performance in grade book.	Provide a peer tutor for assistance.
PREPARATION FOR FUTURE CLASS WORK	Give assignments that are completed entirely at school.	Keep students in at recess to complete the assignment.	Call students' parents.	Provide auxiliary learning aids (e.g., calculator, computer).
	Begin assignment in class without checking for understanding.	Keep students after school to complete the assignment.		Assign work that student can do independently.
		Lower their grade.		Provide a study group.
		Put students' names on board.		Provide extra credit opportunities.
				Adjust (i.e., lower) evaluation standards.
				Adjust due dates.
				Give fewer assignments.

Note: Arranged from most helpful to least helpful.

From "Treatment Acceptability: Determining Appropriate Interventions within Inclusive Classrooms," by E. A. Polloway, W. D. Bursuck, M. Jayanthi, M. H. Epstein, and J. S. Nelson, 1996, *Intervention in School and Clinic, 31*, p. 136. Used by permission.

This collaboration is timely because existing grading systems make success challenging for students who are disabled. Studies on grading patterns have documented generally poor grades for students with disabilities in general education (e.g., Donahue & Zigmond, 1990; Valdes, Williamson, & Wagner, 1990; Zigmond, Levin, & Laurie, 1985). Further, although general education teachers reported that written comments and checklists are most helpful with these individuals, the most common systems in use at the elementary level are letter grades (Bursuck et al., 1996).

In a recent study, elementary general education teachers indicated that adaptations allowing for separate grades for process and product and grades indexed against student improvement were particularly helpful, whereas passing students "no matter what" or basing grades on effort alone was not. Figure 12.6 presents their ranking of grading adaptations.

A related issue is the feasibility of specific adaptations in general education. Bursuck et al. (1996) assessed this question by determining whether teachers actually use these same adaptations with students *without* disabilities. As can be seen in Figure 12.6, three of the four adaptations deemed most helpful for students with disabilities (i.e., grading on improvement, adjusting grades, giving separate grades for process and product) were used by 50 percent or more of the teachers (regardless of grade level) with nondisabled students. On the other hand, basing grades on less content and passing students no matter what are frowned upon.

Questions of fairness also influence the discussion on grading. Are adaptations in grading made only for students with disabilities really fair to other students? Bursuck et al. (1996) report that only 25 percent of general education teachers thought such adaptations were fair. Those who believed they were fair noted that students should "not be punished" for an inherent problem such as a disability, that adaptations for effort are appropriate because the students are "fighting uphill battles," and that adaptations allow students to "be successful like other kids."

CROSS-REFERENCE
Grading issues become more problematic at the secondary level; see Chapter 13 for more information.

1. Grades are based on the amount of improvement an individual makes. (#1)
2. Separate grades are given for process (e.g., effort) and product (e.g., tests). (#3)
3. Grades are based on meeting IEP objectives. (#9)
4. Grades are adjusted according to student ability. (#2)
5. Grading weights are adjusted (e.g., efforts on projects count more than tests). (#4)
6. Grades are based on meeting the requirements of academic or behavioural contracts. (#5)
7. Grades are based on less content than the rest of the class. (#7)
8. Students are passed if they make an effort to pass. (#6)
9. Grades are based on a modified grading scale (e.g., from 93 – 100 = A, 90 – 100 = A). (#8)
10. Students are passed no matter what. (#10)

FIGURE 12.6
Elementary Teachers' Ratings of Helpfulness of Grading Adaptations for Students with Disabilities

Note: Items ranked from most helpful to least helpful by general education teachers. Numbers in parentheses refer to general education rankings of adaptations from *most likely* to *least likely* to be used with *nondisabled* students.

Adapted from "Report Card Grading Practices and Adaptations," by W. Bursuck, E. A. Polloway, L. Plante, M. H. Epstein, M. Jayanthi, and J. McConeghy, 1996, *Exceptional Children, 62,* pp. 301–318.

Those who thought them unfair indicated that other students experience significant learning problems even though they have not been formally identified, that some students have extenuating circumstances (e.g., divorce, illness) that necessitate adaptations, and that all students are unique and deserve individual consideration (i.e., both students with and without disabilities may need specific adaptations). Such attitudes seem to indicate jointly developed adaptations. Finally, a significant minority of general educators believe that classes have standards to uphold; thus all students need to meet those standards without adaptations (Bursuck et al., 1996; Polloway et al., 1996).

Polloway and Patton (1997) suggest these summative considerations about grading:

- Plan for special and general education teachers to meet regularly to discuss student progress.
- Emphasize the acquisition of new skills as a basis for grades assigned, thus providing a perspective on the student's relative gains.
- Investigate alternatives for evaluating content that has been learned (e.g., oral examinations for poor readers in a science class).

- Engage in cooperative grading agreements (e.g., grades for language arts might reflect performance both in the classroom and the resource room).
- Use narrative reports as a key portion of, or adjunct to, the report card. These reports can include comments on specific objectives within the student's IEP.

SUMMARY

- The curriculum for elementary students with disabilities should meet their current and long-term needs, facilitate their interactions with nondisabled peers, and facilitate their transition into junior high school.

- Reading instruction should draw from both direct instruction and whole language approaches to provide a comprehensive, balanced program.

- Math instruction should provide students with concrete and abstract learning opportunities and should stress the development of problem-solving skills.

- Teachers should select programs and strategies that focus on the social skills most needed by students in their classrooms.

- Life skills instruction should be a part of the elementary curriculum through the use of augmentation, infusion, or an integrated curriculum.

- Instructional modifications should be evaluated against their "treatment acceptability"—that is, their feasibility, desirability, helpfulness, and fairness.

- Listening is a skill that requires conscious effort on the part of students and planned intervention strategies on the part of teachers.

- Reading tasks can be adapted through a variety of instructional strategies such as clarifying intent, highlighting content, modifying difficulty level, and using visual aids.

- Written responses can be facilitated through modification of the response requirement.

- Cooperative learning affords teachers a unique opportunity to involve students with disabilities in classroom activities, but should not be used exclusively.

- Modifications in class schedules or classroom arrangements should be considered in order to enhance the learning of students with disabilities.

- Motivation to learn cannot be taken for granted, and educational programs should be designed to reflect its importance.

- Homework creates significant challenges for students with special needs; these should be addressed by using intervention strategies.

- Classroom grading practices should be flexible enough to facilitate inclusion.

RESOURCES

Teaching Exceptional Children

All articles provide practical hands-on suggestions for use in the elementary or secondary classroom. The practical magazine for teachers is available through Council for Exceptional Children at **www.cec.sped.org/**

Deschenes, Cathy, Ebeling, David, and Sprague, Jeffery. (1994). *Adapting Curriculum & Instruction*

in Inclusive Classrooms: A Teacher's Desk Reference. Bloomington, IN: Center for School and Community Integration, Institute for the Study of Developmental Disabilities.

This practical listing of ways to adapt curriculum to have a successful inclusive classroom is an extremely useful resource. See also the Staff Development Kit.

WEBLINKS

Classroom Resources
classroomresources.com
Classroom Resources is an excellent Canadian Web site that offers a variety of classroom resources with Canadian content and representation of Canadian student diversity. It is a must visit for all teachers to see (and download) the latest Canadian Content flyer which reviews in detail different books and classroom resources and states their uses in curriculum design. This material will help teachers to include students from all backgrounds in their daily curricula.

School Psychology Resource
www.bcpl.net/~sandyste/school_psych.html
As a Web site for school psychologists, educators, and parents, this resource covers different exceptionalities, special education procedures (e.g., sample IEPs), and information on all topics relevant to psychology in the schools such as violence, child abuse, suicide, and parent collaboration. Although American based, it has excellent information and materials relevant to Canadian teachers.

The Education Planet—The Education Web Guide
Educationplanet.com
This search engine covers all education-relevant sites. If you want to find specifically Canadian material, you can limit searches to Canadian sources. The highly interesting and rewarding resource provides access to lesson plans, videos, manuals, curriculum materials, and much more!

Teachers.net
Teachers.net
As a huge U.S. Web site, Teachers.net covers a variety of topics of interest to teachers, including curriculum suggestions, resources, and chat rooms with different education issues. It has subject-specific listings of chatboards where ideas, such as teaching secondary school math in innovative ways, are shared. Many resources are available through this Web site for elementary and secondary teachers.

Canadian.Teachers.net
Canadian.teachers.net/
This uniquely Canadian offshoot of Teachers.net provides a specifically Canadian forum with chat rooms, job postings, catalogues, information, professional development with guest speakers, and listings of related sites.

CHAPTER THIRTEEN

CHAPTER OBJECTIVES

- To define the concept of a comprehensive curriculum and discuss curricular alternatives for students with disabilities

- To discuss the ways to determine the curricular needs of secondary school students

- To identify and describe the key elements of effective instruction

- To discuss the roles of general education and special education teachers in ensuring successful secondary school programs for students with special needs

- To identify accommodations and adaptations that can facilitate learning for secondary school students

- To identify and give examples of study skills and learning strategies that can enhance school performance for adolescent learners

Teaching Students with Special Needs in Secondary Schools

Stephanie Hughes went through university loving the study of literature. She majored in English and selected as many courses as she could that focused on literature. Her particular interest was 20th-century Canadian literature, and she completed an honours paper on Robertson Davies. After graduation, she chose to pursue her dream to teach high school English.

For the past three years, Stephanie has been teaching ninth- and tenth-grade English. Because of the trend toward inclusion, her class roll often includes a number of students with special needs, particularly students with learning disabilities. The diversity of her class has led her to question how she can best instill her love of literature in these students while addressing their individual learning needs. She is greatly concerned about the low reading levels of some of the students (several at about third/fourth grade) and their lack of motivation for study in areas that they find neither inherently interesting nor relevant to their future.

1. How can cooperative learning be used to facilitate instruction in this secondary school classroom?

2. What adaptations and modifications will assist the students with special needs in learning important content and in being appropriately evaluated and graded?

3. How can Stephanie make the curricular content more relevant to the future lives of these students when they finish high school?

INTRODUCTION

CONSIDER THIS

Do special education support staff need different skills at the secondary level than they need in elementary schools? If so, what are some of the differences?

Important differences exist between elementary and secondary settings in terms of organizational structure, curricula, and learner variables. These differences create special challenges for successful inclusion. Certainly one concern is the gap found between the demands of the classroom setting and the ability of many students with disabilities. Academically, this gap widens; many students with disabilities exhibit limited basic skills and therefore experience difficulty in performing higher-level cognitive tasks. These basic skills include gaining information from textbooks, memorizing large amounts of information, paraphrasing, discriminating important information from the less important, taking notes, writing themes, proofreading papers, and taking tests successfully (Schumaker & Deshler, 1988).

A second concern is that teachers are often trained primarily as content specialists, yet are expected to present complex material in such a way that a diverse group of students can master the information (National Joint Committee on Learning Disabilities, 1988). Secondary teachers are more likely to focus on teaching the content than on individualizing instruction to meet the unique needs of each student. Further, because there may be reluctance to change grading systems or make other accommodations, it may become difficult for students with disabilities to experience success in general education settings.

A third challenge is the general nature of adolescence. Adolescence is a difficult and trying time for all young people. For students with disabilities, the developmental period is even more challenging. Problems associated with adolescence are exacerbated by the presence of a disability.

Perhaps, given these concerns, it is not surprising to find that secondary teachers have been less positive overall toward efforts at inclusion (Scruggs & Mastropieri, 1996). However, regardless of the difficulties associated with placing adolescents with special needs in general education programs, more students with disabilities are going to depend on classroom teachers to provide appropriate educational programs. Therefore, classroom teachers in secondary schools must be prepared to deal with students who require specialized instruction or modified curricula.

SECONDARY SCHOOL CURRICULA

More curricular differentiation has been advocated at the secondary level to accommodate the individual needs and interests of the wide variety of students attending high school. At the same time, most high schools have a general curriculum that all students must complete. This curriculum, typically prescribed by the provincial education ministry, includes science, math, social studies, English, and French. Often, provinces and local education boards add to the required general curriculum such areas as education on sexuality, drug education, and third languages.

Although the specific curricula offered in different secondary schools vary, they generally follow provincial guidelines. Individual schools, however, do offer unique curricular options that appeal to particular students. The curricular focus that students choose should be an important consideration, because the decision could have long-term implications after the students exit school.

Special Education Curriculum in Secondary Schools

The curriculum for students with disabilities is the most critical programming consideration in secondary schools. Even if students have excellent teachers, if the curriculum is inappropriate to meet their needs, then the teaching may be ineffective. The high school curriculum for students with disabilities must be comprehensive, that is, it must

- be responsive to the needs of individual students;
- facilitate maximum integration with nondisabled peers;
- facilitate socialization;
- focus on the students' transition to postsecondary settings.

In 1979, Alley and Deshler identified five curricular approaches commonly used with secondary special education students: (1) basic skills remediation, (2) tutorial approach, (3) learning strategies model, (4) functional curriculum, and (5) work-study model. A more recent model includes these focuses:

- Basic skills (i.e., remediation of academic deficits)
- Social skills (i.e., stress on social adjustment)
- Tutorial (i.e., receiving support within the regular curriculum)
- Learning strategies (i.e., teaching students to be independent learners)
- Vocational (i.e., job training)
- Life skills (i.e., independent living training)

Each model has a different emphasis. Basic skills and social skills models endeavour to train students to develop the ability to successfully function in the general education classroom. Tutorial and learning strategies models present short-term and long-term solutions, respectively, to provide students with support to retain them in general education. Vocational and life skills programs focus on preparing the student for successful community living and adult adjustment. (See Polloway & Patton, 1997, for a detailed discussion.)

FURTHER READING
For more information on secondary special education models, read "Comprehensive Curriculum for Students with Mild Handicaps," by E. A. Polloway, J. R. Patton, M. H. Epstein, & T. E. C. Smith, 1989, *Focus on Exceptional Children, 21,* pp. 1–12.

Determining Curricular Needs of Students

As noted in Chapter 12, the adoption of a curriculum for any student should be based on an appraisal of desired long-term outcomes and an assessment of current needs. At the elementary level, consideration of the future demands of middle and high school suggests a primary focus on the development and refinement of basic academic and social skills, as well as a beginning emphasis on career awareness and life skills.

Polloway and Patton (1997) suggest that elementary students also be taught specific skills that will facilitate success in high school, such as self-management, study skills, note taking, and homework skills. Still other nonacademic abilities, such as resisting peer pressure, negotiating, accepting negative feedback, and asking questions, should be addressed in the elementary curriculum to facilitate the success of students in secondary settings (Hazel, Schumaker, Shelon, & Sherman, 1982). Although some schools in the process of restructuring are providing learning opportunities in these areas, many schools continue to focus on academics.

Regardless of the seemingly "common" areas that should be included in an elementary curriculum, curricular variation is common. The result is that students arrive in secondary settings with a wide range of academic preparation and varying, often limited, degrees of exposure to transitional subjects such as life skills, career awareness, study skills, and self-management. Since high school represents a final chance for public education personnel to prepare students for their postschool futures, curricular considerations and decisions are critically important. Data on school exit patterns and follow-up studies of students with disabilities have, for the most part, suggested that schools need to improve programs that prepare students with disabilities for life after high school. As many as 50 percent of students with learning disabilities will drop out of high school (Levin, Zigmond, & Birch, 1985). Bender (1998) thinks that the true number of students with learning disabilities who do not finish high school is even higher.

Several studies have shown that adults with disabilities are likely to be employed part-time, underemployed, or unemployed to a significantly greater degree than their nondisabled peers (Edgar, 1988; Edgar & Polloway, 1994). Therefore, regardless of the efforts made in secondary schools to meet the individual needs of students with disabilities, many of these students seem unprepared to achieve success as young adults.

Students themselves are aware that they are not being adequately prepared for post–high school demands. In comparing the transitional needs of high school students with learning disabilities to those of their nondisabled peers, Dowdy, Carter, and Smith (1990) found that, although both groups expressed an interest in help with career decisions, significant differences were noted in their thoughts about the future. For example, students with learning disabilities were far more concerned with learning how to find a job, how to keep a job, and how to live independently. As a group, students with disabilities expressed greater insecurity about their futures than did students without disabilities.

To ensure that students have the optimum chance at success after schooling concludes, transition planning is essential. Transitions represent ongoing challenges that can be identified as horizontal (from a more segregated to a more integrated society) and vertical (across the lifespan) (see Figure 13.1). Of primary concern here is the transition to adulthood from school, which is in itself a multifaceted process (see Figure 13.2 for a model).

One helpful way for the schools to view this process is through the **future-based assessment** and intervention model (see Figure 13.3). In the first step of the model, parents and student have a conference with school personnel to identify the student's interests and goals in terms of postsecondary training, employment, and independent living. During this step, all parties involved in the planning identify the desired future for the student. The appropriateness of these goals is tested in the second step of the model, through administration of a comprehensive assessment battery. In this process, information on the stu-

CONSIDER THIS

What are some things that schools could do to increase the number of students with disabilities who stay in school and graduate? Should schools do these things?

FURTHER READING

For more information on transition planning and other issues, read the special issues of *Journal of Learning Disabilities*, volume 29, issues 1 and 2, published in 1996.

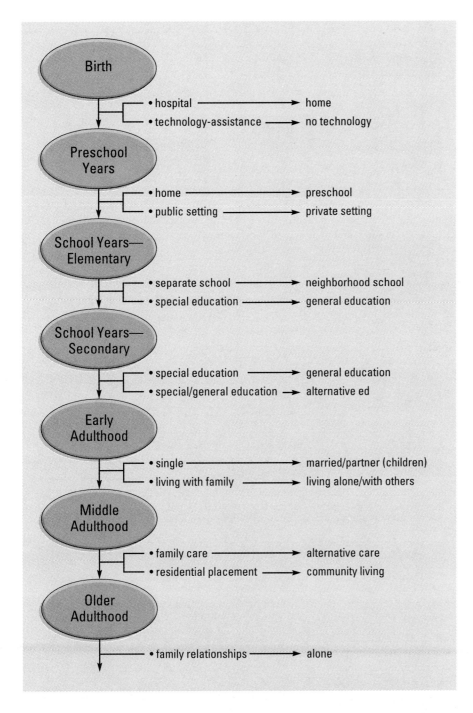

FIGURE 13.1
Vertical and Horizontal
Transitions

From *Transition from School to
Adult Life for Students with
Special Needs: Basic Concepts
and Recommended Practices* (p.
14), by J. R. Patton, 1995, Austin,
TX: Pro-Ed. Copyright 1995 by Pro-
Ed. Reprinted by permission.

dent's future in areas such as academic potential, vocational potential and interests, and social skills is collected. In step 3, the original team is reconvened
to consider the impact of the assessment data on the goals developed during
step 1. Goals might be revised at this time to more accurately reflect the student's ability levels.

FIGURE 13.2
Elements of the
Transition Process

From *Transition from School to Adult Life for Students with Special Needs: Basic Concepts and Recommended Practices* (p. 10), by J. R. Patton, 1995, Austin, TX: Pro-Ed. Copyright 1995 by Pro-Ed. Reprinted by permission.

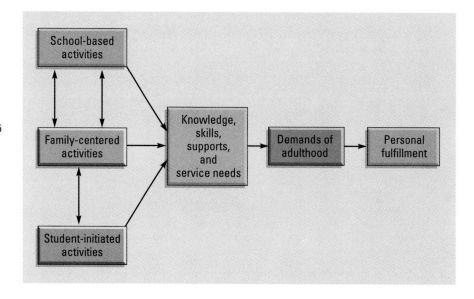

FIGURE 13.3
Future-Based
Assessment and
Intervention Model

From "Future-based Assessment and Intervention for Students with Mental Retardation," by T. E. C. Smith and C. A. Dowdy, 1992, *Education and Training in Mental Retardation, 27,* p. 258. Used by permission.

STEP 1

Student/parent interview: Identify interests and goals for post-secondary training, employment, and independent living.

STEP 2

Conduct comprehensive assessment including academic, vocational, and independent living skills.

STEP 3

Interdisciplinary team meeting: Analyze assessment data and refine future goals.

STEP 4

Determine the characteristics/skills necessary for individuals to be successful in future vocational, academic, and independent living situations.

STEP 5

Identify discrepancies between the characteristics/skills of the student and the skills necessary for success in designated future academic, employment, and independent living situations.

STEP 6

Develop and implement intervention plans (IEPs and Transition plans) to address discrepancies identified in step 5.

STEP 7

Ongoing analysis of student characteristics and future vocational, academic, and social situations to determine if adjustments regarding future needs are to be made (must be done on an annual basis).

In step 4, the skills needed to succeed in the designated goals are identi-fied. These skills are then compared to the current skill levels of the student, and the discrepancies are identified (step 5). After this analysis, in step 6, cur-ricular choices are made: these provide the training and education necessary to facilitate the student's success in each area. For students with disabilities, these goals should be delineated in the IEP and also reflected in individual transition plans (ITPs). See Figure 13.4 for an example of the relationship between IEP and ITP goals.

The final step reflects the constant need for monitoring to affirm that the curricular choices are appropriate. This ongoing review and analysis allows teachers, parents, and the students themselves to know what progress is being made toward future goals. If progress is insufficient, or more rapid than antici-pated, the goals may need to be adjusted.

Although students with disabilities have IEPs that detail specific goals, ob-jectives, and services, the programs must be related to a particular curricular model. As previously noted, without an appropriate curriculum, educational pro-grams necessarily become unfocused. Figure 13.5 summarizes factors related to making curricular decisions for students with disabilities.

TEACHING TIP
Teachers and other school personnel must include students with disabilities and their family members in futures planning.

FIGURE 13.4
Relationship between ITP Goals and IEP Goals and Objectives
Adapted from "Transition and Students with Learning Disabilities: Creating Sound Futures," by G. Blalock and J. Patton, 1996, *Journal of Learning Disabilities, 29,* p. 12. Used by permission.

I. Transition (ITP) Goals
ITP activities or objectives

A. Demonstrating self-advocacy about learning support needs

B. Researching specific university offerings

C. Selecting a major

II. Instructional (IEP) Annual Goals

A. Demonstrate self-advocacy about learning support needs

Objective 1: The student will identify own learning strengths.
Objective 2: The student will identify own learning needs and related supports.
Objective 3: The student will discuss necessary learning supports with high school counsellor.

B. Research five universities' academic and special support offerings

C. Select a major for the freshman year in university

Objective 1: The student will participate in career/vocational and academic assessment.
Objective 2: The student will review findings of all assessment results with teacher or counsellor.
Objective 3: The student will explore five occupational directions that emerge from the assessment, in library and on computer.
Objective 4: The student will select one occupational area that seems most promising and match that area to major areas at the selected university.

FIGURE 13.5

Factors Related to
Curricular Decisions

From "Comprehensive Curriculum
for Students with Mild
Handicaps," by E. A. Polloway,
J. R. Patton, M. H. Epstein, and
T. E. C. Smith, 1989, *Focus on
Exceptional Children, 21* (8), p. 8.
Used by permission.

1. Student variables
   - Cognitive-intellectual level
   - Academic skills preparedness
   - Academic achievement as determined by tests
   - Academic achievement as determined by class grades
   - Grade placement
   - Motivation and responsibility
   - Social interactions with peers and adults
   - Behavioral self-control

2. Family variables
   - Short- and long-term parental expectations
   - Degree of support provided (e.g., financial, emotional, academic)
   - Parental values toward education
   - Cultural influence (e.g., language, values)

3. General education variables
   - Teacher and nondisabled student acceptance
     of diversity (classroom climate)
   - Administrative support for integrated education
   - Availability of curricular variance
   - Accommodative capacity of the classroom
   - Flexibility of daily class schedules and units
     earned toward graduation
   - Options for vocational programs

4. Special education variables
   - Size of caseload
   - Availability of paraprofessionals or tutors in the classroom
   - Access to curricular materials
   - Focus of teacher's training
   - Consultative and materials support available
   - Related services available to students

PROGRAMS FOR STUDENTS IN SECONDARY SCHOOLS

Most secondary students with disabilities are currently included in general education classrooms for at least a portion of each school day. Therefore, the responsibility for these students becomes a joint effort between general education classroom teachers and special education personnel. Unfortunately, many of these students do not experience success in the general classroom setting. They frequently fail classes, become frustrated and act out, and may even drop out of school because they are not prepared to meet the demands placed on them by secondary teachers. There are numerous reasons why many students with disabilities fail in secondary classes:

- Lack of communication between special education personnel and classroom teachers
- Discrepancies between the expectations of classroom teachers and the abilities of students
- Students' lack of understanding about the demands of the classroom

- Classroom teachers' lack of understanding and knowledge about students with disabilities
- Special education personnel's lack of knowledge in working with classroom teachers

Regardless of the reasons why some students with disabilities do not achieve success in general education settings, the fact remains that the majority will be taught in inclusive settings. Therefore, educators, both classroom teachers and special education personnel, must work together to increase the chances that these students will be successful.

Roles of Personnel

As noted, the responsibility for educating students with disabilities in public schools is shared by general classroom teachers and special education personnel. Therefore, educators must improve their skills at working together to help students with various learning and behaviour problems.

GENERAL EDUCATION TEACHERS

The primary role of general classroom teachers is to assume the responsibility for students with disabilities in particular classes or subject areas. Most classroom teachers present information using one general technique, but they will probably have to expand their instructional activities when dealing with students with disabilities. Various accommodations and modifications in instructional techniques and materials will be discussed later in the chapter.

Classroom teachers have five general responsibilities for *all* of the students in their classes:

1. Educating and managing behaviour
2. Making major instructional decisions, determining the pace, and monitoring progress

CONSIDER THIS

The roles of general educators and special educators must change for effective inclusion to occur. What are some likely barriers to these changes, and how can they be overcome?

General education teachers are primarily responsible for students with special needs in their classrooms.

3. Following a curriculum that reflects normal development and identifying any child whose progress is discrepant

4. Managing instruction for a heterogeneous, diverse population through grouping and individualization

5. Seeking, using, and managing assistance for students with educational needs that differ significantly from those of their peers (Jenkins, Pious, & Jewell, 1990)

In addition to these five areas, Rosenshine and Stevens (1986) suggest that classroom teachers focus on equalizing opportunities for students with disabilities in their classes. Teachers should ensure that all students have an opportunity to answer questions and a good chance at achieving at least moderate success in classroom activities. This is not a call for teachers to "give" students with disabilities passing grades, only a request that students with disabilities receive an equal chance at being successful.

Classroom teachers should also do all they can to work effectively with special education professionals. Open communication and dialogue between classroom teachers and special education personnel is crucial if inclusion is to be successful (Mims, Harper, Armstrong, & Savage, 1991). Communication among all individuals providing services to students with disabilities is the most important factor related to the success of inclusion.

When working with students who have disabilities, classroom teachers must realize that no single method always works with these students; teachers have to individualize their efforts. However, some general methods are often effective with students with disabilities. Christenson, Ysseldyke, and Thurlow (1989) describe some of them:

FURTHER READING
For more information on specific techniques to use with students with disabilities in general education classrooms, read *Teaching Adolescents with Learning Disabilities,* by D. Deshler, E. Ellis, and K. Lenz, published in 1996 by Love Publishing.

1. *Classroom management:*   Research has demonstrated that classes in which teachers have effective behaviour management procedures in place have more time for student involvement and instruction. The key is to be proactive in setting up a well-thought-out routine and a few clearly stated classroom rules and procedures. Classroom rules should always be stated in positive terms. Teachers cannot assume that students will know how to act if the rule only tells them how *not* to act. For example, instead of posting a rule that students may not sit on the tops of desks, state that students should sit on their chairs, with feet on the floor.

2. *Positive school environment:*   Students learn more effectively in a classroom in which a humanistic focus combines with an academic orientation (Samuels, 1986). When planning each day's activities, teachers should build in tasks or accommodations that will offer each student a measure of success. All students need to be successful from time to time to maintain their attention and motivation. Using cooperative learning activities, such as those described in Chapter 12, is another way to develop a positive atmosphere.

   Teachers should always set high goals for students and make students feel that the teacher is confident that they can achieve the goals. Students need to believe that their teachers care about them and will support them in their efforts.

3. *Appropriate instructional match:*   The degree of instructional match can be determined by a discrepancy analysis comparing the characteristics of the student and the demands of the task. Analyzing the students' capabilities is often difficult because of the hidden nature of many mild cognitive disabilities.

It is important for teachers to know the unique characteristics of their students, especially those with disabilities or who are at risk of developing behaviour problems or emotional problems. Achievement levels of students are frequently only the tip of the iceberg when it comes to functioning successfully in class. Less obvious characteristics, such as inattention, distractibility, slow work rate, and difficulty processing multiple directions, can be the major culprits preventing successful learning. Accommodations or modifications must address these specific characteristics (see Table 13.1).

4. *Clear teaching goals and expectations:* Effective teachers have a carefully developed master plan that includes teaching goals for each lesson. These goals are important for the teachers, to focus their instruction, but teachers should also communicate these goals to the students frequently and explicitly. Students have a tendency to perform better when they know the specific goals of the instruction. It is better for teachers to say, "Today you are

---

TABLE 13.1

Examples of Accommodations and Modifications

Characteristic	Accommodations and Modifications
DIFFICULTY COMPLETING ASSIGNMENTS	• List or post (and say) all steps necessary to complete each assignment. • Break the assignment into manageable sections with specific due dates. • Make frequent checks for work/assignment completion. • Arrange for the student to have a "study buddy," with phone number, in each subject area.
DIFFICULTY WITH TASKS THAT REQUIRE MEMORY	• Combine seeing, saying, writing, and doing; student may need to subvocalize to remember. • Teach memory techniques as a study strategy (e.g., mnemonics, visualization, oral rehearsal, numerous repetitions).
DIFFICULTY WITH TEST TAKING	• Allow extra time for testing; teach test-taking skills and strategies; allow student to be tested orally. • Use clear, readable, and uncluttered test forms. Use test format that the student is most comfortable with. Allow ample space for student response. Consider having lined answer spaces for essay and short-answer tests.
CONFUSION FROM NON-VERBAL CUES (Misreads body language, etc.)	• Directly teach (tell the student) what nonverbal cues mean. Model them, and have student practise reading cues in a safe setting.
CONFUSION FROM WRITTEN MATERIAL (Difficulty finding main idea from a paragraph; attributes greater importance to minor details)	• Provide student with copy of reading material with main ideas underlined or highlighted. • Provide an outline of important points from reading material. • Teach outlining, main idea versus details, concepts. • Provide tape of text.
CONFUSION FROM SPOKEN MATERIAL, LECTURES, AND AUDIO-VISUAL MATERIAL (Difficulty finding main idea, attributes greater importance to minor details)	• Provide student with a copy of presentation notes. • Allow peers to share carbon-copy notes from presentation (have student compare own notes with copy of peer's notes). • Provide framed outlines of presentations (introducing visual and auditory cues to important information). • Encourage use of tape recorder. • Teach and emphasize key words (the following . . . , the most important . . . , etc.)

going to learn the steps of the scientific method" than to say "Today we are going to study the scientific method." Teachers should set high expectations, monitor achievement continuously, and give frequent, task-specific feedback.

5. *Quality of instruction:* One of the primary roles for all teachers is to provide quality instruction. In order to do this, teachers need to explain lessons clearly, use modelling and demonstration techniques, and monitor whether the concepts are understood by students (Rosenshine & Stevens, 1986). The following outline of steps used in an effective lesson has been adapted from the work of Deshler, Schumaker, Lenz, and Ellis (1984):

   ■ Review the previous lesson.
   ■ Use an advance organizer or graphic organizer to introduce the lesson.
   ■ Obtain student attention and commitment to learn.
   ■ Provide direct instruction (include modelling, demonstration, examples, manipulatives).
   ■ Use a variety of tasks, activities, and questions to maintain interest and generate student response.
   ■ Provide guided practice (monitor boardwork, simple worksheets, small group games with teacher).
   ■ Provide independent practice for generalization (homework, workbooks, regular textbooks, computer, games).
   ■ Ask students to evaluate learning/use informal tests (rapid-fire questioning, brief written assessment).
   ■ Close with a summary and transition to next lesson. Provide student feedback as appropriate. Document observations: student and self-evaluation. (Table 13.2 shows a list of these steps with questions that can be used by teachers for self-evaluation following a lesson.)

6. *Instructional support for individual students:* Instruction is made more effective when teachers monitor students' work frequently and adjust or adapt instruction to meet individual needs of students. Some students require more guided practice, more drill, and more practice to reach automaticity.

TEACHING TIP
Perform self-monitoring (or monitor teachers you may be observing) to determine the amount of time spent in teaching. What are some ways to increase the amount of teaching?

Effective teachers use a master plan for lessons, including specific teaching goals.

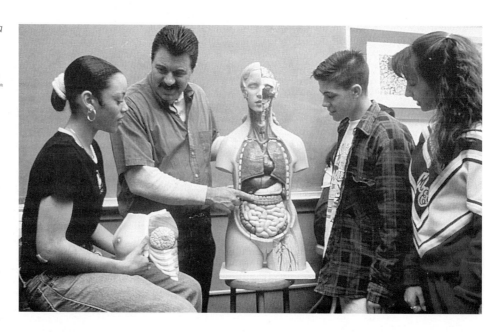

TABLE 13.2

Steps in an Effective Lesson and Corresponding Evaluation Questions

Steps	Questions
1. Reviews previous lesson	Was my transition smooth and meaningful?
2. Uses advanced organizer to introduce new lesson	Were my objectives clear? Did I have the right number of objectives?
3. Obtains student attention and commitment to learn	Was my motivational or attention-getting technique effective? Did I make the lesson relevant to the student?
4. Provides direct instruction (includes modelling, demonstration, manipulatives)	Was my subject matter background okay? Did I use overhead, chalkboard, graphics, models, etc.? Was there a balance between student and teacher talk?
5. Uses a variety of tasks, activities, and questions to maintain interest and generate student responses	Were my questions effective? Did my class ask questions? Did I wait for replies to my questions? Did I involve all students?
6. Provides guided practice (boardwork, simple worksheets, small group games with teacher)	Did I transform students from "passive listeners" to "active participants"? Was teacher activity balanced with student activity? Did I provide timely feedback?
7. Provides independent practice for generalization (workbooks, textbooks, computer, games)	Did I include appropriate homework? Did I use materials that require generalization?
8. Asks students to evaluate learning, uses informal tests (rapid-fire questioning, brief written assessment)	If I didn't know something, did I promise to look it up? Did I ask them what they had learned, to teach self-evaluation? Was my assessment directly related to my objective?
9. Closes with summary and transition to next lesson	Did I have a smooth closing and transition to the next activity?
10. Provides student feedback as appropriate	Did I identify students who needed an individual behaviour change plan?
11. Documents observations: students and self	Was my behaviour management technique effective? Was learning effective and fun?

When students are moved too quickly through the curriculum, they often do not obtain sufficient practice to maintain and then generalize instruction. Waiting until evaluation time may result in several days of wasted instruction. By providing ongoing monitoring and instructional support, teachers can prevent students from sitting in classes without realizing success.

7. *Efficient use of time:* One of the most important roles of classroom teachers is to maximize instructional time with students. The amount of time teachers allocate to instruction, the amount of time students actually spend engaged in academic tasks, and the amount of time students spend in active academic responding are critical in determining a student's opportunity to learn. For students with disabilities, efficient use of time is even more important.

Although the amount of time allotted for instruction is important, the quality of instruction is also critical. Simply having students spend large amounts of time in academic activities does not guarantee learning. An example is having students complete worksheets when they may not under-

PERSONAL SPOTLIGHT

Secondary Teacher ■ AKAPELWA MWEEMBA

Secondary Teacher, Westpark School, Portage La Prairie, Manitoba

Akapelwa Mweemba has been teaching math and science at the junior and senior high levels for more than a decade. He has been involved in a pilot project preparing the Science 10 documents for the Manitoba Department of Education. In 1996 he received the Prime Minister's Award for Excellence in Science Education.

Akapelwa is noted for use of peer tutoring in his inclusive classes. "A great part of my success lies in the use of peer tutoring as a viable and effective teaching strategy. New material is generally taught in conventional ways. Following this, to reinforce the new material learned, the class breaks into groups and peer tutoring ensues. Students who have a firm grasp of the concepts tutor those who are having difficulty. Through this strategy, I have found that the students' abilities to verbally communicate their knowledge improve. The bonus to this method is reversal of roles: the student today will become the tutor tomorrow. It provides every student with a chance to succeed at different points in the course."

Akapelwa speaks at length about the advantages of the peer-tutoring method in his classroom, listing efficiency, structure, a student-centred nature, and, perhaps most important of all, the development of a family atmosphere whereby students help each other. He has made inclusion work in his class but observes that there are hurdles to accomplishing this. "One of the greatest problems associated with inclusion in the secondary class lies in the fact that the pace may be somewhat compromised. The class may tend to move at the pace of the 'slowest'

learner for any given unit. In a fast-paced, finish-the-curriculum-at-all-costs type agenda, the slower learners may not benefit. However, this is *not* an insurmountable obstacle. The challenge would be to create an environment where success for all learners is guaranteed. Success is defined in *personal* terms through what individuals can accomplish with their abilities."

Akapelwa did not always use peer tutoring, initially believing in a more traditional approach to instruction. However, being attuned to problem solving and analytical by nature led him to adopt the practice. "I had been in Westpark School a couple of years when it became evident that a number of students' math skills were below level. To help I tried conducting tutoring after school. Very often this meant repeating previous classes. As I thought about this dilemma, it became clear I needed to change the way I conducted my classes. One student in particular functioned at Grade 5 level in Math when she was in Grade 7. After working with "Patti" for a long time and watching her in class, I realized she often sought the help of a particular student who connected with her. I realized, then, that if I could utilize peers in a more organized fashion, I would maximize my efforts and results. This was the birth of the peer-tutoring program. Subsequently, Patti even stated that math was "fun"! Earlier on in my training I bought into the philosophy that 'anybody can learn anything . . . provided conditions are right.' It has become my mission to provide those conditions to the best of my abilities."

stand the concepts or have already learned the concepts. Teachers must consider allocation of time and the quality of activities designated for each time period.

8. *Substantive student interaction:* Teachers need to facilitate student interaction. Research has shown that the opportunity to engage in active academic responses is positively correlated with academic achievement (Reid, 1986). Effective teachers give cues and prompts that can increase students' correct responses and thus increase the amount of positive feedback they receive. It is important for all students to have an opportunity to actively participate. Because many students with disabilities have slow processing abilities and oral language difficulties, teachers may need to develop strategies to facilitate their interactions. Peer tutoring, choral responding, and cooperative learning offer alternative opportunities for active responding that may benefit students with problems.

9. *Monitoring of student understanding and progress:* Active and frequent monitoring is the key to keeping the total instructional cycle effective (Good & Brophy, 1987). Although teachers plan instruction for groups of students, frequent monitoring of individuals and adapting the instruction help maintain the match between the individual and the instruction. Effective monitoring should require students to demonstrate the learned skill, not simply state that they have no questions. The first items of a practice set should be checked by the teacher. Students should also be asked to explain what they are doing to ensure that an efficient strategy has been selected.

  If teachers wait until a grade-reporting period to evaluate a student's progress, significant amounts of instructional time may be lost. Therefore, constant ongoing monitoring is an important task for teachers with students who have disabilities.

10. *Evaluation of student performance:* Direct assessment of student knowledge is essential for determining whether instructional goals and objectives have been reached. Effective assessment requires frequent evaluation designed to measure exactly what has been taught. Feedback should be explicit regarding the inaccuracy or accuracy of the response, and it should be directly related to the task being completed by the student. For example, "You have really learned the steps in the scientific method" is preferable to "You have really worked hard on this." Through frequent testing, teachers can make better, data-based decisions to determine future goals.

> **TEACHING TIP**
> Evaluation of student performance must be continual in order to provide teachers with feedback to determine the effectiveness of the instructional program and thereby necessary changes.

When teaching content courses, such as history and science, teachers should treat students with disabilities as they treat all other students, remembering that the students with special needs would not be placed in the general classroom setting if an interdisciplinary team had not determined that they could benefit from instruction in that environment.

Within the classroom, teachers can do several things that will facilitate the success of students with disabilities. They can modify the environment, alter the task presentation, vary the student requirements, and make the grading procedures more flexible. However, the realities of the classroom at the secondary level may not permit full individualized instruction or a truly wide range of ways to present instruction (Bryan, Bay, & Donahue, 1988).

Collaborative Role of the Special Education Teacher

The special education teacher plays an important role in the successful inclusion of students with disabilities in secondary schools. In addition to collaborating with general educators, the special education teacher must prepare students for the challenges that occur daily in the general education environment and equip them for future challenges in independent living and employment. Above all, special education teachers play a major support role for general classroom teachers. They should communicate regularly with classroom teachers and provide assistance through consultation or through direct instruction.

FURTHER READING
For more information on collaborative activities of special educators, read Sharon Cramer's book, *Collaboration: A Success Strategy for Special Educators*, published by Allyn & Bacon in 1997.

The specific roles of the special education teacher include counselling students for the personal crises that may occur daily and preparing students for content classes, high school exams, postsecondary training, independent living, and, ultimately, employment (Smith, Finn, & Dowdy, 1993). Special education teachers and general teachers often collaborate in performing these roles.

COUNSELLING FOR DAILY CRISES

Adolescence is a difficult time of change for all children; for children with disabilities, the period is even more challenging. In our society, students are constantly trying to grasp the subtle changes in roles for males and females. They experience more exposure to drugs and alcohol, and pregnancy and AIDS are common issues. The increased tension, frustration, and depression can lead to suicide, the second leading cause of death among adolescents (Guetzloe, 1988; Smith et al., 1993; Spirito, Hart, Overholser, & Halverson, 1990), or a variety of behaviour and emotional problems. Special education teachers need to collaborate with general educators to help students deal with these problems.

PREPARING FOR HIGH SCHOOL CONTENT CLASSES

CROSS-REFERENCE
Review materials in Chapters 3 through 9, and reflect on how different disabilities have an impact on preparation for high school content courses.

The special education teacher should be aware of factors such as classroom teacher expectations, teaching styles, and the demands of the learning environment (Welch & Link, 1991). One way special education teachers can help students deal with the "general education world" is to teach them how to self-advocate. In order to do this, students need to understand their specific learning problems. Therefore, special education teachers may need to have a discussion with their students about the nature of specific disabilities.

Deshler and Schumaker (1988) propose that the primary role of special education teachers should be to teach their students effective strategies for generalization to compensate for their learning deficits and therefore increase the likelihood of success in mainstream classes. They suggest teaching numerous strategies for memorizing, test taking, listening, note taking, proofreading, time management, and organization. Specific techniques for these will be discussed later in the chapter. If students with learning problems know how to use these kinds of strategies, they will have a better chance of achieving success in general classrooms.

When working with students with disabilities in general education classrooms, the role of the special educator expands. It includes informing the general educator as to the unique abilities and challenges presented by each student, providing ongoing support and **collaboration** for the student and teacher, and doing frequent monitoring to ensure that the arrangement is satisfactory for both the student and the teacher.

PREPARING FOR HIGH SCHOOL EXAMS

The requirements regarding final high school credit exams vary across Canada. These exams are monitored by the appropriate ministry of education and are aimed at maintaining a province- or territory-wide standard of performance.

Special education teachers, in conjunction with classroom teachers, have two roles regarding high school exams. On the one hand, they are obligated to help the student prepare for the exam if the student is required to take the exam. On the other hand, they may choose to focus on convincing the student and parents that time could more appropriately be spent on developing living skills rather than on preparing for exams. Information on testing is discussed later in the chapter.

PREPARING FOR POSTSECONDARY TRAINING

Students with disabilities absolutely should aim for postsecondary education if they have the ability and motivation. This is one component of a transition program for students. Postsecondary education does not have to mean attending a university. A community college, vocational-technical school, trade school, or some other form of postsecondary education and training are other possibilities. Teachers, both general and special education, need to inform students about future employment trends and help them select realistic careers with employment potential. The following facts, noted in the report from the Hudson Institute, *Workforce 2000: Work and Workers for the 21st Century* (1987), have several implications for students with disabilities:

1. Higher levels of academic achievement will be required, and very few jobs will be appropriate for individuals deficient in reading, writing, and math.
2. There will be an increase in service industry jobs and a decrease in manufacturing jobs.
3. More than half of new jobs created will require education beyond high school, and more than a third will be filled by university graduates.

PREPARING FOR INDEPENDENT LIVING

Independent living is a realistic goal for the vast majority of individuals with disabilities; however, to live successfully in today's complex, automated world, direct instruction in certain independent living skills may be required. Such instruction is also important in a student's transition program. The following areas may be problematic for persons with disabilities:

- Sexuality
- Managing personal finances
- Developing and maintaining social networks
- Maintaining a home
- Managing food
- Employment
- Transportation
- Self-confidence and self-esteem
- Organization
- Time management

Special education teachers must help students with disabilities achieve competence in these areas. Several curricular guides are available to structure appropriate intervention. Two excellent resources are the Life-Centered Career Education program (Brolin, 1989) and Cronin and Patton's (1993) life skills program. The former presents a comprehensive curriculum for teaching life skills, whereas the latter is a guide for program development. Cronin and Patton (1993) present particularly useful models and strategies for infusing life skills into the regular curriculum. In addition, creative teachers can use community resources, gathering real materials from banks, restaurants, the local court house, and so forth, for developing their own program.

FURTHER READING

For more information on the domains of adulthood, read *The Adult Learner: A Neglected Species* (fourth edition) by M. Knowles, published in 1990 by Gulf Publishers.

FURTHER READING

For more information on the inclusion of life skills into the curriculum, read *Life Skills Instruction for All Students with Special Needs* by M. E. Cronin and J. R. Patton, published in 1993 by Pro-Ed.

TEACHING TIP

For students with disabilities planning to attend university, consult the National Educational Association of Disabled Students for information. Phone 1 (613) 526-8008.

PREPARING FOR EMPLOYMENT

One important goal of education is the employment of graduates at their maximum vocational potential. Teachers need to help students prepare for employment by teaching them the necessary skills for vocational success.

Inclusive vocational and technical programs present a unique opportunity to offer students both a functional curriculum as well as integration with nondisabled peers. These programs can provide appropriate entry into work-study programs, business apprenticeships, and technical and trade school programs.

Teachers must be sure that students with disabilities can communicate their strengths and limitations to persons in postsecondary and future employment settings. Self-advocacy skills will empower individuals to seek employment and independent living opportunities on their own. Woodman (1995) suggests the following tips for teachers to enhance self-advocacy, empowerment, and competence in students with disabilities:

CONSIDER THIS

In what ways can self-advocacy and self-determination affect young adults with disabilities? Should schools help teach self-advocacy skills to adolescents with disabilities? Why or why not?

1. Help students understand their disabilities—not only their weaknesses, but more important, their strengths.
2. Encourage students to develop their strengths into compensatory strategies.
3. Teach students to capitalize on effective study techniques and individualized learning strategies. Model the use of aids such as highlighters, index cards, tape recorders, and spell-checkers.
4. Aid students in developing verbal abilities into a strength.
5. Encourage the development of social skills and self-esteem.
6. Teach students to ask for assistance when it is needed and to know that getting help is not a weakness.
7. Teach [university]-bound students to be aware of the range of services in [university] and to use the support services provided.
8. Instruct students on time-management skills and how to use a calendar to manage their lives.
9. Mentor these students, and give them the gift of confidence; teach them to value themselves and their abilities. (p. 43)

METHODS TO FACILITATE STUDENTS' SUCCESS IN GENERAL EDUCATION CLASSES

TEACHING TIP

For students with intellectual disabilities, consult the local branch of the Canadian Association for Community Living about transition issues.

Students with disabilities traditionally have been placed in general education classrooms for instruction when they were determined to have the requisite academic ability necessary for success. With the advent of the inclusion movement, however, students with disabilities are often placed in such classes for other reasons. For most of these students, there is no need to dilute the curriculum; however, teachers will probably need to make accommodations and students will need to use special learning strategies in order to achieve success.

Accommodations and Adaptations

In most instances, general education teachers are responsible for making accommodations or adaptations to help students with disabilities achieve in the secondary school. This process is hampered by the fact that typically only one fourth to one half of secondary teachers have either taken a class or participated in in-service training in this area (e.g., Bursuck et al., 1996; Struyk et al., 1996; Struyk et al., 1995). Thus, although some studies (Jayanthi et al., 1994; Polloway et al., 1994; Ysseldyke, Thurlow, Wotruba, & Nania, 1990) have indicated that teachers are frequently willing to make adaptations and would find them helpful, many do not have the necessary training. This problem needs to be addressed.

Accommodations can be described as "efforts by the teacher to modify the environment and curriculum in such a way that students with disabilities can achieve success" (Polloway & Smith, 1992, p. 439). Accommodations are usually simple actions that make success for individual students much more likely. For example, allowing visually impaired students to read using Braille is universally accepted. Altering teaching methods or materials for students with other problems is a conceptually similar process. Ysseldyke et al. (1990) found that "altering instruction so that the student can experience success, modifying the curriculum in a number of ways, adjusting the lesson pace to meet a student's individual rate of mastery, and informing students frequently of their instructional needs were viewed as equally desirable by elementary and secondary teachers" (p. 6).

Accommodations should be designed to offer the *least* amount of alteration of the regular programming that will still allow the student to benefit from instruction. This approach is fair to nondisabled students and provides the students with disabilities with a realistic sense of their abilities and limitations. If too many accommodations are made, some students may be set up for failure in a university or other academically demanding environment. Students with too many accommodations may also begin to feel that they bring very little to the class; this assessment can further damage an already fragile self-concept. Modifications used in settings or classes designed to prepare an individual for a future job or postsecondary training program should reflect real conditions present in these future environments.

CROSS-REFERENCE
Review Chapters 3 through 9 to determine specific accommodations suggested for students with different disabilities.

Many different accommodations can be used effectively with students with disabilities. These include altering the way information is presented, the materials used, and the physical environment. Table 13.3 describes sample accommodative strategies.

Teachers can take other actions to accommodate a student's learning difficulties, such as using vocabulary guides, cued text, advance organizers, and a structured overview (Leverett & Diefendorf, 1992). Often, a great deal of a student's grade may be determined by the quality of work on assignments; yet sometimes students with disabilities may not understand an assignment or may lack the ability or time to complete it. Therefore, teachers may need to make some accommodations in the area of assignments. Chalmers (1991) suggests the following:

CONSIDER THIS
Should teachers who refuse to make accommodations for students with different learning needs in their classes be required to do so? What are the consequences for students included in classrooms where teachers refuse to make accommodations?

1. *Preteach vocabulary, and preview major concepts:* Students must have the vocabulary necessary to complete an assignment. If they do not know a particular word, they may not know how to find its definition, causing them to possibly fail the assignment. Similarly, students need to understand the major concepts required to complete the assignment.

2. *State a purpose for reading:* Students need to know *why* they have to do things. Helping them understand the context of the assignment may aid in motivating them.

TABLE 13.3

Sample Accommodative Strategies

Strategy	Description
OUTLINES	Simple course outlines assist pupils in organizing notes and information.
STORY GUIDES	Expanded outlines provide specific information such as assignments and evaluation criteria.
ADVANCE ORGANIZERS	A set of questions or other guides indicate the most important parts of reading assignments.
AUDIOVISUAL AIDS	Overhead projectors, films, film strips, and chalkboard are examples, which can reinforce auditory information and enable students with auditory deficits to access information.
VARYING INSTRUCTIONAL STRATEGIES	Alternative teaching strategies enable students to utilize their most efficient learning style.
SEATING ARRANGEMENT	Place students in locations that minimize problems. Examples: close to front of class for children with auditory and visual problems; away from other children for students with behavior problems; away from windows and doors for those with distractibility problems.
TAPE RECORDERS	Using tape recorders can greatly benefit children with visual problems, memory problems, reading problems, etc. Taped textbooks, tests, and lectures can facilitate learning.

From *Language Instruction for Students with Disabilities* (p. 440), by E. A. Polloway and T. E. C. Smith, 1992, Denver, CO: Love Publishing. Used by permission.

3. *Provide repetition of instruction:* Choral responding, group work, and hands-on activities are examples of providing students with disabilities with the opportunities necessary for learning. One instance of instruction may simply not be sufficient to ensure learning.

4. *Provide clear directions and examples:* "I didn't understand" is a common response from students when they fail. For many students, this response may simply be an effort to evade negative consequences. For many students with disabilities, however, the statement may reflect a true misunderstanding of the assignment. Therefore, teachers need to make every effort to explain all assignments in such a way that they are understandable to all students.

5. *Make time adjustments:* Teachers should individualize the time requirements associated with assignments. Some students may be capable of performing the work successfully, only to become frustrated with time restraints. Teachers should make adjustments for students who simply need more time or who may become overwhelmed by the volume of work required in a particular time period.

6. *Provide feedback:* All individuals need feedback; they need to know how they are doing. For students with disabilities and a history of failure, the feedback, especially positive feedback, is even more critical. Teachers should provide feedback for every assignment as soon as possible after the assignment is completed.

7. *Have students keep an assignment notebook:*   Often, students with disabilities are disorganized; they may need some organization imposed upon them externally. Requiring students to keep an assignment notebook is an example. The assignment notebook not only negates the excuse "I did not have my assignment" or "I lost my assignment," but it also helps some students maintain a semblance of order in their assignments and facilitates their completion of all required work.

8. *Provide an alternate assignment:*   Provide opportunities for students to complete an assignment differently. For example, if a student has difficulty with oral language, the teacher could accept a written book report rather than an oral one. Videotaped, tape-recorded, and oral presentations can be used in conjunction with written presentations.

9. *Allow manipulatives:*   Cue cards, charts, and number lines are examples of manipulatives that can help some students comprehend information. Some students prefer to learn visually, whereas others prefer the auditory mode. Manipulatives can facilitate the learning of all students.

10. *Highlight textbooks:*   Highlight the important facts in textbooks. These books can be passed on to other students with similar reading problems next year. Highlighting material enables students to focus on the important content.

TEACHING TIP
These accommodations are helpful for all students, including those without disabilities who do not need specialized instruction. Many accommodations simply reflect good teaching.

Another important accommodation that teachers can make is the alteration of materials. Ellis and Lenz (1990) describe a way to reduce the content in textbooks. Often, students are capable of reading and understanding, but it takes them significantly longer to read than their peers. Therefore, teachers may wish to reduce the amount of content without altering the nature of the content. When selecting materials, teachers should consider cultural diversity issues. The nearby Diversity Forum feature provides guidelines.

Teachers also have control over how they implement the school curriculum (Carnine, 1991; Simmons, Fuchs, & Fuchs, 1991). They can alter the speed of presentation of the materials, develop ways to inform students that certain information is important, and quickly cover information that is required, but that has limited importance to students. The only limitation in modifying the curriculum is the teacher's creativity. The nearby Inclusion Strategies feature presents creative curricular adaptations. It suggests ways in which students with varied levels of disabilities can be successfully included.

In addition to significant curricular modifications, teachers can make numerous simple adjustments to teach specific information to students:

- Repeat important information several times.
- Write important facts on the board.
- Repeat the same information about a particular topic over several days.
- Distribute handouts that contain only the most important information about a particular topic.

Homework, Grading, and Testing

Homework, grading, and testing stand out as important considerations in students' success within secondary school classrooms. They have become more significant in light of trends toward an increase in academic standards and

DIVERSITY FORUM

Checklist for Evaluating Materials Relative to Cultural Diversity Issues

☑ Are the perspectives and contributions of people from diverse cultural and linguistic groups—both men and women, as well as people with disabilities—included in the curriculum?

☑ Are there activities in the curriculum that will assist students in analyzing the various forms of the mass media for ethnocentrism, sexism, "handicapism," and stereotyping?

☑ Are men and women, diverse cultural/racial groups, and people with varying abilities shown in both active and passive roles?

☑ Are men and women, diverse cultural/racial groups, and people with disabilities shown in positions of power (i.e., the materials do not rely on the mainstream culture's character to achieve goals)?

☑ Do the materials identify strengths possessed by so-called "underachieving" diverse populations? Do they diminish the attention given to deficits, to reinforce positive behaviors that are desired and valued?

☑ Are members of diverse racial/cultural groups, men and women, and people with disabilities shown engaged in a broad range of social and professional activities?

☑ Are members of a particular culture or group depicted as having a range of physi-cal features (e.g., hair color, hair texture, variations in facial characteristics and body build)?

☑ Do the materials represent historical events from the perspectives of the various groups involved or solely from the male, middle-class, and/or Western European perspective?

☑ Are the materials free of ethnocentric or sexist language patterns that may make implications about persons or groups based solely on their culture, race, gender, or disability?

☑ Will students from different ethnic and cultural backgrounds find the materials personally meaningful to their life experiences?

☑ Are a wide variety of culturally different examples, situations, scenarios, and anecdotes used throughout the curriculum design to illustrate major intellectual concepts and principles?

☑ Are culturally diverse content, examples, and experiences comparable in kind, significance, magnitude, and function to those selected from mainstream culture?

From "Toward Defining Programs and Services for Culturally and Linguistically Diverse Learners in Special Education," by S. B. Garcia and D. H. Malkin, 1993, *Teaching Exceptional Children, 26,* p. 35. Used by permission.

accountability in general education classrooms (Hocutt, Martin, & McKinney, 1990; Schumaker & Deshler, 1988). This section explores these problem areas, focusing on adaptations to facilitate student success.

HOMEWORK

Problems in **homework** often become more pronounced at the secondary level. Roderique et al. (1994) report that for school districts with a homework policy, the average amount of homework assigned at the high school level was over 1 hour and 40 minutes per daily assignment, and the frequency was 4.28 nights per week. Struyk et al. (1995) report that 70 percent of the teachers assigned homework two to four times per week; 11 percent assigned it five times per week. The time period needed to complete the homework varied from less than 30 minutes to 1.5 hours per day; 43 percent of the teachers assigned at least

INCLUSION STRATEGIES

Curricular Adaptations: "Real Live Plants"

In a high school biology class, the goal for the class was to learn and understand various aspects of plant characteristics and growth. To ensure that all students had experiences in observing and learning about plants, the teacher and inclusion facilitator planned a visit to a nursery and a project involving growing a variety of plants in the classroom. In addition to the textbook, the team collected a variety of books on plants, such as books with pictures of plants in various stages of development, simple how-to gardening pamphlets, books containing stories about plants, videotapes of plant growth using time-lapse photography, and textbooks containing elementary- to university-level material about plants. Many of the students were responsible for the learning objectives of knowing and understanding types of plants, technical terminology of plant parts, and technical plant life processes such as the photosynthesis process. . . .

During the unit, however, students had varying specific objectives while engaging in group activities with their classmates. For instance, Tammy was unable to read or comprehend the technical words and growth processes of plants. But she still could participate with her classmates . . . by concentrating her studies on learning objectives that included labeling the parts of the plants in everyday language such as the root, stem, and leaves. She also learned along with her peers how to put seeds, cuttings, roots, and young plants into the dirt and was responsible for their care. . . . The teacher asked Tammy questions about plants in everyday language and practical procedures for growing plants during class discussions. In a similar way he asked other students questions about technical terminology and growth processes.

All the students not only learned about plants, but also worked cooperatively together and contributed to the class by growing and nurturing a number of different plants in the classroom for everyone to observe and study. . . . That is, everyone benefited—Tammy learned practical everyday plant parts and how to grow plants, along with picking up a few of the technical words and aspects of the technical growth process by listening to and observing her classmates, while other classmates related the technical terminology, concepts, and ideas they were learning in the biology class to real live plants.

Adapted from "Learning Together in Inclusive Classrooms: What about the Curriculum?" by W. Stainback, S. Stainback, and G. Stefanich, 1996, *Teaching Exceptional Children, 28*, p. 17.

---

30 minutes of homework per night. Given that students typically have 4–6 teachers, assignments represent a significant hurdle for junior and high school students with disabilities. While the amount of homework assigned provides a challenge, the unique difficulties of students with disabilities are underscored by the types of problems they are likely to have. Figure 13.6 lists the highest-rated homework problems of adolescents. Yet each problem carries implicit potential remedies.

Given that students with special needs experience problems with homework, a number of strategies can be pursued. For example, Struyk et al. (1995) found that, with regard to the helpfulness of specific *types of homework*, teachers rated preparation for tests and practice of skills already taught as moderately helpful, whereas enrichment activities and preparation for future class work were seen as least helpful. They rated in-class structures such as checking the level of the students' understanding when beginning an in-class assignment and using a homework assignment sheet or notebook as the most helpful *procedures*. Finally, teachers also rated the helpfulness of specific *adaptations* for students with disabilities. Their responses are summarized in Figure 13.7.

FURTHER READING

For more information on homework and students with disabilities, read "Homework, Grading, and Testing Practices Used by Teachers with Students with and without Disabilities," by L. R. Struyk, M. N. Epstein, W. Bursuck, E. A. Polloway, J. Mc-Coneghy, and K. B. Cole, published in 1995 in volume 69 of *Clearing House* (pp. 50–55).

FIGURE 13.6
Homework Problems of Adolescents with Behavioural Disorders

Note: These are the highest rated problems noted by special educators.

From "A Comparison of Homework Problems of Secondary School Students with Behavior Disorders and Nondisabled Peers," by J. Soderlund, W. Bursuck, E. A. Polloway, and R. A. Foley, 1995, *Journal of Emotional and Behavioral Disorders, 3,* p. 152. Used by permission.

1. Easily distracted by noises or activities of others.
2. Responds poorly when told by parent to correct homework.
3. Procrastinates, puts off doing homework.
4. Fails to complete homework.
5. Whines or complains about homework.
6. Easily frustrated by homework assignment.
7. Must be reminded to sit down and start homework.
8. Fails to bring home assignment and necessary materials.
9. Daydreams or plays with objects during homework session.
10. Refuses to do homework assignment.
11. Takes unusually long time to do homework.
12. Produces messy or sloppy homework.
13. Hurries through homework and makes careless mistakes.

Collaboration among general and special education teachers and parents will encourage successful completion of homework. Teachers should attend to communication problems that can evolve regarding homework. Struyk et al. (1996) cite communication problems as experienced by parents, special education teachers, and general education teachers. Parents' highest-ranked problems were frequency of communication, early initiation of communication, and follow-through. Similar concerns were voiced by special education teachers (i.e., early initiation, frequency, follow-through). Finally, general education teachers cited the following challenges to regular communication: the competing demands of record keeping and paperwork, difficulty in coordinating schedules to set up time to talk with parents, and the large number of students with disabilities in their classes.

Certain policies and procedures can increase students' success with homework. The following ideas have proved effective for general education teachers:

■ Schedule after-school sessions at which students can get extra help on their homework.
■ Provide peer tutoring programs that concentrate on homework.
■ Provide sufficient study hall time during school hours for students to complete their homework.
■ Use community volunteers to assist students in completing homework. (Epstein et al., 1996)

FIGURE 13.7
Homework Adaptations for Adolescents with Disabilities

Note: Items are ranked from most helpful to least helpful.

From "Homework, Grading, and Testing Practices Used by Teachers with Students with and without Disabilities," by L. R. Struyk, M. H. Epstein, W. Bursuck, E. A. Polloway, J. McConeghy, and K. B. Cole, 1995, *The Clearing House, 69,* p. 52. Used by permission.

1. Provide additional teacher assistance.
2. Check more frequently with student about assignments and expectations.
3. Provide a peer tutor for assistance.
4. Allow alternative response formats (e.g., oral or other than written).
5. Provide auxiliary learning aids (e.g., calculator, computer).
6. Adjust length of assignment.
7. Assign work that student can do independently.
8. Provide a study group.
9. Provide extra credit opportunities.
10. Evaluate based on effort, not on performance.
11. Adjust (i.e., lower) evaluation standards.
12. Adjust due dates.
13. Give fewer assignments.

Homework Help on the Internet

Sometimes the questions that students have are not always going to arise during school hours. Wouldn't it be nice for students to have help available during evening hours when many are *doing* their homework? The Internet to the rescue! There are dozens of bulletin boards, chat rooms, and forums that give students the opportunity to ask for help with any number of school-related homework problems. Many of these services have *real teachers online* to answer student homework questions. Commercial service providers often recruit teachers to become online electronic tutors. Teachers are usually reimbursed for their time with free online time with the service provider. Because these tutors are real professionals, adults can worry less about the students who just want easy answers. Online tutors will work through your students' questions, offering tips and explaining procedures—not just doling out answers. Below are listed a few of the places where homework help may be found.

- America Online: Academic Assistance Center. Search word—"homework." Live chat with real teachers between 5:00 p.m. and 1:00 a.m. every day [EST]. In addition to this service, AOL provides a teacher paging service. Search word—"teacher pager." Type in your grade level, your questions, and

click send. E-mail answers are guaranteed within 48 hours.

Homework help is also available for university students if your work is research based. Once in the AAC, enter "research."

- Any Internet Source: Teacher paging on the Internet or with any CSP. Enter this address: homework24@aol.com.

- Compuserve: See the Student's Forum. Search word—"go stufo."

- GEnie: Access the Computer Assisted Learning Center. Homework questions are posted by subject. Real-time chat is available Mondays and Wednesdays, 9:00 P.M.–10:00 P.M. [EST] and Tuesdays and Thursdays, 10:00 P.M.–11:00 P.M. [EST].

- Prodigy: Access the Education Bulletin Board or Homework Helper. Helper is a premium service, and an extra charge is assigned for services rendered.

- For homework help specific to Canada: visit **www.altavista.canada.com** then type in "homework help" and the subject name.

Adapted from *Quick Guide for the Internet for Educators* (pp. 33–34), by J. D. Rivard, 1997, Boston: Allyn & Bacon. Used by permission.

Students can also get help with their homework through the Internet. Secondary teachers need to become familiar with this new source of support and make this information available to students. The nearby Technology Today feature describes homework help available on the Internet.

GRADING

The challenges of inclusion of adolescents with disabilities are perhaps most clearly reflected in the area of grading. The extant research in this area has not shown positive results. For example, Zigmond and her associates (Donahue & Zigmond, 1990; Zigmond, Levin, & Laurie, 1985) report that approximately 60 percent to 75 percent of high school students with learning disabilities received passing grades in their general education classes, but they consistently received below-average grade-point averages (GPAs) (i.e., an overall GPA of 0.99 on a 4.0 scale, or D work). These patterns seem to reflect a persistent lack of academic suc-

CONSIDER THIS

Should school policies on homework be altered to increase the likelihood of success for students with disabilities, or should these students be required to follow a rigid policy set for all students? Why or why not?

CONSIDER THIS

If alternative grading requirements are used with students with disabilities, should these students be eligible for the honour roll and honours programs? Why or why not?

cess, particularly as compared to students without disabilities (e.g., Wood, Bennett, Wood, & Bennett, 1990). Similarly, Valdes, Williamson, and Wagner (1990) report that 60.2 percent of high school students with disabilities had averages of C+ or lower, with a subset of 35.4 percent receiving averages below the C– level. Furthermore, these researchers note that more than one third of students enrolled in graded general education classes had at least one failing grade.

In researching classroom report card practices, Struyk et al. (1995) found that, in determining grades, teachers weighed tests and quizzes highest, and in-class work and homework second highest. Teachers reported that checklists indicating level of competence and skills, supplemented by written comments, were the most helpful apparatus for reporting grades for students with disabilities.

Teachers' responses for grading adaptations for students with disabilities are summarized in Figure 13.8. This list provides a basis for designing grading practices that help adolescents with disabilities succeed in school. In addition, teachers should carefully evaluate the fairness of their grading patterns for students with special needs.

TESTING

The inclusion movement has raised concerns regarding how students with special needs will be assessed. Although some adaptations are being made in standardized instruments, most adaptations for students with disabilities are made at the classroom level (Thurlow, Ysseldyke, & Silverstein, 1993).

Simple adaptations can make the difference between taking a test successfully or poorly. For example, reading a test to a student who is a very poor reader gives the student a chance to display knowledge or skills. If such students have to read the questions themselves, test results will reflect students' poor reading skills and fail to assess knowledge of a particular content area. Teachers can address this situation in the following ways:

- Have another student read the test to the student.
- Have the special education teacher or aide read the test to the student.
- Give the student additional time to complete the test.
- Reword the test to include only words that are within the student's reading vocabulary.

FIGURE 13.8

Grading Adaptations for Adolescents with Disabilities

Note: Items are ranked from most to least helpful.

From "Homework, Grading, and Testing Practices Used by Teachers with Students with and without Disabilities," by L. R. Struyk, M. H. Epstein, W. Bursuck, E. A. Polloway, J. McConeghy, and K. B. Cole, 1995, *The Clearing House, 69,* p. 53. Used by permission.

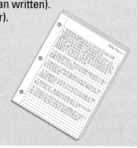

1. Provide additional teacher assistance.
2. Check more frequently with student about assignments and expectations.
3. Provide a peer tutor for assistance.
4. Allow alternative response formats (e.g., oral or other than written).
5. Provide auxiliary learning aids (e.g., calculator, computer).
6. Adjust length of assignment.
7. Assign work that student can do independently.
8. Provide a study group.
9. Provide extra credit opportunities.
10. Evaluate based on effort, not on performance.
11. Adjust (i.e., lower) evaluation standards.
12. Adjust due dates.
13. Give fewer assignments.

A full consideration of adaptations in **testing**, however, extends beyond the consideration of reading ability. Smith et al. (1993) list ways in which teachers can make tests more accessible to students: generous spacing between items on the pages, adequate space allowed for responses, generous margins, readability of text, appropriate test length, logical organization, and clear instructions. The following examples are techniques to adapt measurement instruments:

CROSS-REFERENCE
Review Chapters 3 through 9, and determine specific testing adaptations that might be necessary with students with different types of disabilities.

- Using information about performance outside of school in making evaluations
- Administering frequent short quizzes throughout the course, rather than a few long tests
- Dividing tests or tasks into smaller, simpler sections or steps
- Developing practice items or pretest trials using the same response format as the test (teaching students how to respond), which may help reduce a student's fear of evaluation
- Considering the appropriateness of the instrument or procedure in terms of age or maturity
- Giving open-book tests
- Reducing the number of test items or removing items that require more abstract reasoning or have high levels of difficulty
- Using different levels of questions for different students (i.e., test items for low-functioning children should be at a more concrete level)
- Having a student develop a product or packet of materials that show knowledge and understanding of the content of a unit
- Providing alternative projects or assignments
- Having peers administer tests
- Allowing students to make up tests
- Videotaping a student performing a task and then playing it back to him or her to show skills learned and areas needing improvement
- Videotaping a model performing a task correctly, then videotaping the student completing the task, finally allowing the student to watch his or her performance on videotape to compare it to the performance of the model
- Using a panel of students to evaluate one another on task performance
- Allowing students to type answers
- Allowing small groups to work together on a task to be evaluated (such as a project or test)
- Using short written or verbal measures on a daily or weekly basis to provide more feedback on student progress
- Increasing the amount of time allowed to complete the test, to compensate for slower reading, writing, or comprehension
- Altering the presentation (written, oral, visual) of tests or tasks to be evaluated
- Altering the types of responses to match a student's strengths (written, oral, short answer, or simple marking)
- Having a student review the course or unit content verbally so that he or she is not limited to test item recall
- Limiting the number of formal tests by using checklists to observe and record learning
- Assessing participation in discussions as an indicator of mastery of content
- Giving extra credit for correction of mistakes (Center for Innovations in Special Education, 1990–1991, pp. 5–6)

Testing adaptations raise questions of treatment acceptability. Relative to this concern, Struyk et al. (1995) report that adaptations commonly used for

CROSS-REFERENCE

Refer to Chapter 12 for information on treatment acceptability.

students *without* disabilities include extending the time students have for completing the test (92 percent), giving feedback to individual students during the test (94 percent), and allowing students to take open-book or open-notes tests (96 percent). Since these techniques already are commonly in use, they should be considered as the initial adaptation options for students with disabilities. General education teachers' preferences in testing adaptations for adolescent students with disabilities are summarized in Figure 13.9.

For students to perform successfully on tests, they will need to learn individual test-taking and organizational strategies, which are often difficult for students with disabilities (Scruggs & Mastropieri, 1988). Such strategies are typically subsumed within the area of study skills, discussed in the next section.

Study Skills and Learning Strategies

Teachers' accommodations are insufficient to guarantee that students with special needs will be successful. Students must develop their own skills and strategies to help them overcome, or compensate for, a disability. Understanding how to use study skills will greatly enhance their chances for being successful in future academic, vocational, or social activities. Classroom teachers can help students by helping them acquire a repertoire of study skills.

Study skills can be defined as the "tools used to acquire, record, locate, organize, synthesize, and remember information effectively and efficiently" (Hoover, 1988, p. 10). Examples of study skills include the following:

- Note taking
- Studying for tests
- Reading at a good pace
- Remembering information

FIGURE 13.9
Testing Adaptations for Adolescents with Disabilities

Note: Items are ranked from most to least helpful.

From "Homework, Grading, and Testing Practices Used by Teachers with Students with and without Disabilities," by L. R. Struyk, M. H. Epstein, W. Bursuck, E. A. Polloway, J. McConeghy, and K. B. Cole, 1995, *The Clearing House, 69,* p. 54. Used by permission.

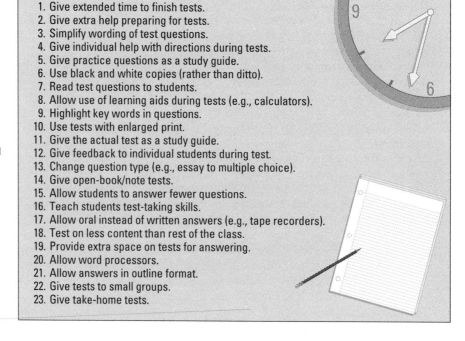

1. Give extended time to finish tests.
2. Give extra help preparing for tests.
3. Simplify wording of test questions.
4. Give individual help with directions during tests.
5. Give practice questions as a study guide.
6. Use black and white copies (rather than ditto).
7. Read test questions to students.
8. Allow use of learning aids during tests (e.g., calculators).
9. Highlight key words in questions.
10. Use tests with enlarged print.
11. Give the actual test as a study guide.
12. Give feedback to individual students during test.
13. Change question type (e.g., essay to multiple choice).
14. Give open-book/note tests.
15. Allow students to answer fewer questions.
16. Teach students test-taking skills.
17. Allow oral instead of written answers (e.g., tape recorders).
18. Test on less content than rest of the class.
19. Provide extra space on tests for answering.
20. Allow word processors.
21. Allow answers in outline format.
22. Give tests to small groups.
23. Give take-home tests.

- Listening
- Managing behaviour and time

Many students have an innate ability in these areas. For example, some students are good readers, adept at comprehension and able to read quickly; other students find it easy to memorize facts. These students may not need instruction in study skills. For other students, however, study skills represent an "invisible curriculum" that must be taught directly if they are to be successful.

Hoover and Patton (1995) note the significance of study skills for learning. For example, the study skill of listening is critical in most educational settings because teachers provide so much information verbally. If students are not able to attend to auditory information, they will miss a great deal of content. Table 13.4 summarizes key study skills and their significance for learning.

There are many ways to teach study skills. For example, in the area of reading comprehension, teachers might teach students to underline facts that are important, pay attention to margin notes, and use SQ3R (i.e., Survey-Question-Read-Recite-Review) (see the later discussion on Multipass). With this technique, students can focus their attention by asking themselves questions and trying to answer them during the reading process. To teach organizational skills relative to assignments, class materials, and time management, teachers can use logs and charts, colour coding of materials, and guided notes (Shields & Heron, 1989).

Closely related to study skills are *learning strategies*—ways to use active learning to acquire and use new information and solve problems ("learning to learn"). Teachers should be alert to ways to teach content and ways to learn and use the content. This dual focus is particularly important in areas such as

FURTHER READING

For more information on study skills, read the 1989 special issue of *Academic Therapy*, volume 24, issue 4, available from Pro-Ed.

Students with special needs often require instruction in study skills.

> ### TABLE 13.4
>
> ## Study Skills and Their Significance for Learning
>
> | Study Skill | Significance for Learning |
> | --- | --- |
> | **READING RATE** | Rates vary with type and length of reading materials; students need to adjust rate to content. |
> | **LISTENING** | Ability to listen is critical in most educational tasks and throughout life. |
> | **NOTE TAKING/OUTLINING** | Ability to take notes and develop outlines is critical in content courses and essential for future study. |
> | **REPORT WRITING** | Written reports are frequently required in content courses. |
> | **ORAL PRESENTATIONS** | Some teachers require extensive oral reporting. |
> | **GRAPHIC AIDS** | Visual aids can help students who have reading deficits understand complex material. |
> | **TEST TAKING** | Students must be able to do well on tests if they are to succeed in content courses. |
> | **REFERENCE MATERIAL/ DICTIONARY USAGE** | Using reference materials makes learners more independent. |
> | **TIME MANAGEMENT** | Ability to manage and allocate time is critical for success in secondary settings. |
> | **SELF-MANAGEMENT OF BEHAVIOUR** | Self-management assists students in assuming responsibility and leads to independence. |
>
> Adapted from *Teaching Students with Learning Problems to Use Study Skills: A Teacher's Guide* (p. 7), by J. J. Hoover and J. R. Patton, 1995, Austin, TX: Pro-Ed.

reading comprehension, error monitoring in writing, problem solving in math, and test preparation. A comprehensive source on numerous strategies for learning (and their use) is provided by Deshler, Ellis, and Lenz (1996). Several sample strategies are discussed in the following paragraphs.

The **COPS** strategy (Schumaker et al., 1981) is an error-monitoring strategy for writing. The acronym stands for four tasks:

C   **C**apitalization
O   **O**verall appearance (e.g., neatness, appropriate margins)
P   **P**unctuation
S   **S**pelling

CONSIDER THIS
What would it be like if all students were provided with instructional strategies that made them more effective learners? How would this affect the number and types of children needing special education?

With this strategy, students review their initial drafts of papers, giving specific attention to these four types of errors. The strategy has proved effective for use with students with learning problems at the upper elementary, junior high, and secondary school levels (Shannon & Polloway, 1993).

Multipass (Schumaker, Deshler, Alley, & Denton, 1982) is a reading comprehension and study strategy originally derived from SQ3R. The term *multipass* refers to the fact that students are taught to make three passes through content reading material. In the *survey* pass, the student reviews, among other things, the title, bold headings, and the summary or conclusion. The *size-up* pass directs students to review the comprehension questions at the end of the chapter. The *sort-out* pass allows students to organize the information in the chapter in a way that helps them form responses to the comprehension questions.

Many learning strategies are best taught in a sequence such as this one:

1. Determine how the skill is currently being used.
2. Teach any preskills that are necessary.
3. Teach the specific study skill.
4. Provide ample opportunity for practice.
5. Help students generalize the skill to other situations. (Beirne-Smith, 1989)

Efforts to validate the use of specific strategies within inclusive classrooms continue. An exciting aspect of instruction in strategies is its potential to benefit students with and without disabilities (Fisher, Schumaker, & Deshler, 1995).

SUMMARY

- Important differences exist between elementary and secondary settings in terms of organizational structure, curriculum, and learner characteristics.

- From a curricular perspective, integrating students with disabilities into general classes is more challenging at the secondary level than at the elementary level.

- The period of adolescence adds to the problems experienced by students with disabilities.

- Curricular options for students at the secondary level with particular relevance for students with disabilities include basic skills, social skills, tutoring, learning strategies, vocational skills, and life skills.

- Future-based assessment offers one method for developing programs for adolescents with disabilities.

- Classroom teachers and special education teachers must collaborate to ensure effective secondary school programs.

- Special education teachers must help prepare students for academic content classes.

- Transition to the secondary level is a major endeavour for students with disabilities.

- Accommodations are changes that teachers can make to facilitate the success of students with disabilities.

- Specific challenges for successful inclusion occur in the areas of homework, grading, and testing.

- Study skills are skills that students with disabilities can use to help them achieve success in general and special education classes.

- Learning strategies enable students to achieve independence as they "learn how to learn."

RESOURCES

Emmer, E. T., Everston, C. M., Clements, B. S., & Worsham, M. E. (1999). *Classroom Management for Secondary Teachers*. 5th ed. Toronto: Allyn & Bacon.

This small book that deals specifically with management issues at the high school level is an invaluable tool for all secondary teachers.

Fisher, D. B., Sax, C., and Pumpian, I. (1999). *Inclusive High Schools: Learning from Contemporary Classrooms*. Baltimore, MD: Brookes Publishing Company.

Since so many inclusive resources focus on the elementary level, this book makes a particularly important contribution. It provides a framework for developing inclusive high schools, illustrated by detailed accounts of high schools that have struggled, strategized, and ultimately achieved success in including all students.

WEBLINKS

Classroom Resources
classroomresources.com
This excellent Canadian Web site offers a variety of classroom resources with Canadian content and representation of Canadian student diversity. It is a must visit for all teachers to see (and download) the latest Canadian Content flyer which reviews in detail different books and classroom resources and states their uses in curriculum design. Such support will help teachers to include students from all backgrounds in their daily curricula.

School Psychology Resource
www.bcpl.net/~sandyste/school_psych.html
This Web site for school psychologists, educators, and parents covers different exceptionalities, special education procedures (e.g., sample IEPs), and information on all topics relevant to psychology in the schools such as violence, child abuse, suicide, and parent collaboration. Although American based, it has excellent information and materials relevant to Canadian teachers.

The Education Planet—The Education Web Guide
Educationplanet.com
A highly interesting and rewarding resource, this search engine covers all education-relevant sites, providing access to lesson plans, videos, manuals, curriculum materials, and much more. If you want to find specifically Canadian material, you can limit searches to Canadian sources.

Teachers.net
Teachers.net
As a huge U.S. Web site, Teachers.net covers a variety of topics of interest to teachers, providing curriculum suggestions, resources, and chat rooms about different education issues. It also has subject-specific listings of chatboards where ideas are posted and shared. Many resources are available through this Web site for elementary and secondary teachers.

Canadian.Teachers.net
canadian.teachers.net/
Derived from Teachers.net, this site provides a specifically Canadian forum with chat rooms, job postings, catalogues, information, professional development with guest speakers, and listings of related sites.

CHAPTER FOURTEEN

CHAPTER OBJECTIVES

- To identify changes in the Canadian family structure that have implications for the public schools of the first decade of the new millennium

- To discuss the particular challenges experienced by parents of individuals with disabilities

- To discuss effective ways to involve the family in education programs

- To list principles of effective communication with parents

- To delineate support roles that parents and family members can play

Working with Families of Students with Disabilities

As advocates for all children, teachers are frequently confronted with difficult family situations in which their assistance is requested and needed. Place yourself in the position of Jody Rinaldi, a primary school educator, who was approached by Josh and Sally Williams with the following concern.

"One month ago, Josh and I were told by our family doctor that our four-year-old daughter, Susie, is not developing as she should be. Her language is deficient and her learning is slow. This problem happened because of an accident. Our doctor suggested that Susie may eventually be identified as having an intellectual disability. Needless to say, this information came to us as a total shock. Since we heard it, we have gone over and over how this could have happened, why this happened, and what we should do about it.

"We haven't really adjusted to the news that our doctor gave us, and I guess we both would admit that our concerns and our disappointments have been a real problem for us. Our biggest worry now is, what lies ahead?

"Some of my 'friends' have said that in the past, a child like our Susie might have been sent away for institutional care. Certainly, we would never consider that, but still we don't know what we can do. Naturally, we would be very grateful for any assistance or information that can help us deal with our concerns and, most important, can help Susie. Thank you very much."

1. Analyze Josh and Sally's current and potential feelings, and discuss their possible reactions upon learning that their child has a disability.

2. What advice, recommendations, and assistance would you provide for these two concerned parents?

3. What would you convey to them about the advantages and challenges of inclusive school programs for their daughter?

INTRODUCTION

Since the 1980s, there has been a significant change in the provision of educational services to students with disabilities: the increased involvement of parents and family. In the past, schools frequently did not encourage parents to participate in the education of their children. As a result, parents were often left out of the decision-making process leading to interventions. Often, they were not even informed of the programs that the school was implementing for their children. Some school personnel did make significant efforts to include parents in the education of their children; others did little or nothing to promote this. Given the numerous concerns that parents may have and the value of parental involvement in the schools, the move to encourage parental involvement is welcome.

Legislation and parental advocacy have established the current high level of parental involvement in the education of students with disabilities. Virtually all school personnel now acknowledge the merit of having parents actively participate in the educational process, including identification, referral, assessment, program planning, and program implementation. Comprehensive programs of family involvement begin when children are young and continue until transition into adulthood. The natural challenge of preparation ultimately for adulthood is aptly stated by the parent of a high school senior:

> I feel my job isn't done. Tell that to a 17-year-old boy who thinks he's adult. I want him to fly—with a parachute. Some of this 'chute comes from school, some from home (Whitney-Thomas & Hanley-Maxwell, 1996, p. 75).

The challenge for educators is to consider diverse, effective ways to involve families in the education of children with disabilities. As an overview, consider the six methods proposed by Dunst, Johanson, Trivette, and Hamby (1991):

- Enhancing a sense of community among the families
- Mobilizing resources and supports
- Sharing responsibility and collaboration
- Protecting family integrity
- Strengthening family functioning
- Implementing proactive human service practices

CROSS-REFERENCE

See Chapter 6 to review how family supports have been provided in the field of intellectual disabilities.

Table 14.1 describes each of these six categories and provides examples of **family support** principles associated with each.

Some families will become more involved with the education of their child than others. For example, Haring, Lovett, and Saren (1991) reported that 23 percent of their survey respondents said they had no involvement in the education of their children in public school special education programs, 43 percent said they were somewhat involved, and only 34 percent said they were actively involved in their children's special education programs. School personnel need to encourage those parents who are active in their children's education to maintain their commitment while developing strategies to increase the active role of other parents.

TABLE 14.1

Major Categories and Examples of Family Support Principles

Category/Characteristic	Examples of Principles
1. ENHANCING A SENSE OF COMMUNITY Promoting the coming together of people around shared values and common needs in ways that create mutually beneficial interdependencies	• Interventions should focus on the building of inter-dependencies between members of the community and the family unit. • Interventions should emphasize the common needs and supports of all people and base intervention actions on those commonalities.
2. MOBILIZING RESOURCES AND SUPPORTS Building support systems that enhance the flow of resources in ways that assist families with parenting responsibilities	• Interventions should focus on building and strengthening informal support networks for families rather than depending solely on professionals' support systems. • Resources and supports should be made available to families in ways that are flexible, individualized, and responsive to the needs of the entire family unit.
3. SHARED RESPONSIBILITY AND COLLABORATION Sharing of ideas and skills by parents and professionals in ways that build and strengthen collaborative arrangements	• Interventions should employ partnerships between parents and professionals as a primary mechanism for supporting and strengthening family functioning. • Resources and support mobilization interactions between families and service providers should be based on mutual respect and sharing of unbiased information.
4. PROTECTING FAMILY INTEGRITY Respecting the family's beliefs and values and protecting the family from intrusion upon its beliefs by outsiders	• Resources and supports should be provided to families in ways that encourage, develop, and maintain healthy, stable relationships among all family members. • Interventions should be conducted in ways that accept, value, and protect a family's personal and cultural values and beliefs.
5. STRENGTHENING FAMILY FUNCTIONING Promoting the capabilities and competencies of families necessary to mobilize resources and perform parenting responsibilities in ways that have empowering consequences	• Interventions should build on family strengths rather than correct weaknesses or deficits as a primary way of supporting and strengthening family functioning. • Resources and supports should be made available to families in ways that maximize the family's control over and decision-making power regarding services they receive.
6. PROACTIVE HUMAN SERVICE PRACTICES Adoption of consumer-driven human service-delivery models and practices that support and strengthen family functioning	• Service-delivery programs should employ promotion rather than treatment approaches as the framework for strengthening family functioning. • Resource and support mobilization should be cosumer-driven rather than service provider–driven or profession-ally prescribed.

From "Family-Oriented Early Intervention Policies and Practices: Family-Centered or Not?" by C. J. Dunst, C. Johanson, C. M. Trivette, and D. Hamby, 1991, *Exceptional Children, 58*, p. 117. Copyright 1991 by the Council for Exceptional Children. Reprinted by permission.

Family participation can and should occur in many areas. These include assessment and IEP development, parent groups, observation of the student in the school setting, and communication with educators. Of these areas, participation in developing the IEP process occurs the most frequently. In a study of 99 families with children with disabilities, 85 families reported that their level of participation in their child's IEP development was either very high or somewhat high. Only 10 families indicated little participation. Sixty-seven of the

CONSIDER THIS

Not unexpectedly, the degree of parental participation in the IEP process is correlated with socioeconomic level. Why do you think this is the case?

Technology Resources for Families

Technology vastly expands families' access to information. The National Rehabilitation Information Center (NARIC) and ABLEDATA Data Base of Assistive Technology (800-346-2742) will conduct computer searches for families concerning products and devices, disability organizations, and funding opportunities. NARIC has more than 20,000 products on its service list, and users can call the electronic bulletin boards to search the database, get messages, and download fact sheets. (At this time the computer dial is 301-589-3563.) Another option for accessing the database is through CD-ROM. NARIC has a directory of national information sources on disabilities, including 42 databases, 700 organizations, and more than 100 resource directories.

Computer list servers provide new and immediate access to information for families. All list servers have unique characteristics. For example, a recent check of the autism list server revealed 30 to 40 daily messages on topics such as teenagers, toilet training, the use of aversive intervention, inclusive education, research possibilities, sign language, and siblings.

Another technology resource is operated by the U.S. Department of Education, Office of Educational Research and Innovation (OERI). Its National Library of Education maintains an electronic repository of education information and provides public access through electronic networks. You can call 202-219-1547 or access the library through e-mail at gopheradm@inet.ed.gov.

Note: Although this information is provided through U.S. sources, it is both available and beneficial to Canadian parents as well.

From *Families, Professionals, and Exceptionality* (pp. 186–187), by A. P. Turnbull and H. R. Turnbull, 1997, Columbus, OH: Merrill. Used by permission.

families said they had some level or high levels of participation in the assessment process, and 52 families indicated they took part in parent groups at some or at high levels (Meyers & Blacher, 1987).

Thus, some families have a very active role in their child's special educational program, whereas others have limited involvement. Schools meet the letter of the law by simply inviting parental participation. However, school personnel should develop strategies to facilitate it. Although some parents create challenges for the school because of their intense level of involvement, for the most part educational programs are greatly strengthened by parental support. This chapter provides perspectives on the family and identifies strategies for enhancing family involvement.

Families are playing a bigger part in special programs for their children. Some families are learning more about special education programs and particular types of disabilities through technology. The Internet offers a wide variety of information about disabilities, educational programs, and how to provide supports for individuals at home. The nearby Technology Today feature provides information on families and technology access.

THE FAMILY

The viewpoint of what constitutes a **family** has changed dramatically in recent decades. Traditionally, a family has been described as a group of individuals who live together that includes a mother, a father, and one or more children. However, this stereotypical picture has been challenged. The **nuclear family** with stay-at-home mother and wage earner father is no longer the typical family structure. Many, perhaps most, families do not resemble this model. Thus the "Leave It to Beaver" or "Ozzie and Harriet" family of the 1950s has given way to the diversity of today's family (Hanson & Carta, 1996).

Currently, numerous family constellations exist. For example, a large number of families are single-parent families, most frequently with father absent. In Canada in 1996, 14.5 percent of families were single-parent families, 83 percent of those female (Statistics Canada, 1996). Some single-parent families are headed by a father, and, in some cases, children live with one or more of their grandparents, without either mother or father present. Other families consist of a husband and wife without children. And, although not as common as they once were, some families constitute extended family units, with grandmother or grandfather living with the parents and child. Some children also live in foster homes, in which the foster parents fill all legal roles as birth parents would. Finally, regardless of individual opinions on this issue, school personnel must also be able to interact with families composed of parents living in gay or lesbian relationships.

The realities of the early 21st century pose further challenges to the family: the increase in both younger and older parents, the increase of families living below the poverty line, the realities of substance abuse, new considerations with regard to HIV/AIDs within the family, the permeation of violence throughout society, and the move away from residential care for children with serious support needs (see Agosta & Melda, 1996; Hanson & Carta, 1996; Lesar, Gerber, & Semmel, 1996; Simpson, 1996). There may never have been a time when family changes and challenges have more clearly called for understanding and support.

Although undergoing major changes in structure, the family remains the basic unit of our society. It is a dynamic, evolving social force. Despite the debate about the current role of families and their composition, the family remains the key ingredient in a child's life. Teachers must be sensitive to the background of the family—see the nearby Diversity Forum feature for a discussion of family values and effective strategies. In addition, it is critical that school personnel remember that students' parents, or grandparents when they are in the role of parents, should take part in educational programs regardless of the specific composition of the family. School personnel must put aside any personal feelings they may have about various lifestyles and work with students' families to develop and implement the best possible programs for the students. School personnel must include the family in all key decisions affecting children—both with special needs and those without.

Families and Children with Disabilities

The birth of any child results in changes in family structure and dynamics. Obviously, a first child changes the lives of the mother and father, but subsequent births also affect the dynamics of the family unit, including finances, amount and quality of time parents can devote to specific children, relationship between the husband and wife, and future family goals. The birth of a child with a disability exacerbates the challenges that such changes bring. For example,

FURTHER READING

For more information on the makeup of today's families, read *Addressing the Challenges of Families with Multiple Risks* by M. J. Hanson and J. J. Carta, published in 1996 in volume 62 of *Exceptional Children* (pp. 201–211).

FURTHER READING

For an extensive discussion of the historical role of families, read Chapter 1 in A. P. Turnbull and H. R. Turnbull's *Families, Professionals, and Exceptionality*, published by Merrill in 1997.

Developing Strategies Sensitive to Diverse Cultures

Western Culture/Values	Family Culture/Values	Strategies for Working with Families
EFFICIENCY		
Value wise use of time; quality of task may be secondary	Efficient use of time not as important; OK to be late	Avoid scheduling parent-teacher conferences too closely together.
Direct approach; get right to the subject; solve problem	Indirect approach; discuss related issues; "talk story"	Avoid "quick fix"; respect quality of the interaction.
Tend to rush, fast paced	More slowly paced, need time to think	Slow pace of meetings with parents; allow "thinking time."
INDEPENDENCE		
Prefer to make own decisions	Interdependence, decisions are made as a family; natural family supports in place	Encourage extended family involvement; work with extended family members.
Individual right to privacy of feelings	Strong family ties; open sharing of personal feelings; actions of individual reflect on entire family	Respect sense of family; identify cultural attitudes or religious beliefs toward disabilities.
Parental responsibility for raising child	Extended family, shared responsibility of childrearing	Identify authority figures; respect deference to authority; allow parents time to take decision to others.
EQUITY		
Parents are equal partners in team	Perceive professionals as "above" family	Professionals need to be aware of and "read" parent perceptions; recognize parents as experts.
Prefer active parent involvement (e.g., input at meetings, work with child at home)	Accept teachers' opinion; teachers are experts	Decrease control of interaction; involve parents in planning, implementing, and monitoring programs.
Information sharing	Passive reception of information	Elicit wants, hopes, and concerns of parents; information sharing versus information giving and question asking; use parent suggestions when possible; provide timely feedback.
Democratic family decision making	Matriarchal or patriarchal family structures	Respect lines of authority

From "Parent and Professional Partnerships in Special Education: Multicultural Considerations," by T. W. Sileo, A. P. Sileo, and M. A. Prater, 1996, *Intervention in School and Clinic, 31*, p. 152. Used by permission.

CONSIDER THIS

What are some problems faced by families following the birth of a child with a disability (or the identification of a child with a disability)?

the almost immediate financial and emotional impact can create major problems for all family members, including parents and siblings.

When a child with a disability becomes a member of the family, whether through birth, adoption, or later onset of the disability, the entire family must make adjustments. Critical problems that may face families of children with serious disabilities include the following:

- Stressful medical treatment, surgery, or hospitalization that may occur repeatedly and for extended periods
- Heavy expenses and financial burdens beyond medical costs, incurred by needs such as special foods and equipment
- Frightening, energy-draining, often recurring crises, as when the child stops breathing or experiences a seizure
- Transportation problems
- Babysitting needs for the other children
- Time away from jobs to get the child to consultation and treatment appointments
- Lack of affordable child care
- Continuous day-and-night demands on parents to provide routine but difficult caregiving tasks (for example, it may take an hour or more, five to six times during a 24-hour period, to feed a child with a severe cleft palate condition)
- Constant fatigue, lack of sleep, and little or no time to meet the needs of other family members
- Little or no opportunity for recreational or leisure activities
- Difficulty (and additional expense) of locating babysitters qualified to care for a child with a disability
- Lack of respite care facilities
- Jealousy or feelings of rejection among brothers and sisters, who may feel the special child gets *all* the family's attention and resources
- Marital problems arising from finances, fatigue, differences about management of the child's disability, or feelings of rejection by husband or wife that he or she is being passed over in favour of the child (adapted from Allen, 1992, p. 321)

In addition to these problems, a primary difficulty is accepting and understanding the child and the disability. Understanding a diagnosis and its implications is critical to a family's acceptance of the child. Parents with a limited understanding of a diagnosis will probably have difficulty in developing realistic expectations of the child, possibly creating major problems between the child and other family members. For example, parents might not understand the nature of a learning disability and therefore accuse the child of being lazy and not trying. Parents who may overlook the potential of a child with an intellectual disability might develop low expectations that will limit the child's success. For example, parents of adolescents might not support a school work program for their son or daughter because they believe that adults with intellectual disabilities are not capable of holding a job.

Families who discover that a child has a disability may react in a variety of ways. Their responses have been compared to Elizabeth Kübler-Ross's stages of grief related to death and dying. Although reactions can differ, they frequently include these stages:

- Shock, disbelief, and denial
- Anger and resentment
- Bargaining
- Depression and discouragement
- Acceptance (Cook, Tessier, & Klein, 1992)

Although it cannot be assumed that all or even most parents experience these particular stages, many must deal with complicated emotions, often experienced

FURTHER READING

For stories by, and about, families with children with disabilities, visit the Lanark County Chapter of the Ontario Association for Families of Children with Communication Disorders Web site at **www.cyberus.ca/ oafccd/**

CROSS-REFERENCE

Review Chapters 3–9, which discuss specific disabilities that can affect children. Then reflect on how different types of problems can cause different reactions.

as a "bombardment of feelings" that may recur over many years (Hilton, 1990). Sileo, Sileo, and Prater (1996) refer to the "shattering of dreams" that underlies many of the feelings. School personnel, including teachers, school social workers, counsellors, and administrators, need to be aware of these dynamics and be prepared to deal with family members who are experiencing various feelings. For example, when parents say that they feel guilt after learning that their child has a disability, school personnel should listen with acceptance to the parents and help them understand the nature of the disability and the fact that they are not responsible for it. Figure 14.1 lists possible parental reactions and interventions that schools can use to help family members.

Switzer (1985) describes a seminar model to help parents adjust to the fact that their child has a disability. The first two seminars focus on definitions. During these sessions, information is provided to help parents understand disabilities and their impact on their children. The third session addresses life at home and how parents can become involved in their child's educational pro-

FIGURE 14.1
Parent Reactions and Possible Interventions

Reprinted with permission of Macmillan Publishing Company from *Adapting Early Childhood Curricula for Children with Special Needs*, Third Edition, by Ruth E. Cook, Annette Tessier, and Diane Klein. Copyright © 1992 by Macmillan Publishing Company.

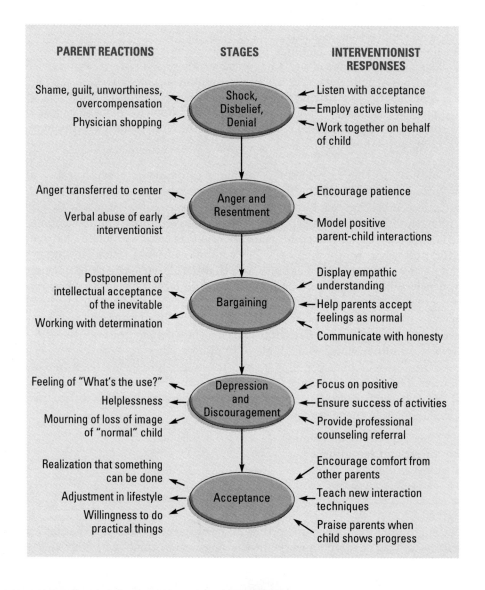

grams. In the fourth session, issues pertaining to the child in school are discussed. Finally, the fifth session targets the future. These seminars are intended to provide factual information, dispel myths, and help parents identify and implement "more responsive treatment options" for their children.

School personnel need to be aware of family members' acceptance level of children with disabilities and make appropriate efforts to support this acceptance. This effort begins with assisting parents in understanding the needs of their child; at the same time, the educator or administrator should listen to the parents in order to better understand the child from their perspective. Summarizing previous research on this issue, Wilson (1995) lists the following things that parents want (and need) from professionals:

- Parents want professionals to communicate without jargon. When technical terms are necessary, they would like to have them explained.
- When possible, they want conferences to be held so both parents can attend.
- They want to receive written materials that provide information to assist them in understanding their child's problem.
- They want to receive a copy of a written report about their child.
- Parents want specific advice on how to manage the specific behavior problems of their children or how to teach them needed skills.
- Parents want information on their child's social as well as academic behavior. (p. 31)

Finally, parents may struggle with the issue of inclusion itself. Educators remain divided on this issue, as do parents and parents' groups. (See Hallahan & Kauffman, 1995, for further discussion.)

Involvement of Fathers

Too often, when people hear that families are taking part in a child's education, they assume that the "family" is really the child's mother. This belief is

CONSIDER THIS

As a teacher, how could you deal with families experiencing various reactions to a child with a disability? What role, if any, should a teacher play in helping parents work through their reactions?

TEACHING TIP

Teachers need to be aware of the different reactions that parents may experience and know some specific strategies for dealing with these reactions.

FURTHER READING

For more information on how parents and professionals view inclusion of students with disabilities, read *The Illusion of Full Inclusion* by D. Hallahan and J. Kauffman, published in 1995 by Pro-Ed.

unfortunate, because the involvement of the entire family is the goal. Often the individual who is left out of the planning is the father.

Hietsch (1986) describes a program that aims at encouraging fathers to get involved in the educational program of their child. The program focuses on Father's Day, when the fathers of children in the class are invited to participate in a specific activity. The following list outlines the Father's Day outing:

1. Make sure that fathers are given sufficient notice to arrange to have the day off from work. (If a day off is not an option, alternative plans should be investigated.)
2. Send a reminder letter home a week to 10 days before Father's Day to rekindle enthusiasm and ensure attendance.
3. Know the first names of the fathers so that introductions are easier.
4. Common denominators help to break the ice. Note similar jobs or interests when introducing fathers to one another.
5. Have children show their fathers special items (e.g., papers, puppets) in the classroom.
6. Make trophies or awards ahead of time for categories related to scheduled activities.
7. On the next day, give individual help to the children in writing and illustrating experience stories to help make Father's Day a learning experience. (adapted from Hietsch, 1986, p. 259)

Involvement of Siblings

Like adults, siblings in a family are important in developing and implementing appropriate educational programs. Since approximately 10 percent of the school population is identified as disabled, the number of children with siblings who are disabled must be significant: a working estimate of 20 percent or more seems realistic. Although not all nondisabled siblings experience adjustment problems, many will have significant difficulties responding to the disability (Gargiulo, O'Sullivan, Stephens, & Goldman, 1989–1990). The mere presence of a child with a disability can have "a profound impact on family structure and dynamics" (Gargiulo et al., 1989–1990, p. 21). On the other hand, these siblings also have a unique opportunity to learn about the diversity of individual needs.

A child with a disability may have an impact on siblings in two primary ways: economic and emotional. As a result of the financial impact, siblings may feel that they are being deprived of certain things. This perception may be based on fact or could simply be mistaken. In either case, nondisabled siblings may feel resentment if they think that the sibling with a disability is draining important economic resources from the family.

Siblings may also feel emotionally deprived. Their parents may spend a great deal more time with the child with the disability than with them. Although doing that may be a necessity, the nondisabled brother or sister may not be mature enough to understand this reality. Parents must convey to the siblings that they are loved just as much as the child with the disability, even though more money and time may be spent on that child (Creekmore, 1988).

There are a number of ways that parents and school personnel can help siblings:

1. *Inform siblings of the nature and cause of the disability.* Often, siblings are concerned that they might become disabled like their brother or sister and

may fear possible genetic influences. In most situations, these occurrences are far from likely, and siblings need to understand that.

2. *Allow siblings to attend conferences with school personnel.* Siblings who are mature enough to understand will be in a better position to help the child with special needs if they are aware of the educational program and their role in it. Siblings may also have useful suggestions for school personnel or other family members.

3. *Openly discuss the disability with all family members.* Trying to be secretive about a family member's disability can only encourage inaccurate conclusions and unwarranted fears. Parents need to share information about a child when siblings are capable of understanding the disability.

One way some schools are involving siblings of children with disabilities is through **sibling support groups** (Summers, Bridge, & Summers, 1991). In addition to disseminating basic information about disabilities, sibling support groups can also provide a forum in which children share experiences and support with other children who have siblings with disabilities. Like parent support groups, sibling support groups can help children cope with having a brother or sister with a disability. Understanding that similar problems exist in other families and learning new ways to deal with them can be very helpful.

Teachers, school counsellors, school social workers, and administrators should work together to provide leadership in developing and maintaining sibling support groups. They should keep the following in mind:

1. Recognize that different disabilities produce different effects in sibling relations. Do not treat all siblings of children with disabilities as if they were experiencing the same thing.
2. Make sure that children feel comfortable in the groups, since sharing feelings and changing behavior can be difficult.
3. Emphasize the importance of prosocial behavior, and encourage children to share prosocial experiences.

FURTHER READING
For more information on sibling support groups, read the article "Sibling Support Groups," by M. Summers, J. Bridge, and C. R. Summers, published in 1991 in volume 23 of *Teaching Exceptional Children.*

TABLE 14.2

Examples of Sessions in Sibling Support Groups

SESSION 1	**Ice breaker:** Involve siblings in various activities to enable them to get to know each other.
SESSION 2	**What it's like to have a disability:** Students go through a series of simulations to better understand what it is like to have a disability.
SESSION 3	**Learn about the sibling's disability:** Students learn about their sibling's specific disability through role-playing, information sharing, and other activities.
SESSION 4	**Exploring feelings:** Students explore their own feelings about having a sibling with a disability. Story sharing, role-playing, and impromptu stories are examples of activities.
SESSION 5	**Sibling observation:** Students get together to observe the sibling in an intervention setting to better understand special programs.
SESSION 6	**Summary session:** Participants are reminded what they have learned. Children may be asked to summarize their new knowledge and feelings.

From "Sibling Support Groups," by M. Summers, J. Bridge, and C. R. Summers, 1991, *Teaching Exceptional Children, 23*, pp. 20–23. Used by permission.

4. Make the group an enjoyable experience as well as an informative one. (Summers et al., 1991, p. 21)

Table 14.2 on page 419 briefly describes a series of six sessions that could be used to get a support group started.

FAMILY AND SCHOOL COLLABORATION

School personnel and families of students with problems need to collaborate in order to maximize educational efforts. All school personnel, classroom teachers, special education teachers, administrators, and support personnel need to be actively involved with families to improve the education of children with disabilities.

Need for Family and School Collaboration

Parents of children with disabilities and school personnel are partners in providing appropriate educational services. Parents actually should be seen as the "senior partners" because they are responsible for the children every day until they reach adulthood. Thus, there are numerous reasons why parents of children with disabilities need to be encouraged to participate in the educational process:

1. Parents are the key individuals in the socialization of their children.
2. Parents know their children better than school personnel do.
3. Members of the child's family can facilitate the transfer of knowledge learned at school to community settings.
4. Children have a much greater chance for success if their parents and school personnel maintain consistent expectations.
5. Parents provide a significant amount of reinforcement to their children for appropriate actions.
6. Children with disabilities make greater developmental gains when parents provide home teaching.
7. Parents participating in programs for their children are in a position to interact and benefit from other parents with children with disabilities. (Allen, 1992)

Family involvement can only enhance educational programs. Figure 14.2 outlines a comprehensive model of parent and family involvement. The nearby Inclusion Strategies feature presents ways to encourage a greater family role, with ideas for addressing multicultural considerations.

Legal Requirements for Collaboration

Although the important role of families in all aspects of child growth and development has been acknowledged for a long time, public schools have historically excluded families from many decisions about the education of children (Kraus, 1990).

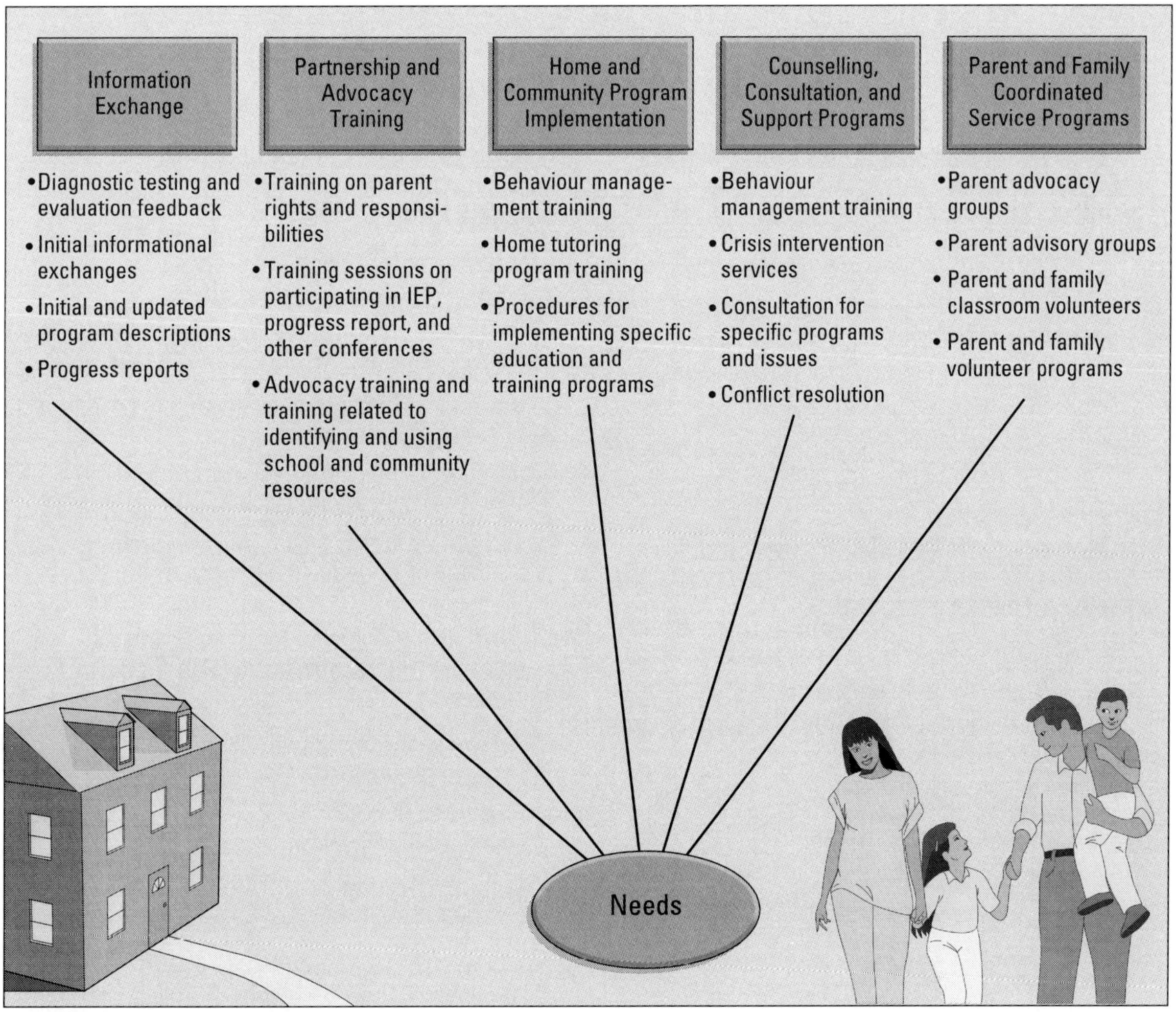

FIGURE 14.2
Model of Family Involvement

Adapted from *Working with Parents and Families of Exceptional Children and Youth* (p. 32), by R. L. Simpson, 1996, Austin, TX: Pro-Ed. Used by permission.

In Canada, parental rights for involvement in the assessment, programming (IEP/IPP), and monitoring of children's school performance vary across the country. William Smith of McGill University's Office of Research on Educational Policy has documented the legal rights of students with disabilities across Canada (Smith, 1994; Smith & Foster, 1996). In his most recent work examining parental rights for involvement, he notes that, as of 1997, there was no legal requirement to include parents in assessment or programming decisions in Alberta, Manitoba, Newfoundland, or Prince Edward Island. In all other provinces and territories parents have the legal right to help make decisions (Smith & Foster, 1997). Furthermore, in New Brunswick and Saskatchewan parents are required to take part in assessment and programming, but not in the ongoing monitoring of the program; in all other provincial/

INCLUSION STRATEGIES

Approaches to Facilitating Family Involvement

PARENT EDUCATION PROGRAMS THAT IMPROVE PARENTS' FORMAL EDUCATION (E.G., BASIC READING, MATHEMATICS, REASONING SKILLS)

- increase parents' self-esteem and self-confidence.

- facilitate positive interactions with school professionals.

- broaden employment opportunities.

- facilitate parent feelings of "being at home" in educational settings.

PARENT EDUCATION PROGRAMS THAT ARE DESIGNED TO INCREASE PARENTS' INFLUENCE ON THEIR CHILDREN'S EDUCATION

- ensure that schools are responsive to school and community values.

- give parents the opportunity to participate in the decision-making process.

- require that educators
  - observe and participate in community activities.
  - listen to parents' concerns to develop mutual understanding.
  - encourage parents to define desired change and to develop an action plan.

AWARENESS TRAINING PROGRAMS THAT PROVIDE OPPORTUNITIES FOR ROLE-PLAYING AND SIMULATION

- increase parent confidence levels for interacting with school personnel.

- facilitate parents' understanding of and shared responsibility for children's education.

- teach new behaviours and skills needed to interact as team members.

- increase family interactions and participation in children's education.

- empower parents and extend leadership abilities in the educational community.

TRAINING AND EMPLOYMENT OF PARENTS AS PARA-EDUCATORS IN BILINGUAL AND BICULTURAL PROGRAMS

- ensure that language and customs will be included as a part of the curriculum.

- help them learn instructional strategies that can be used to benefit their children at home.

- increase the likelihood that parents will choose to further their children's education.

Adapted from "Parent and Professional Partnerships in Special Education: Multicultural Considerations," by T. W. Sileo, A. P. Sileo, and M. A. Prater, 1996, *Interventions in School and Clinic, 31*, p. 148.

---

territorial jurisdictions rights to involvement include the right to monitor the programming.

In summary, the legal rights pertaining to parental involvement vary across the country. In the majority of jurisdictions parents have the right to help make assessment and programming decisions. In all jurisdictions attempts are made to include parents wherever possible.

SPECIFIC COLLABORATION ACTIVITIES

There are numerous ways parents and other family members can become involved with the education of a child with a disability or one who is at risk

for developing problems. The following suggestions focus on areas in which general education teachers can have a positive effect.

Communicating with Parents

A critical element in any collaboration between school personnel and parents is communication. Many parents observe that simply too little communication flows between themselves and the school. Perhaps this is to be expected—

TEACHING TIP

When communicating with parents, avoid using educational jargon and acronyms because they might be meaningless to parents.

approximately 50 percent of both general and special education teachers indicate that they have received no training in this area and consequently rate themselves as only moderately skilled (e.g., Buck et al., 1996; Epstein et al., 1996). This situation is particularly unfortunate, since problems between parents and school personnel often can be avoided by proper communication.

Wilson (1995, pp. 31–32) outlined the following principles of effective communication with the parents of students with disabilities:

- *Accept:* Show respect for the parents' knowledge and understanding, and convey a language of acceptance.
- *Listen:* Actively listen, and make an effort to confirm the perceptions of the speaker's intent and meaning.
- *Question:* Probe to solicit parents' perspectives. Often, questions will generate helpful illustrations.
- *Encourage:* Stress students' strengths along with weaknesses. Find positive aspects to share, and end meetings or conversations on an encouraging note.
- *Stay directed:* Keep the discussions focused on the emphases being discussed, and direct the parents to resources regarding concerns that lie beyond your scope.
- *Develop an alliance:* Stress that the parents and teachers share a common goal: to help the child.

FURTHER READING

For more information on communicating with parents, read *Families, Professionals, and Exceptionality* by A. P. Turnbull and H. R. Turnbull, published by Merrill in 1997.

Effective communication must be regular and useful. Communicating with parents only once or twice per year, or communicating with parents regularly but with information that is not useful, will not facilitate meeting educational goals.

Meyers and Blacher (1987) studied 99 families who had children with disabilities and found that only 11 indicated that they had frequent communication with school personnel; 36 reported regular communication. On the other hand, 18 families responded that they had occasional communication, and 34 families said they had rare or no communication with school personnel. Ap-

Teachers must communicate regularly with parents to keep them informed about their child's progress and needs.

TABLE 14.3

Making Positive Word Choices

Avoid	Use Instead
Must	Should
Lazy	Can do more with effort
Culturally deprived	Culturally different, diverse
Troublemaker	Disturbs class
Uncooperative	Should learn to work with others
Below average	Works at his (her) own level
Truant	Absent without permission
Impertinent	Discourteous
Steals	Takes things without permission
Dirty	Has poor grooming habits
Disinterested	Complacent, not challenged
Stubborn	Insists on having his (her) own way
Wastes time	Could make better use of time
Sloppy	Could be neater
Mean	Has difficulty getting along with others
Time and time again	Usually, repeatedly
Poor grade or work	Works below his (her) usual standard

Adapted from *Parents and Teachers of Children with Exceptionalities: A Handbook for Collaboration* (2nd ed.) (p. 82), by T. M. Shea and A. M. Bauer, 1991, Boston: Allyn & Bacon. Used by permission.

proximately one third of the families in the study had rare or no communication with school personnel. Because collaboration between school personnel and families of children with disabilities is so critical, a major effort is needed to improve communication between these two entities.

Communication between school personnel and parents can take many forms. It does not have to be formal written communication. Effective communication can be informal, for example, telephone calls, written notes, or newsletters. When communicating with parents, school personnel should be aware of how they convey messages. For example, they should never "talk down" to parents. They should also choose their words thoughtfully. Some words convey very negative meanings, whereas other words transmit the message effectively, yet are more positive. Table 14.3 lists words that should be avoided along with preferred alternatives. When communicating with parents, school personnel should also be aware of cultural and language differences. Taking these factors into consideration will enhance the quality of communication with family members.

The following discussion focuses on types of effective communication.

INFORMAL EXCHANGES

Informal exchanges can take place without preparation. Teachers may see a parent in the community and stop and talk momentarily about the parent's child. Teachers should always be prepared to talk to parents about their children, regardless of the setting, but should avoid talking about confidential information in the presence of individuals who do not need to know about it. If the conversation becomes too involved, the teacher should request that it be continued later, in a more appropriate setting.

PARENT OBSERVATIONS

Parents should be encouraged to visit the school to observe their child in the educational setting. Although the parents' presence could cause some disruption in the daily routine, school personnel need to keep in mind that parents have a critical stake in the success of the educational efforts. Therefore, parents should always feel welcome to observe the student in the educational setting. If the teacher feels that one time would be better than another, this information should be conveyed to the parent.

TELEPHONE CALLS

Many teachers use telephone calls a great deal and very effectively to communicate with parents. Parents feel that teachers are interested in their child if the teacher takes the time to call and discuss the child's progress with the parent. When using the telephone for communication purposes, teachers should remember to call when there is good news about the child as well as to report problems the child is experiencing. It makes parents feel very good to get a call from a teacher who says that the child is doing well and not having problems. Again, understanding the language and culture of the home is important when making telephone calls. Giving parents your home telephone number is an option that may prove reassuring to parents.

WRITTEN NOTES

CONSIDER THIS
Some teachers think that daily written communication with parents is too much for them to do. When might this form of communication be necessary, and is it a legitimate responsibility for teachers?

Written communication to parents is also an effective method of communicating about a child's progress. When using written communication, teachers should consider the literacy level of the parents and use words and phrases that will be readily understandable. They should also be aware of the primary language of the home. Written communications that are not understood can be very intimidating for parents. When using written communication, teachers should provide an opportunity for parents to respond, either in writing or through a telephone call.

HOME VISITS

There is no better way to get an understanding of the family than by making a home visit. When possible, school personnel should consider making the extra effort required to arrange and make home visits. When visiting homes, school personnel need to follow certain procedures, including the following:

- Have specific information to deliver or obtain.
- If you desire to meet with parents alone, find out if it is possible to have the child elsewhere during the scheduled visit.
- Do not stay more than an hour.
- Arrive at the scheduled time.
- Dress as a professional.
- Consider making visits with another school system resource person, such as the school social worker.
- Be sure to do as much listening as talking.
- Leave on a positive note. (Westling & Koorland, 1988)

Although we list home visits as an option, we are also cognizant of the low "treatment acceptability" of this practice. General education teachers report that they consider home visits the least effective (and perhaps least desirable) alternative available to them in terms of home-school collaborations (Polloway et al., 1996). Among other possible concerns, home visits for a potentially large number of children may simply be unrealistic.

OTHER FORMS OF COMMUNICATION

Another way for school personnel to convey helpful information to parents is to consider these options:

- Newsletters
- Parent or family support groups
- Open houses

School personnel should use every available means to communicate with parents. Both general and special education teachers have this responsibility. Teachers should never assume that other school personnel will take care of communicating with parents. Effective communication between school personnel and parents should involve many different people.

Parent-Teacher Conferences

Parent-teacher conferences are another excellent method of communication. They can be formal, such as IEP meetings, or informal, arranged when parents call a teacher and request a meeting with one or more teachers about a particular problem. Most schools have twice yearly, or more regular parent-teacher meetings for all children. Regardless of the purpose or formality of the meeting, school personnel should focus attention on the topics at hand. They should send advance information home to parents and make the parents feel at ease about participating in the meeting.

When preparing to meet with parents to discuss children who are experiencing problems, school personnel need to anticipate the components of the discussion. They should gather information about the questions that parents may ask and know what questions to address to the parents. Figure 14.3 provides typical questions raised at such conferences. By anticipating the questions in advance, school personnel will be in a better position to have a successful meeting.

IEP MEETINGS

Parents should be involved in the development of students' individualized education programs for two reasons. First, most provincial/territorial jurisdictions require parental participation. The more important reason for involvement, however, is to gain the input of parents. In most regards, parents know more about their children than school personnel do. They have interacted with the child longer, and beyond the hours of a school day. Schools need to take advantage of this knowledge about the child when developing an IEP.

An example of how parents should be involved in the development of IEPs is described in the future-based assessment and intervention model (Smith & Dowdy, 1992) discussed in Chapter 13. In this model, school personnel, parents, and the student discuss likely "futures" for the student and the necessary interventions that will help the student achieve them. These agreed-upon goals then guide the development and implementation of educational programs for

TEACHING TIP
School personnel might support a parent newsletter that could go out to all school patrons, or at least a column or section in the school newsletter could be contributed by a parent.

CONSIDER THIS
Parents generally do know more about their children than school personnel. In what ways can this knowledge be used to develop programs that meet the needs of children?

QUESTIONS PARENTS MAY ASK TEACHERS

- What is normal for a child this age?
- What is the most important subject or area for my child to learn?
- What can I work on at home?
- How can I manage her behaviour?
- Should I spank?
- When will my child be ready for community living?
- Should I plan on her learning to drive?
- Will you just listen to what my child did the other day and tell me what you think?
- What is a learning disability?
- My child has emotional problems; is it my fault?
- The doctor said my child will grow out of this. What do you think?
- Will physical therapy make a big difference in my child's control of his hands and arms?
- Have you become harder on our child? Her behaviour has changed at home.
- Can I call you at home if I have a question?
- What is the difference between delayed, retarded, and learning disabled?
- What kind of after-school activities can I get my child involved in?
- Can my child live on his own?
- What should I do about sexual activity?
- What's he going to be like in five years?
- Will she have a job?
- Who takes care of him when I can no longer care for him?
- What happens if she doesn't make her IEP goals?

QUESTIONS TEACHERS SHOULD ASK PARENTS

- What activities at home could you provide as a reward?
- What particular skill areas concern you most for inclusion on the IEP?
- What behaviour at home do you feel needs to improve?
- Would you be interested in coming to a parent group with other parents of my students?
- When is a good time to call at home?
- May I call you at work? What is the best time?
- Is there someone at home who can pick the child up during the day if necessary?
- Would you be interested in volunteering in our school?
- What is the most difficult problem you face in rearing your child?
- What are your expectations for your child?
- How can I help you the most?
- What is your home routine in the evenings? Is there a quiet place for your child to study?
- Can you or your spouse do some special activity with your child if he or she earns it at school?
- Can you spend some time tutoring your child in the evening?
- Would you like to have a conference with your child participating?
- When is the best time to meet?

FIGURE 14.3

Questions Asked by Parents and Teachers

Adapted from *The Special Educator's Handbook* (p. 208–209), by D. L. Westling and M. A. Koorland, 1988, Boston: Allyn & Bacon. Used by permission.

the student. Such a focus is critical to the joint development of individual transition plans, which are suggested for all students with disabilities by at least age 16.

School personnel must take steps to ensure parental involvement in their child's education program.

To obtain increased parental involvement in IEP conferences, school personnel need to solicit parental input proactively. Simply inviting parents to attend is not sufficient. In facilitating exchanges between school personnel and parents, de Bettencourt (1987) suggests the following:

1. Hold conferences in a small location that is free from external distractions; hold phone calls and other interruptions so that parents feel you are truly interested in them and their child.
2. Hold conferences on time and maintain the schedule; do not let conferences start late or run late because many parents may be taking time off from work to attend.
3. Arrange the room so that parents and school personnel are comfortable and can look at one another without barriers, such as desks and tables, between them.
4. Present information clearly, concisely, and in a way that parents can understand; do not "talk down" to the parents.

To increase parental participation in the IEP conference, consider having a parent advocate assigned to attend the conference with the parents. The advocate, a member of the school staff, can facilitate parental participation by introducing the parents to the other team members, verbally reinforcing parental participation, directing questions to the parents, and summarizing the discussion at the end of the conference (Goldstein & Turnbull, 1981).

HOME-BASED INTERVENTION

Families can become involved with the education of a family member with a disability through home-based intervention. For preschool children, home-based services are fairly common; however, parents less frequently provide instruction at home for older students. Still, many reports have noted that such instruction can be very beneficial to students with disabilities (e.g., Brown & Moore, 1992; Ehlers & Ruffin, 1990). Parents can be helpful in numerous ways.

Parents and other family members at home can further the student's educational program by providing reinforcement and direct instructional support, and supporting homework efforts.

Providing Reinforcement

CROSS-REFERENCE

A full description of the principles of reinforcement is presented in Chapter 5.

Most students with disabilities experience lots of failure and frustration. Frequently, the more they attend school, the more they fail. This failure cycle becomes difficult to break, especially after it becomes established over several years. Reinforcing success can help break this cycle. Parents need to work with school personnel to provide positive reinforcement for all levels of success. If students are not capable of achieving full success in an area, they need to be rewarded for their positive efforts in the appropriate direction.

Parents are in an excellent position to provide reinforcement. They spend more time with the child than school personnel do and are involved in all aspects of the child's life. As a result, parents can provide reinforcement in areas where a child most desires rewards, such as time with friends, money, toys, or trips. For many students, simply allowing them to have a friend over or to stay up late at night on a weekend may prove reinforcing. School personnel do not have this range of reinforcers available to them; therefore, parents should take advantage of their repertoire of rewards to reinforce the positive efforts of students.

Brown and Moore (1992) describe a method to motivate poor elementary readers at home. It requires that parents listen to their children read four nights each week for a month. Stickers, later redeemable for pizzas, T-shirts, and a pizza party, are used as reinforcers. The entire program is based on reinforcement for students who work at home with their parents.

Parents should also help motivate their older children's efforts in school. Using a reinforcement system can provide incentives for adolescents who need a little extra "push" to get started. School personnel can assist parents in motivating adolescents by discussing potentially desirable reinforcers and by suggesting some home activities.

TEACHING TIP

Regardless of the format, the key element in home-school contingencies is ongoing, effective communication between school personnel and parents.

A special example of reinforcement in the home are *home-school contingencies*. Home-school contingencies can be highly effective and also cost efficient (Pfiffner & Barkley, 1990). They typically involve providing reinforcement contingencies in the home, based on the documentation of learning or behavioral reports from school.

The basic mechanism for home-school contingencies are written reports that highlight a student's behaviour relative to particular targets or objectives. Two popular forms are daily report cards and passports. *Daily report cards* give feedback on schoolwork, homework, and behaviour. They range in complexity from forms calling for responses to simple rating scales to more precisely designed behavioural instruments with formal definitions and designated direct, daily behavioural measures (Dougherty & Dougherty, 1977). *Passports* typically take the form of notebooks, which students bring to each class and then take home daily. Individual teachers (or all of a student's teachers) and parents can make regular notations. Reinforcement is based both on carrying the passport and on meeting the specific target behaviours that are indicated on it (Walker & Shea, 1988).

Providing Direct Instructional Support

For many students with disabilities, direct involvement of family members in instruction can be critical to success. Unfortunately, many family members provide less direct instruction as the child gets older, assuming that the student is capable of doing the work alone. Too often, the reverse is true; students may need more assistance at home as they progress through the grades. Since parents are generally with the child more than school personnel are, it seems logical to ask them to provide direct instruction; with methods such as coincidental teaching, in which parents teach their children various skills in real-life situations, parental involvement in teaching skills is not burdensome and can be truly effective (Schulz, Rule, & Innocenti, 1989).

Advocates for expanding the role of parents in educating their children adhere to the following assumptions (Ehlers & Ruffin, 1990):

- Parents are the first and most important teachers of their children.
- The home is the child's first schoolhouse.
- Children will learn more during the early years than at any other time in life.
- All parents want to be good parents and care about their child's development. (Ehlers & Ruffin, 1990, p. 1)

One effective intervention is a systematic home tutoring program. Thurston (1989) describes an effective program that includes four steps. In step 1, the parents and teachers discuss the area in which home tutoring would be most helpful. Many parents will feel more comfortable with helping their children "practise" skills than with teaching them new skills. Therefore, teachers should help identify topics in which practice would benefit the student. In step 2, family members implement home tutoring procedures: selecting the location for the tutoring, deciding on a time for tutoring, and so on. In step 3, the family member who provides the tutoring uses techniques for encouragement, reinforcement, and error correction. In step 4, family members complete the tutoring session and make a record of the student's accomplishments. Tutoring periods should be short, probably no more than 15 minutes, and should end with a record of the day's activities. A visual chart, on which the student can actually see progress, is often very reinforcing to the student (Thurston, 1989).

Providing Homework Support

In many ways, finishing this chapter with the topic of homework concludes this book with the area that may be most problematic for successful home-school collaboration. The problems of students with disabilities in this area are well documented (e.g., Epstein et al., 1993; Gajria & Salend, 1995) and outline the challenges faced by teachers and parents working together (Patton, 1994). For example, Jayanthi, Nelson, Sawyer, Bursuck, and Epstein's (1995) report on issues of communication problems within the homework process reveals significant misunderstandings among general and special education teachers and parents regarding the development, implementation, and coordination of home-

CROSS-REFERENCE
School-based aspects of homework are discussed in Chapters 12 and 13.

work practices for students with disabilities in inclusive settings. Teachers and parents indicated concerns about failures to initiate communication (in terms of informing the other of a student's learning and behaviour characteristics as well as the delineation of roles and responsibilities) and to provide follow-up communications, especially early on, when problems first become evident. In addition, respondents identified several variables that they believed influence the severity of these problems (e.g., lack of time, student-to-teacher ratio, student interference, not knowing whom to contact).

As Epstein et al. (1996) further reviewed these problem areas, they found that general education teachers reported the following key communication problems: lack of follow-through by parents, lateness of communication, the relative lack of importance placed on homework, parental defensiveness, and denial of problems. These concerns were generally consistent with the reports of special education teachers in a parallel study (Buck et al.). However, these data are open to interpretation—they are survey responses by teachers *about* parents. Also, most of the general education teachers in the study had either primary responsibility for communication with parents of students with disabilities or shared this responsibility with special educators (Buck et al.; Epstein et al., 1996).

Despite the numerous problems in homework, the key is in finding homework solutions. Polloway et al. (1996, p. 136) report that teachers rated the following seven parental communication strategies from most to least effective:

FIGURE 14.4

Effective Strategies Relative to Homework

From "Recommendations of General Education Teachers Regarding Communication Problems about Homework and Students with Disabilities," by W. Bursuck, E. A. Polloway, M. Epstein, & M. Jayanthi. Manuscript in preparation.

Parents' Efforts to Communicate
Parents should
- check with their child about homework daily.
- regularly attend parent–teacher conferences.
- sign their child's assignment book daily.

General Education Teachers' Rules
Teachers should
- require that students keep a daily assignment book.
- provide parents at the start of school with a list of suggestions on how parents can assist with homework.
- remind students of due dates on a regular basis.

Adopting Policies to Facilitate Communication
Schools should
- provide release time for teachers to communicate with parents on a regular basis.
- require frequent written communication from teachers to parents about homework (e.g., monthly progress reports).
- schedule conferences in the evenings for working parents.

Technologies to Enhance Communication
Schools should
- establish telephone hotlines so that parents can call when questions or problems arise.
- regularly provide computerized student progress reports for parents.
- establish systems that enable teachers to place homework assignments on audiotapes so that parents can gain access by telephone or voice mail.

1. Recommend homework strategies for parents to use at home.
2. Send home an assignment sheet or notebook.
3. Require the parent's signature on the assignment.
4. Schedule a conference with parents about homework.
5. Call parents if homework is incomplete.
6. Send home a note.
7. Visit parents at home.

Finally, Bursuck et al. (1996) note the perspectives of general education teachers relative to solutions to homework dilemmas. Examples of strategies ranked most effective are provided in Figure 14.4. Note that many of these strategies have validity for all students, not only those with special needs.

FINAL THOUGHTS

It is a safe assumption that establishing good working relationships with parents and families enhances the school experience of their children. Thus an important objective for the schools should be to achieve and maintain such relationships. Most professionals acknowledge the importance of parent and family involvement in the schooling of their children, and this importance can be especially critical for students with disabilities. But programs that promote home-school collaboration must aim for more than students' classroom success. Often, parental involvement has been focused on their children's goals (i.e., student progress), with less attention given to parental outcomes (i.e., their particular needs). But teachers, parents, and other family members all should gain from cooperative relationships that truly flow in both directions and are concerned with success in both home and school settings. Both general and special education teachers need to help family members understand the importance of their involvement, give them suggestions on how to take part, and empower them with the skills and confidence they will need. Students with disabilities, and those at risk of developing problems, require assistance from all parties in order to maximize success. Family members are critical components of the educational team.

SUMMARY

- The past two decades have see a major change in provision of educational services to students with special needs: the active involvement of families.

- Getting parents to participate in school decisions may be difficult but is nevertheless essential.

- Schools should take proactive steps to ensure the involvement of families of students with disabilities.

- Unlike families of the past, today's families vary considerably in their composition.

- Regardless of their own values, school personnel must involve all family members of a student with special needs, regardless of the type of family.

■ Family members must make adjustments when a child with a disability becomes a family member.

■ Siblings of students with disabilities may also experience special problems and challenges.

■ Families and schools must collaborate to ensure appropriate educational programs for students with disabilities.

■ Most provincial/territorial policies require that schools involve families in educational decisions for students with disabilities.

■ A critical component in any collaboration between school personnel and family members is effective communication.

■ All types of communication between school and families are important.

■ School personnel should encourage parents and other family members to participate during school conferences.

■ Family members should be encouraged and taught how to become involved in the educational programs implemented in the school.

■ A variety of strategies are available to facilitate successful home intervention programs.

RESOURCES

Exceptional Parent

This monthly magazine on parenting a child with a disability or special health needs is an excellent resource, available through the Internet Web site **www.eparent.com/** or by order. An important resource to share with parents of children who have a disability, it will also inform the teacher about relevant organizations and different disabilities.

Alberta Education, Special Education Branch. (1998). *The Parent Advantage.* Edmonton: Author.

This infomative booklet tells how a parent can help a student (Kindergarten to Grade 9) be organized, learn to read, enjoy reading, read textbooks, memorize from reading, write, spell, use

technology, do math, prepare for tests, and complete projects. As a teacher, be sure to have the booklet on hand for parents to refer to—it will save you much time explaining to parents how they can help.

Canter, L., & Hausner, L. (1987). *Homework without Tears: A Parent's Guide for Motivating Children to Do Homework and Succeed in School.* Santa Monica, CA: Lee Canter & Associates.

The authors provide a very practical approach to handling homework issues which, for parents, are always a huge concern. If you, as the teacher, have this excellent resource on hand to refer parents to, it will make homework issues much easier to deal with.

WEBLINKS

Canadian Parents Online
www.canadianparents.com/
A wonderful resource for parents, Canadian Parents Online provides information on all aspects of parenting, with supports, resources, and questions/answers from lawyers, nutritionists, and physicians. It is also a resource for teachers to share with

parents and to read for suggestions about schooling, homework, health, and behaviour.

Child and Family Canada
www.cfc-efc.ca/
The Child and Family Canada Web site provides information on all aspects of the family. There is some

excellent information on parenting children with different special needs, as well as information on child abuse, family supports, and much more. The site is invaluable for teachers who have questions about family issues.

Parentbooks
www.parentbookstore.com/
Parentbooks, a Toronto-based bookstore, offers a huge selection of resources, including books, videos, and manuals in the area of parenting, families, and education. The store has numerous resources specifically for teachers and in the area of special needs.

National Parent Network on Disabilities (NPND)
www.npnd.org/
The U.S. association provides advocacy information for parents of individuals with disabilities. Although much material is specific to the United States, there is some extremely useful information on resources, related Web sites, different disabilities, planning for aging, and much more.

Disability Resource
www.disabilityresource.com
The Disability Resource site provides resources and other Web links to parents and professionals working with children with disabilities. If you have any questions about a disability or its management, this site will direct you to a wealth of information.

Family Education Network
www.familyeducation.com
Although the material on this Web site is intended to be shared primarily with families/parents, it is also useful to the classroom teacher. There are suggestions for educational activities and resources, and tips on managing different special needs concerns.

GLOSSARY

Accelerated schools. Schools that provide optional programming for students considered at risk of failure.

Acceleration. A form of programming for students who are classified as gifted and talented, where the students move through the curriculum at a more rapid pace than their chronological age peers.

Accessibility. The ability of a person with a disability to make use of a physical location or program.

Accommodations. Changes in the way students are taught so that learning will be enhanced; these include changes in instruction, testing, homework, and assignments.

Adaptive behaviour. A way of conduct that meets the standards of personal independence and social responsibility expected from that cultural and chronological age group.

Additions. An expressive language problem characterized by individuals inserting words or sounds into their speech.

Affective education. Educational programs that focus on the emotional health of a child.

AIDS. Acquired immune deficiency syndrome. A sexually transmitted disease that results in a depressed immune system.

Allergens. Substances that individuals are allergic to, such as dust, certain foods, or animal dander.

Alternative communication. Any system of conveying ideas that is used in lieu of human speech.

Alternative schools. Schools designed to provide alternative environments for students with behavioural and emotional disorders.

American Sign Language (ASL). A particular form of sign language used by many individuals with severe hearing impairments.

American Speech-Language-Hearing Association (ASHA). The major professional organization for speech-language and hearing professionals.

Annual goals. Goals for the year that are developed for each student served in special education and made a part of the student's individualized education program (IEP).

Antidepressants. Medications for managing attention deficity/hyperactivity disorder.

Anxiety/withdrawal. A form of emotional/behavioural disorder where children are very anxious and do not interact with their peers.

Articulation disorder. the most common speech disorder, this problem centres around word and sound pronunciations.

Asperger's Syndrome. First listed in 1994 in the fourth edition of the *Diagnostic and Statistical Manual of Mental Disorders* as one of five pervasive developmental disorders. There is significant impairment in social functioning, but otherwise no cognitive delay.

Assessment. The process of collecting information about a particular student to determine eligibility for special services, and strengths and weaknesses for programming purposes.

Assistive technology. Devices that allow students, especially those with specific needs, to participate fully, or even partially, in ongoing classroom activities.

Asthma. A disease that affects breathing that is due to narrowing of the small air passages in the lungs caused by irritation of the bronchial tubes by allergic reactions.

At-risk students. Students who are likely to develop learning or behaviour problems because of a variety of environmental factors.

Attention deficit/hyperactivity disorder (AD/HD). A problem associated with short attention problems and excessive motor movements.

Attention problems—immaturity. A form of behaviour problems associated with attention deficits.

Augmentative communication. Methods used to facilitate communication in individuals, including communication boards, computers, and sign language.

Autism. A severe disorder that affects the language and behaviour of children, caused by neurological problems.

Basal series. The type of reading programs traditionally used in most elementary schools in general education classrooms.

Behaviour management. Systematic use of behavioural techniques, such as behaviour modification, to manage ways of conduct.

Behavioural approach. An intervention model based on behaviourism that is often used with children with emotional problems.

Blind. A category of disabilities characterized by severe visual impairment that usually results in an inability to read printed material.

Braille. A system of writing for the visually impaired that uses characters made up of raised dots.

Canadian Charter of Rights and Freedoms. A part of Canada's Constitution Act which guarantees, among other rights, the rights of all individuals with disabilities.

Career education. A curricular model that focuses on the future vocational opportunities for students.

Cerebral palsy. A disorder affecting balance and voluntary muscles that is caused by brain damage.

Childhood cancer. Any form of cancer that affects children; generally leukemia, bone cancer, or lymphoma.

Chronic health problem. A physical condition that is persistent and results in school problems for the child.

Circle of friends. A peer support network for an individual student fostered by the classroom teacher.

Classroom climate. The nature of the learning environment, including teacher rules, expectations, discipline standards, and openness of the teacher.

Classroom management. A combination of techniques used by teachers in classrooms to manage the environment, including behaviour modification.

Classroom organization. Methods used by teachers to manage the learning environment through physical organization of the classroom, classroom rules, and use of other structure.

Clean intermittent bladder catheterization (CIC). A medical process where a tube is inserted into the catheter to allow for urinary waste to leave the body.

Cochlea. The part of the inner ear containing fluid and nerve cells that processes information to the brain.

Cochlear implant. A technological device inserted in the place of the cochlea that enables some individuals to hear sounds.

Cognitive deficiency. A deficiency in the intelligence processes, including thinking, memory, and problem solving.

Cognitive-behavioural intervention. Instructional strategies that use internal control methods, such as self-talk and self-monitoring, in ways that help students learn how to control their own behaviour.

Collaboration. The process of interactions between teachers and special education teachers to provide instruction to an inclusive classroom.

Communication board. An augmentative communication device that includes letters or symbols that enables a person to communicate either manually or through computer technology.

Community-based instruction (CBI). A model in which instruction is provided in a community setting where skills that are learned will actually be used.

Conduct disorder. A type of behaviour problem that is characterized by negative and hostile behaviours, generally toward authority figures.

Conductive hearing loss. A form of hearing impairment caused by problems with the outer or middle ear that impedes sound traveling to the inner ear.

Consultation. The process where an instructional specialist provides suggestions for other educators to use in their inclusive classrooms.

Contingency contracting. Developing behavioural contracts with students based on their completing specific tasks or meeting certain behavioural expectations in return for positive reinforcers.

Continuous progress. A form of educational programming that allows students to move through a curriculum at their own pace.

Continuum of services. A model that provides placement and programming options for students with disabilities along a continuum of least-to-most restrictiveness.

Cooperative learning. An instructional and learning process that uses teams of children to teach each other and work together on various learning activities.

COPS. An error monitoring strategy for writing.

Creative. A form of intelligence characterized by advanced divergent thinking skills and the development of original ideas and responses.

Criterion-referenced testing. Tests that compare a child to a particular mastery level rather than to a normative group.

Curricular infusion. The practice of infusing various enrichment activities into the general curriculum for students who are gifted and talented.

Curriculum-based assessment. A form of criterion-referenced assessment which uses the actual curriculum as the standard.

Curriculum compacting. An approach used with gifted and talented students where less time is spent on general curriculum activities and more time on enrichment activities.

Curriculum telescoping. An approach used with students who are achieving well academically that enables them to move through a curriculum at a more rapid pace than is typical.

Curriculum. A systematic grouping of content, coursework, extracurricular activities, and materials for students in an educational setting.

Cystic fibrosis. A health disorder that is characterized by fluid and mucus buildup in the respiratory system, resulting in death.

Deaf. A severe level of hearing impairment that generally results in the inability to use residual sound for communication purposes.

Developmental disability. A disability that has a direct impact on a person's mental or physical development.

Developmental period. The period of an individual's life from birth to the 18th year when most cognitive development occurs.

Developmentally appropriate. A level of instruction that meets the developmental level of children being taught.

Diabetes. A health condition where the pancreas does not produce sufficient levels of insulin to metabolize various substances, including glucose.

Diagnostic and Statistical Manual of Mental Disorders (DSM-IV). The diagnostic manual used by medical and psychological professionals.

Diagnostic tests. Tests and other evaluation methods that are designed to result in a diagnosis of a specific problem.

Differential rates of communicative behaviour. Individuals are provided reinforcement as their inappropriate response rates are reduced.

Differential reinforcement of lower rates of behaviour (DRL). A model that provides reinforcement for behaviours that are moving the student in the desired direction.

Differentiated programs. An instructional approach that requires various curricula or programs for different students in the same classroom.

Direct instruction. A technique where the teacher instructs students on a particular topic.

Disability. A condition that affects a person's functioning ability, either physical, mental, or both.

Distortions. Language problems characterized by altering the correct sound of letters and words.

Dual education system. The education model that supports separate programs for students with disabilities and those in general education.

Duchenne dystrophy. A very severe form of muscular dystrophy that results in fat replacing muscle tissue.

Early infantile autism. A term used early in the description of individuals with autism that is currently not used to describe these individuals.

Ecological assessment. Evaluating individuals in the context of their environments and taking into consideration all environmental factors.

Educable mentally retarded (EMR). A term traditionally used to describe students with an intelligence quotient (IQ) in the 50–70 range.

Efficacy studies. Research that investigates the efficacy, or effectiveness, of various programs for individuals with disabilities.

Emotional abuse. A form of child abuse that centers around emotionally abusing a child, such as ridiculing the child in public or always making a child feel like a failure.

Emotional/behavioural disorder (E/BD). The new term used by many professionals to identify children with emotional and behavioural problems.

Enrichment. A variety of methods that are used to facilitate appropriate education for students classified as gifted and talented enabling students to progress beyond the typical curriculum.

Epilepsy. A disability that is caused by random, erratic electric impulses in the brain that results in seizures.

Exceptionalities. Special physical and/or intellectual needs that require special services for the students that have them.

Expressive language. Language that is spoken or written; language that is expressed in some way.

Extinction. The removal of reinforcement from an individual that will result in a particular behaviour being terminated.

Facilitated communication. A controversial method of dealing with children with autism in which an individual provides limited resistance to a child's arm, which then uses a communication board to communicate.

Family. A unit of individuals who are related or who are together through legal means, providing support for each other.

Family support. A model to provide services for individuals with disabilities by providing a wide array of supports for families.

Fluency. The smoothness and rapidity in various skills, such as speech, oral language, reading, and other skills associated with thinking.

Form. The rule systems of language: phonology, morphology, and syntax.

Full inclusion. The movement or trend to fully include all students with disabilities, regardless of the severity, into all general education programs.

Future-based assessment. An evaluation model that focuses on determining the likely future environments of individuals and proceeds to develop intervention programs around those future environments.

Gifted. A term used to describe students who perform significantly above average in a variety of areas, including academic, social, motor, and leadership.

Gifted and talented (GT). A term frequently used to describe high-achieving students as well as students who excel in other areas, such as the arts.

Hard of hearing. A disability category that refers to individuals who have a hearing loss but who can benefit from their residual hearing abilities.

Hearing-impairment. A disability that affects an individual's sense of hearing. The term applies to any level of hearing loss, including being hard of hearing (residual hearing) or deaf.

Homework. A form of individual practice that generally occurs in the home environment after school hours.

Human immunodeficiency virus (HIV). A major fatal disease that is currently impacting all areas of our society, including children in public schools.

Hyperkinetic disorders. Another label to describe individuals who are hyperactive.

IEP. Individualized education program. An IEP is required by most educational jurisdictions for every child receiving special education services.

Inclusion. A practice based on the belief that students with disabilities belong in general education settings, with support services provided in the general classroom by specialists.

Individuals with Disabilities Education Act (IDEA). U.S. legislation that requires states and local schools to provide an appropriate educational program for students with disabilities.

Infusion. An approach to multicultural education in which the multicultural perspective is "infused" into all aspects of the curriculum day.

Inhalants. A group of drugs and substances that can cause hallucinations and other reactions; examples include fingernail polish, paint thinner, and glue.

Integration. A term that has been used to describe the placement of students with disabilities in general education classrooms, at least for a portion of each school day; otherwise known as mainstreaming.

Intellectual disability. An impaired ability to learn which may cause difficulty in coping with the demands of daily life; usually present form birth.

Intelligence. The term used to describe the cognitive capacity of an individual.

Intelligence quotient (IQ). A number used to express the apparent relative intelligence of a person determined by a standardized intelligence test.

Intelligence tests. Tests that are designed to determine an individual's intelligence level, which is usually reported as an intelligence quotient (IQ).

Juvenile delinquency. A legal term used to describe youth who have broken the law.

Language. A formal method of communication used by people that uses signs and symbols to represent ideas and thoughts, and the rules that apply to standardize the system.

Language disabilities. Any number of impairments that interfere with an individual's ability to communicate with others, such as voice disorders, expressive language skills, and receptive language abilities.

Language disorders. Impairments of comprehension or use of language.

Learning disabilities (LD). The disability category that is characterized by students not achieving commensurate with their ability levels.

Least restrictive environment (LRE). The placement of disabled students alongside students without disabilities as much as possible.

Leukemia. A form of cancer that attacks the blood cells, frequently found in children.

Levels of support. The supports that are necessary to enable an individual with a disability to function as independently as possible in the community.

Life skills. A curricular orientation that emphasizes teaching abilities that will be required to function as an adult in a community setting.

Logical consequences. Expected repercussions after a particular behaviour.

Low vision. Students who have a visual impairment but who also have functional use of some residual vision; these students can read print.

Magnet schools. Schools that offer an alternative curriculum to attract students.

Mainstreaming. The term originally used to describe placing students with disabilities in general education classroom settings.

Meningocele. A form of spina bifida where an out-pouching occurs along the spinal cord that has not been closed; there is no paralysis associated with this form of spina bifida.

Mental age. A measure used in psychological testing that expresses a person's mental attainment in terms of the number of years it takes an average child to reach the same level.

Mental retardation. The term preferred in the United States for a disability related to deficiencies in cognitive abilities that occurs before the age of 18 and is associated with deficits in adapted behaviour; this classification generally requires the individual to have an IQ score of about 70 or below.

Mentor program. Program in schools where adults serve as mentors to children, especially children at risk of failure.

Mild mental retardation. A level of mental retardation that usually includes those with an IQ range of about 50 to 70.

Moderate mental retardation. A level of mental retardation that usually includes those with an IQ range of about 35 to 50.

Modifications. Changes in policy that will support students with disabilities in their learning.

Morphologic impairment. An impairment in an individual's ability to use appropriate structure in oral language.

Morphology. The rule system controlling the structure of words.

Motor excess. A level of physical activity that is above expected levels for that age and cultural group.

Multipass. A reading and comprehension strategy whereby students make three passes through content reading material: a survey, size-up, and sort-out pass.

Multiple intelligences. The theory that there are many different types of intelligences, rather than a single, general factor common in all individuals.

Multisensory impairments. Disabilities of both the visual and auditory kind in the same person.

Muscular dystrophy. A progressive disease that is characterized by a weakening of the muscles.

Myelomeningocele. A form of spina bifida where part of the spinal cord is included in the out-pouching, which usually results in lower trunk and limb paralysis.

Natural consequences. The use of consequences typically found in a child's environment as a positive or negative consequence.

Negative reinforcement. The removal of an unpleasant consequence following a student's behaving or responding in the appropriate manner.

Nondiscriminatory assessment. A method of evaluating students that prevents discrimination on the basis of cultural differences.

Norm-referenced tests. Evaluation procedures that are designed to enable the comparison of a child with a normative sample.

Normalization. The process of attempting to make life as normal as possible for persons with disabilities.

Normalization movement. A widely held belief that all individuals, regardless of any disability, should have as normal an education and living arrangement as possible; opposed to institutionalization.

Nuclear family. A reference to the modern family that is somewhat traditional in that there are two parents and children; however, both parents now generally work.

Omissions. A form of speech problem where individuals leave out sounds or words in oral communication.

Ophthalmologist. A medical doctor who specializes in the treatment of vision disorders and disorders of the eye.

Optometrist. An individual who specializes in fitting eyeglasses to individuals with vision problems.

Orthomolecular therapy. The use of dietary interventions to make an impact on learning and behavioural disorders; research does not support these interventions.

Other health impaired (OHI). The U.S. disability category that includes children with health problems that can result in eligibility for special education and related services.

Pediatric cancer. Any form of cancer that occurs in children.

Peer tutoring. An instructional technique that uses children to teach other children a variety of skills.

Peer-mediated instruction. Adaptations in instruction provided by peers, such as reading a section of a textbook orally to a student with a reading disability.

Pharmacological intervention. The use of drugs to combat behaviour or attention problems.

Phonation. The process of putting speech sounds together to form words and sentences.

Phonologic impairment. An impairment in an individual's ability to follow the rules that govern the formation of words and sentences from sounds.

Phonology. the rule system that governs the individual and combined sounds of a language.

Physical abuse. The treatment of children in inappropriate physical ways that are illegal and can lead to disabilities and even death.

Physical disabilities. A variety of impairments related to health problems, such as spina bifida, cerebral palsy, and polio.

Portfolio assessment. A qualitative method of evaluating children that considers their work, in addition to their performance on tests.

Positive reinforcement. Affirmative, pleasant consequences that are given to an individual in recognition of an appropriate behaviour or response.

Prader-Willi syndrome. A rare syndrome, caused by a problem with the 15th chromosome, which leaves an individual with mild intellectual disabilities and an obsession with eating.

Pragmatics. The relationships among language, perception, and cognition.

Prenatal. Occuring prior to the birth of a child, during the approximately 9 months of gestation.

Prereferral interventions. A series of processes that should be attempted by general education teachers for students who are experiencing problems, prior to referring them for special education services.

Preventive discipline. A method of behaviour management where emphasis is placed on preventing behaviour problems rather than reacting to them.

Procedural management. The component of classroom management that deals with classroom procedures, such as rules, expectations, and daily routines.

Procedural safeguards. Rights of children with disabilities and their parents regarding the provision of a free, appropriate public education.

Processing problems. The primary problems experienced by students classified as having a learning disability, including thinking, memory, and organization.

Profound mental retardation. The lowest level of functioning in the traditional classification system for individuals with intellectual disabilities, representing an IQ range below 20.

Psychodynamic approach. An intervention model for students with serious emotional disturbance that focuses on psychoanalytical methods.

Psychosocial management. An intervention model for students with serious emotional disturbance that focuses on the psychosocial elements.

Psychostimulants. The most commonly prescribed medications for attention deficit/hyperactivity disorder.

Psychotic behaviour. Ways of conduct indicative of a serious mental illness, such as schizophrenia.

Punishment. The application of something that is unpleasant to a child after an inappropriate behaviour: the least-desired behaviour management method available.

Pure tone audiometry. The method used to evaluate hearing loss and hearning capabilities of individuals.

Receptive language. Language that is received and decoded or interpreted.

Referral process. The process of identifying and referring a child for special education services.

Reinforcement. The process of providing consequences, positive or negative, following a particular behaviour or response.

Relative isolation. The phase prior to the 1970s during which students with disabilities were served either outside the public schools or in isolated settings within them.

Remediation. The offering of special aid or attention to learners who are struggling in a certain area.

Reprimand. A statement to a student indicating that a certain behaviour(s) is inappropriate.

Residential programs. The way in which many children with intellectual disabilities and with sensory deficits were taught prior to the normalization movement.

Resonance. Tone of voice that is affected by air coming out of the nose—either too much air or not enough—resulting in hypernasality or hyponasality.

Resource room. A special education classroom where students go from the general education classroom for brief periods during the day for specific help in problem areas.

Response cost. A behaviour management technique where rewards or reinforcers are taken away from students who do not exhibit appropriate behaviours.

Restructuring. The process of making major changes in public school programs, including site-based management and co-teaching activities.

School team. The group of individuals, including classroom teachers, who develop an individualized education plan (IEP) for a child.

Self-contained classroom. A special education environment where students are segregated from their nondisabled peers for most or all of the school day.

Self-evaluation. A method that students can use to assess their own behaviours or work.

Self-injurious behaviours. Behaviours exhibited by an individual that result in harm to that person, such as head banging.

Self-instruction. Various techniques that students can use to teach themselves materials.

Self-management. A cognitive strategy that helps individuals with attention or behaviour problems to manage their own problems.

Self-monitoring. A cognitive strategy where students keep track of and record information about their own behaviours.

Self-paced instruction. In this model for serving students who are classified as gifted and talented, students move through a curriculum at their own pace.

Self-recording. A strategy that is used by an individual with a problem to help reduce inappropriate behaviours.

Self-reinforcement. A cognitive strategy where students affirm themselves for appropriate behaviours.

Semantics. The system within a language that governs content, intent, and meanings of spoken and written language.

Sensorineural hearing loss. A type of hearing loss that affects the nerves leading from the inner ear to the brain.

Sensory impairment. A disability affecting either the visual or auditory abilities of an individual.

Sequential phonics program. Intervention program that follows a specified sequence of normal phonics development.

Severe mental retardation. A level of intellectual disability pertaining to an IQ range of approximately 20 to 35.

Sibling support groups. Groups developed for the siblings of individuals with disabilities to provide ongoing supports.

Snellen chart. The chart used by schools and others to screen individuals for visual problems.

Social competence. The ability to use social skills properly in appropriate contexts.

Social skills. Any number of skills that facilitate an individual's successful participation in a group.

Socialized aggression. A form of behavioural disorder affecting children whose inappropriate behaviours are acceptable in a group setting.

Sociological intervention. An intervention model for children with emotional problems based on working with the entire family.

SOLVE-IT. A learning strategy that helps students organize their responses to questions before giving an answer.

Specialized instruction. Any educational activity that is not typical and that is generally utilized for children with particular needs.

Speech. The vocal production of language that is the easiest, fastest, and most efficient means of communicating.

Speech disabilities. Any number of disorders affecting an individual's ability to communicate orally.

Speech disorders. These include impairments of voice, articulation and fluency.

Speech-language pathologist. The professional who works with students who experience speech and language problems.

Spina bifida. A physical disability that results in the spinal column not closing properly, leaving an exposed spinal cord.

Splinter skills. Skills that an individual with a severe disability, such as autism, possess that are beyond explanation.

Strategy. A skill that is taught to students to give them the ability to deal with instructional content and social situations on their own.

Stuttering. A language disorder that results in a person's expressive language being difficult to understand due to breaks and repetitions in speech.

Subject matter acceleration. In this system of providing accommodations for students classified as gifted and talented, students move through a particular subject area at an increased rate.

Subsequent environments attitude. Educators with this attitude consider what will happen to their students in future and how they will need to adapt; they then design curriculum with a focus on these subsequent environments.

Substance abuse. The practice of using illegal or inappropriate substances, such as alcohol, cocaine, or inhalants.

Substitutions. An expressive language problem characterized by the practice of substituting one sound for another.

Supported education. The model of teaching used when students with disabilities are included in general education classes, with the supports necessary for them to achieve success.

Survey tests. Tests that are used to determine general skill levels of students; results from these tests suggest if additional testing is necessary.

Syntax. Various rules of grammar that relate to the endings of words and the order of words in sentences.

Talented. The second component to the category of gifted and talented that includes children who excel in various arts and nonacademic areas.

Teacher-mediated content. Modifications in instruction made by the teacher, such as modifying a homework assignment, that enable students with disabilities to be successful in inclusive settings.

Team teaching. The utilization of more than one professional or para-professional who actually co-teach classes of students or lessons.

Testing. The component of the assessment process where specific questions are asked an individual and a response is recorded.

Time out. A behaviour management technique where the student is isolated from receiving reinforcement.

Tinted glasses. Glasses, with certain colour tints, that have been used with persons with learning disabilities to correct reading problems; research data do not support their use.

Tourette's syndrome. A disorder that results in behaviour tics and inappropriate vocalizations, such as shouting cuss words.

Trainable mentally retarded (TMR). A term frequently used in schools to identify students with IQ ranges of 30 to 50.

Transactional approach. An approach that encourages professionals to understand that a child's difficulties, especially if caused by attention deficit/hyperactivity disorder, will have an impact on the home and family which will then have an impact on the child.

Transition. The process of moving students from one setting to another, such as pre-school programs to Kindergarten, elementary school to junior high school, and high school to work.

Traumatic brain injury (TBI). A disability category that results from an injury to the brain, causing a student to have significant problems in school.

Tremor. A mild form of cerebral palsy that causes trembling.

Tutorial model. Educational approach where students with disabilities receive extra instructional opportunities either from teachers or peer tutors.

Vestibular dysfunction medication. A controversial therapy for treating dyslexia.

Vision therapy. A controversial way to treat individuals with learning disabilities. It is based on the theory that the disabilities are caused by visual defects.

Voice disorders. A typical expressive, oral language affecting pitch, loudness, or quality of sounds.

Whole language. A language arts curricular approach that focuses on teaching language arts as a whole, including written skills, reading, and oral language skills.

Whole language method. Development in areas such as phonics is thought to occur naturally within a wider language context; the teacher teaches specific needed skills through mini-lessons.

REFERENCES

Abikoff, H. (1991). Cognitive training in ADHD children: Less to it than meets the eye. *Journal of Learning Disabilities, 24*, 205–209.

Ackerman, P. T., Dykman, R. A., & Gardner, M. Y. (1990). Counting rate, naming rate, phonological sensitivity, and memory span: Major factors in dyslexia. *Journal of Learning Disabilities, 23*, 325–327.

Affleck, J. Q., Edgar, E., Levine, P., & Kortering, L. (1990). Postschool status of students classified as mildly mentally retarded, learning disabled, or non-handicapped: Does it get better with time? *Education and Training in Mental Retardation, 25*, 315–324.

Agosta, J., & Melda, K. (1996). Supporting families who provide care at home for children with disabilities. *Exceptional Children, 62*, 271–282.

Alberto, P. A., & Troutman, A. C. (1995). *Applied behavior analysis for teachers* (4th ed.). Englewood Cliffs, NJ: Merrill.

Allen, K. E. (1992). *The exceptional child: Mainstreaming in early childhood education* (2nd ed.). Albany, NY: Delmar.

Alley, G. R., & Deshler, D. D. (1979). *Teaching the learning disabled adolescent: Strategies and methods.* Denver, CO: Love Publishing.

American Academy of Ophthalmology. (1984). Policy statement. *Learning disabilities, dyslexia, and vision.* San Francisco: Author.

American Psychiatric Association. (1994). *Diagnostic and statistical manual of mental disorders* (4th ed) (DSM-IV). Washington, DC: American Psychiatric Association.

American Speech-Language-Hearing Association. (1982). Definitions: Communicative Disorders and Variations, *ASHA, 24*, 949–950.

Anthony, S. (1972). *The discovery of death in childhood and after.* New York: Basic Books.

Arc (1993, November–December). Second national status report on inclusion reveals slow progress. *ARC Newsletter,* p. 5.

Armstrong, D. G. (1990). *Developing and documenting the curriculum.* Boston: Allyn and Bacon.

Arnos, K. S., Israel, J., Devlin, L., & Wilson, M. P. (1996). Genetic aspects of hearing loss in childhood. In F. N. Martin & J. G. Clark (Eds.), *Hearing care for children* (pp. 20–44). Boston: Allyn and Bacon.

At-risk youth in crisis: A handbook for collaboration between schools and social services. (1991). Albany, OR: Linn-Benton Education Service Digest.

Atkins, M. S., & Pelham, W. E. (1991). School-based assessment of attention deficit–hyperactivity disorder. *Journal of Learning Disabilities, 24* (4), 197–204.

Austin, J. F. (1992). Involving noncustodial parents in their student's education. *NASSP Bulletin, 76*, 49–54.

Baker, S. B., & Rogosky-Grassi, M. A. (1993). Access to school. In F. L. Rowlley-Kelly & D. H. Reigel (Eds.), *Teaching the students with spina bifida* (pp. 31–70). Baltimore, MD: Brookes.

Banks, J. (1992). A comment on "Teacher perceptions of the Regular Education Initiative." *Exceptional Children, 58*, 564.

Barkley, R. A. (1990). *Attention deficit hyperactivity disorder: A handbook for diagnosis and treatment.* New York: Guilford Press.

Barkley, R. A. (1991). *Attention deficit hyperactivity disorder: A clinical workbook.* New York: Guilford Press.

Baroff, G. S. (1991). *Developmental disabilities: Psychosocial aspects.* Austin, TX: Pro-Ed.

Barr, R. D., & Parrett, W. H. (1995). *Hope at last for at-risk youth.* Boston: Allyn and Bacon.

Barraga, N. C., & Erin, J. N. (1992). *Visual handicaps and learning* (3rd ed.). Austin, TX: Pro-Ed.

Barrish, H. H., Saunders, M., & Wolf, M. M. (1969). Good-behavior game: Effects of individual contingencies for group consequences on disruptive behavior in a classroom. *Journal of Applied Behavior Analysis, 2*, 119–124.

Bauwens, J., & Hourcade, J. J. (1995). *Cooperative teaching: Rebuilding the schoolhouse for all students.* Austin, TX: Pro-Ed.

Beale, I. L., & Tippett, L. J. (1992). Remediation of psychological process deficits in learning disabilities. In N. N. Singh & I. L. Beale (Eds.), *Learning disabilities: Nature, theory, & treatment* (pp. 526–568). New York: Springer-Verlag.

Beirne-Smith, M. (1989a). A systematic approach for teaching notetaking skills to students with mild learning handicaps. *Academic Therapy, 24*, 425–437.

Beirne-Smith, M. (1989b). Teaching note-taking skills. *Academic Therapy, 24*, 452–458.

Beirne-Smith, M., Patton, J. R., & Ittenbach, R. (1994). *Mental retardation* (4th ed.). Columbus, OH: Merrill.

Bender, W. N. (1998). *Learning disabilities: Characteristics, identification, and teaching strategies* (3rd edition). Scarborough, ON: Allyn and Bacon.

Bender, W. N. (1995). *Learning disabilities: Characteristics, identification, and teaching strategies* (2nd ed.). Boston: Allyn and Bacon.

Bender, W. N. (1994). Social-emotional development: The task and the challenge. *Learning Disability Quarterly, 17*, 250–253.

Bender, W. N., & Wall, M. E. (1994). Social-emotional development of students with learning disabilities. *Learning Disability Quarterly, 17*, 323–341.

Bergland, M., & Hoffbauer, D. (1996). New opportunities for students with traumatic brain injury: Transition to postsecondary education. *Teaching Exceptional Children, 28,* 54–57.

Berry, V. S. (1995). Communication strategies for fully inclusive classrooms. In B. Rittenhouse & J. Dancer (Eds.), *The full inclusion of persons with disabilities in American society* (pp. 57–65). Levin, New Zealand: National Training Resource Centre.

Bigge, J. L. (1991). *Teaching individuals with physical and multiple disabilities* (3rd ed.). New York: Macmillan.

Biklen, D. (1990). Communication unbound: Autism and praxis. *Harvard Educational Review, 60* (3), 291–314.

Biklen, D., Morton, M. W., Gold, D., Berrigan, C., & Swaminathan, S. (1992). Facilitated communication: Implications for individuals with autism. *Topics in Language Disorders, 2,* 23.

Blackman, J. A. (1990). *Medical aspects of developmental disabilities in children birth to three* (2nd ed.). Rockville, MD: Aspen.

Blalock, G., & Patton, J. (1996). Transition and students with learning disabilities: Creating sound futures. *Journal of Learning Disabilities, 29,* 7–16.

Blenk, K. (1995). *Making school inclusion work: A guide to everyday practices.* Cambridge, MA: Brookline Books.

Bloom, T. (1996). Assistive listening devices. *The Hearing Journal, 49,* 20–23.

Bowman, B. T. (1994). The challenge of diversity. *Phi Delta Kappan, 76,* 218–224.

Brackett, D. (1990). Communication management of the mainstreamed hearing-impaired student. In M. Ross (Ed.), *Hearing-impaired children in the mainstream* (pp. 119–130). Parkton, MD: York Press.

Breeding, M., Stone, C., & Riley, K. (n.d.) *LINC: Language in the classroom.* Unpublished manuscript. Abilene, TX: Abilene Independent School District.

British Columbia Special Education Branch. (1995). *Special education services: A manual of policies, procedures and guidelines.* Victoria: Author.

Brody, J., & Good, T. (1986). Teacher behavior and student achievement. In M.C. Wittrock (Ed.), *Handbook of research on teaching* (pp. 328–375). New York: Macmillan.

Brolin, D. E. (1989). *Life-centered career education.* Reston, VA: CEC.

Browder, D., & Snell, M. E. (1988). Assessment of individuals with severe disabilities. In M. E. Snell (Ed.), *Severe disabilities.* Columbus, OH: Merrill.

Brown, D. L., & Moore, L. (1992). The Bama bookworm program: Motivating remedial readers to read at home with their parents. *Teaching Exceptional Children, 24,* 17–20.

Bruck, M.(1982). Language impaired children's performance in an additive bilingual education program. *Applied Psycholinguistics, 3,* 45–60.

Bruey, C. T. (1989). Daily life with your child. In M. D. Powers (Ed.), *Children with autism: A parent's guide.* New York: Woodbine House.

Bryan, T., Bay, M., & Donahue, M. (1988). Implications of the learning disabilities definition for the regular education initiative. *Journal of Learning Disabilities, 21* (1), 23–27.

Bryan, T., Bay, M., Lopez-Reyna, N., & Donahue, M. (1991). Characteristics of students with learning disabilities: A summary of the extent data base and its implications for educational programs. In. J. W. Lloyd, N. N. Singh, & A. C. Repp (Eds.), *The regular education initiative: Alternative perspectives* (pp. 121–131). Sycamore, IL: Sycamore.

Buchholz, E. S., & Korn-Bursztyn, C. (1993). Children of adolescent mothers: Are they at risk for abuse? *Adolescence, 28,* 361–382.

Buck, G. H., Bursuck, W. D., Polloway, E. A., Whitehouse, F., & Nelson, J. (in press). Homework-related communication problems: Perspectives of special education teachers. *Journal of Emotional and Behavioral Disorders.*

Bullock, L. (1992). *Exceptionalities in children and youth.* Boston: Allyn and Bacon.

Bullock, L. M., Zagar, E. L., Donahue, C. A., & Pelton, G. B. (1985). Teachers' perceptions of behaviorally disordered students in a variety of settings. *Exceptional Children, 52,* 123–130.

Burnley, G. D. (1993). A team approach for identification for an attention deficit hyperactivity disorder child. *The School Counselor, 40,* 228–230.

Buros Institute of Mental Measurement. (1994). *Tests in print IV: An index to tests, test reviewers, and the literature on specific tests.* Lincoln, NE: Buros Institute of Mental Measurement, University of Nebraska Press.

Buros Institute of Mental Measurement. (1998). *The thirteenth mental measurement yearbook.* J. C. Imara, & B. S. Plake (Eds). Lincoln, NE: Buros Institute of Mental Measurement, University of Nebraska Press.

Bursuck, W., Polloway, E., Epstein, M., & Jayanthi, M. (n.d.). Recommendations of general education teachers regarding communication problems about homework and students with disabilities. Manuscript in preparation.

Bursuck, W. D., Polloway, E. A., Plante, L., Epstein, M. H., Jayanthi, M., & McConeghy, J. (1996). Report card grading and adaptations: A national survey of classroom practices. *Exceptional Children, 62,* 301–318.

Butler-Hall, B. (1987). *Hall's articulation remediation training sheets (HARTS).* Henderson, TX: Creations Publications.

Byrne, J. M., Bawden, H. N., DeWolfe, N. A., & Beattie, T. L. (1998). Clinical assessment of psychopharmacological treatment of preschoolers with ADHD. *Journal of Clinical & Experimental Neuropsychology, 20* (5), 613–627.

Canadian National Institute for the Blind. (1999). *National Consultation on the Crisis in Vision Loss.* Toronto: Author.

Canadian Pediatric Society. (1998). *Children with school problems: A physician's manual.* A F. Mervyn and W. J. Mahoney (Eds.). Ottawa, ON: Canadian Pediatric Society.

Canadian Pediatric Society. (1990). The role of medication in the treatment of AD/HD: Position paper. *Canadian Medical Association Journal, 142* (8), 817–818.

Candler, A. C., & Hildreth, B. L. (1990). Characteristics of language disorders in learning disabled students. *Academic Therapy, 25* (3), 333–343.

Cantu, N. (1993). OCR clarifies evaluation requirements for ADD. *The Special Educator, 9* (1), 11–12.

Carey, S. T. (1987). Reading comprehension in first and second languages of immersion and francophone students. *Canadian Journal of Exceptional Children, 3,* 103–108.

Carnine, D. (1991). Curricular interventions for teaching higher order thinking to all students: Introduction to special series. *Journal of Learning Disabilities, 24,* 261–269.

Carnine, D., Silbert J., & Kameenui, E. J. (1990). *Direct instruction reading* (2nd ed.). Columbus, OH: Merrill.

Carpenter, S. L., & McKee-Higgins, E. (1996). Behavior management in inclusive classrooms. *Remedial and Special Education, 17,* 195–203.

Cartwright, G. P., Cartwright, C. A., & Ward, M. E. (1995). *Educating special learners (*4th ed.). Belmont, CA: Wadsworth.

Cassidy, V. M., & Stanton, J. E. (1959). An investigation of factors involved in the education placement of mentally retarded children: A study of differences between children in regular and special classes in Ohio. Columbus, OH: Ohio State University. (ERIC Document Reproduction Service No. ED 002752).

Cawley, J. (1984). *Developmental teaching of mathematics for the learning disabled.* Austin, TX: Pro-Ed.

Centers for Disease Control. (1988). *AIDS surveillance report.* Atlanta, GA: Author.

Chalfant, J. C., & Van Dusen Pysh, R. L. (1993). Teacher assistance teams: Implications for the gifted. In C. J. Maker (Ed.), *Critical issues in gifted education: Vol 3. Programs for the gifted in regular classrooms* (pp. 32–48). Austin, TX: Pro-Ed.

Chalmers, L. (1991). Classroom modifications for the mainstreamed student with mild handicaps. *Intervention in School and Clinic, 27* (1), 40–42, 51.

Chase, P. A., Hall, J. W., & Werkhaven, J. A. (1996). Sensorineural hearing loss in children: Etiology and pathology. In F. N. Martin & J. G. Clark (Eds.), *Hearing care for children* (pp. 73–88). Boston: Allyn and Bacon.

Cheney, C. O. (1989). The systematic adaptation of instructional materials and techniques for problem learners. *Academic Therapy, 25,* 25–30.

Christenson, S. L., Ysseldyke, J. E., & Thurlow, M. L. (1989). Critical instructional factors for students with mild handicaps: An integrative review. *Remedial and Special Education, 10* (5), 21–31.

Clark, B. (1992). *Growing up gifted: Developing the potential of children at home and at school* (4th ed.). New York: Merrill.

Clark, B. (1996). The need for a range of program options for gifted and talented students. In W. Stainback &

S. Stainback (Eds.), *Contoversial issues confronting special education: Divergent perspectives* (2nd ed., pp. 57–68). Boston: Allyn and Bacon.

Clark, J. G., & Jaindl, M. (1996). Conductive hearing loss in children: Etiology and pathology. In F. N. Martin & J. G. Clark (Eds.), *Hearing care for children* (pp. 45–72). Boston: Allyn and Bacon.

Clary, D. L., & Edwards, S. (1992). Spoken language. In E. A. Polloway, J. R. Patton, J. S. Payne, & R. A. Payne (Eds.), *Strategies for teaching learners with special needs* (4th ed., pp. 185–285). Columbus, OH: Merrill.

Clinkenbeard, P. R. (1991). Unfair expectations: A pilot study of middle school students' comparisons of gifted and regular classes. *Journal for the Education of the Gifted, 15,* 56–63.

Cochran, P. S., & Bull, G. L. (1993). Computers and individuals with speech and language disorders. In J. D. Kindsey (Ed.), *Computers and exceptional individuals* (pp. 211–242). Austin, TX: Pro-Ed.

Cohen, S. B. (1990). A modification perspective of special education curriculum: Introduction. *Academic Therapy, 25* (4), 391–394.

Condition of Education. (1990). Washington, DC: Office of Educational Research and Improvement.

Conroy, J. (1993). Classroom management: An expected view. In C. J. Maker (Ed.), *Critical issues in gifted education: Vol. 3. Programs for the gifted in regular classrooms* (pp. 227–257). Austin, TX: Pro-Ed.

Conte, R. (1991). Attention disorders. In B. Y. L. Wong (Ed.), *Learning about learning disabilities* (pp. 55–101). New York: Academic Press.

Cook, R. E., Tessier, A., & Klein, M. D. (1992). *Adapting early childhood curricula for children with special needs.* New York: Merrill.

Cooke, N. L., Heron, T. E., & Heward, W. L. (1983). *Peer tutoring: Implementing classroom-wide programs.* Columbus, OH: Special Press.

Cooper, H. (1989). *Homework.* White Plains, NY: Longman.

Corn, A. L., Hatlen, P., Huebner, K. M., Ryan, F., & Siller, M. A. (1995). *The national agenda for the education of children and youths with visual impairments, including those with multiple disabilities.* New York: American Foundation for the Blind.

Cosden, M. A. (1990). Expanding the role of special education. *Teaching Exceptional Children, 22,* 4–6.

Council for Exceptional Children. (1992). *Children with ADD: A shared responsibility.* Reston, VA: Author.

Council of Administrators of Special Education. (1992). *Student access: Section 504 of the rehabilitation act of 1973.* Reston, VA: Author.

Cramer, Sharon. (1997). *Collaboration: A success strategy for special educators.* Boston: Allyn and Bacon.

Creekmore, W. N. (1988). Family–classroom: A critical balance. *Academic Therapy, 24,* 207–220.

Crews, W. D., Bonaventura, S., Hay, C. L., Steele, W. K., & Rowe, F. B. (1993). Gilles de la Tourette disorder among individuals with severe or profound mental retardation. *Mental Retardation, 31,* 25–28.

Cronin, J. F. (1993). Four misconceptions about authentic learning. *Educational Leadership, 50* (7), 78–80.

Cronin, M. E. (1988). Adult performance outcomes/life skills. In G. Robinson, J. R. Patton, E. A. Polloway, & L. Sargent (Eds.), *Best practices in mental disabilities* (Vol. 2, pp. 39–52). Des Moines: Iowa State Department of Education.

Cronin, M. E., & Patton, J. R. (1993). *Life skills instruction for all students with special needs.* Austin, TX: Pro-Ed.

Cullinan, D., & Epstein, M. (1985). Teacher related adjustment problems. *Remedial and Special Education, 6,* 5–11.

Cummings, C. (1983). *Managing to teach.* Edmonds, WA: Teaching Inc.

Dagenais, P. A., Critz-Crosby, P., Fletcher, S. G., & McCutcheon, M. J. (1994). Comparing abilities of children with profound hearing impairments to learn consonants using electropalatography or traditional aural–oral techniques. *Journal of Speech and Hearing Research, 37,* 687–699.

Davies, P. W. S., & Joughin, C. (1993). Using stable isotopes to assess reduced physical activity of individuals with Prader-Willi syndrome. *American Journal on Mental Retardation, 98,* 349–353.

Davis, J. (1996). Two different flight plans: Advanced placement and gifted programs—different and necessary. *Gifted Child Today, 19* (2), 32–36, 50.

Davis, W. E. (1993). *At-risk children and educational reform: Implications for educators and schools in the year 2000 and beyond.* Orono, ME: College of Education, University of Maine.

Davis, W. E. (1995). Students at risk: Common myths and misconceptions. *The Journal of At-Risk Issues, 2,* 5–10.

Day V. P., & Elksnin, L. K. (May 1994). Promoting strategic learning. *Intervention in School and Clinic, 29* (5), 262–270.

deBettencourt, L. U. (1987). How to develop parent relationships. *Teaching Exceptional Children, 19,* 26–27.

deBettencourt, L. U., Zigmond, N., & Thornton, H. (1989). Follow-up of postsecondary-age rural learning disabled graduates and dropouts. *Exceptional Children, 56,* 40–49.

Deiner, P. L. (1993). *Resources for teaching children with diverse abilities: Birth through eight.* Fort Worth, TX: Harcourt Brace Jovanovich.

Del Prete, T. (1996). Asset or albatross? The education and socialization of gifted students. *Gifted Child Today, 19* (2), 24–25, 44–49.

DeLong, R. (1995). Medical and pharmacological treatment of learning disabilities. *Journal of Child Neurology, 10* (suppl. 1), 92–95.

Deno, E. (1970). Special education as development capital. *Exceptional Children, 55,* 440–447.

Deno, S. L., Foegen, A., Robinson, S., & Espin, C. (1996). Commentary: Facing the realities of inclusion for students with mild disabilities. *Journal of Special Education, 30,* 345–357.

Deno, S. L., & Fuchs, L. S. (1987). Developing curriculum-based measurement systems for data-based special education problem-solving. *Focus on Exceptional Children, 19* (8), 1–16.

Deshler, D. D., Ellis, E. S., & Lenz, B. K. (1996). *Teaching adolescents with learning disabilities: Strategies and methods* (2nd ed.). Denver: Love Publishing.

Deshler, D. D., & Lenz, B. K. (1989). The strategies instructional approach. *International Journal of Disability, Development and Education, 36* (3), 203–224.

Deshler, D., & Schumaker, J. B. (1988). Learning strategies: An instructional alternative for low-achieving adolescents. *Exceptional Children, 52,* 83–89.

Deshler, D., Schumaker, J. B., Lenz, B. K., & Ellis, E. S. (1984). Academic and cognitive interventions for LD adolescents (Part II). *Journal of Learning Disabilities, 17* (3), 170–179.

Diana v. *State Board of Education,* C-70-37 R.F.P. (N.D., California, Jan. 7, 1970, and June 18, 1972).

Diefendorf, A. O. (1996). Hearing loss and its effects. In F. N. Martin & J. G. Clark (Eds.), *Hearing care for children* (pp. 3–18). Boston: Allyn and Bacon.

Donahue, K., & Zigmond, N. (1990). Academic grades of ninth-grade urban learning disabled students and low-achieving peers. *Exceptionality, 1,* 17–27.

Dorn, L., & Allen, A. (1995). Helping low-achieving first-grade readers: A program combining reading recovery tutoring and small-group instruction. *Journal of School Research and Information, 13,* 16–24.

Dougherty, E. H., & Dougherty, A. (1977). The daily report card: A simplified and flexible package for classroom behavior management. *Psychology in the Schools, 14,* 191–195.

Douglas, V. L., Barr, R. G., Desilets, J., & Sherman, E. (1995). Do high doses of stimulants impair flexible thinking in attention-deficit hyperactivity disorder? *Journal of the American Academy of Child & Adolescent Psychiatry, 34* (7), 877–885.

Dowdy, C. (1990). *Modifications for regular classes.* Unpublished manuscript, Alabama Program for Exceptional Children.

Dowdy, C. A. (1997). Strengths and limitations inventory: School version. In C. A. Dowdy, J. Patton, T. E. C. Smith, & E. A. Polloway. *Attention-deficit/hyperactivity disorder in the classroom: A practical guide for teachers.* Austin, TX: Pro-Ed.

Dowdy, C. A., Carter, J., & Smith, T. E. C. (1990). Differences in transitional needs of high school students with and without learning disabilities. *Journal of Learning Disabilities, 23* (6), 343–348.

Dowdy, C. A., Patton, J. R., Smith, T. E. C., & Polloway, E. A. (1997). *Attention-deficit/hyperactivity disorder: Practical guide for teachers.* Austin, TX: Pro-Ed.

Dowdy, C. A., & Smith, T. E. C. (1991). Future-based assessment and intervention. *Intervention in School and Clinic, 27* (2), 101–106.

Doyle, W. (1986). Classroom organization and management. In M. C. Wittrock (Ed.), *Handbook of research and teaching* (3rd ed., pp. 392–431). New York: Macmillan.

Drug use increasing. (1992). *Youth Today, 1,* 27–29.

Duane, D. D., & Gray, D. B. (Eds.) (1991). *The reading brain: The biological basis of dyslexia.* Parkton, MD: York.

Dunst, C. J., Johanson, C., Trivette, C. M., & Hamby, D. (1991). Family-oriented early intervention policies and practices: Family-centered or not? *Exceptional Children, 58,* 115–126.

Durden, W. G. (1995, October 4). Where is the middle ground? *Education Week,* pp. 47–48.

Dworet, D. H. & Rathgeber, A. J. (1998). Confusion reigns: Definitions of behaviour exceptionalities in Canada. *Exceptionality Education Canada, 8* (1), 3–19.

Dworet, D. H. & Rathgeber, A. J. (1990). Provincial and territorial government responses to behaviorally disordered students in Canada in 1988. *Behavioral Disorders, 15,* 201–209.

Eaves, R. C. (1992). Autism. In P. J. McLaughlin and P. Wehman (Eds.). *Developmental disabilities* (pp. 68–80). Boston: Andover Medical Publishers.

Edgar, E. (1987). Secondary programs in special education: Are many of them justifiable? *Exceptional Children, 53,* 555–561.

Edgar, E. (1988). Employment as an outcome for mildly handicapped students: Current status and future directions. *Focus on Exceptional Children, 21* (1), 1–8.

Edgar, E. (1990, Winter). Is it time to change our view of the world? *Beyond Behavior,* 9–13.

Edgar, E., & Polloway, E. A. (1994). Education for adolescents with disabilities: Curriculum and placement issues. *Journal of Special Education, 27,* 438–452.

Edwards, C. (1996). Educational management of children with hearing loss. In F. N. Martin & J. G. Clark (Eds.), *Hearing care for children* (pp. 303–315). Boston: Allyn and Bacon.

Egel, A. L. (1989). Finding the right educational program. In M. D. Powers (Ed.), *Children with autism: A parent's guide.* New York: Woodbine House.

Eggert, L. L., & Herting, J. R. (1993). Drug involvement among potential dropouts and "typical" youth. *Journal of Drug Education, 23,* 31–55.

Ehlers, V. L., & Ruffin, M. (1990). The Missouri project—Parents as teachers. *Focus on Exceptional Children, 23,* 1–14.

Elam, S. M., & Rose, L. C. (1995). Of the public's attitudes toward the public schools. *Phi Delta Kappan, 77,* 41–56.

Elizer, E., & Kauffman, M. (1983). Factors influencing the severity of childhood bereavement reactions. *American Journal of Orthopsychiatry, 53,* 393–415.

Ellis, E. S. (1994). Integrating writing strategy instruction: Part ll—Writing processes. *Intervention in School and Clinic, 29* (4), 219–228.

Ellis, E. S., & Lenz, B. K. (1990). Techniques for mediating content-area learning: Issues and research. *Focus on Exceptional Children, 22,* 1–16.

Emerick, L. L., & Haynes, W. O. (1986). *Diagnosis and evaluation in speech pathology* (3rd ed.). Englewood Cliffs, NJ: Prentice-Hall.

Emery, R. E. (1989). Family violence. *American Psychologist, 44,* 321–327.

Engelmann, S., & Carnine, D. (1982). *Theory of instruction.* New York: Irvington.

Epilepsy Foundation of America. (1992). *Seizure recognition and observation: A guide for allied health professionals.* Landover, MD: Author.

Epstein, M. H., Patton, J. R., Polloway, E. A., & Foley, R. (1992). Educational services for students with behavior disorders: A review of individualized education programs. *Teacher Education and Special Education, 15,* 41–48.

Epstein, M. H., Polloway, E. A., Buck, G. H., Bursuck, W. D., Wissinger, L. M., Whitehouse, F., & Jayanthi, M. (n.d.). Homework-related communication problems: Perspectives of general education teachers. Manuscript submitted for publication.

Epstein, M. H., Polloway, E. A., Bursuck, W., Jayanthi, M., & McConeghy, J. (1996). Recommendations for effective homework practices. Manuscript in preparation.

Epstein, M. H., Polloway, E. A., Foley, R. M., & Patton, J. R. (1993). Homework: A comparison of teachers' and parents' perceptions of the problems experienced by students identified as having behavioral disorders, learning disabilities, or no disabilities. *Remedial and Special Education, 14* (5), 40–50.

Erickson, J. G. (1992, April). *Communication disorders in multicultural populations.* Paper presented at the Texas Speech-Language-Hearing Association Annual Convention, San Antonio, TX.

Erwin, E. J. (1993). The philosophy and status of inclusion. *The Lighthouse,* 1–4.

Evertson, C. M., Emmer, E. T., Clements, B. J., Sanford, J. P., & Worsham, M. E. (1989). *Classroom management for elementary teachers* (2nd ed.). Englewood Cliffs, NJ: Prentice-Hall.

Fehling, R. H. (1993). *Weekday speech activities to promote carryover.* Austin, TX: Pro-Ed.

Feingold, B. F. (1975). *Why your child is hyperactive.* New York: Random House.

Feldhusen, H. J. (1993a). Individualized teaching of the gifted in regular classrooms. In C. J. Maker (Ed.), *Critical issues in gifted education: Vol. 3. Programs for the gifted in regular classrooms* (pp. 263–273). Austin, TX: Pro-Ed.

Feldhusen, H. J. (1993b). Synthesis of research on gifted youth. *Educational Leadership, 22,* 6–11.

Felner, R., Ginter, M., Boike, M., & Cowan, E. (1981). Parental death or divorce and the school adjustment of young children. *American Journal of Community Psychology, 9,* 181–191.

Ferguson, D. L. (1995). The real challenge of inclusion: Confessions of a "rabid inclusionist." *Phi Delta Kappan, 77,* 281–287.

Fiore, T. A., Becker, E. A., & Nerro, R. C. (1993). Educational interventions for students with attention deficit disorder. *Exceptional Children, 60,* 163–173.

Fisher, J. B., Schumaker, J., & Deshler, D. D. (1995). Searching for validated inclusive practices: A review of the literature. *Focus on Exceptional Children, 28,* 1–20.

Fletcher, J. M., Shayurtz, S. E., & Shankweiler, D. P. (1994). Cognitive profiles or reading disability: Comparisons of discrepancy and low achievement definitions. *Journal of Educational Psychology, 86* (6), 6–23.

Foley, R. M., & Kittleson, M. J. (1993). Special educators' knowledge of HIV transmission: Implications for teacher education programs. *Teacher Education and Special Education, 16,* 342–350.

Forest, M., & Lusthaus, E. (1990). Everyone belongs with the MAPS action planning system. *Teaching Exceptional Children, 22,* 32–35.

Forness, S. R., & Polloway, E. A. (1987). Physical and psychiatric diagnoses of pupils with mild mental retardation currently being referred for related services. *Education and Training in Mental Retardation, 22,* 221–228.

Foster-Johnson, L., & Dunlap, G. (1993). Using functional assessment to develop effective, individualized interventions for challenging behaviors. *Teaching Exceptional Children, 56,* 44–52.

Fowler, M. (1992). *C.H.A.D.D. educators manual: An indepth look at attention deficit disorder for an educational perspective.* Fairfax, VA: CASET Associates, Ltd.

Friedman, D., & Scaduto, J. J. (1995). Let's do lunch. *Teaching Exceptional Children, 28,* 22–26.

Friend, M., Bursuck, W., & Hutchinson, N. (1998). *Including exceptional students: A practical guide for classroom teachers.* Scarborough, ON: Allyn and Bacon.

Fuchs, D., & Fuchs, L. S. (1994–1995). Sometimes separate is better. *Educational Leadership, 52,* 22–24.

Fuchs, L. S., & Fuchs, D. (1986). Effects of systematic formative evaluation: A meta-analysis. *Exceptional Children, 53,* 199–208.

Fuchs, L. S., Fuchs, D., Hamlett, C. L., Phillips, N. B., & Karns, K. (1995). General educators' specialized adaptations for students with learning disabilities. *Exceptional Children, 61,* 440–459.

Fuchs, L. S., Fuchs, D., Hamlett, C., & Stecker, P. (1991). Effects of curriculum-based measurement and consultation on teacher planning and student achievement in mathematics operation. *American Educational Research Journal, 28,* 617–641.

Fulk, B. M., & Montgomery-Grymes, D. J. (1994). Strategies to improve student motivation. *Intervention in School and Clinic, 30* (1), 28–33.

Gajria, M., & Salend, S. J. (1995). Homework practices of students with and without learning disabilities: A comparison. In W. Bursuck (Ed.), *Homework: Issues and practices for students with learning disabilities* (pp. 97–106). Austin, TX: Pro-Ed.

Gallagher, J. J. (1979). *Issues in gifted education.* Ventura, CA: Ventura County Superintendent of Schools Office.

Gallagher, J. J., & Gallagher, S. A. (1994). *Teaching the gifted child* (4th ed.). Boston: Allyn and Bacon.

Gardner, H. (1983). *Frames of mind: The theory of multiple intelligences.* New York: Basic Books.

Gardner, H., & Hatch, T. (1989). Multiple intelligences go to school: Educational implications of the theory of multiple intelligences. *Educational Researcher, 18* (8), 4–9.

Gardner, J. E., & Edyburn, D. L. (1993). Teaching applications with exceptional individuals. In J. D. Lindsey (Ed.), *Computers and Exceptional Individuals* (pp. 264–286). Austin, TX: Pro-Ed.

Gardner, J. F., & O'Brien, J. (1990). The principle of normalization. In J. F. Gardner & M. S. Chapman (Eds.), *Program issues in developmental disabilities* (pp. 39–58). Baltimore, MD: Brookes.

Gargiulo, R. M. (1990). Child abuse and neglect: An overview. In R. L. Goldman & R. M. Gargiulo (Eds.), *Children at risk* (pp. 1–35). Austin, TX: Pro-Ed.

Gargiulo, R. S., O'Sullivan, P., Stephens, D. G., & Goldman, R. (1989–1990). Sibling relationships in mildly handicapped children: A preliminary investigation. *National Forum of Special Education Journal, 1,* 20–28.

Gartland, D. (1994). Content area reading: Lessons from the specialists. *LD Forum, 19* (3), 19–22.

Gearheart, B. R., Weishahn, M. W., & Gearheart, C. J. (1996). *The exceptional student in the regular classroom* (6th ed.). Columbus, OH: Merrill.

Gersh, E. S. (1991). What is cerebral palsy? In E. Geralis (Ed.), *Children with cerebral palsy: A parents' guide.* New York: Woodbine House.

Gerstein, R., Brengleman, S., & Jimenez, R. (1994). Effective instruction for culturallyand linguistically diverse students: A reconceptualization. *Focus on Exceptional Children, 27* (1), 1–6.

Gerstein, R., & Woodward, J. (1994). The language-minority student and special education: Issues, trends, and paradoxes. *Exceptional Children, 60* (4), 310–322.

Geschwind, N., & Galaburda, A. M. (1985). Cerebral lateralization: Biological mechanisms, associations, and pathology: Part 1. A hypothesis and program for research. *Archives of Neurology, 42* (5), 428–459.

Ghosh, R. (1996). *Redefining multicultural education.* Toronto: Harcourt Brace Canada.

Giangreco, M. F., Dennis, R., Cloninger, C., Edelman, S., & Schattman, R. (1993). I've counted Jon: Transformational experiences of teachers educating students with disabilities. *Exceptional Children, 59,* 359–372.

Ginsberg, R., Gerber, P. J., & Reiff, H. B. (1994). Employment success for adults with learning disabilities. In P. Gerber & H. Reiff (Eds.), *Learning disabilities in adulthood* (pp. 204–213). Stoneham, MA: Andover Medical Publishers.

Goldman, R. L., & Gargiulo, R. M. (1990). Child abuse. In R. L. Goldman & R. M. Gargiulo (Eds.), *Children at risk* (pp. 37–49). Austin, TX: Pro-Ed.

Goldstein, S., & Goldstein, M. (1990). *Managing attention disorder in children: A guide for practitioners.* New York: John Wiley & Sons.

Goldstein, S., & Turnbull, A. P. (1981). Strategies to increase parent participation in IEP conferences. *Exceptional Children, 48,* 360–361.

Gollnick, D. M., & Chinn, P.C. (1994). *Multicultural education in a pluralistic society* (4th ed.). New York: Macmillan College Publishing.

Good, T. L., & Brophy, J. E. (1987). *Educational psychology* (3rd ed.). New York: Longman.

Goree, K. (1996). Making the most out of inclusive setting. *Gifted Child Today, 19* (2), 22–23, 43.

Graham, S. (1992). Helping students with LD progress as writers. *Intervention in School and Clinic, 27,* 134–144.

Grant, C. A., & Sleeter, C. E. (1989). *Turning on learning: Five approaches for multicultural teaching plans for race, class, gender, and disability.* Englewood Cliffs, NJ: Prentice-Hall.

Greer, J. V. (1991). At-risk students in the fast lanes: Let them through. *Exceptional Children, 57,* 390–391.

Gresham, F. M. (1984). Social skills and self-efficacy for exceptional children. *Exceptional Children, 51,* 253–261.

Grosenick, J. K., George, N. L., George, M. P., & Lewis, T. J. (1991). Public school services for behaviorally disordered students: Program practices in the 1980s. *Behavioral Disorders, 16,* 87–96.

Grossman, H. J. (1983). *Classification in mental retardation.* Washington, DC: American Association on Mental Deficiency.

Guernsey, M. A. (1989). Classroom organization: A key to successful management. *Academic Therapy, 25,* 55–58.

Guetzloe, E. (1988). Suicide and depression: Special education's responsibility. *Teaching Exceptional Children, 20,* 25–28.

Guterman, B. R. (1995). The validity of categorical learning disabilities services: The consumer's view. *Exceptional Children, 62,* 111–124.

Hallahan, D. P., & Kauffman, J. M. (1991). *Exceptional children: Introduction to special education* (5th ed.). Boston: Allyn and Bacon.

Hallahan, D. P., & Kauffman, J. M. (1997). *Exceptional learners: Introduction to special education* (7th ed.). Boston: Allyn and Bacon.

Hallahan, D. P., & Kauffman, J. M. (1995). *The illusion of full inclusion.* Austin, TX: Pro-Ed.

Hallahan, D. P., Kauffman, J. M., & Lloyd, J. W. (1996). *Introduction to learning disabilities.* Boston: Allyn and Bacon.

Hallahan, D. P., Lloyd, J. W., & Stoller, L. (1982). *Improving attention with self-monitoring: A manual for teachers.* Charlottesville, VA: University of Virginia Press.

Hammill, D. (1993). A brief look at the learning disabilities movement in the United States. *Journal of Learning Disabilities, 26,* 295–310.

Hammill, D. (1990). On defining learning disabilities: An emerging consensus. *Journal of Learning Disabilities, 23,* 74–84.

Hammill, D. D., & Larsen, S. C. (1974). The effectiveness of psycholinguistic training. *Exceptional Children, 41,* 5–14.

Hamre-Nietupski, S., Ayres, B., Nietupski, J., Savage, M., Mitchell, B., & Bramman, H. (1989). Enhancing integration of students with severe disabilities through curricular infusion: A general/special educator partnership. *Education and Training in Mental Retardation, 24,* 78–88.

Hansen, C. R. (1992). What is Tourette syndrome? In T. Haerle (Ed.), *Children with Tourette syndrome: A parents' guide* (pp. 1–25). Rockville, MD: Woodbine House.

Hanson, M. J., & Carta, J. J. (1996). Addressing the challenges of families with multiple risks. *Exceptional Children, 62,* 201–212.

Hardman, M. L., Drew, C. J., Egan, M. W., & Wolf, B. (1993). *Human exceptionality: Society, school, and family* (4th ed.). Boston: Allyn and Bacon.

Haring, K. A., Lovett, D. L., & Saren, D. (1991). Parent perceptions of their adult offspring with disabilities. *Teaching Exceptional Children, 23,* 6–10.

Haring, K. A., Lovett, D. L., & Smith, D. D. (1990). A follow-up of recent special education graduates of learning disabilities programs. *Journal of Learning Disabilities, 23* (2), 108–113.

Harris, D., & Vanderheiden, G. C. (1980). Augmentative communication techniques. In R. L. Schiefelbusch (Ed.), *Nonspeech language and communication: Analysis and intervention* (pp. 259–302). Austin, TX: Pro-Ed.

Harry, B. (1992). *Cultural diversity, families, and the special education system: Communication and empowerment.* New York: Teachers College Press.

Harwell, J. M. (1989). *Learning disabilities handbook.* West Nyack, NY: Center for Applied Research in Education.

Hasbrouck, J. E., & Tindal G. (1992). Curriculum-based oral reading fluency norms for students in grades 2 through 5. *Teaching Exceptional Children, 24* (3), 41–44.

Hasselbring, T., & Goin, L. (1993). Integrated media and technology. In E. A. Polloway & J. R. Patton (Eds.), Strategies for teaching learners with special needs (5th ed., pp. 145–162). Columbus, OH: Macmillan.

Hazel, J. S., Schumaker, J. B., Shelon, J., & Sherman, J. A. (1982). Application of a group training program in social skills to learning disabled and non-learning disabled youth. *Learning Disability Quarterly, 5,* 398–408.

Heath, N. L. (1996). The emotional domain: Self-concept and depression in children with learning disabilities. *Advances in Learning and Behavioral Disabilities, 10,* 47–75.

Heath, N. L. (1995). Distortion and deficit: Self-perceived versus actual academic competence in depressed and non-depressed children with and without learning disabilities. *Learning Disabilities Research & Practice, 10,* 2–10.

Heath, N. L., & MacLean-Heywood, D. (1999). Research highlights: A clinic school partnership program for including students with behavioral problems. In

J. Andrews & J. Lupart, (Eds.), *The inclusive classroom, instructor's manual.* Toronto: ITP Nelson.

Heath, N. L., & Wiener, J. (1996). Depression and nonacademic self-perceptions in children with and without learning disabilities. *Learning Disability Quarterly, 19,* 34–44.

Heaton, S., & O'Shea, D. J. (1995). Using mnemonics to make mnemonics. *Teaching Exceptional Children, 28* (1), 34–36.

Heller, K. W., Alberto, P. A., Forney, P. E., & Schwartzman, M. N. (1996). *Understanding physical, sensory, and health impairments.* Pacific Grove, CA: Brooks Publishing Co.

Herskowitz, J., & Rosman, N. P. (1982). *Pediatric, neurology, and psychiatry—Common ground.* New York: Macmillan.

Hess, R., Miller, A., Reese, J., & Robinson, G. (1987). *Grading-credit-diploma: Accommodation practices.* Des Moines, IA: Department of Education.

Heward, W. L. (1995). *Exceptional children: An introductory survey of special education* (4th ed.). New York: Macmillan.

Heward, W. L., & Orlansky, M. D. (1992). *Exceptional children: An introductory survey of special education* (4th ed.). New York: Merrill.

Hietsch, D. G. (1986). Father involvement: No moms allowed. *Teaching Exceptional Children, 18,* 258–260.

Hill, D. (1991). Tasting failure: Thoughts of an at-risk learner. *Phi Delta Kappan, 73,* 308–310.

Hiller, J. F. (1990) Setting up a classroom-based language instruction program: One clinician's experience. *Texas Journal of Audiology and Speech Pathology, 16* (2), 12–13.

Hilton, A. (1990). Parental reactions to having a disabled child. Paper presented at annual International Conference of the Council for Exceptional Children.

Hobson v. Hansen, 269 F. Supp. 401 (D.D.C.), 1967.

Hocutt, A., Martin, E., & McKinney, J. (1990). Historical and legal context of mainstreaming. In J. W. Lloyd, N. N. Singh, & A. C. Repp (Ed.), *The Regular Education Initiative: Alternative perspectives on concepts, issues, and models* (pp. 17–28). Sycamore, IL: Sycamore.

Homme, L. (1969). *How to use contingency contracting in the classroom.* Champaign, IL: Research Press.

Hoover, J. J. (1988a). *Curriculum adaptation for students with learning and behavior problems: Principles and practices.* Lindale, TX: Hamilton Publications.

Hoover, J. J. (1988b). Implementing a study skills program in the classroom. *Academic Therapy, 24,* 471–476.

Hoover, J. J. (1990). Curriculum adaptations: A five-step process for classroom implementation. *Academic Therapy, 25,* 407–416.

Hoover, J. J., & Patton, J. R. (1995). *Teaching students with learning problems to use study skills: A teacher's guide.* Austin, TX: Pro-Ed.

Housego, B. E. J. (1990). Student teachers' feelings of preparedness to teach. *Canadian Journal of Education, 15,* 37–56.

Hoy, C., & Gregg, N. (1994). *Assessment: The special educator's role.* Pacific Grove, CA: Brooks/Cole.

Hudson Institute. (1987). *Workforce 2000: Work and workers for the 21st century.* Indianapolis, IN: Author.

Huntze, S. L. (1985). A position paper of the Council for Children with Behavior Disorders. *Behavior Disorders, 10,* 167–174.

Hux, K., & Hackley, C. (1996). Mild traumatic brain injury. *Intervention in School and Clinic, 31,* 158–165.

Hynd, G. W., Marshall, R., & Gonzalez, J. (1991). Learning disabilities and presumed central nervous system dysfunction. *Learning Disability Quarterly, 14,* 283–295.

ICD-10: International statistical classification of diseases and related health problems (10th rev. ed.). (1992). Geneva, Switzerland: World Health Organization.

Idol, L. (1983). *Special educator's consultation handbook.* Austin, TX: Pro-Ed.

Infusini, M. (1994). From the patient's point of view. *The Journal of Cognitive Rehabilitation, 12,* 4–5.

Inge, K. J. (1992). Cerebral palsy. In P. J. McLaughlin & P. Wehman (Eds.), *Developmental disabilities* (pp. 30–53). Boston: Andover Press.

Jan, J. E., Ziegler, R. G., & Erba, G. (1991). *Does your child have epilepsy?* (2nd ed.). Austin, TX: Pro-Ed.

Jaquish, C., & Stella, M. A. (1986). Helping special students move from elementary to secondary school. *Counterpoint, 7* (1), 1.

Jastak, S. R., & Wilkinson, G. S. (1984). *The wide range achievement test—Revised.* Wilmington, DE: Jastak Associates.

Jayanthi, M., Nelson, J. S., Sawyer, V., Bursuck, W. D., & Epstein, M. H. (1994). Homework-communication problems among parents, general education, and special education teachers: An exploratory study. *Remedial and Special Education, 16* (2), 102–116.

Jenkins, J. R., & Heinen, A. (1989). Students' preferences for service delivery: Pull-out , in-class, or integrated models. *Exceptional Children, 55,* 516–523.

Jenkins, J. R., Pious, C. G., & Jewell, M. (1990). Special education and the regular education initiative: Basic assumptions. *Exceptional Children, 56* (6), 479–491.

Johnson, L. J., Pugach, M. C., & Devlin, S. (1990). Professional collaboration. *Teaching Exceptional Children, 22,* 9–11.

Jones, V. F., & Jones, L. S. (1995). Comprehensive classroom management (4th ed.). Boston: Allyn and Bacon.

Kamps, D. B., Leonard, B. R., Vernon, S., Dugan, E. P., Delquadri, J. C., Gershon, B., Wade, L., & Folk, L. (1992). Teaching social skills to students with autism to increase peer interactions in an integrated first-grade classroom. *Journal of Applied Behavior Analysis, 25,* 281–288.

Kaplan, P. S. (1996). *Pathways for exceptional children: School, home, and culture.* St. Paul, MN: West Publishing.

Kataoka, J. C. (1987). *An example of integrating literature.* Unpublished manuscript.

Kataoka, J. C., & Patton, J. R. (1989). Integrated curriculum. *Science and Children, 16,* 52–58.

Kauffman, J. M. (1997). *Characteristics of emotional and behavioral disorders of children and youths* (6th ed.). New York: Merrill/Macmillan.

Kauffman, J. M., Lloyd, J. W., Baker, J., & Riedel, T. M. (1995). Inclusion of all students with emotional or behavioral disorders? Let's think again. *Phi Delta Kappan,* 542–546.

Kauffman, J. M., & Wong, K. L. H. (1991). Effective teachers of students with behavioral disorders: Are generic teaching skills enough? *Behavioral Disorders, 16,* 225–237.

Kavale, K. A., & Forness, S. R. (1996). Treating social skill deficits in whildren with learning disabilities: A meta-analysis of the research. *Learning Disability Quarterly, 19* (1), 2–13.

Kazdin, A. E. (1989). Developmental psychopathology: Current research issues and directions. *American Psychologist, 44,* 180–187.

Keating, D. P. (1990). Adolescent thinking. In S. S. Feldman & G. R. Elliott (Eds.), *At the threshold: The developing adolescent* (pp.54–89). Boston, MA: Harvard University Press.

Kerrin, R. G. (1996). Collaboration: Working with the speech-language pathologist. *Intervention in School and Clinic, 32*(1), 56–59.

Kids count data book, Annie E. Casey Foundation. (1996). Baltimore, MD: Author.

King-Sears, M. E., & Bradley, D. (1995). Classwide peer tutoring: Heterogeneous instruction in general education classrooms. *Preventing School Failure, 40,* 29–36.

King-Sears, M. E., & Cummings, C. S. (1996). Inclusive practices of classroom teachers. *Remedial and Special Education, 17,* 217–225.

Kirk, S. A. (1962). *Educating exceptional children.* Boston: Houghton Mifflin.

Kirk, S.A., & Gallagher, J.J. (1985). *Educating exceptional children* (5th ed.). Boston: Houghton Mifflin.

Kirk, S. A., & Gallagher, J. J. (1988). *Educating exceptional children* (6th ed.). Boston: Houghton Mifflin.

Kirk, S. A., & Gallagher, J. J., & Anastasiow, N. J. (1993). *Educating exceptional children* (7th ed.). Boston: Houghton Mifflin.

Kirsten, I. (1981). *The Oakland picture dictionary.* Wauconda, IL: Don Johnston.

Kitano, M. K. (1993). Critique of Feldhusen's "individualized teaching of the gifted in regular classrooms." In C. J. Maker (Ed.), *Critical issues in gifted education: Vol. 3. Programs for the gifted in regular classrooms* (pp. 274–281). Austin, TX: Pro-Ed.

Kluwin, T. N. (1996). Getting hearing and deaf students to write to each other through dialogue journals. *Teaching Exceptional Children, 28,* 50–53.

Knitzer, J., Steinberg, Z., & Fleisch, B. (1990). *At the schoolhouse door.* New York: Bank Street College of Education.

Knoblock, P. (1982). *Teaching and mainstreaming autistic children.* Denver: Love Publishing.

Knowles, M. (1984). *The adult learner: A neglected species* (3rd ed.). Houston: Gulf Publishing.

Koegel, L. K., Koegel, R. L., Hurley, C., & Frea, W. D. (1992). Improving social skills and disruptive behavior in children with autism through self-management. *Journal of Applied Behavior Analysis, 25,* 341–353.

Korinek, L., & Polloway, E. A. (1993). Social skills: Review and implications for instruction for students with mild mental retardation. In R. A. Gable & S. F. Warren (Eds.), *Advances in mental retardation and developmental disabilities* (Vol. 5, pp. 71–97). London: Jessica Kingsley.

Kounin, J. (1970). *Discipline and group management in classrooms.* New York: Holt, Rinehart & Winston.

Krauss, M. W. (1990). New precedent in family policy: Individualized family service plan. *Exceptional Children, 56,* 388–395.

Kuster, J. M. (1993). Experiencing a day of conductive hearing loss. *Journal of School Health, 63,* 235–237.

Lahey, M. (1988). *Language disorders and language development.* New York: Macmillan.

Lang, G., & Berberich, C. (1995). *All children are special: Creating an inclusive classroom.* York, ME: Stenhouse Publishers.

Lapadat, J. C. (1991). Pragmatic language skills of students with language and/or learning disabilities: A quantitative synthesis. *Journal of Learning Disabilities, 24* (3), 147–158.

LaQuey, A. (1981). *Adult performance level adaptation and modification project.* Austin, TX: Educational Service Center, Region XIII.

Larry P. v. *Riles,* C-71-2270 (RFP, District Court for Northern California), 1972.

LDA Newsbriefs. (1996). Toll free access to adult services. *LDA Newsbriefs, 31*(3), 22 and 24.

Learning Disabilities Association of Canada. (1987). *LDAC definition of learning disabilities.* Ottawa, ON: Author.

Lerner, J. W. (1993). *Learning disabilities: Theories, diagnosis, and teaching strategies.* Boston: Houghton Mifflin.

Lesar, S., Gerber, M. M., & Semmel, M. (1996). HIV infection in children: Family stress, social support, and adaptations. *Exceptional Children, 62,* 224–236.

Leverett, R. G., & Diefendorf, A. O. (1992). Suggestions for frustrated teachers. *Teaching Exceptional Children, 24,* 30–35.

Lewis, J. K. (1992). Death and divorce—Helping students cope in single-parent families. *NAASP Bulletin, 76,* 49–54.

Litty, P., Kowalski, L., & Minor, R. (1996). Modifying the effects of physical abuse and perceived social support on the potential of abuse. *Child Abuse and Neglect, 20,* 305–314.

Lloyd, J. (1988). Academic instruction and cognitive techniques: The need for attack strategy training. *Exeptional Education Quarterly, 1,* 53–63.

Lloyd, J. W., Landrum, T., & Hallahan, D. P. (1991). Self-monitoring applications for classroom intervention. In G. Stoner, M. R. Shinn, & H. M. Walker (Eds.), *Interventions for achievement and behavior problems* (pp. 201–213). Washington, DC: NASP.

Lopez, R., & MacKenzie, J. (1993). A learning center approach to individualized instruction for gifted students. In C. J. Maker (Ed.), *Critical issues in gifted education: Vol. 3. Programs for the gifted in regular classrooms* (pp. 282–295). Austin, TX: Pro-Ed.

Lord, J. (1991). *Lives in transition: The process of personal empowerment*. Kitchener, ON: Center for Research and Education in Human Services.

Lovitt, T. C., Cushing, S. S., & Stump, C. S. (1994). High school students rate their IEPs: Low opinions and lack of ownership. *Intervention in School and Clinic, 30* (1), 34–37.

Luckasson, R., Coulter, D., Polloway, E. A., Reiss, S., Schalock, R., Snell, M., Spitalnik, D., & Stark, J. (1992). *Mental retardation: Definition, classification and systems of supports*. Washington, DC: American Association of Mental Retardation.

Luckasson, R., Schalock, R., Snell, M., & Spitalnik, D. (1996). The 1992 AAMR definition and preschool children: Response from the committee on terminology and classification. *Mental Retardation, 34,* 247–253.

Luckner, J. (1994). Developing independent and responsible behaviors in students who are deaf or hard of hearing. *Teaching Exceptional Children, 26,* 13–17.

Lynch, E. C., & Beare, P. L. (1990). The quality of IEP objectives and their relevance to instruction for students with mental retardation and behavioral disorders. *Remedial and Special Education, 11* (2), 48–55.

Lynch, E. W., & Hansen, M. J. (1992). *Developing cross-cultural competence*. Baltimore, MD: Brookes.

Lyon, G. R. (1991). Research in learning disabilities (technical report). Bethesda, MD: National Institutes of Child Health and Human Development.

Lyon, G. R. (1995). Research initiatives in learning disabilities: Contributions from scientists supported by the National Institutes of Child Health and Human Development. *Journal of Child Neurology, 10* (1), 5120–5126.

MacMillan, D. L. (1989). Mild mental retardation: Emerging issues. In G. Robinson, J. R. Patton, E. A. Polloway, & L. R. Sargent (Eds.), *Best practices in mild mental retardation* (pp. 1–20). Reston, VA: CEC-MR.

MacMillan, D. L., & Borthwick, S. (1980). The new educable mentally retarded population: Can they be mainstreamed? *Mental Retardation, 18,* 155–158.

MacMillan, D. L., Gresham, F. M., & Siperstein, G. N. (1993). Conceptual and psychometric concerns about the 1992 AAMR definition of mental retardation. *American Journal of Mental Retardation, 98,* 325–335.

Maker, C. J. (1993). Gifted students in the regular education classroom: What practices are defensible and feasible? In C. J. Maker (Ed.), *Critical issues in gifted education: Vol. 3. Programs for the gifted in regular classrooms* (pp. 413–436). Austin, TX: Pro-Ed.

Mandlebaum, L. H., Lightbourne, L., & VardenBrock, J. (1994). Teaching with literature. *Intervention in School and Clinic, 29,* 134–150.

Mandlebaum, L. H., & Wilson, R. (1989). Teaching listening skills in the special education classroom. *Academic Therapy, 24,* 449–459.

Mangold, S. S., & Roessing, L. J. (1982). Instructional needs of students with low vision. In S. S. Mangold (Ed.), *A teacher's guide to the special educational needs of blind and visually handicapped children*. New York: American Foundation for the Blind.

Manzo, A. V. (1975). Expansion modules for the ReQuest, CAT, GRP, and REAP reading study procedures. *Journal of Reading, 42,* 498–502.

Marchant, J. M. (1992). Deaf-blind handicapping conditions. In P. J. McLaughlin & P. Wehman (Eds.), *Developmental disabilities* (pp. 113–123). Boston: Andover Press.

Markwardt, F. C. (1989). *Peabody individual achievement test—Revised*. Circle Pines, MN: American Guidance Service.

Marston, D., & Magnusson, D. (1985). Implementing curriculum-based measurement in special and regular education settings. *Exceptional Children, 52,* 266–276.

Martini, R., Heath, N. L., & Missiunia, C. (1999). A North American analysis of the relationship between learning disabilities and developmental coordination disorder. *International Journal of Special Education, 14,* 46–58.

Mascari, B. G. & Forgnone, C. (1982). A follow-up study of EMR students four years after dismissal from the program. *Education and Training of the Mentally Retarded, 17,* 288–292.

Mastropieri, M. A., & Scruggs, T. E. (1993). *A practical guide for teaching science to students with special needs in inclusive settings*. Austin, TX: Pro-Ed.

Mather, N. (1992). Whole language reading instruction for students with learning disabilities: Caught in the crossfire. *Learning Disabilities Research and Practice, 7,* 87–95.

Mathinos, D. A. (1991). Conversational engagement of children with learning disabilities. *Journal of Learning Disabilities, 24* (7), 439–446.

Matthews, D. J. (1993). Linguistic giftedness in the context of domain-specific development. *Exceptionality Education Canada, 3,* 1–23.

Mayer-Johnson, R. (1986). *The picture communications symbols* (Book 1). Solana Beach, CA: Mayer-Johnson.

McBurnett, K., Lahey, B., & Pfiffner, L. (1993). Diagnosis of attention deficit disorders in *DSM-IV*: Scientific basis and implications for education. *Exceptional Children, 60* (2), 108–117.

McCarney, S. B., & Wunderlich, K. K. (1988). *The pre-referral intervention manual*. Columbia, MO: Hawthorne Educational Services.

McConnell, J. (1987). Entrapment effects and generalization. *Teaching Exceptional Children, 17,* 267–273.

McDevitt, T. M. (1990). Encouraging young children's listening. *Academic Therapy, 25,* 569–577.

McDonnell, J. J., Hardman, M. L., McDonnell, A. P., & Kiefer-O'Donnell, R. (1995). *An introduction to persons with severe disabilities.* Boston: Allyn and Bacon.

McEachlin, J. J., Smith, T., & Lovaas, O. I. (1993). Long-term outcome for children with autism who received early intensive behavioral treatment. *American Journal on Mental Retardation, 97,* 359–372.

McEnvoy, M. A., Shores, R. E., Wehby, J. H., Johnson, S. M., & Fox J. J. (1990). Special education teachers' implementation of procedures to promote social interaction among children in integrated settings. *Education and Training in Mental Retardation, 25,* 267–276.

McKamey, E. S. (1991). Storytelling for children with learning disabilities: A first-hand account. *Teaching Exceptional Children, 23,* 46–48.

McKeever, P. (1983). Siblings of chronically ill children: A literature review with implications for research and practice. *American Journal of Orthopsychiatry, 53,* 209–217.

McLesky, J. (1992). Students with learning disabilities at primary, intermediate, and secondary grade levels: Identification and characteristics. *Learning Disability Quarterly, 15* (1), 13–19.

McLoughlin, J. A., & Lewis, R. B. (1990). *Assessing special students* (3rd ed.). Columbus, OH: Merrill.

McNeill, J. H., & Fowler, S. A. (1996). Using story reading to encourage children's conversations. *Teaching Exceptional Children, 28* (2), 43–47.

McPartland, J. M., & Slavin, R. E. (1990). *Policy perspectives increasing achievement of at-risk students at each grade level.* Washington, DC: U.S. Department of Education.

McReynolds, L. (1990). Functional articulation disorders. In G. H. Shames & E. H. Wiig (Eds.), *Human communication disorders: An introduction* (2nd ed., pp. 139–182). Columbus, OH: Merrill.

Mercer, C. D. (1997). *Students with learning disabilities.* (5th ed.). New York: Merrill.

Mercer, C., Jordan, L., Alsop, D., & Mercer, A. (1996). Learning disabilities definitions and criteria used by the state education departments. *Learning Disability Quarterly, 19* (2), 217–232.

Mercer, C. D., Jordan, L., & Miller, S. P. (1994). Implications of constructivism for teaching math students with moderate to mild disabilities. *Journal of Special Education, 28,* 290–306.

Meyers, C. E., & Blacher, J. (1987). Parents' perceptions of schooling. *Exceptional Children, 53,* 441–450.

Miller, R. J. (1995). Preparing for adult life: Teaching students their rights and responsibilities. *CEC Today, 1* (7), 12.

Miller, S. P., Mercer, C. D., & Dillon, A. S. (1992). CSA: Acquiring and retaining math skills. *Intervention in School and Clinic, 28,* 105–110.

Mims, A., Harper, C., Armstrong, S. W., & Savage, S. (1991). Effective instruction in homework for students with disabilities. *Teaching Exceptional Children, 23,* 42–44.

Minner, S., & Prater, G. (1989). Arranging the physical environment of special education classrooms. *Academic Therapy, 25,* 91–96.

Mira, M. P., Tucker, B. F., & Tyler, J. S. (1992). *Traumatic brain injury in children and adolescents: A sourcebook for teachers and other school personnel.* Austin, TX: Pro-Ed.

Mirman, N. J. (1991). Reflections on educating the gifted child. *G/C/T, 14,* 57–60.

Moats, L. C., & Lyon, G. R. (1993). Learning disabilities in the United States: Advocacy, science, and the future of the field. *Journal of Learning Disabilities, 26* (5), 282–294.

Moecker, D. L. (1992, November). Special education decision process: For Anglo and Hispanic students. Paper presented at the *Council for Exceptional Children* Topical Conference on Culturally and Linguistically Diverse Exceptional Children, Minneapolis.

Montague, M., McKinney, J. D., & Hocutt, L. (1994). Assessing students for attention deficit disorder. *Intervention in School and Clinic, 29* (4), 212–218.

Moores, D. (1996). *Educating the deaf* (4th ed.). Boston: Houghton Mifflin.

Morgan, S. R. (1994a). *At-risk youth in crises: A team approach in the schools* (2nd ed.). Austin, TX: Pro-Ed.

Morgan, S. (1994b). *Children in crisis: A team approach in the schools* (2nd ed.). Austin, TX: Pro-Ed.

Moriarty, D. (1967). *The loss of loved ones.* Springfield, IL: Charles C Thomas.

Morrison, G. S. (1997). *Teaching in America.* Boston: Allyn and Bacon.

Musselwhite, C. R. (1987). Augmentative communication. In E. T. McDonald (Ed.), *Treating cerebral palsy: For clinicians by clinicians* (pp. 209–238). Austin, TX: Pro-Ed.

Nagel, L., McDougall, D., & Granby, C. (1996). Students' self-reported substance use by grade level and gender. *Journal of Drug Education, 26,* 49–56.

Naremore, R. C. (1980). Language disorders in children. In T. J. Hixon, L. D. Shriberg, & J. H. Saxman (Eds.), *Introduction to communication disorders* (pp. 111–132). Englewood Cliffs, NJ: Prentice-Hall.

National Center on Child Abuse and Neglect. (1986). *Status of child abuse in the United States.* Washington, DC: Author.

National Information Center for Children and Youth with Handicaps. (1990). *Children with autism.* Washington, DC: Author.

National Information Center for Children and Youth with Handicaps. (1991). *The education of children and youth with special needs: What do the laws say?* Washington, DC: Author.

National Joint Committee on Learning Disabilities. (1993). A reaction to full inclusion: A reaffirmation of the rights of students with learning disabilities to a continuum of service. *Journal of Learning Disabilities, 26,* 96.

National Joint Committee on Learning Disabilities. (1988). Letter to NJCLD member organizations.

National study on inclusion: Overview and summary report. *National Center on Educational Restructuring Inclusion, 2,* 1–8.

Nelson, N. W. (1988). Curriculum-based language assessment and intervention. *Language, Speech and Hearing Services in School, 20,* 170–183.

Nessner, K. (1990, winter). Children with disabilities. *Canadian Social Trends,* pp.18–20.

Nowacek, E. J., & McShane, E. (1993). Spoken language. In E. A. Polloway & J. R. Patton (Eds.), *Strategies for teaching learners with special needs* (5th ed., pp. 183–205). Columbus, OH: Merrill.

Olson, J. L., & Platt, J. M. (1996). *Teaching children and adolescents with special needs* (2nd ed). Englewood Cliffs, NJ: Merrill.

Olson, R., Wise, B., Conners, F., Rack, J., & Fulker, D. (1989). Specific deficits in component reading and language skills: Genetic and environmental influences. *Journal of Learning Disabilities, 22,* 339–348.

Owens, R. E., Jr. (1984). *Language development: An introduction.* Columbus, OH: Merrill.

Oyer, H. J., Crowe, B., & Haas, W. H. (1987). *Speech, language, and hearing disorders: A guide for the teacher.* Boston: Little, Brown.

Palinscar, A., & Klenk, L. (1992). Fostering literacy learning in supportive contexts. *Journal of Learning Disabilities, 25,* 211–225.

Parke, B. N. (1989). *Gifted students in regular classrooms.* Boston: Allyn and Bacon.

Patton, J. R. (1994). Practical recommendations for using homework with students with learning disabilities. *Journal of Learning Disabilities, 27,* 570–578.

Patton, J. R., & Cronin, M. E. (1993). *Life skills, instruction for all students with disabilities.* Austin, TX: Pro-Ed.

Patton, J. R., Polloway, E. A., Smith, T. E. C., Edgar, E., Clark, G. M., & Lee, S. (1996). Individuals with mild mental retardation: Postsecondary outcomes and implications for educational policy. *Education and Training in Mental Retardation and Developmental Disabilities, 31,* 77–85.

Pearpoint, J., Forest, M., & O'Brien, J. (1996). MAPs, circles of friends, and PATH. In S. Stainback & W. Stainback (Eds.), *Inclusion: A guide for educators* (pp. 67–86). Baltimore, MD: Brookes.

Pearson, S. (1996). Child abuse among children with disabilities. *Teaching Exceptional Children, 29,* 34–38.

Peck, C. A., Carlson, P., & Helmstetter, E. (1992). Parent and teacher perceptions of outcomes for typically developing children enrolled in integrated early childhood programs: A statewide survey. *Journal of Early Intervention, 16,* 53–63.

Peck, G. (1989). Facilitating cooperative learning: A forgotten tool gets it started. *Academic Therapy, 25,* 145–150.

Pfiffner, L., & Barkley, R. (1991). Educational placement and classroom management. In R. Barkley (Ed.), *Attention deficit hyperactivity disorder: A handbook for*

diagnosis and treatment (pp. 498–539). New York: Guilford.

Pickett, A. L., & Gerlach, K. (1997). *Paraeducators.* Austin, TX: Pro-Ed.

Pierce, C. (1994). Importance of classroom climate for at-risk learners. *Journal of Educational Research, 88,* 37–44.

Plummer, D. L. (1995). Serving the needs of gifted children from a multicultural perspective. In J. L. Genshaft, M. Bireley, & C. L. Hollinger (Eds.), *Serving gifted and talented students: A resource for school personnel* (pp. 285–300). Austin, TX: Pro-Ed.

Podemski, R. S., Marsh, G. E., Smith, T. E. C., & Price, B. J. (1995). *Comprehensive administration of special education.* Columbus, OH: Merrill.

Polloway, E. A. (1984). The integration of mildly retarded students in the schools: A historical review. *Remedial and Special Education, 5* (4), 18–28.

Polloway, E. A., Bursuck, W., Jayanthi, M., Epstein, M., & Nelson, J. (1996). Treatment acceptability: Determining appropriate interventions within inclusive classrooms. *Intervention in School and Clinic, 31,* 133–144.

Polloway, E. A., Epstein, M. H., Bursuck, W. D., Jayanthi, M., & Cumblad, C. (1994). Homework practices of general education teachers. *Journal of Learning Disabilities, 27,* 500–509.

Polloway, E. A., Epstein, M. H., Bursuck, W. D., Roderique, T. W., McConeghy, J., & Jayanthi, M. (1994). Classroom grading: A national survey of policies. *Remedial and Special Education, 15* (2), 162–170.

Polloway, E. A., & Jones-Wilson, L. (1992). Principles of assessment and instruction. In E. A. Polloway & T. E. C. Smith (Eds.), *Language instruction for students with disabilities* (pp. 87–120). Denver, CO: Love Publishing.

Polloway, E. A., & Patton, J. R. (1997). *Strategies for teaching learners with special needs* (6th ed.). Columbus, OH: Merrill.

Polloway, E. A., Patton, J. R., Epstein, M. H., & Smith, T. E. C. (1989). Comprehensive curriculum: Program design for students with mild handicaps. *Focus on Exceptional Children, 21* (8), 1–12.

Polloway, E. A., Patton, J. R., Payne, J. S., & Payne, R. A. (1989). *Strategies for teaching learners with special needs* (5th ed). Columbus, OH: Merrill.

Polloway, E. A., Patton, J. R., Smith, J. D., & Roderique, T. W. (1992). Issues in program design for elementary students with mild retardation: Emphasis on curriculum development. *Education and Training in Mental Retardation, 27,* 142–150.

Polloway, E. A., Patton, J. R., Smith, T. E. C., & Buck, G. H. (1997). Mental retardation and learning disabilities: Conceptual issues. *Journal of Learning Disabilities, 30,* 219–231.

Polloway, E. A., & Smith, J. D. (1988). Current status of the mild mental retardation construct: Identification, placement, and programs. In M. C. Wang, M. C. Reynolds, & H. J. Walberg (Eds.), *The handbook of spe-*

cial education: Research and practice (Vol. II, pp. 1–22). Oxford, UK: Pergamon Press.

Polloway, E. A., Smith, J. D., Patton, J. R., & Smith, T. E. C. (1996). Historic changes in mental retardation and developmental disabilities. *Education and Training in Mental Retardation and Developmental Disabilities, 31,* 3–12.

Polloway, E. A., & Smith, J. E. (1982). *Teaching language skills to exceptional learners.* Denver, CO: Love Publishing.

Polloway, E. A., & Smith, T. E. C. (1992). *Language instruction for students with disabilities.* Denver, CO: Love Publishing.

Polloway, E. A., Smith, T. E. C., Patton, J. R., & Smith, J. D. (1996). Historical perspectives in mental retardation. *Education and Training in Mental Retardation and Developmental Disabilities, 31,* 3–12.

Powers, M. D. (1989). *Children with autism: A parent's guide.* New York: Woodbine House.

Pracek, E. (1996). Software for survival. In J. L. Olson & J. M. Platt (Eds.), *Teaching children and adolescents with special needs* (2nd ed.). Englewood Cliffs, NJ: Prentice-Hall.

Prater, M. A. (1992). Increasing time-on-task in the classroom. *Intervention in School and Clinic, 28* (1), 22–27.

Prater, M. A., Joy, R., Chilman, B., Temple, J., & Miller, S. R. (1991). Self-monitoring of on-task behavior by adolescents with learning disabilities. *Learning Disability Quarterly, 14,* 164–177.

Pratt, S. R., Heintzelman, A. T., & Deming, S. E. (1993). *Journal of Speech and Hearing Research, 36,* 1063–1074.

Pressley, M., & Rankin, J. (1994). More about whole language methods of reading instruction for students at risk for early reading failure. *Learning Disabilities Research & Practice, 9,* 157–168.

Public Law 94–142 (1975). *Federal Register, 42,* 42474–42518.

Public Law 101-476 (1990). *Federal Register, 54,* 35210–35271.

Quay, H., & Peterson, D. (1987). *Revised behavior problem checklist.* Coral Gables, FL: University of Miami.

Reeve, R. E. (1990). ADHD: Facts and fallacies. *Intervention in School and Clinic, 26,* 71–78.

Reid, E. R. (1986). Practicing effective instruction: The exemplary center for reading. *Exceptional Children, 52,* 510–519.

Reid, R., Maag, J. W., Vasa, S. F. & Wright, C. (1994). Who are the children with attention-deficit-hyperactivity disorder? A school-based study. *The Journal of Special Education, 28,* 117–137.

Reif, S. F. (1993). *How to reach and teach ADD/ADHD children.* Boston: Allyn and Bacon.

Reis, S. M. (1989). Reflections on policy affecting the education of gifted and talented students. *American Psychologist, 44,* 399–408.

Reis, S. M., & Schack, G. D. (1993). Differentiating products for the gifted and talented: The encouragement of independent learning. In C. J. Maker (Ed.), *Critical issues in gifted education: Vol. 3. Programs for the gifted in regular classrooms* (pp. 161–186). Austin, TX: Pro-Ed.

Renzulli, J. S. (1979). *What makes giftedness: A reexamination of the definition of the gifted and talented.* Ventura, CA: Ventura County Superintendent of Schools Office.

Renzulli, J. S., & Reis, S. M. (1985). *The schoolwide enrichment model: A comprehensive plan for educational excellence.* Mansfield Center, CT: Creative Learning Press.

Renzulli, J. S., Reis, S. M., & Smith, L. M. (1981). *The revolving door identification model.* Wethersfield, CT: Creative Learning Press.

Reschly, D. (1988). Incorporating adaptive behavior deficits into instructional programs. In G. A. Robinson, J. R. Patton, E. A. Polloway, & L. R. Sargent (Eds.), *Best practices in mental disabilities* (Vol. 2, pp. 53–80). Des Moines, IA: Iowa State Department of Education.

Reynolds, C. T., & Salend, S. J. (1990). Teacher-directed and student-mediated textbook comprehension strategies. *Academic Therapy, 25,* 417–427.

Riccio, C. A., Hynd, G. W., Cohen, M., & Gonzales, T. (1994). Attention deficit hyperactivity disorder (ADHD) and learning disabilities. *Learning Disabilities Quarterly, 17,* 113–122.

Rich, H. L., & Ross, S. M. (1989). Students' time on learning tasks in special education. *Exceptional Children, 55,* 508–515.

Rich, H. L., & Ross, S. M. (1991). Regular class or resource room for students with disabilities? A direct response to "Rich and Ross, A Mixed Message." *Exceptional Children, 57,* 476–477.

Roach, V. (1995). Supporting inclusion: Beyond the rhetoric. *Phi Delta Kappan, 77,* 295–299.

Roberts, C., Ingram, C., & Harris, C. (1992). The effect of special versus regular classroom programming on higher cognitive processes of intermediate elementary aged gifted and average ability students. *Journal of the Education of the Gifted, 15,* 332–343.

Robertson, J., Alper, S., Schloss, P. J., & Wisniewski, L. (1992). Teaching self-catheterization skills to a child with myelomeningocele in a preschool setting. *Journal of Early Intervention, 16,* 20–30.

Robin, S. S., & Johnson, E. O. (1996). Attitude and peer cross pressure: Adolescent drug and alcohol use. *Journal of Drug Education, 26,* 69–99.

Robinson, S. M., Braxdale, C. T., & Colson, S. E. (1988). Preparing dysfunctional learners to enter junior high school: A transitional curriculum. *Focus on Exceptional Children, 18* (4), 1–12.

Rock, E. E., Rosenberg, M. S., & Carran, D. T. (1995). Variables affecting the reintegation rate of students with serious emotional disturbance. *Exceptional Children, 6,* 254–268.

Roderique, T. W., Polloway, E. A., Cumblad, C., Epstein, M. H., & Bursuck, W. (1994). Homework: A study of policies in the United States. *Journal of Learning Disabilities, 22,* 417–427.

Rogers, J. (1993). The inclusion revolution. *Research Bulletin.* Washington, DC: Phi Delta Kappa Center for Evaluation, Development, and Research.

Roller, C. (1996). *Variability not disability: Struggling readers in a workshop class.* Newark, DE: International Reading Association.

Rooney, K. (1989). Independent strategies for efficient study: A care approach. *Academic Therapy, 24,* 389–390.

Rooney, K. J. (1991). Controversial therapies: A review and critique. *Intervention in School and Clinic, 26* (3), 134–142.

Rooney, K. (1993). *Attention deficit hyperactivity disorder: A videotape program.* Richmond, VA: State Department of Education.

Rooney, K. J. (1995). Dyslexia revisited: History, educational philosophy, and clinical assessment applications. *Intervention in School and Clinic, 31* (1), 6–15.

Rosenberg, M. S., O'Shea, L., & O'Shea, D. J. (1991). *Student teacher to master teacher: A handbook for pre-service and beginning teachers of students with mild and moderate handicaps.* New York: Macmillan.

Rosenberg, M. S., Wilson, R., Maheady, L., & Sindelar, P. (1992). *Educating students with behavior disorders.* Boston: Allyn and Bacon.

Rosenshine, B., & Stevens, R. (1986). Teaching functions. In M. Wittrock (Ed.), *Handbook of research on teaching* (3rd ed., pp. 376–391). New York: Macmillan.

Ross, S. M., Smith, L. J., Casey, J., & Slavin, R. E. (1995). Increasing the academic success of disadvantaged children: An examination of alternative early intervention programs. *American Educational Research Journal, 32,* 773–800.

Rosselli, H. (1993). Process differentiation for gifted learners in the regular classroom: Teaching to everyone's needs. In C. J. Maker (Ed.), *Critical issues in gifted education: Vol. 3. Programs for the gifted in regular classrooms* (pp. 139–155). Austin, TX: Pro-Ed.

Ryan, A. G., & Price, L. (1992). Adults with LD in the 1990s. *Intervention in School and Clinic, 28* (1), 6–20.

Safer, D. J., & Krager, J. M. (1988). A survey of medication treatment for hyperactive/inattentive students. *Journal of the American Medical Association, 260,* 2256–2258.

Salend, S. J. (1994). *Effective mainstreaming: Creating inclusive classrooms* (2nd ed.). Columbus, OH: Merrill/Prentice-Hall.

Samuels, S. J. (1986). Why children fail to learn and what to do about it. *Exceptional Children, 53,* 7–16.

Sander, E. K. (1972). When are speeech sounds learned? *Journal of Speech and Hearing Disorders, 37,* 62.

Santrock, J. W., & Warshak, R. A. (1979). Father custody and social development in boys and girls. *Journal of Social Issues, 35,* 112–125.

Sargent, L. R. (1991). *Social skills for school and community.* Reston, VA: CEC-MR.

Savage, R. C. (1988). Introduction to educational issues for students who have suffered traumatic brain injury.

In R. C. Savage & G. F. Wolcott (Eds.), *An educator's manual: What educators need to know about students with traumatic brain injury.* Southborough, MA: National Head Injury Foundation.

Schaffner, C. B., & Buswell, B. E. (1996). Ten critical elements for creating inclusive and effective school communities. In S. Stainback & W. Stainback (Eds.), *Inclusion: A guide for educators* (pp. 49–65). Baltimore, MD: Brookes.

Schaughency, E. A., & Rothlind, J. (1991). Assessment and classification of attention deficit hyperactivity disorders. *School Psychology Review, 20* (2), 197–202.

Scheuerman, B., Jacobs, W. R., McCall, C., & Knies, W. (1994). The personal spelling dictionary: An adoptive approach to reducing the spelling hurdle in written language. *Intervention in School and Clinic, 29* (5), 292–299.

Schewel, R. (1993). Reading. In E. A. Polloway & J. R. Patton (Eds.), *Strategies for teaching learners with special needs.* Columbus, OH: Merrill/Macmillan.

Schiever, S. W. (1993). Differentiating the learning environment for gifted students. In C. J. Maker (Ed.,), *Critical issues in gifted education: Vol. 3. Programs for the gifted in regular classrooms* (pp. 201–214). Austin, TX: Pro-Ed.

Schleichkorn, J. (1993). *Coping with cerebral palsy: Answers to questions parents often ask* (2nd ed.). Austin: TX: Pro-Ed.

Schnailberg, L. (1994, October 19). E.D. report documents "full inclusion" trend. *Education Week,* p. 8.

Schulz, J. B., & Carpenter, C. D. (1995). *Mainstreaming exceptional students: A guide for classroom teachers.* Boston: Allyn and Bacon.

Schulze, K. A., Rule, S., & Innocenti, M. S. (1989). Coincidental teaching: Parents promoting social skills at home. *Teaching Exceptional Children, 21,* 24–27.

Schumaker, J. B., & Deshler, D. D. (1988). Implementing the regular education initiative in secondary schools: A different ball game. *Journal of Learning Disabilities, 21* (1), 36–42.

Schumaker, J. B., Deshler, D. D., Alley, G. R., & Denton, D. H. (1982). Multipass: A learning strategy for improving comprehension. *Learning Disability Quarterly, 5,* 295–304.

Schumaker, J. B., Deshler, D. D., Nolan, S., Clark, F. L., Alley, G. R., & Warren, M. M. (1981). *Error monitoring strategy: A learning strategy for improving academic performance of LD adolescents.* (Research Report No. 32). Lawrence, KS: University of Kansas IRLD.

Schumm, J. S., & Strickler, K. (1991). Guidelines for adapting content area textbooks: Keeping teachers and students content. *Intervention in School and Clinic, 27,* 79–84.

Schumm, J. S., Vaughn, S., & Leavell, A. G. (1994). Planning pyramid: A framework for planning for diverse student needs during content area instruction. *Reading Teacher, 47* (8), 213–217.

Schwartz, S. E., & Karge, B. D. (1996). *Human diversity: A guide for understanding* (2nd ed.). New York: McGraw-Hill.

Schwean, V. L., Saklofske, D. H., Shatz, E., & Falk, L. K. (1996). Achieving supportive integration for children with behavioral disorders in Canada: Multiple paths to realization. *Canadian Journal of Special Education, 11*, 33–50.

Schwean, V. L., Parkinson, M., Francis, G., & Lee, F. (1993). Educating the AD/HD child: Debunking the myths. *Canadian Journal of School Psychology, 9* (1), 37–52.

Scruggs, T. E. & Mastropieri, M. A. (1994). Successful mainstreaming in elementary science classes: A qualitative study of three reputational cases. *American Educational Research Journal, 31*, 785–811.

Scruggs, T. E., & Mastropieri, M. A. (1996). Teacher perceptions of mainstreaming/inclusion, 1958–1995: A research synthesis. *Exceptional Children, 63*, 59–74.

Searcy, S., & Meadows, N. B. (1994). The impact of social structures on friendship development for children with behavior disorders. *Education and Treatment of Children, 17*, 255–268.

Seeley, K. (1995). Classwide peer tutoring. Unpublished manuscript, Lynchburg College (VA).

Semrud-Clikeman, M., Biederman, J., Sprich-Buckminster, S., Lehman, B.K., Farone, S., & Norman, D. (1992). Comorbidity between ADDH and learning disabilities: A review and report in a clinically referred sample. *Journal of American Academy of Child and Adolescent Psychiatry, 31*, 439–448.

Semrud-Clikeman, M., & Hynd, G. W. (1990). Light hemispheric dysfunction in nonverbal learning disabilities: Social, academic, and adaptive functions in adults and children. *Psychological Bulletin, 107* (2), 196–209.

Sexton, D., Snyder, P., Wolfe, B., Lobman, M., Stricklin, S., & Akers, P. (1996). Early intervention inservice training strategies: Perceptions and suggestions from the field. *Exceptional Children, 62*, 485–496.

Shane, H. C., & Sauer, M. (1986). *Augmentative and alternative communication.* Austin, TX: Pro-Ed.

Shaner, M. Y. (1991). Talented teachers for talented students. *G/C/T, 22*, 14–15.

Shanker, A. (1994–1995). Educating students in special programs. *Educational Leadership, 52*, 43–47.

Shanley, R. (1993). Becoming content with content. In C. J. Maker (Ed.), *Critical issues in gifted education: Vol. 1. Defensible programs for the gifted.* (pp. 43–89). Austin, TX: Pro-Ed.

Shannon, T., & Polloway, E. A. (1993). Promoting error monitoring in middle school students with learning disabilities. *Intervention in School and Clinic, 28*, 160–164.

Shields, J. M., & Heron, T. E. (1989). Teaching organizational skills to students with learning disabilities. *Teaching Exceptional Children, 20*, 8–13.

Shimon, D. A. (1992). *Coping with hearing loss and hearing aids.* San Diego: Singular Publishing.

Shore, B. M., Cornell, D. G., Robinson, A., & Ward, V. S. (1991). *Recommended practices in gifted education: A critical analysis.* New York: Teachers College Press.

Siegel, L. (1989). IQ is irrelevant to the definition of learning disabilities. *Journal of Learning Disabilities, 22* (8), 469–486.

Sileo, T. W., Sileo, A. P., & Prater, M. A. (1996). Parent and professional partnerships in special education: Multicultural considerations. *Intervention in School & Clinic, 31*, 145–153.

Silver, L. B. (1995). Controversial therapies. *Journal of Child Neurology, 10* (suppl. 1), 96–100.

Silverman, A. B., Reinherz, H. Z., & Giaconia, R. M. (1996). The long-term sequelae of child and adolescent abuse: A longitudinal community study. *Child Abuse and Neglect, 20,* 709–723.

Silverthorn, K. H., & Hornak, J. E. (1993). Beneficial effects of exercise on aerobic capacity and body composition in adults with Prader-Willi syndrome. *American Journal on Mental Retardation, 97,* 654–658.

Simmons, D. C., Fuchs, D., & Fuchs, L. S. (1991). Instructional and curricular requisites of mainstreamed students with learning disabilities. *Journal of Learning Disabilities, 24*, 354–359.

Simmons, D., Fuchs, D., Hodge, J., & Mathes, P. (1994). Importance of instructional complexity and role reciprocity to classwide peer tutoring. *Learning Disabilities Research and Practice, 9*, 203–212.

Simpson, R. (1996). *Working with parents and families of exceptional children and youth* (3rd ed.). Austin, TX: Pro-Ed.

Sladeczek, I. E., & Heath, N. L. (1997). Consultation in Canada. *Canadian Journal of School Psychology, 1,* 1–15.

Slavin, R. E. (1987). *What research says to the teacher on cooperative learning: Student teams* (2nd ed.). Washington, DC: National Education Association.

Slicker, E. K., & Palmer, D. J. (1993). Mentoring at-risk high school students: Evaluation of a school-based program. *The School Counselor, 40*, 327–334.

Smith, D. D., & Luckasson, R. (1992). *Introduction to special education: Teaching in an age of challenge.* Boston: Allyn and Bacon.

Smith, D. D., & Rivera, D. (1993). *Effective discipline* (2nd ed.). Austin, TX: Pro-Ed.

Smith, D. D., & Rivera, D. P. (1995). Discipline in special and regular education. *Focus on Exceptional Children, 27* (5), 1–14.

Smith, J. D. (1994). The revised AAMR definition of mental retardation: The MRDD position. *Education and Training in Mental Retardation and Developmental Disabilities, 29*, 179–183.

Smith, J. D. (1995). Inclusive school environments and students with disabilities in South Carolina: The issues, the status, the needs. *Occasional Papers, 1*, 1–5.

Smith, S. D., Pennington, B. F., Kimberling, W. J., & Inge, K. J. (1990). Familial dyslexia: Use of genetic linkages data to define subtypes. *Journal of the American Academy of Child and Adolescent Psychiatry, 29*, 204–213.

Smith, S. W. (1990a). A comparison of individualized education programs (IEPs) of students with behavioral disorders and learning disabilities. *Journal of Special Education, 24,* 85–100.

Smith, S. W. (1990b). Individualized education programs (IEPs) in special education: From intent to acquiescence. *Exceptional Children, 57,* 6–14.

Smith, S. W., & Simpson, R. L. (1989). An analysis of individualized education programs (IEPs) for students with behavior disorders. *Behavioral Disorders, 14,* 107–116.

Smith, T. E. C. (1990). *Introduction to education* (2nd ed.). St. Paul, MN: West Publishing.

Smith, T. E. C., & Dowdy, C. A. (1992). Future-based assessment and intervention and mental retardation. *Education and Training in Mental Retardation, 27,* 23–31.

Smith, T. E. C., Dowdy, C. A., Polloway, E. A., & Blalock, G. (1997). *Children and adults with learning disabilities.* Boston: Allyn and Bacon.

Smith, T. E. C., Finn, D. M., & Dowdy, C. A. (1993) *Teaching students with mild disabilities.* Ft. Worth, TX: Harcourt Brace Jovanovich.

Smith, T. E. C., & Hendricks, M. D. (1995). *Prader-Willi syndrome: Practical considerations for educators.* Little Rock: Ozark Learning.

Smith, T. E. C., & Hilton, A. (1994). Program design for students with mental retardation. *Education and training in mental retardation and developmental disabilities, 29,* 3–8.

Smith, T. E. C., Price, B. J., & Marsh, G. E. (1986). *Mildly handicapped children and adults.* St. Paul, MN: West Publishing.

Smith, W. J., & Foster, W. F. (1996). *Equal educational opportunity for students with disabilities.* Montreal, PQ: McGill University, Office of Research on Educational Policy.

Snell, M., & Drake, G. P. (1994). Replacing cascades with supported education. *Journal of Special Education, 27,* 393–409.

Southern, W. T., & Jones, E. D. (1991). Academic acceleration: Background and issues. In W. T. Southern & E. D. Jones (Eds.), *Academic acceleration of gifted children* (pp. 1–17). New York: Teachers College Press.

Sparks, S., & Caster, J. A. (1989). Sex education. In G. Robinson, J. Patton, E. Polloway, & L. Sargent (Eds.), *Best practices in mild mental retardation* (pp. 299–302). Reston, VA: Division on Mental Retardation, CEC.

Spirito, A., Hart, K. I., Overholser, J., & Halverson, J. (1990). Social skills and depression in adolescent suicide attempters. *Adolescence, 25,* 543–552.

Stainback, S., Stainback, W., East, K., & Sapon-Shevin, M. (1994). A commentary on inclusion and the development of a positive self-identity by people with disabilities. *Exceptional Children, 60,* 486–490.

Stainback, W., & Stainback, S. (1984). A rationale for the merger of special and regular education. *Exceptional Children, 51,* 102–111.

Stainback, W. C., Stainback, S., & Wehman, P. (1997). Toward full inclusion into general education. In P. Wehman (Ed.), *Exceptional individuals in school, community, and work* (pp. 531–557). Austin, TX: Pro-Ed.

Staub, D., & Peck, C. A. (1994–1995). What are the outcomes for nondisabled students? *Educational Leadership, 52,* 36–41.

Stehbens, J. A. (1988). Childhood cancer. In D. K. Rough (Ed.), *Handbook of pediatric psychology* (pp. 135–161). New York: Guilford Press.

Stephien, S., & Gallagher, S. (1993). Problem-based learning: As authentic as it gets. *Educational Leadership, 50* (7), pp. 25–28.

Stevens, R., & Rosenshine, B. (1981). Advances in research on teaching. *Exceptional Education Quarterly, 2,* 1–9.

Storey, K. (1993). A proposal for assessing integration. *Education and Training in Mental Retardation and Developmental Disabilities, 28,* 279–286.

Streeter, C. E., & Grant, C. A. (1993). *Making choices for multicultural education.* New York: Macmillan.

Streett, S., & Smith, T. E. C. (1996). *Section 504 and public schools: A practical guide.* Little Rock, AR: The Learning Group.

Struyk, L. R., Cole, K. B., Epstein, M. H., Bursuck, W. D., & Polloway, E. A. (1996). Homework communication: Problems involving high school teachers and parents of students with disabilities. Manuscript submitted for publication.

Struyk, L. R., Epstein, M. H., Bursuck, W., Polloway, E. A., McConeghy, J., & Cole, K. B. (1995). Homework, grading, and testing practices used by teachers with students with and without disabilities. *The Clearing House, 69,* 50–55.

Summers, M., Bridge, J. & Summers, C. R. (1991). Sibling support groups. *Teaching Exceptional Children, 23,* 20–25.

Switzer, L. S. (1985). Accepting the diagnosis: An educational intervention for parents of children with learning disabilities. *Journal of Learning Disabilities, 18,* 151–153.

Tankersley, M. (1995). A group-oriented management program: A review of research on the good behavior game and implications for teachers. *Preventing School Failure, 40,* 19–28.

Tavzel, C. S., & Staff of LinguiSystems. (1987). *Blooming recipes.* East Moline, IL: LinguiSystems.

Teddlie, C., & Stringfield, S. (1993). *Schools make a difference: Lessons learned from a ten-year study of school effects.* New York: Teachers College Press.

Teen drug use is on the rise again. (1996). *Executive Educator, 18,* 7–8.

Templeton, R. A. (1995). ADHD: A teacher's guide. *The Oregon Conference Monograph, 7,* 2–11.

Tennant, C., Bebbington, P. R., & Hurry, J. (1980). Parental death in childhood and risk of adult depressive disorders: A review. *Psychological Medicine, 10,* 289–299.

Tests in Print (1989). Austin, TX: Pro-Ed.

Thomas, P. J., & Carmack, F. F. (1993). Language: The foundation of learning. In J. S. Choate (Ed.), *Successful mainstreaming: Proven ways to detect and correct special needs* (pp. 148–173). Boston: Allyn and Bacon.

Thousand, J. S., & Villa, R. A. (1990). Strategies for educating learners with severe disabilities within their local home schools and communities. *Focus on Exceptional Children, 23,* 1–24.

Thurston, L. P. (1989). Helping parents tutor their children: A success story. *Academic Therapy, 24,* 579–587.

Tirosh, E., & Canby, J. (1993). Autism with hyperlexia: A distinct syndrome? *American Journal on Mental Retardation, 98,* 84–92.

Toliver-Weddington, G., & Erickson, J. G. (1992). Suggestions for using standardized tests with minority children. In J. G. Erickson (Ed.), *Communication disorders in multicultural populations* (1992, April). Paper presented at Texas Speech-Language-Hearing Association Annual Convention, San Antonio, TX.

Torres, I., & Corn, A. L. (1990). *When you have a visually handicapped child in your classroom: Suggestions for teachers.* New York: American Foundation for the Blind.

Trites, R. (1981). Primary French immersion: Disabilities, and prediction of success. *Review and Evaluation, 2.*

Turnbull, A. P., Strickland, B., & Hammer, S. E. (1978). IEPs: Presenting guidelines for development and implementation. *Journal of Learning Disabilities, 11,* 40–46.

Turnbull, A. P., & Turnbull, H. R. (1986). *Families, professionals, and exceptionality: A special partnership.* Columbus, OH: Merrill.

Turnbull, H. R. (1993). *Free appropriate public education: The law and children with disabilities* (4th ed.). Denver, CO: Love Publishing.

Tver, D. F., & Tver, B. M. (1991). *Encyclopedia of mental and physical handicaps.* Austin, TX: Pro-Ed.

U.S. Department of Education. (1989). *11th annual report to Congress on the implementation of IDEA.* Washington, DC: Author.

U.S. Department of Education. (1991). Memorandum: Clarification of policy to address the needs of children with attention deficit disorders within general and/or special education. (Sept. 16). Washington, DC: Author.

U.S. Department of Education. (1993). *15th annual report to Congress on the implementation of IDEA.* Washington, DC: Author.

U.S. Department of Education. (1995). *17th annual report to Congress on the implementation of IDEA.* Washington, DC: Author.

U.S. Office of Education (USOE). (1977). Assistance to states for education of handicapped children: Procedures for evaluating specific learning disabilities. *Federal Register, 42,* 65082–65085.

Valdes, K. A., Williamson, C. L., & Wagner, M. M. (1990). *The national longitudinal transition study of special education students* (Vol. 1). Menlo Park, CA: SRI International.

Van Eerdewegh, M. M., Bieri, M. D., Parrilla, R. H., & Clayton, P. J. (1982). The bereaved child. *British Journal of Psychiatry, 140,* 23–29.

Van Riper, C., & Emerick, L. (1984). *Speech correction: An introduction to speech pathology and audiology* (7th ed.). Englewood Cliffs, NJ: Prentice-Hall.

VanTassel-Baska, J. (1989). Appropriate curriculum for gifted learners. *Educational Leadership, 47,* 13–15.

VanTassel-Baska, J., Patton, J., & Prillaman, D. (1989). Disadvantaged gifted learners at-risk for educational attention. *Focus on Exceptional Children, 22* (3), 1–16.

Vella, D. D., Heath, N. L., & Miezitis, S. (1992). Depression in children and adolescents: Assessment issues. In S. Miezitis (Ed.), *Creating alternatives to depression in our schools* (pp. 95–106). Toronto: Hogrefe & Huber Press.

Victory in landmark "full inclusion" case. (1994). *Disability Rights Education and Defense Fund News, 1,* 6.

Walberg, H. J. (1991). Does homework help? *School Community Journal, 1* (1), 13–15.

Walker, B. (1993, January). *Multicultural issues in education: An introduction.* Paper presented at Cypress–Fairbanks Independent School District In-Service, Cypress, TX.

Walker, J. E., & Shea, T. M. (1988). *Behavior management: A practical approach for educators* (4th ed.). New York: Merrill/Macmillan.

Walker, J. E., & Shea, T. M. (1995). *Behavior management* (6th ed.). Columbus, OH: Merrill.

Wallace, G., Cohen, S., & Polloway, E. A. (1987). *Language arts: Teaching exceptional children.* Austin, TX: Pro-Ed.

Wallace, G., Larsen, S. C., & Elksnin, L. K. (1992). *Educational assessment of learning problems.* Boston: Allyn and Bacon.

Wanat, C. L. (1992). Meeting the needs of single-parent children: School and parent views differ. *NASSP Bulletin, 76,* 43–48.

Wang, M. C., Reynolds, M. C., & Walberg, H. J. (1994–1995). Serving students at the margins. *Educational Leadership, 52,* 12–17.

Warren, D. (1994). *Blindness in children.* Cambridge, MA: Cambridge University Press.

Waterman, B. B. (1994). Assessing children for the presence of a disability. *NICHY News Digest, 4* (1), Washington, DC: U.S. Government Printing Office.

Wayland, L. A., & Sladeczek, I. E. (1999). Work in progress: Conjoint behavioral consultation with children who are socially withdrawn. *Canadian Journal of School Psychology, 14,* 45–50.

Wayman, K., Lynch, E., & Hanson, M. (1990). Home-based early childhood services: Cultural sensitivity in a family systems approach. *Topics in Early Childhood Special Education, 10* (4), 65–66.

Webber, J. (1997). Responsible inclusion: Key components for success. In P. Zionts (Ed.), *Effective inclusion of students with behavior and learning problems.* Austin, TX: Pro-Ed.

Weber, K. (1994). *Special education in Canadian schools.* Thornhill, ON: Highland Press.

Weber, K., & Bennett, S. (1999). *Special education in Ontario schools.* Don Mills, ON: Highland Press.

Wehmeyer, M. (1993). Self-determination as an educational outcome. *Impact, 6* (4), 16–17, 26.

Weinbender, M. L. M., & Rossignol, A. M. (1996). Lifestyle and risk of premature sexual activity in a high school population of Seventh-Day Adventists: Valuegenesis 1989. *Adolescence, 31,* 265–275.

Wiener, J. (1987). Peer status of learning disabled children and adolescents: A review of the literature. *Learning Disabilities Research, 2,* 62–79.

Wiener, J., & Harris, P. J. (1993). Social relations in subgroups of children with learning disabilities. *Enfance, 47,* 295–316.

Wiener, J., Harris, P. J., & Shirer, C. (1990). Achievement and social-behavioral correlates of peer status in LD children. *Learning Disability Quarterly, 13,* 114–127.

Wiener J., & Siegel, L. (1992). A Canadian perspective on learning disabilities. *Journal of Learning Disabilities, 25,* 340–350.

Weiner, Z., Reich, W., Herjanic, B., Jung, K. G., & Amado, H. (1987). Reliability, validity, and parent–child agreement studies of the Diagnostic Interview for Children and Adolescents (DICA). *Journal of the American Academy of Child and Adolescent Psychiatry, 26,* 649–653.

Welch, M., & Link, D. P. (1991). The instructional priority system: A method for assessing the educational environment. *Intervention in the School and Clinic, 27* (2), 91–96.

Wesson, C. L., & Deno, S. L. (1989). An analysis of long-term instructional plans in reading for elementary resource room students. *Remedial and Special Education, 10* (1), 21–28.

West, G. K. (1986). *Parenting without guilt.* Springfield, IL: Thomas.

West, G. K. (1994, Nov. 10). Discipline that works: Part 1. *The News and Daily Advance.*

Westling, D. L., & Koorland, M. A. (1988). *The special educator's handbook.* Boston: Allyn and Bacon.

Weston, D., Ludolph, P., Misle, B., Ruffins, S., & Block, J. (1990). Physical and sexual abuse in adolescent girls with borderline personality disorder. *American Journal of Orthopsychiatry, 60,* 55–66.

Whitney-Thomas, J., & Hanley-Maxwell, C. (1996). Packing the parachute: Parents' experiences as their children prepare to leave high school. *Exceptional Children, 63,* 75–87.

Wicks-Nelson, R., & Israel, A. C. (1991). *Behavior disorders of childhood.* Englewood Cliffs, NJ: Prentice-Hall.

Wiederholt, J. L., & Bryant, B. (1986). *Gray oral reading test—Revised.* Austin, TX: Pro-Ed.

Wiig, E. H. (1986). Language disabilities in school-age children and youth. In G. H. Shames & E. H. Wiig (Eds.), *Human communication disorders* (2nd ed., pp. 331–383). Columbus, OH: Merrill.

Wiig, E. H., & Semel, E. (1984). *Language assessment and intervention for the learning disabled* (2nd ed.). Columbus, OH: Merrill.

Williamson, J. M., Borduin, C. M., & Howe, B. A. (1991). The ecology of adolescent maltreatment: A multilevel examination of adolescent physical abuse, sexual abuse, and neglect. *Journal of Consulting and Clinical Psychology, 59,* 449–457.

Wilson, C. L. (1995). Parents and teachers: Can we talk? *LD Forum, 20* (2), 31–33.

Winebrenner, S. (1992). *Teaching gifted kids in the regular classroom.* Minneapolis, MN: Free Spirit Publishing.

Winners all: A call for inclusive schools. (1992). Alexandria, VA: National Association of State Boards of Education.

Winzer, M. (1999). *Children with exceptionalities in Canadian classrooms* (5th ed.). Scarborough, ON: Prentice-Hall Canada.

Winzer, M. A., & Mazurek, K. (1998). *Special education in multicultural contexts.* Upper Saddle River, NJ: Prentice-Hall.

Witt, J. C., & Elliott, S. N. (1985). Acceptability of classroom management strategies. In T. R. Kratochwill (Ed.), *Advances in school psychology* (Vol. 4, pp. 251–288). Hillsdale, NJ: Erlbaum.

Wolfe, P. S. (1997). Deaf-blindness. In P. Wehman (Ed.), *Exceptional individuals.* Austin, TX: Pro-Ed. pp. 357–381.

Wong, B. (1996). *The ABCs of learning disabilities.* San Diego, CA: Academic Press.

Wong, B. Y. L. (1991). The relevance of metacognition to learning disabilities. In B. Y. L. Wong (Ed.), *Learning about learning disabilities* (pp. 231–258). New York: Academic Press.

Wood, J. W. (1984). *Adapting instruction for the mainstream.* Columbus, OH: Merrill.

Wood, J. W. (1991). *Adapting instruction for mainstreamed and at-risk students* (2nd ed.). New York: Merrill.

Wood, J. W. (1996). *Adapting instruction for mainstreamed and at-risk students* (3rd ed.). New York: Merrill.

Wood, P. H., Bennett, T., Wood, J., & Bennett, C. (1990). *Grading and evaluation practices and policies of school teachers.* (ERIC Document Reproduction Service No. ED 319 782)

Woodman, E., (1995). Transitions: The personal journey of an adult's experiences living with learning disabilities. *LD Forum, 20* (2), 41–44.

Woodrich, D. L. (1994). *What every parent wants to know: Attention deficit hyperactivity disorder.* Baltimore, MD: Brookes.

Woronov, T. (1996). Assistive technology for literacy produces impressive results for the disabled. In E. Miller & R. Tovey (Eds.), *Inclusion and special education* (pp. 9–11). Cambridge, MA: Harvard Educational Letter.

Wright, J. V. (1995). Multicultural issues and attention deficit disorders. *Learning Disabilities Research and Practice, 10* (3), 153–159.

Ylvisaker, T., Szekeres, N., Hartwick, R., & Tworek, L. L. (1994). Collaboration in preparation for personal injury suits after TBI. *Topics in Language Disorders, 15,* 1–20.

York, J., & Vandercook, T. (1991). Designing an integrated program for learners with severe disabilities. *Teaching Exceptional Children, 23,* 22–28.

York, J., Vandercook, T., MacDonald, C., Heise-Neff, C., & Caughey, E. (1992). Feedback about integrating middle-school students with severe disabilities in general education classes. *Exceptional Children, 58,* 244–258.

Young, M. E., Kersten, L., & Werch, T. (1996). Evaluation of patient-child drug education program. *Journal of Drug Education, 26,* 57–68.

Ysseldyke, J. E., Thurlow, M. L., Wotruba, J. W., & Nania, P. A. (1990). Instructional arrangements: Perceptions from general education. *Teaching Exceptional Children, 22,* 4–8.

Zigmond, N., Levin, E., & Laurie, T. (1985). Managing the mainstream: An analysis for teacher attitudes and student performance in mainstream high school programs. *Journal of Learning Disabilities, 18,* 535–541.

Zucker, S. H., & Polloway, E. A. (1987). Issues in identification and assessment in mental retardation. *Education and Training in Mental Retardation, 22,* 69–76.

NAME INDEX

SUBJECT INDEX

Note: Page numbers followed by *t* or *f* indicate tables and figures, respectively.

EDUCATION

DATE DUE

OC